The Capital Budgeting Handbook

Editorial Advisory Board

The Capital Budgeting Handbook

Edited by

Mike Kaufman
Managing Director
Corporate Finance Associates
New York, New York

and
Adjunct Professor of Finance
Pace University
New York, New York

Dow Jones-Irwin
Homewood, Illinois 60430

This publication is designed to provide accurate and
authoritative information in regard to the subject matter
covered. It is sold with the understanding that the
publisher is not engaged in rendering legal, accounting, or
other professional service. If legal advice or other expert
assistance is required, the services of a competent
professional person should be sought.

*From a Declaration of Principles jointly adopted by a Committee
of the American Bar Association and a Committee of Publishers.*

ISBN 0-87094-522-X
Library of Congress Catalog Card No. 85-70803

Printed in the United States of America

1 2 3 4 5 6 7 8 9 K 3 2 1 0 9 8 7 6

To:
   Mom and Mindy,
     George and Steven

Corporate capitalism requires constant recharging with capital and re-invested profits to continue its vibrancy and growth. The capitalist mode of production depends on an abundant supply of cheap raw materials, big markets, and outlets for manufactured goods, constantly improving technology, an efficient market system, consumer confidence, and government support for all but those who abuse the system.

Arthur Jones
The Decline of Capital
Crowell, 1976

Preface

*T*he Capital Budgeting Handbook is designed to help you to think about corporate investment projects—investments in facilities, products, or human resources. The book brings together a broad array of traditional material and current viewpoints. It should be of value to corporate policymakers and those formulating strategy; to those proposing investment projects and those evaluating them; to corporate officers seeking outside funds, as well as prospective lenders and investors; and to those concerned with successful project implementation.

The handbook is intended for practical use by people in business or those serving business. For this reason the chapters have been written by business practitioners or by consultants and university people with broad business experience.

A great deal has been published on the individual aspects of capital budgeting. But this is a first attempt to integrate the many dimensions of the subject. This satisfies a personal ambition of mine to help broaden the treatment of capital budgeting beyond the limits of discounted cash flow analysis.

I've assumed readers have some familiarity with capital budgeting. Ideally, they will use the handbook to review traditional material and to heighten their awareness of important linkages with other corporate functions. I think readers will also be pleased to encounter the newer, more aggressive analytic methods and management techniques that can be used for investment projects.

The chapters of this book have been grouped into five major sections. Part I, Strategic Planning of Capital Expenditures, begins with a state-of-the-art review, summarizing the many facets of capital budgeting, its growing importance as a high-level corporate activity, its problems and controversies, and the broad spectrum of viewpoints on the subject. This introduction is followed by chapters covering methods of formulating business strategies and plans for the allocation of corporate capital. Part II, Preparing the Capital Budget, describes administrative procedures to assemble the capital budget, with references to practices in various sectors. The mathematics of capital rationing and portfolio management each have separate chapters.

Part III, Initiating an Individual Investment Project, deals with the practical details of preparing, evaluating, refining, and authorizing corporate investment proposals. Project evaluation is the best-known aspect of capital budgeting, but it is also the most controversial. Several chapters are devoted to defending different project evaluation criteria and to describing alternative philosophies of capital management. Also included are a chapter on the latest risk analysis methods and one on how to provide for inflation.

Part IV, Financing Capital Expenditures, begins with a chapter on long-term cash forecasting to identify external financing needs. Ensuing chapters cover alternative methods of financing investment projects, and when and how to use each of them.

Finally, Part V, Implementing an Investment Project, covers project management and post-audits. This material is for those responsible for moving a project from the proposal stage to reality.

Organizing and editing this handbook has been a labor of love. My enthusiasm for capital budgeting has grown with my years of corporate and university involvement with the subject. And coordinating the work of 30 authors has been an experience in itself. My thanks to all my authors for their contributions to this handbook.

I'm grateful, too to Joyce Payne, who acted as my personal reference librarian, solving in minutes research problems that would otherwise have consumed days.

Appreciation goes to my students at Pace University for helping with many aspects of the research, and for acting as sounding boards.

Finally, my admiration must be expressed for Carole Healy, typist/ cryptographer, for deciphering my handwriting.

In a way, *The Capital Budgeting Handbook* is more than a handbook. Capital budgeting is not a cut-and-dried subject without controversy and unsolved problems. The book attempts to surface the issues, present the major positions being taken, and leave readers to decide what best fits their situation.

Mike Kaufman

Contributing Authors

Moustafa H. Abdelsamad
Associate Dean for
Graduate Studies
School of Business
Virginia Commonwealth
University
Richmond, VA

Lewis Altfest
Altfest, Young Associates, Inc.
New York, NY

Herbert Berman
Executive Vice President
ORU Group
New York, NY

Harold Bierman, Jr.
Professor
Graduate School of
Management
Cornell University
Ithaca, NY

John F. Childs
Vice President
Kidder Peabody & Co., Inc.
New York, NY

Alan Cody
Mitchell & Company
Cambridge, MA

Harris M. DeWese
President
The DeWese Group, Inc.
Rosemont, PA

Keith B. Ehrenreich
Professor
School of Business
California State Polytechnic
University
Pomona, CA

Charles Frank
Manager of Project Finance
Salomon Brothers
New York, NY

Alan Fusfeld
Vice President and Director
Technical Management Group
Pugh-Roberts Associates, Inc.
Cambridge, MA

David E. Fyffe
Professor
School of Industrial and
Systems Engineering
Georgia Institute of Technology
Atlanta, GA

Bela Gold
Professor
Graduate Management Center
Claremont Graduate School
Claremont, CA

Elbert B. Greynolds
Associate Professor of
Accounting
Southern Methodist University
Dallas, TX

George B. Hegeman
Principal
Arthur D. Little, Inc.
Cambridge, MA

Thomas Henkel
Director
Financial Analysis Division
Conoco, Inc.
Wilmington, DE

David B. Hertz
Director
ICS Research Institute
University of Miami
Coral Gables, FL

Thomas J. Hindelang
Professor of Finance
Drexel University
Kennett Square, PA

Mike Kaufman
Managing Director
Corporate Finance Associates
New York, NY

David Kessler
Senior Technical Analyst
Metropolitan Transit Authority
Office of the Inspector General
New York, NY

Aivars Krasts
Vice President
Coordinating and Planning
Conoco, Inc.
Wilmington, DE

Harvey Leibenstein
Professor of Economics
Harvard University
Cambridge, MA

Bradford C. Lewis
Associate
Arthur Andersen & Co.
San Francisco, CA

Timothy J. McMahon
Consultant
Mitchell & Company
Cambridge, MA

Stephen W. Nagy
Vice President, Finance
Libbey-Owens-Ford Company
Toledo, OH

R. W. Nelson
Manager
General Electric Company
Fairfield, CT

Terry W. Rothermel
Principal
Arthur D. Little, Inc.
Cambridge, MA

Alan Seed III
Principal
Arthur D. Little, Inc.
Cambridge, MA

Nathan Snyder
Vice President—Acquisitions
CBS Inc.
New York, NY

Breffni Tomlin
Professor
University College, Dublin
Dublin, Ireland

David B. Uman
President
Management Advisory Group
Marina del Rey, CA

Stephen C. Wheelwright
Associate Professor of
Business Administration
Harvard Business School
Harvard University
Cambridge, MA

Frederick Enoch White
Tax Partner
Arthur Andersen & Co.
San Francisco, CA

Contents

ing Report. Capital Expenditure Progress Report. Capital Expenditure Audits. Glossary.

The Investment Side of Business Planning. Budgeting for Expansion at the Business Level. The Grand Loop of Overexpansion. Looking for the Second-Order Solution. Options to Expansion. Options for Consolidation. Capital Budgeting as Competitive Strategy. The Conceptual Framework for Business Strategy Expansion. New Directions for Capital Expansion Budgeting. The Role of Anticipation in Competitive Investment Strategy. Countercyclical Capital Expansion Strategies.

Revising the Responsibilities of Corporate Planning. On the Vulnerable Foundations of Capital Budgeting: *Underlying Premises and Estimates. On the Accuracy of Needed Forecasts.* Some Additional Shortcomings of Capital Budgeting Practices: *Widespread Overemphasis on Cost Saving. Foreshortened Horizons. Static Analytical Framework. Undermining Development of Innovational Proposals.* Approaches to Strengthening Capital Budgeting: *Shifting to a "Continuing Horizons" Criterion. Broadening the Coverage of Capital Budgeting Evaluations. Auditing and Improving Capital Budgeting Estimates. The Need for a Strategic Planning Framework.* Some Additional Bases for Major Capital Decisions.

The Budget Problem and Motivation. Why Assessments Are Necessary. Between Design and Result: Discretion, Motivation, and Performance: *Organization, Hierarchy, and Discretionary Effort. Pressure and Effort Choice. Free Riding and/or Adversarial Behavior.* Finding and Reading Motivational Gauges.

Introduction. An Overview of Mathematical Programming Techniques. Linear Programming Representations of the Capital Ra-

Sales Estimation. Estimate Costs. Summary. The Technical Analysis: *Determine Capacity Requirements. Specify the Production System. Determine Space, Structure, and Site Requirements. Select General Location. Estimate Costs. Summary.* The Financial Analysis: *Estimate Costs. Prepare Pro Forma Financial Statements. Evaluate Profitability. Summary.* Writing the Project Proposal.

Contents

Decision Rules. Treatment of Overruns, Underruns, and Supplementary Appropriations. Notification and Appeal. Emergency Requests. Flow of Events. Coordinating Function. Forms Used. How to Design Appropriation Procedures. Documenting the Procedures: *Policy Manual. Procedures Manual. Comprehensive Manual.* Approvals Required. Key Forms: *Preliminary Project Request. Capital Appropriation Request Form. Another Method of Presenting Estimated Cash Flows. Summary Forms and Follow-Up Reports. Cash Flow Estimates. Project Evaluation Sheet. Project Status Report. Simple Capital Expenditure Control Report. Authorization Change Request for New Plant. Executive Summary. Capital Expenditure Project Notice of Completion. Post-Audit Form. Surplus Equipment Report.*

Introduction. Forecasting: *The Business Cycle. Technological Developments. Important Future Events. Seat-of-the-Pants Forecasting. Simple Trend Analysis. Regression Analysis.* Qualitative Approach: *Policy-Level Decisions. Capital Budgeting. External Acquisitions. Dividend Policy. Financial Structure. Corporate Philosophy. Limitations.* The Strategic Plan—Forecasting Overall: *Economic Forecast. Financial Forecast. Industry Forecast. Company Forecast.* Projecting Earnings: *Sales. Cost of Sales. Selling, General, and Administrative Expenses. Depreciation. Interest and Other. Taxes. Net Income.* The Current Position. Statement of Forecasted Cash Flows. Box Jenkins Model: *Class of Model. Specific Model. Implementation.* Evaluation of Quantitative Versus Qualitative Approach. Sensitivity Analysis. Top Executive Review.

Introduction. The Relationship between Financing and Capital Decision Making. The Three Key Ratios in Financial Planning. Long-Term Debt to Total Long-Term Capital: *Summary. Various Types of Securities. Choosing the Right Security. Common Stock. Advantages. Disadvantages. Short-Term Debt Used for Long-Term Purposes.*

I

Strategic Planning of Capital Expenditures

1

Introduction: Capital Budgeting—The State of the Art

Mike Kaufman

Corporate Finance Associates

*A*ny business is a series of capital investment projects. Each investment is an attempt to assure some facet of the company's future well-being. Viewed this way, the subject of corporate investment is the subject of business.

Capital budgeting is the process of allocating the firm's capital to investment projects. It is the planning, financing, and managing of major outlays whose benefits lie in the future. The selection of investment projects and the allocation of corporate capital to them are among top management's primary responsibilities to shareholders. A good corporate investment program can mean sustained growth; failure to invest wisely can impede growth or threaten company survival.

Outlays can be made to modernize facilities; to expand capacity for growing market share; to develop, produce, and market a new product; or to develop human resources. Project objectives can be to maintain operations or improve productivity, to support a long-term growth strategy, or to comply with internal policies or with governmental legislation.

THE CASH FLOW ASSUMPTION

Despite its scope and magnitude as a top-management function, capital budgeting has been treated as a one-dimensional subject. Capital budgeting literature stresses the evaluation of individual investments whose costs and benefits can be expressed as cash flows. Project cash flows include project cost, that is, outlays, offset by disposal of replaced assets; working capital buildup, operating proceeds and operating costs, income taxes, recovery of working capital, and ultimate salvage of project assets. (A major capital project has its own income statement and balance sheet. It's a minibusiness.)

Debate has centered on the relative merits of discounted cash flow methods versus more "traditional" methods of cash flow analysis such as payback. A dissenting voice suggests only occasionally that all such analytic methods work best on trivial projects—those having little strategic impact.

The narrow focus can be explained: capital budgeting evolved as a financial concept, its basic principles formulated by economists. Modern economists favor quantitative analysis, and cash flows lend themselves to quantitative analysis. As technocrats, we analyze what we think we can measure, regardless of its importance, and we ponder, discuss, or turn away from qualitative considerations.

Our business schools have been slow to recognize that capital budgeting is a management function, requiring major contributions from marketing and technical functions as well as from financial functions. Capital budgeting is multidimensional; it warrants comprehensive treatment. Problems arise because many important dimensions, unlike cash flows, defy quantitative analysis. (Perhaps this is why so much capital budgeting literature implies that isolated projects drop from the sky, queueing up to await DCF—discounted cash flow—evaluation. Linkage with an underlying corporate strategy is usually not implied.)

A look at some of the key non-cash flow dimensions of capital budgeting can be very revealing. Learning how to deal with these dimensions is taking on new importance.

THE STRATEGIC DIMENSION

Projects of long-term strategic importance involve more than cash flows. Market-oriented companies invest millions to develop, maintain, or improve market share, often despite no-go recommendations by DCF analysts. Some of these projects succeed, others fail, but so it is with projects that do pass DCF tests.

Problems arise when strategic proposals defy quantification or fall short when quantified. Several solutions to the dilemma have been attempted. One, suggested by the cash flow advocates, is to forecast the costs of not doing a project. The status quo may not be a viable alternative to a market share maintenance project, for example. A second category of attempted solutions employs a procedural linkage between strategic planning and capital budgeting. Once a strategy is approved, the capital to implement it cannot be withheld, although mutually exclusive implementing alternatives are considered. A third method is to subsidize major survival or growth projects until they begin to pay off, 10 or 15 years after authorization. This is often done by parent companies who forgo a subsidiary's earnings for a time, until the subsidiary is on its feet.

Each method has succeeded, and each method has failed. Pragmatic executives consider the strategic dimension of capital budgeting in the context of its other dimensions, described below.

NEW CORPORATE CONSTITUENCIES

The classic financial objective of the firm is to maximize its value to its shareholders. It has recently become apparent that nonshareholder constituencies want to be heard. These new voices include the government and the community as well as those with obvious business connections to the firm.

Peter Drucker and others have made us aware that corporations have multiple objectives. One can associate each of the firm's constituencies with one or more of the firm's capital budgeting objectives. For example, investment in new products, quality improvement, and cost reduction (passed through as lower prices) might all interest the firm's customers and ultimate consumers. Various government agencies are interested in the firm's objective to be a good citizen of the community. Each constituency has its vested interests and exerts its influence regarding the firm's investment strategy. Each interest implies preferences regarding project types, required returns, risk attitudes, size of outlay, and other criteria.

Not much has been done to incorporate multiple objectives into general capital budgeting models. Analytic methods are difficult to apply to qualitative factors. How, then, do American corporations treat investment projects?

CAPITAL BUDGETING, ORGANIZATION, AND PERFORMANCE

Despite its crucial importance as a business function, capital budgeting typically has no organizational identity. Just as most firms have no decision-making corporate planning department, there is hardly ever a single department with responsibility for the ultimate content and success of the capital budget. Below the level of CEO or business unit head, capital budgeting responsibility is very diffuse.

Contrast this with responsibility for working capital investment. Ordinarily, each working capital component is the responsibility of an identifiable division or department—accounts receivable, accounts payable, materials management, cash management. The relative diffuseness of capital budgeting supports the notion that it is synonymous with business management, rather than an element of it.

There are other inherent reasons for the diffusion of responsibility for capital budgeting, compared to working capital:

- The magnitude of a single investment.
- The complexity of choices.
- Uncertainty about the future.
- Irreversibility of decisions.
- The cost of mistakes, compared with working capital decisions.

The Capital Budgeting Process

The ideal capital budgeting process is a complex one. Each element of corporate strategy, whether it be expansion, modernization, or compliance, requires capital. In addition there are tactical requirements for capital, investments necessary for continuity of operations.

Strange to note, the vast literature on strategic planning makes little reference to capital budgeting. A recent exception is Yaritz and Newman's *Strategy in Action,* which devotes an entire chapter to methods of linking the capital budget to corporate strategy.[1] These authors examine four methods—(1) policy constraints on project approvals; (2) written impact statements linking project proposals to explicit strategies; (3) stipulation of projects as part of a strategic program; and (4) separate budgeting for venture units and their needs, as practiced by Texas Instruments and other companies.

In practice, corporations still tend toward ad hoc generation of projects, using combinations of top-down programming and grassroots "wish lists." In a perfect world, ad hoc methods would be confined to tactical projects.

6

As diverse as corporate procedures are in linking strategy and capital budget, they are at least as varied from that point on. Extent of documentation required for appropriating funds, approval limits, criteria for evaluation, methods of financing, and control of implementation are almost unique to a given firm.

Profit Centers

As companies have entered different businesses under one corporate shell, the profit center concept has been widely adopted. Capital budgeting decisions are not handled in any standard way, however.

For example, one important difference among corporate practices has been the degree to which profit centers are assigned balance sheet responsibility. While acquired subsidiaries often retain their own balance sheets, internal divisions frequently are evaluated by income statement criteria alone. Balance sheet responsibility creates an investment center, which is necessary for decentralized decision making on capital investment projects. Without decentralized balance sheets, the corporation will probably use a single corporate hurdle rate for all investments. This practice tends to starve the marginal profit center of capital needed to survive and to discourage aggressive moves by high-performance profit centers.

Performance Evaluation

Closely related to the choice of hurdle rate is the choice of criteria for evaluating investment center performance. Preferences have developed for using accounting ROI (and ROE) for this purpose, raising the interesting question: Is ROI consistent with DCF evaluation of individual projects? Ezra Solomon and others have shown that book ROI usually overstates the DCF rate, particularly for: long project lives; uncapitalized investments (e.g., R&D, marketing, and training); accelerated depreciation; and delayed revenue streams.[2]

It is possible to predict the book ROI of an individual project using its DCF rate (that is, internal rate of return) and the governing accounting conventions. Even this is somewhat complicated by one accounting treatment for cash flows due to tax shields and another for reporting to shareholders. The real difficulty arises when an aggregate book ROI is required to represent a series of IRRs for projects with diverse accounting dimensions: project life, salvage value, capitalization rates, etc.

Alfred Rappaport and others have developed models to determine shareholder value of investment center performance.[3] By estimating

7

future cash flows of an investment project or an entire strategy, one can project their ultimate value to shareholders. Performance standards can be set, and managers' performance can be evaluated against them. This way, strategy and performance depend primarily on margins, sales growth, capital outlays, and risk, not on accounting gamesmanship. Successful corporations, for example, Libbey-Owens-Ford, are using shareholder value measures and are contributing to their development.

Such developments represent progress toward reconciling the evaluation of projects, strategies, and business performance. Their emphasis, however, is still on financial objectives of shareholders. Other constituencies and nonfinancial objectives are not explicitly considered.

Other Ratios

Those who find financial ratio analysis useful for evaluating performance may also note the observations in Table 1. For mature manufac-

TABLE 1

Capital Spending as Percent of Sales, 1979–1983		
(NR)	Agriculture	4.0
(S/CP)	Food processing	4.0
(S/CP)	Personal care	4.5
(BM)	Machinery	5.0
(HT)	Drugs	5.0
(S/CP)	Entertainment	8.0
(BM)	Automobiles	8.5
(BM)	S & P 400	9.0
(BM)	Steel	9.0
(BM)	Chemicals	9.5
(NR)	Energy	10.5
(NR)	Nonferrous metals	11.5
(HT)	Electronics	11.5
(NR)	Forest products	12.0
(S/CP)	Health care	13.5
(HT)	Information	15.0
(HT)	Telecommunications	26.5

NR: Natural resources   BM: Basic manufacturing
S/CP: Services and consumer products   HT: High-technology
Source: Based on "Industry Outlooks 1984," *Business Week*, January 9, 1984.

turing industries a typical capital budget for one year ranges from 5 to 10 percent of reported sales.

Thus, a billion-dollar corporation in basic manufacturing can be expected to invest $50 to $100 million annually in new plant and equipment. (This tends also to be the national percentage of GNP devoted to such investments.)

Natural resource industries, capital intensive by nature, spend 10–12 percent (excluding agriculture). High-tech and other emerging industries spend the most, with telecommunications at 26.5 percent. In general, this percentage is a function of industry maturity, age of plant and equipment, capacity utilization, and competitiveness. As with most other financial ratios, research is lacking on the question of what the capital spending rate should be in a given set of conditions.

Knowing a firm's capital budget, one can spot overly aggressive expansion or unwillingness to replenish existing capital assets. An example: One successful electronics firm I know undertook a capital program amounting to 15 percent of sales. At the time, this struck me as risky. But, the strategy was to upgrade the firm's existing market leadership position by developing new production technology. The rest of the industry would be left in the dust with antiquated margins. However, massive start-up problems and a dramatic decline in total market demand eventually created serious financial problems for the firm.

A second useful ratio is capital budget size as a multiple of depreciation expense. For a given period, this ratio tends to average about 2.5:1. This value implies that a firm is doing something more than replacing existing assets. How much more is a function of the age of that firm's assets and the compounded rate of inflation since the assets were acquired; that is, straight replacement alone requires more than a 1:1 ratio.

THE BEHAVIORAL DIMENSION

Businesspeople are developing a new interest in human behavior. Body language, negotiating strategies, decentralization, quality circles, job enrichment, and executive incentives point in that direction.

The behavioral dimension of capital budgeting is vital but virtually undocumented. It is the way your corporation uses its human resources to make capital budgeting decisions. For example, studies show an important shortcoming of capital budgeting procedures is the failure to consider alternatives—to act prematurely. An explanation lies in the nature of high-level corporate decision processes. Line executives are paid for decisions and action. Staff personnel are paid to

9

evaluate alternatives. But, the development of alternatives depends on effective teamwork, involving a combination of line and staff styles, in marketing, technical, and financial disciplines.

The absence of line-staff cooperation often leads to single-minded party lines and autocratic decision making. This can favor marketing, technical, or financial domination of capital budgeting decisions, depending on conditions (for example, where the firm is in the business cycle). Staff involvement is minimized under all but financial domination; otherwise, competitive deadlines prohibit an exhaustive review of alternatives. One feasible plan is enough to take action. (But it may lead to disaster.)

One answer to this problem has been to promote involvement of staff personnel in the early idea-generation stages of the line organization. Together with decision makers, they can formulate alternatives and keep them alive until they've been properly evaluated. Staff involvement is promoted in three ways: (1) top-management fiat and support; (2) initiative by enlightened line executives to utilize staff resources; and (3) ongoing close relations between staff and their clients in the line in order to permit involvement before party lines are cast in bronze.

Line-staff relations can involve profit center line and headquarters staff, factory line and profit center staff, or any other organizational combination.

A paradox: While the business schools and capital budgeting literature stress quantitative analysis, real corporate decisions can be highly personal and indeed politicized.

IN SEARCH OF EXCELLENT
INVESTMENT PROJECTS

Our penchant for analyzing what we can measure has been extended to management controls. We control what we can measure, without regard to its importance. Perhaps *try to control* is more accurate since controls are often confined to information gathering and reporting—the crucial action element is missing.

Peters and Waterman's chronicle of successful companies, *In Search of Excellence,* is an eye-opener.[4] The authors say that corporations that rely solely on quantitative analysis for their decisions are practicing narrow rationality. This study of excellent companies does not single out capital budgeting for attention, but its observations are relevant. The critique of narrow rationality applies well to the emphasis of business schools and financial literature on DCF analysis. The authors' general contentions are:

1. Narrow rationality limits the scope of analysis. Important issues are left untouched. Cost reduction becomes a higher priority than revenue enhancement.

2. The people element is left out.

3. Narrow rationality ignores the insights of experience.

4. Experimentation is undervalued and mistakes are abhorred, leading to inflexibility.

5. It excludes informality.

6. The rational model denigrates values.

7. It pretends that the future is predictable.

If Peters and Waterman are correct, major decisions in the excellent companies are not shaped through analysis but by corporate *values.* It's likely that these same excellent companies avoid narrow rationality in their capital investment programs.

Future studies may reveal more about capital budgeting practices of excellent companies. Studies to date of corporate capital budgeting practices have not managed to document a broader rationality in more successful companies. This may be because the responsibility for capital budgeting is so diffuse. It is hard to find a single corporate executive who is uniquely in charge of all its aspects.

Since publication of *In Search of Excellence,* I've regularly asked my capital budgeting students to infer from it how the excellent company evaluates investment projects. A summary of these students' observations is enlightening. (The students are MBA candidates majoring in finance, who have been well schooled in DCF techniques.)

- Innovation is encouraged.
- A bias toward action leads to experimentation on qualitative factors.
- They learn from failure and know how to withdraw quickly.
- Closeness to the customer leads to projects stressing quality, reliability, and service.
- Revenue enhancement projects are favored over cost-reduction projects.
- Good information networks keep everyone aware of important developments.
- Hands-on/value-driven teams manage projects from early proposal stages.
- Shared cultural values are used as investment criteria.
- Project evaluations include impacts on personnel, environment, and customers.
- Risk is managed not merely measured.

11

- Experience is utilized.
- Staff groups are small.
- Evaluations are simple and done at low cost.

Earlier authors have recorded the inherent weaknesses of the analytic process.[5] Some contend that these limitations confine analysis to an advisory role. Three major limitations are (1) analysis is necessarily incomplete; (2) measures of effectiveness are inevitably approximate; and (3) ways to predict the future are lacking.

The current back-to-basics movement, characterizing at least some excellent companies, ironically has surfaced at a time when proliferating computers have made analysis somewhat more tractable. A possible explanation is that the new abundance of analytic results has confirmed their futility. For example, with computer assistance, more alternatives can be examined—but if none proves outstanding, perhaps the need is for more creativity and more synthesis, not more analysis.

The back-to-basics movement offers a way out of another analytic dilemma: how do we analyze what we can't measure? For example, consider a market penetration project, a high-risk, high-outlay corporate investment. Not infrequently, the marketing costs of such a project exceed the costs of plant and equipment. First-year advertising alone for a new consumer product may easily cost $40 million to $50 million, while the facility to produce the product is built and equipped for $25 million. It's not uncommon for the advertising expenditure to be authorized on the basis of consultation and subjective research. The smaller plant and equipment expenditure is scrutinized and analyzed in voluminous detail, however. The difference, of course, is the relative ease of quantifying the costs and benefits of production facilities as contrasted with those of a marketing plan. More balanced evaluation methods seem to mark the excellent company.

CAPITAL BUDGETING AND CORPORATE GOVERNANCE

Companies usually set approval limits for capital investment projects. As with other corporate commitments, large outlays require higher-level authorization than smaller ones. A pretty good rule of thumb in my experience: Board approval is required for any outlay greater than 1 percent of the total capital budget (for example, a firm with a $50 million capital budget would require board approval for projects costing $500,000 or over).

Most firms do not regard inclusion of a project in their capital budget as authorization to spend money. The capital budget is considered agreement in principle only and requires minimal documentation. Usually the board must approve the budget per se. Following that, detailed documentation is usually required for funds to be appropriated.

Directors and Shareholders

There have been two notable trends in board composition and function: (1) a sizable increase in outside directors and (2) greater director involvement in management of the business. Neither of these trends truly enhances a board's ability to represent the firm's shareholders and act as their watchdog. Moves by dissident shareholders have surely not decreased.

Even so, direct shareholder approval continues to be required for certain corporate actions. These include consolidations like mergers or acquisitions. Consolidations represent the ultimate capital investment project; for example, Company A makes a multimillion-dollar outlay to acquire Company B.

We might ask: Why isn't direct shareholder approval required for other major corporate investment projects? How might the growth and direction of major corporations be affected by such a requirement? Who would gain? Who would lose?

Manuals

Corporate documentation of capital budget methods is a big variable. Some companies simply have policy manuals; others have procedure manuals or both. The degree to which such manuals reflect reality is another hard-to-pin-down variable. Finally, the correlation between a corporation's performance and the nature of its manuals is tenuous indeed. But the openness and informality of the excellent company would seem to preclude detailed, rigid procedure manuals. Brief statements of policy are more appropriate to the excellent profile.

ESTIMATING, FORECASTING, AND RISK

Many corporations have a risk management function—but it's usually concerned only with insurable risks. The management of project risk is an important but too often neglected facet of capital budgeting. Many practitioners and most business schools stop at project risk analysis. Potentially good projects are rejected for excessive risk when steps could be taken to reduce that risk. (Ruth Mack's *Planning on Uncertainty* is an excellent source of ideas for managing project risks.)[6]

13

We need to better understand the connection between risk and the errors of estimating and forecasting. A project's risk is someone's perception of the range of its possible outcomes, based on the information available. Thus, project risk can be reduced by improving the information available, for example, reducing estimating and forecast errors. This is achieved by doing better research and using more refined techniques.

The use of evolutionary estimating has become more widespread. The idea is that the estimating accuracy should increase as a project develops. Low-cost ±25 percent estimates, using handbook values and cost-capacity curves, are adequate in early exploratory stages. Estimates of ±3 percent are important at the appropriation stage. Such customizing increases the number of screening estimates that can be prepared, thereby encouraging the submission of project ideas without overloading the estimating function.

More needs to be done to connect the ideas of project risk, business risk, financial risk, inflationary risk, and interest rate risk. It is dangerous to divorce the project accept/reject decision from the financing decision. A highly leveraged project is more risky to the firm than one financed with retained earnings and should be evaluated accordingly. But the economics school of finance still advocates determining cost of capital based on a balanced capital structure. Here is one case where new mathematical models and appropriate software are needed to improve our ability to make decisions.

OPPORTUNITY COST AND CORPORATE INVESTMENT OBJECTIVES

Opportunity cost is the lost value of an unused opportunity. To be acceptable, an investment project must have a return at least as great as the firm's opportunity cost, expressed as interest rate of return.

Most people accept the opportunity cost concept, but there is a lot of disagreement about what number to use. (The concept is useful only when financial objectives prevail and projects with cash flows are considered.) In practice, opportunity cost becomes (1) the rate of discount applied to a project's cash flow to determine its net present value or (2) the firm's internal rate of return standard, or hurdle rate.

While more and more large corporations have embraced DCF techniques, few agree on methods for determining discount rates. Models used range from complex derivations of the firm's cost of capital to seat-of-the-pants hurdle rates designed to incorporate someone's perception of risk.

14

Others seek a "true" opportunity cost. Such a notion implies that the firm's cost of capital is less indicative of lost opportunities than is the return available on competing investment projects. That is, if the firm is using retained earnings, lending available funds is a less likely course than reinvesting it in the business—whether for expansion, improvement, or survival. Using the firm's cost of capital as a discount rate implies that the firm would lend available funds if an investment project is rejected.

Even among those who believe that cost of capital represents true opportunity cost, there are differences in preferred methods of calculation. Preferences include the cost of a balanced capital structure, the marginal cost of capital, and ad hoc financing costs, with and without adjustment for risk.

Further disagreement marks the question of whose opportunity cost is relevant. Economics and security market thinking utilizes the shareholder's opportunity cost. That is, if a shareholder isn't satisfied with his return, he can sell his shares and buy those of another firm. Gordon Donaldson and others prefer the notion of corporate opportunity cost, based on the objectives of company management.[7] Donaldson argues that management's fortunes are more closely tied to company success than are those of the shareholder.

Then too, is there a typical shareholder with typical objectives? Most corporations have many shareholders with diverse interests and expectations for their shares, ranging from reliable dividend income to rapid capital gains. Such diversity makes it hard to express a single discount rate in the form of required shareholder return. Existing mathematical models for cost of equity can do no more than determine average cost.

THE DCF DEBATE

If determining opportunity cost and discount rate is controversial, so too is the question of how to apply that rate to project cash flows. Most financial authors still support discounted cash flow methods (DCF) as the surest measure of project return. The time value of money—a dollar today is worth more than a dollar in the future—is etched on the mind of every MBA student. Simply, the dollar today can be invested to become $1.10 one year from now, if the lending rate is 10 percent. Therefore, one dollar is the present value of that $1.10 available one year from now (given a 10 percent rate).

Firms had been slow to adopt the DCF concept to evaluate investment projects. Simple methods like payback and ROI were more popular until recently—they're easier to understand. The advent of cheap

15

financial calculators and computers made DCF models more acceptable. Understanding became unnecessary and calculations were now automated.

But just as acceptance of DCF techniques has grown, new doubts have arisen. Many critics contend that America's industrial decline can be traced to a preoccupation with short-term benefits—the antithesis of the futurity of capital budgeting doctrine. Some of these critics point to DCF models as fostering an emphasis on the short term: Aren't near-term cash flows penalized less severely by discounting than those further out in time?

The reinvestment assumption for DCF methods is an issue that has produced a spate of journal articles and conference papers. Lately, more and more authors have declared that the assumption doesn't exist. Here the question is about the return on reinvested project cash flows, required to validate results of NPV and IRR models. Historically, many authors have contended that reinvestment must return the discount rate used. This became one of the reasons to prefer NPV over IRR, especially for attractive projects where high IRRs seemingly would have to be endlessly duplicated. The NPV discount rate, at the firm's cost of capital, seemed to be easier to reproduce.

A more moderate reinvestment assumption cites the need to reinvest at a project's rate of return for the firm's *overall* yield to equal that of a given project. In this case, the project at hand implies no reinvestment for its own yield to be valid.

Others have asked why they should continue to use IRR at all, considering all the trouble it causes. Trouble includes the possibility of multiple IRR values, the IRR's lack of validity for ranking purposes, and an inability to reflect variable interest rate forecasts. The explanation for the IRR's continued survival is probably its simplicity—characterizing an investment project with a single value. NPV, while superior in many theoretical respects, requires two variables (NPV and discount rate used) to completely describe a project's return. A compromise adopted by some companies is to do project analysis with NPV and to conduct presentations and discussions with IRR.

SECURITY MARKET MODELS

Earlier we noted the widespread project evaluation practice of measuring the measurable and subordinating important qualitative investment project factors. That observation can be extended to read "measurable, using security market investment models." Virtually all important capital budgeting models advocated in the literature were originally developed for investments in securities or other financial instruments. It is important to examine the applicability of these same models to investment *projects*.

DCF Models

A bondholder's IRR is his bond's yield to maturity. A mortgage holder's IRR is the true rate of her mortgage. As financial instruments, bond and mortgage costs and benefits are completely expressable as cash flows. Furthermore, the opportunity costs of a bondholder or mortgage holder are probably the yields of other financial instruments. This is not usually the case for the corporate investment project; yet the IRR model has been adapted without change.

Consider next another of the bond- or mortgage holder's likely objectives aside from rate of return. He probably has made an explicit decision to favor income or to favor capital gain, that is, asset appreciation. He has probably made another decision about how he wants his capital recovered—amortized over the term of the instrument or as a balloon payment at the end of the term.

Now consider the corporate executive and his investment project—assuming it can be well described using cash flows. Virtually all of his business investment benefits resemble amortization of principal and no capital gain. In theory he is like the mortgage holder. But a portfolio of new mortgage opportunities probably represents a small range of returns. The corporate portfolio of new investment opportunities usually represents a wide diversity of returns and an equally diverse set of qualitative costs and benefits that he should also consider.

These are some arguments that can be advanced in behalf of avoiding total dependence on DCF methods for evaluating corporate investment projects. The alternatives are to develop more eclectic models using other appropriate corporate criteria, including cash flow, per se; effects on balance sheet, accounting earnings, and share price plus an array of strategic considerations. For example, a company with a goal of dominating a market within five years might discount fifth-year cash flows less severely than normal DCF models would.

Portfolio Theory

Markowitz's portfolio diversification model has been criticized as a computational nightmare by those using it for securities.[8] Theoretically, forecasts must be prepared for each opportunity in the entire investment universe, and pair-by-pair covariances must be calculated. Targets of other criticisms directed against using Markowitz's model for securities include assumptions that the portfolio decision is a single act and that possible returns are distributed normally.

17

Most capital budgeting texts include a treatment of portfolio theory. One could easily list other assumptions of the model that simply don't apply to corporate investment projects (for example, the additivity of returns, disregarding project interactions; minimum transaction costs; and investment divisibility.) But the principal objection to adopting Markowitz's model is the difficulty of managing the firm's capital budget as an investment portfolio.

Corporate portfolio management is illustrated by the money manager who presides over pension fund investments. It is hard to visualize a second money manager (in the next office?) responsible for the capital budget of an undiversified business. His jurisdiction would have coopted the responsibilities of profit center and corporate management, and the corporation would no longer be an operating company.

Nonetheless, much of the strategic planning of the 1970s was based on the product portfolio matrix conceived by the Boston Consulting Group. BCG recommended milking businesses with high market share in mature industries to feed businesses in fast-growth industries. In mid-1981, after more than a decade of corporate investment in one business after another while modernization of facilities was neglected, BCG's chief executive saw portfolio management being replaced by operating management. A McKinsey director was quoted as saying, "Companies can no longer think of diversifying risk, but rather reducing it altogether."[9] This heralded the back-to-basics movement, which calls for managers to focus on each business as an entity rather than as part of a diversified mix. At this moment, as American industry struggles to regain its international standing, portfolio management seems to hold little promise for capital budgeters.

CAPM

The Capital Asset Pricing Model was developed for securities as an easy-to-use alternative to Markowitz. By calculating the historical beta of a security (that is, its riskiness compared to that of the overall market), one can determine the return to expect from that security. Capital budgeting texts advocate using this model for corporate investment projects. The problem is there is no historical beta for most new projects; therefore, betas of "similar" projects must be sought, which requires a superb intraindustry intelligence system.

Conclusion

While many corporations have developed proprietary models for evaluating their capital projects, there are virtually no general models de-

18

veloped expressly for capital budgeting. The creation of such models is a challenging goal for workers in the field.

FINANCING INVESTMENT PROJECTS

We don't yet agree on the relationship of the economic accept/reject decision for a project and the decision of the method for financing that project. There's not even agreement on the time-honored matching principle or hedging strategy, which says use long-term funds for long-term investments. More and more firms (and many publications) are attempting to forecast changes in long-term interest rates and use short-term money until longer-term rates decline. The old conventional wisdom said this was the road to financial disaster.

The computer industry has a lesson for us. The companies most likely to survive the coming shakeout, according to Stephen McClellan, are those burdened with the least debt.[10] IBM, Digital Equipment, and Hewlett-Packard Co. have little or no debt, and Sperry Corp., Honeywell, and AT&T have over 30 percent debt. The successful computer companies have realized that equity financing is the way to go in an emerging industry. Business risks are high enough without being compounded by financial risks. The juxtaposition of these two risk factors warrants the attention of other emerging or rapidly changing industries investing capital.

Innovations

Project financing has developed as an innovative off-balance sheet source of funds for large, complex investment projects. The idea that investors and lenders look primarily to project cash flow as a source of repayment is a welcome change from the lending officer's traditional stance on equipment loans. Banks tend to regard equipment as security rather than as a source of cash flow. Extension of the project financing concept to smaller-scale projects could have benefits.

PLANNING AND CONTROL

There have been notable advances in the planning and control of capital investment projects. Growth of the venture capital method of financing high-tech start-ups led to the business plan method of documenting investment proposals. A format was required by investors for entrepreneurs to describe the major factors of a business start-up: proposition; management; marketing, technical, and financial plans; financial history; and projections.

19

Investment Project Proposals

Many firms have adopted the business plan format as the basis for documenting all major investment projects whether or not venture capital is required. Where it is used, it can become the context for enumerating both quantitative and qualitative project costs and benefits. Prepared as a selling piece, the project can go far in impressing insiders who authorize project expenditures and outsiders who are prospective sources of funds for the project.

Familiarity with the business plan format has provided project sponsors, analysts, decision makers, investors, and lenders with the ability to recognize the factors leading to project success or failure.

Investment Project Planning

A good investment proposal is at first a feasibility study. Marketing, technical, and financial analyses allow problems and opportunities to surface. Strategies and solutions follow and lead to the final project plan.

We have learned a lot about project planning; we now recognize project scope as a controllable variable along with cost, benefits, and schedule. Scope reduction has become a popular method of reducing potential cost overruns. New York City's contemplated convention center is an example. Exhibit space, seating capacity, and number of elevators were diminished before ground was broken, as inflationary effects and postponements threatened huge overruns.

The abandonment of many nuclear power plant projects before completion might be cited as ultimate examples of scope reduction. But these failures are better examples of abominable project planning, including poor scoping.

One has only to look at Canada's use of nuclear power to see what we might have done with better investment project planning. Five of the world's 10 most efficient reactors are in Canada, and no planned Canadian reactors have been canceled, compared with 105 U.S. orders dropped since 1972. Their reactors take half as long to build as ours. A major Canadian strength: Their 13 completed reactors (and 9 under construction) follow the same design, making technical problems easier to solve. The United States has 4 vendors, 10 engineering companies, and 60 utilities, each wanting a custom-built plant.

It is a pity that in the United States our repugnance for planning at the national level seems to have distorted our understanding of the appropriate role of competition. The U.S. power industry's misadventures with nuclear power are an outstanding, if unfortunate, example of misguided capital budgeting.

Of course, other U.S. industries haven't done much better. But how many of our economic analysts have attributed our failures in steel, automobiles, and consumer electronics to inept capital budgeting? Smarter capital budgeting in these industries would have been more market-oriented, as concerned with the productivity of capital as with that of labor, and more willing to experiment early, for example, with minimills and new technologies.

Does this mean that the Japanese approach to capital budgeting is superior to ours? From what we know, there are great similarities between successful companies in Japan and the excellent U.S. company whose profile was described earlier: market-oriented, informal, participative, and not fixated on quantitative analysis.

Project Control

Government contracts were the first to require rigorous project management methods. (For example, PERT was developed for the Polaris project in 1958.) The techniques eventually were adopted by corporations in all industries. More recently, the proliferation of computers has led more businesses to adopt more effective methods of managing investment projects.

We have learned that while matrix management is not tractable at the firm level, its counterpart—the project team—is very effective for individual capital projects. One reported practice of the excellent company is the formation of multidiscipline project teams, early in the development of a project proposal, to see it through to successful completion.

Excellent companies must manage their investment projects well. Peters and Waterman define excellence in terms of asset and equity growth and return on investment. Superior performance in these areas is not possible without superior management of investment projects. Companies as diverse as IBM, Procter & Gamble, 3M Company, Delta Airlines, Marriott, Boeing, and McDonald's Corporation are esteemed for their team approach and for their financial excellence.

The Post-Audit Paradox

Post-audits are the exit interviews of capital budgeting. A project may not part company with the firm after a post-audit, but the naive implication that a problem situation should be audited after it is beyond redemption is common to both practices.

It is also true in both cases—the discharged employee and the completed investment project—that proper attention early on would have reduced the need for the ex post facto attention. Firms that employ good project management practices can get far better results than those who rely on post-audits alone.

In the right perspective, the post-audit can serve an important purpose. We have learned that third-party intervention by a multidiscipline audit team can get an errant project back on track. But this is only possible when there is still time for action. The notion of postcompletion audits should give way to post-scheduled-completion or post-key-milestone audits.

CAPITAL SPENDING AND THE ECONOMY

We are still confused about what promotes capital spending and what capital spending promotes. We are not quite sure of the productivity role of capital investment. We are puzzled about the relationship of capital spending to capital formation. Is economic growth a cause or an effect of capital spending?

Legislators, regulators, and corporate lobbyists would do well to improve their understanding of these questions. Different investment projects probably require different incentives. So too, different balance sheets require different sorts of investment stimuli.

Of late, signals have been very mixed. Capital spending did not immediately respond to the incentives offered by TEFRA and ERTA, the 1981 and 82 tax acts that laid out simplified and accelerated tax shields for corporate projects. A further puzzler developed when increased capital spending accompanied rising interest rates in the years following. Some corporate sages even suggested that increased market demand might be encouraging capital outlays.

Accelerated depreciation alone cannot assure effective capital spending. In the United Kingdom, capital assets are written off in one year.

And what about recursive capital formation. Does investment by business ripple through other factors of our economy? This has become more difficult to analyze, as investment in new plants is subordinated to investment in equipment—overseas equipment at that.

There is a long way to go before we begin to understand the broad causes and effects of corporate investment. Recently, when short-term money market rates declined, some corporate cash managers diverted available cash to corporate investment projects. This confusion of objectives could be the subject of a rousing roundtable discussion.

The Treasurer's Loop[11]

Coincident with the growth of shareholder value advocates has been the change in the character of the shareholder. Those corporations and consultants who evaluate investment projects according to their impact on stock price are in fact attempting to measure shareholder wealth. But the effect has been alarming. The typical shareholder is no longer an individual investor with a long-term interest in the corporation whose shares he holds. Instead, he is now typically a money manager for an institutional investor.

Many of these money managers have pension funds as clients. The client representative is usually a corporate treasurer. The impact of pension fund performance on a corporation's financial condition has grown substantially. Hence the corporate treasurer watches his pension fund manager closely and presses him to improve his performance.

Given such pressures and favorable tax treatment, money managers have become short-term stock traders. And, ironically, their quest for yield and their broad holdings (60 percent of corporate stocks and bonds, totaling over $1 trillion) has given them great power over corporate investment policy.

The emergence of the money manager as a major shareholder with short-term interests is having these effects on treasurers, CFOs, and CEOs: Earnings must consistently increase, even at the expense of long-range strategies; and reinvestment at the expense of dividends leads to a reduced stock price, closing off equity sources and compelling more borrowing with its attendant hazards.

A BROADER CAPITAL BUDGETING CONCEPT

Given its numerous dimensions and controversies and its huge upside and downside potential, capital budgeting warrants treatment as a broad, coherent discipline. Such a discipline should enlarge upon and differ from conventional treatments of capital budgeting in several important respects:

1. Corporate investment methodology should not be limited to fixed assets (plant and equipment projects) but should include all major outlays for marketing, R&D, training and development of people, and mergers and acquisitions.
2. Major investment projects should be treated as minibusinesses, and the firm as an aggregate of such projects.
3. Strong procedural links should be required between strategic planning and investment project objectives.
4. The multiple objectives of the firm and its constituencies should be incorporated into decision models and pro-

cesses. Marketing and technical needs should share top billing with financial objectives.

5. Project evaluation criteria should provide a means for assessing intangible costs and benefits as well as those expressable as cash flows.
6. Planning horizons should be explicit variables in evaluation models.
7. Evaluation models should not be exclusively quantitative and analytic.
8. Explicit provision for creativity should be considered essential to the capital budgeting process.
9. A financing decision should be associated with each major economic decision.
10. Project teams should be responsible for successful implementation.
11. Post-audits should be insightful, timely, and practical.
12. Consistency should be a less important objective than excellence.
13. Models should not be ruled out simply because they can't be formally documented. Qualitative processes are often difficult to describe.

COMPUTERS AND CAPITAL BUDGETING

The potential benefits of applying computer technology to capital budgeting are huge. But lacking a unified capital budgeting discipline, we have been slow to realize even a fraction of that potential. The possibilities for capital budgeting computer applications can be best viewed in terms of the process stages that are the structure of this handbook:

- Strategic Planning of Capital Expenditures
- Preparing the Capital Budget
- Initiating an Individual Project
- Financing Capital Expenditures
- Implementing a Capital Project

Strategic Planning

There is little general agreement about the best relationship between strategic planning and capital budgeting. The literature tends to neglect the subject entirely, as does much of the corporate community. Some corporations recognize the need for a linkage between planning and

24

budgeting per se, whether for capital outlays or operating expenses. A few companies regard capital budgeting as an element of strategic planning.

Most of the software that is relevant to the planning/budgeting interface is of the "what if" variety. As computers proliferate, scenario planning is growing more popular. Thus the cash flows implied by alternative strategies being considered can be manipulated to reveal the effects of likely scenarios comprising different economic, market, and competitive situations.

Such a process might also combine the analytic and creative aspects of strategic planning. Since computers facilitate "what if" analyses, it becomes more practical to experiment with changes in strategy.

Strategic planning software packages are commercially available for mainframe computers. There is also evidence that a great deal of proprietary work has been done to use computers for improving strategic planning. This extends to the creation of industry- and company-specific data bases comprising data on markets, products, and relevant underlying situations.

As more executives have access to microcomputers, experimentation with strategies will increase, but decentralization will too. It is hard to predict the net effect of computer development on the strategic aspects of capital budgeting. One obvious application is the use of word processors to facilitate redrafting strategic documents.

Preparing the Budget

This is a straightforward job for mainframe computers. Proprietary software is readily developed for mainframes and minis to tabulate capital projects in terms of many key variables. The tendency is to employ generic spreadsheet software for budgeting applications on micros for individual executives. In either case, budgets can be easily redrafted.

Initiating a Project

Most commercially available capital budgeting software is devoted to automating DCF calculations. This, of course, is in keeping with the popular notion that capital budgeting and DCF analysis are synonyms. Proprietary software for this purpose is equally abundant but commonly employs variations on standard techniques.

Once a project is approved and funds are authorized, the fixed asset accounting packages take over. This too is a popular form of application software that does very little for capital budgeting.

Financing Capital Expenditures

Financial software for evaluating alternative capital structures and sources of marginal financing is readily available and easily designed by house staffpeople. Usually these packages, with some proprietary exceptions, do not link the financing decision to the investment project being financed.

Implementing a Capital Project

There is probably more available under the labels "Project Management" and "Project Planning and Control" than there is for any other capital budgeting area.

Conclusion

The potential exists for someone to use computer technology to help create a unified capital budgeting discipline. Appropriate data bases and decision support systems are ideal for the unstructured strategic planning and project development work. These modules could be readily linked with more structured budgeting and evaluation modules. Further links could be created with project management modules so that implementation variances from original concepts could be tracked. Finally, post-audits would be greatly facilitated.

See Appendix B of this book for a brief listing of some relevant software packages that are commercially available.

NOTES

[1] Boris Yaritz and William H. Newman, *Strategy in Action,* (New York: Free Press, 1982).

[2] Ezra Solomon, "Return on Investment: The Relation of Book Yield to True Yield," in *Research in Accounting Measurement*, eds. Robert K. Jaedicke, Yuji Ijiri, and Oswald Neilson (Madison, Wis.: American Accounting Association, 1966).

[3] Alfred Rappaport, "Corporate Performance Standards and Shareholder Value," *The Journal of Business Strategy,* Spring 1983, pp. 28–38.

[4] Thomas J. Peters and Robert H. Waterman, Jr., *In Search of Excellence* (New York: Harper & Row, 1982).

[5] Edward S. Quade, "Cost-Effectiveness Analysis: Introduction and Overview," in *Cost-Effectiveness Analysis,* ed. Thomas A. Goldman (New York: Praeger Publishers, 1966).

[6] Ruth Mack, *Planning on Uncertainty* (New York: John Wiley & Sons, 1971).

[7] Gordon Donaldson, "Strategic Hurdle Rates for Capital Investment," *Harvard Business Review,* March–April 1972.

[8] H. M. Markowitz, *Portfolio Selection: Efficient Diversification of Investments* (New York: John Wiley & Sons, 1959).

[9] Quoted in *Business Week,* June 1, 1981, p. 20.

[10] Stephen T. McClellan, *The Coming Computer Industry Shakeout* (New York: John Wiley & Sons, 1984).

[11] "Will Money Managers Wreck the Economy?" *Business Week,* August 13, 1984, pp. 86–93.

2

Long-Term Forecasting: How to Forecast Factors Affecting Capital Expenditures*

George B. Hegeman
Arthur D. Little, Inc.

INTRODUCTION

The corporate capital budget is a company's ultimate forecast. It anticipates where money can be most usefully invested both to maximize near-term profits and to assure the company's long-term growth and development. In essence, the capital budget is a company's forecast of its future.

It takes all types of forecasts to develop the capital budget and supporting documents. Unfortunately, the key forecasts are usually hidden and only the results are included in the final budget documents

* "How to Forecast Factors Affecting Capital Expenditures," © 1985 by George B. Hegeman.

submitted for top-management and board approval. Nevertheless, the assumptions and forecasts of the future are a key part of the capital budgeting process and, if properly documented, display corporate expectations for the full range of internal and external factors that control the destiny of the projects proposed and the company as a whole. Why are these critical forecasts hidden from view? Peter Drucker provided the best explanation when he asserted that all forecasting is futile and a waste of time since no one can know the future. Experience teaches us that nearly all forecasts will be wrong. Since no executive likes to be proven wrong, the critical business assumptions and forecasts are often deleted from the capital budget, leaving only the expected financial results to support the proposed spending programs.

This book is focused on the methodology of capital budgeting. Before looking at each element in the capital budgeting process and how it is developed, we believe it is critical to look at how to go about the business of developing and using the required long-range forecasts. In this chapter we review the need for forecasting in capital budgeting and then focus on the key factors that should be forecast. For each factor we will also outline an approach to forecasting.

THE IMPORTANCE OF FORECASTING IN CAPITAL BUDGETING

Unless you have been involved in preparing or approving capital budgets, it may seem strange that one of the first chapters in this handbook is about forecasting. Once you have been through the process you will realize that each project proposed and the pattern of spending approved are based on a complex web of forecasts that in total spell out a company's assumptions about the future. Untangling this web at the beginning and laying the groundwork for developing a consistent set of assumptions and forecasts can save hours of debate and delay in the capital budget preparation and approval process.

Where do we begin? We start by recognizing that requests for capital expenditures have different origins within the company and that there are several different types of requests being made simultaneously. Perhaps the easiest way to think about the origin of capital budgets is to take a global view of the company and to move out from the corporate core along three separate axes (see Figure 1). These include (1) business unit capital requirements, (2) major new projects, and (3) corporate investments.

Whether moving along the business unit, new project, or corporate axis, you must start with a consistent set of assumptions about the future. The expectations for all projects and business units must also

FIGURE 1

The Strategic Planning of Capital Budgeting

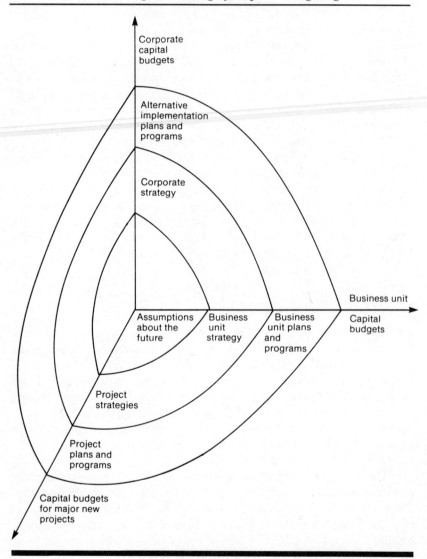

add up to the total corporate strategy. Assuming the base is consistent, then the capital budgets by business, by project, and for the entire corporation will be well matched.

While authorization of all realistic business unit, new project, and corporate requests is common in highly profitable companies experiencing high profits and strong cash flow, companies experiencing constraints on capital spending may have to pick and choose among the proposed projects to produce results that are congruent with their strategic plan.

We also need to recognize that capital budgeting is a time-dependent process which includes developing individual capital appropriation requests, testing requests for congruence with operating budgets and strategic plans, rating and ranking of requests, and approving the capital budget.

Long-range forecasts are required in every step of the process.

FACTORS THAT NEED TO BE FORECAST

To identify which factors need to be forecast for capital budgeting we must consider first the type of capital budget request that will emerge from these three areas.

Business Unit Capital Requests

The most common request will be:

Maintenance and improvement projects. For an individual maintenance or improvement project it is often sufficient to restrict the forecasts to the operating parameters of the individual product/market involved. Assumptions about the macroeconomic environment and even conditions in the industry can often be ignored as long as there are sufficient internal financial rewards through cost savings to justify the project. Among the forecasts likely to be needed for any project are:

Operations Forecasts

Raw material costs	Equipment costs
Utility costs	Transportation costs
Labor costs	Environmental costs
Depreciation	Overhead costs
Marketing costs	Coproduct credits
Product price	Yield or reject rate
Packaging costs	Scrap/salvage value

Expansion projects. For business unit capital requests supporting expansion of an existing business, it is necessary to forecast the microeconomic factors noted above by product area as well as some of the factors relating to the industry, such as:

Industry Forecasts

Demand	Marketing trends
Raw material supply	Competitive position trends
Competitive cost structure	Customer requirement trends
Pricing trends	Maturity
Competitive products	Competitive intensity
Performance trends	Product obsolescence
Price trends	Process obsolescence

Major New Projects

For approval of major new projects, both operations forecasts and industry forecasts are essential. In fact, these forecasts will have to be extended far into the future to encompass the period of profitable operations required to ensure an adequate return on investment. In order to understand the long-term forecasts of operations and industry factors, it is necessary to set these forecasts in perspective with some of the more macroeconomic forecasts, including:

Macroeconomic Forecasts

Regional and national GNP	Capital spending patterns
Demographic trends	Government policy trends
Inflation expectations	World trade trends
Energy outlook	

Then, the financial results of each project need to be evaluated in terms of their impact on:

Corporate Financial Forecasts

Corporate cash flow forecast
Corporate sources and uses of funds forecast
Corporate borrowing plans
Corporate dividend policies
Corporate strategic plans and programs

Seldom are all four sets of forecasts available in a company from the same source with a consistent set of assumptions behind them. Therefore, when the capital requests are being assembled, one of the key tasks for those involved in processing the requests is to check for major inconsistencies in assumptions and forecasts. Typically, companies will publish an annual guideline statement with some of the macroeconomic forecasts included in order to help put all the budgets, plans, and capital requests on an equal footing. Though helpful, it is rarely successful in overcoming the bias, enthusiasm, and myopia of individuals sponsoring major new capital projects.

Corporate Projects

The third major class of capital requests are those based on the need to support corporate projects. These include such diverse capital programs as constructing a corporate headquarters building, investing in a large-scale computer system in support of accounting for all business units, and funding the capital needs of corporate research and development. Here again, a different set of forecasts are required. For example:

Corporate Forecasts

Facilities cost
Communications and transportation costs
Computer hardware costs
Computer software costs
R&D facilities and equipment costs
Accounting and legal costs
Staff productivity trends

FORECASTING TECHNIQUES

Basically there are three approaches to forecasting. These include inertial, inductive, and deductive systems.

Inertial

Inertial forecasts are statistical projections based on historical data. They include conventional statistical forecasts based on time series moving averages, correlation analysis, and special techniques such as exponential smoothing, exclusion charts, and experience curves. The underlying assumption in all of these forecasts is that the future will be controlled by the same events that shaped the past.

Inductive

Inductive forecasts take the inertial forecasts as a base and adjust the projections on the basis of management knowledge and experience. This is a common approach of market research as it modifies statistical forecasts on the basis of knowledge and assumptions about the current and future environments. Delphi forecasts, panel consensus, and typical planning and budget forecasts fall into this category as well.

Deductive

Deductive forecasts use current data and decision rules about alternatives to develop independent long-range forecasts. The deductive approach takes into account the unique characteristics of an industry and requires an intimate knowledge of the business.

In developing any forecast, one must consider the trade-off between the cost of the forecast and the cost of error. The least expensive methods are inertial forecasts, which may provide useful insight into long-range trends without the expense of delving into the cause-and-effect relationships within the market environment. Inductive forecasts require the time and expense associated with a market research effort but provide insight into future industry trends that are not generally available in the industry literature and statistics.

Deductive forecasts are really a totally different type of forecasting system and are based on behavioral simulation models. These forecasts, which incorporate the impact of those variables that are likely to control the future for a specific business, start with current industry data, decision rules about how different competitors act, and the judgment of management regarding future trends in all aspects of the business. These behavioral simulation models also take into account judgments, attitudes, and decision rules regarding future actions because these factors have the most important bearing on how a competitive market evolves. Such models are based on the techniques now being used to develop expert systems as part of the early work in artificial intelligence. There is one problem with such large-scale simulation models: they are very expensive. The result is that most companies opt for inertial forecasts, and for large-scale projects they occasionally seek the input required for the inductive-type forecast. Only when a single product constitutes the life blood of a key division or a whole company will it be justified to spend the time and effort necessary to develop a large-scale industry simulation model.

The principles of deductive forecasting can, however, be applied to creating simplified models of future behavior which are useful for such difficult areas as supply and price forecasting. These simplified models are typically based on rating, weighting, summing, and scaling the factors controlling a situation. The forecast is made iteratively by considering how previous changes in other factors will affect each variable on a year-by-year basis over time. This approach is particularly useful in understanding industry cycles and identifying likely turning points in industry behavior patterns.

A lengthy discussion of how to forecast each of the factors previously identified as significant for different types of capital budgeting items would be a book in itself. To provide a quick reference guide, we have listed each of the key forecasts in Table 1 and identified the primary source of historical data, listed the key factors controlling the future outlook for each item, suggested a forecasting methodology that may be appropriate, and provided comments on critical issues affecting these forecasts.

This display of the large number of forecasts that are inherent in a detailed capital budget suggests the need for major capital budget requests to include a page that identifies the critical assumptions about the future and spells out in detail the forecasts used to justify the project.

TABLE 1

Forecasting for Capital Budgeting

Type of forecast	Primary historical data source	Key factors controlling forecasts	Forecasting methodology	Comments
Operations forecasts				
Raw material costs	Purchasing	Supplier costs/margins, commodity prices	Time series	Pressure to maintain margins important, GDP growth and inflation affect price trends.
Utility costs	Purchasing	Regional energy costs, crude oil prices	Time series	Long-term supply contracts provide stability; tough call.
Labor costs	Payroll	Industry labor contracts, regional labor rates	Time series	Keep contract cycle in mind; compare to national trends.
Depreciation	Accounting	Tax versus book basis, replacement versus historical cost base	Time series	Don't forget to include investment tax credits.
Marketing costs	Marketing	Promotional costs, discounts, allowances; service costs	Market research, trend analysis	Check competitor trends, assess competitive intensity first.
Product price	Sales	Gross sales price versus plant netback	Market research, trend analysis	Market-based price forecasting key; be careful of cost-based forecasts; margin trends better.

Item	Department	Data	Method	Notes
Packaging costs	Purchasing	Package form, filling, labeling costs	Time series	Check marketing for possible changes.
Equipment costs	Purchasing	Maintenance plus installation of new equipment	Time series	Repair frequency often determines replacement rate.
Transportation costs	Sales	Freight rates by type of carrier	Trend analysis	Deregulation has created a free market.
Environmental costs	Production	Operating costs for new equipment changing regulation	Trend analysis	Plan on continuing tightening of regulations.
Overhead costs	Accounting	Staffing plans	Time series	Staffing moves with the business cycle.
Coproduct credits	Production	Coproduct price trends, recovery rates	Market research, trend analysis	Coproduct credits often control profits; spend a little more time on this to improve forecasting results.
Yield or reject rate	Production	Process changes, quality levels	Time series	How tight will specification go? Which ones cost and which ones don't?
Scrap/salvage value	Accounting	Scrap price or age and condition of equipment	Market research, trend analysis	Only applies if there is a real market in scrap or secondhand equipment.
Industry forecasts				
Demand	Marketing	Industry growth including substitution and new uses	Market research, trend analysis	Growth businesses key of market saturation; mature products are tied to the economic cycle.
Raw material supply	Purchasing	Supply/demand outlook for current and alternative materials	Market research, trend analysis	Commodities move in cycles; value-added products move with labor and inflation.

TABLE 1 *(continued)*

Forecasting for Capital Budgeting

Type of forecast	Primary historical data source	Key factors controlling forecasts	Forecasting methodology	Comments
Competitive cost structure	Production	Costs/margins of each producer	Market research, trend analysis	A good analysis here gives you an industry supply curve to work with.
Pricing trends	Marketing	Value to customers, alternatives, supply/demand outlook	Market research, trend analysis	For clues, cross-reference power of buyer/supplier with value to customer and his alternatives.
Competitive products Performance trends	Sales	Product changes, service outlook	Market research, trend analysis	What does the market want versus what can suppliers deliver.
Price trends	Sales	Supply/demand outlook, customer options	Market research, trend analysis	Is this a direct substitution? Have costs or value added controlled prices in its primary markets?
Marketing trends	Marketing	Changes expected for 4 Ps: product/price/performance/place	Market research, trend analysis	Identify future emphasis by competitor; check your strategy and estimate costs.
Competitive position	Marketing	Effectiveness of current market strategy in changing market share	Market research, trend analysis	Current position reflects past strategies; future position based on current strategies.
Customer requirements	Sales	Pressures and constraints affecting customers	Market research, trend analysis	Changes in quality and service requirements are best measured in terms of costs.

Industry maturity	Marketing	Growth rate of demand and potential for change	Market research, trend analysis	Forecasting assumptions and methodology are dependent on business maturity.
Competitive intensity	Marketing	Power of supplier, producer, buyers	Market research, trend analysis	A key analysis to differentiate forces controlling the business environment.
Product obsolescence	Marketing	Customer alternatives; R&D on substitutes	Market research, trend analysis	There is a natural lag time associated with the introduction of a new product or process.
Process obsolescence	Production	R&D on new processes	Market research, trend analysis	Use past experience to help forecast the rate of change.
Macroeconomic forecasts				
National GNP	Planning	Interest rates, money supply	Econometric models, input-output models	Choose your philosophy and state your assumptions.
Regional GNP	Planning	Regional industrial development patterns	Econometric models, input-output models	Structural changes in the economy are critical to regional forecasts.
Demographic trends	Planning	Birth rate, mortality regional shifts	Time series	Once thought to be the easiest of forecasts but not now. Key to product demand forecasts.
Inflation	Planning	Money supply, budget deficits	Panel consensus, Delphi	State your assumptions and move on.
Energy outlook	Purchasing	Crude oil, natural gas, LPG, and coal supply/demand pattern	Panel consensus, Delphi	National policy can distort supply/demand and price outlook; start with the free market outlook and then adjust.

TABLE 1 (*concluded*)

Forecasting for Capital Budgeting

Type of forecast	Primary historical data source	Key factors controlling forcasts	Forecasting methodology	Comments
Capital spending pattern	Planning	National and industry operating rate, profitability, growth	Time series, panel consensus	The "herd instinct" controls both national and industry investment cycles.
Government policy trends	Planning	National development priorities, industry support policies	Panel consensus, historical analogy	Shift from emphasis on employment to emphasis on investment will have a big impact on U.S. future.
World trade trends	Marketing	Regional investment patterns, changing competitive position	Time series, econometric models	Fluctuating currency values can override basic competitive strengths and weaknesses in the short term.
Corporate financial forecasts				
Corporate cash flow	Accounting	Profit and investment trends	Planning and budgets, trend analysis	Compare the corporate plan with past history; then adjust for changing economic conditions.
Corporate sources and uses of funds	Finance	Cash flow, dividends policy, working capital requirements, capital plans	Planning and budgets, trend analysis	Here is where all the forecasting errors are either canceled out or greatly magnified.
Corporate borrowing plans	Finance	Debt-to-equity ratios	Planning and budgets, trend analysis	Keep in mind interest rate cycles to improve forecast timing.

Item	Department	Data	Method	Comment
Corporate dividend policies	Finance	Profit trends, stock values, investment profiles	Panel consensus	A stockholder profile and the background of directors will help in forecasting dividend policy.
Corporate strategy	Planning	Corporate objectives	Panel consensus	This comes first.
Corporate forecasts				
Facilities cost	Accounting	Real estate values, lease costs, corporate growth	Planning and budgets, trend analysis	Corporate image plays a role here.
Communications costs	Accounting	Telephone, telex volume, rates, regional expansion	Planning and budgets, trend analysis	Substantial differences exist between manufacturing and service businesses.
Transportation costs	Accounting	Air fares, car lease costs, trip frequency	Planning and budgets, trend analysis	Is this a controllable cost or a sales cost?
Computer hardware	Accounting	Central computer demand, core and peripheral utilization	Planning and budgets, trend analysis	Purchase versus leasing versus on-line services.
Computer software	Accounting	Diversity of corporate system requirements	Planning and budgets, trend analysis	In-house systems groups versus canned programs.
R&D	Planning	Product/process R&D, trends, and priorities	Panel consensus	Do R&D programs support corporate strategy?
Accounting/legal	Accounting	Accounting and litigation workload	Time series	Meeting internal and external reporting requirements fixes a minimum workload.
Staff productivity	Planning	Staffing trends, corporate workload	Time series	At what level is productivity highest?

3

Business Planning: How to Balance Major Investment Strategies

David B. Uman

Management Advisory Group

*T*his chapter will be concerned with the planning of the business portfolio of a diversified growth company. Here we shall be concerned with the planning of strategy for aggregations of businesses.[1] This topic is further limited to planning issues that arise at the *corporate level* in a diversified growth company. It is important to state the limitations of the topic.

First, by limiting the area of discussion to diversified companies, it is clear that we are concerned with businesses that have two levels of planning: (1) corporate planning and (2) business segment planning.

It is quite obvious that the optimization of corporate objectives is not going to result from aggregating the plans of each diverse element if the plans for each of the separate business segments (or strategic business units, (SBUs) are made on the basis of an optimization of the objectives of each SBU's managers. For this reason, therefore, the corporate level planning has to provide a "portfolio management" function in order to integrate the two levels of planning.

The portfolio management function in corporate level plans (1) formulates objectives, (2) allocates resources, and (3) coordinates actions so that the lower level of planning, the SBU, has a basis for planning in a way that will be optimal for the corporation.

This chapter discusses the aspect of planning that relates to diversified growth companies.

The phrase *growth company* is Wall Street jargon. The universe referred to is the same universe that the securities analyst refers to with this phrase.

The concept of growth implies an increase in something with respect to time. Please note a significant distinction that is incorporated into a definition of a growth company. The term *growth company* describes those companies which achieve an increase in earnings per share over time. According to this definition, an increase in sales, profits, market share, or in any other measurement is not sufficient to characterize a growth company. Only growth of earnings per share counts.

Having given a definition of a growth company, what shall be said about planning for growth is equally appropriate to a diversified or nondiversified growth company.

We will discuss here the set of planning problems that arise when one superimposes planning for earnings-per-share growth on the diversified company. The discussion begins with a review of the earnings-per-share growth objective and then moves to portfolio management problems.

For our purposes, we are looking at the planning process from the viewpoint of the *corporate* level as opposed to the *operating* level. We are drawing a distinction between the planning of the business strategies at each of the diverse components of the company, the SBUs, and the *grand strategy* of the company.

We shall explain the earnings-per-share growth objective in the way that the corporate planner has to explain this objective to his fellows in management. This communication difficulty is a major problem for the planner. It has been useful to explain the earnings-per-share growth objectives in this way.

The basic corporate planning problem in a diversified growth company is that of orchestrating the performance of a number of separate business units into a unified earnings-per-share performance. The effect of each unit's performance has to be coordinated so that the growth results are spaced over time in order to create and sustain

FIGURE 1

Orchestrating a Portfolio of Businesses

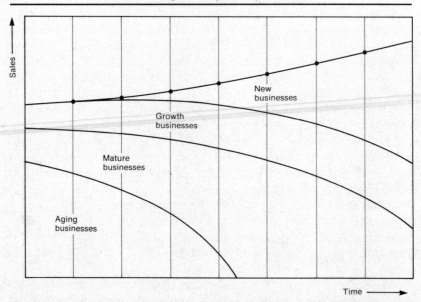

credibility of the investment market's expectations. The effect of the timing of performance is critical to the expectations. Please keep that in mind as we move on.

We will now explore earnings-per-share growth strategies (see Figure 1). We can start by looking at the earnings-per-share equation. The complete form of the equation is as follows:

$$\frac{\text{Earnings}}{\text{Shares}} = \frac{\text{Capital}}{\text{Shares}} \times \frac{\text{Sales}}{\text{Capital}} \times \frac{\text{Earnings}}{\text{Sales}}$$

or

$$\text{EPS} = \text{Capital per share} \times \text{Capital turnover} \times \text{Margin}$$

You will note that the last two terms are those of the ROI equation:

$$\frac{\text{Sales}}{\text{Capital}} \times \frac{\text{Earnings}}{\text{Sales}} = \frac{\text{Earnings}}{\text{Capital}} = \text{ROI}$$

1. We can determine the direction and magnitude of the growth rate of each factor; that is, the sign of and the compound percentage change of profit margins.

2. We can determine the relative contribution of each factor upon the earnings-per-share growth rate; that is, a certain increase in turnover contributed X percent of an earnings-per-share growth of Y percent.

A measurement technique has been developed that enables us, through the use of natural logarithms, to compute growths. Time-sharing systems, new hand-held scientific electronic calculators, and microcomputer systems provide easy access to this technique. In effect, we determine the compound growth rate percentage of each element of earnings-per-share turnover and margin. We then can determine the ratio of the growth of each factor to the growth in earnings per share. These weighted contributions can be added to show the additive influence of the various factors on earnings per share. This technique is called *growth factor analysis*. The following figure is an example of a 10-year growth factor analysis of a typical strategic business unit. As can be seen, it shows the allocation of profit growth from each of the three earnings growth factors: capital per share, turnover, and margin. (See Figure 2.)

Let us now apply this analytic method to the problems of portfolio management in a diversified growth company.

The first obvious observation about the grand strategy of a growth company is that the company has to have a growth objective. That growth objective must be stated as growth rate of earnings per share.

Note that these objective requirements make it imperative that the planning function be very sensitive to the timing of earnings results. We are trying to control earnings changes in respect to time. The *timing* of earnings realization assumes the same degree of importance as the *magnitude* of earnings.

In a diversified company, earnings are the result of the aggregate performance of a number of different businesses. A portfolio of different businesses has to be *balanced* in such a way that their combined results will yield the *timed* stream of earnings increases. Thus, our portfolio management role in planning at the corporate level is one of developing a basis for allocating capital to the SBUs and making policy decisions concerning the earnings affecting strategies of the component units to control the timed earnings of the SBUs. In other words, we balance our portfolio by (1) allocating capital and (2) selecting strategies.

FIGURE 2

Growth factor analysis: 10 years

	1981 actual	1982 actual	1983 actual	1984 actual	1985 est.	1986 plan	1987 plan	1988 plan	1989 plan	1990 plan
Percent net profit growth (decline)	—	(5.15)%	21.61 %	8.91 %	19.80%	14.11 %	21.43 %	17.24%	15.29%	17.81%
Sensitivity index	—	100	100	100	100	100	100	100	100	100
Allocation of profit percent change to asset change	—	6.06 %	21.46 %	18.84 %	10.73%	18.32 %	15.53 %	10.02%	7.27%	8.02%
Sensitivity index	—	(118)	99	211	54	130	72	58	48	45
Allocation of profit percent change to turnover change	—	(.17)%	(9.55)%	(6.44)%	2.89%	.42 %	(.27)%	2.83%	6.57%	7.27%
Sensitivity index	—	3	(44)	(72)	15	3	(1)	16	43	41
Allocation of profit percent change to margin change	—	(11.04)%	9.69 %	(3.48)%	6.18%	(4.63)%	6.17 %	4.39%	1.45%	2.52%
Sensitivity index	—	214	45	(39)	31	(33)	29	25	9	14

How do we define the criteria for portfolio balancing? This task requires us to specify for each given time period how much capital we can make available and what results have to be achieved with that capital. This is easier to do than you may think.

If we have an objective of a particular earnings-per-share growth rate, we can quantify what earnings we are seeking in each future time interval. If we know the earnings objectives by time period, we can derive from that estimates of the capital available in any time interval. If we know how much capital will be available, we can specify what return-on-investment level we have to realize in operations to sustain the growth rate. That ROI rate can serve as a guide to selecting strategies for the SBUs. In other words, we take the earnings-per-share equation for any time period

$$\text{EPS} = \text{Capital per share} \times \text{Turnover} \times \text{Margin}$$

and solve for ROI:

$$\text{Solve for ROI: } \frac{\text{EPS}}{\text{CPS}} = \text{Turnover} \times \text{Margin} = \text{ROI.}$$

Earnings-per-share growth objectives weighted toward dependence upon increases in capital per share are more conservative than those weighted toward increases in ROI, but such a growth pattern is highly dependent upon delivering the right amount of earnings on schedule. This means that investment and development projects have to be completed on time. It further means that the profit flow must be held to a schedule. We feel that such conditions make the use of two management tools essential. These tools are (1) *a project scheduling and control system* and (2) *a flexible budgeting system* wherein failure in performance of one unit can be adjusted for in the performance requirements of other units. In other words, the short-term planning techniques have to be integrated with the long-term planning techniques. The use of flexible budgeting that is reactive to the company's overall performance has major implications for the planning and control system which are not going to be discussed except for one aspect, that of discretionary development expenditures.

A *discretionary development expenditure* is defined as an expenditure undertaken at management's discretion in the expectation that it will enhance the company's future competitive position. When a discretionary expenditure is undertaken, the action reduces current reported profits. Such actions include research and development of new products and processes, market building actions, and so on.

Conceptually, we are looking at the earnings equation in this form:

	Operating profit
Less	Discretionary development
=	Pre-tax profit
Less	Income tax
=	Earnings

The three factors controlling earnings are (1) operating profit, (2) discretionary development, and (3) income tax rate.

From the planning point of view, we are extremely concerned with discretionary expenditures. On the one hand, these expenditures are most readily manipulable to produce short-term earnings improvements. On the other hand, the availability of future growth opportunity and the enhancement of competitive position depend on the allocation and management of discretionary development expenditures.

The formal planning system of almost every company includes procedures for approving and allocating capital expenditures. Capital-per-share and ROI objectives for a corporation are processes relating to the capital allocation system. It is a rare company in which we find a system which can fulfill the analogous functions of (1) quantifying the total amount of discretionary development expenditures of the company that may be possible in the future and (2) allocating these expenditures among the component businesses by reviewing the nature of the discretionary development expenditures and quantifying the magnitude and timing of expected returns from such expenditures.

The key decisions for corporate-level planning in a diversified growth company involve allocating discretionary expenditures so as to realize the earnings-per-share growth objectives. The timing of discretionary development expenditures and the scheduling of the payback from such activities control earnings-per-share performance. It cannot be left to the individual business units of the company to follow their own ideas about optimization of results. *The payoff for the corporation is in terms of corporate performance, not unit performance.*

In order to provide a basis for corporate-level control of growth, it is necessary to:

1. Break down the business for planning purposes into business segments which will be characterized as SBUs.

2. Classify each SBU in terms of the attractiveness of the market environment as an expression of opportunity and then determine the relative competitive position. This entails, among other things: (*a*) assessment of the stage of the life cycle in the market and (*b*) determining the potential payoffs of the three basic strategy options of harvest, hold, and build.[2]

3. We balance the portfolio's earnings-per-share growth expectations by making careful strategy choices for the component SBUs which fit the corporate earnings-per-share growth objectives.

The balancing of a portfolio of diverse businesses in order to yield the optimum corporate earnings-per-share growth performance must necessarily involve the intervention of corporate-level decision making in respect to the choice of strategies in the individual SBUs. The corporate pool of capital is limited, as is the corporate pool for discretionary development spending. Decisions have to be made as to which units will be allocated the scarce resources. The decisions must be made on the basis of the timing of outlays and the schedule of expected results. This necessarily implies a basis for conflict between the corporate-level planner and the operating-level planner. Corporate needs may demand a harvest strategy when the operating manager still perceives that a growth strategy is rewarding.

In a diversified company there is a natural tendency toward decentralized management. Decentralization seems a natural way of shaping the management apparatus to cope with differences in operating units. However, the decentralization tends to have a historical base. In a growing business often the profit centers, which are established as units of administration, tend to develop internal subdivisions, each of which is a separate unit from the point of view of strategy planning. Thus, as times goes on, the historical administrative unit set up as a profit center develops its own portfolio management problems. The successful divisions have money for discretionary development expenditures, but the hard-pressed division does not. In a decentralized company the corporate management can lose control of its power to allocate discretionary expenditures unless it can look at the fundamental units of strategy decision, the SBUs, and decide what strategy options are appropriate to the corporation's grand strategy. This does not mean, however, that corporate-level planning can undertake the role of creating strategy options for the SBUs. This task will continue to be a role of operating-level planning. However, if the corporate growth goals require considering a variety of options, the operating-level planners must present a choice.

Let us look now at how we review our business portfolio. Figure 3 shows the familiar PIMS par matrix.[3] It shows some of the businesses in a diversified company's portfolio. You will note that it includes both good and bad businesses in order to show the diversity of the portfolio.

The par concept is very valuable in assessing a portfolio. It is quite obvious that the businesses in the upper right of the matrix are out-

FIGURE 3

Deviation from Par ROI

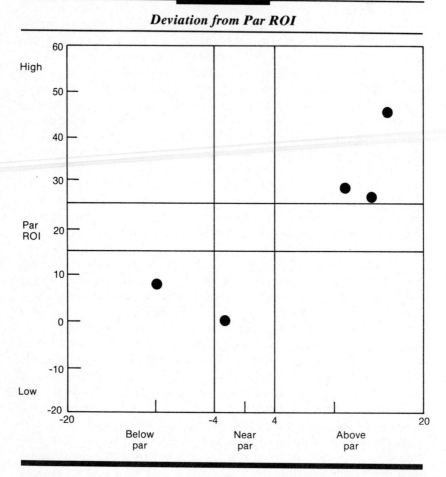

standing performers. Here the corporation concentrates its attention in terms of growth potential and resource allocation—the two key activities aimed at maximizing its earnings growth.

There is another way of reviewing the growth potential of a portfolio. It can be viewed in terms of a series of crosstables that enable an assessment of the relative strengths and weaknesses in a portfolio.

Let's look at these crosstables. The first table (see Figure 4) reviews the portfolio in terms of the attractiveness of the environment and the competitive strength of the business. Factors considered in attractiveness of the environment include short- and long-term market growth rate, industry concentration, and instability of the environment

FIGURE 4

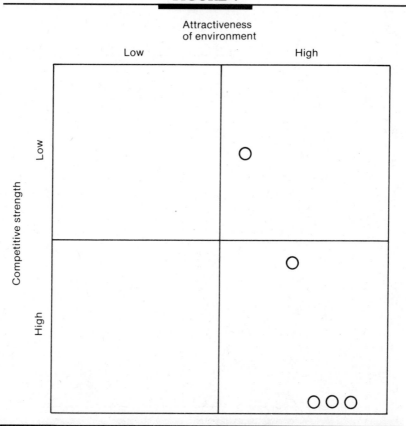

to economic and technological change. Strength of competitive position considers market share, customer dependency, and relative profitability. As you can see, the lower right-hand box is the position to be in.

The second table (see Figure 5) reviews the portfolio in terms of the differentiation of competitive position and the investment return. Factors considered in differentiation of competitive position include relative price and quality, scale advantages of R&D marketing, and the cost structure of the business. Investment return considers the profitability and capital intensity of the business. Once again, you will notice that the good businesses cluster.

The third table (see Figure 6) reviews the portfolio in terms of the attractiveness of the environment and the expansion potential. The attractiveness of the environment has already been discussed. Factors

FIGURE 5

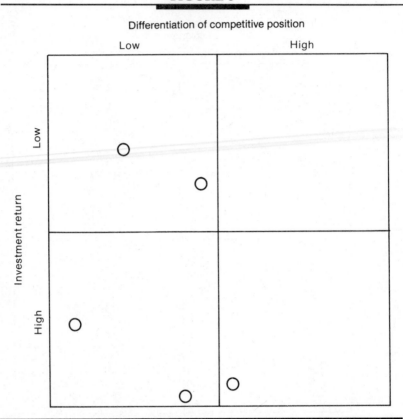

Differentiation of competitive position

considered in expansion potential include capacity utilization, market growth, capital intensity, age of equipment, and return on assets. Here you will note the same clustering.

The fourth table (see Figure 7) reviews the portfolio in terms of the desperation factor and competitive strength of the businesses. We have already discussed competitive strength. The desperation factor relates to how desperate business and economic conditions are within the industry or market segment of the business. It includes value added to investment, market growth, capacity utilization, relative market share, and age of the equipment within a business—factors that relate to how desperate a business is to take radical action in the marketplace.

The final table (see Figure 8) reviews the portfolio in terms of the current strategic trend and signal. The current strategic trend includes factors relating to the current trend of the business such as market share change, vertical integration increases or decreases, changes in

FIGURE 6

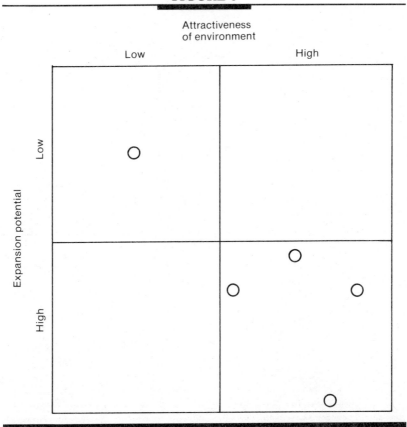

profit, margins, and capital intensity. The current strategic signal reflects the payoff expectations, mostly obtained from PIMS strategy sensitivity reports, of increases in market share, vertical integration, and investment intensity.

Let us review, then, what has been covered.

The success of the diversified growth company is dependent upon its ability to (1) quantify reasonable objectives for each time period as a grand strategy; (2) turn these grand strategy objectives into criteria for setting objectives for the component SBUs; (3) determine the strategy options available to the separate SBUs; (4) assess the outcomes of the capital flows, discretionary development expenditures, and earnings; and (5) then make choices which balance its portfolio to yield the desired objectives over time.

FIGURE 7

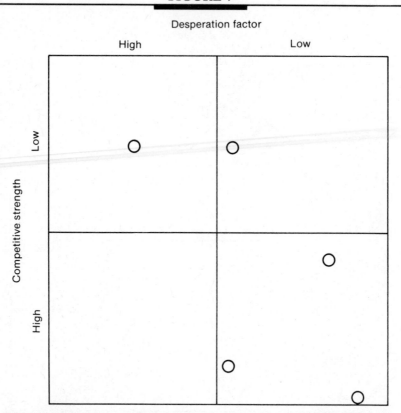

A final observation here is that the corporate-level planner is performing only an analytic role in this process. He is processing information. Most of the information needed for the planning process must be supplied by others. The reliability of the informational inputs is critical. For this reason, great emphasis must be placed on the methods of collecting and assessing the informational inputs. Three techniques of information analysis enhance the reliability of the information we are dealing with: (1) systems that allow us to estimate and control the schedule of operational, capital investment, and development programs such as PERT/CPM; (2) systems that allow us to make independent assessments of market opportunities and competitive posture such as PIMS; and (3) systems for assessing the complex probabilistic outcomes of decisions taken under conditions of uncertainty, such as

FIGURE 8

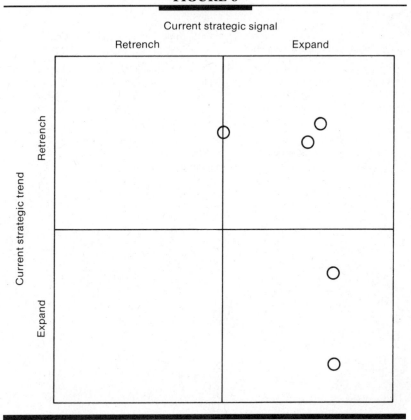

Monte Carlo simulation. Without these tools, the corporate planning job is nearly impossible.

The important thing to note about all of these tools is that they provide an objective analytic process. The sources of the inputs are largely at the operational level of management. The analytic method applies rational techniques of assessing the information. Using such techniques is the key to the successful conduct of the corporate planning role in the diversified company.

NOTES

[1] By *aggregations of businesses* we mean groups of companies, divisions, or separately definable business segments.

[2] These strategy options are used in the long-term PIMS strategic planning study developed by The Strategic Planning Institute, Cambridge, Massachusetts, and explained in detail in the following article: Sidney Schoeffler, Robert D. Buzzell, and Donald Heany, "Impact of Strategic Planning on Profit Performance," *Harvard Business Review*, March–April 1974, pp. 137–45.

[3] The PAR Report used in the PIMS Strategic Planning Study establishes a projected ROI using the PIMS model that can be compared to other firms facing equivalent market and industry conditions and occupying a similar market position.

4

Innovation Planning: How to Plan Major R&D Outlays

Alan Fusfeld

Pugh Roberts Associates, Inc.

Breffni Tomlin

University College, Dublin

INTRODUCTION

*I*nnovation is a process that extends downstream of R&D. It is not complete until a new product or process is successfully commercialized. Thus, it involves engineering, manufacturing, and marketing as well as R&D. Furthermore, R&D is only one route to developing new products and processes: one of the major decisions in innovation strategy is that between independent internal development and use of external mechanisms such as licensing, joint venture, and acquisition. Capital budgeting involves choice, and making decisions about R&D budgets necessarily involves attention to the considerations we mentioned. In choosing a portfolio of projects for funding in R&D, for instance, decision makers must pay attention to the costs, success probabilities, and benefits in manufacturing and marketing. Furthermore, because of the integrated nature of the innovation process, decision making necessarily involves inputs from all the different areas involved and ought therefore to be a group process with diverse participants, rather than to be confined within the R&D function itself.

In summary, we believe that budgetary decisions about R&D are necessarily embedded in a process of decisions about innovation. Our chapter will therefore extend its coverage beyond that implied in the title, to address the topic of capital budgeting for innovation.

The Decision Problem

In principle the set of decisions involved in budgeting for innovation is the most complex in the field of management. To the standard difficulties of capital budgeting are added those springing from the nature of innovation itself.

In practice most companies do not face major problems because the number of businesses in which they are represented and the number of projects they have to consider in any budgetary period are small. However, companies generating large numbers of projects face these problems in all their complexity. Since they are analytically intractable, we shall be describing ways to simplify dealing with them, without producing grossly suboptimal solutions.

The first problem facing a decision unit is deciding how much to spend. Unless some figure is set external to the unit or arbitrarily fixed (both of which we later recommend against), the decision process is necessarily iterative. The unit will attempt to achieve some balance of cost and benefits which is optimal or at least acceptable. At one extreme it might decide to maximize benefits in the cheapest way, that is, to fund all acceptable projects and seek the minimum-cost way of executing them. At the other it might decide to minimize outlay subject to an acceptable level of benefit, that is, to fund only the cheapest acceptable set of projects, done in the most efficient way.

Many companies will be unable to afford the first approach: active firms usually have far more potential projects than they can possibly fund. Most companies will want to do better than the second, since there are often programs that will increase benefits without greatly increasing cost. Whether implicitly or explicitly, therefore, budgeting at any level involves zeroing in on a financial commitment between the extremes.

The difficulty the decision makers face in this situation is that both costs and benefits are uncertain, complex, and interrelated. If the number of projects available relative to resources is small, it will be possible to make near-optimal decisions using simple procedures. However, when the number becomes large, we have the problem described in Galbraith's classic article, "Decision Making: An Information-Processing View." Galbraith suggests that, at a given state of information-processing technology, the load imposed by facing numerous interdependent uncertain events becomes excessive—so that the decision unit must go in one of two ways.[1] One is to increase investment in human resources and hardware in an attempt to deal with the load. This obviously becomes costly. The other is to reduce the load, largely by creating autonomous units that face fewer events. This can be costly in terms of lower performance, caused by ignoring important interdependence or forfeiting economies of scale.

Until recently, the state of the art in information processing was such that most companies were forced to go the second route in making decisions about innovation. This explains in part why most of the literature on R&D management states that management science approaches to the problem are little used in practice, even where they appear promising in principle. However, the increasing power and availability of small computers, the increasing power of analytic approaches and availability of associated software, and the increasing number of executives versed in and comfortable with their use suggest that we will see an increase in the use of these approaches.

In most companies, however, these conditions do not yet exist. So, they go the other route, that is, simplifying the structure of the problem by breaking it into more or less independent parts, using simplified decision procedures within each part. This is the line we will follow, while referring to management science approaches where they appear to be practical and hold promise for dealing with local problems.

Structure of Discussion

Deploying resources for effective innovation involves decision at three levels—strategic, operational, and tactical.

Strategic decisions are long-term decisions about the areas of business and technology in which the corporation will engage, about the nature of its engagement, and hence about the likely calls on its funds in support of its aspirations. Decision making at this level involves also the promulgation of decision rules to guide operational and tactical decisions.

Operational decisions are shorter-term statements of financial intent to fund specific programs of activity. Tactical decisions are ongoing decisions to initiate, terminate, or reschedule specific projects, so as to maximize benefits subject to constraints on real resources.

It could be argued that capital budgeting is an operational decision and that it is unnecessary to discuss strategic decisions. We believe this would be wrong. Operational decisions made without clear strategic guidance will produce bad results, however sophisticated the way in which they are made.

The rest of this chapter deals with strategic decisions. We will discuss the issues involved in designing an appropriate decision process and in using it appropriately: (*a*) what the decision involves, (*b*) who should make it, (*c*) when it should be made, and, most comprehensively, (*d*) how to make it—estimating and matching resource requirements and demands, and choosing combinations of benefits and resource commitments.

STRATEGIC DECISION MAKING

We argued, based on our experience, that strategic guidance is essential to effective budgeting. The most recent study of new product management by Booz-Allen & Hamilton strongly supports our argument.[2] They show that the number of ideas considered in order to produce a commercially successful product has fallen dramatically since their 1968 study, from 58 to 7. They attribute this improvement, and the accompanying drop in funds spent on unsuccessful products, to the fact that most companies began in the interval to use a formal new product process, "usually beginning with identifying the new product strategy."

We say that a clear strategy serves many functions in the innovation process. It directs the search for new ideas to relevant areas. It helps screen out ideas with little hope of later success. And it simplifies the process of more detailed decision making by providing a structured framework within which it can be conducted, together with rules that guide it.

Output of Strategic Decision Making

What will later decision makers know as a result of the strategic decision process? If it is properly conducted, they should have:

1. A statement of the categories of business in which the corporation intends to engage, and the technologies it intends to deploy.

2. The company's strategic intentions and aspirations in each area and their implications for product and process innovation.

3. The general magnitude of spending on innovation in each area and its broad disposition, both between internal R&D and external sourcing, and between long- and short-run R&D.

4. A statement of the broad criteria to be applied in selecting individual projects and project portfolios for funding.

We should emphasize that the spending figures quoted at this stage are preliminary. They represent an estimate of what the corporation is willing to spend to realize its objectives over the planning horizon. They thus serve as a guide to annual budgeting and to more detailed innovation decisions. They represent a statement of broad financial intent, rather than the specific commitment of funds implied in annual budgeting.

The Timing of Strategic Decisions

Strategy implies a degree of continuity. Corporations do not redefine their strategy every day. The time period between strategy definitions will vary from one industry to another, depending on the rate of technological and other changes. We suggest that no corporation can afford to let more than five years go by without a significant radical review of strategy. In the meantime it should formally evaluate its defined strategy in the light of environmental change and company performance.

The length of the strategic planning horizon will obviously vary also with the nature of the industry and the size of the firm. Given the lags inherent in innovation, we suggest that anything less than five years will be inappropriate for most organizations.

Obviously, the ongoing review and periodic redefinition of strategy must take place early enough in the year to allow adequate lead time for the preparation of annual budgets.

Who Makes Strategic Decisions

Decisions about product and process innovation policy affect all corporations in the most fundamental way. The result of these decisions defines the company's concrete relationship with its environment: the products and services it offers, the inputs it needs, and its competitive possibilities.

Decisions as central and as all-embracing as these must obviously issue ultimately from an executive team at the highest level of the corporation, whoever else may be involved in their formulation.

If a company is small and homogeneous, a single team comprising the CEO, the head of R&D, and the executives in charge of marketing, manufacturing, finance, and human resources can be responsible for overseeing the preparation of the strategic financial plan, and for agreeing and ratifying its final content.

In larger, more diversified companies, it will be necessary to conduct the process in two stages because of the size and complexity of the problem. We suggest that the company be divided for purposes of innovation planning into strategic business units, that is, into units that are relatively independent of one another and that are themselves large or complex enough to make strategic planning a substantial chore. In a divisionalized corporation, each division is likely to constitute a unit. In a unitary corporation, significant business areas or product groups can be chosen.

We recommend that planning innovation at the SBU level should be the responsibility of a team comprising executives of appropriate rank from each major function within the unit. For a division, the team responsible for overseeing and accepting the unit's plan would include the divisional CEO, the divisional heads of R&D, marketing, manufacture, finance, and human resource planning. We suggest also that each team include a representative of similar rank from corporate headquarters staff, to ensure a degree of coordination and to prevent obvious suboptimization. In the case where different units are involved in similar marketplaces or technologies, the same representative might be a member of several teams.

Planning strategy within each business unit will, of course, not be enough. In the first place, there may be areas of business or technology the corporation wishes to enter that do not fall within the ambit of any division, or that require investments too large for any division to consider. Furthermore, divisions will often avoid spending on long-run research, especially if they are under tight financial performance control from corporate level. Because of this, it will be necessary to have a team at corporate headquarters that will draw up plans for corporate new business ventures and corporate technology investments. Let us call this team the corporate innovation unit.

The sum of the plans and financial activities drawn up at stage one by these strategic business units and the corporate innovation unit does not constitute a corporate strategic plan or budget. These separate plans must first be reviewed to see if there are significant areas of overlap, significant areas not covered, or significant opportunities for synergy. We suggest that this initial review be carried out in a forum consisting of the chief corporate officers and the heads of each planning unit.

The final stage is the most difficult. It is quite likely, even after the opportunities for combining activities have been examined, that the cost of the plans exceeds what the corporation can afford. The consequent refusals to approve proposals are likely to affect the business units selectively.

Selective cuts are a very sensitive issue, so every effort must be made to ensure that business unit managers believe they were made fairly and in the interests of the corporation as a whole. Divisional managers will be particularly sensitive to what they see as undue influence by staff officers at corporate headquarters. We therefore recommend that these selective cuts be the clear decision of the corporation's CEO. The CEO will, of course, consult with corporate vice presidents for technology, marketing, finance, human resources, and the head of strategic planning. Care should be taken to balance these consultations with detailed discussions with the head of each business unit.

Since the decision to make selective cuts will probably mean that some strategic business units will be hit more heavily than others, the CEO must make a ranking showing the importance to the corporation of each SBU. This topic is dealt with in the subsections below on prioritizing investments. The process of prioritizing plans—at both business unit and corporate levels—will ordinarily require the input of internal staff specialists, and often of external consultants, as well as more junior line management. These plans remain a line responsibility, however, and we have recommended teams whose composition will reflect the fact that the final content of plans, together with the process by which they are arrived at, should be visibly under the control of senior line management, divisional and corporate.

The Process of Strategic Decision Making

The process of making decisions about innovation strategy is iterative, interactive, and incremental. It is iterative because we believe that a company should first examine what it can realistically aspire to do, then see what it can hope to finance, redefining both until it arrives at a statement of strategic intent. The process is interactive because it involves input from and debate among different specialists. And it is incremental because most organizations have existing resources and ongoing commitments which cannot be changed radically in the short term.

The most basic question a consultant can be asked is, "How much should we spend on R&D?'' Companies themselves often answer this question in global terms by applying a simple formula, for example, by comparing themselves with others in the industry in terms of total spending, spending as a percentage of sales, or spending as a percentage of profits. Other companies do not ask the question but simply alter their historic level at the margin, often through a process of political bargaining.

We see two things wrong with these methods, if used alone. First, they are global; and second, they are simplistic and misleading, except as a very rough first cut. *It is a mistake in our view to start by setting an overall budget figure. We believe that the organization's total strategic spending should be built up category by category as illustrated below.* We also believe that the figure within each category should be arrived at as described earlier in this section, that is, by deciding first what the organization wishes to do, and then zeroing in on a level of funding that balances realistic aspirations with financial feasibilities. As Twiss[3] and Martin[4] have argued, use of rules of thumb such as those described above leads to misdirection of effort. In the first place, comparison with other companies can be uninformative. Firms in a single industry often differ in their product mix, in their technology base, and in their innovation strategy, all of which makes their spending a poor guide for others.

Formulas such as percentage of sales can be actively misleading. They result in funds being directed toward businesses with the greatest sales volume, which may be mature areas with little scope for further development. Basing spending on profits leaves it open to short-term fluctuation, especially to panic cutbacks in times of crisis, whereas R&D is necessarily an investment in the company's future, using resources which themselves represent a reservoir of experience that cannot easily be renewed. This is not to say that industry comparisons and present spending have no part to play in strategic decisions. They are useful benchmarks for evaluating the results of the "bottom-up" approach.

We see the process of strategic financial planning as involving four steps:

1. Deciding how to break the total innovation effort into categories.
2. Deciding the categories in which the organization wishes to be active.
3. Deciding for each category the nature of these activities, their likely cost, and their funding possibilities.

4. Summing across categories, and allowing for interrelations between categories, before finalizing the plan.

Categorizing innovation. Before beginning the process of categorization, the organization must first divide itself as we suggested above into strategic planning teams.[5] We recommend that each team proceed to categorize its innovative activities as described below, and to build up its planned spending, category by category, before sending its plan to corporate level for review and approval.

A strategic planning unit's total innovative effort can be broken down into a number of categories, arranged in a nested hierarchy. The purpose of this classification is both to simplify the process of producing a strategic plan and to clarify the thrust of the unit's innovative strategy.

Level 1. Technology planning unit. Producing a sensible strategic plan for innovation involves the choice of markets and technologies in which to compete, and selecting an appropriate strategy for investing in the chosen areas. This requires a process of market evaluation, of technology impact assessment, and of competitive strength analysis. These processes are most easily carried out separately for each technology planning unit, as described by Fusfeld.[6]

A TPU is the intersection of an application ("market") with a technology. What the cell contains depends on how—and how widely—the application and technology have been defined. If the definitions have been very broad and generic, the TPU could comprise an entire industry. If the definitions are very narrow, it might comprise a small component of a single product.

The discussion of where, and how widely, to draw these boundaries goes back at least to Leavitt's famous article, "Marketing Myopia," and to the question, "What business are we really in?"[7] The discussion can often sound like philosophic hair splitting. It is, however, important to define the boundaries well: a careful and creative definition will not only simplify technology forecasting and competitive strength assessment but it can suggest interesting business possibilities previously overlooked.

While the specific boundaries can be set only after detailed discussion in each firm, we recommend starting at a level of aggregation that makes sense in view of the business unit's structure, and working down to whatever level of detail is necessary for accurate forecasting and assessment. In one company, for instance, the technology of particle separation had applications in three areas (industrial pollution, commercial filtration and medical filtration) in which the dynamics of innovation were sufficiently different that they constituted three separate technology planning units.

At a given time, the business unit will be represented in particular TPUs. The first strategic decision it faces in innovation is whether it wishes to remain in them or whether it wishes to diversify, either through meeting existing applications with new technologies, extending its existing technology to new applications, or directing new technology to new applications.

This decision is of great strategic importance to the company, and it has direct implication for innovation. We know that the probability of success falls in the order in which we described the diversification modes. This will affect the criteria used later for project evaluation: the decision to accept or reject a specific project involving new technologies in new applications can only be made properly in the light of the company's strategic decision about its involvement in such areas. And the expectations about success, which enter into project evaluation, can be compared meaningfully only within segments which are relatively similar. Furthermore, the appropriate objectives and mode of investment will vary with the novelty of the area, as Roberts and Berry have shown.[8]

Level 2. Product and process innovation. Having defined the TPUs in which the business unit is—or wishes to be—involved, its strategic planning team must decide within each TPU what emphasis it wishes to place on product as against process innovation. This decision will depend in part on where the industry is in terms of its current product/technology life cycle, and on how long it may be before technology imposes a new cycle. Abernathy and Utterback have argued that as soon as a product attains its definitive basic design, the emphasis shifts from product to process innovation as the competitive emphasis shifts from product performance to price.[9] This will remain so until new technology can obsolete the old design by opening the business again to product competition. Companies must be on the alert to developments in technology so that they can make timely adjustments in the balance of their spending.

Level 3. Targeted and untargeted R&D. The team must next decide, within both product and process R&D, how much effort it will direct toward technical support of existing activities; how much toward new projects with a specified commercial target; and how much toward dealing with more general underlying problems, whose solution can later be incorporated in commercially targeted efforts. These decisions will depend on the rate of change of technology, the company's familiarity with it, its competence vis-à-vis its competition, and consequently on its strategic innovative thrust: whether it can realistically aim to be a leader in the TPU, or whether it will prefer one of the follower strategies. Corporations aiming for a leadership position in emerging technologies will spend more money overall and will devote a greater proportion of it to upstream activities.

Level 4. Commercial targets and time. Finally, the decision unit must decide what its commercial targets are over its planning horizon. In more familiar areas, it will be able to state these with a fair degree of precision: a gap analysis, for instance, may show that a shortfall in sales is likely in three to five years, unless a range of products is developed with specific characteristics, targeted at specific market segments. In new areas, the targets and their implications for innovation will be much more tentative: at very early stages, for instance, the unit may indicate that it is willing to commit resources to explore the possible applications of a developing technology, without specifying those applications or when they are expected to bear fruit.

Choosing categories and approaches. A plan for innovation involves deciding which categories of innovation to be active in and how they are to be approached. Producing such a plan will involve analyzing the attraction of existing and potential markets, forecasting and assessing the impact of technological change, and conducting an assessment of competence and competitive strength in marketing and technology.

Market assessment criteria. The type of market in which it is easiest to succeed is one that is growing;[10] that matches technological and marketing resources the firm already has or can acquire easily; and that promises longevity. Obviously the selection of markets "close to home" will be an important part of strategy. Equally, concentrating on such more easily penetrated markets can lead to strategic failure in the longer run. Cooper has shown that aggressive combinations of market- and technology-driven approaches yield the best long-run results, at least for industrial products.[11] Starting close to home makes sense; staying close to home may not.

Technology forecasts. If a business unit is to manage successfully the technological component of its strategy, it must have a good understanding of the timing, magnitude, and direction of the impact of technological change on its base businesses, and of the opportunities it brings to enter new businesses (Fusfeld[12]). Soundly based programs to bring new technology on board presuppose an understanding of its sources and the channels through which it diffuses. Von Hippel has shown that the sources of innovation vary consideraby by industry, as do the chances of appropriating its benefits.[13]

Competitive strength assessment. One of the major causes of new product failure is underestimating the likelihood and strength of competitive reaction. Any program of innovation must be based on a sound understanding of the identity of the real competitors; of the real basis of competition; and of the company's technical competence vis-à-vis these competitors, in terms of the quality and relevance of its staff's qualifications and experience. Clear-sighted answers to these questions will allow the business unit to decide whether it should enter an area, what strategic posture it should adopt, and what scale of investment it needs to make in new technological and other resources to implement its strategy successfully.

FIGURE 1

Optimum Entry Strategies

Market
Factors

	Base	New Familiar	New Unfamiliar
New unfamiliar	Joint venture	Venture capital or Venture nurture or Educational acquisition	Venture capital or Venture nurture or Educational acquisition
New familiar	Internal market development or Acquisition or (Joint venture)	Internal venture or Acquisition or License	Venture capital or Venture nurture or Educational acquisition
Base	Internal base development or (Acquisition)	Internal product development or Acquisition or License	"New style" joint venture

Technologies or services
embodied in the product

FIGURE 2

Episode Scatter on the Familiarity Matrix

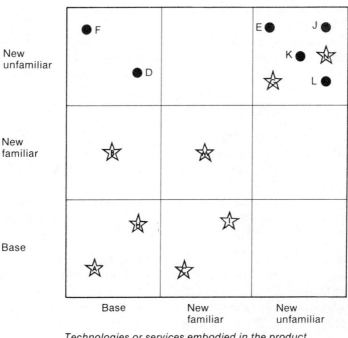

Market
factors

Technologies or services embodied in the product

Key:

☆ = Success

● = Failure

A - F: Internal developments

G - L: Acquisitions

M, N: Minority investments

Selecting an investment mode. When entering a new market or technology the appropriate mode of entry will vary with its novelty. As Figures 1 and 2 from Roberts and Berry show,[14] it is best to enter a very new area in a learning mode, making small initial investments in already established entities (via licensing, joint ventures, and acquisitions) so as to become familiar with the area before making big commitments based on internal R&D.

Costing the strategy. Each strategic planning team must have a clear idea of the resources it needs to implement the provisional strategy and make reasonable estimates of their cost. In applications and technologies with which it is familiar, this will present no real problem: it will have ample historical data on which to base estimates of its spending on targeted, and even on nontargeted, innovation. (The planned spending on targeted innovation will include investments in manufacture and marketing as well as in R&D.) Forecasts of spending on R&D in new areas will have to be based on the best estimates by experienced technologists of what it will cost to achieve the objectives specified for each category of effort. A prudent strategic planning team will at least double even these best estimates if the area is far removed from its current position. (A check ought, of course, to have been made against spending by competitors when conducting the competitive strength assessment. Advice can also be sought from noncompetitive companies applying the same technology.)

When the strategic planning team aggregates its plans and spending estimates across TPUs, it will have a clear idea of the total amount it needs to fund its intended program, of the amount it will spend outside the corporation, and on the size and cost of the R&D establishment it must maintain to implement its strategy.

Confronting corporate financial reality. Even in a decentralized corporation where business units enjoy considerable autonomy in funding their own innovation, there is a need, before finalizing strategic innovation plans, to subject the combined business unit plans to a corporate review. The purpose is three-fold:

1. To see whether items of significant corporate interest have been overlooked by subdividing the planning process.
2. To see whether there is overlap between the separate plans, scope for synergy, or a need for a more determined corporate thrust in a particular direction than any business unit can provide.
3. To see whether the provisional plan can be funded by the corporation without jeopardizing its financial situation, damaging its shareholders' interests, or bringing unwanted changes in control.

It will very likely be true that the totality of divisional plans cannot be funded by the corporation, or that different divisions or business areas wish to be corporate leaders in the same new technologies, or that the sum of the separate divisional efforts in a new technology will not contribute the critical mass and focus needed to give the corporation a significant competitive edge. Even if we assume that each strategic planning team has built up its plans and estimates on the basis of a competent strategic analysis, so that the corporation can decide how to apportion its funds and define responsibilities with some degree of rationality, the discomfort of this process cannot be overemphasized. At this level, the limits of rationality are reached quite early: the uncertanties and difficulty of comparability are so great that the eventual decisions are often reached by a largely political process.

The most painful of these realities is when the plans formulated by the strategic planning teams cannot be financed in full. The way in which this reality is faced and dealt with is likely to depend on the structure of the organization. In a divisionalized corporation where the strategic planning team is likely to be in charge of a financially quasi-autonomous division, each team might prefer to adjust its plan to its own financial possibilities, rather than go to corporate level showing a discrepancy. This can be suboptimal for the corporation, with better-off divisions expanding their plans to use their resources fully, and worse-off divisions cutting much strategically important spending. For this reason we recommended earlier that an executive of appropriate level, from corporate headquarters, be represented with divisional executives on each strategic planning team. In a unified corporation where the strategic planning teams have no financial autonomy, the tendency to adjust plans suboptimally will be less.

On balance, we believe it best if the planning teams produce plans based on their genuine conclusions to a competent strategic analysis, indicating (in the case of autonomous divisions) how much they can afford from their own resources, leaving discrepancies to be remedied at a higher level.

It may be possible to reduce the gap at corporate level by examining areas of overlap or potential synergy between each unit's plans. Thus, different divisions may be planning investments in particular new technologies that could most effectively be handled within a single division or by the corporate R&D facility. We shall assume in what follows that these interdivisional economies have been made and that the corporation is still coming up short.

If the discrepancy between available funds and planned spending is small, a nonselective cut in each decision unit's allocation will be a reasonable way to restore balance. If it is very large (and particularly if the proposed spending on top-priority core programs exceeds what the corporation seems able to afford comfortably), serious consideration must be given to raising additional funds. Assuming the spending plans for core programs have been based on competent assessments of threats to existing businesses, failure to fund them will constitute a

71

threat to the corporation's competitive position and ultimately to its survival.

The most likely situations are where neither small nonselective cuts nor raising additional funds seems appropriate: the discrepancies being too large for one solution and too small for the other (though each can be used as a first cut at reducing the problem). In this case the corporate decision unit will be faced with the need to consider selective cuts in the proposals put forward by the strategic planning teams. This involves first defining the priority of investments, then deciding which to cut most heavily.

Defining investment priorities. As we stated earlier, it may be necessary to cut spending more heavily in some strategic business units than in others. This means that whoever makes this decision must at least have ranked the SBUs in terms of their importance to the corporation.

Whether or not cuts fall more heavily on some units than on others, each unit will probably have to be selective in cutting its own programs since we have assumed that small cuts across the board will not do. Each strategic planning team must therefore rank its priorities, perhaps with the help of general corporate guidelines.

Ranking strategic business units. We have deliberately used the word *ranking* because we believe that, for most corporations, a simple ranking will suffice for strategic decision making. The word *simple* is, however, deceptive, for an attempt at ranking immediately raises the questions of what criteria to use, how to evaluate the units on each criterion, and how to turn these separate evaluations into a single overall score or rank. In short, we encounter here for the first time the problem of multicriteria decisionmaking.

We believe that the same broad criteria apply to evaluating all commercial entities, whatever their level. Thus we believe that roughly the same set can be used to evaluate a whole strategic business unit, a market within an SBU, or a specific product within a market; although, of course, the indicators used and the level of detail involved will vary.

1. *Strategic fit*. The question here is how well the unit fits the general strategic thrust of the business in terms of markets served and technologies employed.
2. *Resource suitability*. The question here is whether the unit has the resources in marketing, manufacturing, and R&D to execute its competitive strategy effectively, or whether it can easily acquire them. An important question, if it has to acquire them, is whether it has the organizational flexibility to integrate them effectively.

3. *Effect on other units.* The question here is whether increasing or decreasing commitment to the unit would have serious negative or positive effect on other units. For example, is it possible to treat the unit safely as a "cash cow"?

4. *Probability of commercial success.* The question here is whether the unit can achieve continuing commercial success by consistently delivering superior products at a competitive price, preferably in growing market segments that it can dominate.

5. *Size of payoff.* This involves rough estimates of the size and timing of sales, profits, cash flow, and returns on investment.

6. *Risk.* This involves consideration of the uncertainty surrounding the payoff estimates, of the size of the investments involved in the unit, and of the dangers of unmanageable competitive response.

The number of strategic units in most corporations is unlikely to be large, almost certainly not greater than 10. With such a small number of objects to be ranked, we suggest that it will be quite easy and quite sufficient to rank the units on each criterion separately, and then to assign them an overall rank. If the number is too large, or if the decision maker finds real difficulty in producing a consistent overall ranking, a more technical method can be considered, for example, the computer-based routine PREFCALC.[15]

It may well be that as a result of this exercise, the decision maker concludes that the SBUs are roughly equal in importance. This simply implies that selectivity must be employed within rather than between SBUs.

We have used the expression *decision maker* in this discussion, and we had earlier suggested that the decision about cuts in plans should rest with the CEO, so as to avoid discontent. This would seem to imply that the ranking of SBUs should be carried out by the CEO alone. The CEO may wish to involve others, but this should be done with care for the consequences: it is probably undesirable that there should be explicit awareness in the corporation of how the SBUs are ranked, unless strategic action necessitates it.

Priorities within SBU. There is a frequent tendency within business units to ration resources by cutting back on research and on long-term development—especially, as we suggested earlier, when they are under stringent financial performance pressure from corporate headquarters. It is by now almost a cliché of business journalism that this practice of eating the seed has hastened the loss of American technical preeminence. Obviously, therefore, a more sophisticated approach is called for.

We recommend that each strategic planning team rank its various business areas or product groups, using the same criteria and the same ranking approach discussed above for assessing SBUs. In this case, however, it will be desirable for each member of the team to carry out a ranking, and then for the team to debate any differences until a consensus is reached.

In the same way the team should rank the various technologies in which it plans to engage, using the following criteria:

1. Probability of technical success in mastering the technology.
2. Commercial impact—size and speed of impact on existing business and breadth of commercial applicability to new business.
3. Timing of results—how long the organization will take to produce results and the readiness of the market to accept them.
4. Proprietary potential—the extent to which the company can hope to master the technology in a commercially defensible way.

Once a rough ranking has been produced, both technologies and markets can be classified as either priority or low priority—a classification as rough as this will do for the decision at hand. The order in which budgetary cuts can be made is shown in Figure 3. (Note in the diagram that nontargeted spending means spending that is not targeted toward producing products or process improvements with defined characteristics. Note also that some spending on technology may not even be designated as serving a particular market, let alone targeted at producing a defined product.)

We suggest that categories of spending be protected against cuts in proportion to their number of stars, that is, the first categories to cut are those marked "0," and so on up to the core programs with three or more stars, for which funding must be found.

It will be seen that we have suggested protection for long-term development and research in priority technologies. Such spending is likely to be a small proportion of the unit's total budget for innovation, so that even small percentage cuts in total spending could have a devastating effect on them if they were singled out. Their small size and long-run importance calls, in our view, for greater protection than larger and less important areas need.

FIGURE 3

	Nature of spending			
	Commercially targeted			Priority for protection[1]
	Short-term	Long-term	Nontargeted	
Priority technologies				
For priority markets	****	***	***	1
For nonpriority markets	**	**	**	2
No market designated	–	–	**	2
Nonpriority technologies				
For priority markets	*	*	*	3
For nonpriority markets	0	0	0	4
No market designated	–	–	0	4

Planning R & D Budget Cuts

[1] Technical support for existing products should also receive high priority for protection against budget cuts.

Choosing investments. We believe that most corporations will seek to minimize conflict by trying to avoid selectivity at the level of the SBU, hoping to "balance the budget" by nonselective cutting of the lowest priority programs of every SBU. We believe that this is a reasonable strategy which needs to be tempered by examining its consequences before finalizing assignments, and we suggest an approach along the following lines.

Step 1. Compare for each SBU the size of its projected spending on priority 4 items with the size of the gap between what it can afford and what it would cost to fund the total strategic plan. If the gap can be closed by cuts in priority 4, make these cuts after checking the following questions:

a. Does the corporation have funds that it could make available to every SBU in order to diminish the size of the cuts?

b. Would the cuts, even in low-priority items, damage an SBU that the corporation feels should be protected? If so, can the corporation channel centrally raised outside funds disproportionately to this SBU? Or can it make selective cuts in SBU plans by permitting some to cut back more lightly than

75

others, and funding the heavier spender out of differential
corporate cash receipts from the SBUs.

If selective cuts are needed, cut the lowest-ranked SBUs most heavily.

Step 2. If cuts in priority 4 items are insufficient to bridge the gap,
go on to contrast the remaining deficit with projected spending on
priority 3 items. Repeat the questions asked in step 1.

Step 3. It is unlikely that it will be necessary to contemplate cuts in
higher-priority items. If this should happen, and especially if priority 1
items are threatened, the company must seriously consider ways of
raising extra finance, as failure to fund at this level constitutes a threat
to its survival.

Conclusion. Decisions to cut whole business units, promising market opportunities, or technical explorations are extremely painful. This
is why we recognize that they are likely to be characterized by a great
deal of emotion, by iterative exploration of different ways to reduce
pain, and by considerable political activity. We recognize that this is
inevitable and that our suggestions on the composition of decision-
making teams, and on the procedures they might follow, will only
inject a degree of rationality into what will always be a difficult process.

The pain and difficulty of drawing up a strategic financial plan for
innovation cause some corporations to flinch away from it. We believe
this is a mistake that increasingly competitive marketplaces and increasingly rapid technical changes will punish severely. Even if the
effort does not result, as we have suggested, in a reasonably detailed
indication of the company's intended efforts in each category of innovation, it will still have helped to clarify the company's situation, and it
will allow some strategic direction to be given to its annual budgeting
and to its technical program management.

If the corporation has worked successfully through this strategic
planning exercise, it will know what order of spending it will incur over
the planning horizon within each business unit (and in its corporate
facilities) and will know within each business unit what categories of
innovation it will fund. Some of this spending will be on external
sources of innovation—joint ventures, acquisitions, purchases of licenses. Most is likely to be on internal development. As a result, each
decision unit—and the corporation as a whole—will know what its
R&D establishment will be: that is, it will know the size and nature of
the facilities it must maintain or build to execute its chosen strategy. To
the extent that this establishment is (put) in place, it will constrain and
simplify annual budgets and program management.

The systematic approach to planning strategic investments in innovation does not preclude rapid, opportunistic responses to fast-moving markets and technologies. However, by thinking through the dynamics of innovation in a particular business, one may perceive such opportunities more readily, and grasp them more realistically, than simply by reacting to events.

Decision Rules for Operations and Tactics

Within the broad strategic framework developed in the previous section, it will be necessary to make annual budgetary dispositions, that is, annual commitments to fund particular portfolios of projects in each spending category. Within this annual budgetary framework, tactical decisions will be made on an ongoing basis, to commit real resources to work on specific projects within each category.

To ensure that these operational and tactical decisions are congruent with the corporation's strategy, it will not be enough to indicate the broad magnitude of funds available to each category of innovation. It is necessary to ensure that the specific portfolios of projects worked on meet the corporation's strategic *performance* criteria, as well as observing its strategic budgetary resource constraints.

Project cost and performance constraints. The corporation may wish to impose performance constraints at the level of the individual project. We suggest that the constraints be developed by the decision units that will apply them, and be ratified at corporate level, after modification if necessary. We suggest that project constraints be stated in terms of cost, success probability, and payoff. Projects that do not fit the corporation's strategy—as indicated in outline by its budgetary intention—will of course be rejected, unless they are of such overwhelming attraction that they should either be accepted by the corporation opportunistically or cause a review of strategy.

The individual *units,* when evaluating projects, may use additional criteria, but the set described here are the only ones for which the *corporation* need consider setting targets.

Cost constraint. Reject any project whose cost is greater than $1/k$ of the budget for its category, where k is a number to be chosen in the light of the category and of the corporation's risk aversion. In a well-understood TPU, the company may feel comfortable spending its whole budget on a single project ($k = 1$); in a poorly understood TPU, it may wish to spread its risks more widely. The corporation may wish to leave some flexibility by adding that expensive projects with low

77

risks and high payoff should be treated as exceptions, to be considered separately rather than routinely rejected.

Success probability constraint. Projects can fail in the marketplace or before they get there. Methods are available for assessing the probability of marketplace success for commercially targeted product developments (Cooper[16]). Obviously, a corporation will reject any project that falls in the category "unlikely to succeed in the market."

It must also concern itself with the probability that a project will fail before it reaches commercialization. Unlike the case of assessing market success, there is no well-founded way to predict the likely success of projects in R&D and manufacture; the best that can be done is to make estimates based on past experience and to compare them with the all-industry average. We know that approximately 33 percent of all targeted product developments which pass the initial screen are killed in R&D, with a further 25 percent failing in manufacture. Thus the average probability of getting to the marketplace is 0.5.

It should be possible to beat this average, however, by better screening. For about half of these failures are caused by unfavorable market information received during development. If the initial assessment of market success is properly done, at least some of these later surprises can be avoided. We therefore suggest that not more than 33 percent of targeted product developments should fail for technical or unforeseeable commercial reasons before reaching the market. The average failure rate for products which reach the market is about 33 percent. This too should be cut by better screening to about 25 percent.

The average success probability for product development ought therefore to be about 0.5 (0.67 before commercialization; 0.75 in the market). This will obviously vary from one category to another: in familiar areas it should be higher; in new and unfamiliar ones it will be much lower. The picture is further complicated by the fact that the probability of technical success can usually be raised by spending more money. We suggest, very tentatively, that overall success probability targets be set as high as 0.8 in very familiar areas, ranging down to 0.2 for very unfamiliar areas, so long as the average is in the region of 0.5. Targeted product development proposals whose estimated probability of success fall significantly below these levels should be rejected, unless they are very cheap to do (substantially below average for the class) and promise high payoffs in the market (substantially above average for the class). Such cases can be treated as exceptions for special consideration.

Projects that are not targeted product developments are more difficult to handle. We have no well-founded methods for estimating their probability of commercial or technical success, and no evidence—

based on overall industry experience—of average success rates, which could be used as targets. In the absence of general guidelines and estimating procedures, it is probably best to avoid setting blanket corporate criteria for nontargeted work or for process developments.

Payoff constraints. These can most easily be stated for targeted projects, whether product- or process-oriented. At a minimum, organizations will wish their expected financial return to be positive, whether measured in terms of expected profit, ROI, or NPV. This will be taken care of reasonably adequately in calculating the probability of commercial success, insofar as commercial success can be equated with an adequate rate of return.

Some corporations may wish to set minimum expected sales targets for product-oriented projects, especially in established or familiar areas. (In the early stages of entry to a very unfamiliar area, the organization should not do so: at this stage it should be content with "learning investments," even if they produce small returns.) Whether a sales constraint and the level at which it should be set are appropriate depend on the size and other characteristics of the individual corporation.

Portfolio performance constraints. Some corporations may feel that it is inappropriate to set constraints for individual projects, preferring instead to set targets which portfolios of projects must meet before getting funding approval. Just as it is only feasible at this stage of our knowledge to set targets for product development *projects,* it is only feasible to set performance targets for product development *portfolios.*

We shall discuss briefly the criteria that might be used for portfolio evaluation and the performance constraints that might be set. Strategic fit is assumed taken care of at the project level, so that no portfolio is likely to include any project not fitting in with strategy, unless in an exceptional case. The cost constraint for portfolios will, or course, be the budget figure ultimately decided on. The remaining criteria have to do with success probability and payoff size.

Success probability constraints. We believe that whatever the category of spending, it should result in a high probability of producing at least one success. Thus, spending on nontargeted projects should have a high probability of producing at least one technical success, while spending on product developments should have a high probability of producing at least one product that goes through from conception to market success. In fact, each broad category of product development should have such a target: this means that companies active in unfamiliar areas, where the probability of getting to the marketplace is low (even for well-screened projects), will need to engage in a substantial number to "guarantee" at least one success.

As we indicated above, average success probability targets based on general experience can be set only for portfolios of product developments. The average success probabilities for all new product developments passing the initial screen are: 0.67 in R&D, 0.75 in manufacture, and 0.67 in the market; that is, 0.33 overall. We suggested above, however, that careful initial evaluation of the eventual probability of commercial success should raise these averages substantially. If projects considered unlikely to succeed in the market are screened out, the average estimated success probability should go to at least 0.67 before marketing (up from $0.5 = 0.67 \times 0.75$), while the average in marketing should similarly rise from 0.67 to at least 0.75. We therefore believe that a reasonable target success probability for a company's overall portfolio—assuming careful screening and effective execution—would be about 0.5; that is, it could expect to succeed with one out of two product development projects, instead of the current average of one in three.

Whether it is worthwhile setting different portfolio constraints for different categories of product development is moot, given the very tentative state of our information, but clearly corporations must be willing to entertain much lower average rates in unfamiliar areas, while expecting higher rates in well-understood businesses.

Payoff constraints. In the course of developing their strategic plans, the different planning teams will undoubtedly have formulated broad sales aspirations for each major product group or business area, together with an overall profit goal, spending estimates, cash flow, and ROI targets. These will all act as portfolio constraints for product and process development, such that any portfolio not keeping the business unit on track toward its sales, profit, and rate-of-return targets will be rejected as inadequate, instigating a search for a better set of projects.

Other Functions of Strategic Planning Teams

The work of the strategic planning teams does not end when the long-term budgetary proposals are finalized and performance standards are set. They will be involved in an annual review and approval process and in some ongoing decisions.

Each unit must routinely review its strategic plan each year and take part in a corporate review so that the process of annual budgeting can proceed within an updated strategic framework. The planning units must review their portfolios to ensure that they are maintaining strategic balance and meeting their performance targets. They will probably draw up, and will certainly approve, the annual budget for the business unit. They will make decisions about exceptional or very large projects which are capable of exerting a strategic influence on the unit's innovation program. In this way they can ensure that technological innovation is consistently integrated into corporate strategy, which is increasingly seen as the key to innovative and corporate success.

NOTES

[1] Jay Galbraith, in *Organizational Planning: Bases and Concepts,* ed. Jay W. Lorsch and Paul R. Lawrence (Homewood, Ill.: Richard D. Irwin, 1972).

[2] Booz-Allen and Hamilton, *New Product Management for the 1980s* (New York, 1982).

[3] Brian Twiss, *Managing Technological Innovation,* 2d ed. (London: Longman Group, 1980).

[4] Michael J. C. Martin, *Managing Technological Innovation and Entrepreneurship* (Reston, Va.: Reston Publishing, 1984).

[5] We shall refer to the teams that are responsible for producing the plans for strategic business units and for the corporate innovation unit as strategic planning teams.

[6] Alan R. Fusfeld, "How to Put Technology into Corporate Planning," *Technology Review,* May 1978.

[7] Theodore Leavitt, "Marketing Myopia," *Harvard Business Review,* September–October, 1975.

[8] E. B. Roberts and C. Berry, "Entering New Businesses: Selecting Strategies for Success," *Sloan Management Review* 26, no. 3 (1985).

[9] W. J. Abernathy and J. M. Utterback, "Patterns of Industrial Innovation," in *Readings in the Management of Innovation,* ed. Tushman and Moore, (Marshfield, Mass.: Pitman Publishing, 1982).

[10] R. G. Cooper, *Project Newprod: What Makes a New Product a Winner?* (Montreal: Centre Quebeçois d'Innovation Industrielle, 1980).

[11] R. G. Cooper, "The Impact of New Product Strategies," *Industrial Marketing Management* 12, no. 4 (1983).

[12] Alan R. Fusfeld, "How Not to Fall on Your Face with Technological Forecasting," *Inside R&D* 7, no. 2 (1978).

[13] Eric Von Hippel, "Appropriability of Innovation Benefit as a Predictor of the Source of Innovation," *Research Policy* 11, no. 2 (1982).

[14] E. B. Roberts and C. Berry, "Entering New Businesses."

[15] PREFCALC™: Eric Jacquet-Lagreze, Euro-Decision, BP 57, 78530 BUC, France.

[16] R. C. Couper, *Project Newprod.*

5

Facilities Planning: Reflecting Corporate Strategy in Manufacturing Decisions*

Steven C. Wheelwright

Harvard University

*I*n spite of the fact that manufacturing frequently accounts for the majority of a firm's human and financial assets, top management often overlooks the role that operations can play in accomplishing corporate objectives. The problem is not that top management ignores manufacturing, but rather that marketing and finance are expected to play a major role in formulating corporate plans, with manufacturing simply reacting to those plans as best it can. This failure to consider manufacturing to be a key resource in realizing corporate objectives seldom represents an explicit decision to restrict it to a reactive role. The

---

* Reprinted from Steven C. Wheelwright, "Reflecting Corporate Strategy in Manufacturing Decisions," *Business Horizons*, February 1978, pp. 57–66.

reasons for such shortsightedness and its consequences have been described by Wickham Skinner:

> Top management unknowingly delegates a surprisingly large portion of basic policy decisions to lower levels in the manufacturing area. Generally, this abdication of responsibility comes about more through a lack of concern than by intention. And it is partly the reason that many manufacturing policies and procedures developed at lower levels reflect assumptions about corporate strategy which are incorrect or misconstrued.
>
> The conventional factory produces many products for numerous customers in a variety of markets, thereby demanding the performance of a multiplicity of manufacturing tasks all at once from one set of assets and people. Its rationale is "economy of scale" and lower capital investment.[1]

Unfortunately, even a company that recognizes these problems and has first-rate managers to work on them faces a major challenge in establishing procedures to ensure that manufacturing decisions mesh with corporate plans and goals. While operating decisions may make sense individually, they may not work cumulatively to reinforce the corporate strategy. The basic problem is that most decisions, particularly those in manufacturing, require trade-offs among various criteria. All too often the trade-offs that are made in such decisions reflect priorities that are internally inconsistent or that run counter to corporate strategy. Management needs a procedure for developing and implementing plans that support and reinforce corporate strategy.

Research and experience suggest that it is not enough just to communicate strategy throughout the organization. Some intermediate mechanism is needed for translating strategy into a form directly applicable to manufacturing decisions. One approach that several firms have applied utilizes a set of criteria that are appropriate for evaluating operations decisions. When the company assigns weights to these criteria that reflect the priorities of corporate strategy, these priorities can be used to ensure that trade-offs associated with operation decisions are consistent with strategy. This approach has been successfully used both by corporate manufacturing staff and by line management charged with making improvements in manufacturing decision making.

The remainder of this article describes and illustrates this approach. The major emphasis is on implementing proven concepts so that the problems cited earlier can be avoided and the full strategic potential of manufacturing can be realized. As a starting point, four typical production decisions are described, and for each one the course of action initially selected by manufacturing management is indicated.

The modifications in those decisions that resulted when a broader corporate perspective was considered are then examined. Following these illustrations of what it means to have manufacturing decisions reinforce corporate strategy, a conceptual framework is described that assists managers to accomplish systematically that desired congruence. Finally, two alternative procedures are presented for implementing that framework. In the first, the corporate manufacturing staff takes the initiative; in the second, line management.

SOME INAPPROPRIATE DECISIONS

In each of the following decision situations, manufacturing management had identified those actions they thought would be most appropriate. However, a subsequent review of each decision's compatibility with corporate goals and strategy indicated that a different course of action would be more appropriate. These four situations suggest the range of operating decisions which are typically made independently, but which have a major cumulative impact on the corporation's success in accomplishing its overall strategy.

Situation A: Major Equipment Purchase

Production output was approaching the capacity of a major piece of equipment at a wholly owned subsidiary of a diversified company. This subsidiary sold 85 percent of its output to other divisions within the corporation. The other 15 percent, which represented outside sales, was an important source of profits for the subsidiary because of the transfer price arrangement established for corporate business and because the in-house business was at the low-priced end of the market. It was agreed that the division would soon need new equipment, and management was about to propose a multipurpose machine. This equipment offered more capacity per dollar invested than other alternatives and promised a chance to expand outside business and thereby increase return on investment. The only question appeared to be whether to buy the new machine at once or to delay the purchase for a year.

As a first step in taking a broader view of this decision, division management determined that the goal for the subsidiary was to be a low-cost source of supply to the corporation for that particular product. Other firms were potential suppliers, but top management had originally established this subsidiary to obtain low-cost materials for specialized, high-volume needs.

Review indicated that purchase of the proposed machine was not the best decision if the subsidiary was to work only for the parent company in the future. The subsidiary's outside customers put quality ahead of cost, but corporate customers emphasized cost. The proposed multipurpose machine would raise the cost on corporate business because of its cost structure. Also, because of the natural desire to utilize expensive equipment as fully as possible, it would probably lead to less emphasis on sales to corporate customers (and on costs) and more emphasis on outside sales (and quality) in order to utilize the equipment's full capability.

Situation B: Quality Control Budget

This company had grown substantially over several years but had recently noted that indirect and overhead costs were growing more rapidly than sales. Management was concerned that these costs were getting out of line. As part of the annual budgeting procedure, manufacturing management proposed that the quality control area be rationalized and streamlined to bring its costs more in line with what they had been historically. The plan was to use more final product sampling (and less components testing) to cut quality control cost per unit.

A broader examination of this situation revealed that the company's products were selling at a premium price with an image of quality and high reliability. In fact, when the use of the product was examined for the major customer segment, it became apparent that the cost of a motor breakdown for even a single day was more than the price of a new motor. Manufacturing concluded that quality had to be maintained and given top priority. Component reliability was identified as an integral part of quality because of the modular product design and customer maintenance procedures. As a result of this review, management decided that more, not less, quality control per unit was appropriate, and that reductions in overhead and indirect costs would have to come from areas other than quality.

Situation C: Labor Negotiations

In six months, the major production facility of a manufacturer of a perishable consumer product (shelf life about three months) would face its first labor contract renewal. The corporate labor relations staff, whose policy had always been one of firmness, considered the existing contract most attractive and wanted to keep the new contract equally favorable to the company. Unfortunately, the union had recently been agitating among employees, emphasizing that the existing contract, unlike most other contracts in that region and industry, had no cost-of-living adjustment clause. A group of employees had become vocal in demands for a substantial "catch-up" adjustment in the new contract. It was assumed that when the contract expired in six months, the normal procedure of having the corporate labor relations staff handle negotiations would be followed. That staff had already recommended that as much extra inventory as possible should be built up in anticipation of a three- to-four-week strike. Given current capacity constraints and the perishable nature of the product, manufacturing had indicated that no more than three weeks of finished goods inventory could be accumulated by the time the current contract expired.

A more thorough examination of this situation indicated that the market was growing at about 60 percent annually and that there were two other major firms in the business. This company and its two competitors each had about the same market share and were seeking to build national distribution as quickly as possible. In addition, recent studies of similar products and their economies suggested that there might only be room for two major firms once the growth rate began to slow. Manufacturing concluded that to achieve reliable, uninterrupted supply was the key task of production if corporate goals were to be met. Consequently, manufacturing decided to take an active role in urging labor relations to open negotiations early and, if at all possible, to resolve the contract issues before a strike became inevitable.

Situation D: Major Capacity Expansion

The established manufacturer of a branded household product suddenly found its market growing rapidly, severely taxing its outdated production process. An engineering firm had been hired to develop process equipment that would improve the consistency of the product and provide substantial productivity improvement. A new process design had been completed and, although the equipment was new to this application, it was based on known technologies from other fields. To meet the coming year's substantially increased capacity requirements, manufacturing management planned to replace the old production process with the new one. This promised twice the output per square foot of plant and per employee, with an investment per unit of capacity that was slightly lower than for the old equipment. The new process appeared to more than meet cost goals, and manufacturing management was planning to move ahead with it as quickly as possible.

In this situation, a broader look at the corporate strategy and the environment identified the critical role of additional capacity. There was no contingency plan in the event that the new production process met unexpected start-up problems, a fact that signaled danger. Further investigation indicated that the cost of excess capacity was minimal compared with the product's gross margin of almost 50 percent, and the maintenance of 30 percent excess capacity would add only 1 or 2 percent to product cost. Management concluded that if the firm was unable to meet all of the demand for its products, the penalty would not only be a loss in market share but a waste of advertising dollars equivalent to the capital investment required for 30 percent idle capacity. Manufacturing concluded that the new process might be appropriate in the longer term; initially, however, it should be added as excess capacity, not as a replacement for the existing process.

A CONCEPTUAL FRAMEWORK

The four decisions described above illustrate a range of situations where individual decisions must be reviewed in the context of corporate goals and strategy if those decisions are to have the desired reinforcing effect. In each instance, manufacturing management thought it had identified the appropriate action; yet a more comprehensive strategic review indicated that a major change in that action was needed. These situations suggest the need to develop a framework that triggers such a review, establishes company-specific criteria to be applied in that review, and provides a means of using those criteria effectively.

The ability of a company's manufacturing function to reinforce corporate strategy is determined by a number of decisions over an extended period of time. Understanding these decisions is the first step in using them to accomplish corporate goals. The following are among the most important factors in determining whether a firm's manufacturing actions will be truly supportive:

Facilities. The rationalization and focus of individual plants and their sizes and locations are major manufacturing commitments. These decisions are often the most visible examples of manufacturing strategy selection, in that options are often first defined at this point.

Choice of process. A major set of manufacturing decisions concerns the matching of the company's choice of equipment and processes with its products' characteristics and competitive pressures. Choices must be made regarding the degree of automation, the level of product-line specificity, and the degree of interconnectedness among different stages in the process.

87

Aggregate capacity. Both type of capacity and the timing of capacity changes are important elements in this category. Should the production rate be level or should it chase demand? Should capacity lead or follow changes in demand? Should overtime, second shift, or subcontracting be used for peak capacity requirements?

Vertical integration. The number of production and distribution stages to be managed by a single firm, and the balance and relationships between vertically linked stages, are critical manufacturing decisions with an impact on corporate strategy.

Manufacturing infrastructure. Molding the bricks, mortar, equipment, and people into a coordinated whole requires that the firm specify policies for production planning and control, quality control, inventory and logistic systems, and work force management. Labor policies and materials-management procedures are important related topics.

Interface with other functions. Manufacturing must work closely with the other corporate functions. The operations manager and the manufacturing executive must facilitate these relations while balancing them against their own priorities.

These six choices determine corporate strategy in a company's manufacturing operations. They are the points at which key trade-offs are made. If they are to support corporate aims, they must consistently reinforce the desired competitive focus and goals—a simple achievement in firms in which the chief executive is involved in all decisions of significance. In larger firms with functional or divisionalized structures, a systematic effort is needed to insure this consistency. This effort is particularly critical as products and businesses grow, develop, or shrink, requiring change in the corporate strategy and in the manufacturing decisions to support that change.

Unfortunately, simply giving manufacturing management a statement of the corporate objectives and strategy is not particularly effective in achieving this desired consistency in decision making. The gap between operating decisions and their impact on corporate strategy is just too great. Some intermediate step is needed.

Manufacturing decisions reflect trade-offs among different performance criteria. Thus, identifying these criteria and prioritizing them has proven effective in bridging this gap. The most important performance criteria are the following:

Efficiency. This criterion encompasses both cost efficiency and capital efficiency and can generally be measured by such factors as return on sales, inventory turnover, and return on assets.

Dependability. The dependability of a company's products and its delivery and price promises are often extremely difficult to measure. Many companies measure it in terms of the "percent of on-time deliveries."

Quality. Product quality and reliability, service quality, speed of delivery, and maintenance quality are important aspects of this criterion. For many firms this is easy to measure by internal standards, but as with the other criteria, the key is how the market evaluates quality.

Flexibility. The two major aspects of flexibility changes are in the product and the volume. Special measures are required for this criterion, since it is not generally measured.

The four situations described earlier illustrate how an initially narrow view may lead to decisions that are not most appropriate for the corporation as a whole. As is frequently the case, in three of those four situations manufacturing management erred initially in assuming that the appropriate trade-offs were those that minimized the production cost per unit. A broader perspective for the last three situations indicated that the single criterion of lowest cost did not identify the best overall decision for those companies.

Every corporate situation is unique; no single procedure will guarantee that manufacturing decisions always reinforce corporate strategy. However, utilizing this framework that seeks to establish manufacturing priorities has been helpful in many situations. A first step in implementing the framework for an individual company is to answer two important questions: *Who* will apply the framework? *When and where* in existing planning and decision-making procedures will it be applied?

Among those who might take responsibility for applying the framework are the division general manager, the director of the corporate manufacturing staff, the division controller, and the division's director of manufacturing. These positions can be grouped into two main categories—line and staff. The division general manager and the director of manufacturing represent line management; the corporate manufacturing manager or a member of the controller's office represents staff. Who can best assume this responsibility depends on the organization of the company and its normal split of staff and line assignments. Even when a staff group facilitates and shepherds the application of this framework, it is always necessary to have the understanding and commitment of line management to make the framework useful.

When and where the implementation of this framework should be monitored depends largely on established management and decision-making procedures. For one company, the most logical time might be the annual budgeting or planning cycle. For another, it might best be incorporated in the periodic corporate review of divisional plans or in the division general manager's quarterly review of operations. How the framework can be used most effectively will depend both on the organization's motivation and management philosophy and on the manager (line or staff) most willing to take responsibility for seeing that significant progress is made.

APPLYING THE FRAMEWORK

Two separate applications of this conceptual framework will illustrate the range of approaches available for its implementation. The first was developed by a corporate manufacturing staff seeking to improve annual manufacturing plans. The second was designed and implemented by a vice president of manufacturing.

A Staff Approach

The corporate manufacturing staff of a large diversified company with several autonomous divisions was concerned that manufacturing was not achieving its potential as a competitive weapon. Historically, the manufacturing staff had consisted of fewer than a dozen people whose major task was to make sure that requests for major capital appropriations were "complete." While the staff's charter continued to call for a limited staff, the vice president who had recently been put in charge of the group wanted to move quickly to help division manufacturing managers take a more active role in the accomplishment of corporate strategy.

As a first step in this direction, he decided that all the divisions had a similar problem: developing annual manufacturing plans consistent with marketing and product strategies. Subsequently, corporate manufacturing assumed responsibility for communicating the framework and concepts related to manufacturing performance priorities and for having each division's manufacturing manager make them operational.

Two major objectives motivated corporate manufacturing's pursuit of this framework in the company. First, the corporate staff wanted to provide the different manufacturing managers from each of the operating divisions with a common set of concepts and language. It was felt that the corporate manufacturing staff and top management, who are not familiar with the technical problems, pressures, and issues facing manufacturing management, would be better able to review and evaluate operations decisions if they mastered these concepts.

A second objective was to help operating managers recognize the specific competitive decisions faced by their division. This could then help such managers make manufacturing decisions and formulate action plans consistent with corporate and division strategies and objectives.

The staff's approach in accomplishing these goals consisted of two phases. The first phase was a two-day seminar for 35 key manufacturing and distribution managers selected from all of the company's divisions. The first step was to introduce the framework presented in Figure 1. Thereafter, through a variety of case studies, the manufacturing managers were able to see the concepts applied to different situations.

FIGURE 1

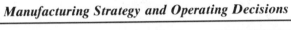

Manufacturing Strategy and Operating Decisions

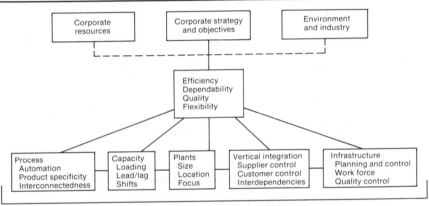

The second phase applied the framework to each of the individual operating units as a part of their annual five-year planning process. After the division's operating plan had been drafted, manufacturing management met for a day with the corporate manufacturing staff. Their purpose was to review the draft plan and to examine the interaction between anticipated operating decisions and the division's strategy. These follow-up sessions consisted of four steps, as illustrated in Figure 2.

Step 1 defined the basic business units of the division—those product-market groupings for which the division had a homogeneous strategy and for which a single set of priorities for the manufacturing performance criteria would be appropriate. Step 2 defined the four performance criteria for that division's manufacturing and marketing setting, determining what constituted quality, flexibility, cost, and dependability. Step 3 identified for each business unit the priorities cus-

FIGURE 2

Application of Manufacturing Criteria by Corporate Manufacturing Staff

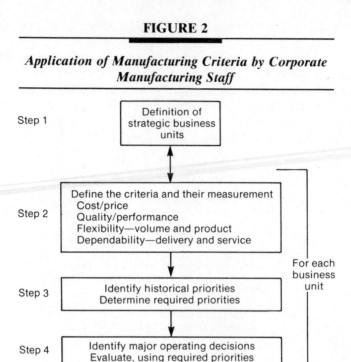

Step 1 — Definition of strategic business units

Step 2 — Define the criteria and their measurement
Cost/price
Quality/performance
Flexibility—volume and product
Dependability—delivery and service

For each business unit

Step 3 — Identify historical priorities
Determine required priorities

Step 4 — Identify major operating decisions
Evaluate, using required priorities

tomarily assigned to the four performance criteria. Identification was accomplished through a review of past manufacturing decisions and the relative emphasis those had given to each criterion. Future priorities for each business unit were also identified during this part of the session. Step 4 identified the key operating decisions to be made in the coming years and evaluated those using the performance priorities specified in Step 3.

In several instances, this process did no more than reinforce the actions tentatively planned by manufacturing management. In other instances, however, the priorities suggested that the proposed decisions should be altered so that actions would better reinforce the division's strategy and have the desired cumulative effect. Situations A, C, and D described earlier were among the proposed decisions that were reviewed and subsequently revised as a result of this exercise.

A Line Management Approach

A second situation where the framework of Figure 1 proved effective did not involve any staff support. It was initiated and guided by the vice president of manufacturing. The company, which manufactured four major industrial products and a line of spare parts, had found itself capacity-constrained for some time. Production bottlenecks were frequent, and manufacturing had been under substantial pressure to improve its performance and its support of the company's goals.

The motivation for this particular application came from the vice president of manufacturing, who had recently attended a two-week seminar on manufacturing in corporate strategy. Upon returning, he was asked, half jokingly, to tell some of the other members of top management what he had learned. He decided to respond by discussing the use of manufacturing priorities to support corporate strategy. He

---

Elements of Manufacturing Strategy as Defined by the Vice President of Manufacturing

Cost. This criterion refers to low cost or even lowest possible cost, including cost of capital employed. This would imply minimum wages, particularly for hourly but also supervision. The amount of supervision would be determined by cost minimization rather than maintenance of quality or dependability levels. Capital equipment selections would be based on acquiring specialized machinery to produce at the lowest cost and would produce parts to the loosest possible acceptable tolerance levels. Equipment would be replaced only when completely worn out and would likely be overhauled once or twice prior to actual replacement. Inventories would be maintained at the minimum level needed to avoid idle shop time but would not necessarily be based upon needs for customer service levels. Emphasis of this criterion maximizes return and minimizes investment.

Quality. This criterion focuses on maintaining high levels of quality. High levels of quality can be defined as significantly higher than competitive products and sufficiently high to support sale of the product based upon its high quality, even if its price is unfavorable with respect to competition. Examples of primary emphasis on quality would be Mercedes automobiles and Hewlett-Packard calculators.

Dependability. This refers primarily to meeting all delivery commitments for new orders and parts. It includes not only the capability to stock products, but also the ability to manufacture replacement parts quickly.

Flexibility. Flexibility refers to the ability to make significant changes in manufacturing volumes and/or products. It entails high responsiveness to either increases or decreases in customer demand in the short term (substantially less than one year). It also may be related to flexibility to changes in product design such as the acquisition of new product lines and/or the significant modification of existing product lines.

also wanted to determine the appropriate priorities for his own operations and to review major operating decisions.

The first step in his approach was to have company vice presidents individually assess current manufacturing priorities. This was done by defining the four criteria described in the accompanying box and having them distribute points among these criteria. The assessment form identified the company's five separate business units and requested that 100 points be allocated for historical (as is) priorities and 100 points for required (should be) priorities for each. (The split into five product categories had been used frequently as part of the planning process.)

As might be expected, responses from the vice presidents varied considerably. To reconcile the differences, discussion sessions were held among all of the members of top management. The result was a consensus as to past priorities and required priorities for each of the company's five business areas, as shown in the accompanying table (see Table 1). This step identified a number of areas in need of a change in emphasis so that manufacturing and its performance priorities would be most supportive of the corporate strategy.

Some of the actions that resulted from the identification of major differences in historical and required emphasis included the following:

> Product 1 should have modest increases in quality and dependability at the expense of manufacturing cost efficiencies.
> Products 2 and 3 should have no significant changes in manufacturing.
> Product 4 should have a significant improvement in manufacturing cost efficiencies at the expense of quality and flexibility.
> Product 5 (parts) should have a significant increase in dependability at the expense of manufacturing cost efficiencies.

As a follow-up, the vice president of manufacturing used the same approach with the manufacturing department heads who reported to him; the results are also shown in the table. This second application of the framework convinced the vice president of manufacturing that his manufacturing managers were motivated primarily by the desire to achieve a high degree of cost efficiency. Since manufacturing's action plan was based on consensus reached by top management, the vice president of manufacturing sought to convince his manufacturing subordinates that it was an appropriate plan of action since it was reached at the policy level in the company.

The vice president was very satisfied with the results he obtained from this process and concluded that his manufacturing people had gained a better understanding of the corporate strategy for each major

TABLE 1

Current and Required Priorities as Assessed by Vice Presidents (VP)* and Manufacturing Managers (MM)*

	Cost		Quality		Depend-ability		Flexibility	
	VP	MM	VP	MM	VP	MM	VP	MM
Product 1								
As is	42	44	17	15	25	26	16	15
Should be	28	46	24	16	31	26	17	12
Needs more (less)	(14)	2	7	1	6	0	1	(3)
Product 2								
As is	26	20	37	43	24	22	13	15
Should be	26	30	36	38	26	20	12	12
Needs more (less)	0	10	(1)	(5)	2	(2)	(1)	(3)
Product 3								
As is	34	36	27	28	23	19	16	17
Should be	34	38	29	24	24	20	13	18
Needs more (less)	0	2	2	(4)	1	1	(3)	1
Product 4								
As is	24	34	30	22	19	17	27	27
Should be	39	44	20	25	23	15	18	16
Needs more (less)	15	10	(10)	3	4	(2)	(9)	(11)
Product 5 (Parts)								
As is	45	37	21	14	18	31	16	18
Should be	22	31	24	13	35	35	19	21
Needs more (less)	(23)	(6)	3	(1)	17	4	3	3

* Criteria totals for VP and MM for each priority = 100.

product segment. He also felt that their ability to use the policies derived from this priority-setting procedure would continue to grow. Situation B described earlier is typical of the impact that this approach has had on his company.

In both of the companies described above, the managers involved found the establishment and application of priorities for manufacturing performance measures to be extremely valuable. This was particularly the case in the second example, where all of the vice presidents had reached a consensus on the priorities for manufacturing. A significant reduction in the conflict resulted between manufacturing and marketing because both areas agreed on a common direction. The exercise also proved to have very useful organizational development benefits, many of which were greater than those obtained from programs designed only for organizational development purposes.

Upon reflection, the corporate manufacturing staff in the first situation felt its approach would have been strengthened had there been feedback to marketing for comment and appraisal. While they were uncertain how best to handle that, given their role as a staff group, they did agree that such marketing involvement should be obtained in future applications.

In both instances, there was some skepticism at the outset about the benefits obtainable from such an approach. In the first case, even the company's president had reservations in the beginning about the value of the exercise. After seeing its results, however, the president subsequently sought to make such an approach a more integral part of the company's annual planning and budgeting process. In the second case, the priorities are being used on an ongoing basis to help both staff and line management more adequately review division operating plans and ensure that major decisions submitted for corporate approval reflect appropriate priorities.

The four decision situations described initially illustrate how the establishment of manufacturing performance priorities allow such individual decisions to be made quickly and effectively in a manner that supports corporate strategy. Also, for those decisions already consistent with corporate strategy, the reinforcement gained through use of these priorities can often advertise their usefulness and appropriateness to other members of top management. By making these concepts an integral part of a company's planning and decision-making process, manufacturing can realize its own strategic potential. Rather than simply being reactive to others' plans, manufacturing can itself be part of the plan.

NOTE

[1] Wickham Skinner, "Manufacturing—Missing Link in Corporate Strategy," *Harvard Business Review,* May–June 1969, pp. 136–45; and "The Focused Factory," *Harvard Business Review,* May–June 1974, pp. 113–21.

6

Human Resources Planning: How to Plan Training and Development Outlays

Harris DeWese

The DeWese Group, Inc.

INTRODUCTION

*T*he return on the dollars that are being invested in training your workers and managers is probably worth more of your consideration than any of your investment alternatives. Most operating managers, who are ultimately responsible for all corporate capital budgeting decisions, either ignore or only superficially calculate the return on training prior to making the investment. After the training occurs there is even less effort to measure or understand the financial yield on the training.

The disinterest in forecasting training return and in measuring the actual is not gross negligence on the part of managers but rather a product of our business environment. For years training has been a "nice thing" to do in good times. Even in bad times, there was always the alternative of on-the-job training. OJT was necessary, if for no other reason than people need rudimentary marching orders in order to run the machine, work the counter, or run the plant.

Our incessantly growing technology, complex new society, and culture have expanded the role of the human being in both the manufacturing and the services sectors. Marching orders no longer suffice. With a decreasing dependence on machines, corporate success or failure now accrues almost entirely from the performance of people. And, training has become the newest source of balance sheet and income statement *leverage*.

Any source of leverage is worth understanding if it is to be used as a predictor of financial outcomes. Leverage must be used systematically and planfully if it is to lift its maximum. Debt financing in inadequate cash flow environments can result in bankruptcy. The future will increasingly require that training leverage, because of its potentially higher yields, be applied without casualness and as carefully as other investment decisions.

The objective is to develop an alternative approach to planning, budgeting, implementing, and measuring training and development investments. Most operating managers regard discussions of the training budget line item as onerous, knotty, "soft," and too small to be worthy of much attention. Worthy subjects are marketing investments, new plant outlays, wages, and benefits. Worthy subjects are more tangible and measurable than the return on dollars invested in the human improvement aims of training.

Training expenditures usually represent less than .5 percent of annual budgets and are easy to slash. Trainers and their departments have been vulnerable to line managers' views of the "real priorities" of running a business. Trainers are forced to keep their résumés current. They attend training conventions with purses and pockets full of business cards. When the axe does fall, and it often does, they always have the option of becoming training consultants and hanging a shingle. They are often forced to exercise this option, and this has contributed to industry's disdain and suspicion for the ubiquity of thousands of training consultants, all peddling a training answer to every business problem.

America's current industrial revolution has already spawned many new and innovative human resources management techniques. The recent economic unpleasantry also forced corporations to make human resources management dramatically more adaptive—more responsive to a work force that time has conditioned to be more self-interested, demanding, and difficult to manage. Finally, the U.S. economy's need to compete with aggressive world competition has inexorably drawn greater human output into the picture.

The generally accepted equation for greater output is too broad to be of much financial value. But it does serve to provide the two strategies for improving productivity.

The equation: Productivity = Automation + Motivation

As in the case of most blackboard oversimplifications, this equation omits too much. That something is the need to *intelligently* invest in greater capacity, or new machinery, or new automation. The principles of intelligent capital investment are contained elsewhere in this volume. This leaves the motivation of workers and managers as the other strategy for productivity gains. The tactics of this strategy range from whips and threats to job security (tactics that don't work so well anymore) to incentives, "cafeteria" benefit offerings, and a variety of worker participation schemes. Newest of all on the right side of the motivational range is the use of improving "corporate culture" as a means of creating an environment that induces people to produce more.

Some of America's toughest and most successful managers are adding a third variable to the right side of the productivity equation. Trainers are thrilled. The new variable is training. The January 23, 1984, issue of *Fortune* featured an article titled, "Why Training Is the Boss's Job." The author was Andrew Grove, a founder and the CEO of Intel Corporation and an engineer. He asserts that "Training is, quite simply, one of the highest leverage activities a manager can perform." *Leverage* is a capital budgeting term. It is unusual to hear it used in the context of training. Dr. Grove continues:

> A manager generally has two ways to raise the level of individual performance of his subordinates: by increasing motivation, the desire of each person to do his job well, and by increasing individual capability, which is where training comes in. It is generally accepted that motivating employees is a key task of all managers, one that can't be delegated to someone else. Why shouldn't the same be true for the other principal means at a manager's disposal for increasing output?

Andrew Grove at Intel, John Opel at IBM, R. W. Miller at Walt Disney, and Fred Turner at McDonald's Corporation are CEOs of some of the companies that Peters and Waterman acknowledged for their vigorous pursuit of excellence in *In Search of Excellence*. All of these leaders have a fundamental belief that training investments should be measured like any other investment.

99

- IBM spends $500 million annually to train some 365,000 employees worldwide. That is 1.5 percent of IBM's total revenue and over $1,300 per employee.
- Walt Disney pays enormous attention to training detail. Teenaged ticket takers at Disney World spend four days in training before they take the first ticket from the theme park's Guests. A significant part of that training is spent just teaching the concept that Guest is spelled with a capital "G," not a lowercase "c" for customer.
- McDonald's has invested heavily in its Hamburger University. That famed institution is the bane of the McDonald's competitors. The installation of McDonald's consistency and quality begins there.
- Intel uses a simple model to measure training return. Grove puts it this way: "Consider for a moment the possibility of your putting on a series of four lectures for members of your department. Let's count on 3 hours of preparation for each hour of course time—12 hours of work in total. Say that you have 10 students in your class. Next year they will work a total 20,000 hours for your organization. If your training efforts result in a 1 percent improvement in your subordinates' performance, your company will gain the equivalent of 200 hours of work as the result of the expenditure of your 12 hours."

These companies sweep others along with their successes. Managers, trainers, and accountants will be forced to adopt systematic capital budgeting techniques as training becomes a more used means of increasing return on investment.

The new productivity equation is:

Productivity = Automation + Motivation + Training

You invest on the right side to gain return on the left side. Productivity is easily measured. Certainly we can measure the investment and return in capital budgeting automation efforts. Major strides are being made by large human resources consulting firms and their clients in the measurement of motivational investments. Systems for financial measurement of training will follow as companies become increasingly dependent on the value that training can add.

The examination of alternatives to maximize the usefulness of this newly important training leverage asks these questions of the expectant practitioner:

1. How are training and development strategies and objectives integrated with marketing, operations, and financial objectives?
2. How is the strategic planning of training done for corporate and SBU functions?
3. How should one prepare an overall training and development budget based on both the corporate strategic plan and its outgrowth—the human resources training plan?
4. And, ultimately, how can operating managers first predict the financial outcomes of training investments and then measure those anticipations against actual?

INTEGRATING TRAINING STRATEGY WITH CORPORATE STRATEGY

Training department managers have been frustrated by countless articles and symposia encouraging that their departmental plans be based on the corporate plan. Their frustration is rooted in the fact that often they are not apprised of the corporate strategy. They are infrequently part of the firm's planning team. It is just as rare that they receive an envelope containing the corporate long-range plan from the CEO.

Without the vital closeness to senior management's strategic decisions, trainers cannot identify training's potential role in implementing the plan. Strategies are the means or routes to the attainment of objectives. Often an objective will read as follows:

Objective: The firm will increase return on equity from 12.1 percent (by 1983) to no less than 16.5 percent by the fiscal year ended December 31, 1986. Progress will be evaluated by returns of 13.2 percent and 14.8 percent for fiscal years 1984 and 1985, respectively.

The objective is often not so difficult to author. Ownership, stock price, competitive factors, and a variety of conditions often demand the objective and the time required for its attainment.

The difficulty for top management is the choice of strategies to attain the objective. The example objective that is provided is so formidable as to require several or even many strategies. Classically, the management team in this example could use one or more of the now-famous Chandler/Williamson five prototype strategies. They are:

1. *Specialized expansion*—The *New York Times* decides to expand its share of the New York market.

101

2. *Related diversification*—The *Times* decides to start or acquire a magazine.
3. *Unrelated diversification*—The *Times* decides to buy or start a chain of fast-food restaurants that are named "All the Food That's Fit to Eat."
4. *Vertical integration*—The *Times* decides to buy the Merganthaler Linotype Company and enter the typesetting business.
5. *Geographic expansion*—The *Times* decides to buy the *Miami Herald* from Knight-Ridder.

Down one level on the strategy hierarchy, management could choose a combination of increasing revenue, reconstructing the firm's financing, and cost containment—three likely choices. These strategies would probably have substrategies. One of them, under increasing revenue, might read:

> *Strategy:* To increase sales we will initiate a branch telemarketing campaign to increase qualified sales leads.

Implicit in this strategy is the need to train branch personnel in telemarketing techniques. Often, however, senior management, content with having articulated the strategy, abdicates and leaves the training to the devices of field management. In this decentralized environment, not one of the regional managers has sufficient budgeted financial resources to successfully train branch personnel in sophisticated telemarketing skills and techniques. The result is that they all spend whatever they have budgeted for training or whatever they can pilfer from other regional line items. In six months top management is frustrated with the failure of 30 regional managers to implement telemarketing and discovers there are 30 different approaches that were installed with 30 different training programs. If we dig deeper, we would likely find that centralized capital budgeting would have cost less and resulted in not only the successful implementation of telemarketing (and hence more leads) but also would have provided a reasonable means for evaluating the return on the training investment.

Robert L. Desatnick, in his book *The Business of Human Resources Management: A Guide for the Results-Oriented Executive,* provides a summation for the dilemma portrayed in our telemarketing case: "The message is clear: Senior management does not understand the function of human resources development. HRD's contributions are not self-evident; its products do not sell themselves. Savvy practitioners may know they have a poor image within their organizations, but even they don't know how to improve it."

As long as the image of trainers is not improved, they will not be injected into the mainstream of the corporate strategy development process. Sometimes the failure to use corporate strategy as the wellspring for training strategy can have disastrous effects for the firm's trainers as well as a big price for management.

A major specialty retailer (several hundred stores) recently fired its entire training department for "empire building" and for conducting countless training needs assessments. No training was happening, just never-ending needs assessments. These questionnaires were consuming months of labor to create, distribute, and tabulate. Nearly a dozen trainers were spending all their time poring over the results and musing about how they would run the company using the insights they had gleaned from store personnel.

At the retail firm's top-management level, however, there was concern for a proliferation of new competitors who were discounters. The new competitors were regional or local and were opening 6 to as many as 20 outlets in their respective markets. In addition, the firm's major competitor was also beginning to discount and had just opened new distribution centers that were reducing transportation costs, inventory, and markdowns.

To counter competition, top management decided on strategies that relied on quality customer service and value-added imaging rather than price competition. Management also decided on fewer layers of field management and a wider span of control for regional managers and district managers—more districts reporting to fewer regions; and more stores reporting to fewer districts. This meant that store managers would get less supervision and would be required to make more decisions in a less centralized environment. Top management also decided that this new organization would require growing district and regional managers from within.

The training of store managers had previously been the responsibility of district managers, who would now be unable to provide the day-to-day on-the-job training requisite to fundamental knowledge required of a new store manager. Some centralized training program was obviously required to implement corporate strategy. At this juncture, the training department began its quest of the ultimate answer. Nearly a year was consumed by the needs assessment process, and management became frustrated by the failure to implement the strategy. An examination of this case and its possible solutions will resume in later sections.

Steps to the Integration of Strategy

It should be useful here, before the onset of total frustration, to set forth steps that should ensure the integration of corporate strategy and training strategy.

1. Training departments *must discipline themselves* to think as if they were outside vendors. Outside vendors' very existence depends on recognizing training needs inherent in corporate strategy. This environment creates a job shop or project mentality. The existence of their "training firm," albeit internal, depends on developing financially measurable solutions to their client's business problems. The solutions must be on time and within budget, or they won't survive.

Line managers, on the other hand, must learn to evaluate the training department just as they would measure an outside custom training vendor. Outside vendors are, after all, an alternative source, and a source that is being used more and more.

These new attitudes will force line managers and training managers to budget as if they were job shops—limiting fixed costs and using capital budgeting techniques to justify projects.

2. The training function *must be informed* about the firm's corporate and divisional (or SBU) planning unit strategies. As has already been demonstrated, trainers must be informed of corporate strategy before they can design and adapt training programs that help realize corporate objectives. This may seem self-evident but, unfortunately, they frequently do not know the organization's strategies. Sometimes this is because human resources development people do not understand or appreciate how they can help achieve strategy; and sometimes this occurs because top corporate management does not understand that training can play a positive role in strategic planning and management.

Trainers were informed when a major steel company changed strategy. For years, only specialists were qualified and allowed to sell coil-coated (prepainted) steel. This product required special technical knowledge and unique sales techniques. When the company opted for a strategy aimed at increasing sales of coil-coated steel, they chose one that required the entire sales force to sell the product. The sales force had to be trained so that each sales representative gained the product knowledge, and the confidence, to aggressively seek new business.

The steel company's training department, working with technical and marketing staffs and using an outside developer of training media, produced a sound/slide film and an illustrated study guide about coil-coated steel. The program explained how it is made, the benefits of coil-coated steel, and how to sell it. The training department then conducted comprehensive seminars complete with question-and-answer periods and role-playing exercises.

Within 60 days, every sales office and 64 percent of the sales force had coil-coated steel customers or serious prospects, and the sales representatives were handling all but the most technical aspects of the sale.

In this case the training department used an outside vendor to develop some of the materials because it had no burning compulsion to maintain fixed-cost capability for every application it might be required to produce. It could concentrate on implementing the strategy rather than fathering its nest with seldom-used video production equipment and people.

3. *Strategies* for the ways in which training programs can help organizations realize that their overall strategies *need to be developed*. Trainers must create their own strategies for helping the larger organization attain its objectives and implement its strategies.

The training department of a leading manufacturer of construction and agricultural equipment created its own strategies that supported corporate direction. The firm distributes its equipment through company-owned retail outlets throughout the United States and has a continuing need for new branch managers. The training department developed a low-cost, print-based self-study program that specifically covered the theory and practice of managing its stores. Topics included cash flow, financial statements, open account credit, used equipment inventory, the branch personnel function, and the service department. Pre- and posttraining comparisons showed the program enabled the learners to reduce their errors by 61 percent.

4. Training operations *need to be organized* to facilitate implementation of the training strategies they have designed to help realize the larger institutional strategies. Here, as in any other organization, structure should follow strategy. In large, decentralized, geographically diverse organizations, it probably makes more sense to decentralize training for the sake of delivery, cost-effectiveness, regional differences, and flexibility.

The training department of a large chain of drugstores decentralized itself when corporate strategy resulted in the electronic linkage of over 600 stores. The training director pointed out that the largest cost in any training program is not the cost of the training materials or program development but how long the learners are away from their

105

jobs. In this case, using the new electronic communications system (which was installed primarily for inventory and accounting purposes) and a willingness to forgo his large central training organization, the former three-day training program was reduced to 12 hours. Testing proved later that it was even more effective than the longer classroom approach.

5. The specific ways in which training programs can teach trainees about organization strategies *must be identified* and articulated. It is never enough for trainers just to know what their organization's strategies are. They must understand the implications in terms of specific needs, constraints, and requirements of the training programs and the trainees. This requires a dialogue between trainers and the operating managers who are supervising the trainees on the job.

This is demonstrated in the example of a multibillion-dollar captive sales finance company. It had been training employees for decades using the "learn-by-watching method." A newly formed training department was given the responsibility of investigating a better way. After studying the situation, the training department and an outside training vendor designed several learner-controlled instruction programs. Learner-controlled instruction outlines what is to be learned and what resources are available. They serve as road maps and allow the employees to discover what they need to know at their own pace.

When the finance company's management evaluated these programs they found that in 57 percent of the cases, less time was required to acquire the basic job knowledge. In 82 percent of the employees, competency was greater. In 67 percent of the students, overall performance was greater after this method of training. The biggest payoff, however, was the reduction of average employee training from eight months to five weeks. It will be shown later, but it should already be evident, that this kind of training evaluation lends itself readily to financial quantification and, hence, to capital budgeting principles.

6. Reward and evaluation *mechanisms* for training personnel *must be adjusted* to reflect newer training strategies, not the least of which is the use of training leverage as a contributor to corporate performance. Return for a moment to the training director at the finance company. During the first year 150 employees were trained in the new learner-controlled method in five weeks versus the previous eight months. The average compensation and benefits for those 150 employees was 30K annually, and the total developmental and production cost was less than 100K. The controller valued the financial mistakes made by these employees at 1.8 million. This oversimplified equation will ignore the supervisory time savings and assume that all training department fixed costs remained the same. Thus we have:

$$150 \times .67 \times 30.0K - 150 \times .10 \times 30.0K - 100.0K + .61 \times 1.8M = 2.466.0M$$

The ingenuity of this training staff accelerated by 23 weeks the time required to bring employees up to speed, and in labor costs alone saved the organization nearly $2.5 million!

This trainer made a very large contribution to his firm's financial performance. Regretably, this specific contribution was not reinforced by a reward specific to the performance that resulted in this saving.

Typically, trainers are measured by criteria like "How many employees were trained during the fiscal year?" This can motivate trainers to use the Chicago feed lot theory of training—process as many cattle as possible. Who cares whether they need it or whether or not the training is any good?

Training managers are like other managers in that they respond to evaluation and reward mechanisms. If a training strategy changes, but the rewards and evaluation criteria for managers and staff do not also change, there is a natural tendency to behave in a way that would meet the previous criteria rather than that required for the success of the new strategy.

7. *Trainers need to be trained* to carry out the strategies that will further the organization's aims. As corporate strategy changes, the training needs of trainers become more dynamic. It should seem obvious that as the firm's training needs evolve and change, so should the training needs of those providing the training that supports the strategy.

HOW TO STRATEGICALLY PLAN TRAINING AND DEVELOPMENT OUTLAYS

Soon, some wordsmith will find an alternative for the words *strategy, strategic,* and *strategically.* He will make millions defining the new words for us with articles, seminars, and books. Others will rush to claim they really invented the new word, and they will hasten to spread the new gospel with even more books and speeches. And we will be at least temporarily relieved to be rid of the old word and so urgent to stay current that we will supply the money for the originator's new-found wealth.

Strategy will be defined here as the means by which we move from point A to point B—as in point Philadelphia to point New York. One could drive, walk, skate, ride the train, ride the bus, or fly by airplane (and this is probably not inclusive). There are even shades of these various strategies. One could walk forward, backward, or sideways. Then there is the question of route. You could walk to New York by way of Bangor, Maine. If there was some entertainment value in walking from Philadelphia to New York, and people would actually pay to watch you do it, they might pay more to see you walk backward via Bangor. The premium they pay might well cause you to examine your forward strategy via the Pennsylvania and New Jersey turnpikes and go for a backward route over the Poconos to Bangor.

Forgive the nonsense and remember the point—strategy development is not an esoteric subject or a difficult task. It is no more difficult for the training manager than for the marketing manager. More than anything else it is disciplined creativity. It requires forcing the planning team to consider its environment (external and internal), determine objectives, consider all the various ways to achieve the objectives, and choose one or some combination of more than one strategy.

As in any capital budgeting process, the strategy chosen should maximize the leverage. Return now to the specialty retailer that we left in a lurch. In order to implement the promote-from-within policy in a rapidly growing field management operation, management obviously needs a trained pool of store, district, and regional management candidates. Recruiting and selection will play a role in this, but we are dealing only with training. Management has many point-A-to-point-B choices in its attempts to maximize training leverage to attain its objective.

For brevity, let's assume that management has determined that its inability to promote from within and the previous layers of field management cost them $6 million last year. That is the total salaries of the eliminated managers, money paid to outside recruiters, downtime while new people learn their way of doing business and the political system, the cost of delayed store openings, buying and inventory mistakes, and several other traceable costs. Training is critical to the achievement and maintenance of the $6 million. They want to attain the $6 million with the least possible training cost. There are 500+ store managers and 500+ assistant store managers. There are also 80 district managers and 12 regional managers. This represents a total audience of nearly 1,200 people.

On the high side, management could hire top consultants in management and retailing to conduct seminars in their area of expertise for all 1,200 managers. These top consultants did not get to the top on stupidity. The first thing they will tell management is, "Learning does not take place in a seminar that contains more than 20 people." They make a good point, but this also maximizes their revenue. This means that the training consultants will do 60 seminars. They will also tell you that they can't teach anything as important as their subject in less than two days. Let's also assume that management has hit on 12 priority areas—so we are dealing with a dozen training consultants. Admittedly, this example is extreme, but it has happened.

If each of these consultants charges $2,000 per day, our retailer is faced with a $2,880,000 expenditure. That doesn't count meeting room expense, a/v equipment, handout materials, participant travel and lodging, faculty travel and lodging, and administration expense. Add all that expense, and this is a $10 million endeavor that will require two years to complete.

Fortunately, this example is about as extreme as people paying to watch someone walk backward from Philadelphia to New York via Bangor. Although unrealistic, it is one strategy that might be used to achieve the $6 million objective. If the training has a life cycle of three years, it might even represent a reasonable payback or training return on investment. In this case that return would be calculated

$$\text{ROTI} = \frac{\text{Revenue}}{\text{Expense}}$$

or

$$1.8 = \frac{18.0}{10.0}$$

The right strategy for the retailer and for any strategist usually occurs in the right environment. Ideas should flow within the boundaries of reasonableness and organizational constraints. The following are the steps to training strategy development. They are also the steps that will help ensure that training leverage is maximized by minimizing training investment and maximizing financial results.

TRAINING STRATEGY DEVELOPMENT

1. Problem Identification

Not all performance problems can be solved by training. Not all objectives can be attained by training. Underlying causes are often obscured by the many factors that affect performance. The need for training may be triggered by many things. Hopefully, the training manager is apprised of a change in strategy and recognizes training required to its

109

success; or perhaps a strategy is faltering due to a lack of training or inadequate training; or someone observes a performance deficiency; or top management requests training in some area.

At this early stage the problem or the opportunity must be quantified. Remember the construction and agricultural equipment manufacturer who was spending eight months training field managers. They were training about 150 people per year with an average salary of 30K. It was taking eight months to make them operational. They were making costly errors in the meantime. Eight months' salary totaled $3 million, and the controller estimated their financial mistakes alone at $1.8 million. The total training revenue opportunity was $4.8 million.

Some organizational development experts will argue against this, but every training project should be subjected to the rigor of this revenue payback test. The test, however, depends on the gathering of baseline data.

2. Establishing Baseline Data

This data should reflect the conditions that have necessitated the training. It should answer the basic question of what to evaluate or measure financially as the training return. Hopefully the data can be collected over a time period long enough to permit a realistic comparison. Examples include the number of grievances over the last six months, the number of errors in claims processing during the last year, the accident frequency rate during the last quarter, or the average monthly sales cost for the previous year.

3. Needs Analysis

During this step a needs analysis is conducted. Whatever spawned the need, the needs analysis should be conducted to determine specific deficiencies in performance or lack of information necessary for good job performance. Needs analyses are usually conducted by means of interviews with potential candidates to be trained, interviews with their superiors, or needs assessment surveys and questionnaires.

4. Audience Profile

The effectiveness of training increases in direct proportion to its ability to relate to the learner. Grill cooks in a fast-food operation may well still be in school or just out of school. They may respond better to highly supervised show-and-tell training. Managers or aggressive sales representatives would balk at this method. An audience profile should

110

be developed that considers levels of education, experience, skill, attitudes, feelings, personal motivations, departmental culture, and corporate culture.

5. Develop Training Objectives

Each training objective should arise from the baseline data that was collected. Part of the baseline data that was collected in the equipment manufacturer example was the controller's valuation of the accounting-related errors that were made. These were errors that resulted in receivables not being collected or earnings that were not realized because of reduced cash flow. They stemmed not so much from inaccurate bookkeeping as from from poor accounting administration due to lack of knowledge. The training objective for this performance deficiency might have been to reduce errors by 40 percent during the first 12 months following the training. Errors were in fact reduced by 61 percent.

The objectives provide direction to the course developers, students, faculty, and management. Management must use these quantified objectives as the criteria by which they make the investment decision. Training objectives should follow the standard for all good objectives. They should be crisp, challenging, timed, achievable, and understood by all the players.

6. Training Research and Content

The challenge of this step is to determine exactly what will make the training effective for the wide range of potential students. The research/designer must then trim that data to only that which will generate optimum performance.

This is probably the most time-consuming part of this process. The content may be determined by subject matter experts who decide, in light of the training objectives, what the participants need to know, such as skill, principles, and facts. This process requires constant review by the responsible managers. Material that is nice to know but not strictly related to the objectives must be eliminated.

The final product of this stage is a detailed design document. This is the culmination of all the research, needs analysis, and audience profiling. It is a blueprint for the creation of the training program. It spells in detail the objectives, the content in very specific terms, the training methodology, the media to be used, and the training logistics (timing, location, and setting). The designer, in most cases, should be a specialist in adult learning theory. Many firms hire outside vendors

111

who have this expertise rather than retaining these skills and knowledge on-staff. It can help to ensure objectivity in the selection of media.

This specialist must deal primarily with the issues of instructional systems in an adult learning environment. The designer must choose among programmed instructions, self-paced or learner-controlled instruction, audiovisual presentations, group discussions, case studies, simulation exercises, lectures, films, reading assignments, interactive video discs, or computer-based simulations. The role is one of orchestra conductor—a careful orchestration of the media most cost-effective to the attainment of the objectives.

The designer will also design the evaluation system during this phase. First, the designer will decide how to evaluate the training. This involves the selection of one or more evaluation methods. Among the methods are pre- and posttests, participant feedback, feedback from others, participant follow-up, action plan audit, performance contrasts, and job simulations.

The designer then selects an evaluation design. The most common are one-shot design; single group, pretest and posttest design; single group, time series design; control-group design; and posttest only, control-group design.

Evaluation strategy is developed next. This step answers the questions of who, where, and when as they relate to the evaluation. Who will do the evaluation? When will it be done? Who will analyze the data? How will observation of new performance be done?

The final evaluation strategy will specify who will evaluate, where it will be done, and when it will be done. These determinations are critical to the credibility of the final measurement of return on training investment.

7. Consideration of Constraints

The managers responsible for the return on training investment must now consider the detailed design document in light of realities. How much time is available? How much money is available? Facilities, and so on? These considerations make the training practical.

8. Budgeting the Training Project

The final version of the design document is the ideal action plan for the easy development of a surprise-free budget. Previous budgets will have been estimated on envelopes and napkins as a part of the sensitivity analysis that any manager goes through before even seriously considering an investment. At this stage, the manager should have developed enough conviction about the promise of return that the project merits a detailed budget.

Figure 1 is a highly detailed training project budgeting form. It's desirability is that it leaves no stone unturned and provides an excel-

FIGURE 1

APPROVED BY:			TRAINING PROJECT TITLE:				

DATES: Target   Actual   Subject(s): _____   Project #: _____

Initialization: __/__/__   Audience(s): _____ Media: _____

Budg. Approval: __/__/__ __/__/__

    Manuscript: __/__/__ __/__/__   **RESPONSIBILITY:**

     Graphics: __/__/__ __/__/__   Project Manager: _____   Writer: _____

    Production: __/__/__ __/__/__   Initialization: _____   Graphics: _____

   Distribution: __/__/__ __/__/__   Editor: _____   Production: _____

			Internal Staff Time			External costs	Totals
Code	Dept./Function	Hours/ Units	Training dept. Rate _____	Sr. Mgmt. Rate _____	Involved dept. Rate _____		

SUMMARY - PROJECT BUDGET

Code	Dept./Function	Hours/Units	Training dept.	Sr. Mgmt.	Involved dept.	External costs	Totals
.1	Administration						
.2	Research						
.3	Copy						
.4	Design						
.5	Production						
.6	Meeting Expense						
	TOTALS		$	$	$	$	$

CREATIVE

Code	Dept./Function						
.0	ADMINISTRATION					TOTAL	($)
.1	Proposal prep.						
.2	Budgeting						
.3	Client consult.						
.4	Administration						
.5	Travel/Ent.						
.0	RESEARCH					TOTAL	($)
.1	Sourcing						
.2	Cross ref.						
.3	Writing						
.4	Editing						

Prepared by: _____

CREATIVE SUB-TOTAL   ($_____)

FIGURE 1 (*continued*)

Code	Dept./Function	Hours/ Units	Internal Staff Time			External costs	Totals
			Training dept. Rate _____	Sr. Mgmt. Rate _____	Involved dept. Rate _____		
			CREATIVE (Continued)	CREATIVE SUBTOTAL		($	)
.0	COPY				TOTAL	($	)
.1	Conferences						
.2	Writing						
.3	Proofreading						
.4	Revisions						
.0	DESIGN				TOTAL	($	)
.1	Conferences						
.2	Design/board time						
.3	Revisions						
.0	CONCEPT TESTING				TOTAL	($	)
.1	Questionairre						
.2	Computer coord.						
.3	Field travel						
.4	Travel/Ent.						
				TOTAL CREATIVE		($_____)	
			PRODUCTION				
.0	GRAPHIC REPRODUCTION				TOTAL	($	)
.1	Color separations						
.2	Paper						
.3	Printing						
.4	Binding						
.5	Postage						
.0	WORD PROCESSING				TOTAL	($	)
.1	Conf./Supervisor						
.2	Data entry						
.3	Proofreading						
				PRODUCTION SUBTOTAL		($_____)	

FIGURE 1 (*concluded*)

Code	Dept./Function	Hours/ Units	Internal Staff Time			External costs	Totals
			Training dept. Rate _____	Sr. Mgmt. Rate _____	Involved dept. Rate _____		
			PRODUCTION (Continued)	PRODUCTION SUBTOTAL			($)
.0	VISUALS				TOTAL		($)
.1	Conferences						
.2	Equipment Rental						
.3	Photography						
.4	Film / Darkroom						
.5	Model fees						
.6	Crew						
.7	Type/Titles						
.8	Quantity Prints						
.0	AUDIO				TOTAL		($)
.1	Conferences						
.2	Director						
.3	Actors/Talent						
.4	Equipment Rental						
.5	Music/Effects						
.6	Edit						
.7	Dubbing/Mixing						
				TOTAL PRODUCTION			($_____)

Code	Dept./Function						
.0	MEETING EXPENSE				TOTAL		($)
.1	Room rental						
.2	Equip. rental						
.3	Lunches/refresh.						
.4	Transportation						
.5	Sleeping rooms						

lent control for investment purposes. It also sets up an internal costing system to ensure that all costs are captured, whether internal or external.

9. Program Development

The program is developed using either inside resources or outside vendors. Very often outside custom training firms or audiovisual production houses offer learning curve, equipment, and experience advantages over existing talent and resources within the firm. Many training managers have been guilty of protecting their turf with the excuse that an outside vendor cannot possibly develop materials that relate to "our people." The detailed design document eliminates this excuse. Good custom training companies will produce whatever their clients demand and they will do it from scratch without using any "off-the-shelf" materials.

10. Validation or Does the Program Work?

Does the program actually produce the specified result? The answer depends on careful measuring against strict standards in a pilot test-run setting. These standards are

- *Integrity*—Does the program teach everything needed for the attainment of the objectives and the desired change?
- *Fidelity*—Does the program contain any points that can be misconstrued?
- *Validity*—Can typical learners perform as predicted?
- *Reliability*—Is the program consistent throughout the full range of the learning audience?

11. Implementation

This requires little discussion, except to note the importance of making students aware of what results are expected. Positive expectations will have a positive impact on the realization of the expected return on training investment.

12. Evaluation Data Collection

A system of data collection must be implemented. A predetermined schedule for data collection must be maintained closely in the actual execution of the evaluation. Plans for the evaluation can fall short if performance data is not collected at the appropriate time.

Evaluators should gather data on evaluation instruments designed during the program design phase. This instrument collects data on attitudes, learning, behavior change, and attainment of the financial objectives. Evaluation instruments may include questionnaires, surveys, attitude surveys, examinations, interviews, observations, job simulations, or record-keeping systems. The instruments should be statistically reliable and easy to use. A reliable instrument is statistically consistent over different measurements of the same behavior.

This data must then be analyzed and interpreted by management. This is often done statistically. The aim is to get back to an accurate accounting of the quantifiable training results in light of the original investment premise.

13. Calculating Return on Training Investment

In this final step the firm calculates and communicates the actual return on training investment. Obviously any value less than 1.0 is disappointing. Training offers huge opportunities for leverage, however, and if done properly should yield results far above those being experienced in other investment alternatives.

The return on training investment formula was previously provided as

$$\text{ROTI} = \frac{\text{Revenue (increased revenue and or cost savings)}}{\text{Cost (total cost of the training project)}}$$

Purists will and should want to apply present value analysis to both the investment and the yield as it unfolds. Those formulas are expressed elsewhere in this volume and should be applied rigorously, if for no other reason than to further enhance the growing credibility of training as a source of leverage.

CONCLUSION

Managers are acutely sensitive to the forces exerted on our human resources by economic conditions that have never previously existed. These forces have cast the responsibility for output squarely on the shoulders of the human beings who work for and manage our institutions. Output can be increased through humans by the fuel of motivation and training.

In this chapter the assertion is made that training investments must now be viewed no differently than we view investments in tangible opportunities—research, capital equipment, plant, land, inventories, or new products. The assertion holds not only for a rigorous and quantified posttraining evaluation, but also for a pretraining capital budgeting process that closely resembles other capital deployment decision processes. One step above the capital budgeting process is the requirement that training be driven and initiated by the organization's strategy.

The 1981–82 recession quieted those corporate training professionals who have allowed training to occur without accountability for results. The new outcry in human resources development books and periodicals is for training that is measured, relevant, and provides a return on investment.

Wickham Skinner, in his 1981 *Harvard Business Review* article titled "Big Hat, No Cattle: Managing Human Resources," portrayed the challenge as follows;

> Acquiring and developing the right talents for the business as it changes strategy, technology, and products requires more shrewd, wise, long-range planning than any other corporate endeavor. The lack of long-range planning in human resources is disastrous. So the ultimate irony is that the personnel function which deals with the most fundamental and central corporate competitive resource and that has the longest-term horizon of any function is left with no long-range strategy and is allowed to react merely to the transient pressures and events.

Some organizations are beginning to make the transition by mainstreaming training and development through relevance to corporate plans, measurement, and accountability. Training managers who are on this course are capital budgeters, entrepreneurs, marketeers, and risk takers. Much of this chapter is devoted to the systems and resulting successes they have developed.

Lawrence Cote of Penn State sums this up very well:

> In the future, companies will have to rely more on internal development training for successful and profitable growth. Companies that lag behind will find themselves lagging behind the competition in productivity as well. Failure to correct productivity problems through training will cost companies more in the long run than training would cost them now.

REFERENCES

Bell, Chip R. "How Training Departments Win Budget Battles." *Training and Development Journal,* September 1983, pp. 42–47.

Carnvale, Anthony Patrick. *Human Capital: A High-Yield Corporate Investment.* Executive Summary for the American Society for Training and Development, National Issue Series. Washington, D.C., 1982.

Connolly, Susan. "Participant Evaluation: Finding out How Well Training Worked." *Training and Development Journal,* October 1983, pp. 92–96.

Dening, Basie S. *Evaluating Job-Related Training.* Washington, D.C.: American Society for Training and Development; and Englewood Cliffs, N.J.: Prentice-Hall, 1982.

Desatnick, Robert L. "Marketing HRD: The Credibility Gap That's Got to Go." *Training,* June 1983, pp. 52–54.

DeWese, Harris. "The Attitudes and Opinions of Southern Chief Executive Officers on Management Training and Development." Master's thesis, Emory University School of Business, 1982.

Eckenboz, Cliff. "Evaluating Training Effectiveness: A Form that Seems to Work." *Training,* July 1983, pp. 56–59.

Jenkins, David. "Half-Trained Managers." *Management Today,* May 1983, pp. 86–90.

Kearsley, Greg. *Costs, Benefits, and Productivity in Training Systems.* Reading, Mass: Addison-Wesley Publishing, 1982.

Nielson, Richard P. "Training Programs: Pulling Them into Sync with Your Company's Strategic Planning." *Personnel,* May–June 1983, pp. 19–25.

Packer, Michael B. "Measuring the Intangible in Productivity." *Technology Review,* February–March 1983, pp. 48–57.

Phillips, Jack J. "Training Programs: A Results-Oriented Model for Managing the Development of Human Resources." *Personnel,* May–June 1983, pp. 11–17.

Rosenheim, John H. "Is Your Training Program Really Paying Off?" *Credit,* April 1975, pp. 4+.

"Why U.S. Workers Are Producing Less." Interview with C. Jackson Grayson, Jr., authority on wages, prices, and productivity, *U.S. News and World Report,* May 1978, pp. 95–96.

7

Financial Planning: How to Determine Financial Feasibility of the Overall Capital Program

Libbey-Owens-Ford Company

INTRODUCTION

Several years ago Libbey-Owens-Ford Company (LOF) began evaluating the strategies of companies and business units in terms of economic or shareholder value creation. The underlying goal of this approach is simply to measure the business unit's potential in terms of the expected cash flows to be generated by the strategy. In the past, LOF management had routinely used discounted cash flow in evaluating individual capital expenditures. However, analyzing the cash flow potential of an entire business unit or company strategy was a new experience.

Proponents of this new evaluation method argued that cash performance was the key measure for any investment activity, whether a single capital project or an entire set of strategies. Furthermore, exceptional cash performance was recognized by investors as the true test of financial success, and anticipated cash generation was the primary force behind the upward movement of a company's stock price. According to market behavior research, the primary factor affecting long-term price movement was not earnings but cash flow, and good earnings performance did not necessarily guarantee good cash performance. This statement is basically true because of the increasingly complex accounting procedures that many companies are required to adopt. Even routine entries such as depreciation expense and LIFO adjustments can cause dramatic swings in earnings while having little or no effect on cash. Cash flow potential, not historical earnings or potential earnings performance, is the key element in long-range stock price increases and the resulting creation of shareholder value.

Actually, the overall shareholder value formula consists of two elements: anticipated dividend payments and stock price appreciation. Of these two elements, only dividends can be directly determined by the company. Evaluating and measuring each business unit's expected cash performance, discounted for time effects and risk, is an approach to controlling the second element of the shareholder value equation.

This is the value approach taken by LOF. Discounted cash flow analysis is emphasized in all evaluation processes. Not only are individual capital projects analyzed in this manner, but also entire strategies, including acquisitions and divestitures. At LOF, our mission statement begins: "Libbey-Owens-Ford Company is a diversified manufacturer that recognizes a primary responsibility to its shareholders and a continuing requirement to increase the value of their investment in the company."

Clearly, a key priority for LOF's success is the creation of shareholder value. This same goal was repeated by the chief financial officer in the 1983 annual shareholders' report:

> Libbey-Owens-Ford has a continuing requirement to increase the value of our shareholders' investment in LOF. This is not just a contemporary business phrase, but the basis for a long-term company strategy. It evaluates business strategies and plans in terms of value to our shareholders, not just [on the] incremental income that the results will contribute to the bottom line. It requires a greater emphasis on developing strategies and plans that will increase shareholder value.

The emphasis in this chapter is on capital expenditures; but while strategic planning of capital expenditures is a critical function, it is merely one part of the overall planning process and, as such, cannot be clearly explained as an isolated function. LOF funds strategies—not projects. Beginning with strategy development and ending with the tracking of actual progress and performance, capital expenditures are analyzed, reviewed, evaluated, and measured on a value basis in every phase.

STRATEGIC PLANS

The mission statement establishes the long-range goals and objectives, the general direction, and the basis for measuring success. Strategic management takes this document and interprets these goals and objectives through the development of individual business strategies. Alternative approaches and sensitivity studies are performed by each business segment, with every scenario measured in terms of its relative value contribution. Strategies are value-driven; each alternative seeks to maximize shareholder value.

Business managers begin the strategic management process with a very limited amount of information, a *strategy profile* (see Figure 1). This process generates a series of base studies, each building to a measurement of the overall value of the strategy (see Figure 2).

At this planning stage, capital expenditures are represented as a one-line item. Other than specifically identified major projects, such as

FIGURE 1

LOF Strategy Profile   Unit strategy _____   Date _____

												80-83%	84-89%
	Information category	Scale	1980	1981	1982	1983	1984	1985	1986	1987	1988	1989	Compound annual growth rates	
A	Market size	$mm												
B	Market potential	%												
C	Major competitor	Name												
D	Our competitive strength or market share	%												
E	Net sales	$mm												
F	Operating earnings	$mm												
G	Operating merger %	%												
H	Net working capital	$mm												
I	Net PP&E	$mm												
J	Return on investment	%												
K	Capital expenditures	$mm												
L	Depreciation	$mm												
M	Employees													

122

FIGURE 2

Strategic Management Process

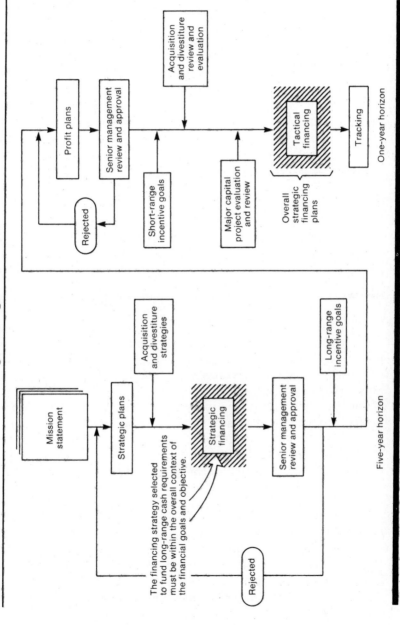

a new production facility or the purchase of a major piece of equipment, this critical one-line cash requirement may be developed through relationship indexes. One such index used by LOF is called the replacement ratio (capital expenditures divided by depreciation). This index is merely a quick indicator of the long-range investment strategy of a business. While year-to-year variations may not be very meaningful, long-range trends can be very informative. Assuming a reasonable rate of inflation compounded over the five-year planning horizon compared to a fixed depreciation charge based on past expenditure activities, the following definitions for capital expenditure levels can generally be implied:

Ratio	Meaning
Less than 1.0	Contraction of business
1.0 to 1.5	Uncertain direction
1.5	Maintenance of business
Greater than 1.5	Expansion of business

A replacement ratio of less than 1.0 may indicate that existing assets are not being replaced at a rate sufficient to maintain the business at its past levels of activity.

Another possibility is that more production has been shifted to outside sources, eliminating the need for continued asset replacement. A third possible explanation is a shift from purchased assets to leased assets, although for analytical purposes both capital expenditures and depreciation could be adjusted to reflect the true movement in this index. Regardless of the reason, the replacement ratio is used as a quick indicator of structural change in the business or its underlying capital expenditure strategy.

While capital expenditures are a major part of a business unit's cash flow, the total cash flow of the business is the basis for shareholder value testing. At Libbey-Owens-Ford, the process of analyzing strategies is greatly enhanced by use of LOF's strategic planning system (SPS). Part of the routine output from this computer model is a set of financial reports, including an income statement, balance sheet, and cash flow statement. In addition to these traditional financial reports, a series of analytical reports are also produced. Included in these special reports are a sensitivity study of key assumptions and a year-by-year analysis of the value creation of the strategy (see Report 1).

REPORT 1

				Cumulative present
		Present	*Cumulative*	*value plus*
Year	*Cash*	*value*	*present value*	*perpetuity*

Present Value of Business Unit Strategy with a Discount Rate of XX.X Percent

Year	Cash	Present value	Cumulative present value	Cumulative present value plus perpetuity
1983	2.218	1.966	1.966	
1984	4.440	3.490	5.456	
1985	13.986	9.745	15.200	
1986	−1.280	−.791	14.410	
1987	11.160	6.111	20.521	75.451
Present value of strategy				$75.451

The last column of this report adds a perpetuity value to the cumulative present value of the strategy. This perpetuity amount represents the ongoing contribution of the plan beyond its final year. There are several alternative approaches that could be used, including the substitution of the residual amount based on book value of the assets or a simple calculation based on a price/earnings multiple (P/E ratio). Other methods of estimating this postplanning horizon residual may also be used as deemed appropriate.

In the previous example, the perpetuity value is $54.930 and is approximately the present value of NOPAT (net operating profit after tax excluding interest) in the year 1987 divided by the discount rate. The assumption used in this example is that the final year's performance will continue indefinitely into the future. Obviously, such a simple assumption could be inappropriate in many situations.

The selection of the analytical horizon, five years in this example, is also a critical assumption that must be made for each individual business. Depending on industry cycles or other unique market characteristics, the analytical horizon used in the strategic planning process may vary, thereby affecting the outcome of the evaluation. The objective, of course, is to select a normalized time period for analysis.

One additional report that is helpful to the strategic planning evaluation is a ratio analysis of the strategy (see Report 2). It provides the reviewer with a snapshot of the business plan. This critical set of measurements and financial relationships also serves as a basis for the development and performance tracking of profit plans.

REPORT 2

Ratio/Growth/Analysis Report

	1980–83 average	1984	1985	1986	1987	1988	Projected average
Profitability							
Operating margin	8.0%	9.1%	9.6%	9.7%	9.7%	9.7%	9.7%
Return on assets	13.6	14.4	17.3	18.7	18.4	15.8	17.2
Sales growth	.1	.4	.1	.5	.2	.2	.3
Earnings growth	11.3	14.0	19.5	48.3	17.1	17.2	19.5
Efficiency							
Working cap turn	7.93	9.49	7.48	7.99	11.97	7.82	8.61
Fixed asset turn	3.87	4.16	4.68	4.69	4.79	4.79	4.79
Total asset turn	2.43	2.89	2.71	2.83	3.00	2.69	2.73
Investment							
Per new sales	$ .21	$ .43	$ .56	$ .20	$ .05	$ .60	$ .28
Replacement ratio	.96	1.71	1.06	1.28	1.31	1.32	1.26
Intensity	11.2%	14.9%	15.8%	15.6%	11.4%	15.9%	14.9%

This report, combined with the traditional financial reports and supporting narratives, serves as the basis for top-level review and evaluation of the individual business units.

RISK ASSESSMENT

Critical to the evaluation of any strategy is the risk associated with the investment. This risk factor is the rate at which projected cash flows are discounted in the value-testing process. In the long run, generating cash sufficient to pay the cost of capital is the absolute minimum requirement of any investment activity. Funding strategies that offer less than this cost cause destruction of shareholder value. Just as entire corporations have unique risk profiles, so do individual business units and different strategies within the same business unit. At Libbey-Owens-Ford, the calculation of the risk-adjusted cost of capital for a particular business unit or strategy consists of a two-step calculation.

- The overall corporate *weighted-average cost of capital* is the first step in calculating risk. This factor is the base risk present in all of LOF's businesses and is represented by the sum of the weighted cost of debt and the weighted cost of equity. The capital asset pricing model (CAPM) has been used as the basis for this estimation. This cost is routinely reviewed, but significant changes within any calendar year are rarely made to this number.
- The second element of the risk calculation is represented by the *risk premium* associated with a particular business unit and/or strategy. The extent to which business strategies are considered risky is determined by the average of objective and subjective risks associated with the business.

Objective risk is determined by the historical variability of earnings and/or cash flow. Variances are measured two ways: on the basis of year-to-year changes and variances from past profit plans. A five-year average variance is used for each measurement to avoid short-term distortions. Each of the variations is then assigned a risk index, and the average of both indexes represents the overall risk class for the strategy. Overall corporate variations for both elements of objective risk serve as the midpoint in determining the risk indexes.

Subjective risk is determined by analyzing the unique characteristics of each business strategy. Included in this evaluation is a determination of the business unit's competitive strength, market familiarity, brand distinction, supplier or customer leverage, international risk exposure, and entry and exit barriers. Each of 16 characteristics is rated on a one-to-five scale of risk perception. A risk ranking of three, for example, would represent an average or moderate degree of risk for the particular element. The average of all factors represents the subjective risk factor for the business.

The overall *risk premium* of a business strategy is an average of both objective and subjective risks. This average is then assigned an overall risk factor:

	Average risk class	Overall risk factor
Low risk	1	.90
	2	.95
Corporate average	3	1.00
	4	1.10
High risk	5	1.20

The final step in determining the risk associated with an individual business strategy is simply multiplying the weighted-average cost of capital by the overall risk factor for the business. Although the determination of risk by this method may seem like a formidable task, the entire process actually takes very little time with use of the strategic planning model.

SENIOR MANAGEMENT REVIEW AND AUTHORIZATION

The review, evaluation, and authorization of strategies and expenditure plans at Libbey-Owens-Ford is an ongoing process. This critical function is carried out by a committee of senior executives and is headed by the chief executive officer. Representatives from each of the operating groups and senior corporate staff members meet periodically to review major proposals and strategic directions. The multidisciplined nature of this group is an essential factor for the balanced evaluation and approval approach required in these major decisions. Included in these decisions are review and approval of strategies, profit plans (budgets), major capital expenditures, acquisitions and divestitures, and incentive compensation goals.

Since this committee is exposed to all aspects of the strategic management process, including strategic planning, any serious deviation in the direction of proposed actual capital expenditures from planned expenditures immediately raises a red flag. It is the responsibility of this group to ensure that the integrity of previously approved strategies and plans is kept intact. Major changes that are proposed must be well-supported and justified. Likewise, acquisitions and divestitures are evaluated within the context of strategic direction and opportunity. All of these proposed transactions are tested for their value-creating potential in the same fashion as the strategic plans themselves. Based on approved strategies, plans, and acquisition activities, long-range incentive compensation goals are established for the planning horizon.

STRATEGIC FINANCING

Up to this point, no consideration has been given to the specific financing approach required to support the cash requirements of the strategic plans, capital expenditure activities, and planned acquisitions. An additional cash consideration that enters the planning process at this time is the corporate-defined dividend policy. At LOF the funding decision is handled as a separate and distinct function from the evaluation process. All strategic expenditure plans are evaluated on the basis of cash flow, exclusive of any financing effects.

Strategic financing is defined as the selection of the most attractive blend of financial instruments to fund all cash requirements. Obviously, this portfolio of financial instruments must be structured in a fashion that is acceptable to existing creditors, will not risk the current bond and commercial paper ratings, contains an acceptable mixture of short- versus long-range instruments that are in line with LOF's exposure to interest rate swings, and will yield the greatest shareholder value.

It should be mentioned that LOF is primarily interested in the long-range financial goals and objectives. Projected short-range peaks and valleys within certain key ratios do not substantially restrict the final balance sheet structure (see Figure 3).

The ultimate objective of this process is to fund *all* value-creating expenditures. However, the risk tolerance of senior management may preclude total funding. Even though cash may be raised to invest in all projects, certain planned strategies or acquisitions may have to be delayed or even rejected outright as being unacceptable business opportunities. Included among the major considerations in this evaluation process are shareholders' value creation, strategic fit or core business protection, and debt capacity creation.

While the process of allocating funds takes into consideration the cash performance of the strategies and plans, it is not purely a numbers

FIGURE 3

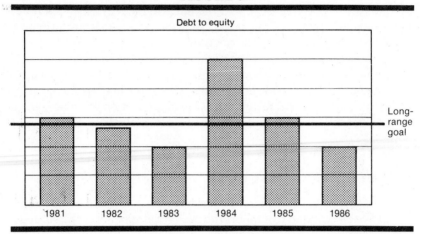

game. Nonfinancial objectives are also included in the evaluation as well. Senior management's understanding and interpretation of our overall mission and the perceived risk of undertaking the project also play critical roles in the funding process. LOF does ration capital but on a business basis and not purely a financial basis.

Not surprisingly, however, funds always seem to be available for those opportunities that will create exceptional value to the shareholder. These projects have generally proven their worth to the overall strategic goals of the corporation and have successfully passed the rigors of evaluation in terms of value creation. All types of projects fall into this group of opportunities, including acquisitions, new products, new processes, promising R&D programs, and divestiture opportunities.

Should it be required to limit or delay funds for certain businesses or capital expenditure programs, these strategies would then be revised. Once the overall long-range financial strategy has been developed in support of the strategic cash requirements and within the general framework of the long-range financial goals and objectives, the stage is set for the profit-planning process or the annual budgets.

PROFIT PLANS

The transition from strategies to profit plans is merely the addition of more detail. The basic planning structure for the corporation has now been essentially established. This is not to imply that the transformation process is an easy task. On the contrary, the profit-planning process is an elaborate and time-consuming function. Specifically, this additional detail is generally in the form of new sales projections that reflect more recent information than was available when the strategies were first designed and approved. This includes more expense detail while maintaining general agreement with previously established cost relationships; more detail, also, in the form of specifically identified major projects and the month-to-month timing of capital expenditures, R&D programs, advertising campaigns, and personnel requirements; and, finally, more detail in the form of step-by-step action plans for achieving the current year's goals and objectives.

As is the case with strategic planning, the process of developing profit plans at Libbey-Owens-Ford is the responsibility of the individual business manager. The "bottom-to-top" profit plan approach better ensures a consistency with the business unit's strategies and affords the manager the opportunity to identify and pursue the long-range direction of his business. Moving from strategies to profit plans, however, is not an exact science, nor is it necessarily a one-to-one relationship. Meaningful profit plans must reflect, among other things, the latest available information regarding sales and price projections, cost structures, and cost quotations for specifically identified capital projects. By nature, strategies cannot and should not be expressed at this level of detail. On the other hand, profit plans cannot be developed in a planning void. Taken out of the strategic management context, profit plans are of little value.

Senior management again becomes involved in the review and approval of the plans. This time, however, profit plans are measured against the strategies to ensure relative compliance with the direction and the realization of shareholder value. Absolute numbers may not agree between the two plans. Relationships, however, must be reasonably similar. Part of this budget critique is to test the realism of the assumptions in terms of margins and investments as compared to historical performance. Sales budgets are also compared with the results of the corporate-developed econometric models for each of the individual business units. Should there be major deviations from historical trends or other projections, these differences must be fully explained and supported by the individual business manager. In addition, if significant structural changes from the strategies occur, or if the levels of projected capital expenditures increase or decrease, or if incremental working capital requirements reflect substantial differences, then further support must be provided for these changes.

Generally, most differences are attributed merely to timing or a

131

more accurate feel for the costs involved in a particular project or strategy. Occasionally, differences are the result of a deliberate change in the approved strategies. In the real world, unexpected problems always occur that require immediate attention. In addition, unforeseen opportunities also happen and should be pursued. In these situations additional evaluation is performed to ensure a proper fit with the long-range plan.

CAPITAL APPROPRIATION REQUEST (CAR)

At this point in the overall planning process, major new capital projects are fairly well defined. The capital expenditure budget now consists of two types of expenditures:

- Current-year expenditures from previously approved projects (prior-year authorizations) for multiyear projects.
- Projected current-year expenditures of new projects (currently unauthorized projects).

It should be noted that despite the fact that the capital expenditure strategies and profit plans have already been reviewed, evaluated, and approved by senior management, no specific authorization has yet occurred. Until this final authorization is provided, no actual expenditure of funds can take place.

By the time a particular major capital appropriation request is received by the senior management committee, all members of the group are familiar with the long-range strategies of the business and short-range profit plans. Most capital expenditure requests come as no surprise, other than those immediate requests that result because of a sudden opportunity or problem. Since the overall strategies and profit plans have previously been reviewed and approved, the primary purpose of this third and final review and evaluation of capital expenditures is to look at alternative approaches to the project in terms of its shareholder value creation. The most attractive scenario in terms of strategic fit, necessity, and discounted cash flow is the approach that is normally approved by the group.

The detailed approach used for this process at Libbey-Owens-Ford is called a capital appropriation request and is supported by an extensive computer model called the capital appropriation system (CAS). The CAR system consists essentially of four forms, the first of which is nothing more than the authorization document itself. The second form is used for a brief review of the expenditure, including a statement of the currently perceived environmental risks plus a listing of the assumptions included in the particular analysis. The third form is a detailed listing of cash requirements by type of asset or expense. The key consideration is *total cash requirements* not just *capital requirements*. Remember, shareholder value is based on total cash flow. The fourth analytical form is the economic cash flow evaluation itself (see Figure 4).

FIGURE 4

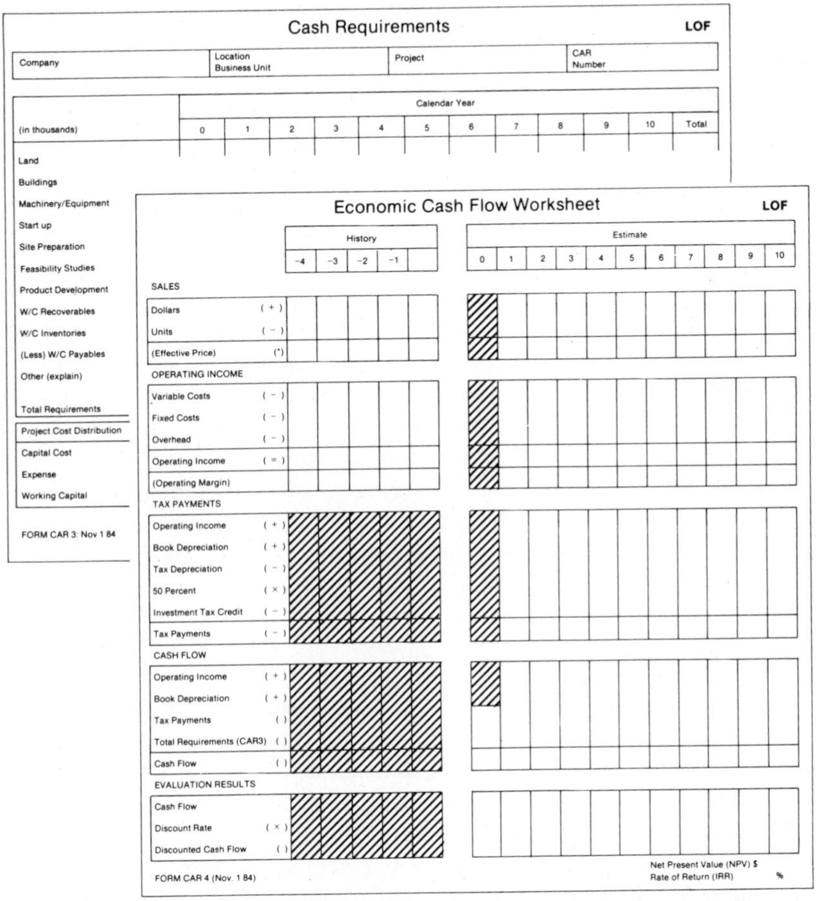

Cash Requirements LOF

Company | Location Business Unit | Project | CAR Number

(in thousands) | Calendar Year: 0 1 2 3 4 5 6 7 8 9 10 Total

Land
Buildings
Machinery/Equipment
Start up
Site Preparation
Feasibility Studies
Product Development
W/C Recoverables
W/C Inventories
(Less) W/C Payables
Other (explain)
Total Requirements

Project Cost Distribution
Capital Cost
Expense
Working Capital

FORM CAR 3: Nov 1 84

Economic Cash Flow Worksheet LOF

History: −4 −3 −2 −1 | Estimate: 0 1 2 3 4 5 6 7 8 9 10

SALES
Dollars (+)
Units (−)
(Effective Price) (*)

OPERATING INCOME
Variable Costs (−)
Fixed Costs (−)
Overhead (−)
Operating Income (=)
(Operating Margin)

TAX PAYMENTS
Operating Income (+)
Book Depreciation (+)
Tax Depreciation (−)
50 Percent (×)
Investment Tax Credit (−)
Tax Payments (−)

CASH FLOW
Operating Income (+)
Book Depreciation (+)
Tax Payments ( )
Total Requirements (CAR3) ( )
Cash Flow ( )

EVALUATION RESULTS
Cash Flow
Discount Rate (×)
Discounted Cash Flow ( )

Net Present Value (NPV) $
Rate of Return (IRR) %

FORM CAR 4 (Nov. 1 84)

This total cash requirement is the basis for evaluating the value performance of each scenario and includes consideration of the proposal's effects on incremental working capital requirements as well as one-time and ongoing expense items. While only the capital portion of the proposal will be capitalized according to generally accepted accounting principles (GAAP), the full *cash* effects are taken into consideration in the evaluation and approval process.

Included as part of the routine corporate staff review of the CARs is an evaluation of the project in terms of:

- Tax issues.
- Legal implications of the investment in terms of contractual arrangements, commitments, and so on.
- Risk exposure in terms of government regulations, safety, security measurements, and environmental compliance.
- Overall financial and accounting review to ensure the structural accuracy of the analytical and accounting approaches plus routine verification of accuracy.

During this review, the corporate evaluation process includes sensitivity analysis on key elements and is essentially the same approach used to test the sensitivity of sales and margins in the strategies.

The final approval and expenditure authorization of the individual projects sets into motion a series of actions:

- The treasury group begins its study of financing options currently available, deciding on those instruments that offer the greatest value to the corporation within the context of the previously structured balance sheet.
- The project is placed on a tracking schedule by the corporate controller's group for routine capital expenditure progress reporting and expenditure auditing at the completion of the project.

TRACKING

The final phase of the planning process is measuring the actual progress and performance of strategies and project expenditures as compared against planned progress and performance. At LOF three distinct forms of tracking are utilized to accomplish this task. Each of these approaches is specifically designed to provide management with a different type of information for decision-making purposes. The first report measures the economic cash performance of the entire business, the second report tracks the progress of total capital expenditures, and the last report is concerned with the individual projects themselves.

STRATEGY TRACKING REPORT

This type of tracking looks beyond the individual capital expenditures and instead evaluates the economic cash flow performance of the entire

REPORT 3

Value Contribution Report (VCR) (six months 1984)

| | Year to date | | Over | Variance due to ($000) | | | |
	Actual	Plan	(under)	Sales	Margins	Invest	Unknown
Income statement							
Sales	21,547	22,179	(632)	(632)	277	—	—
Cost of sales	17,810	18,047	(237)	(514)	277	—	—
Overhead	2,387	2,560	(173)	(73)	(100)	—	—
Operating income	1,350	1,572	(222)	(45)	(177)	—	—
Other—net	(84)	(264)	180	8	172	—	—
Nopat	1,266	1,308	(42)	(37)	(5)	—	—
Cash source (use)							
NOPAT	1,266	1,308	(42)	(37)	(5)	—	—
Depreciation	225	180	45	—	—	45	—
Working capital	(1,564)	(1,767)	203	50	—	153	—
Capital expenditures	(540)	(846)	306	—	—	306	—
Other—net	143	109	34	—	—	—	34
Economic cash flow	(470)	(1,016)	546	13	(5)	504	34
Sales							
Per employee	$ 28.17	$ 29.57					
Per investment dollar	10.24	8.49					
Margins							
Operating	6.3 %	7.1 %					
Nopat	5.9	5.9					
Investment (average)							
Intensity	8.7 %	11.0 %					
Replacement ratio (times)	2.4	4.7					

Totals may not add due to rounding.

business unit. At LOF this report is called the value contribution report (VCR) and is a test of the actual cash performance against the profit plan (see Report 3). It measures not only capital expenditures but also working capital requirements, R&D activity, and the income performance of each business unit. Included with this analysis is a series of measurements that are essentially identical to those used in the strategies and serve to tie the business unit's actual performance to the original strategies. In addition, variances from the profit plan are identified in terms of either sales, margins, or investment activities.

1. *Sales variances* are those changes that have occurred because of sales volume or price differences between actual activity and planned activity.
2. *Margin variances* are those differences that are caused by changes in relationships among the various elements in the income statement.
3. *Investment variances* are cash changes that have occurred solely because of investment activity. These differences are not related to cost margins but are based on a relationship to sales.

Classifying variations in one of these three categories helps the manager to more quickly identify serious variances and initiate corrective action plans.

CAPITAL EXPENDITURE PROGRESS REPORT

The second form of tracking consists of monitoring the expenditure progress of major capital projects (see Report 4). This form of tracking consists of routine monthly reporting and tests projects for variations from authorized expenditure levels and projected completion dates. Only the capital portion of the individual projects is measured on this report.

CAPITAL EXPENDITURE AUDITS

This is the final and most detailed form of tracking and consists of individual and detailed project audits. These expenditure audits are performed on previously approved projects and include a test to ensure that the proper amounts have been spent for the agreed-upon assets or programs. Other tests may include a verification of productivity increases and personnel savings (if these factors were used as a justification for the expenditure). What is not included in this type of capital

136

REPORT 4

	**Libbey-Owens-Ford Company** **Capital Expenditure Progress Report** **(June 1984)**

	Authorization			Expenditures to date			Completion	
	Prior	Current	Total	Prior	Current	Total	Date	Percent
Division A								
Project A	$ 566	$ 911	$1,477	$353	$ 473	$ 826	11/84	85%
Project B	640	—	640	—	—	—	7/84	—
Project C	—	2,081	2,081	—	1,140	1,140	10/84	30
Total	$1,206	$2,992	$4,198	$353	$1,613	$1,966		

expenditure tracking is a measure of cash performance. This type of measurement is extremely difficult to calculate and of questionable value when calculated in such a microenvironment.

CONCLUSION

In summary, it should be repeated that the value approach taken by Libbey-Owens-Ford emphasizes discounted cash flow analysis in all of its business decision-making processes. Not only are individual capital expenditures analyzed in this manner but also entire business strategies, including acquisitions and divestitures. While capital expenditures are certainly a critical element to the future of any manufacturing company, this type of activity represents merely one part of an overall business. To emphasize the analysis and funding of capital expenditures while at the same time ignoring, among other things, the critical implications of working capital requirements, R&D programs, and advertising can only result in faulty or partial answers. Any incomplete approach to expenditure evaluation that includes only capital projects can only serve to provide senior management with a distorted view of the business and its potential for success.

As stated earlier, LOF funds businesses and strategies, *not projects*. Capital expenditures, while they continue to be reviewed, evaluated, and measured as stand-alone projects, simply are not thought of as an isolated function. Capital expenditures, the purpose of which is to increase shareholder value, are part of a much larger strategy at LOF.

GLOSSARY

Operating/nopat margin Operating income (sales less cost of goods sold and overhead) divided by sales. Nopat income equals operating income less the net of other nonoperating income and deductions (exclusive of interest).

$$\frac{\text{Operating/Nopat income}}{\text{Sales}} \times 100$$

Sales/earnings growth Year-over-year changes in sales and earnings. The incremental changes that occurred from the previous year, expressed as a percent. A variation of this measure expressed in terms of new investment is the *investment per new dollar of sales*. This measurement is total investment divided by incremental sales or sales growth.

Sales per employee/investment dollar A measure of productivity as stated in terms of per dollar of sales. This is simply a means of restating personnel and investment numbers in relation to sales activity. This perspective tends to be more easily understood.

Turnover rates Used for measuring the efficiency of certain balance sheet accounts, primarily assets such as working capital, fixed assets, etc.

$$\frac{\text{Annualized sales}}{\text{Average assets}}$$

Replacement ratio A measure of the levels of capital expenditure activity compared to historical depreciation expense (capital expenditures divided by depreciation). Assuming a relatively small inflation rate in new expenditures as compared to historical depreciation expense, the following meanings can generally be implied:

Replacement ratio	Meaning
Less than 1.0	Contraction of business
1.0 to 1.5	Uncertain direction
1.5	Maintenance of assets
Greater than 1.5	Expansion of business

Investment intensity A measure of the relative amount of investment required to support sales activity. Research and development includes engineering expense and is included as an investment for analytical purposes only.

$$= \frac{\begin{array}{l}+ \text{ Increases} - \text{Decreases in working capital} \\ + \text{ Capital expenditures} \\ + \text{ Research and development expense} \\ - \text{ Depreciation expense} \\ \hline \text{Total investment}\end{array}}{\text{Sales}} \times 100$$

8

Expansion Planning: How to Plan Investment in Company Growth*

Terry W. Rothermel
Arthur D. Little, Inc.

THE INVESTMENT SIDE OF BUSINESS PLANNING

At the heart of the study of economics is the relationship that ties price to the intersection or the balance of supply and demand. In business practice the profession of market research has been built around the demand side of this relationship. No similar profession has evolved to deal with the supply side of that relationship, for example, to forecast supply in order to compare it to demand and thereby forecast price (and profits). The focus of market research and its parent profession,

---

* "How to Plan Investment in Company Growth," © 1985 by Terry W. Rothermel.

marketing, is largely on customers and their demand needs. The comparable concern of researching supply would be that of competition and its investment behavior.

In lieu of competitive research and associated supply side information, capital budgets are too often based on an assumption of constant industry capacity against a growing industry demand. It is not surprising that such a process too often results in a perceived need for expansion by several competitors and subsequent overcommitments by all.

As taught by the industry simulation models described in Chapter 2, capacity expansion decisions effectively become pricing decisions at a later time. Again, the connection is through that most basic of microeconomic relationships: price being a function of the supply-demand balance. So, when looking for the causes of the latest price war, don't forget to look back to some earlier expansion decisions.

The industry models described in Chapter 2 also teach that long-term market share is partly determined by capacity share. Hence, implicit in any market share objective should be a capacity share objective. Such a statement in strategic plans is a rarity. Unfortunately, for capital budgeting purposes, expansion is too often assumed to follow demand requirements. In truth, capacity and capacity share expansion must come first if market share goals are to be realized and serviced.

Strategic management means to have a strategy for allocating resources among opportunities just as it means locating and exploiting those opportunities. Budgeting capital simply in reaction to expanded and extrapolated sales is more a response mechanism than one of strategy.

BUDGETING FOR EXPANSION AT THE BUSINESS LEVEL

Company growth and expansion can take many forms. Some of these are categorized in Figure 1. There diversification is identified as growth through new products serving new markets. Selling old products to new markets is market extension. Selling new products to old markets is product line extension. The main focus of this chapter is on that form of company expansion in the sales of current products to current markets. This kind of expansion relates to capital budgeting at the business level. Capital budgeting for expansion at the corporate level embraces all of the cells in Figure 1.

The maturity of an industry also affects capital budgeting for expansion. In embryonic or growth industries, expansions must be planned—sometimes in advance of positive cash flows—in order to capitalize on growth market opportunities. Expansion and growth in

FIGURE 1

Forms of Company Expansion or Growth

<table>
<tr><td colspan="2" rowspan="2"></td><td colspan="2">Markets</td></tr>
<tr><td>Old</td><td>New</td></tr>
<tr><td rowspan="2">Products</td><td>Old</td><td>Expansion</td><td>Market extension</td></tr>
<tr><td>New</td><td>Product line extension</td><td>Diversification</td></tr>
</table>

newly mature industries can mean quite substantial investments because of fast-changing economies of scale.

THE GRAND LOOP OF OVEREXPANSION

When the economies of scale favor larger and larger investments, the seeds of overinvestment cycles are easily planted. In these stages (late growth and early mature) it is difficult for a market to absorb a new, economically sized facility without repercussions in the prices and profits of the industry. It can, of course, be argued that the introduction of larger and larger facilities should be more than adequately cushioned by the larger demand volumes which are available. That might be true if competition were orderly and disciplined. What generally happens is that healthy competitors in a growing market become inclined to maintain their positions by expanding when utilization rates are high and growing demand would appear to easily absorb any new production facility.

Growing demand, shortening supply, rising prices and profits—these would appear to describe the optimum timing for most expansions. And so it would be valid if each competitor was somehow alone in a business, alone in seeing that logical timing, or alone in being able to afford the expansion within its capital budget. But, such is not the case. It turns out that most competitors in such a growing industrial market are tuned in to these same logical but self-destructive wavelengths. Further, potential new entrants can read the trade press as well as anyone and come close to the same timing for their entry.

141

Unfortunately, new entrants tend to react slower, and their plants are wont to appear after overcapacity is already in evidence.

On top of the impact caused by larger, economically sized plants is the impact of having several of these behemoths arriving in the industry at the same time. Such a supply wave is too much for any demand curve to handle in the short term. Panicking suppliers will reduce prices in a desperate attempt first to gain sales and then to hold their own. Economics teaches that with decreasing prices, demands should increase according to classic elasticity. Yet normal price demand elasticities cannot raise demand sufficiently to cushion a glut in supply.

The damage has been done. Logical first-order thinking has led to destructive competitive mistakes in the timing of capital expansion projects, and it takes only one or a few competitors to fall prey to this tendency to make all the industry suffer. At least the industry's customers and their customers will be benefactors of the inevitable lower prices.

So, what we have is the classic beginnings of the "grand loop" of overexpansion, falling operating rates, falling prices, and curtailed investment—until growing demand can heal the industry once more. Thus, it seems that the logical or natural time for expansion may only be a first-order solution to the timing of the expansion. More to the point, it would seem to be an expansion trap of the first order.

What happens as a natural result of industrywide first-order thinking is that industry investment is too orderly, too uniform, too synchronized, and too Pavlovian (that is, too much a response to current market stimuli).

LOOKING FOR THE SECOND-ORDER SOLUTION

In the midst of competition, a second-order investment timing solution is necessary. As the first order of solution was focused unidimensionally on the apparent supply-demand balance, the second-order solution takes competitive behavior into account.

Expansion by second-order thinking, however, is not an easy sell in the capital budgeting process. Second-order thinking means resisting the urge to invest when all the others are taking the bait. It probably means holding off on the current round of expansion, surviving the inevitable down cycle caused by the expansion of others, and maintaining a higher operating rate so that expansion will seem more natural earlier in the next up cycle.

Second-order thinking is also tough to handle within traditional capital budgeting. This competitively sensitive logic preaches restraint at a time when the coffers are full. Then, it will likely suggest action when recent prices and profits are at best only an increase over last year's low point. At worst it will suggest the commitment of resources at the bottom of the cycle—that is, at a time when capital budgeters are the gloomiest, the most tight-fisted, and the least willing to take a risk. These are possible and critical prescriptions in many capital-intensive industries where capital budgeting commitment must precede realized business expansion by a year or more.

What is to be expected of top management, the board of directors, and the decision makers who must approve a capital budget and a second-order strategy for business expansion? Will the business manager have the courage and endurance to persuade both boss and capital budgeting counsel on this kind of competitively sensitive strategy? Will the capital budgeter, in turn, risk a career by endorsing such a strategy to management and the board? Will the general manager risk career and company and invite the criticism of Wall Street and the trade press? It is a tough order. Clearly, the manager who pushes a second-order expansion timing strategy had better believe it's a good bet and have a basis for tracking its success.

Top management and the board of directors may see only the first-order logic. If they are to avoid the first-order timing mistake, they are dependent upon their business managers for a competitively strategic investment. At the time they are asked to be restrained, the industry will herald the new commitments of others. At the time they are asked to make their own commitment, the rest of the industry may look on with woeful disbelief.

There is a lingering question in companies that have gone through the self-destructing grand loop several times. Just when will the board and management say that they have had enough, that there must be an answer, that they must make a commitment to get out of step? The alternative to following first-order logic is too comfortable. Too much capacity in the industry can always be blamed on the other guys, particularly on those new entrants who didn't know what they were doing. Low prices, low profits, and layoffs can be blamed on the general state of the industry or even on the general economy. And after all, everybody agreed that the plant was needed and the time was right. (They sure did!)

OPTIONS TO EXPANSION

Typically, the logical time to expand is already too late to avoid being short of supply at the peak of the up cycle. In capital-intensive industries, major plant expansions simply take too long to come onstream.

A short-term solution is known in some industries as *debottlenecking*. Alternatively, the solution is to run extra shifts, seven days a week or simply overtime. But even seven days a week and round-the-clock operation is not enough in many cases. In such cases debottlenecking may provide the most significant assistance. Debottlenecking means to work on those parts of manufacturing which are capacity limiting. It may mean squeezing in an extra production line or team in a plant of limited space or limited skilled people.

Debottlenecking, like full-out operation, has its penalties. Production economics teaches that marginal variable costs bottom out somewhere short of full-capacity operation and then rise as production exceeds nominal capacity or goes beyond it. This traditional theory reflects the realities of operation. Workers, even the skilled ones, start to make mistakes when things are rushed and there is no time to spare. Product yield and quality go down. People literally begin to run into each other as more and more production is squeezed into available space.

Another option to cushion the blow of tight supply is to have built some inventory against these times. Under normal capital budgeting procedures, however, the "waste" of such strategic inventory is not allowed. After all, we all know that inventory costs money—money that could be earning interest in a bank.

But what of business reality in a cyclic capital-intensive industry? What is the value of having inventory available—and labeled to be used in the time of tight supply? Under normal business practice, excess inventory built up in a time of low operating rates will hardly last through a recovery period, let alone be available in the up cycle. Can inventory produced simply for the purpose of keeping the plant running be mothballed (like a plant is mothballed) for use when it is truly needed, not at the first opportunity?

OPTIONS FOR CONSOLIDATION

Another phase of capital budgeting comes when the business cycle turns down. What then are the options of relieving the pressures of lower operating rates and dwindling margins that can be affected by capital budgeting decisions? One option is a capital disinvestment, that is, the selling of a facility to another party or the permanent shutdown, dismantling, and salvaging of excess or obsolete capacity.

What does cyclic or second-order competitive thinking teach about capital decisions of this kind? The logical or first-order timing for shutdown or divestiture would, of course, be near the bottom of the cycle.

Competitive thinking leads one to expect that all competitors will be thinking in a similar way at that time. Hence, the offers to be received by potential buyers of the facility at such a time are not likely to be very great. Existing competitors are likely to be less interested than a firm looking for diversification or a foreign producer taking any opportunity for a domestic foothold. Certainly Wall Street has long since learned, if not easily practiced, the rule of selling high and buying low (or trying not to sell low). First-order or logical consolidation (negative expansion) doesn't do much for maximizing the value of a capital asset. What is the alternative?

The alternative in cyclic or competitive terms is not really clear. If the divestiture is a long-term intention, it may mean to sell in an anticyclical mode, that is, at the top or just after the top of a cycle. Such a strategy would divest a plant long before market pressures require and at a time when others have a real and present need for it. Even the supplier looking toward an expansion in the next up cycle can benefit from divesting itself of a smaller and obsolete facility at this time. This supplier will go into the down cycle with less excess capacity (assuming its marketing forces hold their own) and will be among the earliest to need more capacity at the next economic plant size at the beginning of the next up cycle.

When does second-order thinking suggest shutting down or mothballing capacity on the down cycle? Clearly, other capital expansion and contraction decisions seem to be recommended ahead of the first-order timing. Pricing and marketing activities that anticipate the down cycle may modulate operating rate damage, albeit at lower margins. Over the longer perspective of an industry cycle, the maintenance or even expansion of market share can mean earlier recovery.

Somewhat surprisingly, second-order thinking seems to call for delaying shutdown beyond the time that others would more naturally take that action. The benefits of delay or even of avoiding this action are quite interesting in both the competitive and cyclic contexts. Competitively, it is easy to understand how competitors who shut down their facilities benefit others in the industry as well as themselves by removing some of the operating rate pressures on prices and profits. The competitor that holds out on shutting down the facility can realize the benefits afforded by such Pavlovian competitors before finally being forced to take that action as well.

Keeping the plant running or bringing a mothballed facility back into operation earlier than others in the down cycle has these cyclic strategy benefits. To produce against growing inventory will pressure the sales force to be active and to hold prices low while demand begins to bring the industry out of its doldrums. This will lead to higher ratios of demand to total capacity (both operating and mothballed) for this supplier in preparation for being one of the first to expand successfully in anticipation of the up cycle. This early-cycle investment move will thus preempt other predictable competitive moves later on.

Clearly, these strategies need to be analyzed in financial terms, but that does not mean "traditional" financial terms. A new financial and capital budgeting calculus needs to be built on cyclic, competitive, and long-term thinking. Financial analysis may show consequences of second-order prescription to be unattractive. Nonetheless, the best financial strategy done on these terms is not likely to be the same as the first-order timing that is too often practiced.

CAPITAL BUDGETING AS COMPETITIVE STRATEGY

What is the opportunity cost of not being able to meet the demand requirements of a good customer or even hard-won marginal customers at a time of short supply? These are the kinds of dynamic considerations suggested by putting capital budgeting into two new contexts. The first is the context of a cyclic industry dynamic: actions taken in one part of a cycle help create the situation in another part of the cycle; the needs of one phase *can* be anticipated at an earlier phase; and the financial gains from the short-term budgeting can mean marketing setbacks or the forced abandonment of market share gains.

The second context is the weaving of a truly *competitive strategy* into the capital budgeting of business expansion. A competitive strategy in this case does not simply mean "remaining competitive." As indicated above, it means making capital decisions in consideration of the actions of competitors. Preemptive strategies of investment will thus reduce, delay, or even prevent later investments by competitors. It means anticipating the expansion moves of competion, and it turns out that that is not really too difficult. It means budgeting capital needs and requirements in a time schedule that will seem unnatural to most corporate experience. But "unnatural" will really mean the achievement of truly rational business decision making. Such rational decision making elevates business above the logical and natural. It is rational in the sense that it takes into account all that it can possibly know—which is far short of the perfect knowledge that economics grants in its competitive models. Not having perfect knowledge, however, we *can* get our hands on a lot more planning information than seems to be used in normal capital budgeting practice.

THE CONCEPTUAL FRAMEWORK FOR
BUSINESS STRATEGY EXPANSION

A forecasting tool capable of providing the insights for second-order expansion strategies was introduced in Chapter 2. A dynamic simulation model of that kind is made of several model sectors that correspond to dimensions of competitive position and behavior. It is appropriate here in a discussion of business expansion to describe the factors and considerations that are typically included in what is called the investment sector of these models. In so doing, a shopping list of information and considerations to guide capital budgeting and planning will result.

The first kind of information shown in Figure 2 may be the easiest: an estimate of current capacity in the industry. Of course, that is not

FIGURE 2

Capacity Acquisition Sector

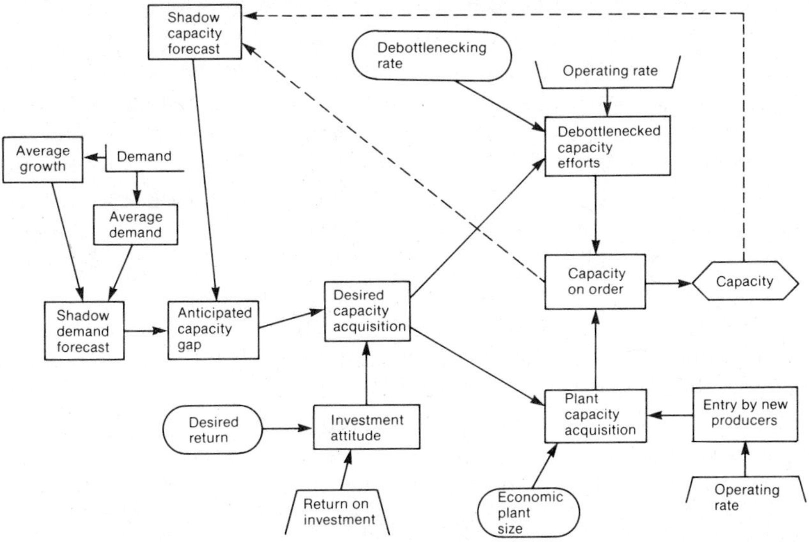

always easy to determine. Nonetheless, decisions are enhanced by finding the best information possible on the capacities of competitors. This means finding out about increased capacity due to debottlenecking, additional production lines, or other changes to original plant de-

147

signs. It means deducing real capacities based on market shares and estimated sales when supplies are tight and everyone is producing as much as possible. Some competitors are known to publish overestimates of their capacity to discourage competitive investments. Others choose to hide their true capacities.

The model logic (Figure 2) considers operating rates for individual producers to stimulate and anticipate the inception of their debottlenecking activities. It is important to determine whether the potential for debottlenecking is different for different competitors and to develop that kind of intelligence through whatever channels of information are available: customers, former employees, or trade gossip.

The delays between the time in which debottlenecking is stimulated and the time that it is available for production are also important. Significant business can be lost or foregone in a tight supply situation in the meantime.

The entry of new producers into an attractive business at the top of its up cycle cannot, of course, be ignored in analyzing the growth of industry capacity. In an early model of an industrial chemical industry, the first projections looked like the forecast of an orderly, disciplined industry. Unfortunately, that bore no resemblance to the actual marketplace. One of the most dramatic steps toward reality was accomplished when new producers were ushered into the industry simply in response to high operating rates and high profits. When those so-called irrational producers were given a role, the behavior of the actual industry was closer to being captured. It has thus far been sufficient to model new producers as responding simply to the state of current or recent business in the industry—much like what one would get from reading the trade press quarterly earning statements and the like.

The heart of the investment sector of a forecasting model (Figure 2) is the simulation of decisions to build major expansions or facilities. This is the mainstream of forecasting industry supply, and it is forecasting supply that allows these models to forecast price and the timing of industry cycles.

An additional step shown in Figure 2 to forecasting competitive expansions is the simulation of how an industry of competitors estimates current capacity and forecasts the need for more capacity (the capacity gap) by comparing it to a forecast of demand. This has been termed *shadow forecasting*.

One form of shadow forecast is the competitive forecast of capacity; the other is a shadow forecast of demand. In the shadow forecast of capacity, competitors can be given a common estimate of existing capacity or given a somewhat clouded view of capacities other than their own. If it is believed that there is at least some sensitivity to the actions of others in making their expansion decision, competitors can be modeled to consider the announced expansion of the competition in determining the need for a new plant—in this case their own. Here, too, there can be an important delay. In modeling investment behavior and overcapacity cycles it is important to know if companies make their commitment to expansion a significant time before it is announced in the marketplace. This increases the chances that several competitors may make simultaneous expansion decisions.

Another factor in modeling competitors' investment decisions is the question of what is called *captive markets* or *captive capacity*. Hence, producers with capacity supporting their own integrated businesses may be viewed as making decisions that are tied more to their own integrated product sales and capacity needs than to the supply-demand balance in the industry itself.

Other producers may be modeled to have a strategy of maintaining or increasing market share primarily through an aggressive investment program and achieving a higher supply share in the industry. Such competitors may be modeled as ignoring the threat of an announced competitive plant in their decision to meet expected future demand with an expansion of their own. The framework in Figure 2 forces a more considered study of individual competitors, their business objectives, and their associated investment behavior. Part of that investment behavior is their standards of profitability and their expectations from the business. These models have demonstrated an interesting interplay between these standards and the cyclic behavior of different kinds of producers.

Take the case of an industry recovering from a down cycle. The producer with a lower standard of profits is likely to be stimulated earlier to invest in the next round of expansion. It will not be so for the producer with a higher standard that waits for the logical, first-order decision time. Thus, there is the chance that those with higher and stricter standards of investment based on recent and short-term returns may pass by the best time for expansion and be the ones that invest in the plants that drive the industry into overcapacity. In addition, those later plants are more likely to come onstream when demands are saturated, prices are falling, and sales are hard to come by. Such a plant is then likely to have its opening delayed until the recovery of the next down cycle. Alternatively, once those producers with lower standards have made their investment, the capacity gap may be recognized by such an industry statesman as not sufficient to justify another plant. As a result, such a competitor may miss this round of investment altogether and be less a factor in the industry in each successive cycle.

149

NEW DIRECTIONS FOR CAPITAL EXPANSION BUDGETING

Business expansion is successful only if a company is able to meet the requirements of both the supply side and the demand side of competition. A company must be able to create demand, respond to customers, and meet competition through marketing. This chapter emphasizes the supply side of competition—providing supply through production capacity and meeting competition on this front as well. Relating marketing to competitive activity is an obvious and accepted association. Viewing investment decisions as another primary competitive activity is less practiced.

Capital budgeting for company expansion is a process of selecting among alternatives for investment. Traditionally, a number of analytical tools are brought to these budgeting decisions. Corporate hurdle rates and business criteria play a major role in choosing between alternatives. Cost estimates and market analyses are among the basic information needs. The bottom line on the decisions comes from a rigorous financial analysis, including the use of present value concepts and projected corporate financial resources.

Financial analysis in capital budgeting is too often against the grain of market realities. From a financial point of view, it is preferred to budget for constantly growing sales, revenues, and resources. It is preferred that the major investments for expansion be spread out as evenly as possible. Very few businesses, of course, enjoy the luxury of achieving these managed outcomes.

The marketplace exerts more power over the conditions of decision, unfortunately, than does a company's decision-making structure. Most markets are cyclical, forcing cyclical results and an uneven pace of investment. Capital budgeting needs to be less a vehicle for flattening expenditure over time and more a vehicle for anticipating and taking advantage of the opportunities for the better timing of investment.

THE ROLE OF ANTICIPATION IN COMPETITIVE INVESTMENT STRATEGY

Better timing comes from better competitive anticipation, and better anticipation is a strategic consequence of better forecasting. Forecasting an industry cycle is an early warning system for company expansion budgets. It is a successful industry forecast that promises the timing for the next important investment decisions for a corporation and its competitors. Such anticipatory decisions are commitments made on a view of tomorrow's market conditions. Making those kinds of commitments in turn requires confidence in the forecast. Such forecasting confidence can come only through using a forecasting tool and understanding the logic by which that tool makes its forecast.

The logic of the industry simulation approach has one major premise: to know the conditions of decision is to know the decision. By simulating the competitive pressures of the marketplace, it has proved possible to anticipate expansion decisions of competitors on the supply side of the marketplace. The decision is deduced through a Pavlovian linkage (i.e., stimulus/response mechanisms). Assuming the competitive decision makers to be prisoners of the pressure of decision is not too bad a predictor. (That is not to say that another industry or future marketplace might require the simulation of more sophisticated investment behavior.)

Competitive anticipation is a broad-based prescription. It means gauging the impact of one's own expansion activity on the actions of competitors. Similarly, it includes anticipating their likely actions in the absence of your own. It also means anticipating the decisions of competitors, understanding and studying their apparent strategies, judging their reactions to reading the same headlines, and being ready to accept the possibility for irrational, Pavlovian, and wrong decisions on their part.

COUNTERCYCLICAL CAPITAL EXPANSION STRATEGIES

Linear thinking clearly needs to be replaced in the capital budgeting process when the cyclicality of the market and competitive action is real and overwhelming. Linear and graduated trends in expansion expenditures may be more desirable than fluctuating ones from a financial management perspective, but the inflexibilities of such linear thinking can be more destructive than constructive if cyclical response is more appropriate.

The prescriptive strategy suggested for cyclical industries is a countercyclical one or is one that at least is out of phase with traditional industry response. The challenge is to avoid the Pavlovian traps lying in an industry's cycles. The challenge is to avoid making an investment along with others at just the wrong time.

Following a countercyclical expansion strategy will seem anachronistic. To management it will instinctively not feel right for the same reasons that it is easy to predict the usual decision under competitive pressures. Hence, these expansion strategies will appear to be ones of either over- or underinvesting in contrast to the behavior of competitors. One may appear to be underinvesting at a time in which new investment is popular. Later one will choose to overexpand at a time before investing again becomes popular.

CONCLUSION

Strategies developed to deal with the competitive problems of cyclicality are only possible for companies that have committed themselves to long-range participation in an industry. Resisting the near-term revenues of logical investment on the upside of the cycle or investing for the future near the downside of the cycle are not acceptable actions if the focus is only on the profits and cash flow of the next six months.

The strategic answer to Pavlovian investment behavior is a capital budgeting process that allows management to resist the immediate pressures of decision. The strategy suggested by this discussion is that of countercyclic investments. In today's business practice such investments are viewed at least at high risk if not impossible—but possibly only because they are counter to prevailing capital budgeting thinking or to the prevailing psychology of an industry. A countercyclic expansion alternative is only one possible competitive strategy. Countercyclic alternatives need to be evaluated carefully in terms of long-term profitability. They will also need to be shepherded through the Pavlovian resistance to such unnatural strategy that will arise in every corporate management and capital budgeting department.

SUGGESTED READINGS

Chambers, John C.; Satinder K. Loeck; and Donald D. Smith. "How to Choose the Right Forecasting Technique." *Harvard Business Review,* vol. 49, no. 4 (July–August 1971), p. 45.

Forrester, Jay W. *Industrial Dynamics.* Cambridge, Mass.: MIT Press, 1961.

Gershefski, George W. "Building a Corporate Financial Model." *Harvard Business Review,* vol. 47, no. 4 (July–August 1969), p. 61.

Jantsch, Erich. "Forecasting and Systems Approach: The Frame of Reference." *Management Science,* August 1973, p. 1355.

MacMillan, Ian C. "Preemptive Strategies." *The Journal of Business Strategy,* Fall 1983, p. 16.

Naylor, Thomas, H., and Horst Schauland. "A Survey of Users of Corporate Planning Models." *Management Science,* May 1976, p. 927.

Porter, Michael E. "How Competitive Forces Shape Strategy." *Harvard Business Review,* vol. 57, no. 2 (March–April 1979), p. 137.

Porter, Michael E. *Competitive Strategy.* New York: Free Press, 1980.

Rothermel, Terry W. "Forecasting Resurrected." *Harvard Business Review,* vol. 60, no. 2 (March–April 1982), p. 139.

Schultz, Robert S. "Profits, Prices, and Excess Capacity." *Harvard Business Review,* vol. 41, no. 4 (July–August 1963), p. 68.

9

Investment Strategy: Strengthening the Foundations of Capital Budgeting

Bela Gold

Claremont Graduate School

*I*n order to maximize its contributions to improving company performance, capital budgeting must revert to its original role as the backbone of corporate planning. Increasing formalization of its procedures has converted large sectors of capital budgeting operations into largely routinized processing of capital goods acquisition and other investment proposals on the basis of the required income and outlay estimates provided by the initiators. Even if such input data were reasonably reliable, however, the results could only be expected to rank the relative magnitudes of the benefits of the competing proposals that were considered. But using these rankings to guide capital allocation decisions might be regarded with some justification as reflecting a policy of rootless improvisation or planlessness, for such an approach need not provide effective bases for answering the two far more critical questions faced by managements and by their corporate planning staffs:

1. What adjustments or improvements are likely to prove necessary to safeguard or strengthen the competitive position of the firm over the next three to five years?
2. To what extent would the proposals to be approved represent the most effective means of utilizing available capital resources to fulfill such emerging needs?

If corporate planning is to provide sound responses to such queries, it must become more comprehensive in coverage; and capital budgeting efforts will have to be restructured in order to help implement the resulting broader perspectives.

REVISING THE RESPONSIBILITIES OF CORPORATE PLANNING

The early monopolizing focus of corporate planning on financial goals and requirements has been widely supplemented in recent decades with output growth and market share targets. But even this expanded scope will continue to fall short of needs until it encompasses all of the major determinants of company performance. Moreover, in order to contribute fully to the development of needed adjustments in management policies, corporate planning must not only formulate improvement goals that promise to strengthen market competitiveness in the future, but it must also suggest the adjustment patterns over time needed to get from here to there.

Such responsibilities center around three requirements. The *first* is to appraise current and prospective market changes and threats to be dealt with over the next three to five years, including (1) likely shifts in the relative competitiveness of each major product's performance capabilities and price in each major market and (2) likely changes in the availability and prices of all needed inputs along with resulting changes in the cost competitiveness of operations. The *second* requirement is to assess the benefits, costs, and risks of alternative means of improving product capabilities and production efficiency in comparison with the probable effects of continuing improvement efforts by competitors. And the *third* is to evaluate needed adjustments in personnel staffing and in organizational arrangements as well as in marketing and finance in order to ensure effective harnessing of the potentials offered by prospective changes in product offerings, procurement policies, and production operations.

155

In order to discharge such added responsibilities, involving penetration beneath the familiar measures of financial performance to the operational determinants of such outcomes, additional types of expertise will be required to supplement those usually provided within capital budgeting staffs. But the needed insights provided by specialists in product design, procurement, production, and marketing are likely to be of limited value if they represent only offhand judgments instead of the considered evaluations that could be crystallized if these specialists were reassigned for a period from their normal tasks to concentrate on exploring longer-term tendencies likely to affect future competitiveness. In addition, it would also be necessary to organize discussions involving interactions among such specialists along with the capital planning staff if the resulting variety of forecasts representing narrowly specialized viewpoints is to be integrated into a coordinated development plan.

The fundamental implications for capital budgeting of such a broader approach to corporate planning are apparent from the fact that the latter may be expected to identify (1) major developmental needs not being addressed by the proposals submitted to capital budgeting and (2) expected changes in products, technologies, and input factor markets that would undermine, or even eliminate, the estimated benefits of current proposals. Accordingly, increasing the effectiveness of capital budgeting would seem to require that it be conducted within the perspectives of corporate planning objectives. In addition, however, it would also seem necessary to revise the underlying premises and criteria as well as the actual methodology of capital budgeting.

ON THE VULNERABLE FOUNDATIONS OF CAPITAL BUDGETING

Because of the strategic importance of managerial decisions involving major investments—whether relating to technological innovations, capacity expansion, or other purposes—they have been a primary target of efforts to develop increasingly sophisticated guides to evaluating relevant alternatives. During the past three decades, these have led first to increasing resort to methods emphasizing the estimated "return on investment" rather than the older "payback period" approach and, more recently, to a further shift of interest in favor of the "net present value" methodology. A number of variants of each of the newer approaches have been developed which offer better adaptations to various kinds of problems and employ different assumptions concerning the cost of capital among other things.[1] But all share the basic foundations whose vulnerability is the initial focus of the following discussion.

156

Underlying Premises and Estimates

The most fundamental of all premises underlying capital budgeting techniques is that it is possible to forecast the time patterns of investment and operating expenditures as well as of revenues and net incomes over the entire life of contemplated projects. Moreover, this must be done within ranges of error so small as to permit meaningful comparisons with alternatives including short-term investments and other long-term projects as well as comparisons with defined minimum rates of return representing "cut-off" levels (below which all projects are to be rejected). In addition, the net present value form of capital budgeting also requires estimates of the discount rates likely to be applicable for the duration of the project.

Although a considerable literature concerning capital budgeting has developed—in economics and accounting as well as finance—surprisingly little attention has been given to:

1. Identifying the considerable structure of forecasts underlying the aggregate estimates entering into capital budgeting calculations.
2. Evaluating the error margins within which such component estimates and their products are likely to range.
3. Appraising the practical value of outcomes subject to such error margins.

Accordingly, the discussion will begin with the first of these: identifying in turn the more immediate determinants of needed estimates of investment requirements, revenues, and costs.

First, forecasts of the investment required to construct planned facilities involve supplementing the initial estimates derived from engineering designs and plans with the additional estimates of:

1. Prospective changes in factor prices during the construction period.
2. Possible delays in the construction schedule due to such factors as labor difficulties, shortages of needed supplies and equipment, or transportation difficulties.
3. Unexpected difficulties in getting new facilities to function properly, especially in the case of innovation.
4. Emerging needs for readjustments in associated sectors of operation to achieve effective integration.

Revenue estimates, a second major component of capital budgeting evaluations, depend on the following three underlying estimates, each of which depends in turn on still others:

157

1. Estimates of the facility's prospective time pattern of output, which are based on:
   a. Forecasts of the industry's total output, product mix, and geographical pattern of demand (reflecting estimates of the needs of major customer groups or industries).
   b. Forecasts of this firm's market share by product and region.
   c. Forecasts of the share of this firm's output likely to be provided by this facility, reflecting its specialized product capabilities and its specific geographical advantages and disadvantages.
2. Estimates of the time pattern of the prices likely to be fetched by this facility's products, which in turn are largely based on such elements as:
   a. Estimates of production and distribution costs (which are discussed below).
   b. Estimates of the time pattern of relationships between supply and demand in its markets, including allowances for the level of inventories and the intensity of competitive pressures from foreign as well as domestic producers.
   c. Estimates of the prospects for gaining (or maintaining) differentially higher prices because of product superiority.
   d. Estimates of changes in general price levels due to broader economic forces as well as governmental policies.
3. Estimates of the facility's economic working life, which are derived from:
   a. Estimates of the likelihood that new or substitute products will displace those which the facility is best suited to produce.
   b. Estimates of the prospects for advances in production technologies and facilities (including increases in scale), or the imposition of higher pollution control standards that would undermine the facility's competitive position.
   c. Estimates of the prospects that major shifts in the sources and availability of needed inputs (for example, raw materials and energy), or in markets, might render the facility marginal because of geographical disadvantages.

The remaining major input into capital budgeting models, in addition to estimates of investment requirements and of prospective revenues, covers estimates of the time pattern of the operating costs and other deductions from revenues that determine net returns to the firm. Such aggregate estimates are based on direct estimates of a variety of components, including:

158

1. Estimates of the time pattern of the average unit variable costs of production, based in turn on estimates of:

    a. Unit input requirements of materials, energy, and labor as affected by efforts to improve efficiency.

    b. Input factor prices (reflecting the effects of changes in input supplies relative to needs, in trade union policies, in market competition among suppliers, and in relevant government controls or restrictions.

    c. Shifts in input factor proportions resulting from the preceding adjustments.

2. Estimates of the time pattern of average fixed costs per unit of output, based in turn on estimates of such factors as:

    a. Depreciation schedules.

    b. Trends in salaried employment costs.

    c. Changes in the cost of working capital.

    d. Estimates of capacity utilization rates.

3. Estimates of the time pattern of changes in marketing and distribution costs.

4. Estimates of adjustments in tax rates and incentives.

There is nothing new, of course, in such a listing; indeed, it has omitted a good deal that would have to be included to approach even reasonably complete coverage. The reason for presenting it, however, is to encourage conscious recognition of the formidable complex of estimates underlying the aggregates with which virtually all capital budgeting exercises begin—and to consider the soundness of these foundations, on which rest decisions that may well be of critical importance not only for the firm but for major sectors of the economy.

On the Accuracy of Needed Forecasts

To provide such an array of forecasts within the margins of accuracy needed to justify the investment choices noted above would patently represent an extraordinary accomplishment even for projects lasting only five years or less. As among the three major forecast aggregates of investment requirements, revenues, and operating costs, the first is usually regarded as the most dependable, and it probably is. Yet industry is awash with projects whose construction costs have far exceeded the estimates entering into the decision to go ahead; and each of the component elements listed above as underlying the forecasts has contributed significantly to such painful errors. Nor can such gross underestimates be attributed to the failure of industry specialists to consider potential future problems, for instances of such difficulties are common features of the industrial landscape. But how is recognition of such possibilities to be translated into quantitative estimates of resulting costs? Within what margins of error can this be done? And on what analytically persuasive basis for the commitment of large investments can such estimates select some quantitatively specified point between the extremes of activist impatience (which minimizes possible difficulties) and of paralyzing pessimism (which exaggerates both the uncertainties and their possible costs)?

In respect to the primary determinants of future revenue expectations, general economic forecasting experience has tended to highlight estimates of changes in output as likely to yield better results than estimates of product price levels. And yet even short-term industry-level output patterns and their associated five-year "trend" extrapolations have been found subject to substantial margins of error.[2] Many still recall the heavy cost of commitments in anticipation of the widely predicted but never realized "soaring 60s"; and the severity of unexpected adjustments during the past two years is widely apparent. More sharply focused evidence of such problems has been provided by Jeckovich, who asked what would have been the effects of introducing major capital expansion programs in the U.S. glass industry at the successive peak output levels marked in Figure 1—and showed the ensuing long periods of underutilization that would have resulted.[3] Figure 2 presents two illustrations of the vulnerability of such relatively shorter-term extrapolations from a study covering 28 industrial and agricultural output series. And it should also be added that this study concluded that these extrapolations had become progressively *more* deviate from actual outcomes in recent decades. Combining such discouraging perspectives even for industry-level forecasts of output with the need to make estimates of the still more highly variable elements listed above as also affecting probable output levels for particular plants suggests that results are likely to be very vulnerable indeed, even within periods of a few years.[4]

The difficulty of forecasting industrial prices over periods of a few years differs widely among industries and even among products in many industries. But it is generally regarded as substantially more difficult than forecasting output, even over periods of only three to five years. The basic problems derive, of course, from the role of prices as the point of interaction among changes in supply-demand relationships, unit cost levels, product design, general price levels, intercompany competition, and interproduct competition. As a result of the great difficulties involved, price forecasts usually focus on the next marketing season, seldom reaching beyond one year. Indeed three- to

FIGURE 1

U.S. Output of Selected Glass Products

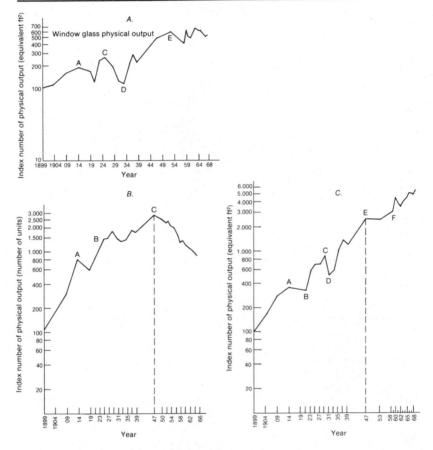

Source: Reprinted from S. Jeckovich, "Technological Forecasting as a Guide for Managerial Planning," *Long Range Planning*, September 1971, pp. 31–33.

five-year forecasts of prices are widely regarded as meaningless. Even in those cases where producers seem able to hold price adjustments within narrow limits, this aid in forecasting revenue tends to be offset by the accompanying tendency of such products to undergo greater fluctuations in output levels.[5]

As for the remaining determinant of total future revenues, the estimated economic life of particular capital facilities, no generally applicable bases for attempting such determinations are available except re-

FIGURE 2

Forecasts Based on Projections of Past Trends into the Unknown Future Compared with Hindsight Estimates of Trends

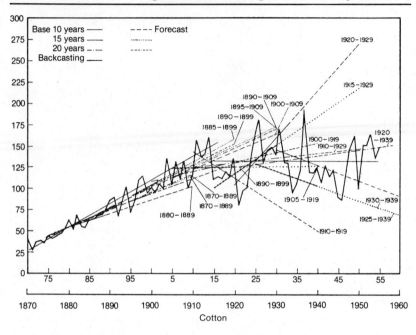

Cotton

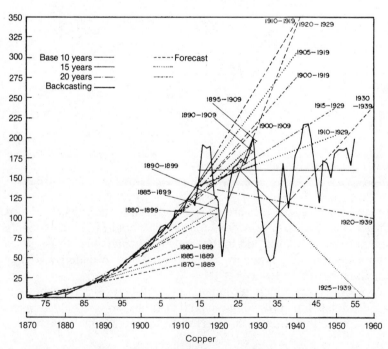

Copper

Source: Reprinted from B. Gold, "From Backcasting to Forecasting," *Omega*, April 1974, p. 216.

sort to the past experience reflected in the allowable depreciable life specified by tax authorities or accepted as reasonable by auditors. But the accelerating pace of technological innovations involving new processes as well as new products, the emergence of material and energy stringencies, the development of increased foreign competition, and substantial changes in transportation costs provide ample basis for unwillingness to extend such historical precedents very far into a turbulent future. It may be argued, of course, that such uncertainties are greater in some industries than in others. One need only attempt to identify major sectors of industry that are relatively free of such prospective disturbances, however, to realize how few are so regarded by their own decision makers.

The estimation of future profit margins also requires forecasts of prospective changes in costs. In respect to production costs, the greatest difficulties probably center around future capital goods prices. There seems to be a widespread belief that materials prices have only recently broken away from less volatile adjustment patterns in the past. But Figure 2 and the study from which it was taken demonstrate that they were virtually unpredictable in the past as well. Capital goods prices are also commonly regarded as having broken loose only in the past few years. But Figure 3 illustrates successive enormous jumps even before 1970. And even if it should be less risky to forecast that wage rates are likely to rise sufficiently to cover both increases in output per man-hour and in consumer price levels, the estimation of these for particular plants is still likely to prove no easy task. As among the remaining determinants of net profits, the costs of working capital, shifts in permissible depreciation policies, and changes in local and national tax rates seem to represent progressively still greater challenges to forecasting efforts.

In short, direct scrutiny of the structure of forecasts that must underlie the commonly required inputs into formal capital budgeting methods suggests that resulting evaluations may easily be subject to error margins of the order of at least 33 to 50 percent, even in respect to capital project estimates covering only five years. And such ranges of error would obviously preclude meaningful comparisons with the precisely determinable rates of return available from relatively riskless short-term investments, or with specified cutoff rates of 15 to 20 percent.

Even more pessimistic conclusions are suggested if one considers the applicability of formal capital budgeting methods to projects involving investments of hundreds of millions of dollars and covering construction periods of 6 to 8 years plus expected effective working lives of at least 25 to 30 years, such as are involved in the construction of

FIGURE 3

Blast Furnaces: Investment Cost Per Gross Ton of Capacity for New and Rebuilt Furnaces

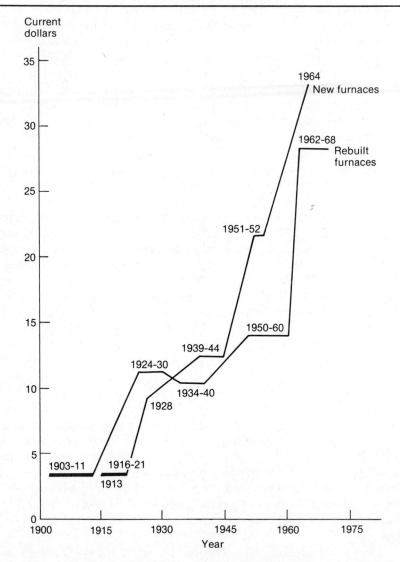

Source: M. Boylan, *Economic Effects of Scale Increases in the Steel Industry: The Case of U.S. Blast Furnaces* (New York: Praeger Publishers, 1975), p. 162.

electric power plants, steel mills, aluminum plants, large-scale mines, and other basic industrial facilities. Specifically, long-range forecasting has thus far proved not only valueless but misleading.

Even in respect to industry-level output patterns alone, the comprehensive pioneering effort by Arthur Burns proved widely at variance with actual outcomes. Specifically, on the basis of studying more than 100 production series covering 45 to 60 years each, he offered three generalizations which are still accepted by many:

1. An industry tends to grow at a declining rate, its rise being eventually followed by a decline.
2. The conception of indefinite growth of industries can be supported neither by analysis nor by experience.
3. Once an industry has ceased to advance—[it] soon embarks on a career of decadence.[6]

In addition, he also estimated long-term growth patterns for each series indicating the year in which its output would reach a peak. The testing of these generalizations and expectations some 25 years later, however, revealed that all were overwhelmingly out of line with actual results.[7] And a comparison of 25-year forecasts of total world consumption of various industrial materials by the President's Materials Policy Commission of the United States in 1950 with actual consumption in 1972–73 showed the latter ranging between 75 percent and 175 percent of the forecasts, with each forecast being in error by not less than 20 percent.[8]

Although much has been made of the seemingly stable growth paths fitted by econometric methods on the basis of hindsight, or "backcasting," there is little evidence of consistent success when efforts are turned around so as to offer long-term forecasts into an unknown future, as shown in Figure 2. Indeed, serious doubts about its feasibility have been expressed by a variety of practitioners.[9]

Thus, there is an absence of supporting empirical evidence as well as analytical doubts concerning the possibility of developing reasonably accurate long-range forecasts even about output alone and even at the aggregative level of major sectors of the economy. Accordingly, there is ample basis for skepticism about being able to provide the wide array of forecasts in respect to the individual plant and firm that is called for by capital budgeting models—and to achieve margins of error narrow enough to provide convincing grounds for commitments involving large investments and having a critical bearing on the future of the company.

In view of the growing popularity of the net present value approach to capital budgeting, it may be worth adding that this technique's fur-

165

ther requirement—that a discount rate be chosen for estimating the net present value of future returns—adds still another source of potential major errors in view of the problem of choosing an appropriate rate for projects of very long duration. For example, looking at Figure 4, it is

FIGURE 4

Return on Short-Term and Long-Term Loans and on Stockholders' Equity

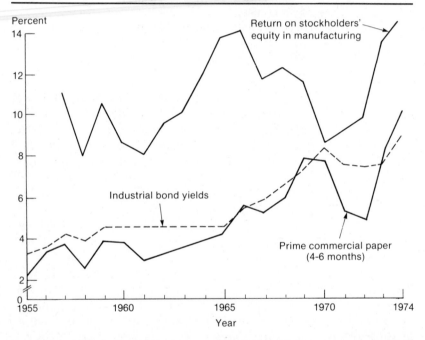

Sources: *Federal Reserve Bulletin*; and Federal Trade Commission and Securities and Exchange Commission, *Quarterly Financial Report for Manufacturing Companies*. Reprinted from B. Gold and M. G. Boylan, "Capital Budgeting, Industrial Capacity, and Imports," *Quarterly Review of Economics and Business*, Fall 1975.

not easy to decide what would have been the most appropriate discount rate to choose for capital budgeting evaluations in 1955, 1960, 1965, or 1970. In the face of such a record, how secure would most managers feel about making such an estimate today in respect to adjustments over the next 30 years or more?

In short, even if the analytical structure of capital budgeting were more fully developed, and its objectives were entirely acceptable, one might still be wary of an approach that promises superior guides to major decisions but whose results seem to be subject to wide margins of error. There is an understandable appeal to prescriptions for dealing with business, economic, and even social problems "rationally" or even "scientifically." But such assertions often outrun performance. In this case, there is a worrisome gap between the extensive literature on technical aspects of capital budgeting methods and the paucity of serious evaluations on the range of errors to which its component estimates are subject. Hence, although it is deemed to be a mark of sophistication to claim reliance on capital budgeting methods, it is not surprising that many such claimants admit to only loose conformance with its specific methodologies.[10] Businessmen who participate in developing the variety of estimates entering into the final capital budgeting calculations are often reluctant to rest their career prospects on any "objective" techniques for combining such soft estimates into hard commitments. Confidential inquiries even suggest that capital budgeting analyses may be more frequently revised to accord with top-level judgments based on other grounds than to serve as the primary basis for managerial decisions.

This does not mean that formal capital budgeting procedures are useless. On the contrary, such approaches tend to encourage a systematic collection and evaluation of whatever information is deemed relevant. They could also provide a methodologically expert approach to identifying the limitations of the assumptions underlying efforts to estimate the possible future adjustment paths of the numerous variables to be covered. And these could then serve as the foundation for, and constraints on, the additional considerations that must enter into the decisions for which senior officials will be held responsible. But, as of this time, capital budgeting methods do not seem to offer a consistently superior basis for evaluating prospective major capital investments even for projects covering only five years—*still less* for projects involving even longer time periods.

SOME ADDITIONAL SHORTCOMINGS OF CAPITAL BUDGETING PRACTICES

Widespread Overemphasis on Cost Saving

One of the most common shortcomings of capital budgeting centers around the notion that the prospective acquisition will serve in large measure as a *replacement* for existing equipment and, hence, that the criterion to be emphasized is cost saving. This may seem reasonable and has actually been the basis for a substantial literature seeking to guide such decisions.[11] But this focus is, nevertheless, wrong, for the essential objective should always be to maintain or to increase profitability.

What is the difference between cost savings and profitability? Simply reducing the costs of product types and of production processes that have been in service for long periods, and that have accordingly been facing progressive obsolescence, is unlikely to prevent declining sales and profitability. During a period when virtually all manufacturing industries are undergoing major changes in technologies and in market pressures, the very concept of "virtual replacement" must be dismissed along with the criterion of "How much more cheaply can we do what we have been doing?" Although this criterion is seldom clearly acknowledged, it is almost pervasively insinuated into the capital budgeting estimates that focus on the magnitude of expected savings (as compared with guess what) relative to required investments.

In order to respond effectively to intensifying competitive pressures, and thus reinforce corporate planning objectives, the basic criteria for evaluation should be determined by answering the question: "In what ways could the future market potentials of our products be increased by what is being done in this and related sectors of our production operations?" To answer this question would require consideration of the possible need for changes in product designs to facilitate manufacturing; in quality specifications; in production methods, including substitutes for machining and other current techniques; in loading and unloading as well as materials handling and inspection; and in the tasks assigned to labor. Thus, practical evaluations should place a heavy weight on the prospective effects of the new equipment on improving the attractiveness of the product to customers, and hence on potential sales and price levels, instead of concentrating on cost levels alone.

Moreover, this approach recognizes the still widely ignored need to keep evaluating the prospective contribution of each newly added operating unit within the context of the larger system of which it is a part, rather than within its own narrow functional boundaries. In carefully integrated manufacturing plants, it is seldom possible to introduce major innovative improvements within any component sector without requiring readjustments in some antecedent as well as subsequent operations in order to reintegrate the system so as to maximize utilization of the innovation's potentials.

Foreshortened Horizons

Perhaps the second most important shortcoming in evaluating the prospective financial benefits of acquiring major innovations in production facilities and equipment is the widespread reliance on capital budgeting methods that use net present value or similar criteria as the basis for recommending decisions. There are several serious weaknesses in this unfortunately popular approach, some of which have only belatedly begun to command increasing attention.[12]

To begin with, one must keep remembering that in buying the long-lasting facilities and equipment that embody major technological innovations, the fundamental objective is not to maximize net *present* value but rather to improve or safeguard profitability over an extended period. Because it involves discounting future net returns back to the present, the net present value approach tends to increasingly foreshorten evaluation horizons as progressively higher interest rates are used in discounting deferred returns. Thus, during periods of high interest rates, virtually all improvements except those promising extraordinarily generous returns within short periods are likely to be rejected as less rewarding than relatively riskless investments in short-term money market instruments. For example, even a 20 percent discount rate would reduce the present value of returns expected to be available after only two years by more than one third, and returns expected to be available after three years by almost one half.

But major innovations can seldom be effectively harnessed within such relatively short periods of time. Even if a firm were to order a copy of a system already functioning effectively elsewhere, it often takes a year or two before it can be built and installed and at least another year before it is likely to have been debugged and integrated into the production processes. And additional time may then elapse before its utilization rate can be brought up to optimal levels. In fact, many major innovations are likely to take even longer before they achieve planned levels of output and efficiency. Consequently, they are likely to invite repeated rejections when evaluated according to net present value criteria, for even waiting until competitors have assumed the potential risks of earlier adoptions may not reduce the time required to achieve effective utilization sufficiently to yield favorable net present returns. Indeed, such waiting may reinforce the unattractiveness of returns because of the concomitant decreasing advantages and profitability available to later adopters of an innovation.

The very innovations rejected by such net present value criteria, however, may provide a necessary basis for strengthening competitiveness over longer periods. After all, the capital goods involved are likely to last for at least a decade, except in rare cases of newly developing technologies. Thus, if they reach increasingly profitable levels after three years, they may make important contributions to productive efficiency and profitability for most of a decade or longer. On the other hand, continuing failure to adopt such innovations can only result in progressively undermining competitiveness and longer-run profitability. After all, the cost-effective productive capacity of plants tends to decline with time, especially after the first five years in most industries. Repeated deferrals of investment in new facilities tends, therefore, to engender progressive reductions in market share relative to competitors using updated facilities. Resulting burdens would include not only the cost of lost sales pending the eventual introduction of new capacity but also the cost of underutilizing the new capacity over whatever period might be necessary to regain the sales volume that it can supply—in the face of increases in the capacity of competitors in accordance with their earlier gains in market share.

Static Analytical Framework

Another widespread shortcoming of capital budgeting, when applied independently of the development perspectives of corporate planning, is the tendency to allow short-term perspectives not only to dominate the definition of the key criterion—net present value—but also to dominate estimates of prospective results through heavy reliance on projections of current relationships and perceptions. Rarely are such evaluations based on serious analyses of possible changes over the next five years in the availability and prices of various relevant types of purchased materials and energy, or in the availability and wage rates of different labor skills. Similarly infrequent are careful studies of prospective changes in product mix and required product qualities. Moreover, such evaluations have commonly assumed the continuation of current high interest rates, thereby further reinforcing deterrents to major long-term improvement projects.

Such an essentially static orientation also manifests itself in other forms. One of these involves concentrating capital budgeting evaluations on each specific proposal by itself, instead of recognizing the need for integration with the strategic perspectives of corporate planning in which current proposals may represent only the initial stages, or infrastructure, of a succession of later proposals that can be expected to prove profitable only after the sequential components of the undertaking have been completed. For example, such a monopolizing concern with immediacies would never recommend support for the introduction of basic research programs, or of a manufacturing technology improvement program, whose initial two years might well concentrate on developing staff, facilities, and work plans without yielding any substantial benefits.

A second form of static orientation is to focus capital budgeting evaluations on ordering projects in terms of their relative net present value as the basis for recommending the most attractive to finance within available resources—without considering possible concomitant decisions by competitors. But this ignores two additional possibilities of potential significance: (1) What would be the effects of rejecting a given innovation if competitors adopt it? (2) What would be the effects of adopting it if competitors do not?

The former raises the possibility that the penalties for falling behind in some aspect of competition might be far greater than the incremental profitability promised by its adoption. An important illustration is the case where failure to acquire the advanced facilities necessary to meet the higher-quality specifications of major customers could lead to serious market losses, although their acquisition might merely enable the firm to retain its past markets.

Firms in roughly the same industry may nevertheless differ in many respects, including product designs, product mix, technological modernity, relative advantages in respect to the availability and prices of needed inputs, as well as in respect to capital resources and managerial capabilities. At any given time, therefore, they may well differ in their priorities in seeking to improve or maintain competitiveness. Nevertheless, in making its choices, each firm must consider not only its own preferences but also the possible effects of rejecting some alternative—for example, a technological innovation—that is adopted by its competitors. Resulting market effects may include a decline in customers' perceptions of this firm's progressiveness and may even lead to a decrease in competitiveness if significant aspects of performance are thereby undermined. The internal implications of having rejected major innovations that have proved highly advantageous to competitors may include a need for early reconsideration of the urgency and means of catching up and also a need to reexamine the reasons for the earlier rejection lest these reflect weaknesses in the evaluative processes that may encourage underestimates of the potential benefits of other potentially important innovations in the future.

Undermining Development of Innovational Proposals

Managerial decisions in respect to major innovational proposals exert a powerful influence both on the kinds of proposals generated and on the performance estimates accompanying them.

Operating supervisors and engineers are obviously sensitive to management's responses to the proposals that have been submitted. If such decisions seem to favor minor over major innovations, or those which can be implemented quickly over those expected to require longer periods to yield expected returns, they may be regarded by prospective sources of proposals as guides to the kinds of efforts most and least likely to reward developmental thought and effort. Even more serious, ambitious, and innovative personnel may well respond to the discouragement of major technological advances by leaving for more promising environments, thereby further reducing the liklihood of proposals with major potentials for strengthening competitiveness.

A quite different problem involves the buttressing of proposals with vulnerable estimates of the magnitude of prospective benefits and the speed and probability of their attainment. On the one hand, these may derive from the overoptimism of those generating the proposals in order to improve the likelihood of approval and in the hope of resulting recognition and rewards, perhaps enhanced by the naïveté of many production and technical specialists concerning the wider determinants of commercial success. On the other hand, the submission of such estimates to other specialists often elicits less encouraging judgments, possibly reflecting some mixture of reasonable doubts and biases rooted in different technical perspectives and organizational motivations. In such instances, capital budgeting evaluators may well be tempted to minimize their own risks by citing these conflicts and uncertainties as reasons for recommending deferral, if not outright rejection of such proposals.

APPROACHES TO STRENGTHENING CAPITAL BUDGETING

Shifting to a "Continuing Horizons" Criterion

In order to safeguard the firm's competitiveness over time, it is obviously necessary to plan for the periodic introduction of improvements in production capabilities to offset the progressive deterioration and technological obsolescence of production equipment and processes as well as changing market pressures. Because substantial periods may be required to install, debug, and bring any resulting major innovations to high levels of utilization, cogent arguments can be adduced for replacing the net present value criterion for evaluating such prospective additions with what I have called a "continuing horizons" approach. Instead of ranking the attractiveness of alternative proposals on the basis of their estimated contributions to maximizing net *present* value at the time of their evaluation, this approach would seek to recommend the adoption of an array of innovations whose contributions to profitability would reach and maintain high levels at successively later periods.

Such an approach could be applied by estimating prospective annual net returns over periods of 5 to 10 years for each alternative proposal *without any discounting*. The analysis would then seek to determine the prospective pattern of profitability over successive years resulting from various combinations of project approvals and rejections. Overconcentration on proposals promising to maximize net present value might thus be revealed to entail growing vulnerability to decreasing net returns beyond the next three to five years as a result of rejecting all major innovations with returns deferred long enough to be severely reduced by discounting to the present, as suggested in Figure 5. Conversely, such a preview of prospective adjustments in undis-

FIGURE 5

"Continuing Horizons" Approach to Evaluating Successive Innovations

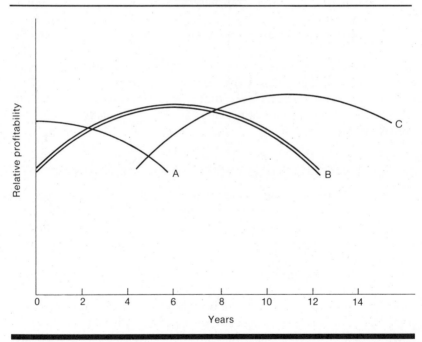

counted profitability rates would also help to identify possible inadequacies in planning for innovations needed to offset prospective declines in intermediate or in longer-term competitiveness. Annual reviews of such conclusions, augmented by consideration of newly emerging proposals and adjusted for changed assessments of prospective opportunities and pressures, would help to keep such innovational portfolios responsive to updated perspectives.

Broadening the Coverage of Capital Budgeting Evaluations

Most currently functioning manufacturing systems embody the results of years of efforts by a variety of technical and managerial specialists to achieve increasingly effective integration of their component operations. Hence, it is seldom feasible to introduce a major innovation into any sector without requiring a variety of adaptive adjustments in antecedent and subsequent stages of the system. Accordingly, effective evaluation of the prospective effects of the innovation would require supplementing the conventional appraisal of the expected effects of the innovation within its immediate area of application with a careful analysis of the nature, location, and magnitude of these further adaptive readjustments in order to estimate their combined impacts on both total production costs and on any additional investments that may be necessary to permit full utilization of the innovation's capabilities. To do so would obviously require enlisting the expertise of specialists in the other operations likely to be affected, as well as in production planning and other supervisory functions, as the basis for possible adjustments to the estimates provided in the initial, usually narrowly conceived proposal.

Auditing and Improving Capital Budgeting Estimates

In view of the tremendous influence on the future competitiveness of firms of the evaluations of prospective innovations by the capital budgeting process, it is obviously important to evaluate the effectiveness of its results. Yet, in contrast to the voluminous literature on predecision evaluations of innovational effects, few publications offer serious evaluations of the actual effects of the innovations that have been adopted—or of the capital budgeting estimates leading to their acquisition. The explanation seems to be that the relevant methods and interpretations are considered so obvious as to offer no analytical challenges. Our research suggests, however, that such efforts are confronted by significant difficulties concerning the appropriate criteria for evaluation, the timing of such appraisals, who should make them, and how the results should be used.

Criteria of evaluation. Most efforts to evaluate the results of major technological innovations tend to concentrate on financial measures,

174

especially on comparisons of outlays and costs with original expectations. But such findings tend to be inadequate and may even be misleading unless account is also taken of all other changes engendered by the innovation. These may include one or more of the following: changes in the quality as well as in the quantities of inputs and outputs, shifts in operating tasks among production stages, alterations in product mix and in the length of production runs, adjustments in reject rates, and increases or decreases in equipment downtime.

Moreover, effective appraisal also requires uncovering the causes of observed deviations from expected results. In particular, management needs to know the extent to which such changes were attributable to equipment characteristics, or to engineering modifications of production methods, or to maladjustments in input and work flows, or to changes in labor capabilities and efforts. In the absence of such analytical determinations, there seems to be a tendency to ascribe any observed deficiencies to external or to unpredictable factors—thereby ignoring internal remedial potentials both in respect to the estimates made and in the coverage of capital budgeting efforts.

In evaluating the cost effects of technological innovations, results may be heavily affected by decisions concerning whether the following are treated as increases in the investment charged to the innovation or as additions to operating costs: the cost of interruptions to production caused by the innovation; the cost of delays before achieving effective functioning of the innovation, including attendant costs of equipment modifications, debugging, operator training, and trial runs; additional outlays in order to improve the capabilities of the new facilities; and the costs and investments involved in readjusting preceding and subsequent operations in order to improve the capabilities and integration of the encompassing production process.

The timing of evaluations. Firms that undertake "post-audits" or "make good" evaluations of installed innovations tend to relay on a single appraisal, usually within 6 to 12 months after project completion. These early appraisals often yield overly optimistic findings, however, because generous allowances are made to offset actual shortcomings on the assumption that these are attributable to temporary problems— such as excessive maintenance, inadequate labor experience, or underutilization due to incomplete integration with adjacent operations.

If such appraisals are to be more effective, they would have to be made repeatedly over three- to six-month intervals for at least the two to three years that the complete absorption of major technological innovations seems to take.[13] Successive evaluations would reveal trends in various performance measures, demonstrate which shortcomings are transitory and which are not, and identify additional sources of improvement through progressively more thorough integration with the larger manufacturing and control systems.[14]

Responsibility for evaluations. One of the critical problems faced in evaluating major innovations is the pressure for biased findings. In the case of very large projects, favorable biases tend to be encouraged by fears that negative findings might reflect on the senior officials who made the basic decisions and be resented by them. Biases may also be generated by assigning evaluations to those who recommended the adoption decision, on the grounds that they alone have the requisite technological competence. Still another source of bias may be the desire of designated evaluators to maintain future cooperative relationships with the project officials involved. As a result of experiences with such problems, some firms have abandoned ex post evaluations entirely, while many others seem to have relegated them to relatively routine financial reporting exercises.[15]

But such carelessness, passivity, or defeatism has already helped to undermine awareness of the shortcomings of past efforts to improve technological competitiveness—and to evaluate proposals more effectively. In addition, such attitudes have also helped to delay recognition of the need to organize more formal, comprehensive, knowledgeable, and regularized evaluations of the effects of the large investments in major technological innovations which may be key determinants of future profitability. Providing the needed objectivity and range of relevant expertise may require that such evaluations be the responsibility of some senior official who is concerned with exacting appraisals of performance, with uncovering any possible means of improving results, and with identifying the sources of errors in predecision appraisals and in the processes of introducing innovations so as to develop more effective guides to such efforts in the future. Such an executive could then secure the contributions of various relevant specialists, and surmount the common self-protective devices of lower-level supervisors and technicians, in seeking to uncover the sources and causes of shortcomings in performance as well as of remedial errors in predecision appraisals.

Formalizing responsibility for the comprehensive evaluation of major technological innovations might yield two additional benefits. First, by providing top management with systematic assessments from an influential official of the potentials, accomplishments, and shortcomings of projects that have absorbed major capital allocations, such periodic reports may help to engender greater sensitivity to the importance of technological improvement efforts throughout the firm. Sec-

176

ond, the very seriousness and scope of such efforts may help to overcome the present widespread failure to make any constructive use of even such postadoption appraisals as are made, either in reexamining means of improving the current results of relatively recent innovations or in strengthening the bases for evaluating future proposals.

The Need for a Strategic Planning Framework

The fundamental purpose of capital budgeting must be recognized as providing one of the basic means of implementing the strategic plans devised to safeguard and improve the firm's competitive strength. In most industries, firms face changing product requirements, continuing improvements in manufacturing technologies, and alterations in the capabilities of production equipment, as well as shifting input availabilities and prices. Each of these developments may stimulate proposals for responsive adaptations involving investment commitments. In the absence of strategic plans based on careful explorations of such alternative adjustment opportunities, capital budgeting evaluations of competing proposals solely on the basis of their own estimated direct effects on prospective costs and revenues cannot ensure progressive improvements even in the short-term cost-competitiveness and profitability of the firm, much less in the effective allocation of available capital resources to strengthen the longer-term performance of the firm.

SOME ADDITIONAL BASES FOR MAJOR CAPITAL DECISIONS

The dominant factor to be remembered in efforts to improve major capital investment decisions is that they necessarily involve large commitments over extended periods into the future in the face of very significant uncertainties. It is usually taken for granted that *objective* bases for decisions are likely to prove more valid than *subjective* bases and that *quantitative* evaluations are better than *judgmental* evaluations. But such terms can easily obscure the realities.

Rather, the bases which are likely to be most persuasive to the decision makers who have to assume resulting risks and responsibilities are those which seem most fully and most realistically to encompass the primary strategic factors involved. The very identification of such factors in a given industrial setting, however, tends to be rooted more heavily in experience and in specialized current judgments than in any standardized analytical formula. Moreover, the evaluation of such factors and the processes by which they are combined into an overall judgment may defy translation into specific numbers and relative weights.[16] Nor is the academic means of dispelling uncertainty by somehow pulling together a sample of subjective estimates of probabilities reassuring to businessmen, who are well aware that entrepreneurial success rarely results from acting in conformance with widely held judgments. On the contrary, such success seems more often to be associated with considering information that is ignored or minimized by many others, or with anticipating developments regarded by others as unlikely, or with taking risks that are unappealing to most.

Nothing in the foregoing is meant to imply any derogation of the need for the fullest possible information attainable within given time, cost, and other constraints. Nor is there any question of the desirability of analyzing such information as effectively as possible. What is being emphasized, however, is the need to recognize the limitations on the completeness and accuracy of the objective and quantifiable information collected, as well as the limitations of any generalized analytical framework when applied to a particular situation, which often involves uncommon conditions, institutional factors, and sensitivities to change. Hence, it would seem necessary to supplement even the best general analytical framework and objective data with an array of experiential judgments and action-oriented or risk-averse subjective inclinations as the basis for making major decisions.[17]

In seeking to strengthen the foundations for making major capital project evaluations, there is obviously great need still for an analytical framework that would provide more effective coverage of the factors to be considered in making decisions. But it is also necessary to develop an increasing understanding of the strategic components of the managerial judgments that are superimposed on available quantitative estimates before decisions are made. Accordingly, it may be useful to present some preliminary findings concerning such actual practices in several industries. Our inquiries suggest that such decisions are based most heavily on top management's judgments concerning the following fundamental issues: (1) the likelihood that demand for the general types of product under consideration will continue for an extended period; (2) the necessity of regularized upgrading of products, facilities, and distribution efforts to remain competitive; and (3) the ability of the firm's staff and the adequacy of its resources to cope with unexpected future developments.

To illustrate the first point, an American mining company officer emphasized that it makes no use whatever of capital budgeting methods, relying instead on the principle that if a mineral deposit can be expected to last at least 75 years at current efficient levels of production, it is worth going ahead. The second point was succinctly illustrated recently by a Japanese steel executive in explanation of his company's decision to expand despite great domestic and international uncertainties: "It all comes down to Hamlet's question: To be or not to be? In an industry subject to continuing changes in the availability of inputs, in technologies, and in markets, we must keep trying to keep up with the leaders or give up." An example of the third point was provided by an official of a European chemical firm who stated, "No one knows what will happen over the next 5 to 10 years, but we want to be there when it does, so that we, too, can try to cope." In short, a qualitative attitude which may be termed *commitment* or perhaps *confidence* seems to serve in many firms as a far more powerful basis for confronting uncertainty than available quantitative estimates based on purportedly sophisticated tools.

Above these foundation determinants of whether to build or not, the bases for deciding the next three elements of a capital project decision seem to have stronger objective roots. How large a capacity to build seems to be determined largely by the availability of resources, the advice of construction and production engineers on unit capacity and unit operating costs, and on the company's market share objectives. What technology to use seems to be determined by the best that is already functioning successfully and that is also adapted to the company's inputs, product mix, and staff expertise. When to build seems to be determined largely by the urgency of needs for new capacity (to overcome capacity limitations, or to adapt to pressures for changes in product or technologies, or to adapt to changes in input availabilities or in geographical market shifts) and, again, by the availability of sufficient resources. And where to build seems to be a less strategic question except in respect to foreign projects, where political assessments vie with economic evaluations.

Thus, one is led to the following tentative hypotheses:

1. Most firms are commited to continued concentration on their established areas of specialization unless these are already reflecting evidence of progressive decline. Hence, they have no option about whether or not to undertake new projects over time—either to upgrade operations or to expand—but can only choose when to initiate such undertakings.

2. Most managements believe that no one can forecast the long-run future effectively enough to yield a consistent competitive advantage and, hence, that the soundest protection against unexpected or adverse developments is to develop strong financial resources, high-quality staff, and reasonable flexibility in policies. Thus, they tend to be dubious about long-range forecasts of factor prices, product prices, profit rates, taxes, and other important elements of their future economic environment. On the contrary, they assume that such changes will tend to be adjusted to one another on economically viable terms.

3. There is general acceptance of the inevitability of mistakes by all competitors, combined with a belief that the only relevant safeguard is alertness to detecting impending errors and penalties as early as possible in order to mitigate their costs. Hence, deferring action until authoritative forecasts are available is less common than intensifying efforts to promptly obtain comprehensive information that may indicate emerging deviations from early expectations. Indeed, many managements seem to believe strongly that the success of long-term projects depends in far greater measure on management's capacity to make strenuous efforts to overcome or adapt to changing pressures and opportunities than on the quality of the original forecasts, that is, on "making it work" rather than on "guessing right."

Lest there be any misunderstanding of the purport of this discussion, it may be worth emphasizing that advances in the effectiveness with which forecasts can be made in respect to the specific elements entering into capital budgeting models would undoubtedly be valuable and welcome. And even if forecasts cannot be made within needed margins of accuracy, decision making would be substantially strengthened by utilizing an analytical framework that ensures more systematic coverage of the variables likely to influence the outcome significantly. But the limited contributions that are available as yet in this area helps to explain why major capital decisions, involving the future of the firm as well as that of its executives, continue to be based primarily on managerial judgments, reflecting their past experience and resulting behavior patterns, rather than on the seemingly refined but largely imprecise estimates entering into modern capital budgeting models. And, of course, such inadequacies tend to be substantially intensified when project proposals involve major technological innovations that broaden the range of uncertainties around many—if not most—of the estimates needed for effective application of such capital budgeting techniques.

NOTES

[1] For example, see J. Dean, *Capital Budgeting* (New York: Columbia University Press, 1951); E. Solomon, ed., *The Management of Corporate Capital* (New York: Free

Press, 1959); E. F. Fama and M. H. Miller, *The Theory of Finance* (New York: Holt, Rinehart & Winston, 1972); and M. Weingartner, *Mathematical Programming and the Management of Capital Budgeting Problems* (Englewood Cliffs, N.J.: Prentice-Hall, 1963).

[2] For example, Zarnowitz's comprehensive analysis of forecasts by several hundred forecasters from industrial firms, banks, government agencies, and universities found "the mean error of one-year forecasts of total industrial production (between 1953 and 1963) was 47 percent of the average annual change." He also noted that, "The overall averages conceal a considerable amount of dispersion among the average errors of different forecasters." See V. Zarnowitz, *An Appraisal of Short-Term Economic Forecasts* (New York: National Bureau of Economic Research, 1967), pp. 4–5.

[3] S. Jeckovich, "Technological Forecasting as a Guide for Managerial Planning," *Long-Range Planning*, no. 4 (1971).

[4] Fama and Miller, *Theory of Finance*.

[5] For early evidence of such price–quantity interactions, see F. C. Mills, *Price–Quantity Interactions in the Business Cycle* (New York: National Bureau of Economic Research, 1946). For relative variations in output and price of different sectors of manufacturing, see W. H. Shaw, *The Value of Commodity Output since 1969* (New York: National Bureau of Economic Research, 1947), p. 23.

[6] A. Burns, *Production Trends in the United States since 1970* (New York: Augustus M. Kelley, 1950), pp. 170–73.

[7] *Explorations in Managerial Economics: Productivity, Costs, Technology, and Growth* (New York: Basic Books, 1971), pp. 250–56.

[8] T. Kono, "Changing Corporate Environment and the World Steel Industry," Nippon Steel Corporation, Tokyo, July 1975, Chart 29.

[9] Norman Robertson, senior vice president of Mellon Bank in Pittsburgh, is an economist who has lost faith in economic forecasting. "I had to do a forecast of the economy in 1980," he relates. "You put together a lot of numbers, and they don't mean a damn thing. There is so much uncertainty and so much instability in the economy that it's impossible to see where we'll be even two years from now. All I can see is very large doses of instability and uncertainty" (*The Wall Street Journal*, May 15, 1975). "Long-term economic forecasting is a notoriously inaccurate undertaking." B. Bosworth, J. S. Deusenberry, and A. S. Carron, *Capital Needs in the Seventies* (Washington, D.C.: The Brookings Institution, 1975), p. 76. For a more fundamental critique of econometric forecasting models, see Karl Brunner, "Review of Econometric Models of Cyclical Behavior," *Journal of Economic Literature*, September 1973, pp. 926–33.

[10] C. F. Carter and B. R. Williams, *Investment in Innovation* (London: Oxford University Press, 1958), p. 60; and B. R. Williams, "Information and Criteria in Capital Expenditure Decision," *Journal of Management Studies*, September 1964, p. 116.

[11] For example, one of the classics in this field was G. Terborgh, *Business Investment Policy* (Washington, D.C.: Machinery and Allied Products Institute, 1958).

[12] For earlier discussions, see B. Gold and M. G. Boylan, "Capital Budgeting, Industrial Capacity, and Imports," *Quarterly Review of Economics and Business*, Fall 1975; and B. Gold, "On the Shaky Foundations of Capital Budgeting," *California Management Review*, Winter 1977. For a recent discussion, see R. H. Hayes and D. A. Garvin, "Managing as If Tomorrow Mattered," *Harvard Business Review*, May–June 1982.

181

[13] For a detailed illustration of such changes, see B. Gold, *Productivity, Technology, and Capital: Economic Analyses, Managerial Strategies, and Governmental Policies* (Lexington, Mass: D. C. Heath, 1980), Chapter 10.

[14] For example, in one computer-aided manufacturing system, it was found that successive minor modifications in operating methods and control yielded a progressive increase in capacity of approximately 40 percent over a five-year period. But such increments were so gradual that management failed to alter production planning and output targets accordingly—leaving the additional capability unutilized until its belated discovery as the result of a strike. See B. Gold, "CAM Sets New Rules for Production," *Harvard Business Review*, November–December 1982.

[15] B. Gold, G. Rosegger, and M. G. Boylan, *Evaluating Technological Innovations: Methods, Expectations, and Findings* (Lexington, Mass.: D. C. Heath, 1980), p. 313.

[16] Williams, "Information and Criteria," pp. 121–23.

[17] The role of values and of preferred directions of change are discussed at length in B. Gold, "The Framework of Decision for Major Technological Innovations," in *Values and the Future*, ed. K. Baier and N. Rescher (New York: Free Press, 1969).

10

Motivation: Some Behavioral Aspects of Capital Budgeting

Harvey Leibenstein

Harvard University

THE BUDGET PROBLEM AND MOTIVATION

At first blush, capital budgeting and motivation seem like rather remote considerations, or at least clearly separable items. The connection is less than obvious. The usual textbook view of capital budgeting is to discuss formulas for (and ways of calculating) returns of different budgetary options and allocations. If for a given budget we can make calculations that tell us on what to spend our capital funds to get the greatest returns, our problem is solved, or so it may appear. But is it solved when what we know are arithmetic procedures or the algebra involved?

Nowadays a good way of looking at the problem would be in terms of a computer program for capital budgeting. Suppose we had such a program. We put the program disk into our handy computer, type in the alternate numbers, and, in a few seconds (or minutes) of computer time, the desired budget items should appear on the screen. The numbers we would punch in would be the alternative capital options available, the anticipated cost of each capital option, the variables that would determine the revenue flows (prices of final products, inputs to be used and their prices, and the alternative production techniques to be employed), and the interest rates and/or the discount rates that are applicable. Whether any of these matters sound technical to the reader is not of great importance since each of them could be explained quite simply. They usually are explained in the standard works on capital budgeting. The basic question is: If we had the right program in the computer, would we get the "right" results? The computer would solve the problem about the appropriate formula to use in order to discount a flow of net revenues to the present period so that we could compare the present value of the net revenues with the cost of capital. Clearly, by doing this for all the options, we can easily work out the allocation scheme that gives us the highest return. But, and it is a big *but,* there is something missing.

What is missing is that we do not really know, or we would not know from the program, how to *evaluate* the various estimated *numbers.* The program is unlikely to tell us whether these numbers are realistic or unrealistic. Are they good estimates or bad estimates? We are likely to be captivated by the flimflam of computer printouts—to believe that rapid calculation somehow is likely to yield the right results. All that the computer does is rapid calculations and the rapid search for data and for procedures put into the machine. The computer does not tell us what to put in or anything about the nature of the numbers that we do put in. But the right results depend very much on the quality of the numbers that we punch into the computer. The main point of all this is that the *quality* of the numbers depends on "who does what," that is, on the nature of the organization that is going to do the doing, and this depends to a considerable degree on intraorganizational motivation.

Before going into detail, let us consider for a moment a significant mechanical consideration. Capital budgeting is normally a "stock flow problem." The stock of money that exists at a point in time and is to be allocated to various projects is, in a sense, known. It represents *hard* data. It is an obvious point, but it is not trivial. By contrast, the flows of revenues or costs are *soft* data. They, of necessity, depend on various estimates about what will happen in the future. It does not help very much to have excellent formulas for determining the present value of the flows in order to compare them with the capital cost (a stock concept) of the investment option if the estimates are not very good. The question, of course, is: How soft is soft data? Could they be "hardened up" to some degree? The argument we put forth here is that this is indeed the case, that hardening up the data involves organizational motivational assessments. It involves searching for and looking at the "motivational gauges."

Let us consider more fully a few aspects of the stock and flow distinction and its significance for our purposes. The amount of money budgeted is a stock. It is a meaningful quantity at a point in time. Any specific allocation to a particular investment option is a stock. It is a quantity that exists at the point the allocation is made. We assume it exists. That is, it is not a problematical amount in any sense. For purposes of the allocation, its existence and accuracy is not at issue. Of course, the money amount will usually be translated into something else, that is, in whole or in part into physical assets. The quality of the physical assets may be somewhat problematical but not the initial budgetary allocation.

The flows are of an entirely different nature. Flows exist over periods of time. Thus the gross revenue associated with a given asset may exist over the lifetime of the asset, say, 20 years. For accounting purposes we usually consider shorter periods such as years or quarters. The important point about flows is that they do not exist now, that is, at a point in time. The flows associated with a certain asset option must of necessity occur in the future from the viewpoint of the time that the allocation is made. Hence the calculation of profitability must of necessity compare a set of uncertain values of future flows with a known investment amount. But the flows themselves must be *guesses*. There is no way of eliminating the uncertainty. They involve the future, and they are guesses about the future. Thus the qualitative nature of the budgeted investments and their consequences—the flow generated by the investments—are very different types of quantities. The flows themselves are assessments of a probabilistic nature.

Before we leave the computer analogy, we have to consider what is involved and what we have to avoid. Essentially we have to avoid being overly impressed and/or being taken in by computational mechanisms. This is true whether the mechanism is inside a computer or whether it follows a formula of some sort, or a set of equations, or is the work of a set of accounting conventions, or some combination of these. In all cases we have to avoid being impressed by the apparent power of a mechanism that appears to produce a precise answer or set of answers.

The mechanism appears to produce a bottom line, but the bottom line is really no better than the quality of the numbers put in. None of this is meant to denigrate calculation or calculating procedures. Calculation is important, and where complexity is involved relatively fast calculation can frequently be useful; but we must keep in mind that the computer maxim "garbage in, garbage out" must always be respected. In general, the numbers inserted will not be pure garbage but will nevertheless be sufficiently problematic as to require caution. We will argue that motivational elements are involved in the assessments, in the determination as to whether the numbers are garbage or reasonably cautious assessments.

In the sections that follow we shall consider (1) why such assessments are necessary, (2) what some of the elements are that we take into account in making such assessments, and (3) how various elements are interrelated with each other. Finally, we shall return to our basic question, can the "motivational gauges" be read?

WHY ASSESSMENTS ARE NECESSARY

On October 13, 1981, the *New York Times* reported a study of two Ford plants, one in the United Kingdom and the other in Germany, that were identical in every respect. Engineering and productivity assessment data indicated that the output should be identical. However, the German plant produced 50 percent more automobiles with 22 percent fewer employees. Clearly, the motivational elements in the two plants were very different.

To see why assessments are necessary, consider the twin plant case in a little more detail. The parent company had the time, expertise, and resources to make the necessary plans (blueprints) in order to calculate the returns on each plant, that is, on each investment. Part of the engineering staff was assigned the job of working out the detailed blueprints of manufacturing the product. Engineers can design the necessary buildings in which the manufacturing process is to take place. Clearly they can also design the machines, work out the routing and processing of the raw material, work out how much personnel is to be used at each point in the manufacturing process, work out the organization of the work processes, and work out the direct labor force as well as the staff necessary to keep records, handle finance, and carry out planning on a day-to-day basis. They carry out motion studies so that in principle the workers can be instructed how to process materials, and they carry out time studies that help to estimate how long it takes to process a given amount of material. Given blueprints of this type, it would not be difficult for an accountant or an engineer to obtain the prices of various materials and the going wage rates for various types of labor, and to calculate the cost per unit of output. All this seems almost straightforward and almost mechanical. It is all mechanical in an important sense.

Now, the type of blueprints we have described would normally yield the numbers to plug into one of the formulas (or into the computer) in order to obtain the bottom-line number. If we had blueprints of this type (and this is much more extensive than what we usually have), we could then compare rates of return for different investment options. This would solve the capital budgeting problem. But there is a fly in the ointment. It is one thing to work out a blueprint, it is something else to put the blueprint into operations, as it were, and have things operate according to the blueprint. Indeed, that is exactly the difficulty with the twin Ford plant example mentioned earlier. The same blueprint applied in different contexts can yield vastly different results. The blueprint numbers, or any numbers that depend only on *design,* cannot tell us what will happen in practice. To put the matter slightly differently, there is a vast difference between blueprinting and doing. The doing need not go according to the blueprint.

My own work in this area resulted from the review of various bodies of literature having to do with attempts to introduce technical change—especially in developing countries. In one case a team of experts visited a plant in India, analyzed its production methods, and suggested some *costless* changes. These involved changing the placement of various types of equipment, changing the routing of materials, and changing procedures, without the necessity of adding space or equipment or personnel. The experts left the plant in the belief that the new procedures, having been introduced and shown to be an improvement, would continue in place. Why not? It seemed a most reasonable thing to believe. However, returning six months later, they found that the plant had reverted to all of the old methods of routing materials and the placement of equipment. The managers and employees were used to the old ways of doing things. It was part of their normal routine. They liked it that way. Why change just because some transitory experts suggested an alternative way of doing things? It is not all that different to rearrange things to the way they were before. Thus here we have a case where a superior method was, in fact, introduced, but the group doing the work had a desire for procedures that were part of their previous experience. Here was a case where people used their discretion in such a way as to employ an inferior method of doing something despite the fact that they were given the knowledge of a superior one. Other variants of this example exist in the literature.

What this and related bodies of literature clearly suggested was that enterprises neither used the best methods of production available nor were they necessarily eager to discover the best methods. Clearly the economists' ideal of a "production function" (the use of optimal methods of production, that is, the use of optimal blueprints) was not in any way realistic. Another body of literature shows that in every industry there is considerable deviation between best-practice methods and average performance. Thus in the same industries plants with approximately the same capital per worker and the same knowledge will frequently have vastly different outputs per worker. Fifty percent differences are not at all unknown. Thus differences in costs are far from trivial.

It doesn't do to say that this is all the result of the "human factor" and leave it at that. While such a remark is frequently trotted out, it tends to trivialize the situation and usually allows us to ignore essentials. Putting it this way frequently represents an attempt *not* to grapple, or even to face, an important class of problems. Giving these problems a name and recognizing them vaguely is not helpful. At the very least we have to appreciate that the so-called human factor does not imply that individuals behave in a completely idiosyncratic manner. Rather, a good deal of behavior in economic organizations represents a response to motivation, to the motivational content implicit in the organization, and to the surrounding circumstances. Furthermore, the motivational elements can be looked into, analyzed, and assessed. In other words, in assessing such elements as sales, costs, and profitability, we have to look at the production processes of an organization not only from a technical and mechanical view but also in terms of motivational analysis. Some of the basic ideas are elaborated in the next section.

BETWEEN DESIGN AND RESULT: DISCRETION, MOTIVATION, AND PERFORMANCE

An allocation of funds will yield a set of flows. These will be flows of something. There are a great variety of possibilities. For the present consider one special case where the essence of the problem is the flows related to the creation of a physical commodity with fixed characteristics. The commodity may be a bar of soap, a drug, an automobile, and so on.

We can visualize a number of stages between the act of investment and the essential flows that end up in the discounted net revenue calculation. To start with there is a planning and design stage of both the commodity and of the means to produce it—such as a factory. Next there is a purchasing and construction stage. Clearly buildings, equipment, and inventories of essential raw materials have to be built and/or

EXAMPLES: PERSONAL MOTIVATION VERSUS COMPANY WELFARE

Motivational elements are important in assessing the activities of the investment project and in determining the investment decisions processes. In many instances the personal motivation of corporate officers may override the numerical data and calculations available for alternative investment options. Most business-people can bring to mind many cases of this sort.

At the time of writing (August 1984), the case of Walt Disney Productions is clearly illustrative. The officers of the company, in order to save or protect their management jobs in the face of a takeover bid, made a number of inappropriate investments. Initially, investments were made which increased company debt in order to decrease the attractiveness of the company to the takeover bidder. In addition, the officers used company funds to purchase the stock from the potential takeover bidder. While the officers succeeded in avoiding the takeover, these decisions were not in the interest of the stockholders.

Another clear-cut case concerns the supersonic aircraft Concorde. The numbers suggested that the investment would not be profitable. But for reasons of French and British nationalistic pride, it was decided to go ahead. In the case of the Boeing Company possibly building an American version of an SST, the numbers were clearly against the economic viability of the project. Neither Boeing nor U.S. government subsidization proceeded. However, some of those involved in consulting on the project—who clearly were aware that the project would not be profitable—nevertheless were in favor of pursuing it in the interests of "developing the technology."

Another case in the last decade involves RCA's entry into the video-cassette recorder market. This was the consequence of the motivation of the founder's son, Robert Sarnoff, attempting to establish a record for himself in building up the company in a different area than the founder had. The venture failed. But the unusual costs and risks could have been foreseen at the outset.

A number of interesting cases are found in Joseph Bower's 1970 study of a large chemical company where the investment decisions were determined, in part, by particularistic motivational considerations.[1] One particular officer was accused of building a factory in East St. Louis that no one really wanted. However, the chief officer in charge decided it was the thing to do. There are a number of other instances where the concern for using advanced technology was considered much more significant than the possibility of cost reductions.[2] As a general matter, it seems that the careers of group vice presidents (and managers of functioning factories) and the history of the divisions they headed determined the priorities they used to make judgments about investment projects.[3]

A striking example of the up-to-date technology investment bias is the case of the Prelude Company.[4] They were in the lobster-catching business. They built a fleet of expensive high-technology boats, but the boats did not catch any more lobsters than their cheaper low-tech counterparts. The company eventually went bankrupt.

There are innumerable additional illustrations. The upshot of all this is that motivational elements are significant in determining investment decisions that are not in the interests of the company. Two classes of consideration are likely to play a role. First, various emotional forces are of significance behind seemingly rational decision making. Second, and perhaps more important, the interests of officers within the corporation are not always the interests of the company and its owners.

Along the lines just mentioned, internal political elements are frequently important. Various levels of management somehow become divided into factions. Showing loyalty to some faction leader or superior is frequently a necessary condition of getting ahead. (It may not always be sufficient.) Thus, people may make decisions not in terms of their actual careful assessments but in terms of what they believe their superior wants, or what they believe will show loyalty to the superior in question. Insiders will frequently understand that the important consideration is not what is the best investment option but rather whose man (or woman) is the person making the decision. Frequently, mutual loyalties between superior and subordinate are involved. Thus, superiors may support a loyal subordinate's proposal even if they believe it is not the best one available. Decisions that do not appear to make sense when examined from an unbiased, objective viewpoint may become transparent when looked at in terms of the internal political games being played.

The bias for the most up-to-date technology has already been illustrated. It is extremely pervasive. In part, it is a bias that exists because some people simply love hardware.

The more complicated the hardware and the more up-to-date, the better. Hardware sells even when we do not understand how it works. Furthermore, hardware appears to promise to replace less reliable and seemingly less pliant human beings. In addition, executives who are primarily trained as engineers are especially likely to be subject to this type of a bias. All of this is likely to be operative despite the fact that at the level of general principles, it is fairly well understood that pieces of equipment that work well in one context when operated by one team of individuals may work poorly in other contexts and with other less mechanized groups. For example, many computerized systems work less well than the systems they have replaced.

Related elements that help to support the "get the latest technology" bias is the feeling that "we must not be left behind in the technology race." If other firms are introducing a certain type of equipment, then it is probably a good idea for us to do likewise. So the thinking of at least some executives is likely to run. This type of orientation is likely to rule in other areas where corporate officers feel they ought to pay serious attention to what other firms appear to be doing. If others attempt to expand in certain lines, then perhaps the firm in question should do likewise. Similarly, if others are diversifying, then perhaps we ought to diversify, whether or not we understand how to operate in widely different areas. There is a fear of being different. Some sense of security is achieved if we act on the view that we can't go too far wrong if we do the same thing that the others are doing. Mistakes will appear to be less terrible if others are making them simultaneously.

An additional motivating element may be the differential attractiveness of the investment versus the motivation to carry it through. Thus, in the short run, individuals may be strongly motivated to invest in certain areas, but they may be much less motivated to carry out the detailed running of the projects that result. Usually, those who make the investment decision do not have to run the resulting economic activity. Such a division of labor can quite readily lead to unfortunate decisions because there is a lack of identification with the problems to be faced by those who eventually have to carry out the details of day-to-day operations.

A significant element behind all of this is the pervasive separation between ownership and management. To a considerable degree, managers make investment decisions but they are not using their own money. Even if the outcome of an investment decision reflects adversely on a manager's performance or record, it will not necessarily throw him or her into bankruptcy or even hurt financially. This last is especially true if the manager is part of a management group making the investment decision. Thus, there is considerable room in the making of such decisions to allow people to let career considerations, professional considerations, or factional politics dominate the elements that enter into investment choices.

[1] Joseph L. Bower, *Managing the Resource Allocation Process* (Cambridge, Mass.: Harvard University Press, 1970).
[2] Ibid., p. 262.
[3] Ibid., p. 276.
[4] Michael E. Porter, *Competitive Strategy* (New York: Free Press, 1980), p. 211.

purchased. At some point the design of the production of the commodity has to be completed. This implies that to some extent the organization of the entity has to be decided on. At the same time employees with a variety of skills have to be hired. The marketing of the final product has to be worked out, and the strategies for doing so have to be designed. Various staff functions such as the keeping of accounts already have to be in place. Also various financial aspects unconnected with the investment allocation have to be arranged. This is not intended to be a complete or definitive list. The main point to note is that there are two major and essential types of activities. One set are "design" and the other are "performance" activities. What happens between design and performance? This is the essential problem at this point.

Our focal idea is that motivation, in a variety of senses, is the critical element in determining the difference between actual performance and design expectations. To indicate why this turns out to be the case, we will consider a number of connected relationships taken from my own work on intrafirm economic analysis. For present purposes it will be sufficient to develop these ideas briefly and in a nontechnical manner. The following are central to our concerns: the relation between organization and hierarchy; between hierarchy and discretion; between discretion and effort; the effect of pressure on effort; the fact that effort may be misapplied for a variety of reasons, among them "free riding" and "adversarial feelings"; and, finally, the influence of conventional decision-making rules and inertia.[1]

Organization, Hierarchy, and Discretionary Effort

An organization, if it is of any significant size, will of necessity have a hierarchy. This implies that some people will be responsible in a direct or remote way for the activities, that is, the doings of others. But what it also means is those who actually work on the product will have to be given some degree of discretion. It is one thing to tell people what to do, or to show them what to do, or to hire people that you believe have the right skills to do the right things, and it is something else for them actually to do it. The best designed automobile may in fact turn out to be a horrible car to operate. Furthermore, whether or not people do their jobs well from a qualitative viewpoint, it also matters at what pace and how assiduously they carry out their activities. Thus the discretion given to individuals will determine the range within which they will carry out their activities, but it is the elements that motivate individuals that will determine how well the work is done within the discretionary range.

Discretion may be given because the superior may believe that the subordinate knows more about some activities or knows certain details that the superior feels he need not care about. We need not go through all the reasons why discretion is given, as it were. It is also important to note that discretion may be taken. A subordinate is almost always in a position to take some discretion because the discretionary boundaries are usually and almost inevitably vague. Thus the discretionary range is usually not determined mechanically in advance. Furthermore, it probably should not be. In any event a discretionary range will exist.

Looking at the matter from the viewpoint of two individuals—one the superior, the other a subordinate—we can see that the subordinate inevitably has discretion to do or not to do what the superior desires. Furthermore, communication is never perfect or complete. There is always the matter of interpretations. Since interpretations are involved, the possibility of misunderstanding is also involved. The superior cannot avoid giving discretionary power to the subordinate.

Another way of looking at it is to suggest that in an organization some people will be the agents of others. While those higher in the hierarchy are not really principals on their own account, they act as if they were. The essential element of the principal-agent problem is that somehow the agent is connected in his activities to the wishes of the principal. Nevertheless, the agent need not do what the principal desires. At the very least, the agent has the choice of not doing what the principal desires even if this may involve consequences for the agent. Thus discretion cannot be squeezed out of the organizational machine. It is always there. In addition, if the agent or a subordinate has information that the superior does not possess, then the agent will inevitably be in a position to use or not to use this information. Thus, once again, some *effort discretion* is part of the organizational situation.

Pressure and Effort Choice

How people handle the discretion available to them will depend on the pressure they face in various circumstances. We can distinguish three types of pressures: (*a*) those internal to an individual, (*b*) those outside the individual but internal to the firm, and (*c*) those that come from outside the firm.

The pressure internal to the individual will depend in part on biological inheritance but mostly on nurture. These elements will determine drive, desire to do work well or poorly, degree and sense of identification with others, capacity and willingness to be cooperative with others, and the extent to which actual or possible adversarial feelings are permitted to dominate behavior. The internal pressures are essentially part of an individual's personality. However, in most cases they will not determine completely how an individual behaves.

Behavior is also likely to depend on how an individual reacts to other individuals in the enterprise. Hence the other two types of pressures are also likely to influence behavior. Nevertheless, the individual with a strong desire to accomplish and to do well is likely to treat discretionary options very differently than one who is uninterested in the work or who is not interested in the objectives of the firm as he or she interprets them.

Every individual is likely to be influenced at work by both peers and superiors. Peers have the capacity to pressure an individual to conform to group desires. This is not to suggest that every individual responds to such pressures, but on the average such pressures are likely to be felt and have an influence. At the same time the individual will be influenced by superiors and whatever authority relations exist between him or her and others. The main point of all this is that under various circumstances peers and superiors will put on pressure for more performance, and under other circumstances they will put on less or none at all.

The circumstances surrounding the enterprise will determine the pressure that emanates from outside the firm. These are best indicated by examples. If a number of new firms enter the industry, and these firms are well managed, innovative, and produce at relatively low cost, they put considerable increases in competitive pressures on the enterprise. On the other hand, if the enterprise is given monopoly power by a local government to run a utility, then it may face very little external pressure. Contracts that operate on a cost-plus basis will also put very little pressure on the enterprise. Similarly, a general expansionary environment will involve less pressure than a recessionary and contracting one. In any event we can easily see that external pressure exists; and furthermore, in any sort of well-functioning enterprise, the external pressure will be transmitted to the firm usually through the higher management levels, which in turn are likely to attempt to transfer this pressure down through the hierarchy. Thus we can visualize a general pressure system which influences the amount and quality of effort people put forward and the extent to which this effort is in the interest of the welfare of the enterprise.[2]

Free Riding and/or Adversarial Behavior

Given effort discretion, two types of behavior are likely to have adverse effects on productivity, output, and profits. In general such behavior depends on how people feel at work and on their interpersonal interactions on the job. Such behavior and the attendant feelings involved can best be described under the rubrics of (*a*) free riding and (*b*) adversarial behavior.

An individual may feel that he would like the company that employs him to do reasonably well, so that neither his job nor his income are endangered. However, if the organization is relatively large, he is likely to know that his particular efforts will not determine the organization's profits or viability. Hence he may feel that there is no reason for him to work especially hard or be especially assiduous on the job. However, almost all individuals in a large organization have reason to think likewise. As a result, a high proportion may choose to put forth only the amount of effort that allows them to get by. Thus many individuals may act as "free riders" with respect to the others. Such behavior is likely to occur where employees do not identify very much with the organization or its objectives, or if they feel disassociated from their fellow workers. Some degree of free riding is fairly common.

It is frequently the consequence of the view that says, "It's just a job."

More extreme forms of behavior are likely to arise where there are strong adversarial feelings toward the organization and its objectives. A visible result or consequence of such feelings may be a bitter strike. In other cases people "work to rule," as it were. Where such feelings affect only a few employees, it is unlikely to be very important; but these attitudes under some circumstances have a tendency to spread and hence may seriously work to the disadvantage of the enterprise. Certainly, employees who have adverse feelings can take advantage of their area of effort discretion in order to "hurt" the firm in some sense. Thus we may view free riding as a somewhat neutral (noncaring) motivation and adversarial behavior as a negative one. Both of these are obviously very different from the sort of positive feelings associated with a clear desire to make a contribution, one that can result in low costs and high revenues.

Effort choice problems are frequently "solved" by the existence of effort conventions. The nature of these conventions usually will depend on the history of the enterprise. Somehow the amount of work an individual is expected to do gets to be determined within the existing culture of the organization. Such ideals as "a fair day's work for a fair day's pay" will depend on some effort convention that a group of workers will visualize as fair because that is what they are used to, that is what they expect to do, and that is what they believe is expected of them. Effort conventions of this type are frequently supported by sanctions. At the very least such sanctions may lead to the signs of approval or disapproval of an employee's effort by her peers, near peers, and/or her superiors.

It is useful to distinguish three types of effort sanctions. In one type there is an upper-bound focus for which those attempting to enforce the sanctions will not care if an individual chooses to work below a certain level but will become concerned if it is above a certain level. This is an "anti-rate-busting" sanction. In a second type there is a lower-bound sanction under which no one seems to care if one works harder or more effectively than some recognized level, but not below that level. This may be designated as a "pull your weight" sanction. In the third type there may be both upper and lower bounds, but between certain bounds the group does not care very much how well an individual works.

In some extreme cases, trade union members are likely to be concerned with anti-rate-busting sanctions. In other organizations people may want their peers to at least pull their weight. The latter seems to be especially true in the large, well-functioning Japanese enterprise. Thus work enterprises are organized so as to induce people to work at a fairly high level of efficiency since everyone is concerned with not disappointing others within the group and showing that at the very least they are putting forth a reasonable amount of effort (both quantitatively and qualitatively) as their contribution to the group effort.[3]

Clearly the type of sanctions that exist is part of the motivational system. In a sense we might say that it is how individuals relate to the effort put forth by others in the group, or within the firm at large, that determines the essentials of the motivational system. These are the elements we have to study in order to make our assessments of those numbers that involve the essential flows that determine the return to an investment.

In most instances people will make effort choices on the basis of some routine. Such routines may involve (*a*) habits, (*b*) rules of thumb, (*c*) standard operating procedures designated by the firm, or (*d*) the type of informal conventions already discussed. All of these routine ways of handling effort choice may be adequate in relatively good times when there is little pressure on the firm and on individuals in it. However, they may be very far from optimal decisions. In other words, there may be more direct decision procedures, as well as other conventions, and other rules of thumb, and so on, that would lead to superior results. Inferior decision procedures persist because there is normally a great deal of inertia within almost any organization when pressures are soft. Essentially the same thing is that under "normal" circumstances, members of the organization attuned to certain routines are likely to resist change.

It usually takes at least a minor crisis to engender change. Resistance to change has already been illustrated in the example in the last section where experts introduced a superior method but, after returning in six months, found that the new methods had been scrapped and all of the old methods were back in place. Another way of looking at this is to suggest that there are "inert area bounds" within which people do not change, and only when the relevant variables (for example, sales, profits, costs, share of market, or jobs) go beyond these bounds do people feel enough of a sense of shock to institute changes that may be required.[4] However, these inert area boundaries may be wide or narrow. In a well-functioning organization motivation is high, and people are confident that change can be absorbed. In such cases the inertial boundaries will be narrow, and the changes will be easily introduced. In the next section, where we look at possible ways to read the motivational gauges, these are some of the elements we have to consider.

FINDING AND READING
MOTIVATIONAL GAUGES

Probably the most important contribution that a chapter of this sort can make is simply to raise the motivation question in connection with capital budgeting. Raising it will lead some to search for answers. Motivation is in some sense ephemeral; nevertheless, it can usually be assessed at least in terms of more or less, or low, medium, or high.[5]

We have seen that any organization will have a hierarchy and the hierarchy will imply discretionary spaces. How people respond to discretionary options will depend on how individuals relate to each other and how they relate to the organization as a whole. Is the attitude of organization members generally one of a high degree of cooperativeness so that individuals are flexible and keen on making contributions to their part of the enterprise? Cooperation may be especially necessary in the interstitial spaces between jobs, that is, between the way people define their jobs and the activities they imply. Flexible and cooperative types are unlikely to define the boundaries of their jobs so rigidly as to have difficulty in taking care of "interjob" problems. This is not a matter of individual psychology. In most cases the culture of the organization will to some degree determine how rigidly people define their jobs, and whether or not people are selected and promoted for flexibilities of this type. Thus, in general, this will be part of the motivational system within the enterprise.

We have indicated various types of behavior associated with different degrees of motivation. Thus clear-cut adversarial feelings are associated with low motivation, free-rider attitudes are associated with low but intermediate motivation, and a positive desire to be cooperative is associated with a high degree of motivation. Probably the highest level of motivation is likely to exist where people have somewhat competitive feelings about the contribution they make to the output of their group. Needless to say, the latter must not be so high that it cannot be maintained over time. These remarks, in general, suggest what one would look for in judging the motivational spirit of a plant or firm or some portion of such an entity.

Knowing what to look for may not be sufficient if one does not have access. We cannot discuss here the strategy of gaining access to information. All we can do is indicate some of the different opportunities that may be available. A lot will depend on whether the investment is going to be handled by (*a*) an outside organization that has a history, (*b*) the organization carrying out the investment, or (*c*) a completely new organization in which the investment is made. If it is an existing organization but different from the investor's enterprise, and it has a

197

past history, then clearly there will be some historical information available. How much of this information is public and readily accessible, and how much of it is private and somewhat more difficult to get at, is something we cannot handle here. To the extent that there is available history, there are certain questions we can raise that suggest elements to look at, for which the history or historical records of the organization may provide answers.

One of the telling aspects is how past crises in the organization have been handled. If some particular crisis has been handled relatively smoothly, and the organization has learned from the crisis experience, and it has made appropriate changes so that the same sort of crisis will not occur again, then the people in such an organization probably (on the average) should get high marks in terms of motivation. In other words, firm members somehow have the capacity to look at the situation that caused the crisis, look at themselves, reorganize, and perform reasonably well under the changed or changing circumstances.

If in the past this organization has introduced new methods of operating, new products, or some other element that is new, then the question can be raised whether its adaptation to the new elements has been relatively short or exceptionally long, or something in between. It may be possible to look at similar activities in other organizations to get some idea about appropriate or reasonable adaptation time. In any event, it is of interest to try to learn how new elements have been handled.

Probably one of the most general motivational aspects is the extent to which the organization learns from experience. Does it learn or does it make the same mistakes again and again? In some cases experience seems to teach the organization in question very little. Changes made are cosmetic rather than real. In any event, assessments of the extent to which the organization seems to learn from experience are an important indicator of the working of the motivational system.

Of a more direct nature is the assessment of effectiveness in the operations of the enterprise by existing executives, former executives, and/or present and former employees. In some research that a colleague and I engaged in, we were able to submit questionnaires to a sample of employees of several firms and to have open-end interviews with middle- and higher-management personnel. We obtained what appeared to be fairly accurate assessments of how much more output the existing employees felt they could produce under different motivational circumstances. We were also able to learn the extent to which the opinions and sanctions of other employees influenced employee behavior. Especially encouraging was that the assessment of managers and the information and assessment obtained from line employees were in accordance with each other. Thus the whole question as to how effective the employees were working vis-à-vis what could be done under more highly motivated circumstances did not turn out to be by any means mysterious. The estimates of how much more could be produced were significantly higher than what was actually produced. How accurate these estimates turn out to be is not of the essence. What is important is that they give clear indication of the order of magnitude as to where the firm is producing at the present time compared to possibilities under superior motivational systems. Thus we felt that measurements could be made. Of course, we had a great deal of cooperation from management and access to information that is not always available. What is clear is that if access is available, then motivational audits can be carried out and reliable motivational assessments made.

Of special interest is that managers who had worked in other companies in the industry seemed to have some fairly clear notions about the motivational structure and its productivity implications in those companies. The point of all this is that such information is clearly obtainable if access exists. Clearly, if questions are not raised and no attempt is made to get information, then of course the significance of various numbers representing future flows will not be obtained. But once the question is raised and significant probing takes place, answers somehow seem to appear.

Different circumstances require adaptations of this general approach. If the enterprise in which the investment is made belongs to the company in question, then of course access is likely to be much easier and more accurate, and relevant historical data will be obtainable. Much greater difficulties exist where investment is to be made in new firms. Here, too, there may be various ways of obtaining some information. If the new members of these enterprises have no motivational concerns whatsoever, then probably there are difficulties. Part of a well-working managerial team is to appreciate the motivational elements in the organization. Other information can be obtained from similar firms that already have a history. In some there may be ways of gleaning some elements in almost all cases. Of course, where the enterprise is completely experimental, and where the nature of the new management is not obtainable, then no assessments could be made. Needless to say, under such circumstances there ought to be a fairly high discount for risk.

SUMMARY

Here is a brief summary of some of main ideas in this chapter. We have emphasized the connection between motivation and effort. To start

199

with, we focused on the discretionary spaces which of necessity exist in hierarchies and on the effort choices made by organization members within their discretionary spaces. How well individuals make those choices depends on how people react to their peers, and/or to their superiors, and how they feel about the firm in general. We distinguished between various sanctions that peers and superiors may use. Of special concern is whether the sanctions have an upper-bound focus, a lower-bound focus, or whether they are neutral. In other words, are effort decision makers encouraged by others to do more than they can, less than they can, or to work within certain bounds? Beyond specific effort levels there is likely to be a feedback mechanism between effort, performance, and pressure. In well-functioning organizations the feedback loop is likely to be narrow in the sense that relatively small declines in effort will lead to increases in pressure and attempts to improve effort. The same will hold for deviations between actual effort levels and firm-expected levels. In organizations where motivation is low, the feedback loops will be wide in the sense that small changes in effort will not result in any changes in pressure or in attempts to change the effort level. Thus, the wider the loop, the greater the association with internal inefficiencies. At the same time the rapidity with which signals of adverse external conditions are transmitted internally is also part of the motivational system. In general, a combination of other-person approval and monetary incentives is likely to work better than negative incentive systems.

Much of the discussion is likely to appear rather abstract in the absence of specific cases. This is somewhat similar to discussing the establishment of a system of accounts for a company without discussing the particulars of the company in question, what the company does, and in what context it operates. Once the particulars are known, then it is not hard for any well-trained accountant to establish useful and specific accounts that reveal the company's financial history. In similar fashion the elements discussed here become relatively concrete when applied to specific situations, even if they perforce must be rather abstract when the exact nature of the enterprise is not specified.

NOTES

[1] For a more elaborate treatment, see H. Leibenstein, *Beyond Economic Man* (Cambridge, Mass.: Harvard Univ. Press, 1976), chaps. 5–10.

[2] For an elaboration of these ideas, see ibid.

³ See Rodney Clark, *The Japanese Company* (New Haven: Yale University Press, 1979); and Ronald Dore, *British Factory—Japanese Factory* (Berkeley: University of California Press, 1973).

⁴ The Chrysler Corporation changed markedly in face of the shock of possible bankruptcy in 1981.

⁵ See Leibenstein, *Beyond Economic Man;* J. W. Atkinson and O. Birch, *Introduction to Motivation* (New York: Van Nostrand Reinhold, 1978); and D. C. McClelland and D. G. Winter, *Motivating Economic Achievement* (New York: Free Press, 1969).

REFERENCES

Arnold, H. J.; M. G. Evans; and R. J. House. "Productivity: A Psychological Perspective." In *Lagging Productivity Growth,* ed. S. Maital and N. M. Meltz. Cambridge, Mass.: Ballinger, 1980.

Leibenstein, H. "X-Efficiency, Intrafirm Behavior, and Growth." In *Lagging Productivity Growth,* ed. S. Maital and N. M. Meltz. Cambridge, Mass.: Ballinger, 1980.

_____. "Property Rights and X-Efficiency: Comment." *The American Economic Review,* September 1983, pp. 831–42.

II

Preparing the Capital Budget

11

Capital Rationing: How to Use Mathematical Programming to Allocate Capital

Thomas J. Hindelang

Drexel University

INTRODUCTION

*O*ther chapters within *The Capital Budgeting Handbook* examine capital budgeting techniques that are appropriate for ranking independent capital investment projects or mutually exclusive projects. However, when firms have a limited amount of capital available for investment in long-term assets (as is true in virtually all firms), the focus of capital budgeting shifts from that of single projects or mutually exclusive sets of projects to that of *portfolios* of projects. Even a moderate number of projects under evaluation leads to an extremely large number of potential portfolios that must be evaluated. Mathematical programming techniques provide an effective methodology for efficiently evaluating portfolios of projects and selecting the best portfolio that satisfies all the constraints or restrictions faced by the firm.

This chapter explores the use of linear programming (LP) and integer programming (IP) to handle the capital rationing problem. In the next section we introduce the approach and terminology of mathematical programming techniques. We also cite several recent surveys that indicate how widely used each of the techniques is in capital budgeting applications. The following sections of the chapter examine the use of LP and IP to assist financial managers in handling the complexities imposed by the necessity to allocate limited resources among competing capital projects.

AN OVERVIEW OF MATHEMATICAL PROGRAMMING TECHNIQUES

Mathematical programming (MP) techniques are a powerful set of "constrained optimization approaches" that can be applied to a wide variety of resource allocation problems in business, industrial, or governmental problem settings. MP models are called constrained optimization approaches because they ascertain the solution to the problem that achieves the best value of the objective that the decision maker is interested in while simultaneously satisfying all of the restrictions that limit the decision maker's options.

Math programming models have been successfully applied in virtually all types of businesses and industries to solve innumerable problems. Some of the applications that have been reported by firms are production management, cost and profit analysis, energy allocation, mixing and refining problems, advertising expenditure allocation, financial and investment planning, transportation scheduling, risk analysis, inventory control, labor force planning, and pollution control.

Two major categories of equations are used in MP models:

1. *The objective function* describes the goal or objective that the decision maker desires to achieve.
2. *Constraint equations* describe any limitations on resources, restrictions imposed by the environment within which the system functions, or managerial policies that the firm will observe.

In formulating both the objective function and the constraint equations used in MP models, two types of variables are used:

206

1. *Input parameters* are values specified by the decision maker to describe characteristics of the system.
2. *Decision variables* will be determined by the model as a part of achieving the optimal solution.

As a brief illustration of these definitions, consider a firm manufacturing and selling two products (X and Y) and desiring to determine that product mix which will maximize total dollar profit. The firm estimates that the unit profit figures are $6 and $18, respectively. The objective function to maximize profit for this firm would therefore be expressed as follows:

$$\text{Maximize profit} = \$6X + \$18Y$$

In this objective function the two values—$6 and $18—are the input parameters since management had to specify these values pertaining to their two products. The variables X and Y, which designate the number of units of product X and product Y that should be produced, are decision variables since the model will determine their values in order to maximize profits.

The most widely used MP model is linear programming (LP). The use of LP imposes four major assumptions on the decision maker.

1. The objective function and all constraint equations can be accurately written by using *linear* equations.
2. The input parameters specified by the decision maker are assumed to be known with *certainty*.
3. The decision maker is able to specify *a single goal or objective* that will be optimized in the objective function.
4. The decision variables in the model are assumed to be *continuous*, which means that they can take on any value within a given range.

These four assumptions are not terribly restrictive for many problem settings. In addition, these assumptions greatly simplify problem formulation and solution via the computer. Virtually all computer manufacturers have software packages available that solve LP problems very readily.

When the capital budgeting problem is formulated using LP, assumption 4 above means that partial projects could be included in the optimal portfolio of projects. Because the acceptance of partial projects may be difficult (that is, the firm would have to seek out a partner for a joint venture), it is often desirable to require that projects be completely accepted or completely rejected. In order to achieve this result, integer programming (IP) can be called upon to represent the capital budgeting problem setting. IP models require that the decision variables are *discrete* rather than continuous variables (as in LP).

Finally, decision makers may desire the flexibility of specifying more than a single goal or objective as in LP. This is accomplished by utilizing goal programming (GP) to assist in the capital budgeting process. GP enables the decision maker to incorporate several relevant goals into the portfolio evaluation process. In addition the decision maker specifies a rank order of importance of the goals and trade-offs that are acceptable among the various goals. GP recognizes that decision makers and firms usually are interested in achieving more than just a single goal in most complex problem settings. The desirable features of both IP and GP can be achieved by calling upon integer goal programming (IGP), wherein multiple goals are reflected in the model and the decision variables are restricted to take on integer values.

The IP, GP, and IGP models entail greater complexity than the LP model. Hence, computerized software packages for these former models are not as readily available as such packages for LP. In addition, additional computer time is required to solve IP, GP, and IGP formulations. However, we would argue that the important degree of realism provided by these more complex models is well worth the added cost of computer solution.

Surveys have indicated an increasing use of LP in capital budgeting through the years. A study done by Klammer indicated that 17 percent of his responding firms used LP in capital budgeting in 1970 while only 8 percent and 5 percent used LP in this area in 1964 and 1959, respectively.[1] About a year after Klammer's study, Professor James Fremgen surveyed 250 financial executives by sampling from Dun & Bradstreet's 1969 *Reference Book of Corporate Managements*.[2] Of the 177 executives who replied, approximately 19 percent said that their firms used LP to handle capital rationing problems. A 1976 study by Petty and Bowlin sampled financial executives from 500 firms who were members of the Financial Management Association in order to determine the degree of familiarity and use of various quantitative decision-making techniques.[3] Of the 227 responses in this somewhat biased sample (even the authors admit that the population consisted of individuals who would tend to be more familiar than executives at large with the sophisticated models that were the subject of the survey), it is interesting to note the differences in familiarity and use of the various mathematical programming models. The results for various techniques are shown in Figure 1. As expected, there are roughly four times as

FIGURE 1

Technique	Extent of use (percent)*						
	1	2	3	4	5	6	7
Linear programming	12.9%	12.0%	17.1%	29.0%	2.8%	25.3%	6.4
Goal programming	35.9	20.7	13.8	7.4	1.4	7.8	13.0
Integer programming	30.9	23.0	13.4	12.9	0.0	7.4	12.4

* 1 = Completely unfamiliar.
  2 = Vaguely familiar.
  3 = Familiar.
  4 = Working knowledge but not currently being used.
  5 = Use being considered.
  6 = Currently in use.
  7 = No response.

many applications of LP as there are of either goal or integer programming; further, about one third of the respondents were completely unfamiliar with all of the mathematical programming techniques except LP; however, these techniques have some hope of being applied in the future, as indicated by 20 to 25 percent of the respondents being familiar with them or have a working knowledge of the techniques.

There is a trend toward greater use of sophisticated MP models, at least by large U.S. industrial firms. This trend is due in part to the complexities faced by such firms in evaluating feasible portfolios of capital investment projects. The significance of the resources required by such projects justifies the use of the most sophisticated techniques available. Furthermore, with the spectacular growth in the mini- and microcomputer fields as well as that of computer service bureaus, it is reasonable to expect a continuing increase in the use of MP techniques by medium-sized and small firms as well. Today, software packages for microcomputers with just 48k of memory can handle small LP problems of up to 30 variables and 30 constraints. In addition, an LP package that can handle up to 255 constraints and up to 2,255 variables on an IBM PC with 128k of memory is available for under $100.

LINEAR PROGRAMMING REPRESENTATIONS OF THE CAPITAL RATIONING PROBLEM

The earliest uses of mathematical programming (MP) techniques to handle the capital rationing problem called upon linear programming

(LP). LP models require that the objective function and all constraint equations can be accurately described using linear equations. The linearities required by LP make it the easiest MP model to solve. This fact coupled with the widespread availability of packaged computer programs to solve LP problems has resulted in the growth in the number of LP applications to finance problems.

The pioneers in the application of LP to the capital budgeting problem were Charnes, Cooper, and Miller in 1959[4] and Weingartner in 1963.[5] Charnes, Cooper, and Miller formulated an LP model to assist the firm in allocating funds among competing uses considering both operating decisions and financial planning. Weingartner's outstanding work formulates the capital rationing problem first as an LP then as an integer programming (IP) model. His work also provided valuable insights concerning the shadow prices and dual variables for the LP and IP formulations.

Since these pioneering works, there have been many advances in the area of mathematical programming applied to the capital budgeting problem. The major extensions have either sought to integrate other financial decision areas with the capital budgeting decision, relaxed the single-goal assumption of LP and IP (mainly through the use of goal programming), or attempted to handle the capital rationing problem under conditions of risk. The focus of this chapter will be to survey the important areas of linear, integer, and goal programming as they apply to the capital rationing problem. Example problems will be formulated in the necessary framework, the optimal solutions interpreted, and sensitivity analysis discussed and illustrated. Due to space limitations, it is necessary to abbreviate our coverage of this highly complex problem area here. The reader seeking a more extensive coverage of mathematical programming applied to the capital rationing problem is referred to our parallel treatment elsewhere.[6]

Formulating the Capital Budgeting Problem Using LP

Based on the introduction to linear programming provided by the previous section, we can proceed to the formulation of the capital rationing problem using the LP model.

$$\text{Maximize NPV} = \sum_{j=1}^{N} b_j X_j \tag{1}$$

Subject to

$$\sum_{j=1}^{N} C_{jt}X_j \le K_t \, t = 1, 2, \ldots T \tag{2}$$

$$X_j \le 1 \tag{3}$$

$$X_j \ge 0 \tag{4}$$

where

X_j = The percent of project j that is accepted.
b_j = The net present value of project j over its useful life.
C_{jt} = The cash outflow required by project j in year t.
K_t = The budget availability in year t.

The following aspects should be noted about the above problem formulation.

1. The X_j decision variables are assumed to be continuous—that is, partial projects are allowed in the LP formulation.
2. As shown in Equation 3, there is an upper limit for each project—that is, it is required that each project have a maximum value of 1.00 or that it is accepted 100 percent (there is only one project of each type available).
3. It is assumed that all of the input parameters—b_j, C_{jt}, and K_t—are known with certainty.
4. The b_j parameter shows the net present value of project j over its planning horizon where all cash flows are discounted at the firm's hurdle rate or required rate of return.

Consider the following classic nine-project, two-period problem originally evaluated by Lorie and Savage:[7]

j	b_j NPV_j	C_{j1} = Cash outflow in period 1 for project j	C_{j2} = Cash outflow in period 2 for project j
1	$14	$12	$ 3
2	17	54	7
3	17	6	6
4	15	6	2
5	40	30	35
6	12	6	6
7	14	48	4
8	10	36	3
9	12	18	3

The LP formulation is as follows:

Maximize NPV = $14x_1 + 17x_2 + 17x_3 + 15x_4 + 40x_5 + 12x_6 + 14x_7 + 10x_8 + 12x_9$

Subject to

$12x_1 + 54x_2 + 6x_3 + 6x_4 + 30x_5 + 6x_6$
$\qquad + 48x_7 + 36x_8 + 18x_9 + S_1 = \$50$ budget constraint year 1

$3x_1 + 7x_2 + 6x_3 + 2x_4 + 35x_5 + 6x_6$
$\qquad + 4x_7 + 3x_8 + 3x_9 + S_2 = \$20$ budget constraint year 2

$$
\left.
\begin{array}{lll}
x_1 + S_3 = 1 & x_4 + S_6 = 1 & x_7 + S_9 = 1 \\
x_2 + S_4 = 1 & x_5 + S_7 = 1 & x_8 + S_{10} = 1 \\
x_3 + S_5 = 1 & x_6 + S_8 = 1 & x_9 + S_{11} = 1
\end{array}
\right\}
\begin{array}{l}\text{Upper limits on} \\ \text{project acceptance}\end{array}
$$

$$
\left.
x_j, S_i \geq 0 \quad
\begin{array}{l}
j = 1, 2, \ldots , 9 \\
i = 1, 2, \ldots , 11
\end{array}
\right\}
\text{Nonnegativity constraint}
$$

The following aspects should be pointed out concerning this formulation. The general approach taken in this example is similar to that shown in Equations 1 through 4. However, slack variables have been added to each less-than constraint so that a fuller interpretation can be given to the optimal solution. Slack variables S_1 and S_2 represent, respectively, the number of budget dollars in years 1 and 2 that remain unallocated to any of the nine projects under evaluation. Slack variables S_3 through S_{11} represent the percent of projects one through nine, respectively, which are not accepted by the firm—the sum of X_j and its corresponding slack variable S_k must equal 1.00 or 100 percent since the entire project must be either accepted or not accepted.

The optimal LP solution obtained from IBM's LINPROG package is shown in Figure 2.

Interpreting the optimal solution, we see that the *basic variables* (variables that are equal to a positive value in the optimal solution) are $X_1, X_3, X_4, X_6, X_7, X_9, S_4, S_7, S_8, S_9, S_{10}$, which are equal to their corresponding values on the RHS of the optimal tableau (that is, $X_1 = 1.0; X_3 = 1.0; X_4 = 1.0; X_6 = .969697$, etc.). Any of the variables in the problem that are not listed as basic variables are, in fact, *nonbasic* variables in the optimal solution, which means that they are equal to zero. Thus, $X_2 = X_5 = X_8 = 0$, which shows that these three projects are completely rejected; in addition, $S_1 = S_2 = 0$, which shows that the entire budget allotment of $50 in year 1 and $20 in year 2 has been spent on the six projects which have been designated for acceptance.

212

FIGURE 2

Optimal Tableau for LP Formulation of Lorie-Savage Nine-Project Problem

		X_1	X_2	X_3	X_4	X_5	X_6	X_7	X_8	X_9	S_1	S_2	S_3	S_4	S_5	S_6	S_7	S_8	S_9	S_{10}	S_{11}	RHS
	X_1	1.0											1.0									1.00
	X_3		1.0												1.0							1.0
	X_4			1.0												1.0						1.00
	X_6		455			5.91	1.0				−.015	.1818	−.364		−1.0	−.273					−.273	.969697
	X_7		1.068			−.114		1.0	.75		+.023	−.023	−.205			−.091					.341	.045455
	X_9									1.0												1.00
Basic	S_4	1.0												1.0								1.00
variables	S_7		1.0														1.0					1.00
	S_8		−.455			−5.91					.015	.1818	.364		1.0	.273		1.0			.273	.030303
	S_9		−1.068			.114			−.75		−.023	.023	.205			.091			1.0		.341	.954545
	S_{10}								1.0											1.0		1.00
	Z	0	3.41	0	0	29.32	0	0	50	0	.1364	1.864	6.77	0	5.0	10.45	0	0	0	0	3.95	70.273

In addition, $S_3 = S_5 = S_6 = S_{11} = 0$ since the projects corresponding to these slack variables (that is, X_1, X_3, X_4, X_9) have been 100 percent accepted. To summarize, projects 1, 3, 4, and 9 have been fully accepted, 97 percent of project 6 is accepted, and only 4.5 percent of project 7 is accepted. These projects require the use of the entire budget in both years and generate the maximum objective function value of $70.273, which is the net present value of the accepted projects.

Of course, it could be asked, do the partial projects in our solution above really make sense? The answer is, maybe. The above LP solution, which was arrived at using only tenths of a second of computer time, does provide considerable insight about the nine projects under evaluation. The fully accepted projects (1, 3, 4, and 9) are clearly attractive to the firm. The two partial projects are only "break-even projects" to the firm. They are the last ones accepted into the firm's portfolio of projects, and the project benefits just cover the costs associated with the project.

Integer programming can be called upon to solve the capital rationing problem where it is desired to eliminate partial projects. It should be mentioned that the above LP formulation of the capital rationing problem is significantly easier to solve than the integer programming formulation (which is discussed below) wherein no partial projects are allowed. Integer programming problems can take up to 100 times longer to solve on the computer than the equivalent LP formulation.

Interpreting Shadow Prices in LP Problems

The optimal solution to the LP provides valuable information concerning the amount that the decision maker should be willing to pay to acquire an additional unit of each resource that was constrained in the problem. Such data are included in the "Z" or the objective function row of the optimal tableau, and the amounts are referred to as *shadow prices*. The shadow price for each resource appears in the objective function row in the column for the slack variable corresponding to the resource in question (these shadow prices are denoted ρ_t^*). For example, the two limited resources in the Lorie-Savage problem are the budget dollars in years 1 and 2; the shadow price for additional year-1 dollars is shown in the S_1 column and denoted ρ_1^*; similarly, the shadow price for year-2 budget dollars is shown in the S_2 column and is denoted ρ_2^*.

The shadow price ρ_1^* shows the maximum interest rate that the firm would be willing to pay to acquire an additional \$1 of budget availability in year 1. The firm would be willing to pay up to the interest rate ρ_1^* because, with the additional budget in year 1, the firm can accept an additional percentage of a partially accepted project which increases the value of the objective function. If the firm has to pay the maximum interest rate ρ_1^* to acquire the additional \$1 of budget in year 1, then it will just break even because the increase in the value of the objective function will just offset the interest paid. If the additional funds can be acquired for less than ρ_1^*, then there will be a net increase in the value of the objective function. Similar interpretations can be attached to shadow prices for other constrained resources.

In addition to the shadow prices for limited resources, the optimal solution for the capital budgeting problem also shows shadow prices that provide the basis to rank accepted and rejected projects. The shadow prices relative to accepted projects are shown under the slack variables that were used in the constraints for the upper limits on project acceptance. These shadow prices could be referred to as the positive goodwill generated by the accepted projects. The positive goodwill refers to the excess of the project's NPV over the implicit cost associated with resources required to accept the project. The implicit cost associated with each of the limited resources is shown by its shadow price in the optimal LP solution. Equation 5 shows the expression for the positive goodwill of project *j*:

$$\gamma_j = b_j - \sum_{t=1}^{T} \rho_t^* C_{jt} \qquad (5)$$

where

γ_j = The positive goodwill associated with accepted project j (shown in the optimal tableau under the slack variables used in the constraint for the upper limit on the acceptance of project j.

ρ_t^* = The shadow price associated with resource t shown in the optimal tableau in the column of the slack variable for resource t.

b_j = The NPV for project j.

C_{jt} = The quantity of resource t required to accept project j.

The rejected projects also have shadow prices that show the amount of negative goodwill associated with such projects. The amount of negative goodwill for rejected projects appears as the shadow prices under the decision variables X_j for the projects. As you might expect, the negative goodwill associated with rejected project $j(\mu_j)$ is expressed by rearranging Equation 5, as shown in Equation 6:

$$\mu_j = \sum_{t=1}^{T} \rho_t^* C_{jt} - b_j \qquad (6)$$

As can be seen, such projects would be rejected because the implicit cost associated with the resources required to accept the project $(\Sigma \rho_t^* C_{jt})$ exceeds the project's NPV (b_j).

For the optimal solution to the Lorie-Savage problem shown in Figure 2, provide a verbal description of each of the shadow prices. In addition, rank the nine projects from most attractive to least attractive.

Figure 3 shows the optimal tableau for the Lorie-Savage problem with the labels for each of the shadow prices.

The interpretation of the shadow prices is as follows:

1. $\rho_1^* = .1364$ or 13.64 percent shows the maximum interest rate that firm is willing to pay to acquire additional budget dollars in year 1; the firm is willing to pay up to this maximum interest rate because, with the additional budget dollars acquired, the value of the objective function will increase by .1364 per dollar of budget acquired.
2. $\rho_2^* = 1.864$ or 186.4 percent shows the maximum interest rate that the firm is willing to pay to acquire an additional budget dollar in year 2.
3. γ_1 to γ_9 show the amount of positive goodwill generated by each accepted project.

4. μ_1 to μ_9 show the amount of negative goodwill generated by each of the rejected projects.

A ranking of the accepted projects would be:

1. $\gamma_4 = 10.45$
2. $\gamma_1 = 6.77$
3. $\gamma_3 = 5.00$
4. $\gamma_9 = 3.95$
5. $\gamma_6 = 0$ ⎱ Marginal or partially accepted projects
6. $\gamma_7 = 0$ ⎰

A ranking of the rejected projects from the least to the most unattractive is as follows:

1. $\mu_8 = .50$
2. $\mu_2 = 3.41$
3. $\mu_5 = 29.32$

The above γ_j and μ_j values provide a ranking of the nine projects from the most attractive to the least attractive. The rankings shown above take the NPV of each project into account as well as the resources required to accept that project (C_{jt}) and the implicit cost (ρ_t^*) of using those resources to accept the project. The shadow prices take the

FIGURE 3

Optimal Tableau for LP Formulation of Lorie-Savage Nine-Project Problem

		X_1	X_2	X_3	X_4	X_5	X_6	X_7	X_8	X_9	S_1	S_2	S_3	S_4	S_5	S_6	S_7	S_8	S_9	S_{10}	S_{11}	RHS
	X_1	1.0									1.0											1.00
	X_3			1.0									1.0									1.0
	X_4				1.0										1.0							1.00
	X_6		455			5.91	1.0					015	1818	364		1.0	273				273	969697
	X_7		1.068			-114		1.0		75		+023	023	205			091				341	045455
	X_9									1.0											1.0	1.00
Basic	S_4	1.0												1.0								1.00
variables	S_7			1.0													1.0					1.00
	S_8		455			-5.91						015	1818	364		1.0	273	1.0			273	030303
	S_9		-1.068			114				75		023	023	205			091		1.0		341	954545
	S_{10}									1.0										1.0		1.00
	Z	0	3.41	0	0	29.32	0	0	50	0	1364	1.864	6.77	0	5.0	10.45	0	0	0	0	3.95	70.273
		μ_1	μ_2	μ_3	μ_4	μ_5	μ_6	μ_7	μ_8	μ_9	ρ_i	ρ_2	γ_1	γ_2	γ_3	γ_4	γ_5	γ_6	γ_7	γ_8	γ_9	

interactions of projects into account as they compete against one another for the limited resources available to accept capital projects.

Finally, we turn to sensitivity analysis.

LP Sensitivity Analysis

One of LP's assumptions that we mentioned above is that the input parameters for the model are known with certainty. For the capital budgeting problem, this means that LP assumes that the values of b_j, C_{jt}, and K_t are known for sure and will not vary in the future. Sensitivity analysis is a vitally important tool that managers can use to determine the ranges for each of the input parameters within which no significant change will take place in the optimal solution. Thus, sensitivity analysis is a hedge against LP's certainty assumption.

As mentioned above, one of the key variables we want to determine in sensitivity analysis is the range of possible right-hand side values for resource constraints. The way sensitivity analysis is performed in LP is to compute a value for Δ^+ and Δ^-. These quantities show the amount by which the original resource availability could either increase (Δ^+) or decrease (Δ^-) and still have the same portfolio of accepted projects. Once the Δ^+ and Δ^- values are determined, the analyst can compute a range for each resource within which the optimal solution will remain unchanged in any significant way. Equation 7 shows how the range is computed.

$$\left. \begin{array}{l} \text{Range of values for} \\ \text{input parameter wherein} \\ \text{optimal solution is} \\ \text{unaffected} \end{array} \right\{ \begin{array}{l} \text{Upper limit} = \text{Original value} + \Delta^+ \\ \qquad\qquad\text{of input parameter} \\ \text{Lower limit} = \text{Original value} - \Delta^- \\ \qquad\qquad\text{of input parameter} \quad (7) \end{array}$$

It should also be mentioned that the range computed using Equation 7 will show the set of values over which the shadow prices will remain valid. That is, only within the ranges determined by sensitivity analysis will the firm be willing to pay the amount shown by the shadow price to acquire additional units of the resource in question. This aspect will be illustrated momentarily.

Most packaged LP programs offer the option of computing the Δ^+ and Δ^- values for the decision maker. Once these values have been determined by the computer, the ranges are immediate and the interpretation of the results is the important aspect for effective management.

The objective function coefficients (b_j) are another set of input parameters for which sensitivity analysis should be performed. Here as well, Δ^+ and Δ^- values are determined by the packaged LP program. We now illustrate the determination of the sensitivity range and its interpretation for management.

For the optimal solution to the Lorie-Savage problem, use the following Δ^+ and Δ^- values to determine the ranges for the corresponding input parameter using Equation 7. Interpret the results for management.

The Lorie-Savage problem as formulated and solved above has only two limited resources reflected in the constraints—dollars of capital budget available in year 1 and in year 2. The following table shows the values determined by the packaged LP program:

	Budget year 1	Budget year 2
Δ^+	$41.50	$0.17
Δ^-	$ 1.98	$5.33

Thus, given that $50 of budget was available in year 1 and $20 of budget was specified for year 2 and using Equation 7, the ranges for the budgets are:

	Budget year 1	Budget year 2
Upper limit	$91.50	$20.17
Lower limit	$48.02	$14.67

The above ranges show that if the budget available in year 1 falls anywhere between $48.02 and $91.50, the same portfolio of projects will be accepted by the firm. As additional budget dollars become available in year 1, greater percentages of the partially accepted projects will be accepted. In addition, within this range, the firm will be willing to pay up to a 13.64 percent (the shadow price for S_1) interest rate to acquire additional budget dollars. A similar interpretation can be placed on year 2.

Turning to the nine projects, let's consider them in three separate groups: the completely accepted projects, the partially accepted ones, and the rejected projects.

Projects 1, 3, 4, and 9 were completely accepted. Their Δ^- and Δ^+ are shown below:

218

	Project 1	Project 3	Project 4	Project 9
Δ^+	∞	∞	∞	∞
Δ^-	6.77	5.0	10.45	3.95

The interpretation of these values is as follows. All of the Δ^+ values are infinite because these projects are all fully accepted and, if their NPVs were increased by any amount, the projects would continue to be fully accepted. The Δ^- value for each project is its positive goodwill shown in Figure 3—the Optimal Tableau for the Lorie-Savage Problem. Hence, if any of these project's NPVs decreased by the amount of its positive goodwill or more, the project would no longer be fully accepted. Of course, the smaller the Δ^- value is (both absolutely and relative to the project's NPV), the more sensitive the project is to downside changes in its NPV value and the more easily it could become only marginally acceptable or unacceptable. For these four projects, project 9 is the most sensitive to decreases in NPVs.

For the two partial projects, we see:

	Project 6	Project 7
Δ^+	$5.0	$11.58
Δ^-	$4.96	$0.67

Hence, the Δ^+ value shows the amount by which each project's NPV would have to increase in order for it to be completely accepted. On the other hand, if the NPV of either of these projects decreased by Δ^-, it would no longer be partially accepted—it would be rejected. Thus, we see that project 7 is very vulnerable to a decrease in NPV value because it would only take a $0.67 decrease before it would no longer be even partially accepted.

Finally, the rejected projects show the following values:

	Project 2	Project 5	Project 8
Δ^+	$3.41	$29.32	$0.50
Δ^-	∞	∞	∞

These values show that the projects' NPVs would have to increase by the amount of their negative goodwill (as shown by the shadow prices under each of these decision variables in Figure 3) before each would be a candidate for even partial acceptance. Thus, project 8 would not require a very significant upward revision in its forecasted NPV before it would be a candidate for at least partial acceptance.

The infinite Δ^- values mean that these projects, which currently are unattractive, would remain so if their NPVs decreased by any amount.

The above discussion provides an illustration of how the optimal LP solution can be further interpreted and how concerned management has to be to potential errors in forecasting the costs and benefits of projects under evaluation.

This section was designed to indicate the potential for applying LP to the capital rationing problem. The LP model can handle constraints of various types showing other resource limitations, management policies, and restrictions imposed by the marketplace or government regulation. In addition, current computer technology (in terms of both hardware and software) enables firms to handle virtually any size LP problem. Large-scale problems involving tens of thousands of projects and tens of thousands of constraints have been reported in the literature.

Next, we turn to an elaboration of the LP model.

INTEGER PROGRAMMING APPLIED TO CAPITAL BUDGETING

As mentioned earlier in the chapter, integer programming (IP) can be called upon to guarantee that all projects accepted by the firm are completely accepted. That is, no partially accepted projects are feasible in IP, as is the case in LP. The general IP formulation for the capital budgeting problem is as follows:

$$\text{Maximize NPV} = \sum_{j=1}^{N} b_j X_j \qquad (8)$$

Subject to

$$\text{Resource limitations: } \sum_{j=1}^{N} C_{jt} X_j \leq K_t \qquad t = 1, 2, \ldots T \qquad (9)$$

$$\text{Project indivisibility: } X_j = \{0, 1\} \qquad j = 1, 2, \ldots N \qquad (10)$$

220

In comparing the IP formulation with the LP general formulation, we see that the two LP constraints shown above as Equations 3 and 4:

$$X_j \leq 1 \tag{3}$$

$$X_j \geq 0 \tag{4}$$

(which show that the decision variable X is continuous) are replaced by the discrete IP condition:

$$X_j = \{0, 1\} \tag{10}$$

The IP constraint states that all projects must either be completely accepted ($X_j = 1$) or rejected ($X_j = 0$).

One of the very beneficial features of IP's project indivisibility is that we can now incorporate into the capital budgeting formulation constraints that convey project interrelationships. Three types of interrelationships among projects are commonly encountered in practice: mutually exclusive, contingent or prerequisite, and complementary or synergistic. Such interactions among projects determine the feasibility of various portfolios of projects. Hence it is helpful to be able to show such requirements directly in the constraints of the capital budgeting formulation. Each of the project interrelationships is examined in turn.

Mutually Exclusive Projects

Mutually exclusive projects are two or more projects wherein the acceptance of one precludes the acceptance of any other. As the reader may expect, it is relatively straightforward to include an IP constraint indicating that from a mutually exclusive set of projects, either (1) *at most* one project can be accepted or (2) *exactly one* of the projects must be accepted. Consider that we have a mutually exclusive set of projects (J), and the two cases are handled by the following two constraints, respectively:

$$\sum_{j \in J} X_j \leq 1 \tag{11}$$

$$\sum_{j \in J} X_j = 1 \tag{12}$$

The $\leq$ sign in Equation 11 denotes that all of the projects in the mutually exclusive set could be rejected, or at most one could be accepted. On the other hand, Equation 12 requires that one of the projects in the mutually exclusive set must be accepted because of the $=$ sign.

To illustrate the use of the above equations, consider that McDonald's is evaluating the construction of a new restaurant somewhere on the northeast side of Detroit. Three locations are under consideration: (1) 8 Mile and Harper roads (designate this location as X_4); (2) 7 Mile and Caudiux roads (call this location X_5); and (3) 7 Mile and Kelly roads (X_6). If at most one of these locations could be selected, the constraint equation is:

$$X_4 + X_5 + X_6 \leq 1$$

Conversely, if McDonald's wanted to require that a new restaurant be built in one of these locations, the constraint would be:

$$X_4 + X_5 + X_6 = 1$$

Constraints similar to those shown in Equations 11 and 12 can be written to indicate that, of a given set of projects, at least some desired number must be accepted or no more than some desired number may be accepted. For example, if Holiday Inns was considering the construction of five new motels off of Interstate 95 in the southeastern United States (call these five projects X_{16}, X_{17}, X_{18}, X_{19}, and X_{20}) and wanted to build at least the best two, the constraint would be:

$$X_{16} + X_{17} + X_{18} + X_{19} + X_{20} \geq 2$$

On the other hand, if among the eight locations under consideration off of Interstate 80 in the northern United States (call these projects X_{70} through X_{77}), Holiday Inns wants to construct no more than three new motels, the constraint would be:

$$X_{70} + X_{71} + X_{72} + X_{73} + X_{74} + X_{75} + X_{76} + X_{77} \leq 3$$

We see that this type of constraint can handle a variety of practical conditions, as is true for the next type of constraint as well.

Contingent or Prerequisite Projects

Contingent projects are two or more projects wherein the acceptance of one necessitates the prior acceptance of the prerequisite project(s). For example, if project A cannot be accepted unless project Z is accepted, then we would say that project Z is a prerequisite project for the acceptance of project A. Alternatively, we could say that the acceptance of project A is contingent upon the prior acceptance of project Z. The IP constraint showing this relationship would be:

$$X_A \leq X_Z \tag{13}$$

Note that if project A is accepted (that is, $X_A = 1$), the constraint would be violated unless the prerequisite project (X_Z) was also accepted. However, project Z could be accepted on its own without regard to whether project A was accepted or rejected.

As with the mutually exclusive constraints illustrated above, there are several variations on the contingency constraint. For example, a project (call it X_6) could be contingent on the prior acceptance of at least two projects from a given set (say projects X_7, X_8, X_9, and X_{10}). The IP constraint conveying this condition would be:

$$2X_6 \leq X_7 + X_8 + X_9 + X_{10}$$

Thus, the constraint would be violated if the firm attempted to accept project 6 without accepting at least two of the projects 7, 8, 9, and 10. Of course, the latter four projects can be accepted irrespective of the disposition of project 6.

Finally, we turn to the treatment of the last type of project interrelationship.

Complementary or Synergistic Projects

If two or more projects become more attractive when accepted together than they would be if accepted singly, then they are called complementary or synergistic. An example of complementary or synergistic projects would be the construction of both a service station and a restaurant at the same exit off an interstate highway rather than constructing them individually at two different exits off the interstate.

In order to handle complementary or synergistic projects in an IP formulation, we utilize the following three steps:

Step 1: Define a new decision variable that denotes the combined acceptance of the projects that make up the complementary set. For example, if projects 7 and 9 are two complementary projects, define a new decision variable, say X_{79}, that will denote the joint acceptance of the two projects. Note that X_7 and X_9 cannot both equal 1 since this would mean that these two projects were accepted together and hence X_{79} must equal 1. Thus, if project 7 is accepted but project 9 is rejected, then $X_7 = 1$, $X_9 = 0$, and $X_{79} = 0$; if project 7 is rejected and project 9 is accepted, then $X_7 = 0$, $X_9 = 1$, and $X_{79} = 0$; if both projects are accepted, then $X_7 = 0$, $X_9 = 0$, and $X_{79} = 1$.

Step 2: Incorporate the new decision variable for the combined project into the objective function and all constraints where it is relevant. The coefficients for the new decision variable will be dependent on the facts of the situation at hand. For example, for the two projects 7 and 9 mentioned in step 1, say that implementing them together will increase the individual benefits by 15 percent and reduce the cost by 10 percent. This would mean that the coefficient for X_{79} in the objective function would be 115 percent of the sum of the coefficients for X_7 and X_9 in the objective function. Similarly, the coefficient for X_{79} in the cost constraint(s) would be 90 percent of the sum of the coefficients for X_7 and X_9 in the cost constraint(s).

Step 3: Write a mutually exclusive project constraint for the complementary set of projects plus the combined project. In our example, this constraint would be

$$X_7 + X_9 + X_{79} \leq 1$$

This constraint states that either (1) X_7 or X_9 can be accepted by itself while the other is rejected; (2) the combined project is accepted, which means that $X_7 = X_9 = 0$ and $X_{79} = 1$; or (3) both projects individually are rejected as well as the combined project—$X_7 = X_9 = X_{79} = 0$.

We now illustrate the formulation of the capital budgeting problem using IP.

The XYZ Company is considering 15 projects with the following cash outflows over three years and NPVs over their entire useful lives:

		Cash flows and NPVs in $000		
				NPV
j	C_{j1}	C_{j2}	C_{j3}	b_j
1	40	80	0	24
2	50	65	5	38
3	45	55	10	40
4	60	48	8	44
5	68	42	0	20
6	75	52	20	64
7	38	90	14	27
8	24	40	70	48
9	12	66	20	18
10	6	88	17	29
11	0	72	60	32
12	0	50	80	38
13	0	34	56	25
14	0	22	76	18
15	0	12	104	28
RHS	$K_1 = 300$	$K_2 = 540$	$K_3 = 380$	

In addition, the following interrelationships exist:

1. Of the set of projects 3, 4, and 8, *at most two can be accepted.*
2. Projects 5 and 9 are mutually exclusive but one of the two *must be accepted.*
3. Project 6 cannot be accepted unless both projects 1 and 14 are accepted.
4. Project 1 can be delayed one year—the same cash outflows will be required but the NPV will drop to $22.
5. Projects 2 and 3 and projects 10 and 13 can be combined into complementary or composite projects wherein total cash outflows will be reduced by 10 percent and NPV increased by 12 percent compared to the total of the separate projects.
6. *At least one* of the above two composite projects must be accepted.

Required:
    a. Define the new decision variables needed for the above problem.
    b. Formulate the problem as an IP.
Solution:
    a. The required new decision variables in addition to X_1 and X_{15} for the original 15 projects described above are as follows:

- X_{16} is a decision variable to denote the delay of project 1 for one year.
- X_{17} is a decision variable to denote the acceptance of the composite of projects 2 and 3.
- X_{18} is a decision variable to denote the acceptance of the composite of projects 10 and 13.

    b. The formulation for this problem is shown below:

$$\text{Maximize NPV} = 24X_1 + 38X_2 + 40X_3 + 44X_4 + 20X_5$$
$$+ 64X_6 + 27X_7 + 48X_8 + 18X_9 + 29X_{10}$$
$$+ 32X_{11} + 38X_{12} + 25X_{13} + 18X_{14} + 28X_{15}$$
$$+ 22X_{16} + 87.36X_{17} + 60.48X_{18} \qquad (a)$$

Subject to

$$40X_1 + 50X_2 + 45X_3 + 60X_4 + 68X_5$$
$$+ 75X_6 + 38X_7 + 24X_8 + 12X_9 + 6X_{10}$$
$$+ 85.5X_{15} + 5.4X_{18} \le 300 \qquad (b)$$

$$80X_1 + 65X_2 + 55X_3 + 48X_4 + 42X_5$$
$$+ 52X_6 + 90X_7 + 40X_8 + 66X_9 + 88X_{10}$$
$$+ 72X_{11} + 50X_{12} + 34X_{13} + 22X_{14} + 12X_{15}$$
$$+ 40X_{16} + 108X_{17} + 109.8X_{18} \le 540 \qquad (c)$$

$$5X_2 + 10X_3 + 8X_4 + 20X_6 + 14X_7$$
$$+ 70X_8 + 20X_4 + 17X_{10} + 60X_{11} + 80X_{12}$$
$$+ 56X_{13} + 76X_{14} + 104X_{15} + 80X_{16} + 13.5X_{17}$$
$$+ 65.7X_{18} \le 380 \qquad (d)$$

$$X_3 + X_4 + X_8 \le 2 \qquad (e)$$

$$X_5 + X_9 = 1 \qquad (f)$$

$$2X_6 \le X_1 + X_{14} + X_{16} \qquad (g)$$

$$X_1 + X_{16} \le 1 \qquad (h)$$

$$X_2 + X_3 + X_{17} \le 1 \qquad (i)$$

$$X_{10} + X_{13} + X_{18} \le 1 \qquad (j)$$

$$X_{17} + X_{18} \ge 1 \qquad (k)$$

$$X_i = \{0, 1\} \qquad i = 1, 2, \ldots, 18 \qquad (l)$$

A few comments should be made concerning this formulation. In Expression *a*, the objective function, the coefficients for X_1 through X_{16} were given in the problem description, and the coefficient X_{17} equals 1.12 times $(38 + 40)$ or 87.36 in order to show the 12 percent increase in NPV over the benefits generated by projects 2 and 3 separately. The coefficient for X_{18} is arrived at in a similar fashion. Expressions *b, c,* and *d* are the budget constraints for years 1, 2, and 3, respectively. The coefficients for projects 1 through 15 are straightforward; the coefficients for X_{16} are those of X_1 delayed by 1 year; for X_{17} and X_{18} the coefficients are 90 percent of the sum of the coefficients for the respective pairs of projects. Expression *e* shows that no more than two of the projects 3, 4, and 8 can be accepted.

Expression *f* shows that either project 5 or project 9 must be accepted but both cannot be accepted since they are mutually exclusive; the strict equality sign conveys that one of the two must be accepted (that is, either $X_5 = 1$ or $X_9 = 1$). Expression *g* shows that in order for project 6 to be accepted, *either* project 1 and project 14 must be accepted or project 1 delayed by one year (that is, project 16) and project 14 must be accepted; it is assumed here that project 1 delayed by one year still satisfies the requirement that both project 1 and project 14 are accepted. Notice also that even if one of the above combinations of projects 1 and 14 is accepted, project 6 can either be accepted or rejected because of the ≤ inequality. Expression *h* shows that *only one* of the two projects 1 or 16 (that is, project 1 delayed by one year) *can be accepted;* if we wanted to force acceptance of one of these two, a strict equality would replace the ≤ sign. Expression *i* and *j* convey that with the two composite projects *at most one of the individual projects or the composite project* can be accepted. Expression *k* indicates that either one or both of the composite projects must be accepted.

If the IP problem formulated above was solved using one of the software packages from computer manufacturers, the printout would only show the optimal value of the objective function and the projects that should be accepted in order to maximize NPV without violating any of the constraints. That is, the solution of IP problems does not yield an optimal tableau as was the case with LP. This discussion leads to our concluding comments on IP.

Limitations of IP Capital Budgeting Formulations

Three major limitations should be kept in mind as IP is evaluated as a tool to assist financial managers in arriving at the optimal portfolio of capital investment projects:

1. Packaged computer programs to solve IP problems are not as readily available as such algorithms to solve LP problems.
2. The solution of IP problems requires significantly greater computer time and memory requirements, which may be an important consideration for small and medium-sized firms.
3. Shadow prices and the ability to perform sensitivity analysis do not exist in IP as was the case in LP. Hence the valuable insight provided by these tools can be obtained only by re-solving the problem several times—which could be very costly in terms of the computer time required.

Thus, IP does have attractive features that recommend its use. However, IP, like all decision-facilitating models, has its limitations or shortcomings as well.

SUMMARY

This chapter has surveyed the important area of mathematical programming applied to capital budgeting. The techniques presented select the portfolio of assets that optimizes the value of the objective function without violating any of the constraints on the firm. We contrasted the LP and IP methodologies for treating the allocation of scarce resources to capital investment projects. LP is the more straightforward of the techniques, and computer software packages are readily available to handle virtually any size problem. Furthermore, the interpretation of shadow prices and the performance of sensitivity analysis is immediate with the LP model. However, the continuous nature of the decision variables for the projects allows the acceptance of partial projects, which is often not feasible, and the possibility of partial projects precludes the treatment of project interrelationships.

IP is a methodology that requires the complete acceptance of projects or their complete rejection. Such a requirement enables the IP model to handle mutually exclusive, contingent, and complementary projects. Although the problem formulations using LP and IP are very similar, the computer time and memory requirements to solve IP problems are significantly greater than those required for LP problems. In addition, another significant shortcoming of IP is that shadow prices do not exist and sensitivity analysis cannot be performed, as is the case with LP. Financial managers will be at a disadvantage without the helpful insight provided by shadow prices and sensitivity analysis.

Both LP and IP are able to handle only a single goal in the objective function. However, goal programming (GP), which was briefly introduced in an earlier section of the chapter, is a very powerful, multicriteria decision model that provides assistance to financial managers in designing portfolios of projects that achieve a hierarchy of goals. Using GP, firms can now handle more realistic conditions and can evaluate trade-offs among goals. Integer GP (IGP) formulations enable the firm to also reflect project interrelationships in the model. Sensitivity analysis in GP shows the impact of varying the priority structure, trade-offs among goals, and desired goal levels. Financial applications of GP reported in the literature have demonstrated the strengths of the approach and very good results.[8]

The surveys cited earlier in the chapter indicate a steady trend of increasing use of math programming models in financial applications in general and capital budgeting in particular. This chapter should provide the foundation for the reader's informed use and interpretation of mathematical programming capital budgeting formulations.

NOTES

[1] T. Klammer, "Empirical Evidence of the Adoption of Sophisticated Capital Budgeting Techniques," *Journal of Business*, July 1972, pp. 387–97.

[2] James M. Fremgen, "Capital Budgeting Practices: A Survey," *Management Accounting*, May 1973, pp. 19–25.

[3] J. W. Petty and O. D. Bowlin, "The Financial Manager and Quantitative Decision Models," *Financial Management*, Winter 1976, pp. 32–41.

[4] A. Charnes, W. W. Cooper, and M. H. Miller, "An Application of Linear Programming to Financial Budgeting and the Cost of Funds," *Journal of Business*, January 1959.

[5] H. M. Weingartner, "Capital Budgeting of Interrelated Projects," *Management Sciences*, March 1966, pp. 485–516.

[6] See J. J. Clark, T. J. Hindelang, and R. E. Pritchard, *Capital Budgeting: Planning and Control of Capital Expenditures*, 2d ed. (Englewood Cliffs, N.J.: Prentice-Hall, 1984), chaps. 19–22; and T. J. Hindelang and M. M. Holland, *The Theory and Practice of Finance* (Reading, Mass.: Addison-Wesley Publishing, 1985), chap. 7.

[7] J. H. Lorie and L. J. Savage, "Three Problems in Rationing Capital," *Journal of Business*, October 1955, pp. 229–39.

[8] The reader interested in the full development of the GP and IGP formulations for the capital rationing problem should see our treatment in Clark, Hindelang, and Pritchard, *Capital Budgeting*, chap. 21; and Hindelang and Holland, *Theory and Practice of Finance*, chap. 7.

REFERENCES

Allen, D. H. "How to Use Mixed-Integer Programming." *Chemical Engineering*, March 1976, pp. 114–20.

Baumol, W. C., and R. E. Quandt. "Investment and Discount Rates under Capital Rationing—A Programming Approach." *The Economic Journal*, June 1965, pp. 317–29.

Bernhard, R. H. "Mathematical Programming Models for Capital Budgeting: A Survey, Generalization, and Critique." *Journal of Financial and Quantitative Analysis*, June 1969, pp. 111–58.

Fabozzi, F. J., and J. Valente. "Mathematical Programming in American Companies: A Sample Survey." *Interfaces*, November 1976, pp. 93–98.

Fourcans, A., and T. J. Hindelang. "The Incorporation of Multiple Goals in the Selection of Capital Investment." Presented at the *1973 Financial Management Association Conference*, Atlanta, October 1973.

Hastie, L. K. "One Businessman's View of Capital Budgeting." *Financial Management*, June 1974, pp. 37–44.

Hirshleifer, J. "Efficient Allocation of Capital in an Uncertain World. *American Economics Review*, May 1964, pp. 188–95.

IBM Mathematical Programming System Extended (MPSX) Control Language User's Manual. Program Number 5734-XM4. White Plains, N.Y.: International Business Machines, 1971.

Kornbluth, J. S. H. "Accounting in Multiple-Objective Linear Programming." *The Accounting Review,* April 1974, pp. 284–95.

Lee, S. M., and A. J. Lerro. "Capital Budgeting for Multiple Objectives." *Financial Management,* Spring 1974, pp. 58–67.

Weingartner, H. M. *Mathematical Programming and the Analysis of Capital Budgeting Problems.* Englewood Cliffs, N.J.: Prentice—Hall, 1963.

————. "Criteria for Programming Investment Project Selection." *Journal of Industrial Economics,* November 1966, pp. 65–76.

————. "Capital Rationing: n Authors in Search of a Plot." *The Journal of Finance,* December 1977, pp. 1403–31.

12

Budget Administration: How to Streamline Budget Preparation*

Moustafa H. Abdelsamad
Virginia Commonwealth University

INTRODUCTION

T he objective of this chapter is to provide some guidelines to capital budget preparers in various firms with emphasis on manufacturing concerns. The reader should modify and tailor the ideas provided here to suit the particular organization at hand. Capital expenditures are non-operating expenditures of large amounts that affect more than one year. These expenditures should exceed a previously established minimum such as $2,500.

---

  * Information provided here is based on general conclusions made by the author based on a study of over 100 capital expenditure written policies and procedures provided by large corporations. The writer is grateful to these corporations for making this information available. Care is taken not to identify any specific corporation.

Examples of these expenditures include land, building, equipment, and major modifications to these items. Long-term leases and leasehold improvements are also included. The term of capital leases exceeds one year and cannot be canceled without a penalty. Operating leases have a term that does not exceed one year and can be canceled within a year without a penalty.

A budget is a written plan prepared in advance. The capital budget contains a list of the various capital investment projects. For each project key information is provided, such as assigned project number, brief description, total investment amount, whether it is a new project or a continuation of an old project, the amount spent to date for ongoing projects, expected completion date, department or division affected, priority rating (high, low, average), and estimate of project profitability.

Thus, the capital budget is a yearly estimate of capital expenditures classified by division and major capital expenditure classification.

The objective of the capital budget is to estimate the total capital expenditures required by the corporation for the next year. Long-range capital budgets for a period of three to five years may also be used. However, the longer the period, the more crude the estimates. The total amount of expenditures needed for capital investments is used to help estimate the financing requirements. The earlier these estimates are made, the better. This information will enable the financial manager to raise the necessary funds on the best possible terms.

Because of the large amounts involved and the effect on years to come, capital expenditures need to be well planned and controlled. A formal capital budget is a necessary tool of planning and controlling capital spending.

OBJECTIVES OF THE BUDGET

The capital budget has many objectives. Here are some of the often-cited objectives:

1. It forces individual managers to think through their ideas more thoroughly and to try to predict the investments needed in their area of jurisdiction.

2. It provides for the coordination of different projects submitted by various parts of the organization. This allows for reconciling conflicting demands, avoiding duplication of capital expenditures, and determining priorities.

3. Early identification of possible capital investments allows the study of these investments in depth. It also allows studying various alternative courses of action. This practice helps avoid delaying action so long that the investment becomes a "must" item for survival.

4. Budget inclusion serves as a notice to various departments, divisions, and other parts of the organization that a capital investment is contemplated. This allows various parts of the organization that could be affected by the proposed investment to provide inputs or be ready to provide the service needed. For example, the tax, accounting, legal, real estate, marketing, engineering, and corporate planning personnel could accordingly be notified that certain projects need their inputs.

5. Annual forecast of capital expenditures helps determine the effect of these expenditures on the operating budget.

6. It provides a rough estimate of funds needed. This amount, in addition to working capital requirements, can be used to determine needed financing beyond funds provided internally. It also ensures staying within the overall cash resources available to the company. Allocation of available funds would be facilitated.

7. It provides for listing and comparing various proposals on common ground. This process helps compare one project to another on a uniform basis. Usually a return-on-investment figure or some other measure of profitability is calculated for each project whenever possible. This return could be measured more accurately when the appropriation request is made.

8. It allows top management to check each investment against established company objectives, policies, and strategic plans.

9. The budget provides a method of controlling expenditures by monitoring each project from beginning to end. Periodic progress reports and budget and appropriations procedures are designed to accomplish the control objective.

Who Should Prepare a Capital Budget

Every organization should prepare a capital budget for a three- to five-year period. This budget is more detailed the next year and less detailed beyond that. Even rough estimates are better than none at all.

Some individuals question the value of a capital budget. They think of it as an unnecessary exercise in futility. However, this is not the case if it is approached as an approximate estimation of need without unnecessary complications and excessive paperwork. Thinking ahead is essential in today's highly competitive and uncertain environment.

Dreams Are Important

Management should not discourage plants and divisions from creative thinking and what is often referred to as preparing a "wish list." Since top management is always in a position to reject or delay projects, inclusion of as many projects as possible allows management to consider and select the best possible proposals. A healthy percentage of projects to be rejected helps ensure that sufficient projects are being considered and that divisions are not placing too many restrictions that discourage innovative and somewhat risky capital investment proposals from being submitted and considered. Many managers argue that funds are not in short supply, but good ideas are.

Budget Inclusion versus Authorization

Inclusion in the capital budget does not imply authorization to spend the money. It simply means approval in principle. Actual authorization is made when the appropriation request is approved. Only then can expenditures be made.

It is not always possible to think of all capital investment projects in time to include them in the capital budget. Accordingly, it is customary to update the budget on a quarterly basis. Appropriation requests may be made for capital investment projects even though they were not included in the budget. Most companies allow submitting individual project requests beyond those included in the capital budget. Appropriation procedures will be covered in more detail in another chapter.

Analysis and Justification

Because budget inclusion does not imply authorization of expenditures or commitment of funds, only preliminary analysis of a capital investment proposal is needed for inclusion in the budget. Detailed justification, analysis, documentation, and evaluation will normally be made when the appropriation request is made. The two key items required at budget time are a description of the project and the approximate cost; other information can be provided whenever possible and improved upon as time passes.

General Economic and Environmental Assumptions

To allow uniformity and consistency in budget estimates, top management should prepare a list of assumptions regarding economic conditions, environmental conditions, and inflation. These estimates should be used by all concerned. Top management—with the help of its own staff of experts—is in a better position to make these assumptions. Deviations from these assumptions by those submitting proposals need to be pointed out and justified.

Inflation

Project estimates should take inflation into consideration whenever possible by using projected-levels inflation factors provided by top management. Reflecting inflation in cost and return calculations makes estimates more realistic.

Often capital expenditure investments that take years to implement, such as building a nuclear power plant, are affected significantly by cost overruns and inflation. The increase in costs due to inflation and other factors can turn the project into a total failure.

TYPES OF BUDGETS

Two major budgeting approaches are followed by companies: financing and rationing. They are described here.

Financing

A financing budget starts with the assumption that money is not in short supply, but good ideas are. Accordingly, a minimum return on investment or minimum return target is established for each major category of investment and risk class. All projects that meet or exceed these minimums are accepted. If a project is profitable enough, it could be financed. The larger the company, the easier it is to raise funds for profitable investment projects.

Rationing

Under the rationing approach, the company starts with a given total amount of funds considered desirable and adequate. Then, all projects compete for the limited funds. In many cases the amount is roughly determined by the amount of depreciation plus an added premium. Some companies may base the total on a percentage of sales consistent with industry position, such as 10 percent of sales.

Unlike the theoretical marginal efficiency of capital assumptions, it is not possible to have all projects identified and listed in advance, and then select the best set of projects that exceed the cost of financing.

Rather, it is customary to use past experience to determine a minimum cutoff rate of return that will limit the investments to the total desirable budget. For example, a company may wish to limit its capital budget for next year to $200 million. Based on past experience, 20 percent aftertax return may be used as a cutoff point for approving individualized appropriation requests. Then, periodically, a check is made to ensure that approved expenditures are within the budget.

Normally, rationing is more common than the financing approach due to management's desire to keep the budget within controllable limits. Also, it is recognized by top management that each investment project takes time. In the short run, top-management time is in short supply. It is argued that beyond a certain limit capital expenditure projects would be too many to effectively manage and control.

Also, some companies prefer to limit their capital expenditure to the amount that could be financed internally and largely from equity funds with little or no debt financing. This practice limits the risk exposure of the company during adverse economic conditions. This practice may be called depression complex.

A company should not religiously adhere to a capital rationing or financing approach. Under capital rationing, a mechanism should be allowed to adjust the total budget limit if conditions warrant it. Also, capital investments should not be allowed to grow uncontrolled. Care should be taken under capital rationing to select the best group of investment projects. Capital budgeting methods have to be used carefully when capital rationing is involved. Using the internal rate of return method to select among mutually exclusive projects of unequal size and life can lead to selecting projects that do not truly maximize the wealth of the owners.

Depreciation as a Base

Depreciation is an allocation of the cost of fixed assets. It is affected by tax and other financial considerations. It does not necessarily agree with actual wear and tear, physical conditions, or productive ability of the assets involved. Nevertheless, many firms use depreciation as a rough estimate of what needs to be invested to ensure the maintenance of the productive capacity of the organization and to adjust capital investments for growth and inflation. It should be used as a rough estimate to be modified by other means. It should be compared to an internal list of needed investments provided by various plants and operating units. Generally, acceptance of capital expenditure projects should be based on return on investment and other nonquantitative benefits and not be strictly tied to depreciation.

CAPITAL BUDGETS: WAYS OF ENHANCING THEIR EFFECTIVENESS

Capital budgets are tools that should be used with care. Here are some ways to prevent budgets from becoming counterproductive.

1. The budgeting process involves planning, executing, comparing actual to forecast (feedback), and replanning. A key element is comparing actual results to the forecast and analyzing the variations or deviations. Deviations from budget estimates can and do occur. Capital budget deviations in particular are expected. Throughout the budgeting and capital appropriation procedure, individual preparers should not be penalized for minor errors in estimates unless they reflect gross negligence. Doing otherwise will result in submitting surefire proposals.

2. Budgets should be realistic. They should not be too optimistic or too pessimistic. Estimates should be checked against those of similar projects undertaken previously. The computer can facilitate checking against past experience.

3. Excessive paperwork should be avoided. Simple, easy-to-understand procedures for preparing the budget are needed. Whenever possible, forms should be simple to fill out and understand.

4. Individual managers should be trained in how to prepare the budgets, with the budget staff ready to answer questions and help when asked.

5. The budget should be regarded as a planning tool rather than an end unto itself. Management should keep this in perspective. The capital budget should be designed to recognize and plan for worthwhile investment projects and to help individual managers both run their operations better and present their departments or divisions in a better light.

6. Budget and appropriation procedures should be evaluated each year or two to find ways of enhancing their effectiveness.

The Computer

Various computer software programs can help reduce the chore of budget preparations. The manager can ask "what if" questions and allow various assumptions to be included with related changes without spending endless hours on these preparations. Also, the computer is a valuable tool in tracking various projects. An increasing number of corporations are using computers (especially personal computers) in budgeting.

ROLES WITHIN THE ORGANIZATION

Two groups of individuals are involved in budget preparations. They may be broadly classified as line personnel and staff support personnel. Line personnel are responsible for identifying projects and preparing estimates. However, planning, budgeting, and other support personnel serve as a source of help to line personnel.

Role of Budget Director/Financial Vice President

The financial vice president or equivalent is ultimately responsible for maintaining the capital budget. He(she) may be aided by a budget director who requests capital investment plans from various units and consolidates them into a budget. Some firms assign the responsibility for checking individual projects to corporate planning development staff.

Staff and Expert Assistance

Help of various experts is especially needed before the actual authorization of capital investment is made. Typically, legal, accounting, tax, industrial engineering, and marketing individuals provide input regarding assumptions and estimates made for an investment proposal. The larger the investment, the more elaborate the analysis. Additionally, outside consultants may be used to provide objective input whenever appropriate, especially for large capital investment projects. This concept will be discussed in more detail under capital appropriation procedures.

ADMINISTRATIVE RESPONSIBILITIES

Budget responsibilities vary from one organization to another, depending on organizational structure. Generally, under the authority of the top financial manager, a budget director (or the controller) or equivalent is made responsible for ensuring that the budget is put together and that communications are flowing between various divisions and the budget office. Capital budget estimates are made by various departments and consolidated by division managers who may change the figures provided by various departments. Then, department or division estimates are consolidated by a group vice president, and all estimates are combined into a capital budget by the budget office.

Project Manager

Each investment project should be assigned to a particular individual who is responsible for following it from beginning to end. This individual will not have formal line authority but instead will have reporting responsibility. He(she) is responsible for the periodic progress reports, ensuring that enough records are kept to allow for postauditing the project, helping with postauditing the project, ensuring that the project is implemented, and alerting appropriate individuals to problems or difficulties.

Postaudit

When a project is completed (that is, fully operational), actual results should be compared to estimates. This is referred to as a postaudit. The purposes of the postaudit are to:

1. Determine the extent to which objectives were achieved.
2. Isolate deviations from actual estimates and explain these deviations. These deviations may be favorable (higher benefits, lower costs) or unfavorable (lower benefits, higher costs). They may be beyond the control of management (such as an unexpected strike or flood that causes excessive price increases of raw materials) or an avoidable type that could have been predicted or considered (such as a better sales estimate that could have been provided by a market survey).
3. Determine action needed. This may include finding a need to change procedures. It may identify poor estimators and possible intentional overestimation of benefits and underestimation of costs by some project sponsors. On the other hand, good estimators could be identified for possible recognition and rewards.

It is generally desirable to have a system of postauditing projects at least using a sampling technique to provide an incentive for project sponsors to be realistic in their estimates.

THE FLOW OF EVENTS

By September of each year, the capital budget should be ready to discuss and review for implementation the following January. The schedule should allow inputs and budget flow from the plant level, to the division level, to the general management, and finally to the board of directors level. Capital budget estimates are integràted with the operating budget. This should be finished by December for the next year.

POLICY ISSUES, ALTERNATIVE POSITIONS

Companies differ in their practices regarding issues addressed by the capital expenditure authorization and control policy. These issues affect both the capital budget and the related appropriation procedures. Each company management should select the position that maximizes the effectiveness of capital investment management and control and that suits the individual preferences of top management and the type of management philosophy it endorses. Here are some of the typical issues to be addressed:

1. The extent of *centralization versus decentralization* of the capital expenditure must be decided. More or less participation could be sought from lower managerial levels. Generally, the more strategic the investment, the higher the degree of centralization of its related decision.

2. What constitutes a capital expenditure? The *established minimum* would differ from one company to another.

3. Project *categories or classifications* must be selected. Some may have a simple classification such as minor or major projects. Some may have an elaborate list, and others may use something in between such as replacement, expansion, new ventures, or mandatory. Other companies may use accounting classifications such as building, land, machinery and equipment, leasehold improvement, tools, furniture, and fixtures.

4. Authorization and *approval levels* represent another policy issue. Some companies require more involvement of top management whereas others reserve top-management involvement to very large projects with a blanket appropriation for other projects. One example often found is:

	Approval required		
Project cost	Group vice president	President	Board of directors
Under $50,000	Discretion of group vice president		
$50,000 to $100,000	Yes	Yes	
Over $100,000	Yes	Yes	Yes

5. The required *reporting and follow-up* policy on various projects, the method presentation of projects, and whether or not a department needs to send a representative to a budget hearing need to be addressed. These policies also address early warning reports, periodic reporting, and postaudit.

6. Another issue has to do with the capital budgeting *evaluation method* to be used, the cutoff or minimum rate of return required, and the size of the capital budget. Many companies specify that the discounted cash flow method must be used for all income-generating projects. One manual states, "Indicators of profitability and risk will be required to provide further insight into the nature and expectation of the projects."

7. What expenditure must receive *special scrutinizing* is another policy issue. Some companies require a special centralized evaluation process for computer acquisitions and leases.

8. Another issue involves the use of *risk analysis*. In some companies investments over $100,000 (except those that fall into the strategic classification) require performance of risk analysis at least in the form of best probable, worst probable, and most likely probable occurrence for each determinable factor. One company manual clearly states, "A rate-of-return calculation should be prepared for each set of circumstances."

9. *Responsibility* for submitting investment requests, preparation of the requests, and postaudits of completed projects need to be addressed.

10. Authority to *approve overruns* of capital expenditures needs to be considered. While practices vary, when the cost of a project is expected to exceed original estimates by 10 percent or more of original appropriations, a supplementary appropriational request is required. For example, the manual of a large glass manufacturer states that overruns need to be approved if they exceed 10 percent or $150,000 of original authorization, whichever is smaller.

11. *Other policy issues* to be considered vary from one company to another. They include designation of the manual that guides the requests, approval and implementation of capital investments; guidelines for disposition of capital facilities; and the responsibilities of each major operating unit, director of capital planning (or equivalent), vice president for manufacturing, other vice presidents, controller, and financial vice presidents. It may also designate the person in charge of interpreting the policy and which manual instructions govern in case of conflict. For instance, one manual states that where instructions are in conflict with regulatory authority requirements, the latter will govern.

241

PREFERENCES AND PRACTICES: VARIATIONS FROM ONE INDUSTRY TO ANOTHER

It is difficult to make generalizations about different industries. However, the following conclusions are reached by the author based on a study of various company manuals.

1. The size and age of the company plays a major role in the extent of sophistication and detailed policies and procedures made available in a manual.

2. Policies and procedures are listed under various titles. They may be part of the accounting manual or another manual. Examples of the titles used are appropriations manual, capital investment policy and procedures, AFE (authorization for expenditure) policy and procedure, policy and procedures for approval and postcompletion evaluation of capital transactions, manufacturing engineering operations manual—economic evaluation of projects, appropriation evaluation manuals, business investments procedure, capital and expenses project appropriation procedure finance memo number X, capital investment manual, capital expenditure procedure, capital programming, and capital expenditures standing instructions. They may also be part of the general policy manual.

3. Some firms provide the instructions as part of a corporate controller's letter.

4. The manual serves as a teaching device of how to prepare and evaluate a proposal. It reflects management philosophy and style.

5. Generally, companies in the industries that are known to use sophisticated planning tools (such as those in the petroleum refining industry) tend to have more elaborate procedures. However, this is not always the case. Some firms that use highly sophisticated production techniques do not use advanced methods for evaluating capital expenditures.

6. Manuals reveal the degree of sophistication and professionalism of management. Family-controlled companies seem to emphasize more subjective evaluation methods than other companies that have widespread stock ownership. While discounted cash flow methods are dominant, they are not as widely used in some of the family-oriented businesses.

7. Companies in industries that are profitable and dominated by a few big companies seem to be using less sophisticated methods and techniques than those that are highly competitive.

8. Companies in the high-tech industry seem to be less structured and concerned with sophisticated capital budgeting procedures and techniques. It seems that the lack of structure in the environment, the highly unpredictable nature of the market, and the difference in the risk makes it difficult to adhere to strict capital budgeting and control procedures.

9. As expected, companies where capital expenditures represent an important percentage of sales and resources use more elaborate policies and procedures than others with small amounts of capital expenditures.

10. Highly regulated industries place a high degree of emphasis on following policies and procedures that will enhance the return on investment allowed under the related regulations.

11. Over the years, more emphasis has been placed on discounted cash flow techniques. However, with the advent of the computer, more than one measure of profitability is calculated.

12. Firms should periodically review their manuals to address the following common faults found in many of them:

- Financing charges are deducted even though they should not be included in discounted cash flow calculations. The net present value or the internal rate of return methods measure the return. Deducting finance charges results in double counting financing costs.
- Risk estimates are not addressed.
- Authorization limits are low. Approval limits need to be periodically revised upward to account for inflation.
- Accounting (or average) rate of return or payback are used as principal methods even though they should be used only as supplementary evaluation techniques. They should not be used as the sole criterion for evaluating capital investment proposals.

13. It seems that the larger the company, the higher the degree of use of committees in the selection and approval of capital expenditure proposals.

POLICY VERSUS PROCEDURE

Capital expenditure policies are designed to provide general decision guidelines to ensure that these expenditures are planned, authorized, implemented, and followed up according to company goals and objectives. Procedures are detailed steps needed to implement the policies. A manual is a collection of such policies or procedures. Written policies and procedures are needed to ensure consistent and uniform application. In the introduction to one manual, five objectives were given for the manual. They are (1) establish discounted cash flow as the method of evaluation, (2) formalize control procedures, (3) establish information bases, (4) inform and guide the divisions in the use of current methods for evaluating appropriations, and (5) facilitate resource allocation.

Examples of Key Policies and Procedures

Policy Statement	*Related Procedures Needed*
• No expenditure or commitment of funds can be made without proper authorizations.	• Steps needed to acquire authorization of funds. • Appropriation request form. • Authorization and approval levels for various size and type investments. • Approvals sequence.
• Overruns and significant additional expenditures must be approved prior to commitment of funds.	• What constitutes a significant increase (for example, over 10 percent or $5,000) is identified with proper forms and necessary approval steps.
• Each project cannot be submitted without proper justification.	• Forms used and attached documents needed to justify a proposed capital expenditure are included and described.
• All computer hardware and software over $10,000 must be approved by the data processing committee.	• Detailed steps needed to acquire such approval and associated forms are described and discussed.
• In one company the policy was "All capital expenditures expected to exceed $100,000 must be approved by Capital Appropriations Committee."	• The procedure refers to information to be completed, approvals, notice of approval, and forms to be used.

244

Policy Statement	*Related Procedures Needed*
• Another company manual states, "It is company policy to develop meaningful plans and goals for capital expenditures, and to establish procedures to provide management, both line and staff, with the necessary information to ensure that these funds are expended in a manner that will fulfill group and corporate goals and objectives."	• The procedure includes a 12-month plan, expenditure categories, appropriation requests, and related forms.
• Each capital expenditure must be identified and periodically reported on.	• Project numbering system is described and explained. • Progress report forms and steps needed to complete them are included. Each report form is provided and explained.
• Veto power is granted to certain individuals.	• Detailed specification of who has power to veto a proposal and under what conditions is listed here. By the nature of their jobs, these individuals can individually discontinue a project.
• Reactivation of old proposals that were rejected cannot be made prior to a given time or significant change in economic conditions or project cost/benefit estimates.	• Details related to who can bring a proposal for a second evaluation and specific justification for such action are described. Forms and other related documents are described.
• Capital budget items must be coordinated.	• Reference is made to steps needed to ensure that all

Policy Statement	*Related Procedures Needed*
	concerned individuals or departments are contacted and kept informed of capital budget proposals and changes thereof.
• Each capital expenditure proposal must be assigned to an individual coordinator. This is done to ensure follow-up and reporting on each investment.	• The details of how a project coordinator is selected are described along with needed forms. Qualifications of the individual coordinator are specified.
• Depreciation method to be used must be realistic and consistent. Taxes must be considered, including investment tax credits and taxes on net income.	• Depreciation method to be used for tax purposes is specified along with reference to how it could be calculated, life guidelines, and the contact person in the accounting department to help in estimating depreciation and tax factors.
• Capital expenditures must be grouped according to similar nature or categories.	• Specific classifications are listed and defined along with different steps and forms needed for each category. Procedures for routine replacement of plant and equipment differ from those pertaining to expansion of existing facilities or entering into new markets. Classification also allows studying and comparing similar items. It also allows applying varying minimum return investment figures to different risk categories.

Policy Statement	*Related Procedures Needed*
• Any expenditure above $1,000 where the benefits extend over one year must be treated as a capital expenditure.	• Steps needed to identify the item by category and balance sheet classification may be cited.
• Except for a few mandatory investments, ROI must be calculated.	• Detailed forms and steps are listed to determine cash flow and calculate ROI using discounted cash flow techniques such as net present value or internal rate of return.
• Generally, property should be bought and not leased.	• Detailed instructions regarding the type of property and justification for leasing it would be listed.
• For approval purposes the total lease amount for the life of the lease must be used.	• Steps needed to evaluate a lease versus purchase are included here. • Forms to be used are provided and explained.
• All major capital expenditure proposals must be accompanied by a formal presentation to the Capital Acquisition Committee of the Board of Directors.	• Detailed requirements are specified. For example, all projects that require $1 million or higher expenditures must be defended before the Capital Acquisition Committee of the Board of Directors. Key items required to be addressed in the executive summary and in the attachments to the summary are listed and explained.
• Method and technique to be used in the evaluation of proposed expenditure.	• It may be specified that net present value will be calculated for all projects with sensitivity

Policy Statement	*Related Procedures Needed*
	analysis conducted on projects over $1 million.
• All company property must be identified as such whenever possible.	• Methods of tagging personal property are described, and responsibility for such a task is fixed.
• Assets cannot be disposed of until careful evaluation is made.	• Steps used to identify and justify disposition of assets are described along with ways of making these items available for other divisions.
• Postaudit of capital addition programs are to be made each year for projects having a full year's commercial operation during the preceding year.	• Detailed explanation of type of reports, format, timing, and financial comparisons for each size category is included.
• Acquisition or replacement of transportation equipment requires corporate approval.	• The procedure includes form to be used, estimating required investment, estimating rate of return, and supporting documents.
• Corporate approval is required for all leases regardless of amount. All lease contracts and agreements must be prepared and approved by the Office of General Council.	• The procedure details the forms to be used and the method of acquiring corporate approval and legal counsel's approval.

LINKAGE WITH STRATEGIC PLANNING AND WITH APPROPRIATION PROCEDURE

No business can be viable unless it can earn a satisfactory return on investment. This return is better achieved through the planning process. General goals are established and translated into specific objectives. These objectives are implemented through policies and strategies. Capital investments must be related to each one of these components since they are needed to accomplish these goals and objectives. Care should be taken to ensure consistency of capital policies and strategies with overall organizational goals, objectives, policies, and strategies.

The linkages with strategic planning occur at different stages. First, through the long-term capital budget estimates, major capital expenditure projects are identified and the needed funds are estimated. Each one of these projects is checked against the overall strategic plan. Each year an update is made, and each capital investment project is checked against the plan before actual implementation is made. As the project is implemented it is periodically checked to ensure that it is still within the plan. Finally, as the project is completed, the results are analyzed and the role it plays in contributing to the plan is evaluated for lesson learning.

PROVIDING FOR TACTICAL AND DISCRETIONARY PROJECTS

Generally, it is not possible nor desirable to identify each single capital investment project in the budget. For a large corporation, this may amount to several thousand items. Accordingly, it is customary to combine minor replacement projects and minor capital expenditures. An approach currently used is to create a blanket appropriation amount for each plant or major division. This category covers the nonstrategic projects, known as tactical or discretionary projects. The amount of each individual investment under this category is not large enough to require higher approval levels. However, a procedure should be established and checked periodically to ensure that these projects are subjected to sufficient scrutiny at the lower level. It is possible to keep the maximum level at $50,000 for each investment for medium-sized companies or $100,000 for larger companies. Naturally, actual amounts will vary depending upon the industry and degree of diversification in the products of the given company.

In a large pharmaceutical company, for example, projects under $20,000 are grouped in the annual forecast as divisional funds.

APPROVAL LIMITS AND HIERARCHIES

Each company establishes approval levels for capital appropriation requests. Higher level of approvals are required for larger dollar amounts and for projects that may affect the company significantly.

For budget purposes, the capital expenditure forecast is sent from the department to the division to the operational vice president to the president. The number of levels will depend upon the size of the company and management preferences. Generally, each higher level groups the requests and modifies them to eliminate obviously undesirable projects and those that should be deferred. At the top level a total budget is established.

Appropriation requests are submitted for each project to get actual approval for undertaking a project and committing the funds. These projects go through predetermined approval levels. These levels vary from one company to another. However, the following suggestions are offered here.

1. The capital budget is used to provide a rough approximation of amounts that could be requested by departments and divisions.
2. Each division is allowed to approve its minor capital expenditures so long as the total is within the limit established for the minor expenditures for that department.
3. Each department and division must submit proposed major projects for approval to higher levels.
4. The finance department (for example, the controller) at the operating level is required to keep track of capital expenditures at their levels and pass the information to the corporate finance department (for example, the corporate controller) that keeps track of all capital expenditure projects. With the advent of the computer, this task is greatly simplified.

When outlays are expected to change for a given project, a supplementary appropriation request is needed if the overrun is significant. Usually, the amount defined as significant is based on both absolute dollar amount and percentage. Typically, a supplemental request is needed if the expected overrun exceeds 10 percent of the original appropriation of $5,000, whichever is higher. Also, the operating unit controller is responsible for ensuring that the supplementary requests are submitted.

The approval process for a major project may be quite involved in some companies. A capital appropriation request in a manufacturing concern requires approval of the following individuals: assistant plant manager, assistant director of engineering, director of engineering, production manager, department manager, operations general manager, assistant director of research, director of research, general manager of manufacturing services, controller, senior vice president, executive vice president, president, and executive committee.

FORMS AND DOCUMENTS

Several forms are used by various companies throughout the capital budgeting and appropriation process. Selected key forms are described here.

Capital Expenditure Proposal Form

The purpose of this form is to notify department, division, and company of the need for a particular capital expenditure and seek approval to submit detailed capital appropriation requests. The approval at this point is in principle only, and rejection is made for obviously poor proposals or those that do not agree with overall company objectives and strategies. Key information needed is a description of the proposed project, classification of expenditures, estimate of needed resources of capital acquisitions and working capital, a preliminary statement of expected benefits, and a crude measure of profitability. No elaborate engineering and other studies are needed at this point. Finally, signature of the originator and other individuals at the department, division, and corporate levels are shown. Figure 1 is shown as an example of this form. This form and all others mentioned here should be modified to suit each particular organization.

Budget Summary Form

The budget summary form may be used to keep track of budgeted projects. Each department, division, and corporate controller should keep a form of this sort to track down various projects. The key information includes capital expenditure item identification number, description of the project, status of the project as to whether it is new or a continuing project, total expenditure authorized, amount to be expended this budget year, and classification of expenditure by major classification category used. Figure 2 provides an example of the form. The column showing expenditure this budget is in essence the capital budget for this year.

The priority column that classifies projects as 1, 2, or 3 may be described as priority 1 for essential projects, 2 for desirable projects, and 3 for deferrable projects.

The return-on-investment column (ROI) is used for that or other measures of profitability and is completed whenever available without

FIGURE 1

XYZ CORPORATION
Capital Expenditure
Preliminary Budget Request

Department _____   Number _____

Division _____   Date _____

Project Classification:
    _____ Replacement/Cost Reduction
    _____ Expansion
    _____ New
    _____ Other _____
               (please specify)

Request (check one):
    ☐ Original
    ☐ Supplementary

Description of Proposed Investment

Amount Needed: $ _____ (as shown below)

$_____ Fixed Assets + $_____ Working Capital − $_____ Net Cash Flow from Replaced Items = $_____ Net Investment

Expected Cash Flow (Benefits):

Expected Time Schedule and Priority:

Expected Benefits and Returns on Investment:

Approvals and Acknowledgements:

	Signature	Date
Project Originator	_____	_____
Department Head	_____	_____
Division Controller	_____	_____
Division Head	_____	_____
Corporate Controller	_____	_____
Director of Budgets	_____	_____
Corporate President	_____	_____

FIGURE 2

XYZ CORPORATION
Capital Budget
For Year 1985

Page Number _____

Department/Division _____

Department	Item number	Description	Status		Total expenditure	Expenditure this budget	Estimated R.O.I.	Priority 1, 2, or 3	Classification			
			New	Cont.					Replacement cost reduction	Expansion	New	Other
Total												

FIGURE 3

XYZ CORPORATION
Capital Expenditures in Process Report

Item number	Description	Approval amount	Original project completion date	Spent to date	Needed for completion	Total	Expected variation	Favorable (F) Unfavorable (UF)	Expected completion date	Comments
Example 84-A-601	Replacement of casting machines	3,000,000	12/31/84	2,000,000	1,100,000	2,100,000	100,000	UF	March 31, 1985	Approval was obtained for 100,000 overrun

much work. This column may be expanded to show more than one factor, such as NPV, IRR, and payback.

Progress Report Form

To keep track of various capital expenditure projects, it may be useful to use a capital expenditure in process report similar to the one in Figure 3. It shows for each project in the budget, number, description, approved amount, amount spent to date, amount needed for completion, total expected expenditure, expected variation, whether the variation is favorable or unfavorable, expected revised completion date, and comments. The comments column indicates approvals for overruns and other observations, such as project is completed at a given date.

SUMMARY AND CONCLUSIONS

The capital expenditure budget is a much needed planning tool. The magnitude of capital expenditures and their impact on years to come make it worthwhile for companies to provide a working system for budget estimates at the department and division levels to be streamlined and combined to form the corporate budget. Budget approval is an approval in principle to be followed by appropriation requests before actual resources are committed.

The ideas presented here should be used as clues and suggestions.

13

Budget Administration: Documenting the Capital Budget

General Electric Company

Administrative practices vary when it comes to documenting a capital budget. Studies by Pflomm[1] and Abdelsamad[2] revealed that some firms employ brief memos for the purpose, others use an array of complex documentation, and a host of companies fall somewhere in between.

The documentation a firm uses for a capital budget and the flow of that information reflect the firm's preferences in several areas:

1. Organizational complexity.
2. Reliance on formal procedures.
3. Criteria employed in evaluating capital proposals.
4. Commitment implied by including a project in the capital budget.

In Chapter 12, Dr. Abdelsamad described the kinds of information firms use in preparing their capital budget and how submissions are usually much more brief than those requesting actual appropriations.

This chapter introduces documentation to employ in preparing an annual capital budget. In this case, the capital budget will be limited to plant and equipment expenditures excluding usage of working capital such as inventories and receivables. It will examine both the role of corporate-level management and the responsibilities of operating-level personnel in preparing what in the end will be a jointly arrived at and agreed upon budget satisfying the corporate "needs" as well as helping the individual components achieve their goals.

ASSUMPTIONS

Following are the key assumptions related to this chapter:

1. The firm is composed of a corporate headquarters and more than one operating component.
2. There are long-range strategic plans for the firm and individual components.
3. Investment policy and practices are clearly defined and understood by operating personnel.
4. The firm has an overall operating philosophy expressed in terms of targets such as (*a*) sales growth should be at least as large as growth in gross national product, (*b*) world cost leadership will be attained, or (*c*) market share of served market will not fall below current level.

ACTIVITY FLOWS

Figure 1 illustrates one flow of activities involved in preparing an annual capital budget. Corporate and operating-level reviews proceed in tandem, assuring strategy-budget linkages as well as practical feasibility. Key considerations are shown at key points in the flow of activities.

Figure 2 represents an activity flow for "continuous capital budgeting." It illustrates the liaison between local functions and head office functions, as well as the flow up the approval hierarchy depending on dollar limits. This flowchart appeared in the Pflomm survey, published in 1963, but except for approval limits it is still effectively employed by many firms. Contrast this budgeting flow with that of Figure 3, the appropriations procedure for the same firm. The latter requires far more detail, backup, and approvals.

FIGURE 1

Short-Term Budgeting Flow Chart for Preparation of the Annual Budget

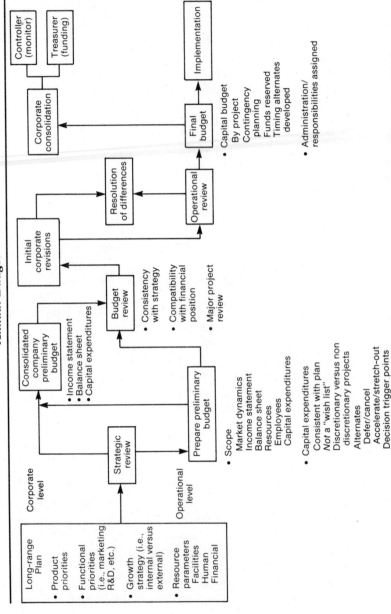

FIGURE 2

Development and Submission of Annual Capital Additions Budget (chart used by a food products company)

(Submit 5 copies of requests for appropriation which may be approved locally and 9 copies of requests for appropriation which may be approved in head office)

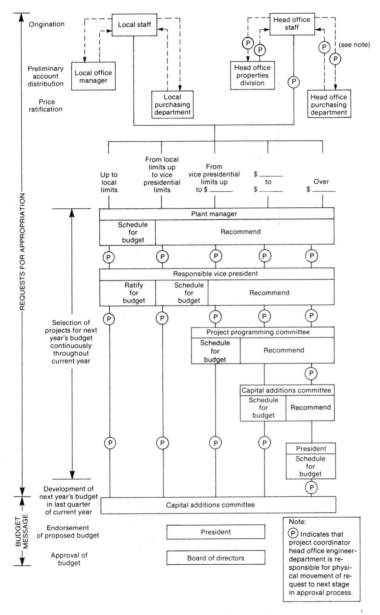

Adapted with permission of The Conference Board, from Norman E. Pflomm, *Managing Capital Expenditures,* Business Policy Study No. 107 (New York: The Conference Board, 1963).

FIGURE 3

Approval of Request for Appropriation Providing Authority to Spend Funds on Budgeted or Interim Capital Additions Project (chart used by a food products company)

(Submit 5 copies for projects which may be approved locally and 9 copies for projects which may be approved in head office)

Origination — Local staff — Head office staff

(P) (P) (P) (see note)
(P)

Preliminary account distribution — Local office manager — Head office properties division (P) — Head office purchasing department

Price ratification — Local purchasing department — Head office purchasing department

Plant manager	
Approve within limits	Recommend

(P) (P)

Responsible vice president		
Ratify local approvals	Approve within limits	Recommend

(P) (P) (P)

Note:
(P) Indicates that project coordinator head office engineer-department is responsible for physical movement of request to next stage in approval process.

Approval or recommendation in accordance with authorization limits

Up to $ — $ To $ — Over $

Project programming committee	
Approve	Recommend

Capital additions committee	
Approve	Recommend

(P) (P)

President
Approve

(P)

Final account distribution and maintenance of approval records

Head office general accounting department

Read office engineering department or plant projects

Sales and traffic department projects

Distribution of copies requests

Head office engineering department or plant projects:
— Head office properties division*
— Local office manager
— Plant manager
— Head office purchasing department
— Project programming committee*
— Chief project engineer*
— Local project manager*
— Plant engineer*
— Head office engineering file

Sales and traffic department projects:
— Head office properties division*
— Local office manager
— Plant manager
— Head office purchasing department
— Project programming committee
— Vice president sales
— Traffic manager
— Plant engineer
— Head office engineering file

*Does not receive copy of request which was approved locally

Adapted with permission of The Conference Board, from Norman E. Pflomm, *Managing Capital Expenditures*, Business Policy Study No. 107 (New York: The Conference Board, 1963).

PROPOSAL FORMS AND FORMATS

Figure 4 is a simple form that one company uses to initiate or dispose of a capital project. The Notification of Initiation (NOI) is used by project sponsors to secure tentative approval before proceeding with the preparation and review of a major plant appropriation request. The NOI establishes the time schedule for review and approval and specifies the

FIGURE 4

Notification of Initiation—Acquisition or Disposition Proposal

1. _____ _____
   (Proposed action)   (Date)

2. _____   3.   Project approval required

   _____Group/division   _____
   _____Component   (Final approving authority)
   _____Location
   _____Product line

4. Summary description of proposed project
   (Objectives/benefits, products, markets, competition, facilities, etc.)

   _____
   _____
   _____
   _____
   _____
   _____
   _____

5. Compatibility with approved strategic plan

   _____
   _____
   _____
   _____
   _____
   _____
   _____

6. Estimated purchase or selling price ranges

   _____
   _____
   _____

7.   Target dates   For approval (as required)

   _____   Meeting of corporate executive office—
                        Operating review
   _____   Meeting of board of directors

FIGURE 4 *(concluded)*

8. Functional reviews—planned and requested

Functional area	Source of contribution: Individual/component/outside firm Critical factors to be considered	Status (b)	Requested reviews (c)	(d)
Accounting (a)				
Legal (a)				
Treasury (a)				
Corporate planning (a)				
International (a)				
Employee relations				
Engineering				
Manufacturing				
Marketing				
Research and development				
Other				

(a) International review is suggested when foreign investment action is involved.
(b) General manager to indicate: C = Completed; I = In Process; P = Planned, not started.
(c) Division general manager to indicate additional reviews.
(d) Group executive to indicate additional reviews.

Initiating general manager   Date

9. Additional instructions _____

10. Approvals to proceed: _____
          Division general manager Date   Group executive   Date

_____   _____
           Date   Date
General instructions

- Sections 1 through 8 to be completed by initiating general manager.
- Send forms through channels for all proposals requiring board of directors' approval.
- Sections 8 and 9 to be completed by intermediate-echelon managers.
- Return completed form through channels to initiating general manager.
- Initiating general manager will make distribution to identified reviewers.

functional staff reviews required. NOIs are helpful in preparing the capital budget.

The lead page stresses qualitative information, including project purpose and capability with an approved strategic plan. Quantitative data are confined to estimated outlays or recoveries, plus target dates for approvals. Page 2 of Figure 4 lists the functional reviews to be performed by various specialist groups. Specific reviews are requested by the initiating general manager.

Figure 5 illustrates the detail required when a plant location initiates a capital proposal. Some firms consider this adequate to actually authorize funds, but others require such detail for budgetary approval and ask for further amplification to authorize funds. An important distinction is the degree of backup required to support the summary information.

The first page of Figure 5 neatly summarizes cash flow and yield information. It provides for cumulative cash flow with and without

FIGURE 5

Plant Appropriation Request (par)

1. Plant appropriation request (PAR)   No. _____

.... Group   Approval required
.... Division
.... Department   ....
.... Product line
.... Project location   (Dollar amounts in thousands)

2. Summary description of proposed project

3. Project expenditures

	This request	Previously approved	Future requests	Total project
Basis for approval				
Related expense				
Total				

4. Key financial measurements

Chart of cumulative funds flow

	Reported	Inflation-adjusted
DCRR	____%	____%
Payback period (years)	____	____

Amount

_____ Reported
...... Inflation-adjusted

0

19 19 19 19 19 19 19 19 19 19

FIGURE 5 *(continued)*

5. Business history and forecast of .... Department/operation

Market	Reported						Inflation-adjusted (c)			
position (a)	Sales		Net income					Net income		
	Amt.	Price index (b)	Amt.	ROS	ROI		Sales	Amt.	ROS	ROI

Year
a. Last five years:
  19
  19
  19
  19
  19
b. Forecast with proposed project:
  Current year
  19
  Next five years
  19
  19
  19
  19
  19

6. Business history and forecast of ....
.... product line

a. Last five years:
  19
  19
  19
  19
  19
b. Forecast with proposed project:
  Current year
  19
  Next five years
  19
  19
  19
  19
  19

c. Increment resulting from project:
  Current year
  19
  Next five years
  19
  19
  19
  19
  19

a- Basis -   Federal income tax rate used -
b- 19 = 100; Basis -
c- Base year -

FIGURE 5 *(continued)*

7. Summary of project expenditures

	This request	Previously approved	Future requests	Total project
Investment expenditures.............................				
Associated deferred charges..........................				
Lease-commitments not capitalized plus lease related expenses...........................				
Subtotal – Basis for approval........................				
Patterns and tooling.................................				
All other related expense				
Grand total				
As a memo:				
All other starting costs................................				
Trade-in value of surplus equipment				

8. Category(s):

	Total	Investment	Expense
Category (prime)			
Category (other)			
Category VII (if applicable)			
Total, this request			

Two calendar years following
project completion

9. Estimated gain (loss)   19____ 19____
in net income to
other G.E. Components:

10. Facility to be replaced

First cost.................................
Year purchased..........................
Book value...............................

Description of facility and
proposed disposition

11. Starting date ....
month/year

Completion date ....
month/year

12. Utilization anticipated in first year
after project completion – 19 ....
........%

Basis ....

13. Number of employees
Location

	Before	After	Before	After
Manufacturing				
All other				
Total				

FIGURE 5 *(concluded)*

14. Performance on closed appropriations

Appropriations
past 3 years (a)

	Total expenditures	Project incremental net income 1st year	2nd year
Forecast (b)			
Actual			
VF% (c)			

Board appropriations
past 5 years

	Total expenditures	Project incremental net income 1st year	2nd year
Forecast (b)			
Actual			
VF%(c)			

(a) – CEO approval and above
(b) – In appropriation requests
(c) – Variance from forecast

15. Principal competitors

Name	Estimated rank or market position This year	Last year

16. Appropriation endorsed and supporting financial data certified by

. . . .
Manager–Finance

Appropriation
endorsed or
approved by . . . .

. . . .

. . . .
Manager–Marketing

. . . .
Manager–Employee relations

. . . .
Manager–Engineering

. . . .
Manager–Manufacturing

. . . .
Legal Counsel

. . . .
Manager–Strategic operational
planning

. . . .
Department general manager   Date

. . . .
Division general manager   Date

. . . .
Group executive   Date

. . . .

266

inflation, per se, as well as for discounted flows. Historical and projected requests and approvals are indicated.

The second page requires a business history and forecast for the department proposing the project and for the project itself. In each case, it calls for market position, sales level, and net income with and without inflation adjustment.

Project expenditures are summarized on page three of the form. Also estimated are start-up losses and impact on other components for the firm.

Track record is summarized on the last page of Figure 5, in terms of performance on prior expenditures. Brief competitive information is included along with the necessary approvals.

FIGURE 6

Capital Expenditure Proposal—Lead Page

Company _____ Proposal no. _____

Unit _____ Management group _____

Proposal amount _____Budget amount _____Budget ref. _____

Descriptive title

Key indicators:			Expenditure details:	
DCF yield in constant terms	_____ %		Capital expenditure:	
DCF yield in current terms	_____ %		To be spent year	_____ _____
Payback period in current terms	_____ years			_____ _____
				later _____
Supplementary indicators:				
DCF yield in constant terms:			Rental/Lease/Hire charges	
—with full share indirect expenses	_____		Cost per year	—
—with full share back-up capital	_____		No. of years contracted	—
			Amount contracted	—
	_____		Engineering services by	
—on corporate funds used (i.e., including receipt of, interest on, repayment of any outside finance)	_____		Signatures: Company/Unit	Date

Other key data:		
Maximum cumulative cash outflow:	_____	
Year in which it occurs	_____	
Date project operational	_____	Management group

Figure 6 is another set of summary documentation that can be used without supporting detail for budgetary purposes or with appropriate worksheets for authorizing appropriations. Lead page content for Figure 6 is similar to that for Figure 5: summary outlay and yield data along with timing and amount of maximum cash outflows. (See Figure 5, p. 1)

FIGURE 7

Capital Investment Proposal
Project title and number: _____

Division or company: _____

1. *General description and justification.* This is, for example, the underlying situation and the solution; assets to be acquired; market profitability.
2. *Classification.* Projects are slotted for ongoing business or as new ventures. They're further classified according to objective, for example:
   a. Reduce costs.
   b. Improve quality.
   c. Increase output.
   d. Improve market position.
   e. Comply with legislation.
3. *Profitability.* The future effect on the firm or unit of the firm.
4. *Inflation.* Indexes used and their sources.
5. *Assumptions.* The main variables affecting the project, plus:
   a. Project yield sensitivity to changes in these variables.
   b. Estimated probabilities of such changes.
6. *Project risk.* Based on the analysis for (5) above, estimate the probability of a significant variance from estimated project profitability.
7. *Alternatives considered.* Include plausible options and the reasons for their rejection.
8. *Staff comments.* Include advisory and service groups and other management groups consulted, and their opinions. Explain where these opinions were not accepted.

A narrative follows covering the points outlined in Figure 7.

Figure 8 is a project schedule, showing year-by-year cash flow projections. Provision is made for net capital outlays, changes in working capital, initial expenses, and aftertax operating proceeds. To pro-

FIGURE 8

Capital Expenditure Proposal—Project Schedule

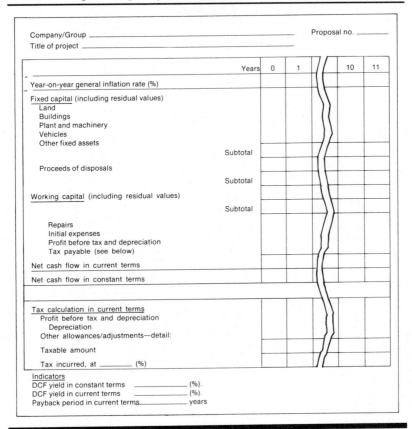

Company/Group _____ Proposal no. _____
Title of project _____

	Years	0	1		10	11
Year-on-year general inflation rate (%)						
Fixed capital (including residual values)						
Land						
Buildings						
Plant and machinery						
Vehicles						
Other fixed assets						
Subtotal						
Proceeds of disposals						
Subtotal						
Working capital (including residual values)						
Subtotal						
Repairs						
Initial expenses						
Profit before tax and depreciation						
Tax payable (see below)						
Net cash flow in current terms						
Net cash flow in constant terms						
Tax calculation in current terms						
Profit before tax and depreciation						
Depreciation						
Other allowances/adjustments—detail:						
Taxable amount						
Tax incurred, at _____ (%)						

Indicators
DCF yield in constant terms _____ (%).
DCF yield in current terms _____ (%).
Payback period in current terms_____ years

vide for inflation, both current dollars and constant dollars are expressed, with a DCF yield calculated for each.

Figure 9 is a simple one-page budget submission form. It relies primarily on a justifying narrative, supplemented by estimated yields. Companies employing this sort of brevity at the budget stage tend to encourage large numbers of submissions, which may then be screened by a headquarters committee, to conform to an established spending level. Amplification of budgeted proposals takes place prior to appropriation.

FIGURE 9

Request for Budgetary Approval—Land, Buildings, Plant, and Equipment

Plant or location _____

Budget center _____

| Project title | Addition ☐ | Starting date completion |
| | Replacement ☐ | Date _____ |

Financial detail—estimated costs			Disposals	
	Capital	Expense 2	Estimated proceeds	Book value
Land _____				
Buildings _____				
Equipment _____				
Totals _____				

Percent expenditures:

First half _____

Second half _____

Thereafter _____

Gross annual savings claimed _____

Other	☐ Legal requirements	☐ Research and development	☐ New products (or changes)
Justification	☐ Safety or labor relations	☐ Product quality improvement	☐ Public relations
(check)	☐ Insurance loss provisions	☐ Increased production capacity	

Description of project

Project sponsor _____ Title _____ Date _____

Approvals		
	_____ Date _____	_____ Date _____
		General engineering manager

Capital expenditures budget

THE CAPITAL BUDGET

The forms used to tabulate all investment proposals for a given budget period also vary widely. Major headings for proposal tabulations might be profit center, project type, or priority. Sorts might be by size of outlay, yield, or other criteria.

FIGURE 10

Request for Budgetary Approval—
Land, Buildings, Plant, and
Research Equipment Location Summary

Location _____

| Description | Capital | | | Memo: |
	Class A	Class B	Class C	Expense #2

Capital expenditures budget

Figures 10 and 11 illustrate forms used for assembling a capital budget. Figure 10 is a simple form that is used to tabulate budgetary items by category, indicating capital outlays and nonrecurring expense. Figure 11 goes further, explicitly requiring carry-overs from existing projects and forecast carryovers into the next budget period.

Other budget formats include quarterly summaries of outlays. Still others require summaries of projected proceeds by period.

271

FIGURE 11

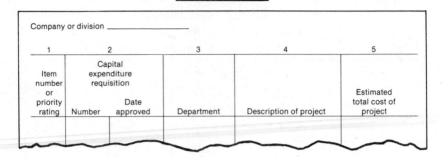

1	2		3	4	5
Item number or priority rating	Capital expenditure requisition		Department	Description of project	Estimated total cost of project
	Number	Date approved			

Date _____

6	7	8	9	10		11	12
				Cash			
Amount previously authorized	Estimated unexpended balance to be carried over into coming year	Capex requisitions to be submitted in coming year	Total 7 and 8	Total estimated expenditures in coming year	Estimated portion chargeable to expense		Estimated unexpended balance to be carried over into subsequent year

Adapted, with permission of The Conference Board, from Norman E. Pflomm, *Managing Capital expenditures,* Business Policy Study No. 107 (New York: The Conference Board, 1963).

CONCLUSION

Since the capital budget usually represents agreement in principle only, for financial planning purposes, documentation tends to be brief and frequently informal. It is at the later appropriation stage where detailed investigation and analysis is an important requirement. For a discussion of appropriation procedures, see Chapter 23, "Project Authorization: How to Design Appropriation Procedures," by M. Abdelsamad.

NOTES

[1] Norman E. Pflomm, *Managing Capital Expenditures,* Business Policy Study No. 107 (New York: The Conference Board, 1963.

[2] Moustafa Abdelsamad, *A Guide to Capital Expenditure Analysis* (New York: Amacom, 1973); and Moustafa Abdelsamad, "How to Streamline Budget Preparation," in *The Capital Budgeting Handbook* Homewood, Ill.: Dow Jones-Irwin, 1986).

14

Portfolio Management: How to Manage the Corporate Investment Portfolio

Thomas J. Hindelang

Drexel University

INTRODUCTION

*C*orporate organizations—much like individual investors—are faced with the problem of managing their portfolio of investments. Viewing the firm's productive capital assets as a portfolio can yield significant benefits in terms of achieving the corporate objectives of earning an acceptable level of return while taking on a constrained degree of risk (or variability in those returns). In order to effectively manage a portfolio of investments, there are at least three relevant dimensions which must be considered: (1) the expected return associated with the individual assets, (2) the degree of risk present in each asset, and (3) the degree of interaction between the assets under consideration and the other investments held in the investor's portfolio. This third aspect is referred to as the *portfolio effects* or the *covariance effects* of the asset under evaluation. As we will see in this chapter, these interaction effects are important in determining the attractiveness of a given investment.

Dr. Harry Markowitz was the first to formally point out the importance of covariance or portfolio effects in constructing a portfolio of assets. In the early 1950s, Dr. Markowitz demonstrated that risk reduction in a portfolio of investments was best achieved by "efficient diversification." Efficient diversification results when the investor selects a portfolio of investments by considering the interaction effects between the investments—the lower the degree of interaction between the investments the better. Intuitively, efficient diversification says that the variability in portfolio returns is reduced by holding assets whose returns move countercyclically to each other—the high returns in one asset offset the low returns in the other, thereby reducing the overall fluctuations in return. We will formalize this discussion later in the chapter.

The purpose of this chapter is to examine the importance of managing the firm's capital investments as a portfolio. This will require that we know how to quantify the three dimensions of project management in a portfolio context cited above. Finally, we introduce the use of the capital asset pricing model (or beta analysis) in the management of the firm's portfolio of capital assets.

RISK AND RETURN ON INDIVIDUAL SECURITIES

It is often helpful to use probability distributions to express possible returns that may be earned on investments based on uncertain future events. The returns on most investments can be tied to the state of the overall economy, and probabilities can be estimated for the likelihood that the economy will experience each of, say, four different states. (The sum of the probabilities over all possible states of the economy must equal one.) Once a probability distribution has been estimated for a given investment, we can determine the expected return and risk or variability in that return.

The *expected return on an investment* is dependent upon the possible returns that could be earned as the economy takes on various states. In fact, the expected return is a weighted average of these possible returns where the weights are the probabilities that the various states occur. Equation 1 shows this relationship.

$$\bar{R} = \sum_{i=1}^{n} (R_i)(P_i) \tag{1}$$

where

$\bar{R}$ = The expected return on the investment.
R_i = The return associated with the ith state of economy.
P_i = The probability that the ith state of the economy will occur.

The *risk or variability in return on an investment* is often measured by the standard deviation of the probability distribution of possible returns on the investment. The standard deviation is a measure of the extent to which the individual returns on the investment differ from the expected return. In comparing two investments, the one with the larger standard deviation is more risky because its individual returns differ by a greater amount from its expected return. The standard deviation (σ) is computed by Equation 2, where all symbols have been previously defined.

$$\sigma = \sqrt{\sum_{i=1}^{n} P_i(R_i - \bar{R})^2} \qquad (2)$$

We now illustrate the use of Equations 1 and 2.

An investor is interested in two securities whose returns can be tied to the state of the economy. The investor believes that the two probability distributions shown in Table 1 accurately portray possible returns that may occur over the coming year.

TABLE 1

State of the economy	Probability	Security X (percent)	Security Y (percent)
Very strong	.1	20%	16%
Strong	.5	15	12
Moderate	.3	11	10
Weak	.1	8	9
	1.0		

Determine the expected return and risk associated with each security. For security X, we find

$$\bar{R} = \sum_{i=1}^{n} (R_i)(P_i)$$
$$= (.1)(.20) + (.5)(.15) + (.3)(.11) + (.1)(.08)$$
$$= .136 \text{ or } 13.6 \text{ percent}$$

Thus, the expected return on security X in the coming year is 13.6 percent.

$$\sigma = \sqrt{\sum_{i=1}^{n} P_i (R_i - \bar{R})^2}$$

$$= \sqrt{\frac{(.1)(.20 - .136)^2 + (.5)(.15 - .136)^2 + (.3)(.11 - .136)^2}{+ (.1)(.08 - .136)^2}}$$

$$= .032 \text{ or } 3.2 \text{ percent}$$

We see that security X has a standard deviation of 3.2 percent. For security Y, we find

$$\bar{R} = (.1)(.16) + (.5)(.12) + (.3)(.10) + (.1)(.09)$$
$$= .1069 \text{ or } 10.69 \text{ percent}$$

$$\sigma = \sqrt{\frac{(.1)(.16 - .1069)^2 + (.5)(.12 - .1069)^2 + (.3)(.10 - .1069)^2 + (.1)}{(.09 - .1069)^2}}$$

$$= .02 \text{ or } 2 \text{ percent}$$

Thus, we see that security Y has an expected return next year of 10.69 percent and a standard deviation of 2 percent.

Comparing the two securities, it can be noted that security X has both greater expected return than security Y (13.6 percent versus 10.69 percent) and greater risk (3.2 percent versus 2 percent). Intuitively, we would expect investors who would be willing to hold higher-risk securities such as security X would also demand a greater expected return. In fact, if a security simultaneously had less risk but a higher expected return than some other security, it would be said to dominate that security and no rational investor would hold the latter security.

As mentioned earlier, in addition to the measures of expected return and risk on the individual securities, portfolio construction also necessitates an evaluation of the interaction effects between the securities. There are two frequently used measures for quantifying the extent of these interaction effects: (1) the correlation coefficient and (2) the covariance between the two securities. The *correlation coefficient* conveys the nature and strength of the relationship between the two securities. This relative measure has a range of values between +1 and −1. The sign of the correlation coefficient shows the nature of the relationship between the two securities—a positive value means that as the returns on one security increase, the returns on the other security increase also; conversely, a negative value means that the returns of the two securities move in opposite directions. The numerical value of the correlation coefficient conveys the strength of the relationship between the two securities—the closer the value is to one, the stronger is the relationship between the two securities; conversely, the closer the value is to zero, the weaker is the relationship. With a correlation coefficient of zero, the two securities do not exhibit any systematic relationship to one another in their returns—they are said to be independent to or uncorrelated with one another.

The covariance between the returns on two securities (Cov_{xy}) is equal to the product of the correlation coefficient between the returns on the securities (r_{xy}) and each security's standard deviation. Equation 3 shows this calculation.

$$\text{Cov}_{xy} = r_{xy}\sigma_x\sigma_y \tag{3}$$

Based on our discussion above, the covariance between two securities can be positive, negative, or zero depending on the sign of the correlation coefficient and whether that value or either of the standard deviations on the securities is zero (a security with a standard deviation of zero would be a risk-free security). As we will see in the next section, the covariance between securities will have significant impact on the risk of a portfolio of securities.

Equation 3 denotes the conceptual meaning of the covariance between two securities. Equation 4 presents a relationship which will facilitate the calculation of the covariance.

$$\text{Cov}_{xy} = \sum_{i=1}^{n} P_i(R_{ix} - \bar{R}_x)(R_{iy} - \bar{R}_y) \tag{4}$$

where

P_i = The probability that the ith state of the economy will occur.

R_{ix} = The return on security X that will occur if the ith state of the economy occurs.

$\bar{R}_x$ = The expected return on security X.

R_{iy} = The return on security Y that will occur if the ith state of the economy occurs.

$\bar{R}_y$ = The expected return on security Y.

Note in Equation 4 that the product $(R_{ix} - \bar{R}_x)(R_{iy} - \bar{R}_y)$ can be positive or negative depending on how the values R_{ix} and R_{iy} fall relative to their respective expected returns; if these two values are *both* above or below the expected returns, the covariance term will be positive; otherwise, it will be negative. Of course, each negative term reduces the value of the covariance while each positive term increases it. As we shall see shortly, the smaller the value of the covariance, the smaller will be the contribution of a given pair of securities to the overall portfolio risk.

Let's illustrate the use of Equation 4 on the two securities shown in Table 1. Table 2 shows the calculations required by Equation 4. Recall that based on our earlier calculations $\bar{R}_x = .136$ and $\bar{R}_y = .1069$; these values will be needed, respectively, in columns 4 and 5 of Table 2.

TABLE 2

	1	2	3	4	5	6
State of the economy	P_i	R_{ix}	R_{iy}	$R_{ix} - \bar{R}_x$	$R_{iy} - \bar{R}_y$	$1 \times 4 \times 5$
Very strong	.1	.20	.16	.20 − .136	.16 − .1069	+.0003398
Strong	.5	.15	.12	.15 − .136	.12 − .1069	+.0000917
Moderate	.3	.11	.10	.11 − .136	.10 − .1069	+.0000538
Weak	.1	.08	.09	.08 − .136	.09 − .1069	+.0000946
	1.0					+.0005799

Substituting the total from column 6 into Equation 4, we obtain:

$$\text{Cov}_{xy} = \sum_{i=1}^{n} P_i(R_{ix} - \bar{R}_x)(R_{iy} - \bar{R}_y)$$

$$= +.0005799 \text{ or } .05799 \text{ percent}$$

It is difficult to intuitively interpret the meaning of the covariance between the returns on two securities until we see how the covariance is used in determining the risk on a portfolio of assets. This is the purpose of the next section.

RISK AND RETURN ON A PORTFOLIO OF ASSETS

Once the expected return and risk on each security or asset has been determined as shown in the previous section, we can turn our focus to portfolio construction. As mentioned, the covariance between pairs of securities or assets will also come into play. The two measures of importance in portfolio analysis are the expected return on the portfolio and the risk or variability in the return on the portfolio. These measures are examined in turn.

The *expected return on a portfolio of securities* is a weighted average of the expected returns of the securities which make up the portfolio where the weights are the proportions of the investor's funds allocated to the securities. Equation 5 quantifies the relationship.

$$\bar{R}_p = \sum_{j=1}^{n} X_j \bar{R}_j \tag{5}$$

where

$\bar{R}_p$ = The expected return on the portfolio of securities.

X_j = The proportion of the investor's funds allocated to security j; it should be noted that

$$\sum_{j=1}^{n} X_j = 1.$$

$\bar{R}_j$ = The expected return on security j.

Consider that an investor wants to allocate the following proportions of investable funds to each of the three securities shown in Table 3.

TABLE 3

Security	X_j	$\bar{R}_j$ (percent)
1	.2	12%
2	.5	16
3	.3	20
	1.0	

The investor is interested in determining the expected portfolio return. Using Equation 5 he would find

$$\bar{R}_p = \sum_{j=1}^{n} X_j \bar{R}_j$$

$$= (.2)(12 \text{ percent}) + (.5)(16 \text{ percent}) + (.3)(20 \text{ percent})$$

$$= 16.4 \text{ percent}.$$

Thus, with the allocations shown in Table 3, the investor can expect to earn 16.4 percent on the average. A more conservative investor (who would allocate a greater proportion of funds to security 1 which has less risk and less return than the other two securities) would find that the expected portfolio return would be less than that found above. For example, if an investor wanted to allocate 0.7 of his funds to security 1, 0.2 to security 2, and 0.1 to security 3, his $\bar{R}_p$ would equal 13.6 percent.

Next, we turn to portfolio risk. The variability in the return on a portfolio is often measured by the *standard deviation of the portfolio returns*. This standard deviation depends on (1) the standard deviations of the individual securities which make up the portfolio, (2) the proportions of the investor's funds invested in each security, and (3) the covariances between all possible parts of securities held in the portfolio. We illustrated how to determine the first and third elements in the previous section. The second element is determined by the investor or the firm so as to achieve relevant risk and return objectives. Formally, the standard deviation of the returns on the portfolio (σ_p) is found by Equation 6:

$$\sigma_p = \sqrt{\sum_{j=1}^{n} X_j^2 \sigma_j^2 + 2 \sum_{j=1}^{n-1} \sum_{i=j+1}^{n} X_i X_j \, \mathrm{Cov}_{ij}} \qquad (6)$$

where

σ_j = The standard deviation of the return on security or project j.

X_j = The proportion of the investor's funds allocated to security or project j.

Cov_{ij} = The covariance between security i and security $j = r_{ij}\sigma_i\sigma_j$.

Note in Equation 6 that there are two components of σ_p—the first term under the square root is the sum of the weighted variance of the securities which make up the portfolio, and the second term is the sum of the weighted covariances between all possible pairs of securities which make up the portfolio. Recall from our discussion in the previous section that the covariance between two securities can be positive, negative, or zero. We see from Equation 6 that σ_p will be minimized. Thus, in order to reduce portfolio risk, investors or firms should select securities or projects which have small covariances between them.

Let's illustrate the use of Equation 6 by expanding on the information given in Table 3. In Table 4 we consider the same three securities shown in Table 3 but we provide the σ_j values and the r_{ij} values for all pairs of securities.

TABLE 4

Security	X_j	$\bar{R}_j$ (percent)	σ_j (percent)	r_{ij} 1	2	3
1	.2	12%	3%	+1.0	−.2	+.4
2	.5	16	8	−.2	+1.0	+.3
3	.3	20	15	+.4	+.3	+1.0
	1.0					

Determining the risk on the portfolio of these securities, we find

$$\sigma_p = \sqrt{\sum_{j=1}^{n} X_j^2 \sigma_j^2 + 2\sum_{j=1}^{n-1} \cdot \sum_{i=j+1}^{n} X_i X_j \, Cov_{ij}}$$

$$= \sqrt{\begin{array}{l}(.2)^2(.03)^2 + (.5)^2(.08)^2 + (.3)^2(.15)^2 + 2[(.2)(.5)(-.2)(.03) \\ (.08) + (.2)(.3)(+.4)(.03)(.15) + (.5)(.3)(+.3)(.08)(.15)]\end{array}}$$

$$= \sqrt{0.004673} = 0.684 \text{ or } 6.84 \text{ percent.}$$

Thus, we see that given the proportions invested in each of the three securities, the risk on the portfolio is 6.84 percent. It should be noted that the risk on the overall portfolio is less than 7 percent even though 50 percent of the investor's funds are invested in a security which has a standard deviation of 8 percent, and an additional 30 percent of the investor's funds are allocated to a security which has a standard deviation of 15 percent. The reason for the low σ_p value is the *low correlation and low covariance between the pairs of securities in the portfolio.*

Consider the impact of holding three securities in a portfolio that have the same characteristics as those shown in Table 4 with the exception that the off-diagonal r_{ij} values were all +.9 instead of the values shown. This change increases σ_p from 6.84 percent to 8.85 percent—a very significant 29 percent increase in portfolio risk. The bottom line is that the *correlation and covariance between pairs of securities or projects is a highly important determinant of the degree of risk present on the portfolio.*

PORTFOLIOS OF CAPITAL ASSETS VERSUS PORTFOLIOS OF SECURITIES

In our discussion thus far we have used the words *securities* and *assets* and *capital investments* interchangeably. We have argued that firms should view their set of productive capital assets as a portfolio of investments much like individual investors view their portfolio of investments. Nonetheless, questions might arise concerning how firms should arrive at the data inputs for a group of potential capital investments in order to call upon Equations 5 and 6 to determine the expected return on the portfolio and the standard deviation of the returns on the portfolio.

To recap, the firms must have reliable estimates of the following values in order to call upon the portfolio model developed: (1) the expected return on each project under evaluation, (2) the standard deviation in the returns on each project, and (3) the correlation coefficient between the returns on each potential pair of projects under evaluation. Our recommendation is that the firm subjectively assess a probability distribution of possible internal rates of return (IRR) that could be earned on capital projects under evaluation. These possible IRRs can be tied to the "state of the economy" much like the two securities shown in Table 1. If probability distributions can be so developed for each project under evaluation, the firm can rather easily arrive at each of the three sets of required data inputs specified above. In today's computer age very straightforward programs can be written to carry out all of the calculations. In addition, sensitivity or "what if" analysis can be performed on any of the project probability distributions to determine the impact on the project's expected IRR and standard deviation in IRR.

Given these data inputs, the firm can call upon Equations 5 and 6 to determine $\bar{R}_p$ and σ_p for potential portfolios of capital projects. The X_j values in Equations 5 and 6 would be the proportion of the firm's total capital budget that would be allocated to project j. The cash outflows required by the various projects along with the size of the overall budget will determine which portfolios of projects are "feasible." In addition, the various types of project interrelationship constraints which we discussed in Chapter 11—"Mathematical Programming Techniques Applied to the Selection of Strategic Investments"—will also limit the number of potential portfolios of projects. Again computer hardware and software packages greatly facilitate the portfolio evaluation process.

One caution should be mentioned relative to the above methodology. Namely, the internal rate of return has been suggested as the criterion to evaluate capital projects and to select portfolios of projects. This criterion was suggested because of the convenience of using an annual percentage return figure in evaluating portfolios of projects and because the IRR criterion has found widespread use in practice. However, as we have illustrated in-depth elsewhere, the IRR method has an implicit reinvestment assumption that specifies that estimated cash inflows can be reinvested by the firm to earn an annual rate of return equal to the IRR on the project under evaluation; if the firm is unable to earn the implicitly assumed rate of return on the reinvested cash inflows, then the IRR on the original project has been overstated.[1] This shortcoming of the IRR method can be overcome by either using the net present value method or by modifying the IRR method to reflect a more achievable reinvestment rate of return on the project's cash inflows.

Given the above caveats, once the firm has evaluated several feasible portfolios (that is, ones which satisfy budget and project interrelationship constraints), a convenient mechanism for ranking the portfolios is required. Dr. Harry Markowitz, in addition to formalizing the risk and return measures for portfolios of assets, also recommended that portfolios be plotted on risk and return axes in order to discern "dominated" and "undominated" portfolios.

As shown in Figure 1, as investors evaluate possible portfolios of securities, they are faced with the diagram as shown. Any portfolio within the feasible region is attainable with the amount of funds the investor has available. The upper boundary of the region between points A and B is referred to as the Markowitz Efficient Frontier (MEF). The MEF is the set of portfolios which maximizes the expected portfolio return for a given level of portfolio risk or minimizes the portfolio risk for a given level of expected return. All rational investors will select a portfolio on the MEF rather than somewhere within the shaded feasible region. Consider a portfolio such as that labeled X in Figure 1. An investor could increase the expected return by continuing to take on the same degree of risk but moving up to point Q on the efficient frontier. Conversely, if the investor was willing to accept the current level of expected return at point X, he could reduce his level of risk by moving to point P on the efficient frontier. Furthermore, by moving from point X to any point on the efficient frontier between point P and point Q, the investor will simultaneously increase the expected return and reduce the level of risk.

Therefore, the Markowitz Efficient Frontier provides a convenient mechanism for dividing portfolios of securities into two groups—those that *dominate* since they maximize return for a given level of risk and those that *are dominated* since a portfolio on the efficient frontier offers one of the following: (1) a greater expected return for the same level of risk, (2) less risk and the same level of expected return, or (3) a greater expected return and a smaller degree of risk simultaneously.

Given that the MEF describes the set of dominant portfolios, the investor basically has to address the issue of where on the MEF it is

FIGURE 1

The Markowitz Efficient Frontier

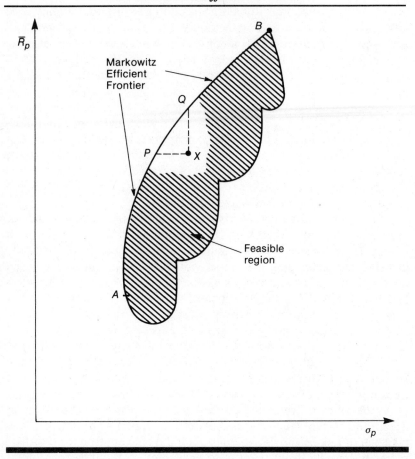

preferable to be. This issue is probably most conveniently addressed by specification of the level of σ_p that the investor is willing to take on or a specification of the level of $\bar{R}_p$ that the investor wants to earn. Realistically, the investor will probably specify a range of acceptable values of σ_p or $\bar{R}_p$. This will in turn imply a set of optimal portfolios on the efficient frontier. Finally, the investor can select the preferred portfolio by examining the candidate optimal portfolios and their component securities to determine which meets the other objectives (besides risk and return) and preferences.

Again, there is a parallel conceptual framework and selection process for firms selecting their optimal portfolio of capital investment projects. The major difference is that the efficient frontier is not a smooth curve as shown in Figure 1. Since capital projects have to be accepted completely or rejected, the MEF for capital investment projects is a disjointed set of points denoting the optimal portfolios. The MEF for capital projects is shown in Figure 2 and is made up of the points labeled *A* through *G*. As shown in Figure 2 also, the feasible region is made up of a disjointed set of points showing feasible portfolios of capital projects.

FIGURE 2

The Markowitz Efficient Frontier for Capital Investment Projects

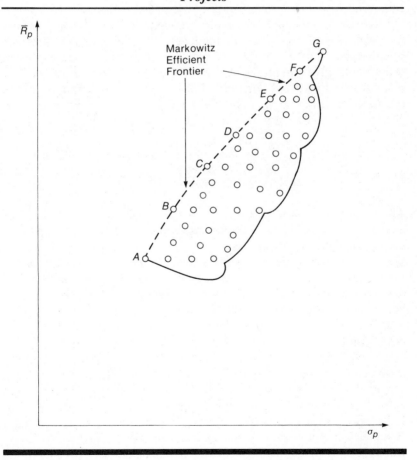

The firm would then examine the portfolios on the MEF (for example, points *C, D,* and *E*) that satisfy management's perceptions of the risk and return objectives. Upon examining the component capital projects, the firm can then select the overall optimal portfolio which best meets its risk-return objectives, its other objectives, and its other constraints.

The approach provided by Dr. Markowitz enables firms to effectively select the optimal portfolio of capital projects.

THE CAPITAL ASSET PRICING MODEL

About 10 years after Dr. Markowitz developed modern portfolio theory, a student of his, Dr. William Sharpe, pioneered the development of capital market theory. Capital market theory (CMT) establishes an equilibrium rate of return for any risky asset based on its level of "systematic" or "nondiversifiable" risk. CMT argues that investors should not be compensated for the level of "total risk" (as measured by the standard deviation) that they take on because rational investors should hold investments in well-diversified portfolios. If an investor holds a well-diversified portfolio, then any asset's contribution to the risk of the portfolio is the asset's systematic risk. Thus, we can disaggregate an asset's or a portfolio's total risk as follows:

$$
\begin{array}{llll}
\text{Total} & \text{Systematic or} & \text{Unsystematic or} & \\
\text{risk} & = \text{Nondiversifiable} & + \text{diversifiable risk} & (7) \\
\text{on the asset} & \text{risk on the asset} & \text{on the asset} &
\end{array}
$$

All assets held in well-diversified portfolios will have a zero level of unsystematic risk. Thus, the only relevant risk on an asset is its systematic or nondiversifiable risk.

In order to determine an asset's level of systematic risk, it is necessary to first establish a "market portfolio of risky assets" and second to determine the relationship between the asset and the market portfolio. In theory, the market portfolio of risky assets should consist of all risky assets that exist—all stocks, bonds, options, futures, gold, silver, other commodities, antiques, art, real estate, all productive capital assets, etc. Of course, such a market portfolio would be enormous, and it would be very difficult to track return and variability of return of such a portfolio. In practice, because the true market portfolio does not exist, financial analysis must use a surrogate for the market portfolio. In analyzing securities traded on an exchange, the Standard & Poor's 500, the New York Stock Exchange Index (consisting of approximately 1,800 securities), and the Wilshire 5,000 Index have been used as surrogates for the market portfolio. When it comes to analyzing productive capital assets, the determination of an appropriate market portfolio is more difficult. It is often recommended to use one of the surrogates for the market mentioned above or to use a broad-based index of economic activity. Although imperfect, these recommendations are probably acceptable.

The second requirement for the use of CMT is the determination of the relationship between the returns on the asset and the returns on the market index. This relationship is quantified by the widely cited *beta factor* which shows how responsive the returns on the asset are relative to the returns on the market. A beta value of 1.4 for a given security, say, Ramada Inns, means that if the returns on the market are expected to increase by 10 percent in the coming year, the returns on Ramada will increase by 14 percent (1.4 × 10 percent). Assets with betas greater than one are more volatile than the market; those with betas less than one are more conservative than the market.

Mathematically, the beta coefficient for asset $j(\beta_j)$ is computed by Equation 8.

$$\beta_j = \frac{\text{Cov}(R_j, R_m)}{\sigma_m^2} \tag{8}$$

where

$\text{Cov}(R_j, R_m)$ = The covariance between the returns on assets j and the returns on the market index.

σ_m^2 = The variance in the returns on the market index.

The value of $\text{Cov}(R_j, R_m)$ can be found using Equation 4 where the returns on asset j take on the identity of R_{ix}, and the returns on the market index take on the identity of R_{iy}. The beta coefficient is the capital asset pricing model's (CAPM) standard measure of systematic risk. The greater the value of β, the more volatile are the returns on the asset in question and the greater is the asset's level of systematic risk.

The final step in CAPM's development is the derivation of the security market line (SML). The SML shows the rate of return required by investors to take on the level of systematic risk present in assets. There is a positive linear relationship between the required rate of return on an asset and its level of systematic risk. The SML posits that the required rate of return on an asset is the risk-free return which compensates the investor for delaying consumption plus a risk premium to compensate the investor for the level of systematic risk present in the asset. The equation for the SML is

$$R_j^o = r_f + (\bar{R}_m - r_f)\beta_j \tag{9}$$

where

R_j^o = The required rate of return on asset j.
r_f = The risk-free rate of return.
$\bar{R}_m$ = The expected return on the market portfolio.

We can plot the SML on coordinate axes where β is shown on the horizontal axis and return on asset j is shown on the vertical axis. The SML would then depict the required rate of return for each level of systematic risk. Figure 3 shows the SML and the area labeled "attrac-

FIGURE 3

Project Evaluation Using the SML

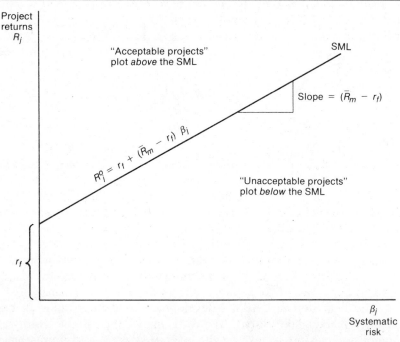

tive investments" *above* the SML as well as that labeled "unattractive investments" *below* the SML. Each asset whose *expected* return is *greater* than its *required* return (that is, the asset plots *above* the SML) is a candidate for acceptance; the reverse is true for assets which do not offer an expected return which at least equals the required return for the level of systematic risk present in the asset.

Next, we turn to an illustration of using the SML to evaluate capital projects. Table 5 provides probability distributions for returns on the market (R_m) as well as two capital projects, R_A and R_B. The risk-free rate at present is 7 percent. First, compute $\bar{R}_m$ and σ_m. Then,

TABLE 5

State of economy	P_i	R_m	R_A	R_B
Strong recovery (S_1)	.10	.35	.40	.32
Mild recovery (S_2)	.30	.20	.24	.18
Stable economy (S_3)	.35	.10	.16	.10
Mild recession (S_4)	.15	−.10	.00	−.10
Major recession (S_5)	.10	−.25	−.28	−.30
	1.00			

compute $\bar{R}_A$, σ_A, $\text{Cov}(R_A, R_m)$, β_A, and R_A^o as well as the same measures for security β. Finally, recommend whether each of the projects is acceptable or unacceptable.

We begin by determining $\bar{R}_M$ and σ_M in the following table.

State of the economy	Probability	R_M	Probability × R_M	$R_M - \bar{R}_M$	$(R_M - \bar{R}_M)^2$	Probability × $(R_M - \bar{R}_M)^2$
S_1	.10	.35	.035	.265	.070225	.0070225
S_2	.30	.20	.060	.115	.013225	.0039675
S_3	.35	.10	.035	.015	.000225	.0000788
S_4	.15	−.10	−.015	−.185	.034225	.0051338
S_5	.10	−.25	−.025	−.335	.112225	.0112225
	1.00		$\bar{R}_M = .085$			

$$\sigma_M^2 = .027425$$
$$\sigma_M = .165605$$

Thus, we see that the market index has an expected return of 8.5 percent and a standard deviation of 16.56 percent. Next, we turn to projects A and B.

The calculations required for each project are shown in Table 6. Using this data, we can next determine R_j^o for each project using Equation 9.

$$R_j^o = r_f + (\bar{R}_M - r_f)\beta_j$$
$$R_A^o = .07 + (.085 - .07)1.036 = .0855$$
$$R_B^o = .07 + (.085 - .07)1.010 = .0852$$

Finally, we compare the required returns for the two projects with their expected returns computed in Table 6. The table below presents the data and the appropriate decision.

Project	Required return (R_j^o)	Expected return $(\bar{R}_j)$	Decision
A	.0855	.14	Project is acceptable
B	.0852	.076	Project should be rejected

The results shown in the above table are also shown graphically in Figure 4. Note that the expected return for Project A plots above the SML since given project A's β of 1.036, its required return is .08.

FIGURE 4

Summary Plot of Two Projects plus the Market

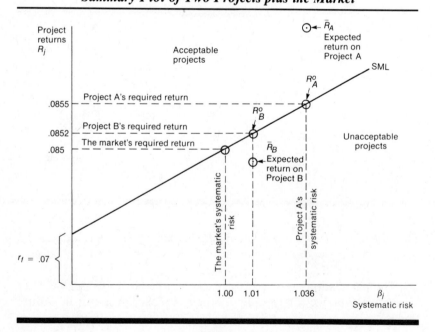

290

TABLE 6

Calculations for Projects A and B

Project A

State of the economy	Probability (P_i)	R_A	$P_i \times R_A$	$R_A - \bar{R}_A$	$(R_A - \bar{R}_A)^2$	$P_i(R_A - \bar{R}_A)^2$	$(R_A - \bar{R}_A) \times (R_M - \bar{R}_M)$	$P_i(R_A - \bar{R}_A) \times (R_M - \bar{R}_M)$
S_1	.10	.40	.04	.40 − .14	.0676	.00676	.0689	.00689
S_2	.30	.24	.072	.24 − .14	.01	.003	.0115	.00345
S_3	.35	.16	.056	.16 − .14	.0004	.00014	.0003	.000105
S_4	.15	.00	.00	.00 − .14	.0196	.00294	.0259	.003885
S_5	.10	−.28	−.028	−.28 − .14	.1764	.01764	.1407	.014070
	1.00		$\bar{R}_A = .14$			$\sigma^2_{R_A} = .03048$		$\mathrm{Cov}(R_A, R_M) = .0284$
						$\sigma_{R_A} = .1745852$		

Project B

State of the economy	Probability (P_i)	R_B	$P_i \times R_B$	$R_B - \bar{R}_B$	$(R_B - \bar{R}_B)^2$	$P_i(R_B - \bar{R}_B)^2$	$(R_B - \bar{R}_B) \times (R_M - \bar{R}_M)$	$P_i(R_B - \bar{R}_B) \times (R_M - \bar{R}_M)$
S_1	.10	.32	.032	.32 − .076	.059536	.0059536	.06466	.006466
S_2	.30	.18	.054	.18 − .076	.010816	.0032448	.01196	.003588
S_3	.35	.10	.035	.10 − .076	.000576	.0002016	.00036	.000126
S_4	.15	−.10	−.015	−.10 − .076	.030976	.0046464	.03256	.004884
S_5	.10	−.30	−.030	−.30 − .076	.141376	.0141376	.12596	.012596
	1.00		$\bar{R}_B = .076$			$\sigma^2_{R_B} = .028184$		$\mathrm{Cov}(R_B, R_M) = .02766$
						$\sigma_{R_B} = .1678809$		

Conversely, project B has an expected return of .076 but a required return of .0852; thus, project B plots below the SML, designating it as unacceptable.

The evaluation of capital projects using CAPM as just illustrated has strong supporters in the field of finance. However, informed use of this financial model requires recognition of at least three major short-comings. First, the CAPM is a static, single-period, partial equilibrium model; this implies that the underlying parameters of the model (r_f, $\bar{R}_M$, $\sigma^2_{R_M}$, and β_j) all remain constant over time. Unfortunately, this is at variance from observed reality. Second, a reliable market index for real capital assets does not exist; this creates problems for the accurate application of the model to capital project evaluation. Finally, CAPM was developed under the assumption that assets are perfectly divisible. This assumption does not create great difficulties for the evaluation of securities in the capital markets, but it does present problems in the evaluation of capital projects which usually must be either accepted or rejected in their entirety. Ongoing research in finance is attempting to overcome these and other shortcomings that flaw the application of CAPM to capital project evaluation.

SUMMARY

This chapter has surveyed the treatment of risk and portfolio effects in the capital budgeting process. We began with the examination of the quantification of risk and return on individual assets. Here we illus-trated the use of expected value, standard deviation, correlation coeffi-cient, and covariance in capturing the important dimensions of risk and return. Next, as we turned to the construction of portfolios of assets, we saw that the individual asset measures contributed to the determi-nation of the expected return and risk on the portfolio. Then, we ex-plored the differences between building portfolios of capital assets and building portfolios of securities. We also presented the Markowitz Effi-cient Frontier for both types of portfolios. Finally, we illustrated the use of the capital asset pricing model to evaluate capital investment projects. We discussed the importance of systematic risk in a CAPM framework and showed how the security market line could be used to make decisions for capital projects.

NOTE

[1] J. J. Clark, T. J. Hindelang, and R. E. Pritchard, *Capital Budgeting: Planning and Control of Capital Expenditures,* 2d ed. (Englewood Cliffs, N.J.: Prentice-Hall, 1984), chaps. 6 and 7.

SELECTED REFERENCES

Ben-Horim, Moshe, and Haim Levy. "Total Risk, Diversifiable Risk: A Pedagogic Note." *Journal of Financial and Quantitative Analysis,* June 1980, pp. 289–98.

Blume, M. E. "Betas and Their Regression Tendencies: Some Further Evidence." *Journal of Finance,* March 1979, pp. 785–96.

Clark, J. J.; T. J. Hindelang; and R. E. Pritchard. *Capital Budgeting: Planning and Control of Capital Expenditures.* 2d ed. Englewood Cliffs, N.J.: Prentice-Hall, 1984.

Copeland, Thomas E., and J. Fred Weston. *Financial Theory and Corporate Policy.* 2d ed. Reading, Mass: Addison-Wesley Publishing, 1983.

Elgers, P. T.; J. R. Haltiner; and W. H. Hawthorne. "Beta Regression Tendencies: Statistical and Real Causes." *Journal of Finance,* March 1979, pp. 65–84.

Epstein, Larry G., and Stuart M. Turnbull. "Capital Asset Prices and the Temporal Resolution of Uncertainty." *Journal of Finance,* June 1980, pp. 580–602.

Everett, James E., and Bernhard Schwab. "On the Proper Adjustment for Risk through Discount Rates in a Mean Variance Framework." *Financial Management,* Summer 1979, pp. 61–65.

Fama, Eugene F. "Risk, Return, and Equilibrium: Some Clarifying Comments." *Journal of Finance,* March 1968, pp. 29–40.

Friend, L.; R. Westerfield; and M. Granito. "New Evidence on the Capital Asset Pricing Model." *Journal of Finance,* June 1978, pp. 622–45.

Hamada, R. S. "Investment Decisions with a General Equilibrium Approach." *Quarterly Journal of Economics,* November 1971, pp. 667–83.

Harrington, Diana R. *Modern Portfolio Theory and the Capital Asset Pricing Model: A User's Guide.* Englewood Cliffs, N.J.: Prentice-Hall, 1983.

Harrington, Diana R. "Stock Prices, Beta, and Strategic Planning." *Harvard Business Review,* May–June 1983, pp. 157–64.

Hindelang, T. J., and M. M. Holland. *The Theory and Practice of Finance.* Reading, Mass: Addison-Wesley Publishing, 1985.

Levy, H. "The CAPM and Beta in an Imperfect Market." *Journal of Portfolio Management,* Winter 1980, pp. 104–22.

Lin, Winston T., and Frank C. Jen. "Consumption, Investment, Market Price of Risk, and the Risk-Free Rate." *Journal of Financial and Quantitative Analysis,* December 1980, pp. 845–65.

Lintner, John. "The Valuation of Risk Assets and the Selection of Risky Investments in Stock Portfolios and Capital Budgets." *Review of Economics and Statistics,* February 1965, pp. 13–37.

Markowitz, H. M. "Portfolio Selection." *Journal of Finance,* March 1952, pp. 77–91.

Markowitz, H. M. *Portfolio Selection: Efficient Diversification of Investments.* New York: John Wiley & Sons, 1959.

293

Mossin, J. "Equilibrium in a Capital Assets Market." *Econometrica,* October 1966, pp. 768–83.

Mullins, D. W. Jr. "Does the Capital Asset Pricing Model Work?" *Harvard Business Review,* January–February 1982, pp. 102–9.

Myers, S. C., and S. M. Turnbull. "Capital Budgeting and the Capital Asset Pricing Model: Good News and Bad News." *Journal of Finance,* May 1977, pp. 321–32.

Perrakis, Stylianos. "Capital Budgeting and Timing Uncertainty within the Capital Asset Pricing Model." *Financial Management,* Autumn 1979, pp. 32–40.

Rendleman, Richard J. Jr. "Ranking Errors in CAPM Capital Budgeting Applications." *Financial Management,* Winter 1978, pp. 40–44.

Roll, R. "Ambiguity When Performance Is Measured by the Securities Market Line." *Journal of Finance,* September 1978, pp 129–76.

Roll, R. "A Critique of the Asset Pricing Theory's Tests: Part I: On Past and Potential Testability of the Theory." *Journal of Financial Economics,* March 1977.

Ross, S. A. "The Current Status of the Capital Asset Pricing Model (CAPM)." *Journal of Finance,* June 1978, pp. 885–901.

Rubenstein, M. E. "A Mean Variance Synthesis of Corporate Financial Theory." *Journal of Finance,* March 1973, pp. 167–82.

Stapleton, R. C. "Portfolio Analysis, Stock Valuation, and Capital Budgeting for Risky Projects." *Journal of Finance,* March 1971, pp. 95–118.

Van Horne, James C. "An Application of the Capital Asset Pricing Model to Divisional Required Returns." *Financial Management,* Spring 1980, pp. 14–19.

Weston, J. Fred. "Investment Decisions Using the Capital Asset Pricing Model." *Financial Management,* Spring 1973, pp. 25–33.

III

Initiating a Capital Project

15

Proposing a Project: How to Assemble a Capital Proposal

David E. Fyffe

Georgia Institute of Technology

*T*he preparation of an effective capital project proposal is a vital step in the capital budgeting process. There are three major categories of proposals:

1. *Internal tactical.* An internally funded project for maintenance of operations.
2. *Internal strategic.* An internally funded project having long-term implications for company survival or growth.
3. *External.* A project funded from outside the organization.

Internal proposals recommend an investment project to top management and corporate directors. They are not addressed to outsiders and include primarily project-related information.

An external proposal is designed to persuade outside sources of financing to fund a project. The ideal external proposal is a complete business plan, regardless of the method of financing sought.

Business plans were originally for venture capitalists who needed a quick way to identify promising propositions and to screen out others. With the growth of entrepreneurism within large corporations, business plans have become the preferred way of packaging major capital projects.

The material in this chapter applies equally well to small, independent start-ups and large corporate marketing or technical projects. Business plan elements relate directly to project justification and are suitable to internal proposals, as well.

A bank lending officer, underwriter, or venture capitalist must pass judgment on dozens of proposals each week. Their screening decisions as to which proposals will receive serious consideration are often made in five minutes or less. What can you do to increase the odds that your proposal will be impressive enough to survive the initial screening and receive favorable action?

WHAT A LENDER OR VENTURE CAPITALIST LOOKS FOR IN A PROJECT PROPOSAL

Any potential investor will look to the project proposal for answers to the following questions:

- What is the proposition?
- What are the characteristics of the product, the company, and the industry?
- What are the qualifications of the people involved?
- Is there a market, or can the venture successfully create a market?
- What is the growth potential?
- Can the company produce the product competitively?
- What is the profitability potential?
- What are the risks?

Both the loan officer and the venture capitalist will focus on the product and the competency of management. A loan officer will consider three analyses: high side, middle of the road, and low side. The officer will be concerned about whether or not your cash will be sufficient to support the company if it booms and whether or not you can meet payments if things go badly. Other considerations relate to the product and the management group.

- *Will the product benefit society, and is it properly positioned?* The product must not be aimed at a market that is either too narrow or too well developed.
- *Have you had related business experience?* Previous successful experience is always a big plus.
- *Does the management group possess the necessary talent?* In particular, does management have the marketing skill, financial skill, and technical skill to make the project successful?
- *What is the extent of your personal and financial commitment?* Any potential investor will hold the view that you should have enough faith in the project to commit *all* your personal resources before he or she will be willing to invest.

A venture capitalist has a very similar set of criteria. The most important decision factors are extent of management commitment, product, market, management marketing skill, management technical skill, marketing plan, and management financial skill. Like the loan officer, the venture capitalist will be concerned about the appropriateness of experience of the entrepreneur and management group. If the management team does not demonstrate the skills listed above, the project is unlikely to survive the initial screening.

The product and its market must offer the potential for rapid growth. Ideally, the venture capitalist expects a 5- to 10-fold return in about five years. This requires something unique about the business—an advantage that tends to be proprietary.

Finally, the proposal should be well prepared. It must create an impression that the entrepreneur knows precisely what to do and how the project will be carried out. The information needed to prepare the proposal is developed by three major analyses that constitute the project feasibility study. These are the market study, technical analysis, and financial analysis.

The procedures for conducting each of these analyses are presented in the following sections. An outline for the preparation of a project proposal is presented in the final section.

THE MARKET STUDY

The market study must establish that there is a viable market and that your product or service can successfully compete in that market. If the market is presently served, the market study must provide convincing reasons why your product will be more attractive to customers than

299

competing products. In addition, market trends and potential threats must be analyzed in order to evaluate downside market risks.

The market study must also establish a proposed pricing policy along with selling and distribution plans. The latter include distribution channels and a sales organization structure. These provide the basis for estimates of product sales and of costs related to selling and distribution.

The information outputs from the market analysis that are necessary for the technical and financial analyses are (1) sales estimates and (2) the estimates of selling and distribution costs.

A suggested approach to market analysis is shown in Figure 1. The major steps are discussed in the following sections of this chapter.

Define the Market

This part of the market analysis is concerned with defining clearly the general population that comprises the market. The questions that must be answered are:

1. Who are the potential customers? (For example, types of industries or demographic characteristics of consumers.)
2. What geographic area will be served?

The answers to these questions will establish market boundaries.

Failure to correctly define the market is very likely to result in erroneous estimates of the total potential market and sales. Suppose that the product is high-purity, sharp silica sand. The potential users include glass makers, fertilizer producers, sand blasting contractors, construction contractors, filter manufacturers and service, golf courses, and beaches. Certainly, we should delete from this list the potential customers whose needs are not adequately met by your product and those whose needs can be easily met by a product of lesser value. It is best, however, to include "marginal" users until further steps in the market analysis have been completed.

The identification of potential customers may require a survey. In the case of a "Cinema and Draft House" project, for example, a telephone survey and personal interviews were conducted. These techniques helped to identify a market segment consisting of college-age singles and young married couples with low to moderate incomes.

Market Estimation

With customer characteristics defined and geographic boundaries established, we next attempt to estimate the market—currently and in

FIGURE 1

Steps in the Market Study

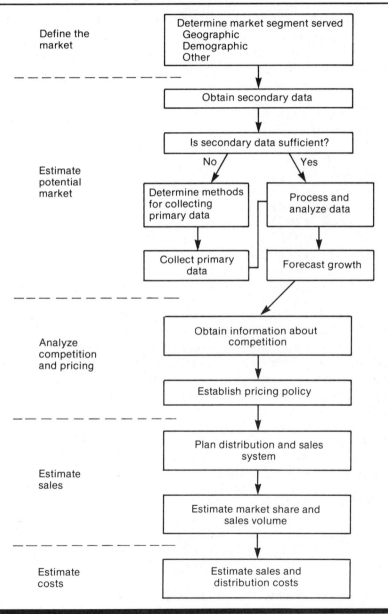

the future. Our major concern is whether or not the market can sustain your project. The precise questions to be answered are (1) What is the potential market size? (2) What is the present demand? and (3) How will the demand behave in the future?

There is a vast amount of secondary data to help us obtain information concerning the size of the population of potential customers and historical demand. Secondary data consists of published information that is available to the general public. A few of the more important publications are listed below.

Customer population. The primary sources are the following U.S. Department of Commerce publications.

- *County Business Patterns*
- *Census of Population*
- *Census of Housing*
- *Survey of Current Business*
- *Census of Business—Retail Trade*
- *Census of Selected Service Industries*
- *Census of Manufacturers*
- *Census of Mineral Industries*
- *Census of Construction Industries*

In addition, individual states publish manufacturing directories which provide a listing by SIC number of all manufacturers in the state.

Detailed information such as mailing address, telephone numbers, and company officers may be obtained from trade directories, telephone directories, and the *Thomas Register of American Manufacturers* and the *Thomas Register Catalog File* (Thomas Publishing Company, New York).

Historical consumption, production, and end use. Statistical data on past consumption, production, and end use are available from numerous sources. Some of the major publications are the following:

- Census reports (see listing above)
- *Current Industrial Reports,* U.S. Department of Commerce
- *Minerals Yearbook,* U.S. Bureau of Mines
- *Standard & Poor's Industry Surveys,* (McGraw-Hill, New York)

Projected consumption, production, and end use. Projections of demand for many products (classified by SIC number) may be found from the following sources.

- *Predicasts,* Predicasts, Inc., Cleveland, Ohio
- *U.S. Industrial Outlook,* U.S. Department of Commerce

In addition to these secondary data sources, various trade associations may be willing to provide demand data. *The Encyclopedia of Associations* lists associations, their addresses, telephone numbers, names of officials, and other information concerning the scope of their operations.

The search of secondary data sources may provide sufficient information for estimating the potential market and predicting market trends. If not, primary data must be obtained. Primary data is collected directly from the population of customers (or potential customers) by the analyst.

Primary data is collected through telephone surveys, mail questionnaires, and personal interviews. The choice of survey technique will be influenced by (*a*) the objective of the survey, (*b*) the type of market, (*c*) the number of potential customers, and (*d*) the time and money available.

Mail surveys are generally less expensive than either telephone surveys or personal interviews. A mail survey is a logical choice if a large number of people are to be queried and if the questions are easily understood. The principal disadvantages of mail surveys are (1) the low proportion of respondents (typically 20 to 30 percent) and (2) the time required to obtain responses.

Telephone surveys are used when response time is important and the number of customers to be queried is not prohibitively large. A telephone survey is frequently used in conjunction with a mail survey in an effort to determine whether or not the mail survey respondents are representative of the total population.

Personal interviews are costly. Their advantage, however, is that they permit great flexibility. Customer product preferences and other information may be obtained during the interview. For this reason, personal interviews are used most often when questions of product characteristics and pricing are to be examined.

Regardless of the choice of survey technique, a survey instrument (or plan) must be designed and tested, the sampling units identified, and the sample size determined. The questions in the survey instrument are field tested with a small group of respondents to ensure that they are unambiguous and will provide the desired information. Sampling units (that is, individuals to be included in the survey) are selected from a population list for the defined market. Such a list may be compiled from telephone directories, business directories, trade association lists, and other sources. Sampling units may be selected randomly from this list. However, if the total population consists of a number of such groups, each having some characteristic of interest in common, stratified sampling is used. Stratified sampling ensures that the number of sampling units from each subgroup is proportional to the relative size of the subgroup. The sample size can be calculated using statistical sampling techniques.[1]

The final step in market estimation is the analysis of both secondary data and primary data (if collected) to answer the three questions posed at the beginning of this section. If the data clearly indicates sufficient sales for the project, further analysis may be unnecessary. For most projects, however, it will be necessary to estimate the total market and to develop market forecasts.

Sales Estimation

At this step in the market analysis we are concerned with estimating the sales levels over time, in dollars and units, that the project can achieve. We seek to answer the following questions: (1) What selling price shall we establish? (2) How many units can we sell each month over the next five years?

These are the most difficult questions to answer in the entire project analysis—and they are quite likely the most important. Factors that must be included are product quality and value, competition, distribution, and market growth.

Competition. Know as much about the competition as you possibly can. Who are your competitors? Where are they located? What is their sales volume? What is their production capacity? Do they enjoy a cost advantage? What is their pricing structure? How does the quality of their product compare to yours? Some information concerning competitors will be available (for example, employment level, prices, and possibly sales). Information related to most of the above questions, however, is very difficult to obtain.

Pricing. Although many managers believe that prices cannot be established until costs are determined, the truth is that competition, not costs, should determine prices. This does not mean, however, that prices should be set with no knowledge of costs. It is important, for example, to know the relationship between fixed and variable costs and which costs vary with volume. Unfortunately, at this stage in the project analysis, cost information has not yet been developed.

The usual approach to product pricing at this stage is to establish a price that is competitive when the product is compared with similar products. If time permits and product is available, market tests can be conducted to determine demand at various price levels. Also, consumer surveys can be conducted to provide an indication of what consumers would be willing to pay.

Distribution and sales organization. The distribution system and sales organization affect sales volume and vice versa. The task of estimating sales volume, therefore, also necessitates consideration of alternative approaches to selling and distribution. If the project involves a product that is merely an expansion of the current product line, these considerations may center on advertising and promotion. On the other hand, if the project is a new venture or involves a totally new product, a distribution system and sales organization must be designed.

Sales projections (the marketing plan). The sales projections made in this phase of the market analysis are the basis for income projections and cash flow planning. In addition, the sales volume projections are a primary input to the technical analysis. It is necessary, therefore, to provide a marketing plan that shows units and dollars of sales by products and by geographic area. The projections should be monthly or quarterly for the first year and annually for at least another four years.

Estimate Costs

In addition to sales estimates that are input to both the technical analysis and the financial analysis, the market analysis must provide cost estimates of sales and distribution costs for the financial analysis. These costs should include (*a*) advertising and promotion costs, (*b*) selling and distribution expenses, and (*c*) aftersales facilities and services (if required).

Selling and distribution expenses are all expenses, except advertising and promotion, that will be incurred in contacting customers, delivering products, and collections. These include costs that vary with sales such as packaging, sales commissions, shipping, and storage. Other costs such as salaries, travel, and entertainment are considered fixed for a particular sales volume.

Aftersales facilities and services costs are important for a wide range of products. These may include field service facilities, service personnel salaries, warranty costs, and more.

Summary

The market analysis should provide convincing arguments that a viable market exists—or can be created—and that your product can successfully claim a share of that market. It should examine market threats such as demand stability, price stability, and possible actions by competitors.

THE TECHNICAL ANALYSIS

The market analysis has provided a demand schedule and finished goods inventory requirements. The technical analysis accepts these inputs and provides a manufacturing plan. The end results from the technical analysis are listed below.

1. Assurance of technical feasibility of the project.
   a. Adequacy of technology.
   b. Availability of inputs.
   c. Conformance to environmental requirements.
2. Facilities location.
3. Production system design.
   a. Civil works specifications.
   b. Process design.
   c. Equipment and tooling specifications.
   d. Facilities layout.
4. Production work force, organization, and staffing needs.
5. Pro forma estimates of investment and operating costs.
   a. Fixed asset costs.
   b. Preproduction capital expenditures.
   c. Operating costs (materials and inputs, wages, and salaries, overhead).

The effort and cost that should be expended on the technical analysis depend on the project size, the technological novelty of the product, and the desired accuracy of the cost estimates. In the case of a well-established product for which production technology and costs are readily available, the technical analysis will require minimal effort. A new, high-tech product, on the other hand, will likely necessitate extensive work for the technical analysis.

Inadequacies in the technical analysis usually result from failure to include all relevant start-up and production costs. In particular, overhead costs such as indirect labor, scrap losses, and maintenance are often overlooked. The resulting understatement of operating costs will cause the project to look deceptively attractive. A thoroughly done technical analysis is never a waste of time. The steps for a technical analysis are shown in Figure 2.

306

FIGURE 2

Steps in the Technical Analysis

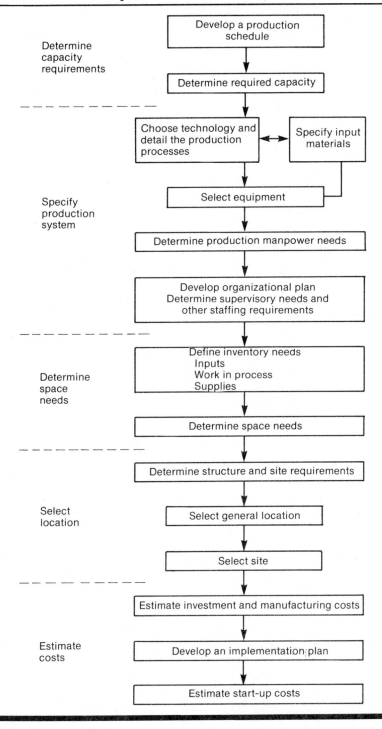

Determine Capacity Requirements

Before any work can be done toward developing production cost estimates, the question "What production capacity should we provide?" must be answered. The projected demands from the market analysis do *not* constitute a production schedule. Certainly the maximum monthly demand is not likely to be the same as the plant production capacity.

Prior to determining a planned capacity for the production facility, we must first determine a production schedule. The production schedule must meet the projected market demands, but the two are not the same. The additional factors to be considered in developing the production schedule are finished stock inventory build-up and workload leveling.

Additional factors that must be considered in determining the capacity are projected growth trends and relative costs of incremental capacity increases if acquired now versus at a later date. We must also decide whether the planned capacity shall be based on one, two, or three shift operations.

Specify the Production System

Specifications for the production system are required for estimating certain fixed costs (machinery and equipment, working capital, and preproduction costs) and operating expenses. A preliminary task is to completely specify all purchased input materials, the quantities needed, and sources of supply. The remaining tasks are as follows: (1) detail the production process, (2) select equipment, (3) determine direct and indirect labor requirements, and (4) develop an organizational plan and determine supervisory and staff needs. Each of these tasks is discussed in the sections which follow.

Detail the production process. The production process is the sequence of operations, inspections, transports, and storages used to convert purchased inputs to finished products. A typical process flow chart is shown in Figure 3. Printed forms such as shown in Figure 3 are generally available from engineering bookstores. A separate chart should be made for each component, subassembly, and assembly produced.[2]

The presentation of a complete set of process charts is clearly a time-consuming task. The alternative is to select equipment and roughly estimate the number of direct and indirect workers required. As we shall see, process charts provide a much more precise tool for estimating equipment and work force needs.

308

FIGURE 3

Process Chart

| Process Chart | Page ____ of ____ |

Part name _____

Process description _____

Department _____

Plant _____

Recorded by _____ Date _____

Summary	No.
Operations	
Transportations	
Inspections	
Delays	
Storages	
Total steps	
Distance traveled	

Step	Operations	Transport	Inspect	Delay	Storage	Description of _____ Method				
	○	⇨	□	D	▽					
	○	⇨	□	D	▽					
	○	⇨	□	D	▽					
	○	⇨	□	D	▽					
	○	⇨	□	D	▽					
	○	⇨	□	D	▽					
	○	⇨	□	D	▽					
	○	⇨	□	D	▽					
	○	⇨	□	D	▽					
	○	⇨	□	D	▽					
	○	⇨	□	D	▽					
	○	⇨	□	D	▽					
	○	⇨	□	D	▽					
	○	⇨	□	D	▽					
	○	⇨	□	D	▽					
	○	⇨	□	D	▽					
	○	⇨	□	D	▽					
	○	⇨	□	D	▽					
	○	⇨	□	D	▽					
	○	⇨	□	D	▽					

Select equipment. Equipment and tooling must be specified for each operation, transportation, and inspection shown on the process chart. If there are alternative methods for accomplishing the operation, an economic analysis should be made to select the "best" alternative. Information concerning equipment may be obtained from equipment manufacturers. Sources for identifying equipment manufacturers include the following:

- Trade Association publications. Trade Associations are listed in the *Encyclopedia of Associations,* Detroit: Gale Research Company.

309

- *Thomas Register of Manufacturers,* New York: Thomas Publishing, 1980.
- *Sweet's Catalogs,* New York: Sweets Division, McGraw-Hill Information Systems Company.

Data for equipment capacities can be compared with the desired production capacity in order to obtain the quantity of equipment required. Auxiliary equipment such as work benches, air compressors, or electrical generators must be included.

The primary end result of this task will be a complete listing of production, material handling, and inspection equipment and tooling required to support the desired plant capacity. The production rates for individual pieces of equipment should be noted for later use in calculating work force needs.

Determine production work force requirements. Process flow charts also provide a convenient and thorough approach for determining direct and indirect production work force requirements. The questions that must be answered are

- How many employees are needed?
- What skills must these employees have?

The best approach for answering these questions is to designate a set of work centers for the production activities. Each operation, transportation, and inspection is then assigned to a work center, and a skill level is specified. The time required to produce the *scheduled output* is then calculated. (Note that equipment quantities are based on capacity; work force needs are based on scheduled output.) In this way, we obtain the total workhours for each skill level at each work center. This information is converted to work force requirements in the form of work force tables, as shown in Figure 4.

Determine supervisory and staff needs. After estimating work force requirements, a production organization structure must be designed. The use of work centers, as recommended previously for estimating work force requirements, will facilitate the design of a production organization. Individual work centers or work center groups can be used as functional units, and a supervisory position can be assigned to each functional unit. The number of workers reporting to a supervisor depends upon the complexity of the work and the physical dispersion of the work group. As a general rule, this number ranges from 5 to 15.

FIGURE 4

Workforce Planning Table

Workforce Planning Table
(variable and fixed labor)

Work center:

Job function		Hours per week				
		Yr. 1	Yr. 2	Yr. 3	Yr. 4	Yr. 5
1	1					
	2					
	3					
2	1					
	2					
	3					
3	1					
	2					
	3					
4	1					
8	1					
	2					
	3					

In addition to supervisory positions, the number and type of staff and service positions must also be estimated. These vary according to the nature and size of the business. Functional activities that should be considered are janitorial, maintenance, receiving, shipping, warehousing and inventory control, quality control, production planning, methods, tool room, clerical, and machine shop.

This task is facilitated by the use of service cost centers similar to the work centers used for estimating production work force needs. The number of employees and their skill requirements is itemized in the form of a work force table for each service cost center.

Determine Space, Structure, and Site Requirements

The next set of tasks is the estimation of the total space required for the project and identification of special structural and/or site requirements.

Space requirements. The total space requirements for the project consist of production space (work stations, inspection, storage, and factory offices), production support activity space, auxiliary equipment space, and office and services space (staff functions, employee services, other services, general and administrative, marketing and sales, etc.).

Estimates of production space needs can be made by using the process charts. Each work station and inspection activity should be identified and the following space needs estimated: physical equipment—including auxilary equipment and tooling, worker and work space, and in-process materials storage. These estimates should be aggregated by work centers. The sum should then be multiplied by 1.5 in order to provide adequate space for aisles and material handling. This approach will provide a suitable estimate of production floorspace needs.

Additional production-related space will be required for storage of raw materials and other inputs and for storage of finished products. In order to estimate these space requirements, it is necessary to determine maximum inventory levels. In general, inventory levels of raw materials and inputs should be kept low. Purchased materials inventories will depend on economic order quantities and procurement lead times. Finished stock inventory depends on such factors as customer service objectives, demand variability, and the distribution system.

Production support activities for which space must be provided are tool room, machine shop, maintenance, laboratory, supplies, receiving and shipping, and purchased materials inspection.

Auxiliary equipment space needs must also be considered. These include air compressors, transformers, pumps, heating and air conditioning, waste disposal, and power generation.

Finally, office and services space needs must be estimated. The following is a checklist for these needs.

- Manufacturing staff
  Methods and standards
  Production planning
  Maintenance
  Quality control

- Engineering
    Product design and development
    Research
    Manufacturing engineering
    Facilities design
    Drafting
- Plant services
    Lavatories and showers
    Eating facilities
- Health facilities
    Security
    Safety
- Personnel
    Wage and salary administration
- Finance
    Financial accounting
    Managerial accounting
    Personnel accounting
    Auditing
    Financial management
- Data processing
- Marketing
    Sales
    Customer service
    Market analysis
- General administrative
    Administrative offices
    Conference rooms
    Reception areas

At the same time that space requirements are being estimated, special structural and site requirements can be identified. These, of course, will depend on the production processes. However, they include the following:

- Structural requirements
    High ceilings
    Special flooring
    Special foundations
    Sound and heat isolation
    Controlled atmosphere
    Heavy-duty electrical service

313

- Site requirements
  - Rail siding
  - Fuel storage
  - Highway access
  - Sewage treatment
  - Waste storage

These factors affect the choice of location. They also influence rental expense or, if a building is to be constructed, the construction costs.

After space requirements have been estimated, a tentative area layout should be constructed. This layout permits a visual overview of total space allocations and helps to ensure that major needs have not been overlooked.

Select General Location

Quite possibly, the project is to be an addition to existing facilities, and its location is already fixed. If not, the location decision is very important. The general location alternatives must be selected and analyzed for their effects on costs. Evaluation of intangible factors also influences the location decision. A checklist of factors affecting the choice of a general location is given below.

- Capital investment
  - Land cost
  - Construction
  - Site development
- Taxes
  - Income tax
  - Property tax
  - Inventory tax
  - Sales and use tax
- Industrialization incentives
  - Jobs credit
  - Tax credits
  - Training
  - Other
- State and local government
  - Environmental controls
  - Labor laws
  - Attitude toward industry

314

- Labor factors
    - Wage patterns
    - Availability
    - Union and labor attitudes
    - Productivity
- Utilities (power, gas, water)
    - Rate structure
    - Availability
    - Reliability
    - Quality
- Waste disposal
    - Disposal facilities
    - Treatment facilities that must be provided by the project
- Supporting industry and services
    - Suppliers
    - Transportation costs
- Market factors
    - Competitor's locations
    - Transportation costs
- Community factors
    - Schools
    - Recreational facilities
    - Cultural activities
    - Local transportation
- Living costs
- Proximity to major airport
- Climate
- Local transportation

The major considerations are those affecting investment and operating costs.

Information concerning location alternatives is available from a large number of sources. Industrial development organizations in each of the 50 states provide such data. Information may also be obtained from:

- *Area Wage Survey,* U.S. Department of Labor, Bureau of Labor Statistics
- *Statistical Abstracts of the United States,* U.S. Department of Commerce, Bureau of the Census
- *Site Selection Handbook,* Atlanta: Conway Publications
- *Industrial Development,* Atlanta: Conway Publications

In order to adequately evaluate location alternatives, a pro forma income statement should be prepared for each potential location. The "bottom line" can then be compared.

Estimate Costs

The three major cost areas for which the technical analysis provides estimates are (1) fixed investment, (2) preproduction capital expenditures, and (3) factory costs (both fixed and variable).

Fixed investment costs. Fixed investment consists of land and site preparation, buildings and civil works, machinery and equipment, and property rights.

Precise estimates for land and buildings are site dependent. However, adequate estimates can be obtained from realtors, industrial development departments of state and local governments, and industrial development departments of other organizations (for example, power companies, railroads).

Machinery and equipment costs can be obtained from equipment manufacturers and suppliers. Cost estimates should include transportation, installation, debugging, initial tooling, and spare parts. As a rule, these estimates are slightly higher than actual prices that can be negotiated. They therefore tend to be slightly conservative.

Costs of property rights (for example, easements) depend upon the nature and value of the right. They do not usually constitute a major cost element.

Preproduction capital expenditures. Every project incurs project implementation expenditures prior to actual operation which must be capitalized. Examples of such expenditures related to the technical aspects of the project are preparatory studies, salaries and fringe benefits, travel, training, consulting fees, and trial runs. Failure to include these costs is a major blunder and can jeopardize the project.

Factory costs. Factory costs are direct material and inputs (variable), direct labor wages and salaries (variable), and factory overheads (fixed). Direct materials and inputs consist of purchased raw materials and components. Quantity estimates, as noted previously, will be based on the planned production schedule. Costs can be obtained from various suppliers.

Estimates of direct labor wages and salaries are based upon the Manning tables shown previously in Figure 4. Wage estimates can be obtained from *Area Wage Surveys*.[3]

These wages, however, are *not* the total wage cost. Surcharges on wages should be calculated as follows: (*a*) FICA, (*b*) federal and state unemployment tax, (*c*) worker's compensation, (*d*) retirement contribution, and (*e*) insurance contribution. The total surcharges are approximately 25 to 30 percent. Wage rates, increased by the amount of the surcharges, must be multiplied by the total time units (hours, months) worked per year to arrive at estimated annual costs.

Factory overhead costs are incurred in the production of goods and/or services but cannot be directly identified with each individual unit of output. Typical cost items are wages and salaries, indirect material, office supplies, utilities, repair and maintenance, and other.

These costs are easily overlooked. The most thorough approach is to itemize the costs for each service cost center (for example, quality control, production planning, maintenance, security).

Summary

The technical analysis produces a detailed manufacturing plan. It ensures that potential technological problems are dealt with and that all production costs are enumerated. A thorough technical analysis is essential to the validity of project feasibility analysis. Inadequate analysis of production technology and environmental impacts, failure to consider alternatives, and omission of production support costs are the most common sources of errors. Such errors are a major threat to the success of the project.

THE FINANCIAL ANALYSIS

The market study has produced estimates of sales income and of selling and distribution costs. The technical analysis has produced cost estimates for fixed asset costs, preproduction capital expenditures, and operating costs. In the financial analysis remaining cost elements are estimated, pro forma financial statements and cash flows constructed, and the potential profitability is scrutinized. Financial analysis represents the culmination of the project analysis efforts.

The outputs from the financial analysis are (1) cash flow tables, (2) pro forma income statement and balance sheet, (3) pro forma measures of project profitability and performance, and (4) analysis of risk. The steps for a financial analysis are shown in Figure 5.

Estimate Costs

The major cost categories for which complete estimates have not yet been made are (1) total investment costs, (2) general and administrative

FIGURE 5

Steps in the Financial Analysis

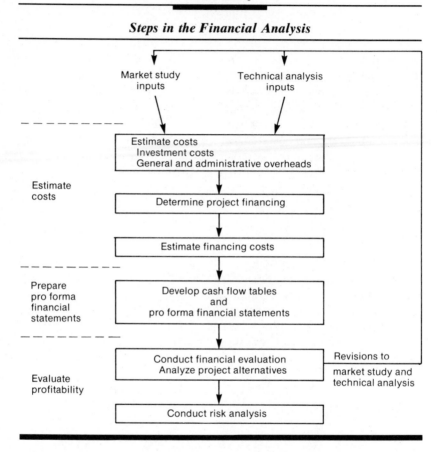

overheads, and (3) financing costs. The first two of these may be incorporated into the technical analysis. We have chosen to include them as a part of the financial analysis simply because, unlike the other cost estimated produced by the technical analysis, they are not a direct result of technical considerations.

Total investment costs. The total investment costs for a project consist of fixed investment (land and site preparation, buildings and civil works, and equipment), preproduction capital expenditures, and working capital. Estimates for the fixed investment costs and for some elements of preproduction capital costs were obtained from the technical analysis. Quite likely, however, there will be additional preproduction capital expenditures.

318

In addition to the technology-related project implementation costs listed earlier, other possible preproduction capital expenditures include costs for feasibility studies, product promotion, interest on construction loans, office expenses, communications, and legal fees.

Preproduction costs that are directly attributable to specific assets may be added to the cost of the asset, and the total cost may be amortized over the life of the asset. Otherwise, preproduction capital costs are amortized over a time period as permitted by IRS regulations.

Working capital is the money needed to operate the project according to plan. Although these funds continually "flow," so long as the project remains in operation they are as permanently committed as are fixed investments. Working capital may be defined as either net or gross.

Net working capital = Current assets − Current liabilities

Gross working capital = Current assets

There are arguments to support the use of either in project analysis. The use of gross working capital results in a conservatively high estimate of total investment.

Current assets that should be included in estimating working capital and the approximate minimum requirements for each are listed below.

Current assets	Minimum requirements
Cash	15 days
Accounts receivable	15–30 days
Inventory	
Purchased inputs	10–15 days
Maintenance parts	30 days
Work in process	5 days (at factory cost)
Finished products	15 days (at factory cost plus administrative overhead)

Current liabilities will consist primarily of accounts payable for purchased inputs (that is, raw materials, purchased components, and utilities). An estimated value of 15 to 30 days is appropriate.

Working capital requirements should be estimated for each year in the planning horizon (typically 5 to 10 years) for the project, and year-by-year increases or decreases should be calculated. Similarly, estimations of fixed investments and preproduction capital expenditures must be time-phased. The result is a schedule for total investment costs over the planning horizon for the project. Additionally, a schedule for total asset expenditures (that is, fixed investments, preproduction capital expenditures, and current asset increases) can be prepared.

General and administrative overhead. The factory overhead costs discussed earlier are only a portion of the total overhead costs. Additional overhead is generated by administrative components. These overhead costs consist of wages and salaries, travel and entertainment, property taxes, insurance, communications, postage, and office supplies. As with factory overhead, the most thorough approach is to itemize the costs for each administrative/staff component of the organization.

Estimate financing needs. Project financing must be considered at this time in order to prepare pro forma financial statements. The total investment schedule has been prepared; and the total initial costs for the project can be calculated. The basic question to be answered is, "Where will the money come from?" Certainly the project will be financed by equity and loans. Discussions concerning the advantages, disadvantages, and sources for each are beyond the scope of this chapter. They may be found in many books dealing with business financing. What is important for the purposes of financial analysis is the split between equity capital and borrowed funds and the anticipated interest rate for borrowed funds. This information is necessary for preparing pro forma financial statements.

Prepare Pro Forma Financial Statements

All cost estimates that are required for pro forma financial statements have now been made. The work to assemble and organize these costs is a major task of the financial analysis. The pro forma statements of interest are cash flows, net income, and balance sheet.

Cash flow table. A cash flow table is essential for financial planning and the timing of funds acquisitions. The purpose of the cash flow table is to ensure that the anticipated timing and amount of cash inflows are adequate to meet anticipated cash outflows. Cash flows should, therefore, be projected monthly for the first year of the project and yearly for the rest of the project planning horizon (typically 5 to 10 years). A suggested format for the cash flow table is shown in Figure 6.

FIGURE 6

Cash Flow Table

	Year 1 (months)											Year 2	Year k
Cash receipts													
1. Sales revenues													
2. Capital inputs													
a. Equity													
b. Long-term loans													
c. Short-term loans													
d. Supplier's credits													
Total cash receipts													
Cash disbursements													
1. Fixed assets													
2. Preproduction captial expenditures													
3. Operating costs													
a. Factory costs													
b. Administrative overhead													
c. Selling and distribution													
4. Debt service													
5. Taxes													
6. Dividends													
Total cash disbursements													
Cash balance													
Cumulative cash balance													

Income statement. For any project, the most important financial projection is the income statement. This statement shows whether or not the project, as planned, will be profitable. It provides information for further analysis in the form of financial ratio tests and break-even analysis. The pro forma income statement, like the cash flow table, should show monthly periods for the first year and annual periods for the remainder of the project planning horizon. Income and expense elements are as follows:

1. **Gross sales (from market study)**
   Less sales returns and allowances
2. **Net sales**
3. **Cost of goods sold**
   a. Finished goods beginning inventory
   b. Cost of goods manufactured
      i. Factory costs (from technical analysis)
      ii. General and administrative (from financial analysis)
   c. Goods available less finished goods ending inventory
   d. Total cost of goods sold
4. **Selling and distribution expense (from market study)**

321

5. Financial costs interest (from financial analysis)
6. Depreciation (from financial analysis)
7. Total costs
8. Gross taxable profit (net sales less total costs)
9. Tax
10. Net profit after tax

Balance sheet. The balance sheet for an operating business shows its assets and liabilities at a particular point in time. The pro forma balance sheet for a proposed project attempts to predict assets and liabilities at specified time points in the future. All information required to prepare the balance sheet is available from previously prepared schedules and statements.

I. Assets
  A. Current assets
    1. Cash (from cash flow table)
    2. Accounts receivable (from working capital calculations)
    3. Inventory (from working capital calculations)
  B. Fixed assets
    1. Fixed investments (from total investment calculations)
    2. Preproduction capital expenditures (from total investment calculations)
  C. Losses (from income statement)
II. Liabilities
  A. Current liabilities (from working capital calculations)
  B. Loans (from estimates of financing)
  C. Equity (from estimates of financing)
  D. Retained earnings (from income statement)

It should be noted that annual depreciation must be considered in arriving at the value of fixed investments.

Evaluate Profitability

The pro forma financial statements and the cash flow table provide the necessary financial information to evaluate the project. The basic question to be answered is "Will the return on equity capital be sufficient to justify this project?"

Financial evaluation. Since the financial analysis is based on a *planned* financing structure, it is usually desirable to consider several alternatives with different capital structures. In fact, the analyst may also evaluate other alternatives such as product mix, production processes, and locations.

The commercial profitability of a project may be evaluated by one or more of the following:

- Payback period
- Simple rate of return
- Net present value
- Internal rate of return

The *payback* period is defined as the period required to recover the initial investment when the project is operated at full production. It is obtained by successively subtracting the annual profits from the initial investment until the remainder reaches zero. *Profit* is here defined to be the aftertax net income plus interest and depreciation. The project is judged on how quickly the initial investment is recovered.

The only advantages of payback evaluation are (1) it is easily calculated and (2) it includes some inherent consideration of risk. Its major disadvantage is that it overemphasizes near-term cash flows and leaves unanswered the important question of how the project will perform over a longer horizon.

The *simple rate of return* on total investment is taken as the ratio of profit (at full production) to the initial investment. The simple rate of return on equity capital may be calculated in a similar manner. In these calculations, *profit* may be defined as the aftertax net income. When computed in this way, the simple rate of return shows period-by-period financial performance. It may vary considerably from one period to the next. Moreover, it ignores the timing of earnings.

Unlike the two simple methods described above, *net present value* calculation is a ''discounting method.'' The net present value of a project is defined as the discounted present value of all net cash inflows and outflows over the life of a project. The discount rate is usually based on the cost of capital in the long-term capital markets. If the net present value is positive, the project's profitability is greater than the discount rate. Thus, if desired, discount rate can be arbitrarily set at a specified value in order to determine whether or not the project will achieve that rate.

Compared with the payback period and the simple rate of return, the net present value has the advantage that it considers the entire life of the project (or at least a much longer horizon) and the timing of cash flows. The major problem in using this method is the selection of the discount rate.

323

The internal rate of return approach is somewhat similar to net present value. The *internal rate of return* is defined as the discount rate at which the present value of *all* net cash flows over a specified time horizon is exactly zero. The net cash flows from the cash flow table are used for these considerations. The internal rate of return, then, indicates the actual profit rate for the total investment or, if proper adjustments are made, the equity capital. The project is considered to be financially attractive if the internal rate of return exceeds an arbitrary "minimum attractive" rate of return. This method is widely used. It is a very satisfactory approach for evaluating the profitability of a project alternative.

In addition to measures of profitability, financial analysis should include several financial ratios that are based on the pro forma statements. The ratios that are commonly used are the following:

1. Balance sheet ratios
   a. Current ratio
   b. Quick ratio
   c. Fixed asset to tangible net worth
   d. Total debt to tangible net worth
   e. Current debt to tangible net worth
2. Mixed ratios
   a. Working capital turnover
   b. Net profits on tangible net worth
   c. Inventory turnover
   d. Collection period
3. Operating ratios
   a. Net profit to net sales

Financial ratios for many industry groups are published in *Annual Statement Studies* by Robert Morris Associates and by Dun & Bradstreet. Discussions of the methods for computing these ratios and their interpretation may be found in Clifton and Fyffe, *Project Feasibility Analysis*.

Risk considerations. Obviously, the entire project analysis has been built on a foundation of estimates and assumptions. Forecasts of sales and estimates of many cost elements may not be exact. It would be foolhardy, then, to accept the results of the project analysis without examining uncertainties. For example,

- What would be the effect on profitability if demand were 15 percent less than expected?

- If production costs were 5 percent more than estimated?
- If the inflation rate were greater than expected?

Such uncertainties can be examined by the use of break-even analysis and sensitivity analysis.

Break-even analysis is a method for examining how changes in cost, production volume, and price affect profits. The *break-even point (BEP)* is defined as the volume (physical units or sales) at which sales revenues equal production costs. For example,

$$BEP = \frac{\text{Fixed costs}}{\text{Unit sales price } - \text{ Variable unit costs}}$$

expresses the value of the break-even point in terms of physical units. The break-even point in terms of sales is obtained if this quantity is multiplied by the selling price. Dividing the above BEP value by the planned capacity produces the percent capacity utilization at which the project will break even (provided that fixed costs remain unchanged at this production volume). In a somewhat similar fashion, the selling price at which the project breaks even (for a specified demand) can also be determined.

Break-even analysis provides a way to examine threats related to volume and selling price. In essence, it determines how easily fixed costs are recovered.

Summary

The financial analysis generates those cost elements that were not obtained from the market study or technical analysis. Revenues and costs are then organized to produce pro forma financial statements that are the bases for profitability evaluation. When needed, pro forma statements are prepared for project alternatives (for example, location alternatives). Also, the financial data are used to examine the consequences of estimation errors (for example, demand, price, costs) and other risks.

WRITING THE PROJECT PROPOSAL

The contents of the project proposal will differ somewhat depending upon whether it is being prepared for the purpose of obtaining borrowed funds or equity financing. The major difference, as discussed earlier, is that a bank lending office will be concerned with security for the loan, while the venture capitalist will be interested in downside risk and the potential for rapid growth. In either case, a screening decision is likely to be made after a brief perusal of the proposal.

In order to prepare a good project proposal, the detailed studies and analyses described in preceding sections must be done. However, much of the detail—particularly from the technical analysis—should be omitted from the project proposal or else placed in an appendix. The body of the proposal must impress the loan officer or venture capitalist with the soundness of deal (from their point of view) and the competence of the management team.

A suggested outline for the project proposal follows.

1. *Summary of proposed financing.* The first thing the loan officer or venture capitalist wants to know is "What is the deal?" This section should contain the following:

- Name and address of the company.
- Characteristics of the company and industry and overview of project justification.
- Proposed financial structure of the company.
- Financial needs.
- Use of funds.
- Additional capital acquisition plans.

2. *The company and its management team.* Provide historical information on the company, such as date and state of formation, founders, product line(s), operating history, and current financial statements (if these exist). Most important, present information concerning the management team, board of directors, investors, and outside professional services. If the company has no operating history, include financial statements for principal officers and investors. This section must convince the loan officer or venture capitalist that the management group is capable.

3. *Market analysis.* A suggested outline for the market analysis section follows.

   I. Project justification—the importance of the product or service and its advantages or unusual features that will provide a significant lead over competition

   II. Market potential
      A. Market definition
      B. Current demand
      C. Growth projections

III. Competition
  A. Identification of competitors
  B. Capabilities and market share
  C. Competitive threats
IV. Pricing policy
 V. Selling and distribution plan
VI. Sales projections

4. *Technical analysis.* Describe the production process, input materials, and present cost estimates for production of the company's product.

  I. Plant capacity and the production plan
 II. Production processes and technology
III. Materials and inputs
  A. Specifications
  B. Sources and availability
IV. Environmental impact
 V. Cost estimates
  A. Fixed assets
  B. Operating costs
  C. Preproduction expenditures
VI. Project implementation plan

5. *Financial analysis.* Present pro forma statements and a commercial profitability analysis for the project.

  I. Project investment costs
  A. Fixed investment
  B. Working capital
  C. Preproduction capital costs
 II. Proposed financing schedule
III. Pro forma financial statements
  A. Cash flows (monthly for the first year and quarterly or annually for succeeding years)
  B. Operating statements
  C. Balance sheets
IV. Financial analyses
  A. Profitability measures
  B. Performance ratios
 V. Risk analyses
  A. Break-even analyses
VI. Future financing needs

NOTES

[1] William G. Cochran, *Sampling Techniques* (New York: John Wiley & Sons, 1953); and David S. Clifton and David E. Fyffe, *Project Feasibility Analysis: A Guide to Profitable New Ventures* (New York: John Wiley & Sons, 1977).

[2] Instructions for completing a flow process chart can be found in Clifton and Fyffe, *Project Feasibility Analysis*.

[3] U.S. Department of Labor, Bureau of Labor Statistics, *Area Wage Surveys* (Washington, D.C.: U.S. Government Printing Office).

16

Tax Treatment: How to Maximize Tax Benefits

Frederic Enoch White

Bradford C. Lewis

Arthur Andersen & Co.

*N*o capital investment can be effectively analyzed without taking into consideration the effect of federal and state income taxes. A significant portion of any expenditure made by a company will be recovered at some time through income tax savings as the investment is deducted for tax purposes through depreciation or amortization. In addition, some part of an investment may be immediately recovered through investment or other tax credits where the investment is made in qualified assets. The earlier the year in which the credit or deduction becomes available, the lower the net cost of the investment, taking into consideration the time value of money.

Soft costs, which are attributable to and therefore tax deductible in the period incurred, are less expensive costs than those which are required to be capitalized and deducted over a period of time. In analyzing the real cost of an investment, the discounted present value of the right to receive the potential tax benefits of an investment will always be greater where tax deductions and credits are immediately available. Accordingly, much of the tax planning in the capital budget decision-making process involves accelerating potential tax benefits to the earliest year possible. The various concepts and techniques discussed below illustrate the effects of tax planning on capital budgeting, financial statements, and income tax reporting.*

CAPITAL COST RECOVERY THROUGH DEPRECIATION, AMORTIZATION, AND TAX CREDITS: TAX AND FINANCIAL ACCOUNTING CONSIDERATIONS

Depreciation Methods

The depreciation of fixed assets has historically provided one of the most fruitful opportunities for accelerating cost recovery. Depreciation is an accounting technique for systematically allocating the cost of an asset over its economic useful life. Prior to 1981 most corporations used straight-line depreciation in their published financial statements but employed some form of accelerated depreciation for tax purposes.

In an attempt to stimulate capital investment and simplify methodology, Congress enacted new depreciation provisions which are incorporated in the Economic Recovery Tax Act of 1981 (ERTA). The accelerated cost recovery system (ACRS) substantially reduces the amount of time required for enterprises to recover the cost of their capital expenditures. State tax policy has not been fully consistent with federal policy; some states have adopted the ACRS provisions, but many have not conformed.[1]

ACRS is a completely new, mandatory cost recovery system for tax purposes. This new system replaces the asset depreciation range (ADR) and "facts and circumstances" depreciation systems for all property acquired after December 31, 1980.[2] ACRS abandons traditional depreciation concepts of estimated useful lives, salvage value, and used-property rules. Instead, ERTA created five property classes that include all property defined as recovery property.[3] The Tax Reform Act of 1984 created a sixth class. Cost recovery allowances are computed on the unadjusted basis of recovery property in accordance with tables provided in the law (see Table 1). ACRS provides a limited

---

* Tax effects are subject to changing legislation. The material covered here accounts for tax acts through 1984. Previews of 1985 legislation portend reduction in corporate incentives (eg., ITC, ACRS).

number of elections to give taxpayers flexibility in using the benefits of the new system. Straight-line depreciation may be elected in lieu of the specified cost recovery allowances.[4]

As a limited alternative to capitalizing and depreciating assets under ACRS, The Internal Revenue Code, Section 179, provides that a certain amount of recovery property may be deducted currently as an expense. The annual maximum deductible amount under this provision is phased in as follows:

Taxable year beginning in:	Amount
1985, 1986, or 1987	$ 5,000
1988 or 1989	7,500
1990 and after	10,000

To the extent an asset is expensed under Section 179, no investment tax credit may be taken on that property.

To illustrate the benefits of ACRS, assume that a corporation acquires an asset that costs $1.2 million and has an estimated 12-year life. The company decides to depreciate the asset on a straight-line basis for financial reporting purposes, resulting in a yearly depreciation book charge of $100,000. Under ACRS the asset falls within the five-year class; accordingly, the total cost of the asset is deducted over five years. The total depreciation charged off under any method cannot exceed asset cost so, after 12 years, the total written off for both book and tax purposes equals $1.2 million. This is illustrated in Table 2. The table also demonstrates that in the early part of an asset's life, ACRS provides differentially higher tax deductions which are exactly offset by lower write-offs in later years. Thus, during the first year ACRS provides an extra $36,800 in cash by way of deferred taxes. In the sixth year the pattern reverses, and book depreciation exceeds tax depreciation by $100,000—resulting in $46,000 less cash available.

Although the stream of cash savings net out to zero over the 12-year period, the fact that money has a time value means that the earlier use of the extra cash made available by the higher tax depreciation yields a present value that far exceeds the negative value of the lower charge-offs in the later years. In this particular case discounting the entire stream of cash savings over the 10-year period by a 10 percent rate yields a present value of $110,497. This present value figure repre-

TABLE 1

ACRS Cost Recovery Tables

Personal property
Placed in service after December 31, 1980

	Class of interest			
Ownership year	3-year (percent)	5-year (percent)	10-year (percent)	15-year utility (percent)
1	25	15	8	5
2	38	22	14	10
3	37	21	12	9
4		21	10	8
5		21	10	7
6			10	7
7			9	6
8			9	6
9			9	6
10			9	6
11				6
12				6
13				6
14				6
15				6
	100	100	100	100

Real estate (all real estate except low-income housing)*
Placed in service after March 15, 1984

(Use the column for the month in the first year the property is placed in service)

Ownership year	1 (percent)	2 (percent)	3 (percent)	4 (percent)	5 (percent)	6 (percent)	7 (percent)	8 (percent)	9 (percent)	10 (percent)	11 (percent)	12 (percent)
1	9	9	8	7	6	5	4	4	3	2	1	0
2	9	9	9	9	9	9	9	9	9	10	10	10
3	8	8	8	8	8	8	8	8	9	9	9	9
4	7	7	7	7	7	8	8	8	8	8	8	8
5	6	7	7	7	7	7	7	7	7	7	7	7
6	5	6	6	6	6	6	6	6	6	6	6	6
7	5	5	5	5	6	6	6	6	6	6	6	6

(cont.)	(percent)	(percent)	(percent)	(percent)	(percent)	(percent)	(percent)	(percent)	(percent)	(percent)	(percent)	(percent)
8	5	5	5	5	5	5	5	5	5	5	5	5
9	5	5	5	5	5	5	5	5	5	5	5	5
10	5	5	5	5	5	5	5	5	5	5	5	5
11	5	5	5	5	5	5	5	5	5	5	5	5
12	5	5	5	5	5	5	5	5	5	5	5	5
13	4	4	4	5	4	4	4	4	4	4	4	4
14	4	4	4	4	4	4	4	4	4	4	4	4
15	4	4	4	4	4	4	4	4	4	4	4	4
16	4	4	4	4	4	4	4	4	4	4	4	4
17	4	4	4	4	4	4	4	4	4	4	4	4
18	4	4	4	4	4	4	4	4	4	4	4	4
19	0	0	1	1	1	2	2	3	3	3	4	4
	100	100	100	100	100	100	100	100	100	100	100	100

Low-income housing
Placed in service after December 30, 1980

(Use the column for the month in the first
year the property is placed in service)

Ownership year	1 (percent)	2 (percent)	3 (percent)	4 (percent)	5 (percent)	6 (percent)	7 (percent)	8 (percent)	9 (percent)	10 (percent)	11 (percent)	12 (percent)
1	13	12	11	10	9	8	7	6	4	3	2	1
2	12	12	12	12	12	12	12	13	13	13	13	13
3	10	10	10	10	11	11	11	11	11	11	11	11
4	9	9	9	9	9	9	9	9	10	10	10	10
5	8	8	8	8	8	8	8	8	8	8	8	8
6	7	7	7	7	7	7	7	7	7	7	7	7
7	6	6	6	6	6	6	6	6	5	6	6	6
8	5	5	5	5	5	5	6	5	5	5	6	6
9	5	5	5	5	5	5	5	5	5	5	5	5
10	5	5	5	5	5	5	5	5	5	5	5	5
11	4	4	4	5	4	5	5	5	5	5	5	5
12	4	4	4	4	4	4	4	4	4	5	5	5
13	4	4	4	4	4	4	4	4	4	5	5	5
14	4	4	4	4	4	4	4	4	4	4	4	4
15	4		4	4	4	4	4	4	4	4	4	4
16			1	1	2	2	2	3	3	3	4	4
	100	100	100	100	100	100	100	100	100	100	100	100

The official table to be published by the Treasury Department may differ from the percentages shown above.
* These tables do not apply for short taxable years of less than 12 months.

TABLE 2

Present Value of Tax Deferral Using ACRS (years 1–12)

	1	2	3	4	5	6	7
Book depreciation	$100,000	$100,000	$100,000	$100,000	$100,000	$100,000	$100,000
Tax (ACRS depreciation)	180,000	264,000	252,000	252,000	252,000	—	—
Excess	80,000	164,000	152,000	152,000	152,000	(100,000)	(100,000)
Income tax deferrals at 46 percent	36,800	75,440	69,920	69,920	69,920	(46,000)	(46,000)
Present value of tax deferrals at 10 percent interest rate	36,800	68,582	57,785	52,532	47,756	(28,562)	(25,966)

	8	9	10	11	12	Total
Book depreciation	$100,000	$100,000	$100,000	$100,000	$100,000	$1,200,000
Tax (ACRS depreciation)	—	—	—	—	—	1,200,000
Excess	(100,000)	(100,000)	(100,000)	(100,000)	(100,000)	0
Income tax deferrals at 46 percent	(46,000)	(46,000)	(46,000)	(46,000)	(46,000)	0
Present value of tax deferrals at 10 percent interest rate	(23,605)	(21,459)	(19,508)	(17,735)	(16,123)	110,497

sents the benefits of deferring the tax that would have been payable had a straight-line method been used for tax purposes.

Investment Tax Credit

As a further stimulus to capital investment, Congress has provided an investment tax credit, which allows 10 percent of the cost of qualifying property as a credit against tax.[5] The rules governing the amount of qualified investment were changed in 1981 to conform with the ACRS recovery periods. In the case of 5-, 10-, and 15-year property, 100 percent of the property's cost is considered a qualified investment; for 3-year recovery property, 60 percent of the cost is a qualified investment.[6] Only tangible personal property qualifies for investment tax credit; real estate or buildings will not qualify. Any credit which is unused during the year, due to an operating loss or other limitation, may be carried back 3 years and carried forward 15.[7]

In addition to property purchased and placed in service during the year, advance investment credits may be claimed for construction progress payments made on qualified property with a normal construction period of two or more years.[8]

Under the Tax Equity and Fiscal Responsibility Act (TEFRA), changes were made to the amount of tax benefit realized through the investment tax credit. Congress perceived that the combined effects of ACRS and the investment tax credit could, in certain situations, produce results more beneficial than expensing the asset in the year it is purchased. To assure that cost recovery benefits are no better than expensing, the new rule provides that the basis of a depreciable asset will be reduced by one half the amount of the credit taken on the property.[9] As an alternative to basis reduction, a taxpayer may elect to reduce the amount of investment tax credit taken on property by two percentage points. Present value analysis indicates that there is practically no difference in the two methods for ACRS five-year property, while reducing basis and claiming the higher credit is more advantageous for ACRS three-year property. Publicly held companies may choose to take the higher credit due to its effect on earnings per share.

Two options are available for treatment of investment tax credit in a company's financial statements: the flow-through method[10] and the deferral method.[11] The flow-through method flows through all of the income statement benefits of the credit in the year of acquisition, as opposed to the deferral method which spreads the benefit over the life of the acquired asset. Both methods are acceptable under generally accepted accounting principles.

Rehabilitation Credit

Short depreciation lives encourage investment in new property but may have the effect of reducing the attractiveness of investing in older business structures. Accordingly, an income tax credit is presently available for costs incurred in rehabilitating commercial structures.[12] The amount of the credit ranges from 15 to 25 percent, depending upon the age and character of the property. The benefit of the credit is diluted by the requirement that the depreciable basis of the property must be reduced by the credit. However, the credit is still a significant inducement since it allows a company to recover a significant portion of the cost of a rehabilitation building in the year the costs are incurred.

Rehabilitation Credit Example

Depreciable basis

Purchase of building	$ 40,000
Rehabilitation expenditures	360,000
	$400,000
Rehabilitation credit	
(20 percent × $360,000)	(72,000)
Adjusted basis of building	$328,000

Cash flow—first year

Purchase of building	$(40,000)
Interest on loan	(54,000)
Tax benefit of interest expense	27,000
Rehabilitation credit	72,000
Tax benefits of depreciation (½ year)	4,525
Net aftertax cash flow	$ 9,525

Amortization

The cost of and related expenditures to acquire intangible assets with a useful life of more than one year are capital costs and may not be currently expensed for tax purposes. Expenditures for intangibles such as copyrights or patents are generally amortized on a straight-line basis over the useful life of the intangible. In the case of a patent, this is generally 17 years (the legal life of a patent); however, a patent may be amortized over a shorter life if the facts so indicate. Financial accounting treatment of intangibles is, in general, very similar to the tax treatment. Potential differences may arise in the treatment of items such as goodwill which is never amortizable for tax purposes but must be amortized for financial accounting purposes.

Financial Accounting for Book/ Tax Differences

Accounting for cost recovery under generally accepted accounting principles does not necessarily correspond to tax concepts. To the extent that the same method is used for both book and income tax purposes, the accounting treatment is relatively simple. However, the difficulty arises in the usual case where the corporation uses straight-line depreciation for financial statement purposes and ACRS for income tax purposes. The resulting "timing differences" between book income and taxable income give rise to interperiod tax accounting adjustments. Historically, there has been substantial disagreement (especially among public utilities) regarding how these timing differences should be properly treated for accounting purposes.

There are currently two major accounting treatments used: flow-through and normalizing. Flow-through reports net income on the books in accordance with the cash accounting concept; that is, book income is reduced by the amount of income tax that is actually payable for the year. If depreciation expense on the books is shown on a straight-line basis, but tax expense is determined by using ACRS, the tax benefits of ACRS depreciation are "flowed through" to reported income.

Normalizing, on the other hand, reduces book income by a provision for income tax based on book income rather than taxable income. This is achieved by setting up a deferred tax liability account for taxes not currently payable. Where the tax advantage of ACRS over straight-line depreciation in the early years results in a current tax liability that is less than the book tax provision, a credit to the deferred tax reserve account offsets the corresponding debit entry to the tax provision. Later in the asset's life, when ACRS depreciation falls below straight-line depreciation and tax depreciation is less than book depreciation, the reserve for deferred taxes is reduced (debited) and the current liability is increased (credited). The normalizing method is required by the Accounting Principles Board but is currently under reconsideration.[13]

FINANCING CAPITAL COST EXPENDITURES

Leasing

Leasing should be considered particularly whenever the tax benefits associated with ownership of an asset cannot be fully utilized by a corporation. The objective in a leasing transaction is often the transfer of tax benefits such as depreciation and investment tax credits to a lessor with a high incremental tax rate in exchange for a lease rate that is lower than the lessee's available borrowing rate. For example, assume an airline will pay little or no tax for the foreseeable future due to large operating losses. If the airline purchases a new aircraft, the depreciation and investment tax credit associated with that aircraft will be wasted. If, however, the airline sells the aircraft to another taxpayer who can utilize the tax benefits and leases it back, the lease rate charged to the airline will reflect the use of these benefits and will be correspondingly lower.

There are other business and financial considerations in the lease-or-buy decision. One of those in favor of leasing is the ability to circumvent restrictions under loan covenants. Leasing also provides 100 percent financing, while an equipment loan would typically require an initial down payment. Furthermore, leasing avoids budget restrictions in that lease payments may be structured as operating expense. Level payments under a lease may improve cash flow in the early years of a lease as compared with an equipment loan which will typically require higher payments of interest in the early years. Finally, short-term operating leases can shift the risks of obsolescence from the lessee to the lessor.[14]

Some of the major areas of concern in a leasing transaction are the definition of a lease for tax purposes and the lessor's ability to use investment tax credits. A functional definition of a lease for tax purposes cannot be found in either the Internal Revenue Code or the Regulations. The IRS has provided guidelines for what it will consider a lease in one of its procedural announcements.[15] This definition is important because a purported lease could be recharacterized as a sale—which would cause the lessor to lose the tax benefits associated with ownership. The IRS guidelines include the following:

1. *Equity commitment.* The lessor must have a minimum unconditional equity investment of 20 percent of the property's cost, both at the initiation of the lease and over the lease term.
2. *Residual value and useful life.* The fair market value of the property at the end of the lease must be at least 20 percent of

the original cost. The leased asset must have a remaining useful life of the greater of one year or 20 percent of the original useful life.

3. The lessee must not have a bargain purchase option at the end of the lease term.

4. No part of the original cost of the property can be furnished by the lessee, nor may the lessee lend funds to acquire the property or guarantee any loans in connection with the acquisition.

5. *Economic substance.* The lessor must expect to receive a profit from the transaction, apart from tax considerations.

Another consideration is the restriction placed on a noncorporate lessor's ability to use investment tax credits.[16] In general, noncorporate lessors will not be entitled to the investment tax credit on leased property unless: (1) the property is manufactured or produced by the lessor, or (2) the lease term is less than 50 percent of the property's useful life and the lessor's deductions (other than depreciation, interest, and taxes) attributable to the leased property exceed 15 percent of the rental income from the property.

Financial reporting for leases is governed primarily by FASB Statement No. 13, "Accounting for Leases."[17] The statement distinguishes between operating leases (lessee expenses lease payments) and capital leases (transaction is treated as purchase of an asset by the lessee). If any of the following criteria are met, the lessee must recognize the lease as a capital lease.

1. Ownership of the leased property is transferred to the lessee at the end of the lease term.

2. The lease contains a bargain purchase option.

3. The lease term is for 75 percent or more of the remaining useful life of the asset.

4. The present value of the lease payments is 90 percent or more of the FMV of the leased property.

The classification of the lease as a capital or operating will have several effects on the lessee's financial statements. A capital lease is recorded on the balance sheet as an asset with a corresponding "lease payable" liability. The lease payable is separated into a current and long-term portion due. The current portion does not reflect the interest portion of payments coming due; this is an expense affecting the income statement only. In an operating lease no amounts are required to be capitalized; lease expense affects the income statement only. Assuming all other items are constant, these differing treatments will cause liquidity ratios (current, quick) to be higher under an operating lease than a capital lease. Correspondingly, leverage ratios (debt/equity) will be higher under a capital lease than an operating lease. On the income statement side expenses under a capital lease will generally be higher (at least in the early years of the lease) than expenses under an operating lease. This can be explained by the fact that the combination of interest and depreciation expense required under a capital lease is generally greater in the early years of a lease than the level payments under an operating lease. This means that profit margins, return on equity, and earnings per share will all generally be higher under an operating lease than a capital lease.[18]

INDUSTRIAL DEVELOPMENT BONDS

Industrial development bonds (IDB) are bonds issued by state or local municipalities, the proceeds of which are used to finance private developments. For example, a real estate developer might use the proceeds of an IDB issue to finance the development of an airport. Alternatively, a chemical company might use the proceeds of an IDB issue to build pollution control facilities. The tax law provides that interest on IDBs may be tax exempt if the proceeds of the offering meet certain requirements.[19] Obviously, to the extent interest on an obligation is tax exempt, a lower yield will be required to induce potential creditors to purchase bonds. The offering restrictions fall into two main categories: (1) restrictions on the use of the offerings and (2) offering size restrictions.

If substantially all of the proceeds of an IDB obligation are used to finance one of several types of facilities, the interest on that obligation will be tax exempt. Among the eligible facilities are (1) low-income residential rental property; (2) sports facilities; (3) convention or trade show facilities; (4) airports, docks, wharves, mass commuting facilities, and parking facilities; (5) sewage and solid waste disposal facilities; (6) local electrical- or gas-furnishing facilities; (7) air or water pollution control facilities; (8) certain facilities for the furnishing of water; (9) qualified hydroelectric generating facilities; (10) qualified mass commuting vehicles; and (11) industrial parks.

If the offering will not be used to finance any of the above, it may still qualify for tax-exempt status under the "small issue" exception. This applies to issues of $1 million or less, provided that substantially all of the proceeds are used for the acquisition, construction, or improvement of land or depreciable property. At the election of the issuer, the limitation may be raised to $10 million.

Restrictions under TEFRA and Tax Reform Act of 1984

Legislation was passed under the Tax Equity and Fiscal Responsibility Act of 1982 (TEFRA) and the Tax Reform Act of 1984 in response to congressional concerns over the tremendous increase in volume of IDBs and the effect of this increase on capital markets. Both TEFRA and the 1984 act introduced a number of restrictions, so in spite of the new restrictions IDBs may still provide an attractive means of financing large capital expenditures.

INVENTORIES

LIFO versus FIFO

In periods of high-rate inflation, the method of accounting for inventory costs can dramatically affect the earnings and the current tax liability of a corporation. Generally, a corporate taxpayer uses one of the two more popular methods of accounting for its inventory costs: FIFO—where the oldest inventory is deemed to be sold first (first in, first out); and LIFO—where inventories are charged to the income statement on the basis of last in, first out.

Table 3 indicates that the pretax earnings of a company using FIFO would be $20,000 greater than if LIFO were used. This is because cost

TABLE 3

Comparison of LIFO with FIFO				
	Lifo		Fifo	
	Amount per unit	$ amount	Amount per unit	$ amount
Beginning inventory				
50,000 units	$2	$100,000	$2	$100,000
Purchases				
20,000 units	3	60,000	3	60,000
		$160,000		$160,000
Ending inventory				
20,000 units	2	40,000	3	60,000
10,000 units	2	20,000	2	20,000
Total		$60,000		$80,000
Cost of goods sold		$100,000		$100,000

of goods sold is charged with the lower cost of the earlier inventories. As the same inventory method must be used for both book and tax purposes, the current tax liability of the company is accelerated.[21] Consequently, FIFO has two great shortcomings. First, it overstates profits by including inventory profits (which are arguably not true operating profits). Second, it accelerates a tax liability that could be deferred with the use of LIFO.

The emphasis on earnings per share, however, often makes management reluctant to convert to an inventory method which will reduce earnings. On the other hand, it should be kept in mind that a corporation using LIFO may, by footnote, indicate the effect on earnings if FIFO were used in the year of change.[22] Also, there is some question as to whether the reduction in earnings as a result of switching to LIFO affects the price of the corporation's stock. The sophisticated investor realizes that in a period of rising prices, inflated inventory values artificially inflate profits. As the investing public becomes more sophisticated, the emphasis will increasingly be on quality of profits rather than quantity. Accordingly, LIFO may continue to gain as the more popular inventory method.

The company that charges current inventory costs against current sales, benefits by deferring income taxes and more correctly stating its income statement. Its balance sheet, on the other hand, suffers in that inventories are stated at amounts substantially below current costs. LIFO, thus, represents price-level accounting for the income statement but not for the balance sheet. No one method represents the answer. The best alternative is to allow LIFO for tax purposes and FIFO for book purposes, with any difference being reflected in an interperiod tax allocation. Unfortunately, this alternative is not currently available.[23]

RESEARCH AND DEVELOPMENT COSTS

For financial statement purposes, research and development costs are treated as period costs deductible as incurred, under the theory that their future benefit is indeterminable.[24] The income tax rules are far more flexible. Research and experimental expenditures (which may not correspond definitionally to research and development costs) may be deducted currently, deferred and written off over 60 months, or capitalized and recovered through depreciation.[25] Although most companies will be motivated to deduct research and developmental expenditures currently to reduce taxable income in the current period, there may be a variety of tax planning reasons for deferring or capitalizing the expense.

For a number of years there has been some concern that U.S. companies were falling behind their competitors in developing new technology. With this in mind, a new provision was added to the tax law in 1981 to allow companies incurring research costs to claim a 25 percent credit for incremental increases in research expenditures incurred after June 30, 1981.[26] Assuming a 46 percent corporate tax rate, 71 percent of incremental research expenditures (46 percent corporate tax rate plus 25 percent credit) will be recovered through tax savings immediately.

There are several planning ideas which might be considered in the R&D credit area. To the extent an enterprise does not have in-house facilities, research expenditures qualifying for the credit can be "farmed out" on a contract basis to universities or private institutions. Depreciation expense on assets used in research and development is not a qualified expenditure. Leasing would be a more prudent vehicle to finance this type of investment, as lease expense on R&D property will qualify for the credit.[27]

ACQUIRING ALL OR PART OF A GOING CONCERN

One of the most significant investments a company can make (if not in terms of dollars, at least in terms of analysis required) is the acquisition of a going concern. In addition to acquiring fixed assets, the buyer may purchase inventory, accounts receivable, prepaid costs, deferred charges, goodwill, and other unrecorded intangibles, while at the same time assuming both short-and long-term debt. As part of the acquisition the purchase agreement may include employment contracts and covenants not to compete. Tax considerations abound. Assuming that the target company is a corporation, the buyer will have the option of purchasing all of the capital stock or all of the underlying assets of the company. If stock is acquired the target company can be retained as a subsidiary, merged into another subsidiary, or liquidated into the acquiring parent company. One common acquisition technique is to form a new corporation and use it as the acquiring vehicle—either merging it into the target company or vice versa.[28]

While grappling with the technical tax alternatives, the acquiring company will have to consider how the acquisition will be recorded for financial statement purposes. Different acquisition structures will have significantly different effects on future earnings. Should the company be bought with cash, debt, common stock, preferred stock, nonvoting common or preferred, hybrid instruments? The seller, of course, may be the most important factor since his requirements may dictate, for example, that the target company be sold in a tax-free transaction.

Because of the numerous variables involved in acquiring a going concern, analyzing the financial impact of the investment is a difficult exercise. If the deal is a taxable acquisition, the acquiring company may obtain a future tax deduction for a material part of the purchase price thereby reducing the net cost of the investment. On the other hand, financial statement earnings may have to be reduced accordingly. The essence of an acquisition, however, is whether it will be taxable or nontaxable and whether it will be recorded as a pooling or purchase for financial statement purposes.

Tax Considerations

Tax-free acquisitions are structured using stock of the acquiring company, either common or a combination of common and preferred, to acquire assets or stock of the acquired company. If cash or debt is used, the acquisition will become partly or fully taxable.[29] From the acquiring company's standpoint, there may be strong tax reasons for making the deal taxable. First, in a nontaxable acquisition the tax cost basis of the target company's assets carry over.[30] Therefore, if the acquiring company pays $10 million in stock for the assets or stock of a target company which has assets with a tax cost basis of $2 million, no tax deduction will be received in the future for the $8 million difference. If cash or debt is used in a taxable deal, the acquiring company would get a step-up in the tax cost basis of the target company's stock or assets resulting in a tax deduction at some time in the future. If assets that turn over in a short period of time (such as inventory) are acquired (or deemed to be acquired), the net cost of the investment will be reduced immediately as a result of the tax refund arising from the deduction. Certain assets are not "wasting assets" in that they are considered not to have a determinable economic useful life. Inherent in any acquisition of a going concern is the presence of some going concern value, that is, goodwill or other intangibles. To the extent the purchase price is attributable to these assets, which have an unlimited useful life, no tax deduction is available until the business is terminated.[31] If the acquisition is taxable and results in a step-up in the basis of underlying assets in the target company, the acquiring company will have to allocate the purchase price among the various assets acquired on the basis of relative fair market value.

After deciding whether to structure the transaction as taxable or nontaxable, the parties must determine whether the transaction should be cast as an acquisition of stock or of assets. Except in a statutory merger, the buyer may avoid exposure to the target's contingent or unknown liabilities by casting the transaction as either a taxable or nontaxable asset acquisition.[32] A seller, on the other hand, will generally prefer a stock sale when a sale of assets would result in substantial depreciation or investment tax credit recapture.

If the buyer purchases the stock of the target, and if certain conditions are met, he may be able to increase the tax basis of the target's assets to account for the difference between the purchase price of the stock and the tax basis of the underlying assets.[33]

Another factor in any merger or acquisition is the ability of the acquiring corporation to purchase the target's tax attributes, specifically, net operating losses. For tax purposes, the form of the acquisition will control in this area. Assume corporation A is contemplating the acquisition of corporation B, which has a history of operating losses. Both corporations are engaged in the same line of business. If A attempts to avail itself of B's operating losses through a taxable purchase of B's stock (and then liquidate B or file a consolidated return), it will have major hurdles to overcome.[34] Alternatively, A could acquire the stock or assets of B in a nontaxable exchange of A's stock for B's stock or assets. In this case B's NOLs would generally be available for A's utilization, assuming that the shareholders of A retain at least a 20 percent continuing interest in the combined business.[35] The tax principles in this area are quite complicated. If a consolidated return is contemplated, an additional level of analysis is required.[36]

Financial Statement Considerations

Tax considerations occasionally take the back seat to management concerns about future effects on financial statements and earnings per share. The acquiring company has two alternatives: pooling or purchase accounting.

A pooling is accounted for as if the target company and acquiring company had always been commonly owned. Assets, liabilities, and profit and loss are added together and carried over at preacquisition costs. Pooling of interest accounting may only be used where voting common stock is used to acquire substantially all of the voting common stock of the target company.[37]

Purchase accounting must be used when the requirements for pooling of interest accounting are not met. The purchase price is required to be allocated to all of the assets required, including goodwill. Amounts allocated to goodwill and other similar intangibles must be amortized over a period of not more than 40 years.[38] Because purchase accounting "steps up" the target company's asset value, depreciation charges

345

will generally be higher than under a pooling of interest which reports the assets of the combined entity on a preacquisition historical cost basis. Earnings per share will generally be higher in postacquisition years under pooling of interest accounting than under purchase accounting.

Generally, an acquisition that qualifies as a tax-free reorganization for tax purposes will be treated as a pooling of interests, and a taxable purchase will be reported as a purchase for financial statement purposes. However, although these two treatments correspond conceptually, there are differences between the tax rules and the financial accounting rules. For example, a tax-free acquisition using voting preferred stock would be treated as a purchase under the accounting rules.[39]

CONCLUSION

Accelerating deductions, deferring income, and realizing credits are the key elements in reducing the net cost of any investment. To be really effective, the capital budget decision-making process must take into consideration these tax planning and deferral techniques. Frequently the simultaneous goals of favorable income tax consequences and favorable financial statement treatment will be in conflict. However, the real economic cost of a capital expenditure can be effectively analyzed only in the light of income tax consequences; short-term financial statement benefits should not be controlling. To the extent that a manager can reconcile the conflict between financial statement impact and income tax savings, companies can significantly reduce their capital costs.

NOTES

[1] California, for instance, has not conformed to ACRS.

[2] ADR was available for assets placed in service in years beginning after 1970.

[3] Internal Revenue Code (IRC); §168(c). ERTA created five property classes that include all property defined as recovery property. The Tax Reform Act of 1984 created a sixth class. The classes have recovery periods of 3, 5, 10, 15, and 18 years.

Three-year property means "Section 1245 property" (generally defined as personal property or other tangible property used in certain activities) with an ADR midpoint life of four years or less. This category consists primarily of automobiles, light-duty trucks, and special tools used in various manufacturing operations. The three-year property class also includes assets used in research and development activities and certain horses.

Five-year property includes all Section 1245 property not specifically included in the 1-, 10-, and 15-year classes. Because of changes in the definition of Section 1245 property in the new law, the five-year class now also includes (*a*) single-purpose agricultural and horticultural structures and (*b*) storage facilities for petroleum and its primary products. Most depreciable property of U.S. businesses falls within the five-year class, including public utility property with an ADR midpoint life of 4.5 to 18 years.

10-year property is (*a*) Section 1245 public utility property with an ADR midpoint life of 18.5 to 25 years, (*b*) "Section 1250 property" (which generally includes real estate) with a present ADR midpoint life of 12.5 years or less (primarily theme parks), (*c*) railroad tank cars, (*d*) manufactured (mobile) homes, and (*e*) coal conversion boilers and equipment.

15-year public utility property is Section 1245 public utility property with an ADR midpoint life greater than 25 years.

15-year low-income housing is real property entitled to special subsidies under federal, state or local law.

18-year real property is any Section 1250 property that is not a 10-year property and is not low-income housing. This class includes most depreciable real estate of U.S. businesses.

[4] IRC §168(b)(3). Under the straight-line election, the asset may be depreciated under the following class lives:

3-year property	3, 5, or 12 years
5-year property	5, 12, or 25 years
10-year property	10, 25, or 35 years
15-year utility property	15, 35, or 45 years
18-year real property	18, 35, or 45 years

This election may be beneficial in the case of real property, as ERTA provided that all accelerated depreciation on real property is subject to recapture. Under prior law, only depreciation in excess of straight-line was recaptured. (IRC §1245(a)(5)).

[5] IRC §46, §48, §38.

[6] IRC §46(c).

[7] IRC §39.

[8] IRC §46(d).

[9] IRC §48(q).

[10] This method was accepted by the Accounting Principles Board in *APB Opinion No. 4* (1964).

[11] *A.P.B. Opinion No. 2* (1962).

[12] IRC §46(a)(3).

[13] AICPA, *A.P.B. Opinion No. 11*, "Accounting for Income Taxes" (New York, December 1967); AICPA, *A.P.B. Opinion No. 23*, "Accounting for Income Taxes—Special Area" (New York, April 1972).

The Financial Accounting Standards Board is currently engaged in a major project to reconsider APB Opinion No. 11. The FASB's project will also involve reconsideration of other related areas, including those relating to investment tax credits, net operating losses, etc. A Discussion Memorandum was issued on August 29, 1983. Among the possible solutions included in the Discussion Memorandum are (1) eliminating interperiod tax allocation, (2) providing deferred income taxes for some but not all timing differences, and (3) retention of the present rules under APB No. 11. An exposure draft is due to be issued in 1984 and a final statement is due in 1985.

[14] Arthur Andersen & Company; Specialized Tax School—Leasing, Participant Manual ©1980.

[15] IRS Revenue Procedure 75-21; 1975-1 CB 715

[16] IRC §46(e)(3).

[17] FASB, *Statement of Financial Accounting Standards No. 13,* "Accounting for Leases" (as amended and interpreted through May 1980).

[18] Amembal and Isom, "Leasing for Profit," American Management Associations—Extension Institute; ©1980.

[19] IRC §103(b).

[20] The restrictions fall primarily in the following areas:

Public approval—the issue must be approved by the applicable elected representative of the applicable governmental unit after a public hearing or by a voter referendum. This applies to obligations issued after 12/31/82.

Reporting requirements—the issuer must file with the Treasury Department a statement indicating (*a*) the name and address of the issuer, (*b*) terms of the issue, (*c*) the name of the elected official who approved the issue, and (*d*) the name and address of the principal user of the facility.

Limitation on maturity—for obligations issued after 12/31/82, the average maturity of the obligations of an issue cannot exceed 120 percent of the average reasonably expected economic life of the facilities financed with the proceeds of the issue.

Depreciation limitations—to the extent facilities are financed using tax-exempt IDBs, ACRS or any other accelerated method may not be used to depreciate the facility. Straight-line depreciation over the applicable ACRS class life must be used on such property. This applies to property placed in service after 12/31/82. Certain exempt categories of property were provided under TEFRA, but all but one, multi-family housing, may use ACRS under the Tax Reform Act of 1984.

Elimination of small issue provisions—the most significant change under TEFRA was the elimination of the small issue ($1 million or less) exception for obligations issued after 12/31/86. The Tax Reform Act of 1984 delayed the sunset date to 12/31/90, but only for manufacturing facilities.

State volume gap—an annual per-capita limit of $150 is imposed on the volume of IDBs that can be issued in any state, but the CAD in any state will not be less than $200 million.

Federally guaranteed bonds—tax exempt status is denied for any IDB directly or indirectly guaranteed by an agency or instrumentality of the United States. Exemptions are provided for guarantees provided through insurance programs administered by certain government agencies.

[21] Income Tax Regulations, §1.472–2(h).

[22] Revenue Ruling 73-66,IRB 1973. SEE also Rev. Proc. 75-10, Rev. Rul. 75-49 and Rev. Rul. 75-50. Reg. §1.472(e)(1) outlines specific instances where non-LIFO inventory methods will not violate the LIFO conformity rule.

[23] IRC §472(c) requires that a taxpayer using the Lifo method for tax purposes must also use the Lifo method for annual report purposes. However, Rev. Proc. 77-33 liberalized this requirement somewhat by allowing financial statement footnote disclosure of the net income effect of a Lifo layer penetration during the year.

[24] FASB, *Statement of Financial Accounting Standards No. 2*, "Accounting for Research and Development Costs (October 1974).

[25] IRC §174 (current expense or 60-month amortization). IRC §168(c)(2)(A) (depreciation).

[26] IRC §30.

[27] IRC §30(b)(2)(A).

[28] IRC §368(a)(2)(D); §368(a)(2)(E). These are commonly called "triangular" mergers.

[29] Cash or debt is treated as "boot" under the reorganization rules. If both stock and boot are exchanged in an acquisition, IRC §356 will require gain to be recognized to the extent of the boot transferred.

In a stock-for-stock acquisition (368(a)(1)(B)) the receipt of any boot will disqualify the entire transaction as a tax-free reorganization. In other acquisitive reorganizations (stock for assets, assets for stock), a limited amount of boot may be used without destroying the tax-free status of the entire transaction.

[30] IRC §362.

[31] Reg. §1.167(a)(3).

[32] The buyer may also avoid exposure to these liabilities by structuring a merger as a triangular reorganization. (Supra note 28.) In these acquisitions a new subsidiary is formed solely for the acquisition, and it is either merged into the target or the target is merged into the newly formed subsidiary. Any hidden liabilities are thus shielded from the acquiring parent.

[33] IRC §338. In general, the acquiring corporation must make an election under this code section within 8 months and 15 days after the acquisition to step up the basis of the assets to that of the stock. The acquiring corporation must obtain at least 80 percent of all of the target's outstanding classes of stock within a 12-month period. Depreciation and the ITC recapture will be triggered upon making this election.

[34] IRC §269(b) could limit the utilization of B's NOLs if B was liquidated; if A filed consolidated returns with B, §269(a) and §382(a) would be major hurdles to overcome.

[35] IRC §§381, 382(b). The requisite percentage of continuing interest for A's shareholders is increased to 40 percent beginning in 1986.

[36] In addition to the limitations outlined above, a newly acquired subsidiary of an affiliated group filing a consolidated return may be subject to the Separate Return Limitation Year (SRLY) and the Consolidated Return Change of Ownership (CRCO) rules. (Regs. §§1.1502-1(c) and 1.1502-1(g)) A discussion of these rules is beyond the scope of this paper.

[37] *A.P.B. Opinion No. 16*, "Business Combinations."

[38] *A.P.B. Opinion No. 17*, "Intangible Assets."

[39] *A.P.B. Opinion No. 16* requires the exchange of solely common stock for common stock of the acquired company in order to qualify as a pooling of interest.

REFERENCES

AICPA, *A.P.B. Opinion No. 11*, "Accounting for Income Taxes (New York, December 1967).

AICPA, *A.P.B. Opinion No. 16,* "Business Combinations" (New York, 1970).

AICPA, *A.P.B. Opinion No. 17,* "Intangible Assets" (New York, 1970).

"Accounting and Tax Considerations for Business Combinations in the United States." ©Arthur Andersen & Company.

Amembal and Isom, "Leasing for Profit," American Management Associations—Extension Institute ©1980.

Danos & Imhoff, "Intermediate Accounting"; ©1983 by Prentice-Hall, Inc., Englewood Cliffs, New Jersey.

Davidson & Weill, "Handbook of Modern Accounting"; ©1983 by McGraw-Hill, Inc.

FASB, *Statement of Financial Accounting Standards No. 13,* "Accounting for Leases" (as amended and interpreted through May 1980).

The Internal Revenue Code of 1954, as amended.

"Specialized Tax School—Leasing"; Participant's Manual; ©1983 by Arthur Andersen & Co.

17

Evaluating a Project: In Defense of Net Present Value

Harold Bierman

Cornell University

It is very surprising that, as we approach the end of the 20th century, it is still necessary to defend the net present value (NPV) calculation. One very large consulting firm declares "DCF is obsolete," and two professors from a large eastern business school warn us that there are real dangers in using NPV. An operating manager has to be confused by the fact that modern finance books strongly recommend the use of NPV, but headlines in business periodicals warn of its use.

The critics of NPV say that it focuses excessively on short-term considerations. While U.S. management may pay excessive attention to the short term, it is not because of the NPV calculation. The NPV calculation takes into consideration the entire life of the investment being considered. While it is true that a dollar to be received at year 10 is valued less using NPV than a dollar to be received immediately, no valid economic analysis would do otherwise.

This paper will consider two aspects of capital budgeting. One is the matter of taking time value of money into consideration. The second is to compare three widely used methods of evaluating investments. To remove the suspense, let there be no doubt that there follows a defense of taking the time value of money into consideration when making decisions, and an advocacy of using the net present value calculation as the way to accomplish this. It should be obvious that the analysis to be described applies to any investment for which we are able to estimate cash flows. Without reasonable cash flow estimates, we cannot use the NPV calculations described in this chapter.

We will define NPV as a method of analyzing investment decisions where future cash flows are brought back to their present value equivalents using a discount rate that appropriately measures the time value of money. An investment is acceptable if its NPV is equal to or larger than zero.

TIMING AND DECISIONS

Assume an investment will earn $100 of cash flow 30 years from now. Assume further that the firm considering this investment refuses to accept it even though it only costs $30. Assume further that this investment is socially desirable (like growing a tree). Why would a firm not be willing to pay $30 to earn $100?

The answer to the above question is that the outlay takes place now, and the benefits are not received until time 30. The timing of the benefits can cause the investment to be undesirable.

Assume the firm can borrow funds using a zero coupon bond at a cost of .12 per year. A calculator or a table tells us that the present value now of a dollar to be received in 30 years is $.0334:

$$(1.12)^{-30} = .0334$$

The present value of $100 to be received at time 30 is only .0334 × $100 = $3.34 now.

The firm was correct to reject the investment. We cannot guess whether or not investing $30 now to receive $100 in 30 years is desirable. Only intelligent application of good finance—and in this type of situation the calculation of NPV is good finance—will tell us whether to accept or reject the investment. The net present value is a negative $26.66 (that is, 3.34 − 30.00 = −$26.66), and the opportunity to invest $30 and earn $100 should be rejected.

But how can we convince someone who rejects NPV as a method of analysis that the investment is not acceptable? Assume that we accept the $30 investment and finance it with .12 debt coming due in 30 years. At the end of 30 years, the firm will owe $898.80, that is, $30(1.12)^{30} = 30(29.96) = 898.80.

Since the investment earns $100 at time 30, and the amount the firm has to pay is $898.80 to repay the debtholders, we regret having made the decision to invest.

It could be argued that the investment could not be financed 100 percent with debt, and we should have considered the investment using the higher-cost common stock. Given that we rejected the investment using the .12 borrowing rate, we would also reject the investment using a higher discount rate arising from considering the cost of common stock capital.

The mechanics of the NPV calculation are deceptively simple, given all that the calculation accomplishes. The steps for evaluating independent investments are:

1. Define the investment's cash flows.
2. Define the appropriate discount rate.
3. Compute the present values of all cash flows and add all the present values to obtain the NPV.
4. Reject the investment if the NPV is less than zero and accept otherwise.

The mechanics of the calculation are simple; but, if the facts being used are valid, the results of the calculation are theoretically correct and will lead to valid accept or reject decisions.

In the above situation we have:

Present value of benefits	$100 × .0334 =	3.34
Outlay		−30.00
Net present value		−26.66

Using .12 as the discount rate, this investment should be rejected since it has a negative net present value. If funds are borrowed at .12, the investment will not lead to enough funds to repay the loan.

Now let us assume that the benefits are received at time 10. The present value of the cash flow is:

$100(1.12)^{-10} = 100(.3220) =$		32.20
Outlay		−30.00
Net present value		2.20

353

The net present value is positive, and the investment is acceptable. Let us assume the investment is accepted, and $32.20 is borrowed. This is again a zero coupon debt paying interest at maturity so that the investor earns .12. The amount to be paid at time 10 is $100:

$$\$32.20(1.12)^{10} = \$32.20(3.1058) = \$100$$

The investment earns just enough to repay the loan when the amount borrowed is equal to the present value of the positive cash flows.

Note that $32.20 was borrowed, and the investment only cost $30. There was $2.20 from the loan available for spending or investing in any fashion that the firm wished. The $2.20 is also the amount that could be spent at time 0 for the investment in addition to the basic cost of $30 without the investment becoming unattractive.

We could also prepare an income statement at time 10 by subtracting the investment cost from the $100 of revenue earned at time 10. The investment cost has to include the interest cost on the $30 investment as well as the original investment. The interest cost is:

$$\$30(1.12)^{10} - 30 = \$93.18 - 30 = \$63.18$$

The income statement would be:

Revenue		$100.00
Depreciation*	$30.00	
Interest cost	63.18	93.18
Income		6.82

* Equal to the outlay cost of the original investment at the time of acquisition.

The present value of the income is:

$$\text{PV of income} = \$6.82(1.12)^{-10} = \$6.82(.3220) = \$2.20$$

The present value of the income measured carefully as above is equal to the net present value of the investment as previously computed.

The net present value calculation is very powerful in that it does so many things so well. It tells us whether we will have enough funds to repay the debt; and, as illustrated above, it is logically linked to a measure of income.

If an investment costs $30 and if we ignore the time value of money, then any future cash flow greater than $30 in any time period would be sufficient to justify the investment. This failure to consider the cost of money in a theoretical (and practical) manner would cause the decision process to be fatally flawed.

Does this mean that those who criticize NPV are completely wrong? In one sense yes, and in a second sense no.

They are completely wrong in the sense that future cash flows have to be multiplied by $(1 + r)^{-n}$ to find their present value equivalent (it is a trivial change to multiply the cash flows by $(1 + r)^n$ to find their future value) if we are to evaluate investments in a systematic theoretically correct way. You might be able to evaluate a simple, relatively short-lived investment using a "seaman's eye," but a long-lived asset with changing cash flows is much more difficult to evaluate without computing the net present value. It is necessary to do the calculations.

What can we say in defense of the critics? Most important, it is possible to use the theoretically correct tool of NPV and use it in such a manner that it gives about as many incorrect decisions as if you had used a known incorrect decision process.

Let us consider the situation where an investment costs $100, and it will pay $144 at time 2. The firm can borrow $100 using a zero coupon debt at .12 per year. The cash flows are:

	0	1	2
Investment	−100	0	+144
Debt	+100	0	−125.44
Net	0	0	+ 18.56

Looking at the cash flows, we can conclude that the investment is obviously acceptable as long as .12 debt money is used to finance it. The net present value using .12 as the discount rate is:

$$\$144(1.12)^{-2} = \$144(.7972) = \$\ \ 114.80$$
$$-100.00$$
$$\text{NPV} = \$\ \ \ \ 14.80$$

355

The present value of the $18.56 obtained above for time two is also $14.80 since the borrowing rate is being used as the discount rate.

$$\$18.56(1.12)^{-2} = \$14.80.$$

While the above analysis indicates the investment is acceptable, few firms are willing to assume the investment is financed 100 percent with debt. They would require further analyses. Let us assume the actual financing will be .3 debt costing .12 and .7 common stock costing .20. The weighted average cost of the capital is:

	Proportion	Cost	Weighted cost
Debt	.3	× .12 =	.036
Common stock	.7	× .20 =	.140
	Weighted average cost =		.176

Using the .176 weighted average cost of the capital to compute the present value of the cash flows, we have a NPV of $4.12 and the investment is still acceptable.

$$\$144(1.176)^{-2} = \$ \ 104.12$$
$$-100.00$$
$$\text{NPV} = \quad 4.12$$

At time 2 the capital contributors will receive:

Debtholders	$30 × 1.12² =	$ 37.63
Common stockholders	$70 × 1.20² =	100.80
		$138.43
Residual (excess)		+5.57
	Cash flow at time 2 =	$144.00

The investment is again acceptable.

Now assume the firm is not satisfied with requiring a return of .176 and, for one of many possible reasons (the reasons being used are not necessarily correct reasons), requires a .25 return.

356

Now the NPV is a negative $7.84, and the investment would be rejected.

$$\$144(1.25)^{-2} = \quad \$\ \ 92.16$$
$$-100.00$$
$$\text{NPV} = \$-\quad 7.84$$

The use of an arbitrary high discount rate by a firm can have disastrous results in evaluating investments with cash flows in the reasonably distant future. The distortions increase the longer the time until the cash is received.

Assume a new innovation in equipment would cost $900,000 and would return labor savings of $200,000 per year forever. It can be shown that the present value of a perpetuity of $1 per period is equal to $\dfrac{1}{\text{Interest rate}}$. Thus, with an interest rate of .10, the present value of a perpetuity of $1 per year is $10.

If .10 is the borrowing rate and if .10 is used as the discount rate, we have a net present value of $1,100,000 and the investment is accepted.

PV of benefits:	$200,000 $\left(\dfrac{1}{.10}\right)$ =	$2,000,000
Immediate outlay:		−900,000
	NVP =	$1,100,000

But assume the firm has higher aspirations than merely earning its borrowing rate and sets a required return of .25. We then have:

$$\$200,000 \left(\frac{1}{.25}\right) = \$\ \ 800,000$$
$$-900,000$$
$$\text{NPV} = \$-100,000$$

The NPV is negative, and the innovation would be rejected.

Here we have a prime example of NPV being used in a manner that results in a very bad decision.

Failure to buy the equipment will likely result in the firm not being able to compete because its costs are too high compared to its competitors and will ultimately force it from the market.

There is an extremely high cost in using a decision-making process that employs an excessively high discount rate. It is not a conservative practice. In fact, it is just the opposite. Using high hurdle rates to evaluate efficiency-type of investments is a very risky investment strategy. It jeopardizes the economic viability of the firm since in the long run it wi'l cause the firm to become a high-cost producer.

If firms were to persist in escalating reasonable costs of money upward so that the discount rate did not accurately reflect the cost of the capital being used but rather artificial goals of management, then it would be valid to say that the use of NPV was not effective. The rejoinder is that one is not using NPV if the discount rate does not represent the costs of obtaining capital or the returns from investing capital in other uses (the opportunity cost). A firm might be using the formula $(1 + r)^{-n}$ to transform the future cash flows but, if r is not correctly defined, the numbers obtained are not present values and the NPV method is not being used.

Another difficulty, of a somewhat more minor nature because it is easily fixed, arises when different time periods have different interest rates. Let us return to the example where a $100 investment will return $144 at time 2. Now we will assume that the interest for one period at time 0 is .12, but the one-period interest rate at time 1 for period 2 is .25. Instead of using $(1 + r)^{-2}$ to compute the present value of the $144 received at time 2, we will use $(1 + r_1)^{-1}(1 + r_2)^{-1}$, where r_1 is the one-period rate at time 0 for period 1 and r_2 is the one-period rate at time 1 for period 2. We now have

$$\$144(1.12)^{-1}(1.25)^{-1} = \$ \quad 102.86$$
$$\underline{-100.00}$$
$$\text{NPV} = \$ \qquad 2.86$$

The NPV is now $2.86.

Assume a second investment also costing $100, but this investment will earn cash flows of $40 at time 1 and $96 at time 2. The investment also earns a .20 internal rate of return.

Assume the firm can borrow one-year money at .12, but two-year money costs .22. If we use .12 as the discount rate, the investment would be accepted; but if we used .22, the investment would be rejected. Since the investment has a life of two years there is a temptation to use .22; but this is not correct since some cash flows will be received at time 1. A correct calculation would be:

$$\$96(1.22)^{-2} = \$ \quad 64.50$$
$$\$40(1.12)^{-1} = \qquad 35.71$$
$$\overline{\qquad 100.21}$$
$$\underline{-100.00}$$
$$\text{NPV} = \$ \qquad .21$$

The investment is marginally desirable.

Assume we have computed the one-period rate at time 1 for period 2 to be .329. We then have:

$$\$96(1.12)^{-1}(1.329)^{-1} = \$ \quad 64.50$$
$$\$40(1.12)^{-1} \qquad\qquad = \quad \underline{35.71}$$
$$100.21$$
$$\underline{-100.00}$$
$$NPV = \$ \quad .21$$

This is the same result we obtained previously. Using .22 as the discount rate for cash flows received at time 2 is equivalent to using a discount rate of .12 for period 1 and .329 for period 2.

The NPV method is not restricted to the use of one interest rate. The method is very flexible, and we can easily modify the calculations to incorporate any assumption we wish as to different interest rates in different time periods.

So far the entire discussion has been centered on NPV. The most widely used discounted cash flow procedure is the internal rate of return method (IRR), not NPV. We need to understand IRR and then use it correctly in conjunction with NPV. There is no essential conflict between NPV and IRR, but there is the possibility of introducing errors into the analysis unless we understand how to use IRR.

INTERNAL RATE OF RETURN

The NPV method leads to a dollar measure of value. Many managers prefer a percentage measure because they find they have difficulty interpreting a dollar measure. They claim it is easier to evaluate an investment if they are told that the investment has an internal rate of return (IRR) of .20 than if they are told the net present value is $1,000.

Fortunately, there is no need to disagree on the relative merits of NPV and IRR. In evaluating independent investments with conventional investment-type cash flows, the two measures lead to consistent decisions. In some situations (such as where there are different interest rates in different time periods) the NPV method can be used but IRR cannot be used.

The basic definition of IRR is that it is the rate of interest that causes the NPV of the investment to be equal to zero. Thus the IRR is a very special rate of interest, one that leads to a zero net present value for the investment. Consider the following investment.

359

Time	Cash flow
0	−2,000
1	+1,200
2	+1,440

The investment has an internal rate of return of .20.

Time	Cash	Present value factors	Present values
0	−2,000	1.20^{-0}	−2,000
1	+1,200	1.20^{-1}	+1,000
2	+1,440	1.20^{-2}	+1,000
		NPV =	0

The most useful method for illustrating the economic characteristics of an investment is the net present value profile. Figure 1 shows the net present value profile of the investment being considered.

Figure 1 shows that the investment has a positive present value as long as the rate of discount is less than .20.

FIGURE 1

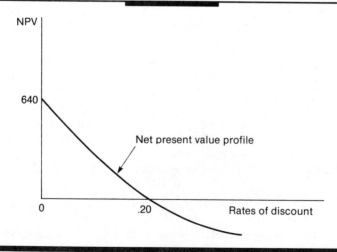

Assume the firm has a hurdle rate of .10. The investment is desirable since its IRR of .20 is greater than the .10 required rate of return. The investment is also desirable since its NPV is positive using .10.

With a conventional independent investment (one or more outlays followed by benefits) both NPV and IRR lead to the same decision. There is not conflict.

Note that the IRR of an investment is the intersection of the net present value profile with the X axis. This is where the NPV is equal to zero.

CALCULATING NPV AND IRR

We are assuming that the cash flows are known with certainty so that we can concentrate on the several discounted cash flow methods that are used.

Let us continue the example where the cash flows of the investment are:

Time	Cash flow
0	−2,000
1	+1,200
2	+1,440

With the net present value method the first step is to decide on a rate of discount and use it. The rate of discount may be called the required rate of return or the hurdle rate. Sometimes it is the borrowing rate and sometimes the weighted average cost of capital. The important thing is that the discount rate is chosen before the cash flows are defined and is then applied to the cash flows of the investment. Assume it is decided that .10 is the correct discount rate to apply to the cash flows of the above investment. We then have:

Time	Cash flow	Present value factors	Present values
0	−2,000	$(1.10)^{-0}$	$−2,000
1	+1,200	$(1.10)^{-1}$	1,091
2	+1,440	$(1.10)^{-2}$	1,190
		Net present value =	$ 281

The net present value is positive, and the investment is acceptable using the net present value method.

But now assume that management wants to use the internal rate of return; therefore, we have to compute it.

The method of solution is to use a trial-and-error approach where different discount rates are used. Assume the first trial uses a .10 rate of discount, and we find that the net present value is $281. Applying the basic definition of the internal rate of return, we want to find the discount rate for which the net present value is equal to zero. Since the net present value using .10 is a positive $281 and since the positive cash flows are all after time 0, we can decrease their present value by increasing the rate of discount being used to discount the cash flows.

Assume the next discount rate that we use is .30. The objective is to find the discount rate for which the net present value is either zero (in which case we have found the internal rate of return) or negative (in which case we will lower the rate of discount to be used on the next trial).

Using .30 as the discount rate we obtain:

Time	Cash flow	Present value factors	Present values
0	−2,000	$(1.30)^{-0}$	$-2,000
1	+1,200	$(1.30)^{-1}$	923
2	+1,440	$(1.30)^{-2}$	852
		Net present value =	$ −225

The net present value is a negative $225.

Now we know that the internal rate of return is between .10 and .30. If we continue the search process, we will narrow in on the .20 that is the internal rate of return.

With the net present value method we chose .10 and then computed the net present value. Frequently, management will want to know how sensitive the net present value is to the choice of the discount rate. When we determine the internal rate of return we go a long way toward answering questions about the sensitivity of the investment to the choice of the discount rate. The advantage of the net present value profile graph is that it shows graphically the effect on net present value of choosing different discount rates (see Figure 2).

FIGURE 2

Net Present Value Profile

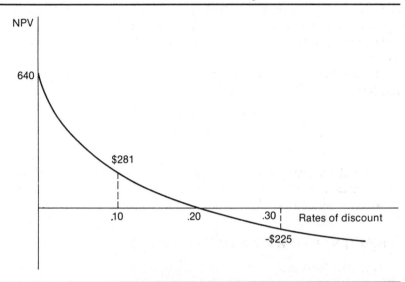

RETURN ON INVESTMENT (ROI)

Several measures of investment worth ignore the time value of money. Is it possible for such measures to be used effectively?

It is possible but not likely. It is more likely that the measures will mislead the decision makers.

Let us return to the investment with the following cash flows:

Time	Cash flow
0	−2,000
1	+1,200
2	+1,440

The measures of income and ROIs of the two periods of use are:

Period	Beginning investment	Revenue	Depreciation	Income	ROI
1	2,000	1,200	1,000	200	.10
2	1,000	1,440	1,000	440	.44

363

The average ROI is $\dfrac{.10 + .44}{2}$ = .27, while the IRR is .20. If the firm required a rate of return of .25, the IRR indicates that it should be rejected, but the average ROI indicates it should be accepted. The average ROI does not have a reliable economic interpretation and should not be used. It does not take into consideration the time value of money.

One incorrect solution that is used to solve the above problem is to compute the ROIs using the gross investment.

Period	Gross investment	Income	ROI
1	2,000	200	.10
2	2,000	440	.22

Now the average ROI is .16. Again, the average ROI is misleading since the IRR is .20, and the smaller average ROI can lead to mistakes in decision making.

SOME INTERPRETATIONS OF IRR

The primary interpretation of an investment's internal rate of return of .20 is that it is analogous to the return earned on a bank account earning .20. The fact that it is the rate of interest that causes the net present value to be equal to zero does not impart a great deal of intuition.

A very good intuitive definition is that the internal rate of return is the highest rate at which funds can be borrowed to finance the investment with the funds used from the investment to repay the loan.

For example, assume the following investment with a .20 internal rate of return:

Time	Cash flow
0	−2,000
1	+1,200
2	+1,440

If $2,000 is borrowed at a cost of .20, we would owe $2,400 at time 1. If $1,200 is repaid, we still owe $1,200. At the end of period 2 we owe $1,200(1.20) = $1,440, and the investment generates exactly enough cash to repay the remaining balance of the debt.

If funds are borrowed at a lower cost than .20, there will be something left over for the investors to consume or invest after repaying the debt.

If an investment has an internal rate of return of .20 and if funds can be borrowed at less than .20, then—by using the right amount of debt—the residual stock equity investment can be made to equal any amount greater than the borrowing rate.

For example, if the above investment is 50 percent, financed with .10 debt, we have:

	0	1	2
Investment	−2,000	+1,200	+1,440
Debt	+1,000	−1,100	—
Stock equity	−1,000	+ 100	+1,440

The internal rate of return of this stock equity stream is a little larger than .25.

If the investment is 90 percent financed with debt, we have:

	0	1	2
Investment	−2,000	+1,200	+1,440
Debt	+1,800	−1,200	− 858
Stock equity	− 200	0	+ 582

The stream has an internal rate of return of .706. As we change the amount of debt or change the rate of debt repayment, we will change the internal rate of return of the stock equity stream. It is dangerous to use the stock equity stream to evaluate investments since it is difficult to evaluate the effect of the changing capital structure.

A POSSIBLE CONFLICT

So far it would appear that there is no possible confusion in the use of internal rate of return. However, there is one very important common complexity that should be understood.

We will define mutually exclusive investments to be two or more investments that are competing for acceptance where only one can be accepted because of basic physical reasons (land can only be used in one way) or because economic logic dictates that only one be used (for example, a house will only have one roof).

Consider the following two mutually exclusive investments:

	Time				Net present
	0	1	2	IRR	value (.10)
A	− 2,000	+1,200	+ 1,440	.20	$281
B	−10,000	+1,200	+11,645	.15	715

Assume the firm's required return is .10. Which investment is more desirable? B requires an additional investment of $8,000 and gives

$10,205 more cash flows at time 2. If $8,000 is borrowed at time 0, the loan can be paid at time 2 with $9,680. The firm accepting B will have $525 more cash at time 2 to spend as it wishes.

Investment A has an internal rate of return of .20 and thus appears to be more desirable than B (with an internal rate of return of .15). But B has a net present value at .10 of $715, and A only has a net present value of $281. B is preferred.

We can use the internal rate of return to compare the two investments but must compute the internal rate of return of the incremental cash flows (B − A or A − B) to determine whether the increment is desirable. For example, B − A gives:

		Time			
	0	1	2	IRR	NPV (.10)
B − A	−8,000	0	+10,205	.129	$434

Investment A is acceptable, and investment B − A is also acceptable. By taking both B − A and A as being acceptable we are really undertaking B.

	Time		
	0	1	2
A	− 2,000	+1,200	+ 1,440
B − A	− 8,000	0	+10,205
A + (B − A)	−10,000	+1,200	+11,645

This bottom line is investment B.

If A is undertaken, there will be $8,000 left over to invest to earn .10. This will lead to $9,680 at time 2. By adding this $9,680 to the $1,440 from investment A we would have $10,120. Investment B gives $11,645 at time 2, thus B is better than investing in a combination of A plus a return of .10 on the leftover $8,000. The $1,200 at time 1 occurs with both A and B and thus can be left out of the calculations.

THE REINVESTMENT RATE

The internal rate of return can be computed without making an assumption about reinvestment rates. But if in the above example we choose A or B, we are implicitly making an assumption about the return earned on invested funds.

Assume that leftover funds can be invested at time 0 to earn .14 for two years, and funds invested at time 1 for one year will earn .14. Investing $10,000 in B will lead to:

$$\$1,200(1.14) + \$11,645 = \$13,013$$

at time 2.

Investing \$2,000 in A plus \$8,000 in a two-year .14 investment will lead to:

$$\$8,000(1.14)^2 + 1,200(1.14) + 1,440 = 10,397 + 1,368 + 1,440 = \$13,205.$$

Investment A plus the .14 yielding investment of \$8,000 is better than a \$10,000 investment in B. This verifies the fact that we determined above that B − A was only acceptable if the cost of money was less than .129.

OTHER COMPLEXITIES

We want to review other complexities with the use of internal rate of return.

1. Changing interest rates through time.
2. Investments with more than one internal rate of return.
3. The internal rate of return does not consider the length of time the funds are invested.

If each time period has a different interest rate, then the application of the net present value method is straightforward. Instead of $(1 + r)^{-n}$, one multiplies the cash flow by the present value factor $(1 + r)^{-1}(1 + r_2)^{-1} \ldots (1 + r_{n-1})^{-1}(1 + r_n)^{-1}$. If the internal rate of return method is used, we might or might not be able to define the required rate of return. The procedure would be very hard (or impossible) to implement.

If the cash flows of successive periods change signs (for example, go from an outlay to positive cash flows back to negative cash flows), it is possible that the cash flow stream has more than one internal rate of return. Consider the following investment:

	Time	
0	*1*	*2*
−100	+300	−200

This stream has two internal rates of return. One is zero (indicating a very bad investment), and the other is 100 percent (indicating a very desirable investment). Rather than attempting to unravel this confusion, a switch to net present value indicates that the net present value

367

is positive as long as the rate of discount being used is between 0 and 100 percent.

The failure of the internal rate of return to consider the length in time of the investment is illustrated by the choice between an investment of $1,000 with an internal rate of return of 50 percent but where the investment matures the next day, and an investment of $1,000 with an internal rate of return of 20 percent maturing in one year. A high return for a very short period may be less desirable than a long-lived investment with a smaller return. The net present value method can easily solve the problem.

There is one problem that we have to face with the use of net present value. If the lives of the alternatives are unequal, it may be necessary to make the alternatives comparable with respect to the time periods studied.

Consider the following two alternatives:

	0	1	2	NPV (.10)
A	−1,000	1,210		100
B	−2,000	1,265	1,210	150

B would seem more desirable than A. But now consider what happens if at time 1 it is possible to reinvest $1,000 and earn $1,210 at time 2.

0	1	2	NPV (.10)
−1,000	+1,210		100.00
	−1,000	+1,210	90.90
−1,000	+ 210	+1,210	190.90

Investment A with reinvestment at time 1 has a net present value of $190.90, and this is better than investment B. One has to be careful to compute the present value of the appropriate set of cash flows.

TERMINAL VALUE

Instead of computing the net present value, one can compute the net terminal value. If the net present value is positive—indicating that the investment should be accepted—the net terminal value will also be positive.

Under what circumstances might we want to use the terminal value? The net terminal value will be larger than the net present value, thus it might be more persuasive. For example, assume that the net present value using a .20 interest rate is $10 million for a 20-year investment. The net terminal value would be

$$\$10 \text{ million } (1.20)^{20} = \$38,338,000.$$

To have $38,338,000 at time 20 might impress top management more than having $10 million of net present value.

WHICH PROCEDURE?

Which procedure should a company use to evaluate investments? Is IRR or NPV preferred?

The recommendation is clear. Use the net present value profile and label clearly the internal rate of return and the net present values for interesting interest rates.

If the investment decision is to make an accept or reject decision for an independent investment with conventional cash flows (one or more outlays followed by periods of benefits), the net present value method and the internal rate of return will give the same accept or reject decision. Figure 3 shows that if an investment is acceptable with net present value, it is also acceptable using the internal rate of return. To be explicit, assume an investment has positive cash flows of $1,200 at time 1 and an outlay of $1,000 at time 0.

FIGURE 3

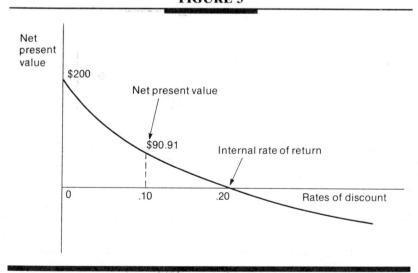

Figure 3 shows that both the net present values (for several rates of discount) and the internal rate of return can be indicated, and a decision maker should not be confused by the information.

When we consider mutually exclusive investments, it is possible to be confused by the recommendations of the net present value method and the internal rate of return method. It is possible to prefer the investment with a higher net present value and a lower internal rate of return than a second investment. Figure 4 shows a situation where

FIGURE 4

Two Mutually Exclusive Investments

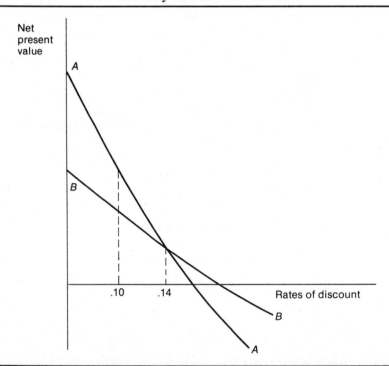

there are two mutually exclusive investments, and A is preferred to B if .10 is the appropriate discount rate, even though B has a larger internal rate of return. At a discount rate larger than .14, investment B is preferred to investment A.

If the independent investment being considered has more than one internal rate of return or where the firm wants to use different discount rates for different time periods, the net present value method dominates the internal rate of return method.

If we shift from certain to uncertain cash flows, some managers will prefer to know that the internal rate of return is .20 when there is a .10 required return, rather than knowing that the net present value is $1 million. Both measures have information, and it would be foolish not to give both measures to the managers making the decision.

We can conclude that the choice between internal rate of return and net present value methods is much less important than understanding the calculations of both methods.

If we are comparing any method that uses discounted cash flow with a method that does not use discounted cash flow (such as return on investment), then there is a clear preference. ROI (income divided by investment) should not be used to evaluate investment alternatives. Since it omits time value considerations, it is a flawed calculation.

OTHER DIFFICULTIES

Some critics of NPV cite the difficulties of forecasting interest rates and inflation rates.

The interest rate problem can be solved by borrowing funds with the same duration as the investment. If interest rates then go down, the value of the debt goes up—but the present value of the asset goes up about the same amount. If interest rates go up, the present value of the debt goes down—and the present value of the investment's cash flows also goes down.

If this type of hedging is not attractive because of the inherent risks of debt, then it is true that there is an interest rate risk. But this risk exists because the investment has a life longer than one year—not because of using NPV as the method of analysis.

While the future rate of inflation is difficult to forecast, we are helped somewhat by the fact that inflation will affect both revenues and costs.

Assume we have made the following forecast:

Revenues	120
Costs	110
Net cash flow	10

The net cash flow is forecasted to be $10. Now assume a 20 percent surprise inflation takes place, and the following cash flows take place:

Revenues	144.00
Costs	123.20
Net cash flow	20.80

371

The revenues go up by $24, but the net cash flow only increases by $10.80. Taxes would further decrease the absolute change in cash flows.

But, more important, if the forecast of inflation and interest rates is difficult to make, this is no reason to abandon the most effective means of incorporating the best forecasts into the decision process.

CONCLUSIONS

We stop short of considering the primary problem of applying the net present value—uncertainty. But with the assumption of certainty we find that the net present value is an extremely powerful tool. If we shifted to an uncertainty assumption, we would find that any sensible procedure would build on some discounted cash flow procedure. One has to take the timing of the cash flows into consideration if sensible decisions are to be made.

If we are going to be intelligently critical of practice, then we have to be critical of how the method is being applied. The use of excessively high discount rates can lead to bad decision making.

REFERENCES

Bierman, Harold Jr., and Seymour Smidt. *The Capital Budgeting Decision.* 5th ed. New York: Macmillan, 1980.

Gitman, Lawrence J., and John R. Forrester, Jr. "Forecasting and Evaluation Practices and Performance: A Survey of Capital Budgeting." *Financial Management,* Fall 1977.

Hayes, R. H., and D. A. Garvin. "Managing as if Tomorrow Mattered." *Harvard Business Review,* May–June 1982, pp. 71–79.

Klammer, Thomas. "Empirical Evidence of the Adoption of Sophisticated Capital Budgeting Techniques." *Journal of Business,* July 1972, pp. 387–97.

Levy, Haim, and Marshall Sarnat. *Capital Investment and Financial Decisions.* Englewood Cliffs, N.J.: Prentice-Hall, 1978.

Lorie, James H., and Leonard J. Savage. "Three Problems in Rationing Capital." *Journal of Business,* October 1955, pp. 227–39.

Petty, J. William; David F. Scott, Jr.; and Monroe M. Bird. "The Capital Expenditure Decision-Making Process of Large Corporations." *Engineering Economist,* Spring 1975, pp. 159–72.

18

Evaluating a Project: The Use of Stock Price as a Criterion*

Alan M. Cody

and

Timothy J. McMahon

For Mitchell and Company

INTRODUCTION

*I*n a recently published survey of over 600 chief executives, *Business Week* found that 60 percent believe that their companies are undervalued by the stock market.[1] The growing number of leveraged buyouts of publicly held firms, whose management feels that private stock ownership of the company is preferable to being public, is further evidence of this undervaluation.

Executives blame the short-term earnings per share orientation of institutional investors for their own reluctance to pursue investments

---

 * "Evaluating a Project: The Use of Stock Price as a Criterion," © 1985 by Mitchell and Company.

and programs of long-term value to their companies. In the August 13, 1984 cover story of *Business Week,* the chief executive officer of Gulf + Western Industries, Martin Davis, is quoted as saying, "There are no long-term stockholders anymore."

Operations-oriented executives do not always agree that stock price improvement can or should be made. They often feel that stock price is determined by irrational forces beyond their control. Or they may believe that actions taken by management to raise stock price are unethical attempts to manipulate the market. Some may argue that stock price is simply an external measurement to watch rather than manage.

Mitchell and Company's research has shown that Wall Street, however irrational it sometimes may seem, reacts predictably and rationally to certain strategies to improve operations and stock prices. Nor are many stock price improvement efforts unethical. The market is not fooled by and does not reward substanceless financial schemes. The investment community does, however, respond to actions which produce solid economic benefits. Management's being responsive to how the stock market values companies should be viewed as part of its obligation to shareholders. Finally, those who consider stock price as just an external measure providing feedback overlook its role in determining performance. The need for America to reindustrialize would not be as pressing today if higher stock prices had already given more companies access to lower-cost equity capital for reinvestment in operations. Improving stock price contributes powerfully to the ability to form new capital and to expand borrowing power.

Many companies whose executives believe they are undervalued are profitable and growing their earnings. If so, why aren't they being valued more highly by investors? Or, to put it another way, why do some companies and not others have high valuations that give them access to lower-cost equity capital? Recent research on the stock price performance of similar companies reveals new findings which can be applied to capital investment decisions.

VALUATION INFLUENCE—AN EXAMPLE

The following example compares the stock price performance of Kimberly-Clark Corporation to that of James River Corporation from 1975 to 1983. These two companies operate in the same industry. Yet, the differences in the financial policies which they practice have led to an average annual growth rate in the price of the stock of James River of 36.91 percent—nearly three times that of Kimberly-Clark over the same period (13.16 percent).

FIGURE 1

Kimberly-Clark Compared to James River: James River Objectives

1. Maintain return on equity at 20 percent level.
2. Produce products that balance cyclicality.
3. Produce products with a high degree of value added.
4. Maintain high growth through acquisitions and operating strategies.

Source: *James River 1982–83 Annual Report.*

As Figure 1 shows, James River emphasized in its objectives a return on equity of 20 percent, growth, and producing products with high value added, which balance the cyclicality of commodity paper products. In Figure 2, Kimberly-Clark, by contrast, emphasized growth in earnings per share and real growth in dividends per share and maintained debt at 28 to 32 percent of capital.

FIGURE 2

Kimberly-Clark Compared to James River: Kimberly-Clark Objectives

1. Growth in earnings per share of 11 to 14 percent.
2. Have real growth in dividends per share after inflation.
3. Total debt is 28 to 32 percent of capital.

Source: *Kimberly-Clark 1982 and 1983 Annual Reports.*

As Figures 3, 4, and 5 show, James River leveraged a lower return on capital into a higher return on equity and grew its book value per share faster by paying lower dividends as a percent of income than did Kimberly-Clark. The higher stock price growth, which James River has achieved by emphasizing high return on common equity and growth in common equity per share, reflects a pattern of valuation for large pulp and paperboard companies, as shown in Figure 6.

375

FIGURE 3

Performance Comparison

	Stock Price	
	Kimberly-Clark	James River
1975	$15.28	$ 2.68
1976	20.36	3.31
1977	21.56	3.48
1978	22.26	6.86
1979	22.18	8.92
1980	23.58	9.40
1981	31.92	11.90
1982	32.14	18.56
1983	41.09	33.09
Average annual compounded growth	13.16%	36.91%

FIGURE 4

Performance Comparison
1975–1983

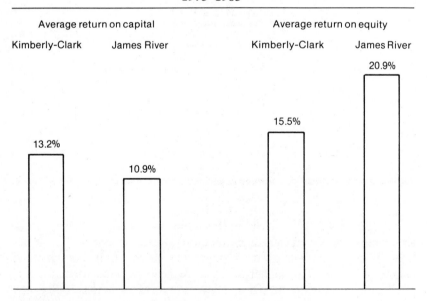

Average return on capital — Kimberly-Clark 13.2%, James River 10.9%

Average return on equity — Kimberly-Clark 15.5%, James River 20.9%

Source: © 1984 Mitchell and Company.

FIGURE 5

Performance Comparison
1975–1983

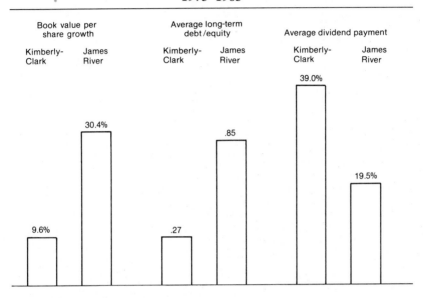

Source: © 1984 Mitchell and Company.

VALUATION ANALYSIS

This relative equity valuation chart can be computed for any one of the many industry groups into which the investment community classifies companies for trading in their stock. The vertical scale measures average annual stock price divided by common equity per share plotted on a logarithmic scale. The horizontal scale measures an average return on common equity over several years. The weighting of the average reflects the particular manner in which investors form expectations about the future performance of companies in that industry from recently reported results. A line fitted to the points in the chart estimates the valuation accorded to each company in the industry as a function of its average return on equity, as shown in the lower-righthand corner of the chart. Companies in the industry have the majority of sales, earnings, and assets in the paper industry.

This value relationship has been confirmed from extensive observation of the trading and value patterns for the common stock of pub-

FIGURE 6

Pulp and Paper/Paperboard Companies
Revenues over $2 Billion
Relative Equity Valuation—1983

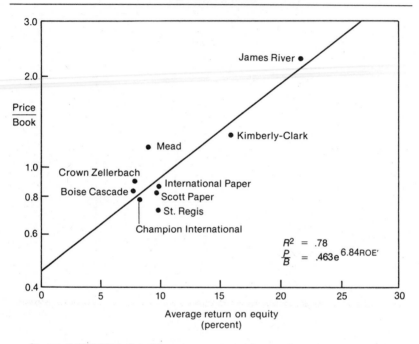

Source: © 1984 Mitchell and Company.

licly owned companies. This occurs even for diversified companies involved in several businesses. For example, Figures 7 and 8 show that the valuation of Varian Associates follows closely the pattern of valuation for other electronics companies despite the fact that approximately half of Varian's sales are derived from other industries (instruments and medical products) and markets. The large percentage of earnings derived from the electronic devices segment leads investors to value and trade this company's stock together with other similar companies in the electronics industry. Where a majority of activities are not concentrated into a stock market category, as in Varian's case, a diversified company will often trade in a conglomerate grouping.

FIGURE 7

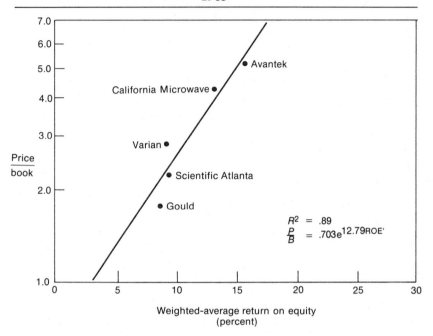

Electronics Industry
Relative Equity Valuation
1983

Price/book vs. Weighted-average return on equity (percent)

- Avantek
- California Microwave
- Varian
- Scientific Atlanta
- Gould

$R^2 = .89$

$\dfrac{P}{B} = .703e^{12.79ROE'}$

Weighted-average return on equity
(percent)

Source: © 1984 Mitchell and Company.

FIGURE 8

Varian Associates
Results by Industry Segment
1983

	Percent of total		
	Sales	Pretax Operating Profits	Identifiable Assets
Electronic devices	47.9%	72.8%	42.7%
Semiconductor equipment	15.8	11.1	20.7
Analytical instruments	16.3	3.7	18.1
Medical and industrial products	20.9	16.1	18.5
Adjustments and eliminations	(0.9)	(3.7)	0.0
Total	100%	100%	100%

Source: Varian Associates *1983 Annual Report.* © 1984 Mitchell and Company.

THE IMPORTANCE OF COMPANY FOCUS

Mitchell and Company has identified more than 450 industry stock price groups. Each group is characterized by a stock price curve which relates each company's price-to-book ratio to its historical weighted-

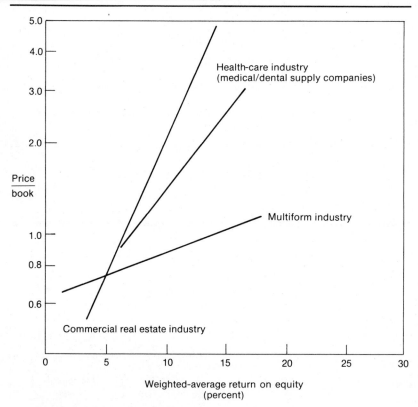

FIGURE 9

Industry Curves
Relative Equity Valuation
1983

Source: © 1984 Mitchell and Company.

average return on equity (Figure 9). Some industries have steep-sloped curves which make gains in return on equity highly leveraged in stock price growth. Industries having flat-sloped curves mean a change in return on equity does not lead to a change in price-to-book ratio.

380

Acquisitions and divestitures can be useful in changing the market's perception of a company so that it moves from a flat-sloped industry to a steep-sloped one. Gould Inc. is a good illustration of this. By divesting its battery division and several other electrical businesses, Gould has gone from being valued as a traditional electrical equipment manufacturer to trading as a high-technology electronics company. Of course, companies can go the other way as well. When Sun Chemical Corporation had acquired approximately 20 percent of Chromalloy American Corporation, a highly diversified conglomerate, it changed its industry identity from chemicals to multiform, moving from a fairly attractive industry to a less attractive one.

Because the valuation patterns vary by industry, investment policies which change the mix of the company's business and hence its industry identity with the investment community can dramatically alter shareholder value. Direct measurement of the valuation patterns of companies in hundreds of different industry segments allows management to assess the impact of its financial policies on the valuation of its company.

In the case of large pulp and paperboard companies, 78 percent of the variation in the ratio of market to book value is explained by changes in average of return on equity, while in the case of electronics equipment companies, 89 percent of the variation is explained. Thus, policies which lead to higher book value per share growth and return on equity for a company tend to increase its valuation. No two companies will have the same sensitivity for these variables due to differences in profitability and industry valuation. These policies can include swapping preferred for common stock to reduce the common equity base on which earnings grow or allowing dividends to grow more slowly in an economic recovery, building book value per share faster from profitable investments in new assets.

Comparisons of similar companies in hundreds of different industry groups show that stock performance is best when return on equity and book value per share grow rapidly, and a company is identified with an industry for which performance is given high value by investors. The relative importance of book value per share growth and return on equity varies considerably by industry, as shown in Figure 9.

Many conglomerates and companies in below-average attractiveness industries have highly profitable subsidiaries in above-average attraction industries which, as a result of being part of the parent, are undervalued. The stock price of a conglomerate may even reflect what has been called a "conglomerate discount"—a kind of penalty investors assess for being unable to make sense out of a diversified combination of businesses.

381

CHANGING COMPANY FOCUS

Companies that change their industry identity—either through investment policies which emphasize one business segment versus another or through acquisitions—can realize large changes in valuation. Monsanto Company dramatically increased its ability to reward its shareholders by reducing its dependence on fibers and becoming a specialty chemical company (based on its agricultural chemicals businesses) where the shareholder rewards for better performance are higher than in basic petrochemicals. (See Figure 10.)

Even if other businesses are a significant share of a company's total earnings, its value is usually determined by the pattern of its predominant (60 percent or more) business area. Capital investment programs, which alter this mix, change valuation. Diversified companies, with businesses whose industry valuation patterns are different, usually can improve their valuation significantly by developing (through internal investment or acquisitions and divestitures) a predominant industry business. With nearly 30 percent of companies selling below all book value in mid-1984, the possibilities for value improvement should be very great indeed.

KEY LESSONS OF VALUATION IMPROVEMENT

There are, therefore, three major variables which can lead to improved valuation of a publicly held company. A company must have consistent and growing return on equity; it must grow its book value per share; and it must associate itself with industries where success in the first two measures will produce maximum gains in valuation. An awareness of how a company's investment decisions will impact these three variables allows a company to set investment objectives and select a portfolio of investment projects which produce the greatest gains in stock market valuation, thus reducing the company's cost of capital relative to competitors.

THE IMPACT AND COMPANY FOCUS ON CAPITAL BUDGETING

Traditional approaches to investment analysis and capital budgeting emphasize present value and internal rate of return analysis. Adding a perspective on industry identity and valuation to these project-by-project financial analyses allows management to achieve greater gains in value by choosing profitable projects and managing the mix to keep all profits valued in the industry of greatest investor attractiveness.

FIGURE 10

Monsanto Became a Specialty Chemical Company through Reducing Dependence on Fibers

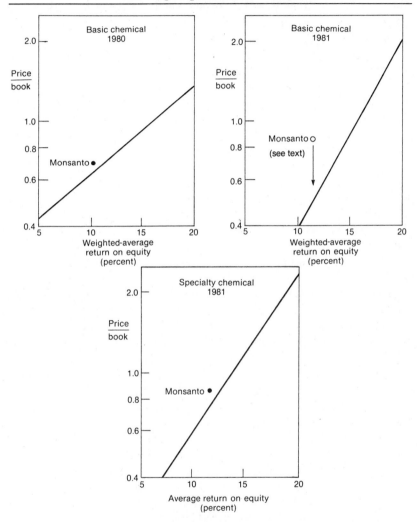

Source: © 1984 Mitchell and Company.

While high growth in book value per share and high return on equity lead to higher valuation, excessive short-term management of earnings, investment communications programs without action, and expensive acquisitions which confuse industry identity do not. Companies like James River which manage to achieve consistently high returns on equity and rapid growth in book value per share outperform their competitors and reward their shareholders handsomely.

Understanding how the stock market values companies, as described above, allows management to assess the impact of its alternative investments on its valuation and ability to create rewards for its shareholders. This methodology assumes that a separate and complete financial analysis has been made for each individual investment project, so that the contribution of each project to the future net income of the entire company can be estimated.

Because the valuation of a company is so closely affected by its industry identity, grouping investment projects by business segment and assessing the extent to which they would tend to change the industry with which the company is currently associated by the investment community is the logical starting point for evaluating the impact on valuation of these projects.

Generally speaking, a company will tend to be identified (and valued) within an industry group (such as specialty chemicals) which corresponds to the business segment from which it derives approximately 60 percent of its sales, earnings, and assets—with earnings being the most important. Therefore, the investment valuation described here will be most useful to companies that are diversified or have more than one line of business. Even the valuation of a company participating in a single line of business, however, will be affected by the extent to which its chosen investment projects alter its return on equity and growth in book value per share—a function of the profitability of the project and the method of financing it.

For a company with two or more lines of business, the potential exists to choose investment projects which, by virtue of their contribution to earnings by business segment, alter the percentage of total revenues, assets, and earnings by industry group—thus affecting the way in which the company is valued and perhaps also the return on equity and book value per share.

Therefore, the purpose of a valuation analysis of capital spending programs is to determine the change (if any) in the industry from which the company derives approximately 60 percent of its sales, earnings, and assets after any proposed combination of investment programs is chosen for the capital budget.

Figure 11 shows several major investment projects for a hypotheti-

FIGURE 11

Diversified Holdings, Inc.
($ millions)

	1985	1986	1987	1988	1989
Revenues					
Real estate					
Investment 1	$110.0	$137.5	$178.8	$200.5	$222.5
Investment 2	90.0	99.0	108.9	125.2	225.0
Investment 3	120.0	132.0	147.8	184.8	249.5
Health care					
Investment 1	65.0	81.3	101.6	130.1	169.1
Investment 2	50.0	57.5	71.9	93.5	129.2
Operating profit*					
Real estate					
Investment 1	5.3	6.7	8.7	9.7	10.8
Investment 2	4.9	5.4	5.9	6.8	12.2
Investment 3	7.1	7.8	8.8	11.0	14.8
Health care					
Investment 1	7.0	8.8	11.0	14.0	18.3
Investment 2	5.4	6.2	7.8	10.1	13.6
Identifiable assets					
Real estate					
Investment 1	115.5	144.4	187.7	210.5	233.6
Investment 2	94.5	104.0	114.3	131.5	236.3
Investment 3	126.0	138.6	155.2	194.0	262.0
Health care					
Investment 1	61.8	77.2	96.5	123.6	160.6
Investment 2	47.5	54.6	68.3	88.8	119.9

* Operating profit includes interest cost incurred when financing investments.

Source: © 1984 Mitchell and Company.

cal company—Diversified Holdings, Inc.—grouped by business segment and their contribution to revenues, earnings, and assets projected by year for the next five years. Each project also is identified by the industry group with which it would tend to identify the company were it a majority of the company's business.

The relative attractiveness of each of these industry groups or business segments also is shown in Figure 9. As should be readily obvious, highly profitable projects which are associated with less attractive industries can be highly valuable to a company by virtue of their contribution to improved return on equity and growth in book value per share if the company maintains an overall identification with an industry group which has a high valuation pattern.

Selection of projects must be done with a view toward maintaining at least 60 percent of sales, earnings, and assets within an industry group with the highest valuation pattern of any of the company's business segments. Therefore, the most profitable projects from the most attractive industry group should be chosen until the profitability of the most profitable project from the next most attractive industry segment exceeds the last project chosen in the most attractive industry group. Then these projects should be chosen from all remaining industry segments as long as the projects exceed the company's cost of capital, which is calculated based on its principal industry identification.

As shown in Figure 12, Exhibit B, were the company to accept two

FIGURE 12

Exhibit A
Diversified Holdings, Inc.
($ millions)

	1985	1986	1987	1988	1989
Revenues					
Real estate	$180.0	$201.6	$229.8	$264.3	$306.6
Health care	130.0	145.6	166.0	190.9	221.4
Specialty chemical	90.0	100.8	114.9	132.1	153.3
Total	$400.0	$448.0	$510.7	$587.3	$681.3
Operating profit					
Real estate	$ 10.7	$ 12.0	$ 13.7	$ 15.7	$ 18.2
Health care	14.0	15.7	17.9	20.6	23.9
Specialty chemical	7.3	8.2	9.3	10.7	12.4
Total	$ 32.0	$ 35.9	$ 40.9	$ 47.0	$ 54.5
Identifiable assets					
Real estate	$207.0	$231.8	$264.3	$303.9	$352.6
Health care	123.5	138.3	157.7	181.4	210.3
Specialty chemical	99.0	110.9	126.4	145.4	168.6
Total	$429.5	$481.0	$548.4	$630.7	$731.5

Source: © 1984 Mitchell and Company.

FIGURE 12

Exhibit B
Diversified Holdings, Inc. with Two Additional Investments in Commercial Real Estate*
($ millions)

	1985	1986	1987	1988	1989
Revenues					
Real estate	$410.0	$471.1	$556.4	$ 649.6	$ 778.6
Health care	130.0	145.6	166.0	190.9	221.4
Specialty chemical	90.0	100.8	114.9	132.1	153.3
Total	$630.0	$717.5	$837.3	$ 972.6	$1153.3
Operating profit					
Real estate	$ 23.1	$ 26.5	$ 31.2	$ 36.4	$ 43.8
Health care	14.0	15.7	17.9	20.6	23.9
Specialty chemical	7.3	8.2	9.3	10.7	12.4
Total	$ 44.4	$ 50.4	$ 58.4	$ 67.7	$ 80.1
Identifiable assets					
Real estate	$448.5	$514.8	$607.2	$ 708.4	$ 848.2
Health care	123.5	138.3	157.7	181.4	210.3
Specialty chemical	99.0	110.9	126.4	145.4	168.6
Total	$671.0	$764.0	$891.3	$1035.2	$1227.1

Assumes: Real estate investments 1 and 2.
* A company is valued in the industry from which approximately 60 percent of revenues, profits, and assets is derived. In this particular example, the operating profit of the company's real estate business falls short of 60 percent. However, the revenues and assets exceed 60 percent; and, in the real estate industry in particular, this schedule would clearly qualify Diversified Holdings, Inc. as a real estate company.
Source: © 1984 Mitchell and Company.

---

investment projects in commercial real estate, this would most likely change the company's valuation pattern from the multiform to the commercial real estate industry. This will allow the company to realize a much more attractive valuation for their shareholders of the changes in performance implied by the projected profitability of its investments. This is exemplified in Figure 13, Exhibit B, by the pro forma projections of net income, book value per share, and return on equity. The company can realize substantial gains in valuation from this schedule of investments when compared to a base case forecast, Exhibit A, or to

FIGURE 13

	Exhibit A Diversified Holdings, Inc.*				
	1985	1986	1987	1988	1989
Net income	$ 32.0M	$ 35.9M	$ 40.9M	$ 47.0M	$ 54.5M
Common equity	$206.5M	$242.4M	$283.3M	$330.3M	$384.8M
Return on equity	15.5%	14.8%	14.4%	14.2%	14.2%
Weighted-average return on equity	15.2%	15.0%	14.9%	14.6%	14.5%
Price to book	1.07	1.06	1.06	1.04	1.04
Market value	$221.0M	$256.9M	$300.3M	$343.5M	$400.2M

* Valued on multiform industry curve, as shown in Figure 9.
Source: © 1984 Mitchell and Company.

FIGURE 13

	Exhibit B Diversified Holdings, Inc. with Two Additional Investments in Commercial Real Estate*				
	1985	1986	1987	1988	1989
Net income	$ 44.4M	$ 50.4M	$ 58.4M	$ 67.7M	$ 80.1M
Common equity	$ 286.5M	$ 336.9M	$ 395.3M	$ 463.0M	$ 543.1M
Return on equity	15.5%	15.0%	14.8%	14.6%	14.8%
Weighted-average return on equity	15.1%	15.1%	15.1%	15.0%	14.9%
Price to book	5.67	5.67	5.67	5.56	5.46
Market value	$1,624.5M	$1,910.2M	$2,241.4M	$2,574.4M	$2,965.3M

Assumes: Real estate investments 1 and 3 from Figure 11.
* Valued on commercial real estate industry curve, as shown in Figure 9.
Source: © 1984 Mitchell and Company.

FIGURE 13

Exhibit C
Diversified Holdings, Inc. with an Additional Investment in Commercial Real Estate and an Additional Investment in Health Care*

	1985	1986	1987	1988	1989
Net income	$ 43.9M	$ 50.1M	$ 62.0M	$ 72.7M	$ 90.7M
Common equity	$283.2M	$333.3M	$395.3M	$468.0M	$558.7M
Return on equity	15.5%	15.0%	15.7%	15.5%	16.2%
Weighted-average return on equity	15.2%	15.1%	15.3%	15.4%	15.7%
Price to book	1.07	1.06	1.07	1.07	1.08
Market value	$303.0M	$353.3M	$423.0M	$500.8M	$603.4M

Assumes: Real estate investment 2 and health investment 1.
* Valued on multiform industry curve, as shown in Figure 9.
Source: © 1984 Mitchell and Company.

a second case, Exhibit C, associated with a choice of one investment in the health-care business and one in commercial real estate.

FINANCING TECHNIQUES AND VALUE IMPROVEMENT

Finally, the choice of financing vehicles for funding the entire set of investment projects can have a dramatic impact on valuation by using debt, preferred stock, and even other forms of off-balance-sheet financing—discussed below—to allow earnings to grow on a smaller base of shares outstanding and total equity than if common equity were to be issued any more than necessary to preserve borrowing power and take advantage of favorable market conditions.

Recent evidence suggests that companies can make use of special issues of preferred stock to raise funds required for investments and retirements of common stock. This is especially useful to companies that have little unused debt capacity but nevertheless wish to obtain the benefits of the secondary leverage which preferred stock can provide. These issues of preferred stock can be designed with special features such as adjustable rates, growth-adjusted dividends, and foreign currency dividends which lower the required dividend yield to a point close to the aftertax cost of debt. Because the valuation of the company's common equity per share is so heavily dependent on return on common equity, the leverage provided by the use of these special issues of preferred stock creates additional benefits for the common equity shareholders of the company. This also allows current shareholders, who may have different risk and return objectives, to continue to participate in the company's growth and performance.

SUMMARY

Current research on valuation of publicly held companies suggests that three variables are important in understanding how investment policy may affect the valuation of the company.

1. The investor attractiveness of the industry from which the company derives approximately 60 percent of its sales, earnings, and assets.
2. The average return on equity of the company over the past several years with special weight given to the most recent years.
3. The growth in common equity per share of the company.

Investment projects and overall investment programs should be carefully chosen and evaluated to determine the extent to which they and the way they are financed affect these variables. Of central importance is the need to set objectives for investment policy in diversified companies which ensure that at least 60 percent of sales, earnings, and assets are associated with the most investor-attractive industry group of all the business segments in which the company participates. At the same time, continued development of other businesses with high returns, even though derived from less attractive industry groups, contributes to higher return on equity and greater value by virtue of the company's overall identification with a high-value industry.

None of these findings should be interpreted as constraining the development of promising businesses which take more time to generate profits, are small, and have a minimal overall impact on a company's earnings and return on equity; they can be pursued with little danger of shareholder value destruction. In the case of emerging businesses with larger losses, alternative ways ranging from the use of limited partnerships to joint ventures can be used to separate the financial reporting of these ventures from the company until they can generate a significant contribution to value. These and other methods listed in Figure 14 have the advantage of eliminating or minimizing the impact of the ventures on current profitability and raising funds directly from investors whose

FIGURE 14

Financing Strategies for Promising Businesses Which Are Currently Unprofitable

1. Enter into a joint venture.
   Equity infusion.
   Off parent's financial statements.
   Additional expertise.

2. Secure advanced contracts (that is, OEMs).
   Capital future revenues.
   Future revenues.
   Provides financing opportunities.

3. Sell/license the rights to provide an integral or add-on product or service.
   Capital.
   Future revenues.
   Provides financial opportunities.

4. Establish a limited partnership.
   Off parent's financial statements.
   Shift risk of the venture.
   Capital.
   Some income to parent.

5. Set up as a separate entity and seek funds from corporate and institutional investors.
   Capital.
   Lower risk.

6. Utilize government funds and programs set up for the research and commercialization of new ideas and technologies.
   Source of funds/incentives.
   Lower risks.

7. Acquire a related company that enhances the prospects and profitability of the business.
   Horizontal/vertical integration.
   Improved financial condition.
   Provides financing opportunities.

8. Raise capital by restructuring parent's balance sheet and portfolio of businesses.
   Sale of businesses.
   Partial spin-off.
   Growth adjustable.

9. Reassess potential value of the business to the company versus its value to some other company.
   Takeover target.
   Opportunity costs compared to other businesses in the portfolio.
   Divestiture.

Source: © 1984 Mitchell and Company.

risk orientation better matches these projects than the average share-holder's does.

NOTE

[1] *Business Week,* "Companies Feel Underrated by the Street," February 20, 1984, p. 14.

19

Investment Appraisal: How to Develop a Comprehensive Appraisal Program

Mike Kaufman

Corporate Finance Associates

*I*nvestment appraisal is the heart of the capital budgeting process. But there is wide disagreement as to purposes, methods, and criteria. While a good deal has been written supporting or attacking various schools of thought, not much has been done to organize the tools that are available. This chapter is an attempt to fill that gap. It's designed to help the capital budgeting practitioner tailor specific methods for appraising proposed capital investments. The practitioner might be a staff analyst, a policy or decision maker, or a prospective source of funds.

THE VARIABLES

The method we choose to appraise a capital proposal should be sensitive to at least these factors:

1. Project type.
2. Project stage.
3. Organizational role of the appraiser.
4. Values of the firm.
5. The situation.
6. Quality of the information available.

Project Type

Each corporation has its own means of classifying capital proposals. Some schemes distinguish economic and noneconomic projects. *Economic* projects comprise revenue-enhancing or cost-reducing investments. *Noneconomic* projects are represented by compulsory investments with no clear financial return. Other schemes distinguish *strategic* projects with comprehensive long-term effects on the firm from *tactical* or routine projects that are necessary to maintain operations.

A further means of project classification is by type of *business*. Multibusiness firms sort their projects by profit centers according to the primary business impacts of the investments.

Project *purpose* is the usual lowest level of classification:

1. Improvement of operations.
   a. Replacement of worn and obsolete assets.
   b. Productivity improvement.
   c. Other cost reduction.
2. Expansion of capacity.
   a. For existing products.
   b. For new products.
3. Compliance.
   a. With legislation or regulations: EPA, OSHA, etc.
   b. With internal policy, for example, product quality and working conditions.

A given project can be further typed by the *size* of its investment outlay and its relative risk. These characteristics usually determine the organizational level that approves expenditures. The choice of an appraisal method or methods should account for all of a project's important characteristics.

Project Stage

The magnitude and complexity of a project usually determine the number of stages it passes through, from initial conception to start-up.

A major capital project usually goes through some version of this common sequence:

1. Project definition.
   a. Strategic plan.
   b. Research and development.
   c. Business plan.
   d. Project alternatives.
2. Economic decision.
   a. Capital budget.
   b. Capital appropriation.
3. Execution.
   a. Design, procurement, and construction.
   b. Start-up.

The Appraiser

Project appraisal takes place at several levels of the firm. It is also done by outsiders, for example, prospective lenders or investors. For our purposes the following organizational roles are representative.

1. Project sponsor—for example, an operating division manager.
2. Division staff analyst—the sponsor's analytic resource.
3. Intermediate approving authority—for example, business unit general manager.
4. Final approving authority—a policy-level executive or board member.
5. Corporate staff analyst—the approving authority's analytic resource.

Although in some cases similar appraisal methods may serve several organizational roles, one can begin to appreciate the many permutations of requirements placed on project appraisal methods.

Company Values

A more general concept is that of the firm's *values,* as embodied in policy statements, expressed or implied. Values include these considerations:

1. *Objectives*—marketing, technical, and financial standards of performance.

2. *Constraints*—limits of action based on internal policy or technological or environmental restrictions.
3. *Needs*—requirements for survival or growth, or simply continuity of operations.
4. *Priorities*—a hierarchy of values.
5. *Conflicts*—disparate views among policymakers of the firm.
6. *Goals*—concrete targets, which in the aggregate represent a strategy of the firm.

The Situation

The internal situation, comprising the firm's strengths and weaknesses, its place in the business cycle, etc., and the external situation, comprising problems and opportunities, will also affect appraisal methods. Factors include:

1. *Product market conditions*—the competitive situation, demand trends, etc.
2. *Technical conditions*—product, process, and end user technologies and trends.
3. *Economic-financial conditions*—the state of the economy and the capital market.
4. *Organizational setting*—the culture and politics of the firm; dominant factions.

Information

The appraisal method selected should be sensitive to the quality of the information available for the project to be assessed and its setting. One type of information is that required to define the variables we have identified: project type, project stage; the appraiser; and values of the firm. A second type of information is the set of forecasts, estimates, and assumptions that describe the project itself and *the situation:*

1. Conditions, situations, and practices—past and present experience.
2. Alternative scenarios—projected.
3. Project costs and benefits, tangible and intangible.
4. Sources of uncertainty.
5. Contingencies and likelihoods.
6. Alternative ways to achieve the purpose of the project.

Ideally, the project appraisal method should determine the type and quality of information to be gathered. We introduce information quality as a prerequisite to take note of probable restrictions on the *availability* of *complete* and *accurate* information, and its effect on the choice of appraisal method. (Note also that information quality determines project risk.)

Given this complex of considerations affecting the choice or design of a project appraisal method, one could conclude there is no one best method for evaluating a capital project. What we need is a mixed bag of techniques that is versatile enough to cover rather diverse needs.

One might also conclude that capital budgeting is not simply a job for financial analysts. It involves contributions from marketing, technical, and financial management, but it is ultimately the responsibility of general management.

Summary and Procedure

The important variables that affect the choice of a project appraisal method are:

I. Project type
   A. Economic versus noneconomic
   B. Strategic versus tactical
   C. Purpose
      1. Improvement
      2. Expansion
      3. Compliance
   D. Size

II. Project stage
   A. Exploration
   B. Project definition
   C. Economic decision
   D. Execution

III. Project appraiser
   A. Project sponsor
   B. Division analyst
   C. Intermediate approver
   D. Final appraiser
   E. Corporate analyst

IV. Company values
   A. Objectives
   B. Constraints/policies
   C. Needs
   D. Priorities

    E. Conflicts
    F. Goals

V. Situation (internal/external)
    A. Product market conditions
    B. Technical conditions
    C. Economic-financial conditions
    D. Organizational setting

VI. Quality of the information available (risk)
    A. Experience
    B. Projections
    C. Costs and benefits
    D. Uncertainties
    E. Contingencies and likelihoods
    F. Alternatives

Procedure. The variables interact. Project type and stage should be some reflection of the firm's goals and objectives. In turn, type and stage usually dictate the appraiser and the information available.

The corporation can benefit from an analysis and update of its policy manual for capital budgeting. By studying the variables identified and their interactions, it is possible to pose some challenging questions:

1. Do major projects reflect the firm's goals and objectives?
2. Are appraisers consistent with project type and stage?
3. Is the information available and its quality consistent with project type and stage?
4. What specific demands should be placed on the corporate organization to make the answers to questions 1, 2, and 3 more acceptable?

CRITERIA TO CONSIDER

The choice of a particular project appraisal method is ultimately based on the criteria that the method incorporates. Criteria act as a link between the project variables we have identified and the appraisal method chosen. Although the criteria nominally available for consideration are limited in number and scope, many corporations have not formally examined their options.

But, project appraisal criteria needn't be restricted to those advocated in the financial literature. If one thinks of capital budgeting as a tool for implementing corporate strategy, the list of criteria grows. Viewing the firm as a business having marketing, technical, and financial functions with appropriate objectives and strategies, our list of criteria comprises (1) marketing criteria, (2) technical criteria, and (3) financial criteria.

These criteria are the standards for advancing a capital project to its next stage. They incorporate the goals, objectives, and other values of the firm, along with the information available on the project itself and the prevailing situation. In making a specific decision, criteria are weighted to reflect relative importance. Assigning maximum weight to a criterion means it is a compelling reason for or against an alternative. Subject to project type, project stage, and role of the appraiser, project criteria can be classified as marketing, technical, or financial.

Marketing Criteria

Many firms have experienced the difficulties of evaluating a marketing-oriented project, particularly when the project fails financial tests. While financial criteria are commonly part of explicit corporate policy, this is often not the case with marketing criteria. The formalizing and documentation of marketing criteria is a good beginning in the development of comprehensive project appraisal methods.

Useful criteria reflect corporate values, the prevailing situation and conditions, and the quality of the information available. This means that formal marketing criteria for project evaluation should account for the following strategic considerations:

1. Corporate values respecting competitive position.
  a. Markets to be served.
  b. Long-term market share objectives.
  c. Specific goals for market penetration and share maintenance.
  d. Product concepts.
  e. Preferred distribution channels.
  f. Pricing strategies.
  g. Communication strategies.
  h. Conflicts with technical and financial values.
2. The marketing situation and conditions.
  a. Market size and other dimensions.
  b. Entry barriers.
  c. Strength and other characteristics of the competition.
3. Quality of the information available.
  a. Product market analysis and forecasts.
  b. Industry analysis and forecasts.

    c. Competitive analysis and forecasts.
    d. Buying practices analysis and forecasts.

Applied to a specific project proposal, these criteria will measure the extent to which corporate marketing objectives will be supported in the projected competitive environment and the likelihood of success, given the quality of the analyses performed. What remains is to integrate these marketing criteria with other criteria in the technical and financial realms.

Technical Criteria

The technical functions of a business comprise research and development, engineering (product and process), and operations. In turn, operations comprise production and logistics. Production represents those operations that convert raw material to product; logistics deals with the management and flow of all materials.

    A management group may wish to invest in a forward-looking technological advancement. It may be product-oriented or process-oriented. If the firm's financial standards are not met, the culture and politics of the organization will probably dictate the project's disposition. As with marketing criteria, technical criteria are too often not stated as part of explicit corporate policy; formalizing technical criteria for project evaluation is a *second* important step toward developing an eclectic approach to project evaluation. These criteria should also reflect corporate values, prevailing conditions, and the quality of information available:

    1. Corporate values respecting product and process technology.
      a. The relative importance of innovation.
      b. Nonfinancial concerns about productivity.
      c. The firm's attitudes toward its various constituencies.
      d. Specific technological goals.
      e. Product and process concepts.
      f. Objectives for maintenance and replacement of assets.
      g. Availability of resources or implement project proposals.
      h. Needs for capacity.
      i. Technical priorities.
      j. Conflicts with marketing and financial values.
    2. The technological situation and conditions.
      a. Projected availability of new developments.
      b. Access to innovative resources.
      c. Resources of competitors.

3. Quality of information available.
   a. Technological forecasts.
   b. Feasibility studies.
   c. Intangible strategic value of innovation.

The criteria applied to a project proposal will measure the degree to which corporate technological objectives will be supported. Together with marketing and financial criteria they represent the link between project proposals and evaluation methods.

Financial Criteria

The firm's financial objectives may override its marketing and technical objectives; but financial criteria, per se, cannot be applied until marketing and technical proposals have been developed. Although financial criteria are usually the most formal and most consistently applied of all project criteria, there is no general agreement regarding (1) how to match financial criteria to corporate values and situational variables or (2) how to integrate financial criteria with marketing and technical criteria in assessing a capital investment project.

The *third* step, then, toward a comprehensive project evaluation program is the formalizing of financial criteria for investment project evaluation. Such criteria should account for:

1. Corporate financial values.
   a. The relative importance of increasing shareholder value.
   b. Liquidity and solvency constraints.
   c. Costs of debt and equity.
   d. Specific goals for return on assets and equity.
   e. Dividend policy.
   f. Capital rationing policy.
   g. Attitude toward project risk and other business risks.
   h. Policy constraints on financing methods.
   i. Conflicts with marketing and technical values.
2. The financial situation and conditions.
   a. Interest rate projections.
   b. Inflation rate projections.
   c. Business unit contribution forecasts.
   d. Projections of true opportunity costs, that is, practical investment alternatives.
   e. Corporate borrowing and lending rates.
   f. Projected costs of equity, including retained earnings.
   g. Cash flow projections.

h. Debt capacity.
  i. Potential for new equity.
3. Quality of financial information available.
  a. Economic forecasts.
  b. Pro forma income statements and balance sheets.
  c. Financial statements of the competition.
  d. Presentation of the project proposal.

DEVELOPING PROJECT ALTERNATIVES

One of the serious shortcomings of investment project proposals is the failure to consider alternatives. Positions for and against a proposal harden as available decision time diminishes. This commonly results in an accept-or-reject decision, without regard to the possibilities for improving the project proposal.

Once project evaluation criteria have been formally established along with a system for weighting them, opportunities for proposal improvement will suggest themselves. Since proposals are typically assembled by business unit or operating management but ultimately evaluated by corporate financial management, proposal improvements are often needed to improve the financial returns on an operationally viable project. Failure to accomplish this early in the life of the proposal can lead to increased conflict and reduce cooperation between opposing corporate factions. If one thinks of a financially acceptable project as having appropriate risk-return characteristics, project alternatives can be developed using trade-offs, including the following:

I. Improving project risk.
  A. Delaying a project to reduce risk.
  B. Hedging or ensuring against risk.
  C. Innovating less to reduce risk.
  D. Avoiding head-to-head competition to reduce risk.
  E. Accepting lower project return to reduce project risk.

II. Improving project return.
  A. Reducing or delaying project outlays, for example,
    1. Construction costs.
    2. Working capital build-up.
  B. Increasing or accelerating project inflows, for example,
    1. Reduced start-up times via early debugging.
    2. Steeper learning curves.
  C. Accepting greater project risk to increase project return.

It is important to understand that a major value of a good project evaluation process is the ability of the corporation to identify proposals needing improvement and to suggest the means for doing so. In some respects the ability to improve a project is a greater resource than the ability to make an accept/reject or ranking decision.

PROJECT EVALUATION METHODS

Until recently, capital budgeting was a synonym for the financial evaluation of investment proposals. The subject had only the most tenuous links to corporate strategy. The catalog of project evaluation methods was restricted to traditional financial methods (payback, accounting ROI, etc.) and the more modern discounted cash flow methods (internal rate of return, net present value, terminal value, profitability index, etc.).

Later, methods of measuring, comparing, and evaluating project risk were introduced, mostly borrowed from the literature of the securities market. These included risk analysis models using utility theory, probability theory, simulation, network analysis (decision trees), sensitivity analysis, portfolio management, and capital market models.

Some contemporary financial writers and a few corporations have lately recognized the need to overcome the conflicts between product-market competitive objectives and classical capital market financial objectives. This has led to a variety of strategic planning-oriented evaluation methods. Several of these more recent methods will be described. Following that, suggestions will be offered for integrating financial and strategic methods to form a comprehensive evaluation procedure.

Virtually all of these methods are described elsewhere in this handbook, but a quick review of each will serve to set the financial evaluation methods in a broader context of comprehensive corporate values. In addition, a brief critique will accompany each method, along with suggestions for overcoming inherent weaknesses.

Straight Financial Methods

Capital budgeting is intellectually appealing partly because of the many controversies it harbors. While disagreement characterizes much of financial management theory, capital budgeting has more complex implications stemming from its nonfinancial dimensions.

Payback and ROI. The so-called traditional methods of project profitability analysis exclude the principle of the time value of money—a dollar today is worth more than a dollar in the future. Yet many corporations continue to use payback and accounting ROI to evaluate investment proposals. It is not uncommon for some major corporations to reject projects whose proceeds take longer than three years (or four, etc.) to pay back their investment. Note that ROI is simply the reciprocal of payback.

Example.

A. Project outlay	$100,000
B. Annual proceeds	25,000
C. Payback period = A/B:	4 years
D. Project return on investment = B/A:	25 percent

There are a number of variations of each of these models, mostly dependent on data employed. For example, proceeds can be before- or aftertax earnings, cash flows, or discounted cash flows.

Payback period is a popular method because it's simple and often revealing with regard to project risk. Other things being equal, projects with short payback periods have lower cash exposure and make capital available for reinvestment more quickly than projects with longer paybacks.

DCF methods. Capital market theory eventually led to the use of discounted cash flow methods for evaluating investment projects. Bondholders were accustomed to the yield-to-maturity concept which accounted for the time value of money. Early advocates of capital budgeting as a financial discipline applied the yield-to-maturity model to corporate investments and renamed it internal rate of return. Both YTM and IRR are the discount rates which set the present value of investment proceeds equal to the value of the initial outlay. In the case of mortgages or other debts with uniform repayments, the cost of the loan is the discount rate that sets the present value of all loan payments (including principal and interest) equal to the original loan principal. Thus, investments with vastly different cash flow profiles can have the same nominal returns.

Examples. Three investments with three-year lives and 10 percent returns.

	a. A bond	b. A mortgage	c. A fixed asset
Investment	−$1,000	−$1,000	−$1,000
Proceeds			
Year 1	100	402	300
2	100	402	400
3	1,100	402	530

The shortcomings of the IRR concept (see Chapter 17) eventually led to the substitution of the net present value concept as the favored

DCF model among financial writers. NPV represents the present value of revenue income less the present value of outlays. Discounting is performed using the firm's cost of capital or the true opportunity cost of a business unit. Although NPV is theoretically more sound for ranking project alternatives than the IRR, it has the practical weakness of requiring the selection of a discount rate.

More recently, NPV itself has come under attack (see Chapter 9). The discounting concept is said to favor short-term cash flows over future cash flows. Suggestions for improvement include artificially altering discount rates to favor future years critical from a strategic viewpoint.

Other financial methods. Some capital budgeting practitioners believe there are more direct methods for testing project costs and benefits for impact on shareholder wealth. Some of these methods stress accounting earnings and balance sheet effects; others have developed specific models for shareholder value (see Chapter 7) and forecast effect on stock price (see Chapter 18). These firm-level methods are usually applied to complete business strategies rather than to individual projects.

Financial Methods Incorporating Risk Analysis

The foregoing methods of project evaluation all assume that project costs and benefits can be expressed deterministically as cash flows (that is, there is no uncertainty or risk). Other methods are used to incorporate risk analysis.

Simple methods. A variety of techniques is being used for measuring, comparing, and combining project risks (see Chapter 21). These include the following (it is important to note the correspondence of relative information quality and project risk):

Measures of estimating quality. Managers of large capital projects are tailoring estimating accuracies to suit the stages of a project. Figure 1 shows an example of this method in use. Relative risk of a project can then be improved via selectively refined estimates of cash flows, as shown in Figure 2.

Delphi method. Originally developed to produce technological forecasts, this method employs a panel of experts and statistical analysis of their opinions. It is now used for forecasts of a wide class of variables, including project cash flows. The resultant distribution of individual forecasts represents the expected value and relative risk of the variable involved. *Shortcoming:* input values are still estimates.

FIGURE 1

Summary of Estimating Method Characteristics

Information required	Probable accuracy ½ range*	Approximate cost per $1 million†	Process equipment, including instruments	Installation material for process equipment—piping, wiring, fnd., etc.	Building, distribution, site material	Labor	Design cost	Field expense
I. Detailed unit cost method								
General project basis Process design Site information Engineering design Detailed design	±3%	$11,000 to $33,000 (excluding design)	Based on firm bids, includes freight, corrected for probable escalation.	Based on completed and priced bills of material or lump-sum bids.	Based on completed and priced bills of material or lump-sum bids.	Based on detailed worker-hour estimate and expected labor rates corrected for job conditions, or lump-sum bids.	Actual plus estimated design cost of changes.	Detailed budget
II. Material takeoff method								
General project basis Process design Site information Engineering design Partial detailed design	±6%	$3,200 (excluding design)	Based on quotes or recent purchase, includes freight, corrected to probable index.	Based on preliminary priced bills of material, plus allowances for stores material.	Based on preliminary priced bills of material plus allowances for stores material.	Based on standard labor-material ratios for detailed work classifications, corrected for job conditions and using expected labor rate for each work classification.	Actual plus estimated design cost to complete.	Preliminary budget

Method and basis	Accuracy	Cost†	Process equipment	Installation	Process piping	Instrumentation / labor	Engineering / drawing	Other costs
III. Defined equipment ratio method General project basis Process design Site information Engineering design	±12%	$320	Based on quotes or recent purchase, includes freight, corrected to probable index.	By ratio to value of process equipment.	From layouts and line diagrams on a unit-price basis.	Based on standard labor-material ratios for similar work, corrected for job conditions and using expected average labor rates.	Based on complete drawing list.	Per cent of physical plant cost from experience records.
IV. Preliminary equipment ratio method General project basis Process design General site information	±25%	$80	Major process equipment based on capacity-cost graphs corrected to probable index. Auxiliary equipment and instruments by ratio to value of major process equipment.	By ratio to value of process equipment.	By ratio to value of process equipment; ratio built to fit expected needs.	Based on standard labor-experience ratios for similar work, corrected for job conditions and using expected average effective labor rates.	Worker-hour/$ of material cost from experience records at average cost per design worker-hour	Per cent of physical plant cost from experience records.
V. Capacity-cost curve method Plant type, capacity	Variable	Negligible	Total cost from curve					

* For projects costing more than $100,000. For smaller projects, accuracy ranges will be wider.

† For projects costing about $1 million. Does not include cost of project design on which estimate is based.

Source: Adapted from John W. Hackney, *Control and Management of Capital Projects* (New York: John Wiley & Sons, 1965).

FIGURE 2

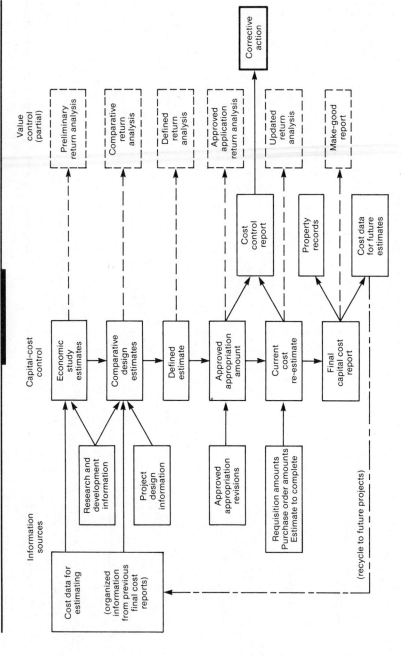

Source: John W. Hackney, *Control and Management of Capital Projects* (New York: John Wiley & Sons, 1965).

Dominance methods. This is a powerful set of elegant analytic methods for comparing two alternatives. Its chief value is for early pair-by-pair screening of a large number of choices. An alternative A is said to dominate alternative B when A is *always* superior to B. It becomes unnecessary to consider B any further. Examples of dominance methods include:

1. *Mean-variance analysis.* If two alternatives have equal returns (for example, expected NPV), the one with the lower risk (for example, variance of NPV) is dominant. Discard the other. If they have equal risks, discard the one with the lower return.

2. *A fortiori analysis.* Make all unfavorable assumptions about A and all favorable assumptions about B. If A is still superior to B, A is dominant. Discard B.

3. *Sensitivity analysis.* If the distribution of a key decision variable (for example, sales volume) is entirely above or below the point of equal returns, the choice of an alternative is not sensitive to assumptions for that variable. The higher return alternative can be said to be dominant.

Shortcoming: Dominance methods are elegant and conclusive—when they work—but the likelihood of a dominance relationship is small.

Refined methods. Other techniques for assessing risk employ utility theory or capital market theory. However, critics assert that required estimates of utility and risk factors are subject to the same bias as are deterministic cash flow estimates. This, they believe, negates the benefits of risk analysis, with the possible exception of dominance methods. Examples of refined project risk analysis methods include the following:

Certainty equivalent. This model employs the decision maker's utility function to compare investment project alternatives. The certainty equivalent of a risky project is a hypothetical risk-free project that could be exchanged for it; that is, the certainty equivalent is the minimum selling price for the risky project. The ratio of certainty equivalent to the expected return of the risky project is used to reduce the project cash flows, offsetting the decision maker's perception of risk. *Shortcoming:* Whose certainty equivalent to use?

Risk-adjusted present value. This is based on the distribution of external conditions (states of nature) affecting project cash flows and costs of capital. The aggregate effect is to reduce present values of cash flows. *Shortcoming:* Risk adjustment requires additional estimates and is subject to wide errors.

Discount rate risk premium. This is a popular method in many firms. Normal discount rates are arbitrarily inflated to correspond to different risk categories. For example, plant cost-reduction projects might be discounted at 15 percent, while market penetration projects are discounted at 25 percent to account for risk differential. *Shortcoming:* It's harder for a decision maker to perceive a risk premium than a certainty equivalent.

Decision trees. This popular network technique is invaluable for organizing a complex set of alternatives and applying dominance analysis. By rolling back the branches of the tree, means and variances of returns can be associated with choices of project alternatives.

Simulation. Share of market distributions of alternative cash flow elements (for example, market size, growth rate, SOM, price) are entered into a computer. Points are randomly selected from the distributions and functionally combined (for example, to create the cash flow: project revenue). Ultimately, subject to certain constraints to exclude unrealistic combinations, a distribution for project NPV is developed. This represents expected project return and risk. *Shortcoming:* Distributions for cash flow elements are still estimated.

Abandonment theory. It is often practical to consider abandoning a project before the end of its useful life. Abandonment is preferable whenever it yields a value greater than the present value of all normal subsequent cash flows (the question may have profound implications regarding the firm's values). Decision trees facilitate analysis of the abandonment option.

Portfolio methods. Other techniques borrowed from the securities market and based on capital market theory include Markowitz's portfolio model and the capital asset pricing model. These are techniques for comparing risks of alternatives and taking steps to manage aggregate portfolio risk and return.

Portfolio theory. This is based on the statistical relationship of project alternatives, ranging from perfect negative correlation to perfect positive correlation of project outcomes. Individual variances and pair-by-pair covariances must be calculated for all alternatives being considered in order to determine aggregate portfolio risk, expressed as overall variance. For example, for a three-investment portfolio:

$$\text{Var}(X_1 + X_2 + X_3) = \text{Var } X_1 + \text{Var } X_2 + \text{Var } X_3 + 2[\text{Cov } X_1 X_2 + \text{Cov } X_2 X_3 + \text{Cov } X_1 X_3]$$

410

Whereas ROI is used for security portfolios, NPV is more practical for fixed asset investments; therefore portfolio return is simply the sum of individual investment returns:

$$NPV(X_1 + X_2 + X_3) = NPV\ X_1 + NPV\ X_2 + NPV\ X_3$$

The investor's objective is to create an efficient portfolio by diversification of investments, that is, selecting investments whose returns are independent or negatively correlated. (An efficient portfolio is one whose risk cannot be decreased without decreasing return and whose return cannot be increased without increasing risk.) *Shortcoming:* A long list of assumptions (see Chapter 1) underlies the portfolio model; it is particularly tenuous for capital budgeting applications.

Capital asset pricing model. This is based on capital market theory. CAPM addresses systematic risk (inherent in the market) and excludes nonsystematic risk (a property of the investment itself, and therefore diversifiable).

The *capital market line* is used to determine the return required of a specific portfolio, given its risk relative to that of the market.

$$CML:\ r_p = r_f + \frac{\sigma_p}{\sigma_m}(r_m - r_f)$$

where

r_p = Expected portfolio return.

r_f = Return on a risk-free investment.

$\dfrac{\sigma_p}{\sigma_m}$ = Portfolio risk relative to market risk.

$(r_m - r_f)$ = The premium placed on expected market return to offset its inherent risk (so-called "excess return").

In the case of capital budgeting, the concept of the *market* must be modified to include those investments made by the firm and its industry competitors.

The *security market line* is used to determine the return required of a specific risky investment, given its risk relative to that of the market.

$$SML:\ r_* = r_f + \beta(r_m - r_f)$$

where

r_* = Expected return from the investment.

r_f = Risk-free return.

β = The investment risk relative to market risk.

$(r_m - r_f)$ = The market premium.

411

For capital budgeting applications, β (beta) must be determined using the history of returns of similar projects versus that of the overall market (industry).

Note that

$$\beta = \frac{COV(r_m, r.)}{\sigma_m^2}$$

where

$COV(r_m, r_*) =$ Investment risk.
$\sigma_m^2 =$ Market risk.

Thus the SML and the CML are seen to express risk in different terms. *Shortcoming:* Market return and risk, as well as β, are difficult to determine in the capital budgeting context.

Methods for Evaluating Intangibles

Still other methods are employed to assess intangible costs and benefits of an investment project, that is, those that cannot be expressed as probabilistic cash flows.

Cost-effectiveness analysis. Index numbers are used to specify the relative effectiveness of mutually exclusive projects in achieving some intangible objective. Cost-effectiveness is the ratio of project cost to effectiveness.

Example. Two alternative investments are offered for improving plant safety. Investment A costs $100,000 and will reduce time lost due to accidents by 20 worker days per year. Investment B costs $50,000 and will save 15 worker days per year. A's cost-effectiveness is $5,000 per worker day. B's cost-effectiveness is $3,333 per worker day. Therefore, A is more cost-effective than B, with respect to reducing lost-time accidents. *Shortcoming:* Cost-effectiveness is a relative measure that cannot be used to compare independent prospects with unlike objectives. For example, dollars per worker days for a safety project are not comparable with dollars per decibel reduced by a noise abatement project.

Cost-benefit analysis. Whereas cost-effectiveness can only compare one factor at a time, cost-benefit analysis combines ratios by using a common denominator, usually dollars. This leads to an overall ratio of dollars expended to dollars in benefits achieved. *Shortcoming:* It is often difficult to associate dollars with benefits.

412

Effectiveness rating schemes. Various other methods have been used to assess mutually exclusive alternatives with intangible benefits (or costs). One popular method assigns numerical importance ratings to individual project goals. Project alternatives are scored using numerical effectiveness ratings. Relative overall effectiveness of alternatives is calculated by summing the effectiveness ratings weighted by the importance ratings.

Example.

Goals	Importance rating (scale of 1 to 5)	Effectiveness rating (scale of 1 to 5)		Weighted scores (scale of 1 to 25)	
		Alternative A	Alternative B	Alternative A	Alternative B
1. Lower accident frequency	4	4	2	16	8
2. Lower accident severity	5	1	4	5	20
3. Reduced noise level	2	2	4	4	8
Overall effectiveness				25	36

Results may be refined using interactions. By singling out the key goals distinguishing alternatives, one can compare goal importance ratings and revise them to make relationships more realistic. For example, is lower accident frequency really only twice as important as reduced noise level? New judgments may lead to revised evaluations. *Shortcoming:* As with other utility-oriented methods, an important question is whose preferences to employ.

Methods Linking Strategy and Capital Budgeting Decisions

There lately has emerged a new family of appraisal methods that attempt to evaluate a capital proposal in a more strategic context than do earlier methods. These methods generally acknowledge the contribution of a healthy competitive position toward a long-term increase of shareholder wealth.

Opportunity cost grid. The corporation with multiple business units, profit centers, or investment centers strains the versatility of

413

corporate cost of capital as an all-purpose discount rate. It becomes necessary to somehow distinguish the business whose capital proposal is being appraised. The reasons are practical. Global use of corporate capital cost can sink the marginally performing unit through capital starvation; it can create complacency among high-performing units.

An opportunity cost grid is one method of acknowledging such differences. Tactical capital investment needs should be segregated from strategic issues; business units are segregated by performance, that is, current return.

Example.

Investment Type	Marginal	Corporate cost of capital: 15%	
		Business Unit Discount Rates	
		Acceptable	Superior
Tactical	8%	15%	20%
Strategic	17	20	25

In this example of three business units, the marginal business unit, for tactical projects (that is, day-to-day needs), is expected to return its present level. This keeps the unit alive, precluding its willy-nilly dissolution. Also for tactical needs, the acceptably performing unit is expected to return the corporate cost of capital; the superior unit is measured against competition.

The strategic decision for the marginal unit is whether or not to liquidate it. When this decision is addressed, the return due to redeployment of assets to the other units is employed. A strategic decision to expand the acceptable unit is based on returning the equivalent of the superior unit; expanding the superior unit is pitted against external opportunities, for example, acquiring an ongoing business. *Shortcoming:* The model, as with other DCF models, attempts to encompass a variety of value criteria in a single number—a discount rate.

Shareholder value methods. The firm's financial objective of creating shareholder wealth is addressed directly with these models (see Chapter 7). The essence of these methods is the DCF analysis of complete strategies rather than of individual projects. Once a strategy has passed the DCF criteria, all those projects necessary to implement it are accepted, in one form or another. *Shortcoming:* The method appears to beg the question of how to appraise an individual project.

Key factor checklists. The most rudimentary schemes for linking individual projects to corporate strategy are checklists incorporating a variety of considerations. One such scheme is shown in Figure 3.

FIGURE 3

Key Factor Checklist

I. Operating factors
  1. Will it produce significant operating results? (Decrease costs, improve product quality or customer service?)
  2. Is it cost-effective? (Will benefits exceed costs?)
  3. Can it be implemented? (Does the company have the facilities, personnel, and expertise?)
  4. Will there be other departmental benefits?
 	
II. Planning factors
  1. Is it consistent with company strategy? (Strengthen resources and capabilities for growth and development?)
  2. Is it consistent with company policies? (Within guidelines and constraints?)
  3. Will it meet other company needs? (Other departments?)
  4. Is there a compelling reason to do it? (Mandated by government, necessary to avoid a strike or takeover?)
 	
III. Financial Factors
  1. Is the return satisfactory?
  2. Is the risk acceptable?
  3. Is the payback period satisfactory?
  4. Is the return satisfactory?
 	
Source: Adapted from Thomas Petit and Tony Wingler, "Key Factors in Capital Budgeting," *Managerial Planning*, May–June 1981, p. 21.

Shortcoming: Checklists are by nature superficial. Substantial backup is needed to support the checklist elements.

Stages of evaluation. In 1970, Joseph L. Bower of Harvard published *Managing the Resource Allocation Process: A Study of Corporate Planning and Investment.* In it Bower argues that selecting investments with the highest net present values is theoretically correct but practically irrelevant. "In fact," he says, "the set of problems corporations refer to as capital budgeting is a task for general management rather than financial specialists."

415

Bower examined a series of actual cases and concluded that capital budgeting is a sequential process, ideally evolving through a series of meetings:

1. *Strategic plan evaluation.* Block out the extent of the need for a facility. Review the strategic assumptions of the business.
2. *Business plan evaluation.* Is this specific project needed? What strategic setting will it serve? Use the corporate information network to help with project definition.
3. *Project evaluation.* Outline alternative facilities to consider.

This sequential process is consistent with the shareholder value method. It avoids the binary accept/reject approach in favor of developing a preferred solution of implementing a carefully scrutinized strategy. *Shortcoming:* Bower's study shows that self-serving interests and other behavioral obstacles often govern the actual decision-making process.

Systematic linking. There are two basic approaches to initiating capital project proposals—top-down or bottom-up. When top executives know their operations in detail, this permits them to formulate strategy and to think of concrete projects to implement it. In large, diversified corporations top executives are forced to set criteria for evaluating projects proposed by operating people. Most capital proposals do originate in the business units. Necessary projects, improvement projects, and natural expansion projects fit into this category; they can be neatly appraised with textbook DCF methods. But usually absent is a systematic linking of capital proposals to strategic plans.

Two ways to tie capital proposals to strategy are:

1. *Establish policies.* Policy constraints can screen out proposals not consistent with strategies. These can be in the realms of marketing, technical, or financial issues.
2. *Require impact statements.* A written description of important contributions to current strategy becomes necessary for project approval.

These devices are natural adjuncts to the concept of stages of evaluation. *Shortcoming:* Policy constraints must be formulated with care and continually brought up to date.

A COMPREHENSIVE PROGRAM FOR PROJECT APPRAISAL

Summarizing the weaknesses of available project appraisal methods highlights these points:

1. "Hard," quantitative capital budgeting methods suffer from our inability to gather foolproof information.
2. They also preclude qualitative intuitive judgments, often required to support corporate strategy.
3. "Soft," qualitative strategic planning techniques used alone could compromise the corporate objective of increasing equity value—winning in capital markets as well as product markets.
4. They also lend themselves to personal, political, and social objectives that may conflict with corporate interests.

What is needed for a comprehensive appraisal program is a finely tuned mix of hard and soft techniques; improved information management; and a basis for linking product-market strategies to strategies in the capital market. This is a very tall order, but the basis for a beginning is available.

The Hard-Soft Mix

Some conditions clearly require primarily hard analytic techniques; others must depend on soft methods. If we define these two extremes in terms of the capital budgeting variables listed earlier, that will leave the gray center of the hard-soft spectrum to be fine-tuned with some sort of mix.

Conditions dictating hard financial analysis. There are still a host of situations that justify the use of standard or modified capital budgeting methods. In terms of the key variables, these conditions include:

Project type. Projects whose costs and benefits are primarily economic, and are also (*a*) not required for continuity of operations, (*b*) cost improvement, rather than revenue enhancement, or (*c*) expansion of capacity for existing products.

Project stage. For economic projects DCF analysis is appropriate at each major stage.

Appraiser. The use of financial analytic methods should be the province of the financial analyst.

Corporate values. Obviously, the greater the corporate emphasis on financial values, the more suitable are the "hard" financial methods (for example, DCF, cash flow per se, balance sheet analysis).

The situation. When capital market pressures outweigh product market pressures, hard financial analysis is important.[1]

Information quality. When experience is limited, uncertainties are great, and alternatives are abundant, "hard" financial analysis can help with screening (for example, sensitivity analysis, other dominance techniques, decision trees). Poor information quality is common in early project stages.

Conditions dictating soft analysis. In other cases the qualitative, intuitive, creative approach is usually warranted, sometimes essential, and often the only choice. These conditions include:

Project type. Projects whose costs and benefits are primarily noneconomic, and are also (*a*) tactical, that is, required for continuity of operations, or (*b*) compliance projects, tactical or strategic.

Project stage. For noneconomic projects, final approval at policy level should usually be based on qualitative considerations, unconstrained by hard financial analysis.

Appraiser. Soft decision-making methods should be the province of sponsors and policy makers, not analysts.

Corporate values. The greater the corporate emphasis on competitive position, the more suitable are the creative nonfinancial methods.

The situation. When product market pressures outweigh capital market pressures, qualitative and nonfinancial judgments are important.

Information quality. When information quality is good, that is, risks are low or can be hedged, intuitive techniques are warranted.

The above judgments may not evoke a consensus. Readers may substitute their own; but the format employed is offered as a convenient framework for beginning to formulate hard-soft mix guidelines.

Conditions requiring a mix of hard and soft methods. The gray area remains—where neither hard nor soft techniques can dominate.

Project type. Major strategic projects with both economic and noneconomic costs and benefits.

Project stage. Any stage of the process.

Appraiser. Teams of analysts and decision makers working closely, across organizations and levels.

Corporate values. Product market and capital market objectives are in perspective. Long-term growth and development strategies are called for.

The situation. Competitive and capital market pressures are in balance.

Information quality. Projections are difficult to make, risks cannot be defined in probabilistic terms.

This gray area represents the conditions best suited to a method for linking strategy and capital budgeting described earlier. To summarize, there are three sets of conditions:

- Type I conditions: Indicate "hard" capital budgeting analysis.
- Type II conditions: Indicate "soft" strategic planning techniques.
- Type III conditions: Both strategic planning and capital budgeting techniques.

Improved Information Management

Information quality is one of the key capital budgeting variables. Our understanding of each of the other key variables is improved when information quality is improved.

The dimensions of information management for capital budgeting are several. Recognition of the need to link capital budgeting to strategic planning—indeed, to incorporate strategic planning considerations into project appraisal—expands the information issue further.

Considered separately, the *capital budgeting* information problem deals with estimating and forecasting methods, proposal content, capital budget administration, and capital appropriation procedures.

Improving these information categories tends to reduce project risk and increase the return of projects selected.

Second, *strategic planning* information needs include the strategic planning process, marketing data bases, technical data bases, and financial data bases.

Improving these categories facilitates the use of planning techniques for capital allocation as well as the linking of product market and capital market strategies.

Capital budgeting information. Most of these considerations are covered in detail in other chapters. A brief word about each category may help to place the subject in the perspective of an appraisal program.

Estimating and forecasting. When costs and benefits can be expressed as cash flows, estimating (internal variables) accuracies should improve as a project moves from stage to stage. Techniques are available to match estimating accuracies to project stages; for example, cost-capacity curves for order-of-magnitude exploratory estimates, major parts design and handbook ratios for intermediate accuracies, final design and vendor quotes for ±3 percent appropriation estimates. Such techniques should be used for all cash flows, that is, project outlays, working capital changes, operating revenues, operating costs, and residual values such as salvage and working capital recovery.

Estimates of internal variables require forecasts of external variables, for example, market size or growth rate. Forecasting procedures should be formalized and interdisciplinary. In this way communication is improved at all project stages (see Chapter 2).

Proposal content. Here again formality improves communications, clarifies project definition, and fosters improvement of a weak proposal rather than immediate rejection. When mixing of capital budgeting analysis with strategic planning issues is important, appropriate proposal formats can be helpful, for example,

1. Recommendation.
   a. Project description.
   b. Investment required.
2. Summary of key data.
   a. Criteria used, financial and other.
   b. Alternatives considered.
   c. Basis for recommendation.
   d. Execution plan and timetable.
3. Execution plan.
   a. Marketing.
   b. Technical.
   c. Financial.
4. Impacts of recommendations.
   a. Assumptions.
   b. Impacts.
      1. Operations.
      2. Financial condition.
      3. Growth, etc.
5. Examination of alternatives.
   a. Descriptions.
   b. Summary analysis.
   c. Basis for rejection.
6. Appendixes summarizing worksheets.

(See Chapter 15.)

Capital budget administration. The use of project teams to shepherd a project through the system is a good idea for major projects (see

420

Chapter 28). Wide dissemination of corporate policies and investment objectives should be achieved via published manuals or memos. Awareness at all levels of what drives the firm to invest can help to improve cooperation, ease coordination, and create common understanding about individual roles and measures of performance. (See Chapter 12.)

Capital appropriation procedure. Here is where the proposal development process is specified. All executives and managers should know and understand the process and the roles of all service and staff groups in amplifying, refining, and reviewing a proposal. (See Chapter 23.)

Strategic planning information. Capital budgeting practitioners in a firm must join forces with the strategic planners. Such interaction will improve communications and facilitate linking the disciplines. Some specific strategic planning information needs related to investment planning are described below.

Strategic planning process. Here again, formalization will improve communications and understanding. Ultimately, there should be explicit provision for linking the strategic planning process, at key stages, with both the preparation of the capital budget and the capital appropriations procedure. The crucial linkage, respecting investment in fixed assets, is at the point of development of the company facilities plan. This plan is drawn up by the firm's *technical* people to implement a manufacturing strategy in support of strategies prepared by *marketing* people.

The facilities plan should form the basis for most of the capital budget. It describes the location, size, and technology of projected production locations, distribution points, sales and administrative offices, and R&D labs designed to service and support the activities proposed in the marketing strategy.

Marketing data bases. A good deal of strategic planning in the competitive product market realm begins with marketing. (Some may begin with R&D.) Improved information management requires that data about markets, products, prices, channels, media, competitors, possible new entries, as well as data on the economy be organized into formal data bases and kept current. Timely knowledge about customers and their customers leads to pace-setting strategies and innovation and ultimately requires investment support.

Technical data bases. The technical organizations of the firm are R&D, engineering, and operations. Together they develop the strategies to support the company's marketing efforts. Technical data bases should include history and projections for all relevant technologies, that is, those involving product design, production processes, and end use of the product. (Equivalent concepts apply to service businesses.) Specific data should include technical feasibility, unit modules, costs, lead times, capabilities, and capacities.

Manufacturing science is coming of age. This applies to planning and managing with computers, accurately measuring and utilizing capacity, and knowing how to expand. PERT and other techniques assure the smooth integration of marketing and technical functions at the project execution stage. Linking up marketing and technical data bases can produce models that economically match planned operating technologies to projected marketing plans.

Financial data bases. The firm's financial function should be responsible for capital market data and analysis. The financial feasibility of marketing and technical strategies can then be realistically appraised at appropriate levels and stages. Financial data bases should include all available financial information on the firm, its competitors, major customers and suppliers, sources and costs of capital, and other financial opportunity costs.

Linking Product Market Objectives and Financial Goals

A comprehensive investment appraisal program has to integrate financial goals and product market objectives. It is not only possible but essential to test the compatibility of, for example, ROE, market share, and growth rate objectives with earnings growth goals.

Managers and executives as well must understand that a product market success adds value to their firm only if the required investment returns more than the cost of capital. While such requirements can be balanced among business units (compare to opportunity cost grid.), the aggregate corporate effect must be positive.

The key factor in making this crucial strategic linkage is to appraise major business strategies, not their specific projects, as investments. This requires a simple three-step procedure for market penetration or share growth strategies:

1. *Make careful projections.* Forecast market growth rate and competitors' behavior, including capacity changes.
2. *Appraise each alternative strategy.* Determine all investments required over the planning period (marketing, working capital, plant, and equipment); determine pricing strategy given rivals' behavior; calculate profitability and increase in the value of the firm using DCF.
3. *Select the most profitable strategy.*

While there is no single formula for appraising business strategies in terms of financial goals, the concept is one that must be embraced for all major investment programs.

Exhibits 1 through 9 illustrate the ways various firms are attempting to link strategic planning and capital budgeting. They include planning goals for investment decisions, resource allocation processes, investment objectives and criteria, investment categories, delegation and decision processes, evaluation forms, and a strategic planning and budgeting cycle.

NOTE

[1] It's interesting that soft techniques are considered creative in deciding on the marketing aspects of business strategy, and they frequently override hard analysis, for example, contrary market research. Moderation is warranted here as well.

EXHIBIT 1

Corporate Planning Department Goal for the Capital Investment Decision Process—A Lumber Products Company

Maintain a capital investment decision process which achieves optimum return to the shareholders in the strategic allocation of capital and other resources.

[The company's] capital investment decision process has three general phases. The first phase determines the amount of capital available for investment. Simply stated, this amount is projected cash flow plus new debt or equity less projected dividend payout requirements. Cash flow projections will include all reasonable downside risks. Outside capital will be obtained on the basis of the company's financing policy.

The second phase, during which capital is allocated among the company's investment alternatives, is the culmination of each annual cycle of the strategic planning process. The primary information source for the allocation decision has been the "bottom-up" process in which the performance projections, strategic options, and capital needs are prepared by the business units. These are based on strategic plans and are presented for analysis and discussion in the business plans and capital budgets. Other sources of input to the allocation decision are the alternatives offered by the corporate planning functions, past performance of the business units, and the independent judgments of senior management. The corporate planning staff provides independent critical analysis and recommendations as input to senior management in the capital investment decision process. Capital is allocated to business units on the basis of approved investment programs. Capital may also be disallocated from existing investments by pruning assets which do not consistently meet the long-term performance standards of that business.

The third phase of the capital investment decision process contains the detailed analysis and the actual approval of capital spending for specific projects which make up the broad investment programs. During the preparation and approval of authorizations for capital expenditures (ACEs), a number of criteria are considered. The most important are the degree of necessity, consistency with the strategic objectives of the business unit, the degree of risk, and the internal rate of return. The corporate planning staff will maintain a system of forecasting the costs of capital. Discretionary investments will normally be made when the return is higher than the internal rate of return criteria.

Source: "Resource Allocation and Strategic Planning," *Information Bulletin No. 99* (New York: The Conference Board, 1981).

EXHIBIT 2

Planning and Resource Allocation in an Oil Company

"There are several steps to our annual planning process, all of which contribute to our eventual resource allocation decisions.

1. The corporate senior executive issues corporate objectives which provide general expectations for our future performance and position in our major business areas.

2. Operating managements in our various businesses develop and propose alternative strategies to satisfy these corporate objectives, including the capital funding requirements associated with each.

3. The corporate senior executive reviews these various strategy proposals and, after considering the various trade-offs presented, both between businesses and in terms of corporate performance (e.g., growth versus returns), makes a corporate choice from among them which is composed of the selected strategy for each business. Based on this corporate choice, the senior executive issues planning guidelines for each business, which include capital spending guidelines.

4. Operating management then develops detailed business plans, which include specific capital programs.

5. The senior executive then reviews these plans and programs and approves a capital budget.

6. Operating management implements the approved plan. Individual capital projects are approved by corporate management based on the [financial and other] criteria. The net result of these project approvals may vary up or down from the approved plan, but it is generally in the same ballpark.

This may seem like a cumbersome process, and it would be, if we attempted it all from scratch each year. However, our annual plan looks out 5 to 10 years. So each year we are really only examining additions to, or changes in, the plan in place from the previous year. This allows for evolutionary changes in strategies and their capital allocations from a corporate perspective. In any given business, however, in any particular year, we may do a complete strategy revision, scrubbing the plan in place entirely, if environmental and competitive conditions seem to warrant doing so."

Source: "Resource Allocation and Strategic Planning," *Information Bulletin No. 99* (New York: The Conference Board, 1981).

425

EXHIBIT 3

Investment Objectives and Criteria for Acceptance—A Business Forms Company

Corporate investment objectives

1. To diversify and grow within [the stated definition of the business].

2. To provide a safe and healthy workplace for employees, a reliable product for customers, and a fair return on stockholder investment.

3. To maintain and improve the productive capability of each operating unit of the corporation.

4. To obey all governmental regulations within the jurisdictions in which the corporation operates.

5. To maximize corporate return on investment.

Criteria for acceptance

1. The proposal achieves one or more of the corporate investment objectives.

2. It meets the specific strategic plans of both the corporation and the operating unit.

3. It achieves at least the minimum rate of return according to the consideration of risk.

4. It can be funded within accepted financial opportunities and constraints.

5. Alternative capacity is unavailable or uneconomic.

6. It cannot be deferred without harmful impact on corporate operations.

7. The social, political, and economic situation in the locations affected by the investment will allow long-term security for the investment and a reasonable opportunity for business success.

In order to provide a guideline for judging financial feasibility, the corporation must achieve a return on investment that exceeds its cost of capital by an amount which allows for future unanticipated investment in mandatory *nonproductive* projects and a provision for risk. This return must be accomplished within the investment's anticipated useful life.

The corporation does not intend to avoid high-risk projects per se. The opportunity loss of not undertaking a project may be more significant than the risks inherent in the project itself. However, it is most important that a quantitative assessment be part of all significant capital investment projects so that an informed decision may be made.

As a general rule, the proposed investment must achieve [the minimum return on capital employed (ROCE) according to its appropriate classification].

Source: "Resource Allocation and Strategic Planning," *Information Bulletin No. 99* (New York: The Conference Board, 1981).

EXHIBIT 4

Resource Allocation System at a Large Diversified Corporation

"Each month, requests for capital appropriation (RCA) are submitted to corporate headquarters; advance notice of submission is received in the prior month. A 'corporate reviewer' (or several, depending on the importance or complexity of the project) is assigned to represent corporate management's interest. The corporate reviewer acts as an adversary, questioning the rationale for the investment and making a recommendation on the project. The corporate reviewer is generally a senior executive on the appropriations committee (the 'A' committee is a senior-level management committee which votes on forwarding the proposed project to the board of directors) with broader business expertise in the area for which the investment is proposed, but without a stake in the outcome of the decision.

"Each RCA is also circulated for comment to other 'A' committee members and corporate staff departments. Responses by the management sponsoring the project are also circulated to reviewers, 'A' committee members, and staff departments so full exposition is given to all issues.

"Once the issues have been aired, the 'A' committee meets and debates the merits of the project, with a vote being taken to indicate disposition. If approved, the project is forwarded to the board of directors for its consideration and discussion. Final authority for the decision ultimately rests with the board, which is assured of the quality of the presentation by the rigors of the approval process."

Source: "Resource Allocation and Strategic Planning," *Information Bulletin No. 99* (New York: The Conference Board, 1981).

EXHIBIT 5

Investment Categories—A Chemicals Company

Category I: Projects with measurable profits

> *Category IA*
> Projects which increase profits through additional sales revenue resulting from new or existing products.

> *Category IB*
> Projects which increase profits through cost savings.

Category II: Projects without measurable profits

> *Category IIA*
> Investments which are indirectly necessary for maintaining and increasing profits, but which may be postponed (e.g., projects for R&D; purchase of land; administration, social, and welfare buildings).

> *Category IIB*
> Projects which are necessary due to legal obligations or for reasons of management policy (e.g., development of infrastructure, safety measures, ecological requirements).

Source: "Resource Allocation and Strategic Planning," *Information Bulletin No. 99* (New York: The Conference Board, 1981).

EXHIBIT 6

Investment Measures—A Diversified Manufacturer

Investment measures	Investment categories/key investment measure	Investment measure		
		Description	Purpose	Applicability
Return on investment (ROI) Incremental profit after tax (before interest) Return on average invested capital	New products/programs	The year-by-year incremental returns to the corporation (after tax, but before interest charges) expressed as a percent of the average capital investment computed for each of the first five years of the project's life. (Note capital investment is equivalent to total net asset requirements.)	To establish an investment measure that can be related directly to corporate goals for (incremental) return on invested capital.	All discretionary investments.
Internal rate of return (IRR) Incremental discounted cash flow/internal rate of return	Expansion	The rate of return (percent) which equates the net initial investment to the present value of subsequent annual cash flow (after tax, but before interest charges) over the life of the project. Cut off at 10, 15, or 20 years if necessary and add the total net assets at that point to the cash flow in the final year of the projection.	To account for the time value of money, particularly when an investment transaction will result in irregular cash flow.	All discretionary investments.

Measure	Category	Definition	Purpose	Application
Payback (PB) incremental, aftertax cash flow, payback period	Cost improvement	That period (in years) for the cumulative, net, incremental cash flows (after tax, but before interest charges) accruing to the corporation to reach the break-even point (i.e., zero).	To provide a simple measure of the period required to return the original investment (in cash).	All discretionary investments.
Return on assets (ROA) performance based fully accounted, profit before tax return on average net assets employed		The before-tax return on assets (ANAE) which would be expected to result after making the proposed investment considering: 1. *This project* on a fully accounted stand-alone basis if feasible; and if not possible, then 2. The *business unit* of which this project will represent a substantial part. This measure should be constructed consistent with normal performance reporting conventions, recognizing all applicable allocations for expenses and assets.	In effect, this measure reflects the commitment to future results that will or could be identified in the corporation's performance reporting system.	Required for *all* investment projects which will comprise a substantial portion of a business unit's activity.

Source: "Resource Allocation and Strategic Planning," *Information Bulletin No. 99* (New York: The Conference Board, 1981).

EXHIBIT 7

Delegation and Decision Process—An Automotive Products Firm

[The company] prefers to delegate decision authority and to accompany this authority with adequate decision guidelines and appropriate management controls. The provisions below apply to decisions to invest company financial resources.

1. Company financial resources include stock and cash generated either in the normal course of business, by the sale of assets, or by a financing transaction.
2. Investment decisions should normally be proposed at the organizational level having the direct responsibility for their implementation. They should be approved at each organizational level whose performance will be significantly affected by the outcome.
3. Investment decisions should be made using informed judgment and decision guidelines that apply equally to all [company] investments. The decision guidelines include:
   a. Use of [the company's] standard valuation policy (SVP) or an approved adaptation. [The provisions of the SVP cover the development of cash flows for valuation purposes, the calculation of the internal rate of return (IRR), and the determination of the range of IRRs.]
   b. Consideration of available alternatives and proposal of the best alternatives as part of an explicit strategy.
   c. Disclosure of the assumptions underlying cash flow estimates.
   d. Evaluation of the risks of not achieving the assumed conditions.
   e. Consideration of qualitative factors such as capability of personnel, political factors, etc., which might affect the proposed investment.
4. Investment decisions should be made using evaluation practices and procedures appropriate to the type of investment. All such practices and procedures should meet the following standards:
   a. Provide adequate visibility of each proposed investment and the process leading to investment decisions.
   b. Accommodate the range of circumstances expected for the type of investment.
   c. Facilitate early identification of promising investment candidates as well as those not meeting [the company's] standards.
   d. Provide decision guidelines consistent with [the company's] investment policies.
   e. Provide constructive and selective postaudits. These provisions will include disclosure of the assumptions that underlie investment proposals to facilitate constructive comparisons with subsequent events.
5. All of [the company's] investments are designated as one of the following two broad types:

EXHIBIT 7 *(continued)*

a. Strategic investment—produces a sustainable change in the strategic competitive position of [the company], or of a [company] business, or a significant and sustainable change in the magnitude or timing of its earnings or cash flow.

b. Reinforcing investment—continues, extends, or improves an established strategy that has proved successful and profitable for [the company].

6. Differences in the delegation and decision process between the two types of investments include:

a. For strategic investments (*i*) the decision maker is determined on a case-by-case basis, (*ii*) standard company decision guidelines are used directly, and (*iii*) the decision process employs a standard company practice and procedure adapted to the circumstances of the [company] unit.

b. For reinforcing investments (*i*) the size of the investment generally determines the decision maker, (*ii*) the standard company decision guidelines may be adapted to the circumstances of the [company] unit, and (*iii*) the decision process may employ practices and procedures not standard throughout [the company].

Source: Resource Allocation and Strategic Planning," *Information Bulletin No. 99* (New York: The Conference Board, 1981).

EXHIBIT 8

Investment Evaluation Form—A Transportation Company

Nine block – Positioning Elements

Industry attractiveness

Weighting

Element	Less than GNP	Equal to GNP	Greater than GNP
Industry growth	2.0	4.0	6.0
Industry return on revenue (net)	Less than___% / .5	___% / 1.0	Greater than___% / 1.5
Industry return on investment	Less than___% / 1.0	___% / 2.0	Greater than___% / 3.0
Competition	Many small with___% share / .5	Mixture / 1.0	Two or three major with___% share / 1.5
Economic dependence of industry	Highly dependent/cyclical / .5	Average / 1.0	Stable / 1.5

Business unit strength

Weighting

Element	Less than #1 share	Equal to #1 competitor	Greater than next major competitor
Share of served market	2.0	4.0	6.0
Revenue growth rate	Less than GNP / .5	Equal to GNP / 1.0	Greater than GNP / 1.5
Return on revenue net	Less than___% / .5	___% / 1.0	Greater than___% / 1.5
Return on investment	Less than___% / 1.0	___% / 2.0	Greater than___% / 3.0
Internal resources or strengths (versus competition)	Poor-fair / .5	Good / 1.0	Excellent / 1.5

Nine block – Risk Factors
(Reductions to nine block position)

Legend
B = Business unit
I = Industry
✓ = Reduction

	Affects
"Served" segment small compared to total market	I
Supplier dependence	B
Major customer dependence	B
Host-country political stability and/or currency	I
Management depth	B
Competitive ease of entry	I
Fuel	I
Government regulation	I
Business reductions	
Industry reductions	
Total net reductions	

Nine block – Investment Implications

	Industry →		
Business ↓	1	2	4
	3	5	7
	6	8	9

1–Major investment for maximum growth in excess of industry growth.
2-3–Selective investment for growth with industry or greater in a segment.
4-5-6–Selective investment to achieve high earnings. Hold.
7-8–Harvest—reduce investment to sustenance level—divert to growth opportunities.
9–Divest in prudent manner.

Source: Resource Allocation and Strategic Planning," *Information Bulletin No. 99*

EXHIBIT 9

Strategy Planning and Budgeting Cycle— An Industrial Manufacturer

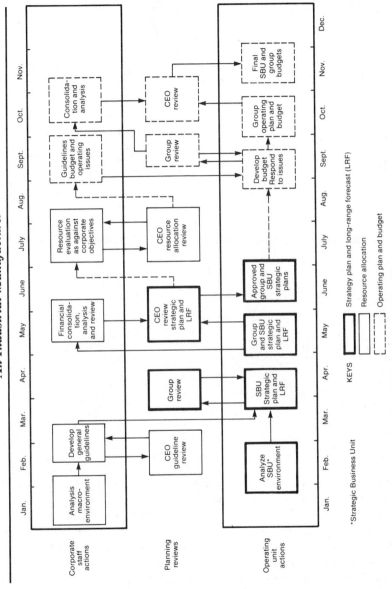

Source: Resource Allocation and Strategic Planning," *Information Bulletin No. 99* (New York: The Conference Board, 1981).

20

True Opportunity Cost: How to Set Realistic Hurdle Rates

Alan Seed, III

Arthur D. Little, Inc.

*A*t least once a year, the senior executives and directors of many corporations address the problem of establishing a capital spending budget and selecting the projects that will be undertaken during the following year. The usual practice is for proposals to be submitted up through the organization; top management selects the most promising proposals, and the directors approve the selection. Some projects are selected for economic reasons; other selections are largely based on nonfinancial considerations such as environmental compliance.

Regardless of the common threads of this process, considerable controversy surrounds the appropriate methodology to be applied to the selection.

Allen H. Seed, III, "Structuring Capital Spending Hurdle Rates," *Financial Executive,* February 1982, pp. 20–26.

One of the focal points of this controversy is the determination of capital spending hurdle rates:[1] Should they even be used, and if so, how should they be calculated?

This article explores alternative practices and points of view and suggests a new broad approach that provides a methodology for quantifying the factors that should be considered and one that can be applied in a practical manner to most business situations. The factors involved are as follows:

1. The cost of capital.
2. The inherent risk of the project.
3. The relative importance of spending for different strategic and tactical purposes.

By using a different debt to equity mix and cost of equity assumptions, it is possible to simulate the cost of capital that would apply in varying financial risk and strategic business circumstances.

THE VALUE OF HURDLE RATES

A survey of 136 companies by The Conference Board[2] showed that 62 companies (46 percent) do not specify minimum cutoff rates for their capital investments. These proportions correspond with my own experience. Many companies do not establish capital spending hurdle rates for three reasons:

1. Management wishes to reserve the prerogative of determining which proposals should be accepted and which should be turned down or deferred. They do not wish to discourage the submission of any capital proposals. However, all proposals should be ranked in the order of their desirability.

2. It is difficult to determine what "cutoff" or "hurdle rate" should apply, as risks, capital costs, and strategic considerations vary among projects. Moreover, some projects should be considered on a noneconomic basis.

3. If a hurdle rate is made known to operating management, the figures used in proposals may be "massaged" to pass this rate rather than present the project on an objective basis.

There is merit to the point of view of not using hurdle rates. Good proposals should indeed not be discouraged, particularly those that cannot be supported by strictly a financial basis. It *is* difficult to determine the cost of capital and the impact of risks. Simplistic, arbitrary rates are not a solution either, and operating management *will* tend to play games with capital proposals if hurdle rates are known.

However, not establishing cutoff rates imposes some important disadvantages. Operating managers are not informed about the basic economics of the business. The absence of information encourages the submission of proposals that do not support these economics. It is akin to asking managers to prepare budgets without budget guidelines or objectives, or marketing managers to set selling prices without cost information. Each individual is left to his own devices without any common focus or sense of direction. Unofficial yardsticks as to "what will fly" often emerge from this vacuum. Such yardsticks are communicated through the grapevine and are as apt to provide misinformation as they are to constructively assist with the capital spending proposal and selection process.

SINGLE HURDLE RATES

Some companies that use capital spending cutoff rates use single hurdle rates. The underlying concept is that returns from any prospective capital expenditures should exceed this cost if the enterprise is to enhance its overall return to its stockholders. Half of the 74 companies included in The Conference Board study follow this practice. However, this proportion may be on the low side for business, in general. The companies that participated in The Conference Board study had a median sales volume of $484 million. Thus, they tend to represent the practices of some of the larger members of the corporate community. An informal study by Samuel L. Hayes, III of Harvard University[3] suggests most companies use a single rate (if any), and the derivation of this rate often does not take inflation into account. Moreover, the process of capital allocation appears to be highly politicized.

Commonly, the hurdle rate is a round number that ends in a zero, or five. Some years ago 10 percent returns after taxes were considered to be a satisfactory cutoff for capital expenditures, but more recently 15 and 20 percent cutoff returns seem to be more typical. This rate may be arbitrary, or it may be based on a calculation of the company's cost of capital.

One definition of the cost of capital is that it consists of the risk-free rate of return plus an allowance for risk, inflation, and expenses of marketing and servicing the capital. While this definition seems straightforward on face value, it is fraught with practical difficulties in determining just what this cost is in most enterprises. Consider the elusiveness of the components of this formula: What is the risk-free rate of return in a free capital market? Should the yield of U.S. government securities approximate this value, and if so, why do these yields fluctuate so widely in relation to real or prospective inflation rates? What premium should be assigned for risk? As swings in the stock market have indicated, the factor is also subject to the vagaries of the market and the supply of capital that is available for investment. And what about inflation? Two years ago, a survey of financial executives[4] indicated that something in the order of a 6 percent inflation rate was expected. Now (in May 1979), the government's "guidelines" are at a 7 percent level, and many economists are predicting domestic inflation rates in an 8 to 10 percent range.

A practical approach to determining the "cost of capital" (a concept widely used in utility rate making) is to add up the weighted cost of each of its components, debt, deferred charges, and preferred and common stock. While each component has an apparent measurable cost, as with the case of the theoretical approach, a problem immediately arises as to what this cost really is. Should debt be valued at its historical cost or a replacement basis? (We suggest the latter.) How should deferred charges be treated; is this free capital and how should it be considered? What is the cost of equity capital; should it be based on present markets, and if so, over what time frame? Should equity costs be based on the market for the company's existing stock or the cost of new stock? And what mix of capital components should be assumed—the present mix or a mix adjusted for the financial norms of the industry concerned? I believe that there are workable solutions to this dilemma, but the fact still remains that one must choose between imperfect alternatives.

There are two reasons for using a single hurdle-rate approach:

1. It is relatively easy to understand and apply throughout the organization. More complex multiple hurdle rates contain more variables and hence require heightened understanding and additional analysis.

2. All calculations of prospective cash flows from capital spending projects are often rough approximations at best. Why attempt to refine the cost of capital calculation when a rough yardstick will serve in this imperfect environment?

These reasons for a single hurdle rate have appeal; however, they do not reflect the differences in risk that are inherent in certain types of expenditures, nor do they reflect differences in the strategic impact of the cost of capital that is inherent in different types of businesses. These latter differences can lead to significant shifts in capital spending with consequent important strategic and financial consequences to the enterprise.

THE NEED FOR MULTIPLE HURDLE RATES

The use of multiple hurdle rates is not new. Several companies use different rates for different types of projects. These rates typically reflect differences in project size, capital cost including business and financial risk, and priorities. What we believe is new, however, is an effective, organized method for linking hurdle rates to the current cost of capital, to risk, and to strategic impact. This approach is not intended as a substitute for sensitivity and risk analysis for major projects. It is a tool that can be readily applied in any organization to help screen proposals and sharpen capital spending decision making.

Gordon Donaldson prescribes strategic hurdle rates for capital investments related not to the cost of capital but to the actual investment alternatives available to the business.[5] He makes a distinction between tactical and strategic hurdle rates. "The hurdle rate for tactical decisions would be the ROI[6] standard reflecting the current potential of the profit center based on demonstrated performance. Strategic hurdle rates for any division would be the best ROI performance among other divisions, and for all divisions, the most attractive ROI on new products or markets."

One way of dealing with the issues of relating capital spending with strategic objectives is to ration the amount of capital available to each division or business unit.

Harold Bierman Jr. suggests that strategic objectives are obtained if past performance is used as a basis for allocation of at least part of the funds available for capital spending.[7] The track record of management is often an important indicator of capital expenditure desirability. All other things being equal, betting on a winning jockey is more productive than betting on losers. The man who has delivered before is most likely to deliver again. However, both of these approaches tend to minimize the importance of cost of capital and the individual contributions that can be derived from specific capital expenditures. Most companies have a wide range of capital spending opportunities available to them, and the challenge is to select amongst these competing opportunities.

Several years ago I was associated with a large packaging manufacturing business that was losing money. One of the actions that led to the subsequent dramatic improvement in profitability of this business was the construction of efficient new plants and the acquisition of high-speed automated equipment. Even in a mature business surrounded with red ink, there are usually a number of opportunities to make judicious capital expenditures where the potential returns exceed the cost of capital. The point is that the cost of capital should be factored into the hurdle rate, and that this rate should be modified to reflect differences in risk and strategic priorities.

As previously implied, there are three dimensions to the multiple hurdle rate structure that I propose:

Base Cost of Capital

Anticipate replacement cost in years of expenditure for normal capital structure for type of company concerned. This element should reflect the current cost of debt and equity based on the existing capital market and anticipated inflation rates. Deferred charges and other "free" capital should be excluded from this calculation.

Risk Adjustment

Normal, above normal, and below normal based on type of proposed expenditure. This element adjusts the pro forma mix of debt and equity to reflect the realities of the financial risk involved.

Strategic Impact

High, medium, and low. This factor reflects the positions of the business in its life cycle and can be equated to the relative growth rates (business risk) of the industry served. A "high impact" means that a business is in the ascending part of its life cycle with above average growth. "Medium impact" means that the industry is near the top of its life cycle with average growth. "Low impact" implies industry maturity with limited expansion potential.

The concept here is that the cost of equity would reflect a different price-earnings (P/E) multiple depending on how the business evolves as a result of the expenditure. For example, a capital expenditure that is designed to help migrate from a low P/E ratio (no growth) business to a higher P/E ratio (growth) business would have a lower cost of equity assigned to it than a capital expenditure that was designed to maintain the status quo. The underlying rationale here is that given a normal financial structure, investors will pay a higher premium for equity in a growth industry, and thus a company's cost of capital stock will decrease as the balance of its portfolio of businesses shifts from a mature to a growth state.

439

Determining the cost of capital for different strategic purposes does not preclude the need to allocate capital for strategic investments or to evaluate strategic investments in their totality. Most companies find that capital resources are limited, and thus available capital must be allocated to support different strategies as part of the strategic planning process. These requirements, and their associated returns, should be calculated for the strategy as a whole. Spending for fixed assets is ordinarily only part of this investment. However, when the prospective returns for the strategy are quantified, they can be compared with different costs of capital depending on the nature of the strategy.

The first step in quantification is to assign values to the normal (base) case for the industry concerned; the second step is to adjust these values for the variation of each dimension. These amounts may be obtained by analyzing debt-equity ratios, price-earnings ratios, and new issue costs of various types of comparable businesses. Published market values may be adjusted to reflect flotation costs to determine new issue costs. Reasonableness is more important than precision in this instance because the resulting hurdle rates are used as a basis for rough sorting rather than for detailed analysis.

For example, let us assume that the corporation involved is a large diversified manufacturing company. Regardless of its existing financial structure, such a company might be expected to maintain a $1:2$ debt/ equity ratio. new debt would cost about 12 percent before taxes and 6.5 percent after taxes based on a 46 percent effective tax rate. New equity would cost about 12.5 percent after taxes based on a $8 \times$ P/E ratio. On a weighted basis this works out to a composite aftertax replacement cost of capital of 10.5 percent ($0.67 \times 12.5 + 0.33 \times 6.5$). This becomes the base case (normal risk, medium strategic priority) cost of capital for this corporation.

Values for the risk dimension are determined by modifying the mix of debt and equity to reflect the normal financial structure required to support the type of expenditure to be considered. Lower-risk businesses with predictable cash flows (such as real estate and finance companies) typically support debt/equity ratios of $4:1$, whereas high-risk businesses are normally entirely financed by equity. Thus, the cost of capital for below-normal risk projects (for medium strategic priority businesses) might be calculated to be 7.7 percent ($0.20 \times 12.5 + 0.80 \times 6.5$). The inherent cost of capital for high-risk projects would be 12.5 percent because this type of project should be entirely financed by equity.

Values for the strategic impact dimension are determined by adjusting the cost of equity to reflect the P/E ratios of independent companies that are engaged in the industry associated with the strategic purpose of the expenditure. In this instance, it might be reasonable to assume that the corporation's P/E ratio (in today's market terms) will increase from 8 to 12 times if the corporation's strategic objectives are obtained. Conversely, capital expenditures required for low-priority strategies (for example, to maintain mature businesses) would cause the P/E to slip from eight to five times. In the first instance, the cost of equity would be 8.3 percent after taxes and, in the second instance, the cost of equity would be 20 percent after taxes.

All of these elements can be arrayed in a manageable matrix as illustrated in Table 1.

TABLE 1

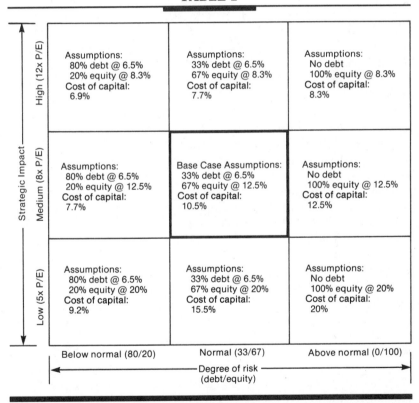

It should be emphasized that the foregoing values are shown for illustrative purposes only. Each organization will have its own notions of relevant debt/equity mixes and the cost of each element of capital. These costs will also change over time to reflect changes in the rate of inflation and the money market. Some organizations may also wish to

441

add a contingency factor to their calculations to offset optimistic projects, allow for the unknown, and partially compensate for limited capital availability.

The matrix of hurdle rates that are developed should be used by all business units of a corporation for all projects that are to be evaluated on an economic basis. Each business unit should be classified by strategic impact, as most of the internal proposals of any business unit will ordinarily fall into the same category. This means that different business units will use different hurdle rates. The effect of this approach is to favor the growth business units (with a lower incremental cost of capital) and penalize the business units in mature industries (with a high incremental cost of capital). However, capital expenditure proposals from business units in mature industries that lead to strategic growth opportunities would be subject to lower (high strategic impact) hurdle rates even though the host business has a low strategic impact. The governing concept is that it is the purpose of the expenditure—not the proposer of the expenditure—that determines the appropriate strategic impact to be selected.

Rates of return using the discounted cash flows or ROI methods may be compared with the appropriate cost of capital contained in the hurdle rate matrix to help ascertain the value of the proposed expenditure. Of these two methods for calculating actual returns, the discounted cash flow method is preferred because it reflects the time value of money. The discounted cash flow rate of return is the discount rate that equates the present value of cash receipts from a capital investment with the present value of the cash outlays made to support the investment. Cash receipts are ordinarily assumed to be the year-by-year incremental profit contribution after income taxes, but before depreciation (cash flow) from the project. Cash outlays should be incremental requirements for working capital as well as capital expenditures.

Hurdle rates can also be used as the discount rate in performing net present value or benefit-cost ratio calculations. The difference between the present value of the outlays and receipts of a proposed investment based on the discount that is applied is the present value of the project. A benefit-cost ratio is determined by dividing the net present value of receipts by the present value of outlays.

CONCLUSION

Meaningful multiple hurdle rates should be used as benchmarks to help with management decision-making. Executives of many large and medium-size businesses typically consider hundreds of capital proposals

442

each year. These proposals often involve many millions of increasingly scarce and expensive capital and have an impact on the strategic course of the business. Structuring capital spending hurdle rates on a matrix to reflect cost of capital, degree of risk, and strategic impact can help make this process more manageable and can improve the effectiveness of the resultant decisions.

NOTES

[1] A hurdle rate is the rate of return that must be generated by a capital spending project for it to be a desirable economic undertaking. In theory, this is the point where marginal revenue is just equal to marginal cost.

[2] Patrick J. Davey, *"Capital Investments: Appraisals and Limits"* (New York: The Conference Board, Inc., 1974), p. 6.

[3] Samuel L. Hayes, III, "Capital Commitments and the High Cost of Money" *Harvard Business Review,* May–June 1977.

[4] Allen H. Seed, III. *Inflation: Its Impact on Financial Reporting and Decision Making.* Financial Executives Research Foundation, 1978.

[5] Gordon Donaldson, "Strategic Hurdle Rates for Capital Investment," *Harvard Business Review,* March–April 1972.

[6] Return on investment.

[7] Harold Bierman, Jr., "Strategic Capital Budgeting," *Financial Executive,* April 1979.

21

Project Risk: How to Assess the Risk of Project Failure

Intelligent Computer Systems Research Institute

Of all the decisions that business executives must make, none is more challenging—and none has received more attention—than choosing among alternative project opportunities. What makes this kind of decision so demanding, of course, is not the problem of projecting return on investment under any given set of assumptions. The difficulty is in the assumptions and in their impact. Each assumption involves its own degree—often a high degree—of uncertainty; and, taken together, these combined uncertainties can multiply into a total uncertainty of critical proportions. This is the element of risk for which the executive has been able to get little help from currently available tools and techniques.

There is a way to help the executive sharpen key project decisions by providing him or her with a realistic measurement of the risks involved. Armed with this gauge, which evaluates the risk at each possible level of return, the executive is then in a position to measure more knowledgeably alternative courses of action against corporate objectives.

BASIC CONCEPTS

The evaluation of a project starts with the principle that the productivity of capital is measured by the rate of return we expect to receive over some future period. A dollar received next year is worth less to us than a dollar in hand today. Expenditures three years hence are less costly than expenditures of equal magnitude two years from now. For this reason we cannot calculate the rate of return realistically unless we take into account (*a*) when the sums involved in an investment are spent and (*b*) when the returns are received.

Comparing alternative projects is thus complicated by the fact that they usually differ not only in size but also in the length of time over which expenditures will have to be made and benefits returned.

These facts of investment life long ago made apparent the shortcomings of approaches that simply averaged expenditures and benefits, or lumped them, as in the number-of-years-to-pay-out method. These shortcomings stimulated students of decision making to explore more precise methods for determining whether one project would leave a company better off in the long run than would another course of action.

It is not surprising, then, that much effort has been applied to the development of ways to improve our ability to discriminate among project alternatives. The focus of all of these investigations has been to sharpen the definition of the value of projects to the company. The controversy and furor that once came out in the business press over the most appropriate way of calculating these values have largely been resolved in favor of the discounted cash flow method as a reasonable means of measuring the rate of return that can be expected in the future from an investment made today.

Thus we have methods which are more or less elaborate mathematical formulas for comparing the outcomes of various projects and the combinations of the variables that will affect the projects. As these techniques have progressed, the mathematics involved have become more and more precise, so that we can now calculate discounted returns to a fraction of a percent.

But the sophisticated executive knows that behind these precise calculations are data which are not that precise. At best, the rate of return information is based on an average of different opinions with varying reliabilities and different ranges of probability. When the expected returns on two projects are close, the executive is likely to be influenced by intangibles—a precarious pursuit at best. Even when the figures for two projects are quite far apart and the choice seems clear, there lurk memories of the Edsel and other ill-fated ventures.

In short, decision makers realize that there is something more they ought to know, something in addition to the expected rate of return. What is missing has to do with the nature of the data on which the expected rate of return is calculated and with the way those data are processed. It involves uncertainty, with possibilities and probabilities extending across a wide range of rewards and risks.

THE ACHILLES HEEL

The fatal weakness of past approaches thus has nothing to do with the mathematics of rate of return calculation. We have pushed along this path so far that the precision of our calculation is, if anything, somewhat illusory. The fact is that, no matter what mathematics is used, each of the variables entering into the calculation of rate of return is subject to a high level of uncertainty.

For example, the useful life of a new piece of capital equipment is rarely known in advance with any degree of certainty. It may be affected by variations in obsolescence or deterioration, and relatively small changes in use life can lead to large changes in return. Yet an expected value for the life of the equipment—based on a great deal of data from which a single best possible forecast has been developed—is entered into the rate of return calculation. The same is done for the other factors that have a significant bearing on the decision at hand.

Let us look at how this works out in a simple case—one in which the odds appear to be all in favor of a particular decision. The executives of a food company must decide whether to launch a new packaged cereal. They have come to the conclusion that five factors are the determining variables: advertising and promotion expense, total cereal market, share of market for this product, operating costs, and new capital investment.

On the basis of the "most likely" estimate for each of these variables, the picture looks very bright—a healthy 30 percent return. This future, however, depends on whether each of these estimates actually comes true. If each of these educated guesses has, for example, a 60 percent chance of being correct, there is only an 8 percent chance that all five will be correct (.60 × .60 × .60 × 60 × .60). So the "expected" return actually depends on a rather unlikely coincidence. The decision maker needs to know a great deal more about the other values used to make each of the five estimates and about what can be gained or lost from various combinations of these values.

This simple example illustrates that the rate of return actually depends on a specific combination of values of a great many different variables. But only the expected levels of ranges (worst, average, best; or pessimistic, most likely, optimistic) of these variables are used in formal mathematical ways to provide the figures given to management. Thus, predicting a single most likely rate of return gives precise numbers that do not tell the whole story.

The expected rate of return represents only a few points on a continuous curve of possible combinations of future happenings. It is a bit like trying to predict the outcome in a dice game by saying that the most likely outcome is a seven. The description is incomplete because it does not tell us about all the other things that could happen. Now suppose that each of eight dice has 100 sides. This is a situation more comparable to business project investment, where the company's market share might become any 1 of 100 different sizes, and where there are eight factors (pricing, promotion, and so on) that can affect the outcome.

Nor is this the only trouble. Our willingness to bet on a roll of the dice depends not only on the odds but also on the stakes. Since the probability of rolling a seven is one in six, we might be quite willing to risk a few dollars on that outcome at suitable odds. But would we be equally willing to wager $10,000 or $100,000 at those same odds, or even at better odds? In short, risk is influenced both by the odds on various events occurring and by the magnitude of the rewards or penalties that are involved when they do occur.

To illustrate again, suppose that a company is considering an investment of $1 million. The best estimate of the probable return is $200,000 a year. It could well be that this estimate is the average of three possible returns—a one-in-three chance of getting no return at all, a one-in-three chance of getting $200,000 per year, and a one-in-three chance of getting $400,000 per year. Suppose that getting no return at all would put the company out of business. Then, by accepting this proposal, management is taking a one-in-three chance of going bankrupt.

If only the best-estimate analysis is used, however, management might go ahead, unaware that it is taking a big chance. If all of the available information were examined, management might prefer an alternative proposal, with a smaller but more certain (that is, less variable) expectation.

Such considerations have led almost all advocates of the use of modern capital investment index calculations to plead for a recognition of the elements of uncertainty.

How can executives penetrate the mists of uncertainty surrounding the choices among alternatives?

ALTERNATIVES

A number of efforts to cope with uncertainty have been successful up to a point, but all seem to fall short of the mark in one way or another.

1. *More accurate forecasts.* Reducing the error in estimates is a worthy objective. But no matter how many estimates of the future go into a project decision, when all is said and done, the future is still the future. Therefore, however well we forecast, we are still left with the certain knowledge that we cannot eliminate all uncertainty.

2. *Empirical adjustments.* Adjusting the factors influencing the outcome of a decision is subject to serious difficulties. We would like to adjust them so as to cut down the likelihood that we will make a "bad" investment; but how can we do that without at the same time spoiling our chances to make a "good" one? And, in any case, what is the basis for adjustment? We adjust, not for uncertainty, but for bias.

For example, construction estimates are often exceeded. If a company's history of construction costs is that 90 percent of its estimates have been exceeded by 15 percent, then in a project estimate there is every justification for increasing the value of this factor by 15 percent. This is a matter of improving the accuracy of the estimate.

But suppose that new product sales estimates have been exceeded by more than 75 percent in one fourth of all historical cases and have not reached 50 percent of the estimate in one sixth of all such cases? Penalties for such overestimating are very real, and so management is apt to reduce the sales estimate to "cover" the one case in six— thereby reducing the calculated rate of return. In so doing, it is possibly missing some of its best opportunities.

3. *Revising cutoff rates.* Selecting higher cutoff rates for protecting against uncertainty is attempting much the same thing. Management would like to have a possibility of return in proportion to the risk it takes. Where there is much uncertainty involved in the various estimates of sales, costs, prices, and so on, a high calculated return from the investment provides some incentive for taking the risk. This is, in fact, a perfectly sound position. The trouble is that decision makers still need to know explicitly what risks they are taking—and what the odds are on achieving the expected return.

4. *Three-level estimates.* A start at spelling out risks is sometimes made by taking the high, medium, and low values of the estimated factors and calculating rates of return based on various combinations of the pessimistic, average, and optimistic estimates. These calculations give a picture of the range of possible results but do not tell the executive whether the average result is more likely to occur than either of the extremes. So, although this is a step in the right direction, it still does not give a clear enough picture for comparing alternatives.

5. *Selected probabilities.* Various methods have been used to include the probabilities of specific factors in the return calculation. L. C. Grant discussed a program for forecasting discounted cash flow rates of return where the service life is subject to obsolescence and deterioration. He calculated the odds that the investment will terminate at any time after it is made depending on the probability distribution of the service-life factor. After having calculated these factors for each year through maximum service life, he determined an overall expected rate of return.

Edward G. Bennion suggested the use of game theory to take into account alternative market growth rates as they would determine rate of return for various options. He used the estimated probabilities that specific growth rates would occur to develop optimum strategies. Bennion pointed out:

> Forecasting can result in a negative contribution to capital budget decisions unless it goes further than merely providing a single most probable prediction. [With] an estimated probability coefficient for the forecast, plus knowledge of the payoffs for the company's alternative projects, and calculation of indifference probabilities, the margin of error may be substantially reduced, and the businessman can tell just how far off his forecast may be before it leads him to a wrong decision.[1]

Note that both of these methods yield an expected return, each based on only one uncertain input factor—service life in the first case, market growth in the second. Both are helpful, and both tend to improve the clarity with which the executive can view project alternatives. But neither sharpens up the range of "risk taken" or "return hoped for" sufficiently to help very much in the complex decisions of capital planning.

SHARPENING THE PICTURE

Since every one of the many factors that enter into the evaluation of a decision is subject to some uncertainty, the executive needs a helpful portrayal of the effects that the uncertainty surrounding each of the significant factors has on the returns likely to be achieved. Therefore, I

449

use a method combining the variabilities inherent in all the relevant factors under consideration. The objective is to give a clear picture of the relative risk and the probable odds of coming out ahead or behind in light of uncertain foreknowledge.

A simulation of the way these factors may combine as the future unfolds is the key to extracting the maximum information from the available forecasts. In fact, the approach is very simple and uses a computer to do the necessary arithmetic. To carry out the analysis, a company must follow three steps:

1. Estimate the range of values for each of the factors (for example, range of selling price and sales growth rate) and within that range the likelihood of occurrence of each value.

2. Select at random one value from the distribution of values for each factor. Then combine the values for all of the factors and compute the rate of return (or present value) from that combination. For instance, the lowest in the range of prices might be combined with the highest in the range of growth rate and other factors. (The fact that the elements are dependent should be taken into account, as we shall see later.)

3. Do this over and over again to define and evaluate the odds of the occurrence of each possible rate of return. Since there are literally millions of possible combinations of values, we need to test the likelihood that various returns on the investment will occur. This is like finding out by recording the results of a great many throws what percent of sevens or other combinations we may expect in tossing dice. The result will be a listing of the rates of return we might achieve, ranging from a loss (if the factors go against us) to whatever maximum gain is possible with the estimates that have been made.

For each of these rates we can determine the chances that it may occur. (Note that a specific return can usually be achieved through more than one combination of events. The more combinations for a given rate, the higher the chances of achieving it—as with sevens in tossing dice.) The average expectation is the average of the values of all outcomes weighted by the chances of each occurring.

We can also determine the variability of outcome values from the average. This is important since, all other factors being equal, management would presumably prefer lower variability for the same return if given the choice. This concept has already been applied to investment portfolios.

FIGURE 1

Major Steps of Risk Analysis

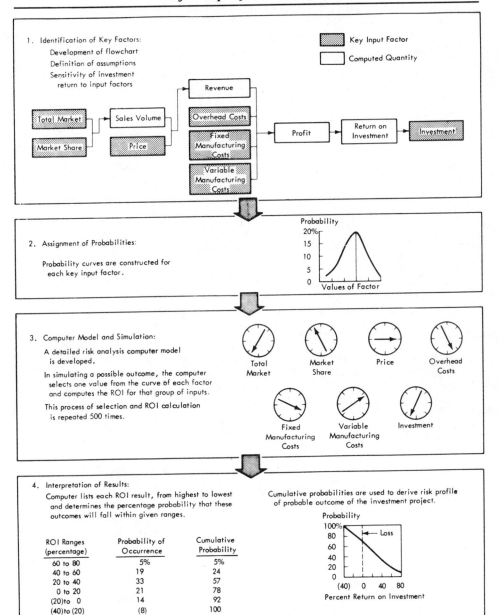

Source: David B. Hertz, "Incorporating Risk in Capital Expenditure Analysis," in *Controller's Handbook*, ed. Sam R. Goodman and James S. Reece © 1978, Dow Jones-Irwin: Homewood, Ill., p. 436.

451

When the expected return and variability of each of a series of investments have been determined, the same techniques may be used to examine the effectiveness of various combinations of them in meeting management objectives. The entire process is depicted in Figure 1.

TRADITIONAL RISK ANALYSIS METHODS

A project's intrinsic worth is measurable in terms of the stream of values (including salvage) it returns to the investor over its useful life. The prospective worth of a project, therefore, can be evaluated by the stream of net returns (in whatever form) that is expected to be forthcoming once it has been made. The investment inputs and returns usually (but not always or necessarily) are measured in monetary units. The times at which the various parts of the investments are made and at which the returns are anticipated need to be taken into account in order to compare the values of a dollar spent or received today with those that may be spent or received in the future.

A consensus of dictionary definitions of *risk* is "exposure to the chance of injury or loss, and the degree of probability of such loss." Managers are well aware of the fact that projects involve a greater or lesser degree of risk—either by virtue of the size of the potential loss (a loss that could bankrupt a business will be viewed in a different light than one which simply could reduce earnings by a few percent) or because of the likelihood of such loss (the greater the size of potential loss, the more critical for the decision maker becomes the probability of its occurrence). And most businesspeople, either intuitively or analytically, evaluate both of these elements of risk. But, whether or not the decision maker accounts for risk in making investment choices, if the risk exists it is a factor.

Suppose that a project whose cost is $4,000 is expected to yield a $1,000 annual pretax return over out-of-pocket cost for seven years. Given a 32 percent tax rate, straight-line depreciation, and no salvage value, the post-tax discounted internal rate of return (DCR) would be 11.6 percent. If the investment lasts only six years, instead of seven, then the return drops to 9.1 percent; if the pretax return turns out to be $800 annually, then the DCR falls to 6.5 percent, or only 56 percent of the original estimate. The variability of the return over ranges of uncertainty in the elements of the investment can be very significant.

For example, in a simplified conventional analysis of a project where the best-guess estimates of the input elements are to be compared with the best (optimistic) and worst (pessimistic) cases, it should be clear that there is no way to make a prudent decision. Using a simple ROI measure, we obtain the following.

452

$$\text{ROI} = \frac{(\text{Price} \times \text{Unit sales}) - \text{Costs}}{\text{Investment}}$$

	Best-guess estimates	Likely ranges
Price	$5.00	$5.00 to $5.50
Costs	$800,000	$700,000 to $875,000
Sales	200,000 units	175,000 to 225,000 units
Investments	$1,000,000	$950,000 to $1,100,000

Best guess: $\dfrac{5.0 \times 200,000 - 800,000}{1,000,000} = 20$ percent ROI

Worst case: $\dfrac{5.0 \times 175,000 - 875,000}{1,100,000} = 0$ percent ROI

Best case: $\dfrac{5.5 \times 225,000 - 700,000}{950,000} = 56.5$ percent ROI

What is significant here is not so much the fact that the possible ROIs range from 0 to 56.5 percent (although if the range were, say, from 18 to 22 percent for the worst to best cases, the uncertainty involved probably would be acceptable) but that the chances a specific ROI will occur are completely unspecified. It should make a great deal of difference to the decision maker to know that 0 percent ROI has a 1 in 100 chance of occurring, while at least 20 percent ROI could occur 1 in 2 times, and 56.5 percent ROI, 1 in 20 times; versus 0 percent ROI at 1 in 15 chances, at least 20 percent ROI, 1 in 10 times, and 56.5 percent ROI, 1 in 100 times. With the same ranges, the prospects for each of these projects would look entirely different.

Only the most naive managers act as though there were no risk in every project. At the very least they make one or more of the following adjustments to aid in their decision to make what they consider a risky investment, depending on their view of the risk:

1. Require a higher than normal return.
2. Require a shorter than normal payback period.
3. Adjust estimated return on investment to account for probabilities of varying results—for example, assess the range of outcomes by using low, most likely, and highest values of factors to calculate result.
4. Adjust estimated return, or some of the input factors, on a purely subjective or intuitive basis.

453

There are two kinds of risks to be taken into account:

1. The risk implicit in the wider range of outcomes (the difference between the ranges 0 to 56 percent and 18 to 22 percent) is one of greater risk of low return coupled with possibly higher returns for the former, and a high degree of comfort or safety (that is, freedom from risk) with the latter.

2. The risk of a greater probability of an unfavorable outcome (a project that has only one chance in three of not being successful is inherently less risky—at the same cost—than one that has four chances out of five of not being successful).

In either of these kinds of cases, in order to understand the nature of the risks, it is necessary to attach some numerical probabilities to each of the outcomes in order to develop an average for these outcomes, weighted by the probability of their occurrence. This average then will be the expectation or expected value of the particular project. Thus, to calculate the expected value of the project investments, we should determine the payoff for each of the possible outcomes. There is some probability of winning a contract that could make a project attractive. That probability presumably will vary from manager to manager, depending on his "risk preference" or "risk aversion" viewpoints—in other words, on what is called his utility function.

GROUP UTILITY

Frequently a group assessment has to be made. In these circumstances the Delphi technique may be a useful vehicle for obtaining probability estimates. In the Delphi technique, a panel of experts is interrogated by a sequence of questionnaires in which the summarized responses to one questionnaire are used to produce the next questionnaire. The rationale is that as a result of several rounds of the procedure, most of the assumptions and information about the problem should have been exchanged among the participants. Eventually, it is argued, the process leads to an acceptable group consensus. This technique also attempts to eliminate the bandwagon effect of majority opinion.

There are a number of possible voting procedures for accomplishing agreement between group members, and bargaining procedures can be devised where individuals "give way" on the evaluations of some outcomes in return for their own evaluations being accepted. There is, however, no reason to suppose, a priori, that there exists any voting or bargaining process which will result in a single unique group utility enabling the group, whatever the decision procedures it adopts, to act as a whole "rationally" and to maximize the expectation of a single consensus utility function.

The measurement of group utility is clearly an important practical problem, particularly because utility evaluations of individuals cannot be simply aggregated to obtain a group utility—it being a relative and not an absolute measure. As an illustration of a possible procedure, consider the formulation of a risk policy for making capital investment decisions in a corporation.

1. Present a number of executives in the company with a series of hypothetical investment decisions and, from their answers, plot utility functions (one for each executive).
2. Agree with the help of further questioning on a functional form to fit the utility plots (the same functional form, but with different parameters being used for each executive).
3. Reinterview, allowing each executive to spend a great deal of time on a few questions, and determine each executive's parameters for the functional form from the results.
4. Present the results to top management, attempting to form in discussion with them the best parameters for a corporate risk policy.

Basically, step 4 argues that a group utility is best obtained by a consensus process of "thrashing out" the inconsistencies of individual decision makers at the level of the top decision-making group. In most cases it is found that, at all levels of investment, the final corporate utility function is far less conservative than the average for the individual executives interviewed. (This can be regarded as a particular example of the "risky shift phenomenon," that is, a willingness to be more risky in group situations, which has been well documented by psychologists.)

The main identifiable advantages accruing from a study like the one discussed above are, first, that it is educational in the sense that executives are forced to consider their individual risk attitudes; second, that the premature rejection of risky projects by middle management is avoided; and, finally, that it allows the development within the corporation of a way of communicating risk by means of utility evaluations, and of identifying a rational form of corporate risk policy which can be compared to the organization's perceived goals, for example, the maximization of shareholder wealth.

There appears to be little doubt that the only realistic and practical approach for obtaining a group utility structure is for the group to meet and approach a group utility view through a consensus process. The

455

method of conducting such a meeting is, however, of crucial importance in order to ensure that the final view which emerges is that of the group.

DECISION TREES—INCORPORATING PROBABILITY INTO INVESTMENT ANALYSIS

The decision paths to possible outcomes under alternative states of nature or external events can be described by a *decision tree*. The simplest case is one in which there is only one investment decision involving two or more alternatives and two or more states of nature—a "single-stage" decision. Figure 2 illustrates such a case, comprising alternative plant investments and market conditions. The decision tree simply makes explicit the decisions and the uncertain elements facing the investor. The expected monetary return (EMV) for each decision is calculated by tracing back the outcomes weighted by the probability of their occurrence to each *node* where chance (for example, a competitor's action) or nature (for example, rainfall during a growing season) takes over.

Multiple Decision Stages

The same methodology applies to the multistage investment problem, that is, one in which a series of decisions is required, the ultimate outcomes from which depend both on the various choices made and the uncertainties of future events or states of the world. The method requires that the EMVs be calculated back from the end of the tree to each chance event node, with the decision yielding highest EMV at the node then being selected for the immediately previous decision stage. This decision stage then is treated as though it were the end of the tree and "rolled back" to the preceding chance event nodes, where the appropriate preceding decision is once again selected. The process is continued through all decision stages until all decisions but one have been eliminated. This one will have the highest EMV.

The possible decisions for a two-stage plant investment and subsequent expansion under conditions of uncertainty as to whether additional market share will become available are as shown in Illustration 1. There are two key uncertainty factors in the future: (1) under expansion, will the company capture a greater market share (probability estimated at 20 percent) or only maintain its present share (probability 80 percent); and (2) with no expansion, can the present product sales mix be upgraded to increase profits (probability 10 percent) or not (probability 90 percent)? Other questions include sensitivity of the

456

FIGURE 2

Use of Decision Tree to Analyze New Plant Investment Alternatives

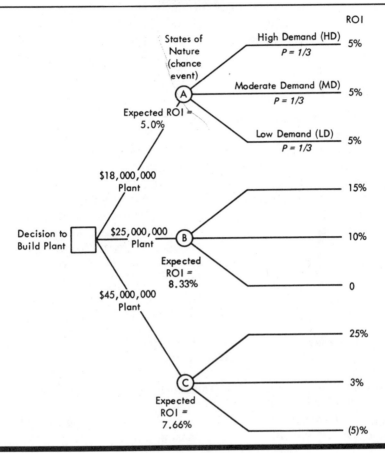

ILLUSTRATION 1

1. At first decision point:
   A. Large plant—$40 million investment
   B. Small expandable plant—$25 million investment
   C. No new plant—$0 investment
2. After three years—second decision point:
   B–1. Expand plant B—$15 million investment
   B–2. Do not expand
   C–1. Expand plant C—$25 million investment
   C–2. Do not expand

present values of the alternative decisions to changes in these probabilities and to postponement of the decision to expand beyond three years. The completed decision tree for this two-stage investment decision problem is shown in Figure 3. In order to reflect the time value of money, we will use net present value (NPV) as the decision criterion.

The first step in the calculation of the expected NPVs for the various decision points, after having laid out all the alternative possibilities along the branches of the tree, is to determine the net present value (or other criterion that a manager may wish to use) using the accepted methods for determining that value. Thus, there are 16 paths through the decision tree in Figure 3. Each one has its own NPV at the end of the 10th year, depending upon the decisions taken at the starting year and at the third year (decision points 1 an 2 on the decision tree). Thus, for example, branch number (1) involves a $40 million outlay for a large plant, the assumption that an increased share of the market would ensue and would yield an NPV (if the assumption held true) of $25 million. However, it is counterbalanced by the possibility of no new share of market—branch (2)—which would lead to overinvestment and an NPV of only $500,000.

Therefore, "rolling back" from these end points, as before, the expected NPV of a decision to build a large plant in the starting year is:

$$\text{Expected NPV}_A = (0.2 \times 25,000,000) + (0.8 \times 500,000)$$
$$= 5,400,000$$

Similarly, for the small-plant decision (B), working backward to decision point 2 (which did not enter into the calculation relating to the large plant since there was only one decision to be made), we find the expected NPV for the second expansion to be:

$$\text{Expected NPV}_{B-2} = (0.2 \times 20,000,000) + (0.8 \times 4,000,000)$$
$$= 7,200,000$$

which must be balanced against no expansion at decision point 2, or:

$$\text{Expected NPV}_{B-2} = (0.2 \times 10,000,000) + (0.8 \times 1,500,000)$$
$$= 3,200,000$$

Thus, if we had reached decision point 2 along the branches from a decision to build a small plant and had achieved increased share of market, the best decision (as we look at it in the starting year) would be to expand. Therefore, the manager can discard the no-expansion possibility (indicated by the two lines "chopping off" that branch) and

458

FIGURE 3

Two-Stage Decision Tree for Plant Investment

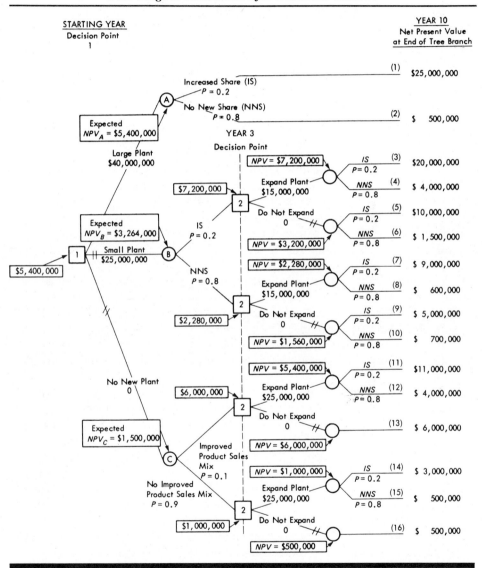

consider only expansion. However, the increased-share possibility only has a 20 percent chance of occurring; thus, the *no-increased-share branch* also must be considered, one of its alternate possibilities discarded, and the best result combined with the $7,200,000 expectation at decision point 2. As Figure 3 indicates, expansion branches (7) and (8) yield an NPV of $2.28 million; whereas the no-expansion branches (9) and (10) result in only $1.56 million and therefore are discarded.

The possibilities of the small-plant expansion may now be combined to compare it with the other alternatives:

$$\text{Expected NPV}_B = (7,200,000 \times 0.2) + (2,280,000 \times 0.8)$$
$$= 3,264,000$$

Similarly, for no new plant (possibility C), the expected NPV is calculated at $1.5 million. Thus, the large-plant alternative has the highest expectation ($5.4 million) and should be chosen, given a satisfactory degree of confidence in the assumptions.

The sensitivity of the decision to invest in the large plant (alternative A) to the assumption of a 20 percent probability of increased market share can be checked by substituting larger and smaller values for this event in the tree. It happens that any probability larger than 20 percent would increase the relative desirability of the large plant; and even at 10 percent probability of increased share, the large plant still remains the most desirable. To determine the sensitivity of the result to the timing of either the first or second decision, additional branches that represent alternative timing possibilities can be constructed to this tree.

As many stages and alternatives may be included in such a tree as seems desirable and practical to the manager. Weak strategies (in terms of their expected yields) can be "pruned out" to simplify the calculations. But the basic methodology remains the same, no matter what the size of the tree: (1) laying out in sequence all the alternatives; (2) assessing the chance events or states of nature that will affect them; (3) determining the payoff criterion at the end of each branch; (4) calculating the expected payoffs by rolling back through each chance event node to the relevant decision point; (5) selecting the strategies at the respective decision points with the highest payoff; (6) continuing to calculate through the chance event nodes; and (7) resulting eventually in an expected payoff that is equivalent to the decision maker to the entire problem depicted by the tree.

A decision tree permits the evaluation and comparison of monetary expectations (EMVs) under the general circumstance that the number of branches leading from chance event nodes is relatively small; otherwise a decision tree may become impractically unwieldy. This means that the distribution of chance events at those nodes is represented by only a few point estimates (for example, 20 percent chance of increased and 80 percent chance of decreased market share). As a result of this "condensed" representation, the decision tree's expected value for the decision criterion may not be an adequate representation of the average that would result if more complete estimated distributions of these chance events were taken into account. A more complete representation for each alternative investment decision, or strategy, would be a probability-type distribution of the payoffs (such as NPV, payback, ROE, and so on). Using these representations to compare business opportunities provides a more complete insight into the nature of specific risky investments. This method of incorporating uncertainty into investment evaluations is called *risk analysis* and will be discussed in the following section.

SCREENING FOR RISKY VENTURES: DOMINANCE APPROACHES

If the outputs of decision analyses are presented in the form of probability distributions of a financial measure, such as net present value, two issues emerge for the decision maker who is confronted with a series of projects evaluated in terms of probability distributions: (*a*) reduction or screening of the options into a feasible or efficient set— rules of stochastic dominance and (*b*) deriving a choice criterion, for example, expected utility for determining the "most preferred" option within that feasible set.

The simplest approach for screening under uncertainty consists of identifying the "efficient" set of options. The efficient set excludes all "dominated" options. An option is said to be dominated (in a mean-variance sense) in the set if there exists either another option with the same mean but lower variance or with the same variance but higher mean.

This concept of dominance is founded in the principle of minimizing variance (a surrogate for risk) for risk-averse decision makers. It can be summarized as follows for two alternatives (X_1 and X_2) with means $E(X_1)$ and $E(X_2)$ and variances $V(X_1)$ and $V(X_2)$.

1. Alternative 1 is preferred to alternative 2 if

$$E(X_1) \geq E(X_2) \quad \text{and} \quad V(X_1) < V(X_2).$$

2. Alternative 1 is preferred to alternative 2 if

$$V(X_1) \leq V(X_2) \quad \text{and} \quad E(X_1) > E(X_2).$$

461

It can be shown that these rules hold if the probability distributions for the outcome of X_1 and X_2 are reasonably symmetrically (strictly normally) distributed, and if the decision makers' preferences for outcomes are of the quadratic form.

The mean-variance approach summarized above involves certain assumptions, and for screening purposes we have to question how robust these assumptions are in identifying the best subset. Less restrictive constraints in the form of implicit function can be dealt with using screening models developed from the concept of stochastic dominance. *Stochastic dominance* is said to occur if the expected utility of an option is greater than that of another over a whole class of utility functions.

To illustrate the application of stochastic dominance criteria, a simple example is given below.

It should be noted initially that the stochastic dominance approach examines the entire range of likely outcomes from an investment project, rather than concentrating upon parameters of the distribution of outcomes such as the expected value (mean) and the standard deviation (variance).

Therefore, the stochastic dominance approach may be employed as an additional refinement to the mean-variance type of analysis or as

FIGURE 4

Pdfs for X *and* Y

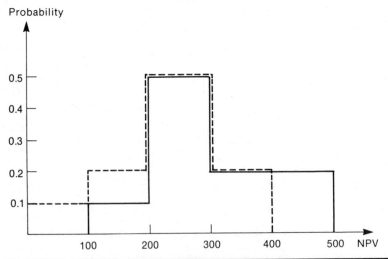

an alternative method. However, it is important to remember that if the stochastic dominance approach is used as an additional analytic vehicle to mean-variance analysis, the rules of stochastic dominance may reduce the number of portfolios in the mean-variance efficient set of projects. Equally, if the rules of stochastic dominance were applied before mean-variance rules, it would be possible to find that some portfolios not included in the mean-variance efficient set were members of the efficient set determined from the stochastic dominance rules. Generally, therefore, the efficient sets determined from both approaches will not normally be equivalent.

Now let us consider two project portfolios X and Y (valued in NPV terms), both of which are members of the mean-variance efficient set.

| X | | Y | |
Probability distribution		Probability distribution	
X(NPV) $m	Probability	Y(NPV) $m	Probability
$100 \leq X < 200$	0.1	$0 \leq Y < 100$	0.1
$200 \leq X < 300$	0.5	$100 \leq Y < 200$	0.2
$300 \leq X < 400$	0.2	$200 \leq Y < 300$	0.5
$400 \leq X < 500$	0.2	$300 \leq Y < 400$	0.2
Mean $E(X) = 300$		$E(Y) = 230$	
$V(X) = 8500$		$V(Y) = 7600$	

Figure 4 gives a visual representation of these two probability distributions in terms of histograms or probability density functions (pdfs).

If we follow the decision analytic route and assume that both constant risk aversion and independent events hold, we can show that an important simplification for the portfolio selection problem is available to us. We can treat multiple projects separately, whereas in most situations in project evaluation, both the overall portfolio and all possible subset combinations must be evaluated and treated in detail (in general, the assumption of risk aversion requires that all possible combinations should be evaluated).

Therefore, individual project selection and portfolio selection coalesce under this set of assumptions. The extent to which this set of assumptions can be considered realistic is, however, a matter for examination in the actual problem situation.

For the record, we should note that the assumption of constant risk aversion means that the risk premium (the absolute value of the difference between the certainty equivalent and the EMV) depends only on the size of the difference between the outcomes and not on the absolute values of those outcomes. In mathematical terms, constant risk aversion implies a utility function (u) for wealth (x) of exponential form. Specifically, $\mu(x) = \alpha - \beta e^{-\mu x}$, where μ is a measure of risk aversion, and α and β are constants. Screening procedures can be distinguished: those which attempt to reduce the set of options or those which attempt to simplify the structure of the decision model. In conceptual terms it might appear that these are two distinct stages in a rational decision analysis framework. The options are first reduced to a minimum, and the final decision model is then simplified to the most realistic structure. However, options or alternatives cannot be adequately "screened" without a simple decision model; and furthermore, in "screening" the structure of that model, extraneous options would fall out anyway as additional complications. There is, therefore, a simultaneity in screening options and structural assumptions, and this should always be recognized.

Some decision analysts agree that an initial prior analysis of the rough decision tree as well as the use of sensitivity analysis to test and question assumptions can help to screen out both in terms of structural reduction and refinement of the set of alternative options.

THE MEASUREMENT OF UNCERTAINTY AND THE CERTAINTY EQUIVALENT

The process of making assessments of uncertain events involves three distinct parts, which together form a logical structure. Initially, the individual assessor must have some experience of, and training in, the available methods of assessing probabilities. This phase is sometimes referred to as the pre-encoding phase. The second phase of encoding relates to the actual quantification of the decision maker's judgment in probabilistic terms. The appropriate methods are those which the assessor can understand, use, and is comfortable with. In addition, a third phase of verification and calibration is needed in which the responses obtained in the encoding phase are checked for internal consistency and amended, if inconsistency manifests itself. The overall process is depicted schematically in Figure 5.

As probability assessment is one of the important measurement tasks to be undertaken in the decision analysis approach, it is therefore assumed that the analyst and decision maker have discussed the decision problem and the set of underlying assumptions, and have reached the point at which a realistic decision tree has been constructed. At the same time, a crude sensitivity analysis of the tree will also have been

FIGURE 5

The Process of Probability Assessment

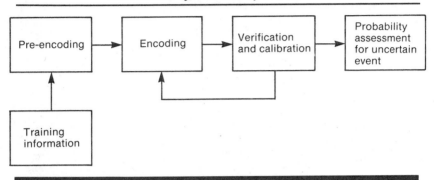

performed. This will have identified the important features of the problem and, in particular, the areas in which uncertainty plays a crucial part. The aim is then to proceed to a careful assessment of the probabilities for the uncertain events on the decision tree.

The equivalent urn (EQU) method for discrete probabilities is described in terms of the following example. Suppose the probability of the successful development of a new product by 1985 is required. The assessor is offered the choice between gamble A or gamble B, shown in Figure 6 in terms of probability trees. Under gamble B, one ball is drawn from the urn at the end of 1985 (the urn contains 900 black balls and 100 white balls).

If the assessor chooses A, the assessment is repeated, but with more black balls (and correspondingly fewer white balls) in gamble B. If he chooses B, it is repeated until the proportion of black balls in gamble B is such that he is indifferent between the two gambles. The required probability is then taken as the final proportion of black balls in B. At no time in this process is it necessary to ask a more difficult question than "do you prefer this gamble, or that one, or can't you say?" Numerical measurement of an individual's degrees of belief can thus be obtained simply by asking questions of preference.

In the foregoing discussion an urn with colored balls was used to vary the probabilities. Such a decision aid (or standard device) as the urn is intended to help the manager in probability assessment tasks. However, although many executives have made use of such standard devices, not all have felt totally at ease using them. The main objection seems to be the close analogy drawn between business and gambling.

Furthermore, for a complex problem with many probabilities to be

FIGURE 6

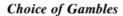

Choice of Gambles

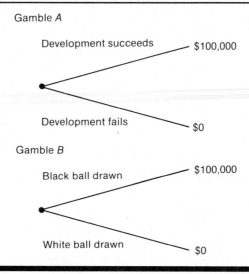

Gamble *A*

Development succeeds — $100,000

Development fails — $0

Gamble *B*

Black ball drawn — $100,000

White ball drawn — $0

estimated, they find that the discipline imposed is tiring—they get stale and hence are not so certain that later assessments are realistic. Therefore, although these methods are quick and easy to use, they are probably best used as initial training aids. Care must be exercised to ensure that the assessor does not react unfavorably to the standard device and, as a consequence, produce ill-considered judgments.

Other standard devices have been popular. A pie diagram, or spinner, is a favorite with the Decision Analysis Group at the Stanford Research Institute. A circle is divided into two sectors, and the relative sizes of the sectors can be adjusted. A spinner randomly selects one of the two sectors. Thus, the larger a sector, the greater its chance of being chosen. The same bets as those shown in the earlier figures can be offered, but the outcomes for bet B are determined not only by drawing a ball from an urn but also by noting which sector is chosen. The relative sizes of the sectors are adjusted until the indifference point is reached; the sector sizes then represent the probabilities of the event being assessed and its complement.

We should, at this point, note quite explicitly that the indirect estimation of probabilities from gambling preferences makes strong behavioral assumptions. Quite often, it is assumed that the individual is behaving so as to maximize expected monetary value. Thus, returning to the development gamble presented here, a statement by the decision maker of his certainty equivalent (CE) for gamble A (that is, his minimum selling price for that gamble) allows the probability of development success to be imputed as the CE/$100,000.

However, in order to have any confidence in this imputed value as a predictive probability, we should determine whether the decision maker's preference function is in fact a linear form over the relevant range of assets. If trouble is to be taken in measuring the individual's utility curve in the first place, there is no reason why the payoffs should not be appropriately mapped into utility values in order to obtain consistent subjective probabilities. If a Von Neumann-Morgernstern utility function is derived using standard devices to articulate the probabilities presented in the artificial gambles, then the subsequent use of this function in the derivation of subjective probabilities should give valid estimates provided that the individual acts in a coherent and consistent manner. Unfortunately, individuals react and behave differently in gambling situations. Some people pay more attention to the chance of winning, others to the chance of losing, while a further group seems to look mainly at the size of the payoffs.

In summary, I believe that standard devices should primarily be used as training aids for the probability assessment process. Thus, managers can be alerted to the nature of probability but are not asked to treat business decisions as forms of gambling.

CAPITAL ASSET PRICING (CAP) IN THE FACE OF RISK

The underlying market equilibrium model on which risk-adjusted capital asset pricing (CAP) is based can be stated in terms of the following equation:

$$E(R_j) = R_F + \beta_j[E(R_M) - R_F] \tag{1}$$

where

$E(R_j)$ = Expected return on a project investment (asset).

$E(R_M)$ = Expected return on a market index of investments (for example, the Dow-Jones or Financial Times 500 Index).

β_j = Measure of systematic nondiversifiable risk, that is, the regression coefficient of R_j on R_M.

R_F = A risk-free interest rate (usually to be found from prevailing interest rates on government or gilt-edged securities).

467

Put simply, the equation above indicates that the expected return on a given investment (asset) is the sum of two terms: a risk-free rate and a term which represents a required risk premium.

Further, the theory indicates that the risk premium should be calculated from the formula $\beta_j[E(R_M) - R_F]$, and this means that the risk premium is the market's risk premium $[E(R_M) - R_F]$ weighted by the index of volatility, or systematic risk, β_j, of the given investment. This quantity, β_j, is often called the beta coefficient and measures the sensitivity of the investment's returns to market returns. For example, a beta value of 0 would indicate no correlation between investment j and the market, whereas a beta of 1 would imply that the investment would have a risk exactly equivalent to the market risk. A beta value greater than 1 would, on the other hand, imply an aggressive type of investment which has more risk than a market portfolio. In other words, beta takes account for a given investment of factors such as the overall economy and industrial structure, which reflect risk sources that have not been diversified away.

One of the key assumptions of CAP is that perfect efficient capital markets exist, and that investors have homogeneous expectations. The market appears to be neither unduly optimistic nor pessimistic, and it does not seem to exhibit any generalizable sources of bias. The general mathematical relationship of CAP given in Equation 1 can be graphed as shown in Figure 7.

It is further argued that for a well-diversified portfolio of projects (say of 20 or more randomly selected investments), the total risk of the portfolio is reduced to the point where only systematic risk remains. Therefore, the only important source of risk for a particular investment is the sensitivity of its returns to those of the market portfolio—the so-called beta risk or, in other words, the undiversifiable risk that has not been eliminated by an efficient diversification process. Thus, for a particular investment, beta is a sufficient measure for its risk and, more specifically, it can be shown that risk premiums are proportional to beta risk. (This differs from the certainty equivalent view which argues that the risk of the project is its marginal contribution to firm risk, as measured by the covariance of the project's return with that of the firm's portfolio of projects.)

One of the advantages of the model described by Equation 1 is that the only factor which needs to be estimated is the beta coefficient. Every other factor has a market-determined value and can be obtained relatively easily from existing data sources.

How then does CAP relate to project investment decision making? It is agreed that the stated aim of management is to maximize the

FIGURE 7

Graphical Description of the Basic Model

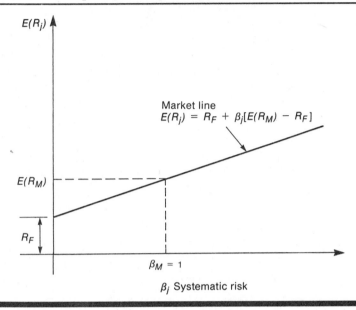

firm's value, as measured by a maximization of shareholder wealth objective. Further, assets are priced in such share markets by discounting cash flows at a risk-adjusted rate, which reflects both the market's risk premium and the investment's volatility relative to the market. Therefore, for capital project appraisal, an individual project's expected cash flows should first be discounted by the required risk-adjusted rate of return determined from CAP. Any project which then increases the value of the firm, that is, has an NPV $\geq$ 0 when discounted at the required risk-adjusted rate (which equals the opportunity cost of capital), should be accepted. If we return for a moment to the graphical depiction of the model in Figure 7, we can translate the logic of CAP for project appraisal into visual terms. Recall for a moment that Equation 1 gives us a formula for the expected return of a project or investment in terms of the risk-free rate and the market's risk premium weighted by the beta coefficient. If we can determine, in reality, that the expected return for investment j exceeds the sum of the risk-free rate and the beta-weighted market premium, then we should clearly accept the j investment. In graphical terms, this means that

469

projects with expected return-systematic risk characteristics (which ensure that they lie above and to the left of the market line) must be acceptable to the firm.

Let us now compare this criterion with the test discount rate or hurdle rate approach which is often used in corporate finance to determine acceptable projects. There is, apparently, a commonly held view that the application of a single cutoff or hurdle rate (reflecting the firm's weighted average risk) for all investment projects will lead to correct and sensible capital investment decisions. Let us examine this in graphical terms. Figure 8 shows the now familiar market line and also a hurdle rate, R_o, which is the minimum "average" return for any investment.

FIGURE 8

CAP and the Hurdle Rate Method Compared

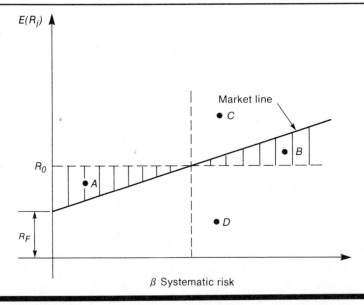

The drawback of a constant cutoff rate is that it does not take account of risk as effectively or directly as the CAP approach. Indeed, it could be argued that each project belongs to a different risk class and that, therefore, there should be a different hurdle rate for each risk class. The weighted-average cost of capital approach therefore needs some procedure for screening projects into risk classes and also for determining hurdle rates for each of these classes. Even if all this were done, however, it would not be clear how the accept/reject decisions offered by the cutoff procedures would connect satisfactorily with a valuation objective of maximizing the overall value of the firm.

We should note that the CAP approach for project appraisal implies that the required rate of return for a particular investment project does not only depend upon the policy of the company contemplating that investment possibility. Since investment projects should be evaluated solely in terms of their systematic risk, the market will expect and require a return from that project which would be at least as good as for any other firm in the same industry confronting such a project. Some firms, because of internal reasons of capital structure, efficiency, or cash flow potential, may derive greater benefit from a given project once accepted; but at the decision stage, acceptance or rejection should only be made in terms of the market's required rate of return. This may be calculated for the relevant industry if acceptable firm beta information is not available.

CAP states that the risk inherent in an individual project can be diversified into two components: systematic risk or beta (the non-diversifiable risk) and the diversifiable risk (often called the unsystematic risk). In other words, in efficient markets investors can eliminate the unsystematic component through a sensible diversification process and need concentrate only on the beta factor. It is important to recognize that the total risk approach looks at the total business risk for the firm by evaluating the portfolios of investments for a firm in relation to a corporate trade-off (typically in terms of a subjective utility function and not the functional capital market line trade-off given by CAP) between risk and return. Any individual project is reviewed in relation to its marginal impact on the total return (expected value) and total risk (standard deviation) of the firm as a whole. It is then the management's task to judge the best firm portfolio in terms of a total risk perspective. Therefore, some of the approaches for single project evaluation (for example, simulation, risk analysis, Hillier model) are useful as input information for evaluation in terms of a total risk perspective.

The total risk approach should clearly be useful in situations in which the CAP approach may be shaky, such as bankruptcy. Furthermore, it is extremely valuable for firms whose shares are not traded in markets, and this would tend to be the case for a large number of small to medium-sized private companies.

Perhaps the most sensible suggestion for the practical analyst is that whenever there is uncertainty about the decision context (such as when the CAP assumptions do not apply), the total risk analysis should be carried out. In addition, it might also be useful to carry out other approaches, such as an incremental risk analysis, as a backup and a guideline. The results of such alternative approaches can then be discussed with management, and advice can be given when different approaches offer conflicting suggestions about whether to accept or reject a particular investment.

While I believe that the CAP approach is an increasingly useful one, I also feel that risk simulation procedures provide insights about total risk, about cash flow forecasting (particularly in relation to strategic management), and about the risk classes of projects. Such additional information is usually very valuable in relation to financial decision making.

I would like to stress the importance of using several approaches in decision-making contexts. Indeed, the need to develop flexible, interactive project investment decision-making procedures becomes increasingly evident when we confront case study evidence of the practical implementation of risk concepts in decision making.

This discussion should not be closed, however, without reminding readers of the survey evidence presented earlier regarding the implementation of financial decision-making techniques. Although techniques such as DCF are now widely used, it took considerable time and managerial education before they were successfully adopted. Though the treatment of risk is becoming necessary in such contexts, the implementation of risk analysis procedures lags far behind the theoretical developments of risk analysis and the CAP. The role of the practical analyst must surely be to educate the manager about the assumptions and merits of each approach and to develop procedures which are both theoretically sound and also capable of implementation by practicing managers.

I propose a two-stage procedure. The first stage involves risk determination and positioning, and the second stage involves a project risk evaluation process. The schematic diagrams for each follow. Having examined various approaches for risk analysis, I now offer an alternative approach. This approach consists of a mixture of conventional risk analysis and risk simulation but includes the modern asset pricing theories of finance.

During stage I (see Figure 9) we seek to identify the risk associated with the project. During this phase I believe that a probabilistic type of risk simulation should be used to forecast the likely cash flows and earnings projections, (narrowly for the project and more broadly for the firm as a whole). This is so that the manager can develop an understanding of the project's intrinsic riskiness. By the use of sensitivity analysis in association with this forecasting procedure, the manager can also gain an increased understanding of the relationships between factors affecting project cash flows.

472

FIGURE 9

Risk Determination and Positioning Phase

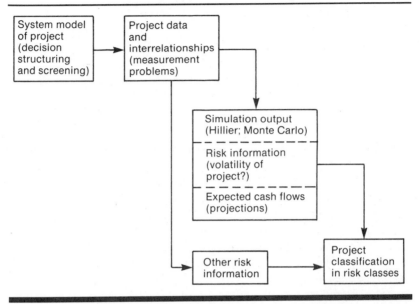

The basic idea at this stage is that the manager develops a procedure to screen projects into ranges of perceived risk from low to high. Simulation is a fundamental part of this screening process, and as a consequence, it is extremely important for a manager to learn how to interpret the output of risk simulations, so that projects can be meaningfully classified into risk bands. From time to time, other information about risk is also valuable, and this can be culled from evidence of the experience of other comparable firms undertaking similar projects. Such information will provide additional backup for establishing a project's risk class.

We should note that the purpose of simulation at this point is to develop project understanding and also to classify projects according to the degree of perceived nondiversifiable risk of each type of project. Such nondiversifiable risk refers to the project's exposure to the spectrum of economic risks and, in particular, the project's volatility in relation to project cost and revenue expectations. Thus, a high-risk project would be highly sensitive to cost and revenue variations in relation to economic activity.

Stage 2 (see Figure 10) of the process is to identify the appropriate risk-adjusted rate which should be associated with each project risk

FIGURE 10

Project Evaluation Process

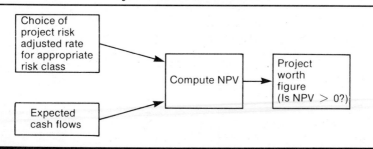

class. This rate should take account of the relevant capital market risk premium according to the CAP approach, noting that it may be difficult to determine betas for projects or divisions of a company in order for the basic CAP formula to apply.[2] The final risk-adjusted rate should then be the sum of the after-tax risk-free rate (obtained, say, from returns on government bonds) and the risk premium calculated for each risk class.

The procedure for calculating a project's NPV would then involve discounting the project's period-by-period expected cash flows by the risk-adjusted rate previously calculated. The NPV figure obtained from this calculation can predict the likely marginal net effect of a project on the firm's value. Only if the NPV figure is positive can we say that the project will increase the value of the firm.

Stage 1 and stage 2 together give us a procedure in which simulation is a necessary first step for risk evaluation of projects. Indeed, such a procedure should be able to provide a basic approach which can be accommodated within the firm's managerial decision-making process.

A simplified initial structure to conceptualize managerial decision making for capital investment is shown in Figure 11. Basically, the risk analyst provides the manager with a project worth measure, the NPV, and some sensitivity analyses connected with the NPV measure which the manager or his team may request. There is a managerial desire to capture risk more formally in the decision process yet to have available for decision purposes simple, intuitive measures of worth which can be relatively easily understood. I believe the stage 1 process views simulation results as a managerial framework for understanding the influence of uncertainty on projects. Thus, stage 1 is a broad, risk-screening phase, before a "collapsed" measure, NPV, is obtained in stage 2.

FIGURE 11

Decision-Making Process

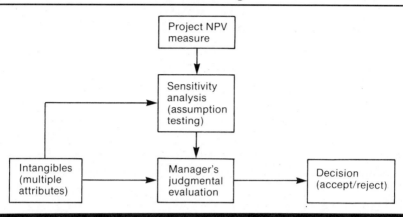

However, it should also be remembered that appraisal processes are dynamic and change rapidly with experience, intangible or unquantifiable factors, and new information. Top managers look at three main factors in their decision process. First is project risk, which is identified in the risk analysis process and which leads to the NPV measure. Second are project interdependencies with the other activities of the firm. This is handled partially through a positive NPV value which indicates a potential increase in the firm's market valuation, and partially by managerial assessment of the relationships between projects. Managers should be especially concerned about whether such an addition would fit well in terms of the firm's growth and strategy path. Third, managers also need to consider attributes other than purely financial measures. Such factors might include strategic issues, the need to develop new products, and to maintain expertise and employee morale within the organization.

CONCLUSION

I believe that many organizations may find it useful to divide responsibility, on a mutually agreeable basis, in the conduct of the investment decision-making process. It may be sensible, for example, for the project sponsor or functional manager to carry out a risk simulation, thereby undertaking some preliminary risk screening for the project. If the project does not fail on this screen, it should be passed for further appraisal, say, by the divisional manager who might perform the risk-adjusted NPV calculations and any relevant sensitivity analyses jointly with the financial manager. The divisional and functional managers would then be in a position to discuss the results with top management and, during a final project appraisal task, may consider any additional information which might need to be reviewed. Included in the discussion at this stage might be the issue of satisfying a number of alternative goals. Management, at this level, would probably wish to judge the potential impact of the project on the firm's future value and growth. It is perhaps also appropriate to mention at this point the problem of bias associated with such judgment tasks. It is to be hoped that such biases can be lessened by sensible interactive decision processes. However, it is possible that such interactive decision making may introduce other biases. For example, lower-level managers may distort information channels and bias the assessment of risk classes in order to influence the ultimate decision.

NOTES

[1] Edward G. Bennion, "Capital Budgeting and Game Theory," *Harvard Business Review,* November–December 1956, p. 125.

[2] The suggested procedures are to identify βs (betas) for firms carrying out similar projects and with similar financial structures. Thus, for example, in a pharmaceutical investment situation, a firm would look for βs for firms investing in projects in essentially similar pharmaceutical areas.

22

Providing for Inflation: How to Measure the Effect of Inflation on Project Yield

Aivars Krasts and Thomas R. Henkel

Conoco Inc.
Subsidiary of E. I. duPont de Nemours and Company

INTRODUCTION

*T*here is a broad consensus that discounted cash flow techniques such as net present value, the discounted cash flow rate of return,* and the capital productivity index provide the best measurements of investment worth. Consequently, the inflation adjustment techniques pertaining to individual project evaluation discussed in this chapter deal exclusively with adjusting anticipated net cash flows. To understand the need for making such adjustments, it is helpful to examine how inflationary government policies affect the financial condition of private enterprises and how inflationary expectations affect forecasts of

---

* We prefer the term, "discounted cash flow (DCF) rate of return" to the less specific "internal rate of return." Of course, the terms are synonymous.

cash flows generated by proposed investments in new production capacity.

During most of the 70s, in spite of rising earnings, many U.S. industrial companies experienced a "cash squeeze." Among the chief reasons for this were the unprecedented rapid increases in the cost of purchasing and erecting industrial equipment and increases in working capital requirements, which outstripped the increases in internally generated cash flow. This situation, in turn, implied for most companies a more rapid escalation of the prices of things they bought than that of prices for the products they sold. Such a discrepancy can be maintained for a surprisingly long time as long as prevailing economic policy is focused on efforts to maintain consumers' standard of living in the short run. Under such policy, efforts to contain the inflation generated by massive income redistribution from savers to consumers rely to a considerable degree on direct price controls on producers, or threats of price controls and other punitive actions. The effect of enacted or threatened price controls is to inhibit increases in production costs from being fully passed on to the consumer sector of the economy, while at the same time higher production costs are being fully reflected in the prices of capital goods. Simultaneously, income redistribution increases the rate of consumption, dampening savings in all sectors of the economy. As practiced over most of the 70s, these policies led to a shortage of capital and increases of the cost of both debt and equity capital to peak rates. Furthermore, persistence of these conditions imbedded in the public's mind the expectation that a high rate of inflation would continue indefinitely.

The symptom of this condition that surfaced in corporate capital budgeting was a shortage of internally generated funds for new investment and difficulty in borrowing, at a time when investment opportunities as measured by traditional discounted cash flow methods appeared to be more attractive than ever. Closer examination, however, revealed that the record high DCF rates of return being forecast for many investment projects were spurious. The people making the cash flow forecasts correctly sensed that the disparity in price escalation rates between capital goods and consumer goods could not last indefinitely. Inflationary expectations led them to escalate the product prices that determine revenue streams at an accelerated rate. In many forecast cash flow patterns expressed in nominal dollars, projected high inflation increased cash inflows that come later in time far more than it affected the bulk of cash outflows made in the front-end construction phase of the project. Thus, inflationary expectations alone increased projected internal rates of return. Some form of deflating was needed to get a better fix on the real return.

478

In the early 80s, disinflation accompanied changing government policies and a deep recession. The rate of general inflation was cut by more than half. Prices for some capital goods and services as well as key commodities declined in real terms. The forecasts of the 70s proved inaccurate, although expectations of the return of higher rates of inflation continued. It is probably unreasonable to expect that the experience of the early 80s could have been accurately forecast in the early 70s. However, our experience with disinflation following accelerating inflation confirms the need for a prospective investment project profitability measure in terms of constant purchasing power that can provide comparable benchmarks for capital budgeting decisions under varying rates of inflation.

As we approach the second half of the 80s, a number of observers are expressing the fear that disinflation may evolve into outright deflation with a broadly based decline in nominal prices, particularly for commodities. If such expectations were to be projected for the life of a new investment proposal, they could lead to a very low discounted cash flow return for similar reasons to those that led inflationary expectations to inflate returns. In that case the adjustment factors needed to convert to a constant purchasing power profitability measure may have to be inflators instead of deflators. The general concept would remain unchanged. However, the probability of protracted deflation appears to be low since central banks are more adept at expanding liquidity than controlling it. The response to a serious danger of deflation would likely bring on another bout with inflation.

CASH FLOW DEFLATION PROCEDURE

Choice of Index

The procedure for eliminating inflationary distortions in the discounted cash flow technique of evaluating prospective investments involves deflating the forecast nominal (or current) dollar cash flows of a prospective project to dollars of equal purchasing power. Then, to calculate the constant purchasing power internal rate of return, one need only find the discount rate at which the present value of the deflated cash flow stream is zero.

The next question that arises is what index to use for the deflator. Conventional capital budgeting theory includes in the cost of capital the shareholder's anticipated rate of inflation. The shareholder is considered to be an individual with a consumer's interest. Thus, forecasts of the Consumer Price Index would represent the shareholder's perception of inflation. However, during much of the 70s, the cost of capital goods escalated much more rapidly than consumer prices, and using the Consumer Price Index to adjust forecast cash flows could have resulted in undertaking projects that would not return to the company the purchasing power invested in them if that purchasing power is measured in terms of the ability to buy capital equipment. Consequently, companies that produce products with growing or stable demand and wish to reinvest funds in these business areas to sustain their productive capacity should use a company-specific purchasing power index rather than the Consumer Price Index or other index of general inflation. It is not appropriate to use an index based on the projections for any one specific business in a diversified company because the company may not wish to replace its productive capacity in a mature or declining business area.

Developing a Company's Purchasing Power Index

For companies that are as diversified as most large corporations are today, it will be difficult to find any single published price index that reasonably closely reflects the price changes of all the capital inputs they buy. Consequently, each firm may have to develop its own unique purchasing power index. This process must begin with developing the company's own "market basket" of the capital goods and construction services it buys. The purchasing and engineering departments are usually good sources of information on the kinds of equipment bought and their past and present prices. Past capital budgets and capital expenditures records are also very helpful in building up a historical data base. If the company has a long-range strategic plan that specifically forecasts its anticipated capital investment program, this projection provides the needed data base for the future.

Using these and other sources of information, it is possible to construct a company's own purchasing power index by (1) estimating the physical volume of each kind of capital equipment or construction services the company has bought or plans to buy during each year of the period covered, (2) collecting the prices of items bought or to be bought, (3) weighting the price of each item in the annual market basket by the proportion of the market basket that the specific item represents, (4) adding together all the weighted prices for each year, and (5) converting the resulting series to an index.

The most useful way to estimate the physical volume of equipment and services is in terms of constant dollars. This approach makes the data directly applicable in weighting the prices of individual items that compose the index.

The method of estimating the corporate purchasing power index is best illustrated by a simple example. Suppose a diversified company expects to operate in only three basic business areas over the next five years. For convenience, we shall label these as business areas Alpha, Beta, and Gamma. For simplicity, assume also that the capital equipment used in these three areas is fairly standard and that a single projection is adequate to describe the company's expectations of cost escalation for its equipment in each of these areas. Schedule I shows

Schedule I

Business area	Constant dollar capital expenditure forecast ($000)					
	Year 1	Year 2	Year 3	Year 4	Year 5	Total
Alpha	$ 90	$ 70	$125	$ 60	$ 50	395
Beta	50	50	100	30	100	330
Gamma	60	34	75	80	50	299
Total	$200	$154	$300	$170	$200	1024

this company's five-year projection of its constant dollar capital expenditure program, indicating a relatively stronger investment program for business area Alpha than areas Beta and Gamma.

Schedule II shows the company's current projections for the increases (or decreases) in the prices of the capital goods for each of the three business areas. Clearly, the company expects the prices of the

Schedule II

Business area	Expected rate of equipment cost escalation (percent)				
	Year 1	Year 2	Year 3	Year 4	Year 5
Alpha	30.0%	25.0%	8.0%	2.0%	2.0%
Beta	20.0	15.0	5.0	2.0	0.0
Gamma	15.0	8.0	4.0	2.0	0.0

capital goods in business area Alpha to increase much faster than in areas Beta and Gamma.

Schedule III illustrates the simple calculation necessary to obtain the corporate purchasing power (CPP) index. For each year, each busi-

Schedule III					

	Contribution to corporate purchasing power rates (percent)				
Business area	*Year 1*	*Year 2*	*Year 3*	*Year 4*	*Year 5*
Alpha	13.50%	11.36%	3.33%	0.71%	0.50%
Beta	5.00	4.87	1.67	0.35	0.00
Gamma	4.50	1.77	1.00	0.94	0.00
CPP escalation rates	23.00	18.00	6.00	2.00	0.50
CPP index	1.2300	1.4514	1.5385	1.5693	1.5771

ness area's proportion of the total constant dollar capital expenditure is multiplied by the expected equipment cost escalation rate in that year, obtaining as a result each business area's contribution to the change in the total corporation's purchasing power. The year-by-year sum of these individual contributions represents the change in CPP. The CPP index is then produced by compounding these changes over time.

Applying the Index

Two hypothetical five-year projects in business area Alpha were developed to show how the relative price changes in the capital goods a company may purchase can affect the ranking—and relative anticipated attractiveness—of projects, depending on whether constant dollar, nominal (current) dollar, or constant purchasing power measures are used.

The zero escalation, constant dollar case is shown in Schedule IV. Project 1 describes a $70 million plant that will produce 25 million units of product over its life. Production for project 1 declines over time, resulting in higher operating cash flows early in the project life. Project 2 is a much more capital-intensive project. Its $160 million (constant dollar) investment is spread fairly evenly over three years. Project 2

Schedule IV
Business Area Alpha—Project 1

Project year	Capital investment ($000)	Working capital ($000)	Total production (000)	Unit price ($)	Unit cost ($)	Pretax margin ($000)	Tax depreciation ($000)	Total tax ($000)	Net cash flow ($000)
0	$70,000	$ 0	0	$ 0.000	$ 0.000	$ 0	$ 0	$ 0	$−70,000
1	0	37,725	7,000	25.000	19.195	40,632	14,000	13,316	−10,409
2	0	−5,389	6,000	25.000	19.195	34,827	14,000	10,414	29,803
3	0	−10,778	4,000	25.000	19.195	23,218	14,000	4,609	29,387
4	0	0	4,000	25.000	19.195	23,218	14,000	4,609	18,609
5	0	−21,557	4,000	25.000	19.195	23,218	14,000	4,609	40,166
Totals	$70,000	$ 0	25,000			$145,113	$70,000	$37,556	$ 37,556

DCF = 12.0000   NPV @ 8.0% = 10256   PI = 1.13

Schedule IV
Business Area Alpha—Project 2

Project year	Capital investment ($000)	Working capital ($000)	Total production (000)	Unit price ($)	Unit cost ($)	Pretax margin ($000)	Tax depreciation ($000)	Total tax ($000)	Net cash flow ($000)
0	$ 50,000	$ 0	0	$ 0.000	$ 0.000	$ 0	$ 0	$ 0	$ -50,000
1	60,000	4,425	1,000	25.000	13.597	11,403	10,000	701	-53,724
2	50,000	8,850	3,000	25.000	13.597	34,208	25,000	4,604	-29,246
3	0	17,700	7,000	25.000	13.597	79,818	41,667	19,076	43,042
4	0	0	7,000	25.000	13.597	79,818	41,667	19,076	60,742
5	0	-30,976	7,000	25.000	13.597	79,818	41,667	19,076	91,718
Totals	$160,000	$ 0	25,000			$285,065	$160,000	$62,532	$ 62,532

DCF = 12.0000   NPV @ 8.0% = 16419   PI = 1.11

also differs from project 1 in that it sacrifices early production for a sustained high level of production in years three through five. This production and investment schedule results in much higher operating cash flows in the later years for project 2 than for project 1. Like project 1, however, project 2 produces a total of 25 million units over its five-year life, and both projects sell their product for the market price of $25 per unit. Project 2 has a pretax operating margin of about $11.40, while the more labor-intensive project 1 earns a lower margin of about $5.80.

Using the assumptions outlined in Figure 1, and assuming no inflation, both projects would earn a 12 percent discounted cash flow (DCF)

FIGURE 1

Assumptions Used for Project 1 and Project 2 Analyses

1. End-of-year discounting.
2. A 50 percent tax rate.
3. Straight-line depreciation for tax purposes.
4. Escalation of prices and costs at 80 percent of the escalation for capital goods in the business area.
5. Working capital equal to 30 days net receivable less payables, 20 days cash costs, plus 72 days of inventory (a turnover rate of five times yearly). A year is assumed to be 360 days long.
6. The cost of capital excluding the inflation component is 8 percent and is 15 percent including the inflation component. The 8 percent rate is assumed to equal the risk-free rate plus the appropriate risk premium for the firm.
7. The unit cost for project 1 is $19.195492. The unit cost for project 2 is $13.597405.
8. The productivity index (PI) is the result of dividing *a* by *b*, where *a* is equal to the net present value of the operating cash flow, and *b* is equal to the net present value of the capital expenditures and working capital, discounted at the cost of capital.

rate of return. The net present value (NPV) at 8 percent (the assumed "no inflation" cost of capital) of project 2 is higher than that of project 1, and for those who believe in constant dollar investment appraisal, project 2 would probably be preferable to project 1.

Schedule V shows how both projects can be affected by changes in absolute and relative price levels. In this case, both prices and costs were escalated at (an arbitrary) 80 percent of the capital good escala-

Schedule V
Business Area Alpha—Project 1

Project year	Capital investment ($000)	Working capital ($000)	Total production (000)	Unit price ($)	Unit cost ($)	Pretax margin ($000)	Tax depreciation ($000)	Total tax ($000)	Net cash flow ($000)
0	$70,000	$ 0	0	$ 0.000	$ 0.000	$ 0	$ 0	$ 0	$ -70,000
1	0	46,778	7,000	31.000	23.802	50,383	14,000	18,192	-14,587
2	0	1,337	6,000	37.200	28.563	51,823	14,000	18,911	31,575
3	0	-13,985	4,000	39.581	30.391	36,760	14,000	11,380	39,365
4	0	546	4,000	40.214	30.877	37,348	14,000	11,674	25,128
5	0	-34,676	4,000	40.858	31.371	37,945	14,000	11,973	60,648
Totals	$70,000	$ 0	25,000			$214,258	$70,000	$72,129	$ 72,129

DCF = 19.5790   NPV @ 15.0% = 11594   PI = 1.14

Schedule V
Business Area Alpha—Project 2

Project year	Capital investment ($000)	Working capital ($000)	Total production (000)	Unit price ($)	Unit cost ($)	Pretax margin ($000)	Tax depreciation ($000)	Total tax ($000)	Net cash flow ($000)
0	$ 50,000	$ 0	0	$ 0.000	$ 0.000	$ 0	$ 0	$ 0	$ −50,000
1	78,000	5,487	1,000	31.000	16.861	14,139	10,000	2,070	−71,418
2	81,250	14,267	3,000	37.200	20.233	50,901	29,500	10,701	−55,316
3	0	29,288	7,000	39.581	21.528	126,371	56,583	34,894	62,189
4	0	785	7,000	40.214	21.872	128,393	56,583	35,905	91,703
5	0	−49,826	7,000	40.858	22.222	130,447	56,583	36,932	143,342
Totals	$209,250	$ 0	25,000			$450,251	$209,250	$120,500	$ 120,500

DCF = 17.4034   NPV @ 15.0% = 10659   PI = 1.06

tion forecast shown in Schedule II for business area alpha. The nominal dollar DCF return for project 1 increases by over 7.5 points to 19.6 percent, while for project 2 the DCF return rises by about 5.4 points to 17.4 percent. With a nominal dollar cost of capital of 15 percent, the net present value, profitability index (PI), and DCF analyses confirm that both projects 1 and 2 are attractive investment opportunities for the firm, although project 1 is clearly preferable to project 2.

This example demonstrates the problem inherent in using constant dollar economics for making investment decisions. The prices and costs of different components that determine the future net cash flows from the project are likely to escalate at different rates, and projects with dissimilar components in their cash flow streams are affected quite differently by escalation of the components. For example, depreciation is unaffected by relative price changes, while additional investments in working capital are required due to changes in the prices and costs of the manufactured goods. Without capturing the impact of these differential effects, misleading results will be obtained and inappropriate decisions made.

			Schedule VI			
Project year	Nominal $ project 1 cash flow ($000)	Nominal $ project 2 cash flow ($000)	Purchase power rates (%)	Purchase power index	CPP $ project 1 cash flow ($000)	CPP $ project 2 cash flow ($000)
0	$−70,000	$−50,000	0.000%	1.0000	$−70,000	$−50,000
1	−14,587	−71,418	23.000	1.2300	−11,859	−58,063
2	31,575	−55,316	18.000	1.4514	21,755	−38,112
3	39,365	62,189	6.000	1.5385	25,587	40,422
4	25,128	91,703	2.000	1.5693	16,013	58,438
5	60,648	143,342	0.500	1.5771	38,456	90,889

Project 1: CPP − DCF = 6.402   CPP − NPV @ 8.0% = −4076   CPP − PI = 0.952
Project 2: CPP − DCF = 8.109   CPP − NPV @ 8.0% =   462   CPP − PI = 1.003

Schedule VI describes the calculation of the CPP–DCF returns for these same two projects. Project 1, which was preferable under current dollar analyses, has a CPP–DCF rate of return of only 6.4 percent, resulting in a negative CPP–NPV and a CPP–PI of less than one at an 8 percent cost of capital. Conversely, project 2 has a CPP–DCF rate of return of 8.1 percent, a positive CPP–NPV, and a CPP–PI of slightly over one. *Project 2 will, therefore, return the purchasing power invested in it to the corporation while project 1 will not.* A company that accepts a project like project 1 obviously cannot grow in any real sense. The most striking thing to note is that the relative ranking of the projects is affected by relative price and cost changes.

The appropriate cost of capital for constant purchasing power-type calculations is the inflation-free stockholders' cost of capital. Clearly, in no case should a company invest money in a project that returns *less* than the stockholders' expected rate of return. However, it can, when confronted with alternative investments that all promise returns above the cost of capital, choose those projects that promise real growth for the company as opposed to real decline and gradual liquidation.

Schedule VII

	Expected rate of equipment cost escalation (percent)				
Business area	Year 1	Year 2	Year 3	Year 4	Year 5
Alpha	6.0%	8.0%	10.0%	15.0%	20.0%
Beta	−4.0	0.0	4.0	17.0	22.0
Gamma	−4.0	3.9	4.0	17.3	18.0

Schedule VIII

	Contribution to corporate purchasing power rates (percent)				
Business area	Year 1	Year 2	Year 3	Year 4	Year 5
Alpha	2.70	3.64	4.17	5.29	5.00
Beta	−1.00	0.00	1.33	3.00	11.00
Gamma	−1.20	0.86	1.00	8.16	4.50
CPP escalation rates	0.50	4.50	6.50	16.46	20.50
CPP index	1.0050	1.0502	1.1185	1.3025	1.5696

489

Schedule IX
Business Area Alpha—Project 1

Project year	Capital investment ($000)	Working capital ($000)	Total production (000)	Unit price ($)	Unit cost ($)	Pretax margin ($000)	Tax depreciation ($000)	Total tax ($000)	Net cash flow ($000)
0	$70,000	$ 0	0	$ 0.000	$ 0.000	$ 0	$ 0	$ 0	$ −70,000
1	0	39,535	7,000	26.200	20.117	42,582	14,000	14,291	−11,244
2	0	−3,479	6,000	27.877	21.404	38,835	14,000	12,417	29,896
3	0	−10,096	4,000	30.107	23.117	27,961	14,000	6,980	31,076
4	0	3,115	4,000	33.720	25.891	31,316	14,000	8,658	19,543
5	0	−29,076	4,000	39.115	30.033	36,327	14,000	11,163	54,239
Totals	$70,000	$ 0	25,000			$177,021	$70,000	$53,510	$ 53,510

DCF = 15.5910   NPV @ 15.0% = 1402   PI = 1.02

Schedule IX
Business Area Alpha—Project 2

Project year	Capital investment ($000)	Working capital ($000)	Total production (000)	Unit price ($)	Unit cost ($)	Pretax margin ($000)	Tax depreciation ($000)	Total tax ($000)	Net cash flow ($000)
0	$ 50,000	$ 0	0	$ 0.000	$ 0.000	$ 0	$ 0	$ 0	$ -50,000
1	63,600	4,638	1,000	26.200	14.250	11,950	10,000	975	-57,263
2	57,240	10,165	3,000	27.877	15.162	38,144	25,900	6,122	-35,383
3	0	22,500	7,000	30.107	16.375	96,123	44,980	25,572	48,051
4	0	4,476	7,000	33.720	18.340	107,658	44,980	31,339	71,843
5	0	-41,780	7,000	39.115	21.274	124,883	44,980	39,952	126,711
Totals	$170,840	$ 0	25,000			$378,759	$170,840	$103,959	$ 103,959

DCF = 17.3679   NPV @ 15.0% = 9120   PI = 1.06

This same switching phenomenon can be observed when company projections suggest *increasing* instead of *decreasing* escalation in prices and costs. The example below uses the same forecast of future constant dollar corporate expenditures as shown in Schedule I, the same two projects 1 and 2, but a projection of rising escalation as shown in Schedules VII and VIII. Schedules IX and X show that, while

	Nominal $ project 1 cash flow ($000)	Nominal $ project 2 cash flow ($000)	Purchase power rates (%)	Purchase power index	CPP $ project 1 cash flow ($000)	CPP $ project 2 cash flow ($000)
Schedule X						
Project year						
0	$-70,000	$-50,000	0.000%	1.0000	$-70,000	$-50,000
1	-11,244	-57,263	0.500	1.0050	-11,188	-56,978
2	29,896	-35,383	4.500	1.0502	28,467	-33,691
3	31,076	48,051	6.500	1.1185	27,784	42,961
4	19,543	71,843	16.455	1.3025	15,004	55,156
5	54,239	126,711	20.500	1.5696	34,557	80,731

Project 1: CPP − DCF = 8.265   CPP − NPV @ 8.0% =   649   CPP − PI = 1.008
Project 2: CPP − DCF = 7.490   CPP − NPV @ 8.0% = −2053   CPP − PI = 0.988

project 2 appears preferable to project 1 using current dollars, only project 1 returns its invested purchasing power when the CPP rates are used to deflate the cash flows to dollars of constant purchasing power.

It should be noted that two short-lived projects were used as examples in this chapter for brevity. In reality, project lives are usually much longer, and the same set of expectations will accentuate the impacts of inflationary or disinflationary environments.

INTRODUCING AND USING CONSTANT PURCHASING POWER INVESTMENT APPRAISAL MEASURES

It is unlikely that most organizations, particularly large ones, will accept inflation-adjusted methods of investment appraisal without considerable internal debate. Therefore, it may be useful to review the arguments usually raised in opposition to this technique as well as to note the observed benefits. (The arguments in favor have already been discussed earlier in this chapter.)

The Arguments

By far the most common argument raised against the use of constant purchasing power discounted cash flow techniques is that the rates of cost escalation for plant and equipment cannot be forecast by anyone with a reliable degree of accuracy. Thus, the deflation of the cash flows would merely introduce one more potential source of error in the calculations.

This should not be considered sufficient reason for abandoning the method. It has been difficult to forecast any variable in the economic environment during the past 10 or so years, as the records of most forecasters show. The cost escalation rates of new plant and equipment are nothing special. The impact of changing prices and costs is a risk affecting the economic performance of investments that is intensified during times of rapid change. By ignoring it we may simplify our calculations, but not reality. It is not easy to construct a satisfactory corporate purchasing power index and project it into the future, but the effort is worth it. One side benefit of this effort can be understanding with greater specificity than before the forces that move these costs. This understanding can lead to considerable savings to the company through judicious timing of construction and equipment purchases.

A second source of opposition is likely to be people who will argue that the same purpose can be served by simply using today's costs and prices in project economics, thereby calculating a "constant dollar rate of return." The problem with this zero escalation approach is that it fails to recognize that various costs and prices will escalate and deescalate at widely varying rates and that various components of the net cash flow are affected differently—such as working capital and depreciation. Some of the risks affecting the project's economic performance are embodied in unanticipated differences among these escalation rates. The assumption of zero escalation does not produce a constant dollar return but a return for what probably is the least likely scenario of all, the assumption that years from now the relative relationships among all prices and costs will be the same as today.

The most carefully thought-out line of criticism of adjusting cash flows for changes in corporate purchasing power comes from fundamentalist market theoreticians. They point out that financial markets impute the expected rate of inflation into each company's cost of capital. Therefore, as long as the estimated cost of capital is used as the basis for establishing cutoff rates for project acceptability, there is no need to adjust the projected nominal net cash flow for changes in corporate purchasing power.

There is nothing wrong with this theoretical construct. The problem encountered in applying it is that the market does not tell what the company's cost of capital will be 5 or 10 years from now, when the full net cash flow from today's investments will be reaped. Some theoreticians will retort that the equity component of today's cost of capital fully reflects the market's expectations regarding the company's future. Similarly, the debt component fully reflects the market's expectations regarding the future course of interest rates. Therefore, today's cost of capital is all that is needed.

This collapsing of time is convenient for developing theory but should leave business managers uneasy when they recognize that the market's assessment of the cost of equity capital is a fickle thing, as evidenced by wide swings in stock prices for reasons that are never explicit and are often unknown. Similarly wide swings have been experienced in the cost of debt, as government authorities have attempted to manipulate it in pursuit of specific macroeconomic policy goals. Usually, as inflation intensifies, these manipulations become more frantic with increasingly unpredictable results.

How then can managers using prevailing theory obtain some comfort that their decisions to undertake large investment projects will, over the economic lives of these projects, enhance the company's value? One approach is to see if the prospective internal rates of return of proposed new projects exceed the company's average cost of capital over a protracted historical time period. The risk in this approach is that at crucial turning points in the long-term economic outlook, this reliance on looking at past cost of capital to make judgments about the future will be totally invalid. In most instances this approach would have led to bad decisions if applied during the past decade.

The other alternative is to try to forecast the cost of capital along with all other variables relevant to investment decisions. This is a formidable task because the company's future cost of capital is likely to be significantly affected by the investment decisions currently under consideration. It is not a variable independent of those decisions, particularly if they involve large amounts of capital and are strategically important decisions. Nevertheless, it can be tried.

In the effort to introduce some constant purchasing power measures into the arsenal of a company's investment appraisal tools, it is not necessary or even desirable to win all arguments with the fundamentalist market theoreticians. After all, they represent the best available thinking on the theory of the value of the firm on which all modern capital budgeting is based. It is only necessary to get them to modify the excessively doctrinaire position that no useful insights can be obtained about a project's value to the company by analysis other than the straight comparison of unadjusted DCF rate of return with an unadjusted estimate of the company's cost of capital, or alternatively by calculating the net present value at that cost of capital. Nobody can justify being that doctrinaire and mechanical in reaching decisions in an uncertain world where no economic forecasts and estimates are ever correct and markets are less than perfect. If one were to find that the same proposed project promises to yield an unadjusted DCF rate of return well in excess of the estimated cost of capital, but has a constant purchasing power DCF rate of return barely above the cost of capital excluding inflation, one should recognize the result as inconsistent and adjust one's views of either forecast inflation or the estimated cost of capital before making the investment decision. The expanded analysis can reduce the risk of making a blunder and is therefore a useful supplement to the more traditional methods for capital allocation.

The authors' experiences suggest that the availability of capital in relation to a broad range of investment opportunities can have a greater impact on the size of capital budgets than the estimate of a company's cost of capital. Capital has been scarce and promises to remain so, leading to rationing before the prospective returns of available investment opportunities reach the estimated cost of capital. Thus, the actual cost of capital committed to a project is the return that could have been earned by investing in a competing opportunity that was foregone. Because of the estimating difficulties mentioned previously and the fact that wide dissemination throughout a company of a hurdle rate can lead to suppression of ideas before they reach the corporate level, or to liberal forecasting of costs and revenues to clear the hurdle rate, the authors do not recommend excessive reliance on that single number called the cost of capital in budgeting. It is better to let the projected rates of return fall where they will without explicit guidance on where they should be, and to let senior management decide whether the rewards promised by each specific project are greater than the risks.

Experience and Benefits

Both experience and financial modeling have shown that changing rates of inflation significantly affect the measures used to determine the attractiveness of proposed investments in new production facilities. In an environment where capital is a scarce resource, it is helpful to see which among a number of proposed projects promise the greatest real economic benefits. The constant purchasing power measures described in this chapter do so by providing comparable yardsticks for measuring investment worth under a wide range of plant and equipment cost escalation rates. The use of these measures permits those charged with making corporate investment decisions to develop rule-of-thumb reference levels for judging what constitutes attractive investments in various businesses that need not be altered in response to changing inflation rates. During the inflation of the 70s, our experience was that the method of deflation described here reduced forecast internal rates of return for oil and coal investment proposals by 5 to 10 percentage points, and in a number of instances changed our perspective about the relative attractiveness of specific projects.

Experience with making inflation-adjusted project profitability calculations brings to the attention of operating management the various ways in which inflation affects their operations. For example, even a relatively superficial examination of these calculations reveals that during times of rapid inflation it is necessary to increase margins, not merely keep them constant in terms of nominal dollars, in order to retain any given level of constant purchasing power profitability. This alerts the sales force to make margins, not merely prices, subject to escalation clauses in sales contracts, whenever market conditions permit. A widespread understanding of this need throughout an organization can be a significant help in maintaining adequate levels of cash inflow when costs appear to be inexorably rising. When real costs are falling, declines in unit margins may be tolerable.

Similarly, these calculations draw attention to the importance of controlling working capital. It becomes clear that unless the rising cost of inventories is recovered through rising prices *before* the purchase of new inventories, working capital requirements for maintaining the same physical sales volume will increase, leading to new financing requirements and costs with no accompanying expansion in business. If inflation is protracted, a lag in recovering working capital increases will increase working capital permanently. This is one mechanism by which inflation impairs balance sheets and threatens cash shortages. To survive and grow, a company needs to follow pricing and cash management policies that try to avoid this trap by recovering working capital increases from customers, suppliers, and governments (by delayed remittance of sales taxes) whenever possible.

As noted before, careful work on developing the corporate purchasing power index can lead to greatly improved understanding of how inflation and other factors affect the markets for capital goods and services a company buys. This understanding can save a company significant amounts of money by making it possible to make certain purchases at times when prices are more favorable, rather than letting construction schedules alone determine the time of purchase. For example, when heavy demand and continually escalating prices for certain equipment are anticipated, it may pay to place an order early and buy a place in line for later delivery if the order cancellation charge is modest relative to the anticipated price increase. The authors have seen several million dollars made by such early ordering even when the project for which the equipment was to be used was subsequently canceled. The company involved was able to sell its place in the order line to a third party at a tidy profit. It is, of course, also possible to forecast incorrectly and lose money on such transactions. They should be entered only when there is high confidence in the quality of the projections of certain components of the corporate purchasing power index.

In the case of deflation, some of these relationships would be working in reverse. Assuming that capacity replacement costs, cash operating costs, and the prices of products produced are all declining in nominal terms, it seems safe to say that contractual terms that lead to heavy burdens of fixed nominal dollar cash costs for a sustained time period should be avoided in developing investment opportunities as well as running existing operations. Such obligations would have to be met with dollars of increasing purchasing power which may be increasingly difficult to generate in an environment of falling prices. Longer-term fixed price sales contracts would spread margins if costs are kept flexible. It may be worthwhile to pay all bills promptly and extend terms for receivables to solvent customers as long as the amounts to be collected are fixed. Deflation would bring about an environment with which the current generation of managers, including ourselves, has no experience. It is therefore difficult to provide general insights, emphasizing the need in such an environment for careful analysis of proposed investment projects in both nominal and constant purchasing power terms.

INFLATION-ADJUSTED PERFORMANCE APPRAISAL

It is always a sound business practice to compare objectives and forecasts with actual performance. Therefore, a company that adopts inflation-adjusted measures to supplement its other capital budgeting techniques should also consider some form of follow-up to test whether the forecast constant purchasing power returns are actually attained. This can be achieved by setting up a post-audit program.

Methodology

A continuing post-audit program requires maintaining accounting records for each major investment a company undertakes in the same format as the forecast budget economics used in justifying the decision to make the investment; that is, all costs and revenues for each major project should be kept separately so that the books would show the annual cash flow generated by each major facility. As time passes, each of these accounting modules becomes a cash flow time series, which permits line-by-line and year-by-year comparison of actual results to date with the results that were anticipated at the time the project was approved. Performance during the remaining economic life of the project can be reforecast in the light of actual performance to date and adjusted expectations about the future.

Similarly, the corporate purchasing power index should be updated annually to reflect actual costs of the items in the corporate market basket as well as any changes in expectations of future price trends.

Uses

The extra bookkeeping effort required to maintain updated post-audits can have a high payoff in terms of useful information on performance that is directly applicable to setting financial performance goals and making future investment decisions.

When performed several years after it was anticipated to have reached production at full capacity, a post-audit provides the best possible measure of a project's profitability while it is still in operation. The project's actual construction and start-up costs are known. The annual production and sales volumes, prices, costs, financial earnings, and cash flow for the first several years of operation are known. Forecasts of these variables for the remaining life of the facility can be made with as much confidence as is ever possible in the real world. Thus, the post-audit cash flow estimates represent a bridging of several years of past performance, present conditions, and future expectations that have been refined by experience.

Since the process of discounting places a higher present value on the early-year cash flows that are already known, the project's post-audit DCF rate of return is as reliable a measure of the profitability of a particular activity as can be obtained while this information is still relevant to decisions regarding modification of existing operations and making new investments. If a post-audit reveals impairment from anticipated results, examination of the reasons for the impairment may suggest needed remedial actions to improve profitability. To the extent that the post-audited investment represents a program generating continuing new opportunities, the post-audit internal rate of return is a relatively reliable measure of the prospective profitability of additional similar investments in this activity. Profitability data extracted from post-audits with a very long history is not useful for making current decisions because the world is changing.

The corporate purchasing power index can be used to deflate post-audit net cash flow in the same way as it was applied to forecast net cash flow in proposed project economics. If the resulting constant purchasing power post-audit DCF rate of return exceeds the company's prevailing real cost of capital, the profitability of the project in question is adequate. The real cost of capital is the company's prevailing weighted-average cost of capital less the prevailing rate of inflation as measured by the implicit GNP price deflator. If the constant purchasing power return is significantly below this level for a protracted period, the project in question is not generating enough purchasing power to provide for future growth of production capacity and is not enhancing the real value of the company to its stockholders. The calculation of these measures must take into consideration all corporate taxes.

In the economic sense, the entire company is but an aggregate of investment projects burdened by the overhead of the corporate services departments and the salaries and expenses of top management. Ideally, post-audits can be expanded to cover all of a company's major business units and ultimately the entire company. If a company's management information system can achieve this level of sophistication, it will enable the company to set unequivocal financial goals. Its post-audit internal rate of return must exceed its cost of capital in order to make the equity value of the company grow. Similarly, its post-audit constant purchasing power DCF rate of return must exceed its inflation-adjusted cost of capital to give shareholders real growth in the value of their business and concurrently permit the business to continue growing.

23

Project Authorization: How to Design Appropriation Procedures

Moustafa H. Abdelsamad

Virginia Commonwealth University

*C*apital expenditures usually represent large sums of money and affect years to come. Due to their importance and possible serious impact on the corporation, they must be closely monitored and controlled. Top management must ensure that no commitments or expenditures are made without prior approval and that throughout the organization procedures are established to ensure that these capital expenditures are in line with company objectives. The capital budget was discussed in another chapter. This chapter addresses the appropriation procedures. Appropriation procedures refer here to all procedures related to authorizing capital expenditures.

Authorization for Funds

The official vehicle for getting authorization to commit or spend funds is known as an *appropriation request* or an *authorization for funds* or a *capital outlay request.* The request may be original or supplemental. A supplemental request is related to a previously approved request (such as overrun). Ensuring that no funds or resources are committed or spent without prior approval is the heart of the appropriation procedure.

Who Needs Them

All firms need some procedures to control and properly manage capital investment projects. The procedures need to be understood by all concerned and must fit the needs and the type of individuals employed by the organization. Formal procedures are needed since informal procedures may result in inconsistent and careless handling of capital expenditure proposals.

Administrative Aspects Vary

It is impossible to specify detailed capital appropriation procedures that fit all companies regardless of size, industry, experience, or circumstances. Because each company is somewhat different from other companies, it is important to continuously develop and update the administrative procedures to suit each particular company. Accordingly, the ideas presented here are meant to be used as suggestions and clues for each company management to use to design or reevaluate and modify its own appropriation procedures.

The ideas presented here are based to a great extent on ideas found in over 100 written policy and procedures manuals of large industrial corporations that were kind enough to provide them to the author for use in his research. Special care has been taken not to identify any company or to draw heavily from a particular company.

Objectives

Appropriation procedures are designed to accomplish the following objectives:

Control expenditures. Corporations need to limit capital expenditures to those authorized in advance. This is done to ensure that the corporation lives within its means. Capital expenditures cannot exceed the limits established by top management.

Control cash flow. The capital appropriation procedures are designed to facilitate the estimation of cash needs, raise the necessary funds needed economically, and allocate the funds to the most worthwhile set of proposals.

Obtain managerial approval. Appropriation procedures are designed to ensure that commitments or expenditures receive proper evaluation by specifying approval levels needed for various sized expenditures. The larger the size, the higher the level of approval needed. This is so because of the impact on the corporation and the need to inform, prepare, and involve various managerial levels in the authorization of expenditures that have an impact on them.

Ensure consistency with objectives. Appropriation procedures are designed to ensure that each project to be undertaken fits nicely within the goals and objectives of the corporation.

Select the best alternatives. The procedures enable the company to consider other alternative ways of undertaking a capital investment and to select the best possible alternative based on return on investment and other considerations. The procedures must encourage project sponsors to think of various alternative ways of accomplishing the objective.

Ensure careful, consistent, and uniform evaluation. The procedures aim to ensure careful and thorough evaluation of each proposal in a consistent and uniform way that will recognize key elements and allow comparisons of various projects. This evaluation should include quantitative, and nonquantitative analysis. It should allow for considering risk factors.

Develop audit records. Procedures provide the mechanism for keeping adequate records of project data to allow for auditing the results when the project is completed.

Develop monitoring techniques. Procedures aim to follow up the progress of each project from beginning to end. Periodic progress reports provide constant feedback necessary to take corrective action and keep management informed of project status. The procedures should allow for tracking any given project and be able to determine its status at any given time.

Avoid unnecessary delays and roadblocks. The procedures should be designed to avoid complex and excessively cumbersome administrative routines that may cause unnecessary delays and roadblocks to undertaking worthwhile investment projects. Excessive paperwork is costly. Emphasis should be placed on providing understandable documents throughout. These documents should emphasize essential elements of the proposals.

Encourage submission of worthwhile proposals. The procedures should not be so formidable that they discourage the submission of good proposals.

Various Stages

Capital expenditures go through various stages that need to be addressed by appropriation procedures. They are:

Idea stage. It is often said that money is not in short supply but good ideas are. The corporate environment and procedures need to be conducive to encouraging capital investment ideas. The smaller the size of the company, the larger the need to encourage project generation.

Capital budget. Each year, responsible managers are asked to submit their estimates of capital expenditure needs. These needs are combined, modified, and put in the capital budget. This budget is an estimate of capital expenditure projects for next year (both new and continuing). Inclusion in the capital budget only signifies an approval in principle. It does not give the authorization to commit the resources or undertake the project. Accordingly, only preliminary and crude justification is needed.

Authorization stage. At this point, details of the project are included along with the necessary analysis and documentation. Authorization requests are not limited to projects included in the budget. Once authorization is made, the funds can be committed. Procedures, here, govern the actual implementation such as placing purchase orders, acquiring and installing equipment, and other activities needed to get the project underway and be fully operational.

Execution stage. At this stage the project is actually implemented.

Follow-up and monitoring stage. From the beginning to the end, periodic progress reports are needed. Follow-up of each project identifies problem areas and allows for a timely response. If needed, supplementary appropriation requests can be submitted. Also, if warranted, a decision may be made to abandon the project. Part of the follow-up is informing key individuals of what is happening throughout the life of the project.

Post-audit stage. This is the last stage when the project is fully operational. It requires comparing actual costs and benefits to the estimates and isolating and explaining deviations. This stage is very important to maintain the seriousness of the process. It helps in keeping project advocates from grossly overestimating benefits and underestimating costs of the proposal. It also helps in identifying good estimators for recognition, promotion, and rewards.

MAJOR VARIABLES AFFECTING THE DESIGN OF APPROPRIATION PROCEDURES

Appropriation procedures differ from one company to another. Some of the key industry variables that may affect the design of these procedures are explained below, followed by other major variables.

Industry Variables

Capital intensity. Chemicals, airlines, and heavy-industry companies require large amounts of capital expenditures. Accordingly, in these industries, the procedures need to be more formalized and detailed than in other industries that do not make sizable capital expenditures, such as banks. However, lack of capital intensity should not be used as an excuse for having sloppy procedures.

Technological stability. High-technology companies that change drastically cannot have as strict and detailed capital appropriation procedures as those companies in old and technologically stable industries.

Regulation. The extent of governmental regulation in a particular industry has a bearing on capital appropriation procedures. Projects need to be checked against current regulations. For example, industries that use nuclear plants must allow for regulations that can create delays and have a high cost of compliance.

Sophistication. The petroleum refining industry, for instance, has used various sophisticated techniques in production that can easily be extended to capital investment procedures. Sophisticated risk analysis and detailed organized appropriation procedures seem to be more common in these industries.

Profitability and stability of earnings. Often profitability is used to justify sloppy and less formal appropriation procedures. Competition tends to emphasize the need for better capital expenditure control.

Predominant project type. Industries that have expensive major projects as part of their normal operations need more elaborate procedures than those that have routine replacement or expansion projects.

Corporate Objectives

Corporate objectives are translated into a combination of operating and capital budgets. The objectives influence appropriation procedures. The required return on investment needs to be tied to the evaluation of capital expenditures and the minimum cutoff for accepting various projects.

Corporate Strategy

To accomplish various objectives, a company adopts strategies. These strategies influence capital expenditure procedures and evaluation. Strategies such as having the latest plant and equipment, buying instead of leasing equipment, making decisions at the highest or lowest levels, involving top management in certain projects, or adopting a financing budget influence procedures.

Corporate Image and Market Position

A corporation may wish to create an innovative or dominant corporate image. The image the corporation wants to create affects the capital appropriation procedures. They may be designed to encourage new products, high-quality furniture and decoration, and faster replacement of plant and equipment.

Corporate Organization and Management Style

The corporate organization and management style influence the design of the appropriation procedures. A conglomerate must depend more heavily on the judgment of various divisions and must monitor progress by results. Top management may delegate more decisions to lower levels or it may reserve most of the approval power for capital expenditures at the top. The style is reflected in the authorization levels and the reporting mechanism.

Profitability and Financial Strength

A profitable, financially strong company can allocate more decision-making power to lower managerial levels. The company can afford the mistakes that may occur as a result of such delegation. Companies in financial difficulty must have more control over capital expenditures and, therefore, must keep a tighter grip on the funds and monitor projects more carefully.

PARAMETERS OF APPROPRIATION PROCEDURES

Many parameters need to be addressed in developing and changing appropriation procedures. Selected key parameters are discussed here.

Project Concept

Capital appropriation procedures must emphasize the "project concept" to avoid circumventing approval limits. For instance, if a proposal of up to $50,000 can be approved at the plant level, a replacement decision concerning 10 pieces of equipment costing $50,000 each can be submitted as 10 separate requests rather than going through the higher approval level needed for projects of $500,000. This idea was ably expressed in one company manual that states that a project is

> a complete, self-contained program involving the acquisition of capital assets. Its completion or effectiveness is not dependent on approval of additional expenditures. It is unrelated to other projects in the sense that it cannot be construed as a phase of a larger program.

Project Classification

Projects need to be grouped in similar categories. This classification process facilitates the evaluation, monitoring, and allocation of funds. It also helps in recognizing different degrees of risk, urgency, and funding of various investments.

Projects may be classified as replacement or new acquisition. Replacement projects can be evaluated with the benefit of accumulated data about assets to be replaced, while new acquisitions have to be approached with more care. Another classification is capacity maintenance versus growth. Capacity maintenance refers to investments that keep the company at its current production capacity level. These are less risky investments and usually are essential for continuing in business. Growth investments are more risky, involve larger expenditures, and require more extensive market studies and more top-management attention.

Cost reduction is a category used to describe a set of projects that often can be implemented with less risk. However, this classification should alert the project reviewer to carefully examine the estimates of benefits and costs with regard to savings in labor since union problems, litigation, and other personnel problems play a significant role in the realization of benefits from these projects. Estimators tend to underestimate the costs involved and overestimate the personnel savings to be realized.

The environmental classification has appeared regularly in company manuals. Often, the investment must be made or the company must close down the plant. Savings are often negligible in these projects. The evaluation should emphasize finding the best alternative to accomplish the desired results while using the least amount of resources.

Another common classification of projects is minor versus major. A minor project has a small effect on the firm and does not require a large investment of funds. Major projects (also referred to as front-office projects) are of key importance, influence the company's survival, and must be treated accordingly. Examples of classifications found in selected manuals are:

- *Company 1*. Capacity maintenance, growth, cost reduction, and environmental.
- *Company 2*. Cost savings, replacement (noncost savings), new plant or product, increased capacity, equipment leases, other nonincome-producing projects.
- *Company 3*. Expansion, replacement, cost reduction, process/product quality improvement, employee welfare, obligatory, other.

Evaluation Process

A topic often addressed in the literature is the economic evaluation of capital investment projects. It is covered in more detail in other chapters. However, it will be addressed here as it relates to capital appropriation procedures and manuals.

Methods. The objective of economic evaluation is to determine the economic consequences of an investment decision. Methods of evaluating capital expenditure proposals try to measure the profitability of such proposals. The four commonly used methods are payback, average rate of return, net present value, and internal rate of return. The latter two methods are known as discounted cash flow methods. Over the years, discounted cash flow methods have received an increasing amount of attention. One company manual after another states that the key method to use is discounted cash flow. The net present value (NPV) uses a discount rate (a desirable minimum rate of return) to compute the present value of future cash flows. Then, the net present value is found by subtracting the initial investment from the present value of future cash flows.

The company manual addresses the discount rate to be used in calculating the NPV. Some companies use more than one discount rate to show the effect of using different rates on the NPV. Also, some companies require different discount rates for different project classifications. The more risky the investment, the higher the discount rate used. These rates should be updated at least annually. Some companies do not reveal the rate to be used for projects evaluated by the corporate office so that as many investments as possible can be considered. Company manuals usually explain how to use the NPV and provide several forms to facilitate the calculations. Those that have computer programs explain them and provide examples to show what key entries must be made and what the output means.

The other discounted cash flow method used is the internal rate of return method (IRR). It uses trial-and-error techniques to find the rate of return that will make the discounted future cash flows equal to the initial investment. The IRR is more difficult to calculate than the NPV and should be used with care due to its nature and the possibility of getting multiple yields for unconventional investments (conventional investments are those that have a negative cash flow followed by positive cash flows or vice versa). The NPV is more theoretically sound than the IRR. However, the IRR is more often used because it is easy to interpret and compare to the cost of capital and it avoids the need for precisely determining the discount rate to use (which is essential in NPV calculations). When the IRR method is used, a minimum cutoff rate is established based on the cost of capital and is often called the hurdle rate. Many procedure manuals provide forms with columns to be used in trial-and-error calculations.

The average rate of return is an accounting concept found by dividing average income by average investment. It is not very applicable for capital expenditure evaluation. It is useful as a supplementary evaluation method to help measure the effect of the proposed expenditure on the financial statements.

The payback method does not measure profitability or risk. It instead measures how long it takes to recover the original investment. Accordingly, it measures how long capital is invested with risk. This method is the most commonly used method in practice. It should be used as a supplementary method and not as the primary acceptance criterion. It is useful in identifying the cash break-even point in numbers of years. It is important in very risky investments such as foreign investments, highly competitive constantly changing markets such as that of toys, and where cash flows are highly unreliable.

The introduction of the computer facilitates easier evaluations. Therefore, more than one evaluation measure should be used. Company manuals should explain each method, why it is used, what it measures, how it is used, and how to interpret the results. Standard forms should be provided to ensure uniform and consistent evaluation.

Cost of capital. Each company should specify the discount rate (or rates) that should be used in the calculations of NPV or the hurdle rate when IRR is used. Companies may explain the concept of a weighted-average cost of capital and how it relates to the accomplishment of targeted rates of returns.

Some firms show how to calculate the cost of each individual long-term source of funds (bonds, other long-term debt, preferred stock, and common equity). It is advisable here to explain, especially for nonfinancial managers, that the lower cost of debt cannot be used instead of the higher overall average cost of capital because debt cannot be obtained without underlying equity.

The cost of capital must be an aftertax estimate. At best, it is a close estimation. It is never known with certainty due to the numerous variations in assumptions used in calculating its components and combining them into an overall cost figure. The discount rate used for capital expenditure evaluation is often the cost of capital adjusted upward to accommodate projects that must be undertaken with little or no return (such as projects to comply with environmental regulations or to protect employee health or welfare). Also, some rates may be adjusted for risk and applied to various project categories, with higher-risk projects penalized by the use of higher discount rates.

Risk treatment. Since the future is never known with certainty, expected project cash flows are never known with certainty. The larger the expected variation in cash flows, the greater the project risk. Recently a number of firms have recognized the importance of dealing

509

with risk in capital expenditure proposals. Techniques for dealing with risk differ in their level of sophistication and cost. Accordingly, it is customary to increase attention to risk as the size and importance of the investment project increases. Some companies find it useful to specify that risk analysis will be performed on projects that cost at least $1 million.

The techniques described in the manuals reveal the following practices in order of sophistication. They are described briefly here.

Ignore it. Some manuals fail to mention risk at all. The assumption is that other calculations deal with it implicitly.

Informal techniques. Some managers argue that dealing with risk is an art and a very complicated subject. Accordingly, they find that informal, subjective methods of dealing with risk that are subject to each manager's discretion are sufficient. Written descriptions of risk factors are also used to make the reviewer cognizant of risk elements inherent in a project.

Favorable, unfavorable, and most likely. A large number of firms acquire three sets of data for each project. One set measures the results under the most favorable conditions, another measures the results under the worst possible conditions, and the last set measures the most likely results. The collected data help comparing one investment project to another.

Sensitivity analysis. This technique takes each one of the key estimates of a project and measures the effect of a small change in each element on the profitability measure. If a small change (5 to 10 percent) in a given factor results in a much larger change in the profitability of the project, then the project is judged to be sensitive to the factor. The factors are then listed in order of sensitivity. Additional data may be acquired to reduce the estimated error in sensitive factors. The technique is costly and understandably used for larger projects. It has two key drawbacks. First, it does not consider a combination of changes at one time. Instead, a change in each factor is considered separately. This is unrealistic since changes do occur simultaneously. Second, it does not use probability estimates. If one factor is not likely to change as much as another factor, it is not logical to treat them equally.

Risk analysis. This technique is more advanced than sensitivity analysis. It allows for considering changes simultaneously and uses subjective probability. Due to the large number of possible outcomes from changes in various estimates, the use of computers is needed in risk analysis. The computer is used to simulate the probability distributions of key estimates; then it randomly selects a set of numbers following these probability distributions and combines these numbers to determine the NPV or IRR on the project for a given trial. The com-

510

puter runs thousands of these trials (iterations) to arrive at a collection of results that are shown as a distribution with expected average and standard deviation along with the highest and lowest expected values.

This technique is expensive and time consuming. It is reserved for very large investments. The results could be used to reach conclusions regarding the possibility that the project will lose money or exceed a certain return on investment. A better measure of risk is hereby achieved. This technique is less frequently mentioned in capital expenditure evaluation manuals than the other less sophisticated techniques.

Estimating cash flows. The most important aspect of capital expenditure evaluation is that of estimating the cash flows associated with the proposal. If this part is wrong, all evaluation results are also wrong. Therefore, special attention must be directed to this activity. Companies provide help in this regard by using forms that identify the key estimates needed to arrive at annual cash flows. They start with revenue and follow the accounting system to arrive at net income per year, which is then adjusted by adding depreciation to arrive at an estimate of cash flows.

The key assumptions used in making the estimates must be stated in the proposal to allow for more realistic evaluation of project cash flows.

Evaluation criteria. Evaluation criteria should consider both quantitative and other nonquantitative factors. One company explicitly addressed this issue by stating that the general broad criteria considered in evaluating capital expenditure proposals are long-range objectives, government regulations, capacity, cost and financial returns, and personnel considerations.

Consistency

To be able to compare one project to another, criteria must be consistently and uniformly applied. The forms used help in this regard. Also, by using procedures manuals, some consistency can be maintained.

Judgment

Judgment is needed throughout the capital appropriation process. The information and data gathered are not substitutes for judgment. However, judgment should not be used as an excuse for sloppy procedures that do not consider known factors in an organized manner.

Interpretation of the Results

The more information the better—so long as this information means something and is interpreted correctly. The manual should emphasize the meaning and significance of each measure and answer. Capital expenditure returns are not precise statistical measures. At best, they are close approximations to be used with judgment and care.

Executive Summary

Each capital appropriation request should consist of two parts. The first part is a summary of the proposal. The second part is more detailed and includes the supporting documents. The first part should be written in language that a nonexpert can understand. As a summary sheet, it should be short—one or two pages. Key items that should be included in the summary are:

1. Identification number and data regarding the division.
2. Brief description of the proposed expenditure.
3. Brief description of the expected benefits such as increase in sales or reduction in costs, etc.
4. Classification of the project such as replacement, growth, new venture, etc.
5. Amount of the investment and form. A differentiation is made between investment in fixed assets and working capital because working capital is recoverable.
6. Expected cash flow each year from the first to the last. Often companies limit the estimates to a 20-year period with the assumption that the project will be liquidated at that time.
7. Brief reference to alternatives considered and why they were disregarded in favor of the current project.
8. A brief description of nonquantitative aspects of the project and their importance.
9. Summary of the measures of profitability of the project (for example, the payback, average rate of return, net present value, and IRR). Whenever possible, three estimates for each item (most favorable, least favorable, and most likely results) should be provided, especially for larger projects.
10. Summary of risk factors and an assessment of the likely effect on the organization.
11. A brief statement on the assumptions used.
12. A brief statement of how this project fits into the total goals, objectives, and strategies of the corporation.

512

13. Consequences of rejecting or delaying the project need to be stated. This sense of urgency and consequences can provide a valuable input.
14. Approval and review signatures and dates showing all key individuals that must review the project depending on size, classification, and importance.
15. Index of supporting documentation and attachments. Detailed studies may be attached or referred to with an indication of where a copy could be acquired. Copies of the proposal and the attachments may vary, with detailed engineering documentation given to those that need it and are technically qualified to judge it.
16. One useful attachment is a photograph of what the item would look like, if available and feasible.
17. Reference is also made to how the copies of the forms are to be distributed.
18. The name of the sponsor and the project manager or individual responsible for following up and monitoring project progress should be included.

Supporting Documentation Required

Supporting documentation will vary from one project to another. The larger and more important the project, the greater the amount of documentation required. The following are examples of the type of documentation needed for major projects.

Economic assumptions. A listing of economic assumptions used is provided. Assumptions are key to realization of the objectives of the project. The more realistic the assumptions, the better the chances for the success of the project.

Detailed economic studies and detailed cash flows. These documents show in detail how the cash flows are arrived at and any studies that were conducted to show the economic viability of the project.

Detailed calculations of project worth. These calculations are shown in more detail here, with the results summarized on the cover sheet.

Market research studies. These studies are important in evaluating new markets or new product likelihood of success.

513

Alternatives considered. This is a more detailed description of alternatives that were considered and disregarded along with reasons why they were deemed inferior to the proposed project. Only key alternatives are described. Some companies limit it to one or two alternatives. There is always an alternative to doing something—which is doing nothing.

Engineering studies. These will demonstrate the practicality of the proposed project whenever it is technically oriented. They will also address the ease of maintenance, amenability to modifications, and other factors such as economic life.

Environmental factors. These factors reflect a change in the times. A profitable project is no longer as desirable if it hurts the environment. Also, reference will be made here to other governmental regulations that must be met.

Risk studies. These studies will vary in methodology and detail depending upon the type of investment and its potential impact on the corporation.

Noneconomic consequences. These factors are frequently as important to the success of the project as the quantitative aspects of a project. A listing and explanation of key nonquantitative costs and benefits can help make the reviewer aware of the total impact of the proposed investment.

Roles of Operating and Staff Groups

For the capital appropriations system to work, it must be supported by all concerned. However, operating line individuals are primarily responsible for following the capital appropriation procedures with staff support and help. Operating personnel can ask for the help of various staff specialists with regard to taxes, legal, engineering, marketing research, and other technical subjects. Finance and planning personnel can help with preparation of the documents, instructions on calculations, use of computer programs, and interpreting the results.

To ensure objectivity, the ultimate responsibility for post-auditing projects should be given to a department other than the one in which the project resides. However, the latter must be responsible for seeing that records are kept to make the post-audit possible.

The corporate planning or capital acquisitions department may help with projects reviewed by top management by checking calcula-

514

tions and assumptions and providing a list of questions raised and a critique of the proposal.

Roles of Committees and Top Management

It is useful to make use of committees at different levels to evaluate capital expenditure appropriation requests. Capital expenditure proposals lend themselves to evaluation by individuals with different viewpoints. Representatives from marketing, engineering, manufacturing, research, legal, and financial departments can check the worthiness of the underlying project assumptions from their different vantage points.

Top management must see to it that it has an overall satisfactory system that encourages the submission of sufficient worthwhile projects, that these projects are evaluated adequately and consistently, that the best set of projects is selected, that those selected are executed, that a representative sample of those executed are post-audited, and that enough records are kept to keep track of what is happening and to constantly check these projects against long-range plans and objectives.

Top management must be ultimately responsible for capital expenditure programs and for ensuring that delegation of the responsibility is taken seriously and that the benefits of such delegation outweigh the potential cost of making wrong or shortsighted decisions.

Top management has an especially tough job here because a choice must be made between maximizing short-run earnings that reflect well on the price of the stock in the short-run and long-run earnings that enhance the company's future. Top management is under constant pressure to push short-term income statement immediate earnings per share at the expense of the long run. A delicate balance must be maintained.

Top management also has a special responsibility to see that the capital appropriation system is sound. Also, top management must see that the underlying philosophy of management is reflected and that the assumptions used throughout the process are realistic.

Interface with the Capital Budget

While capital budget inclusion is not a prerequisite for undertaking the expenditure or committing the funds, capital appropriation requests are prerequisites for such action. For budget inclusion, only preliminary estimates are needed. Thus, when the appropriation request is submitted, updated budget figures can be made. When approved, requests for appropriations for projects not included in the budget need to be added to the budget.

Both capital expenditure appropriations previously included or not included in the budget must not exceed the total amount allocated for that particular classification, division, or the total capital budget target.

Approval Limits

Capital expenditure appropriation requests must go through various levels of approval depending upon their size. While practices vary drastically, a typical example is provided here.

Needed approval	*Amount*
Board of directors	Over $1 million
President	To $1 million
Group vice president	To $300,000
General managers	To $100,000

Another example from a large diversified company is:

Needed approval	*Amount*
Board of directors	Over $20 million
Executive committee	Up to $20 million
President	Up to $1.5 million
Group vice president/staff vice presidents	Up to $300,000

Many companies base their approval levels on the size of the total capital budget. The amounts allowed for every level of approval are made as a percentage of the total capital budget.

Decision Rules

Practices vary from one company to another regarding the degree of specificity of capital expenditure appropriation decisions. The rules

516

can be too broad or too specific. Some of the questions which should be addressed include:

1. What is the minimum required rate of return to be used as the cutoff point or hurdle rate when the internal rate of return method is used and as a discount rate when the net present value method is used?
2. How much adjustment, if any, should be made to the required return to allow for projects that must be undertaken with little or no return?
3. How would risk be considered? Should a risk-adjusted rate of return be used? If so, how much is the adjustment needed for different risk classifications?
4. What size investment proposal requires elaborate risk analysis studies?
5. Which method or combination of methods would be used to select among competing projects?
6. Should financing be used to accept worthwhile projects? If so, what corporate debt level must not be exceeded?
7. What percentage of undertaken projects should be audited, and how should these projects be selected?
8. How much guidance should be given to project sponsors and departments regarding assumptions used by the company and corporate goals and objectives?

Treatment of Overruns, Underruns, and Supplementary Appropriations

No one can accurately predict the future all the time. The future is never known with certainty. Events beyond the control of project originators can occur to change project costs and benefits. Realizing that deviations from estimates will occur, a mechanism must be developed to deal with these changes. Usually overruns are more serious to handle. Allowance should be made for projects to vary in a small range (such as 5 to 9 percent) without having to request extra appropriations. However, when the amount of deviation exceeds 10 percent or a given dollar figure such as $100,000, a supplementary appropriation request is needed. The purpose of this request is to alert management that a significant change is needed, to allow studying the variation and taking necessary corrective action, and, when necessary, abandoning the project (if enough problems are expected to change a project to a nonprofitable investment).

A project may also be more profitable than expected. Small deviations could occur on both the high and the low sides. If a significant underrun is expected, management should be alerted to find out whether the project is being executed as planned or if inferior materials are being used. If the savings are significant, the extra funds may be allocated to other projects or the debt could be reduced.

The level of approval needed for supplementary appropriations should parallel that of the original appropriation. The request should explain why the changes occurred and why it is still advisable to continue the project.

Notification and Appeal

Project authors need to be kept informed of the status of their proposals. As soon as a proposal is approved, the originator is promptly notified. If a proposal is disapproved, the originator should also be notified.

Some firms allow a disapproved project to be resubmitted after a given period of time such as a year or two has elapsed. Others allow an appeal mechanism. The appeal should be handled by a committee that makes recommendations to the division head or the president.

Emergency Requests

Appropriation request procedures must include an allowance for emergency requests. A plant production line cannot be stopped while the department waits to replace a piece of equipment because an appropriation request is being processed. This type of procedure allows for unforeseen circumstances when action is needed in a hurry. Some companies allow the department head to get phone approval with the request submitted after the expenditure is made. One company states that "emergency requests may be approved by the executive committee or the chairman of the board."

Flow of Events

A company may decide to follow a plan whereby each profit center or department submits its capital expenditure requests to the division by September of each year. The division reviews all requests, combines them, and prepares an overall budget request by October 1. Divisional requests are then submitted to the corporate planning committee (or equivalent review board) for approval of large projects or getting a blanket approval (lump sum) for other projects. Then, each originator of a capital expenditure request is notified of the preliminary evaluation. If the review board approved the budget, an appropriation request is then prepared. The appropriation request is accompanied by a number of supporting documents and studies that vary in length and detail directly with the size and importance of the project.

Preparation of the appropriation request may take as little as a few weeks or as long as several months. The originator should start early enough to allow time for preparing the request, for the evaluation and notification of outcome, and to be able to implement the project at the desirable date.

Progress reports are made throughout the life of the project, preferably on a quarterly basis. Finally, post-audit reports are made on completed projects (or a sample of these) as soon as a project is completed or fully functioning.

Copies of reports or a summary thereof need to be distributed to the project manager (for follow-up), project manager supervisor, corporate budget office and financial officers, and management's groups (division heads, president, and board of directors). The number of copies vary and may go as high as 22 copies or more. Also, the details sent to various individuals will vary depending upon each specific individual's need for details.

Example. One company holds quarterly meetings at the corporate level. The mid-year objective is to discuss and review overall guidelines and broad budget features. In September a meeting is held to prepare budget estimates for next year, including amounts allocated for various divisions and capital expenditure categories against which authorization requests are to be made. In December a yearly budget review is made. At each quarterly meeting, specific appropriation requests are approved for the next quarter, and the budget is updated accordingly.

Coordinating Function

The coordinating function of capital expenditures is done at several points. A project coordinator is assigned to each project as soon as the appropriation request is approved. This individual is responsible for following the project through from beginning to end. Throughout the whole budgeting and project evaluation process various committees also perform a coordinating function. Department, divisional, and corporate capital expenditure committees provide inputs at various levels that can better estimate the impact of the project from different perspectives and evaluate its realism. Members of these committees are also kept aware of projects that will impact on their departments or divisions.

It is often argued that committees are extremely valuable in capital expenditure evaluation where projects need to be looked at from various viewpoints. Experts in engineering, marketing, production, finance, legal, accounting, tax, and others can provide much needed inputs.

Committees, however, need to be used with care to avoid excessive delays, stifling innovation, and making undesirable compromises that may lead to the selection of routine and less than optimal sets of capital expenditure projects.

Forms Used

Selected key forms used in the appropriation process will be discussed at the end of this chapter.

HOW TO DESIGN APPROPRIATION PROCEDURES

There is no single best method of designing or changing appropriation procedures. However, the designer may start by specifying the objectives to be accomplished by the appropriation procedures, preparing a draft of the procedures that recognizes the organizational structure and the business environment, sending the draft to key individuals for comments, preparing revised procedures, obtaining top-management approval, implementing the procedures, monitoring the results, and making necessary changes. The procedures need to be reevaluated periodically to meet changing needs of the organization and the environment within and outside the organization. Here are some examples of the desired objectives and their effect on the appropriation procedures.

Objective	*Examples of implications*
Control expenditures	• The procedures should prevent individuals from making unauthorized capital expenditures. Controls should also be established at the purchase order and payment levels.

Objective	*Examples of implications*
	• To allow for effective time management, the approval level must vary with the size of the expenditure. In highly diversified companies, more autonomy should be given to the plant or individual unit.
	• Authorization for expenditure forms must show needed authorizations.
Control cash flow	• The procedures should ensure that expected timing of expenditures and receipts are communicated to all concerned. This will allow better utilization of cash, more effective fund raising, and, when necessary, changing the timing of major expenditures to coincide with expected cash receipts. The routing of forms needs to be tied to the cash budget mechanism.
Obtain managerial approval	• Procedures need to ensure that projects are adequately considered by various managerial levels. Timetables can be designed to allow review and approval without unnecessary delays. The approval mechanism needs to be carefully designed.

Objective	*Examples of implications*
Ensure consistency with objectives	• An initial screening process needs to be established to ensure that projects that are inconsistent with corporate objectives are excluded prior to going through the expensive and time-consuming evaluation process.
	• The appropriation request form needs to tie projects to corporate objectives. A statement of purpose of the project and consistency with corporate objectives may be required of each project originator. Classification of projects may be used to facilitate relating projects to corporate objectives.
	• The procedures should be designed to allow for project objectives to be communicated throughout the organization.
Select the best alternatives	• The procedures need to be designed to force the project originator to look at alternative ways of undertaking the project. A brief description of the best alternatives considered and disregarded and why they were deemed inappropriate may be requested to accomplish this objective. Attention of

Objective	*Examples of implications*
	reviewers, evaluators, and consultants needs to be directed to whether the proposed expenditure is the best alternative from the long-run perspective as well as the short-run. If the expenditure is not advantageous in *both* the long and short runs, the conflict and the reasons for selection of one over the other should be explained.
Ensure careful, consistent, and uniform evaluation	• The procedures need to prevent hasty, inconsistent, and careless evaluation of proposals.
	• Discounted cash flow techniques should be used. Forms need to be designed to facilitate including key estimates and calculating the economic worth of proposed projects in a way that would allow comparisons and recognition of economic and other consequences. Some individuals need to be designated as a source of help with preparing the appropriation request and its attachments. Training in capital budgeting is needed by all managers involved in these projects.

Objective	*Examples of implications*
Develop audit records	• The procedures need to assign responsibility for keeping sufficient records for following up on the completed projects. The accounting system should be checked to ensure that it can provide needed data on a project basis.
Develop monitoring techniques	• Periodic progress reports need to be installed to keep track of various projects. This procedure will deal with project overruns, underruns, and encountered problems. The purpose of these procedures is to take corrective action when needed, including abandoning the project. Included here are the questions of who should receive various reports and at what level of detail.
Avoid unnecessary delays and roadblocks	• The procedures need to make the evaluation process thorough but speedy. Maximum time for processing requests needs to be established. Assigning responsibility for tracking projects is needed. The level of computerization of the process is a decision variable here.

Objective	*Examples of implications*
Encourage submission of worthwhile proposals	• The procedures should be detailed and specific enough to be helpful but not too detailed or too specific to be stifling and counterproductive. Thus, appropriation procedures should not be so formidable as to discourage submission of worthwhile projects. The procedures should not ignore the mechanism of providing a sufficient supply of projects for consideration. Procedures should be periodically updated to recognize changing needs and circumstances.

DOCUMENTING THE PROCEDURES

Procedures need to be written to avoid confusion, misunderstanding, and excessive waste of time guessing what should or should not be included and how to go about getting approval for a capital expenditure proposal. However, procedures need not be put in a manual. Various methods may be used to document the appropriation procedures. A collection of similar procedures may be put together in the form of a manual. The manual may be made exclusively for capital facilities acquisition or it may be a section of a larger manual. Some companies prefer to use a letter of memorandum to be sent once a year to ask for budget estimates and provide the latest policies and procedures. Other companies collect all policies in one manual, with the procedures printed in a separate manual. Generally, policies are fewer in number than procedures and are often combined in one place, with the policy statement followed by more detailed procedures to implement that policy.

Periodic revisions of policies and procedures need to be made to keep track of changes. Loose-leaf pages may be used to allow inserting revised pages easily. With the advent of word processing equipment, revisions can be made without having to retype everything. The following format was found useful in tracking down revisions of policies and procedures.

XYZ Corporation *Capital Expenditure* *Policies and Procedures* *Guide*—Authorization levels	No: 200 1001 00	Page 2	of 10
	Originally issued: 10/11/83	Latest revision: 12/31/85	

The items listed mean:

Item	Explanation
XYZ	Corporation name.
Capital Expenditure Policies and Procedures Guide	Title of policies and procedures manual.
No: 200 1001 00	Policy number for tracking purposes.
Page 2	Refers to specific page.
of 10	Refers to number of pages for that section.
Originally issued: 10/11/83	This policy and procedure was issued on 10/11/83.
Latest revision: 12/31/85	Refers to the last time revised. This is needed to keep track of the various revisions.

No manuals. As mentioned above, some companies handle capital appropriations by an annual letter that asks various managers to submit requests. This letter identifies the procedures required and details the needed work. This practice necessitates sending other supplementary letters and forms with detailed instructions.

Manuals. A brief description of policy and procedure manuals will be made, with emphasis placed on the latter. Then a detailed outline of key items included in a comprehensive manual will be provided. A brief explanation is made when necessary. (Many of the items included in the outline were explained elsewhere in the chapter.)

Policy Manual

Policy refers to general and broad-standing answers to recurring questions in capital expenditure management. It includes statements regarding who is ultimately responsible for the capital expenditure program, policy on capitalization of physical property, long-range planning cycle, short-range planning cycle, significance of budget approval, appropriateness of leasing, corporate return on investment objective, and monitoring and post-auditing projects.

Procedures Manual

Procedures are detailed steps needed to implement the policies. These procedures must be consistent with the policies. The amount of detail and specificity needed will depend on the individuals working for the company and the amount of freedom given to individual proposal authors and departments.

Comprehensive Manual

An example of items in a rather complete policy and procedures manual is provided to aid those who need to prepare a new manual or update their current manuals. Generally, problems and mistakes that occur frequently need to be addressed. The final test of a good manual is in its actual use by those who need it. The main objective of the manual is to provide factors that need to be considered by all and to provide clues for those who prepare and administer capital expenditure projects. It can also help in selling and maintaining better communications and understanding of what management is doing. The manual may reflect the degree of awareness and competency of company management and understanding of capital expenditure management.

Item	*Brief explanation*

• Introduction
   Purpose of manual
   Intended reader
   Program objectives
   Management philoso-
      phy
   How to use this manual
	• The purpose of the manual
	is stated along with a
	description of for whom
	the manual is made,
	objectives of the capital
	expenditure program, a
	statement expressing
	management philoso-
	phy on degree of in-
	volvement of various

Item	*Brief explanation*
	individuals, and how capital expenditure management as a whole is structured and viewed. It may also specify where to go for additional help or explanation and how this manual relates to other manuals.
● Company objectives	● The key objectives of the company as a whole are stated. This will help make it known to all concerned what the company aims to accomplish. It is useful in emphasizing the team approach of viewing objectives as "ours" instead of "theirs." Objectives may include market share, ROI target, sales total, degree of plant modernization, as well as others.
● Economic and environmental assumptions	● General economic and environmental assumptions are better and less expensive to make when made for the company as a whole. They are treated as given to save each project originator from preparing assumptions that could be made more accurately and professionally by the company experts.

Item	*Brief explanation*
• Definitions	• A glossary of terms used may be useful to readers who may be unfamiliar with the terminology. For example, terms that may be included are capital expenditure, budget, appropriation, cash flow, working capital, NPV, IRR, risk, cost of capital, discount rate, financing versus rationing budget, and post-audit.
• Capital expenditure policies	• These are general statements that apply to recurring questions. They should be limited in number (10 to 15).
• Responsibility for capital expenditures	• This section lists the key individuals involved in the capital expenditure program and delineates the responsibility of each. The individuals include project originator, department head, division or general manager, project engineer, marketing managers, manufacturing director, financial planning manager, controller, budget director, treasurer, vice president of finance, president and board of directors, and various committee chairpersons.

Item	*Brief explanation*
• Capital budget	• The capital expenditure budgeting process is described along with detailed procedures and forms to be used. Budget calendar may also be included.
• Who can make a proposal	• The procedures list who can make a capital expenditure proposal. Generally, any individual can submit a capital expenditure idea. However, ideas must be screened by the department involved. Emphasis should be placed on encouraging innovation and a healthy supply of ideas.
	• The procedures should list the route that an idea must go through from beginning to end.
	• Incentive programs can be explained here. Some companies give awards to those who submit ideas that result in savings or profit improvement. The rewards could be substantial or small. One large tobacco company provides a token monetary award but lots of recognition with the assumption that, through profit sharing, everyone will benefit from the new idea.

Item	*Brief explanation*
• Appropriation request	• The details of how an appropriation request should be prepared are found along with appropriate forms. Other questions related to appropriation procedures that are included in other parts of the manual are referenced. The reader of this section should be able to find who is qualified to submit an appropriation request, how to prepare it, the channels it follows for approval, and what level of authorization and documentation is needed. Additionally, specific appropriations versus blanket appropriations are discussed.
• Preparation for evaluation	• This is a detailed section that expands upon the appropriation request. It includes: *A. Classification of projects.* Projects are grouped according to some logical basis such as new products, capacity increase, cost reduction, replacement, safety, office equipment, and facilities and other. *B. Authorization levels and routing of forms.* Some companies use a matrix that lists various authorization levels on

| *Item* | | | *Brief explanation* | |

one heading and type of
capital expenditure on
another, with an "X"
placed beside the neces-
sary approvals for each
major classification. An
example follows which
groups replacement pro-
jects by dollar amounts.

	Up to $50,000	Up to $250,000	Up to $2 million	Over $2 million
Division	X	X	X	X
Group vice president		X	X	X
President			X	X
Board of directors				X

*C. How to complete
the appropriation request.*
This is a detailed section
that has several items to
help the preparer of an
appropriation request. It
may be divided further
into the following subti-
tles:

1. *Estimating invest-
   ment cost.*
2. *Estimating working
   capital needs.*
3. *Depreciation guide-
   lines.*
4. *Economic life guide-
   lines.*
5. *Tax consideration
   and rates.*
6. *Preparing cash flow
   by year.*

Item	*Brief explanation*

7. *Alternatives considered and abandoned.*
8. *Statement of key assumptions used and how they were determined.* If the assumptions differ from those provided by management for the economy and environment, an explanation for deviations is needed.
9. *Cost/benefit analysis.* Each capital expenditure analysis method, how to compute it, and how to present the results are included. Emphasis is placed on preparing data for evaluation. Often detailed work sheets are included to help determine the cash flow estimates needed in the calculation and to facilitate actual calculation of the measures of economic worth determined by these methods.
10. *Risk analysis.*
11. *Use of computer programs.* An explanation is made of computer programs available for use in facilitating calculation of economic

Item	*Brief explanation*
	worth of projects. When risk analysis is used, there is a greater need for explaining how to use computers in simulating probability distributions and repeating iterations to try to predict expected outcomes, averages, and standard deviations.
	12. *Attachments and supplementary data.* Economic, engineering, and market studies are described and explained.
	13. *Use of consultants and outside experts.* This is especially needed for major projects where objectivity is important.
• Approval and notification	• This section details how each proposal author will be notified of the progress of the proposal, appeal mechanism if any, notice of project approval and assigned number, and what to do with rejected projects.
• Evaluation and selection	• A description is given of how a project will be evaluated and selected for implementation.
	• Selection is more of an art than a science since

Item	*Brief explanation*
	both quantitative and qualitative factors have to be considered along with intuition and feel for the market and what is possible. Selection should never be viewed as a routine exercise.
• Execution and implementation	• This section describes how to implement approved projects in a timely manner.
• Monitoring progress	• These procedures make reference to steps needed to keep track of various projects until they are completed and fully operational. These procedures include: A. Summaries of authorized projects. B. Supplementary requests, overruns, and underruns. C. Project status reports (usually monthly or quarterly). D. Cancelation of projects. E. Project completion notice. F. Summary of projects completed.
• Post-audits	• This is the last step needed. It compares actual results to those provided by projects' originators. It is needed for lesson learning and

Item	*Brief explanation*
	to keep people honest. Sampling techniques may be used to select projects.
• Special items	• This section may include details regarding: A. Emergency requests. B. Dates and deadlines/calendar of events. C. Reference to other manuals. D. List of names and telephone numbers to call for clarification of information and help.
• Index	• The index is needed to facilitate using the manual.
• Appendixes	• Forms to be used and present value tables are examples of items that may be included in an appendix.

APPROVALS REQUIRED

A more detailed example of approvals required for capital expenditures found in one manual is presented in Figure 1.

KEY FORMS

Forms used in capital expenditure evaluation vary in number and detail, depending upon company needs and preferences. A selected set of key forms is described here. They are designed to encourage uniformity, consistency, and completeness of documentation, and to help in making the submission, evaluation, control, monitoring, and post-audit of capital expenditure projects as painless as possible. They also can help save time for busy executives. Each user must modify the forms,

FIGURE 1

Approvals Required for Capital Expenditure Appropriations

Approval	From: $0 To: $10,000	$10,000 $25,000	$25,000 $50,000	$50,000 $100,000	$100,000 $200,000	$200,000 $500,000	$500,000 and over
Plant manager	X	X	X	X	X	X	X
Operations manager		X	X	X	X	X	X
Division engineer		X	X	X	X	X	X
Division controller		X	X	X	X	X	X
Division manager			X	X	X	X	X
Director of corporate engineering				X	X	X	X
Treasurer				X	X	X	X
Vice president, administration					X	X	X
President						X	X
Board of directors							X

add additional ones, or eliminate some to tailor these forms to each company's needs.

Preliminary Project Request

This is a request to proceed with submitting the appropriation request and collecting necessary data. It is designed to save unnecessary ef-

FIGURE 2

Preliminary Project Request

Project title _____ Project no. _____

Department and division _____

Is it included in annual capital budget? _____yes _____no

Description and classification

Estimated investment

Land _____, Building _____, Machinery and equipment _____,
Facilities
total _____, Working capital _____, Total investment _____,

Expected benefits

Requested by _____ Phone _____

Review	Authorization to submit final report
yes/no Signature Date	yes/no Signature Date
Engineering _____	Division _____
Marketing _____	Group vice president _____
Production _____	President _____
Financial _____	

forts by eliminating obviously poor or undesirable capital expenditure projects (see Figure 2).

Capital Appropriation Request Form

This form contains all the information needed to evaluate a capital expenditure proposal (see Figure 3). Typical items included are:

1. **Project number.** It may be divided so that first two digits designate year, the third digit designates type of expenditure, and the fourth through sixth digits would designate division and department.
2. **Brief description of project.** The purpose of the project should be properly defined.
3. **Alternatives considered** and why they were rejected.
4. **Assumptions used** with regard to sales, pricing, service, economic life of machinery, etc.
5. A statement on the effect of the project on existing business should be required. Some projects can adversely affect existing business. This should not mean that such a project would be rejected. If the company does not introduce a new product to avoid competing with its current products, its competitors will definitely not hesitate to do so.
6. **Estimated required investment.** One company manual details it in the following categories.

Property, plant, and equipment	XXX
Transportation and installation	XXX
Gross cost to be capitalized	XXX
Deduct: Disposal value of replaced facilities	(XXX)
Net capital investment	XXX
Additional funds required for working capital	XXX
Total investment	XXX

7. **Priority.** In one company, a project is classified as absolutely essential, economically desirable, or general improvement. In another company, a project is classified as essential, desirable, deferrable. A statement is needed to answer

the question, "What would happen if the project is not undertaken?"

8. Justification. Project justification can be made on economic grounds (increase return on investment), or another basis, or both. Some reference needs to be made to what could best be done with abandoned machinery and equipment, if any.

Another Method of Presenting Estimated Cash Flows

A more detailed and useful way of presenting cash flows and their timing within each year was found in some manuals. This approach helps in cash management by providing data on specifically in which quarter cash is expected to be received or paid, rather than the typical approach of lumping cash on an annual basis. An example is provided below.

Summary Forms and Follow-Up Reports

Four forms used to summarize appropriations requests and approvals and to keep track of projects during different stages of their progress are provided here as examples.

Capital appropriation request status. This form may be used by department, division, or central office to show what happened to appropriation requests that were submitted (see Figure 4).

Chronological list of approved projects. It lists approved appropriation requests by date of approval. With the advent of the computer, a variety of reports could be made by sorting according to desired item. For example, a report may be prepared to show approved projects by return on investment in descending order, by size of investment in

FIGURE 3

Appropriation Request for Capital Expenditure

Original request/supplemental request   Project assigned number _____

Plant name _____   Date of request _____

Division name _____   Revision number _____

Subsidiary name _____   Prepared by _____

Location of plant _____   Classification of expenditure (replacement, expansion, new product, other):

_____

Description of project: _____

_____

Justification: _____

Amount in current budget for this project:
     Authorized $_____   Spent $_____   Balance $_____

Estimated, start-up date: _____;   Completion date: _____
Investment:
Capital facilities $_____,   Working capital $_____,   Total $_____

Estimated cash flows:

Year end	0	1	2	3	4	5		20
Amount								

Financial indicators of worth:

IRR	NPV			Payback in years	Discounted payback	Effect on accounting income
	@ __%	@ __%	@ __%			

Risk factors
    Describe worst possible outcome and effect on NPV: _____

    Describe best possible outcome and effect on NPV: _____

    Realistic assessment: _____

Assumptions used in calculations: _____

What are the consequences of delaying the project? _____

_____

Special attachments and schedules:
____ Detailed engineering studies   ____ Detailed economic assumptions
____ Market research studies   ____ Alternatives considered and rejected
____ Detailed cash flow and project   ____ Effect of project on existing business
     calculations

Project author's name: _____   Telephone: _____

Approvals:	Yes	No	Signature and date		Yes	No	Signature and date
Division head	—	—	_____	Corporate controller	—	—	_____
Area/Sub. president	—	—	_____	Executive vice president	—	—	_____
Regional/Group vice president	—	—	_____	President	—	—	_____
Board of sub.	—	—	_____	Chairman of appropriations committee	—	—	_____
Manager of capital assets	—	—	_____	Board of directors, chairman	—	—	_____

FIGURE 4

XYZ Corporation
Capital Appropriation Request Status
Department/Division/Central Office

| Item number | Description | Amount requested | Date received | Date sent for approval | Approval | | | Disapproval | | Special comments |
					Date received	Amount approved	Date originator notified	Date received	Date originator notified	

descending order, by priority or by classification (such as all replacement projects or new ventures). The reports should be designed to serve management's needs (see Figure 5).

Capital expenditure summary worksheet. This form is designed to list all capital expenditure projects approved for a given year, classified by major expenditure category (see Figure 6).

Work-in-process summary. This list maintains an updated record of approved projects that are still in the process of being completed (see Figure 7).

Cash Flow Estimates

A variety of forms are used to help calculate annual cash flows. Four forms are provided here as examples.

Investments needed. This form details the investments by showing the key components and the amount of cash flow to be expected at the end of the project's life. For example, working capital is expected to be recovered by the end of the project's life.

	Investments Needed	
	Investment	*Recovery, end of period*
Fixed assets		
Land and buildings		
Machinery and equipment		
Furniture		
Working capital		
Cash		
Accounts receivable		
Inventory		
Expenses		
Start-up		
Moving and relocation		
Employee training		
Other	_____	_____
Total	_____	_____

FIGURE 5

Chronological List of Approved Projects

| Date | Number | Classification | Priority* | Estimated | | | Investment | | | Description and comments |
				ROI	NPV @ ___%	Payback (in years)	Facilities	Working capital	Total	

* List appropriate priority as follows: must, desirable, deferrable.

FIGURE 6

Capital Expenditure Summary Worksheet

Year_____

Project name and number	Land	Building and imprvmts.	Machinery and equipment	Furniture and fixtures	Small tools	Vehicles	Computers and telecomm.	Other	Total

FIGURE 7

Work-in-Process Summary

Report date: _____

Project number	Description	Date project started	Amount appropriated	Amount spent to date	Balance remaining	Degree of physical completion	Estimated total cost	Variance	Estimated completion date	Comments

Cash flow estimates. This is one way of computing cash flows by listing the key income statement items to help determine accounting income, then adjusting the figure by adding noncash charges (depreciation) to compute cash flows. The top part of the form is the total investment (or cash outflows) presented in a summary form. The years of project life are listed horizontally (see Figure 8).

Computation of net cash flow. This is another way of computing cash flows by listing the years vertically and the categories of net income horizontally. The last column adjusts net income by adding noncash charges to arrive at cash flows.

Computation of Net Cash Flow						
Year	Benefits	Costs	Depreciation	Before-tax earnings	Net earnings	Cash flow
1						
2						
3						
4						
5						
6						
7						
8						
9						
10						
11						
12						
13						
14						
15						
16						
17						
18						
19						
20						

Project Evaluation Sheet

To facilitate the computation of net present value and internal rate of return of projects, a form similar to the one provided here may be used (see Figure 9). The actual cash flow is listed in the second column. The present value factor for a given interest rate is multiplied by a cash flow

FIGURE 8

Cash Flow Estimates

Department _____ Division _____ Project No. _____ Date _____

	−4	−3	−2	−1	0	1	2	3	4	5	6	7	8	9	10	11	12	13	14	15
											Life of capital expenditure									
Capital outlay																				
Working capital (additions, subtractions)																				
Total																				
Changes in revenues Quantity increase Volume change																				
Changes in costs and expenses (List) (Depreciation, labor costs, maintenance, power, inventory, safety, flexibility, supplies, etc.)																				
Net effect on operating income																				
Income taxes																				
Effect on income taxes																				
Add back noncash charges Depreciation																				
Cash flow																				

FIGURE 9

Excerpts from a Project Evaluation Sheet

Period ending	Cash flow Amount	Trial 1 15% interest rate PV factor	Trial 1 15% interest rate Present value	Trial 2 ___% interest rate PV factor	Trial 2 ___% interest rate Present value	Trial 3 ___% interest rate PV factor	Trial 3 ___% interest rate Present value
1st year		.8696					
2nd year		.7561					
3rd year		.6575					
4th year		.5718					
5th year		.4972					
6th year		.4323					
7th year		.3759					
8th year		.3269					
9th year		.2843					
10th year		.2472					
11th year		.2149					
. . .							
20th year		.0611					
Total							
Less present value of investment							
Net present value							

to arrive at the present value. The total of each column will show the present value of the project at the given interest rate. When the net present value method is used, the investment is subtracted from the present value of cash flows to arrive at the net present value. When the profitability index is used, the present value of cash flows is divided by the present value of the investment. When the internal rate of return method is used, a series of trials are made to find the rate of discount that will make the present value of future cash flows approximately equal to the investment. Interpolation may be used to determine the rate.

Project Status Report

A progress report, also called a work-in-process status report, is a periodic report (quarterly or monthly) to show amount spent to date, amounts needed for completion of the project, how the actual amounts differ from the estimates, and whether an overrun is expected (see Figure 10). The status report should alert management to potential problems.

Simple Capital Expenditure Control Report

This form may be useful in keeping track of total amounts authorized and spent for each project on a quarterly basis (see Figure 11).

Authorization Change Request for New Plant

This form may be used as a supplement to the appropriation request form to summarize the change requested and the total amount resulting when a major change in investment is warranted (see Figure 12).

Executive Summary

This report is prepared at least once a year for top management to monitor selected projects of special importance (see Figure 13). Others may be combined in a total appropriation amount that shows for each division the amount authorized/spent to date and a brief statement of major concerns or problems.

Capital Expenditure Project Notice of Completion

This form should be completed as soon as the project is operational. It should be updated annually until the project life is ended (see Figure 14).

FIGURE 10

Project Status Report

Project no.: _____   Date of report: _____
Project title: _____   Period covered: _____
Plant: _____
Location: _____
Project manager: _____

Investments

	Authorized to date	Spent this quarter	Spent to date	Projection This quarter	To date	Explanation
	$_____	$_____	$_____	$_____	$_____	_____

Projections
    Amount needed for completion: $_____, Projected overrun/underrun: $_____
    Explanation: _____

Cash Flow
    This year: Expected for year $_____, Results so far $_____
                    Expected by year end $_____

    Explanation: _____

Cash Flow Summary to Date

Year	Projected	Actual	Year	Projected	Actual	Year	Projected	Actual
0			7			14		
1			8			15		
2			9			16		
3			10			17		
4			11			18		
5			12			19		
6			13			20		

Description of how project is proceeding: _____
_____
_____
_____

Warnings/need for action: _____
_____
_____

Signatures/acknowledgments
    Project preparer _____ Date _____
    Department Head _____ Date _____
    Plant Manager _____ Date _____

Post-audit Form

The purpose of a post-audit form is to accomplish the objectives of a post-audit (see Figure 15). Post-audits aspire to learn from past mistakes, to identify poor projects and unsuccessful projects, and to put sponsors of proposals on notice that estimates will be checked when the project is actually undertaken. Thus, good estimators will be recognized and rewarded, and poor estimators will also be recognized. No

FIGURE 11

Simple Capital Expenditure Control Report
Quarter Ended _____

Project number	Description	Amount authorized	Amount spent	Estimated total cost

FIGURE 12

Authorization Change Request for New Plant

	Change requested	Previous authorization	Total
1. Land			
2. Building and land improvements			
3. Machinery and equipment			
4. Small tools			
5. Vehicles			
6. Computers and telecommunications			
7. Other			
Total			

FIGURE 13

Executive Summary for Project Status

Project number	Division and department	Amount authorized	Amount expended	Life	Year now	Problems Yes	Problems No	Brief description of project, explanation of status, and comments
100016	1-056	$2 million	$1 million	10	2		X	Replacement of 10 pieces of equipment. The project is proceeding as planned.
100017	1-059	$10 million	$4 million	20	1	X		Building a new plant for XYZ product line. The project is 20 percent complete, but the expenditures exceed estimates. A special committee is investigating the project.
100018	1-060	$14 million	$14 million	10	5		X	New machinery to replace manual assembly line. Proceeding as planned. Actual cash flows exceed expectations.
100019	2-201	$3.5 million	$.5 million	5	2	X		Introducing a new computer in production line 7 on experimental basis. It is a total failure. Machine is causing several production problems. Cash flows are less than estimated. Project is abandoned.

FIGURE 14

Capital Expenditure Project
Notice of Completion

Title: _____ No.: _____ Date: _____ Location: _____

Date authorized: _____ Date completed: _____

	Equipment	Working capital	Total
Cost estimate per original request	_____	_____	_____
Cost estimate per supplemental requests	_____	_____	_____
Total estimated cost	_____	_____	_____
Actual cost	_____	_____	_____
Variation: Favorable (F), Unfavorable (UF)	_____	_____	_____

Explanation of variation: _____

Cash flow	Actual	Estimate	Variance	F/UF	Explanation
Investments Year ___ Year ___ Year ___					
Cash flows: End of year 1 2 3 4 5 6 7 8 . . . 20					

Acknowledgments

Responsible person	Signature	Date
Plant Manager		
Plant Auditor		
Sales		
Production		
Engineering		
Vice President, Finance		
President		

FIGURE 15

Capital Expenditure Project
Post-audit Report

Year of project life _____

Project name: _____ No.: _____ Location: _____

Date authorized: _____ Date fully operational: _____ Report date: _____

(Attach an updated copy of the Notice of Completion)

1. Why and how this project was selected for post-audit: _____
   _____
   _____

2. Did the cost of investment agree with the projection? yes / no
   If no, please explain: _____
   _____
   _____

3. Overall, how did the actual annual cash flows compare with the projected cash
   flows? If different, please explain the difference: _____
   _____
   _____

4. Overall, was the project a success? If so, explain: _____
   _____

   If failure, explain: _____
   _____

5. Please state lessons learned that could be used in future projects: _____
   _____
   _____

6. What changes should be made in the Capital Expenditure Policies and Procedures
   Manual to enhance the capital expenditure program effectiveness? Please attach
   copies of the pages that need correction. Provide explanation: _____
   _____
   _____

Individual doing post-audit: Signature   Telephone   Date
                            _____   _____   _____

Acknowledgments

  Responsible person   Signature   Date
    Plant Manager   _____   _____
    Plant Auditor   _____   _____
    Sales   _____   _____
    Production   _____   _____
    Engineering   _____   _____
    Vice President, Finance _____   _____
    President   _____   _____

FIGURE 16

Surplus Equipment Report

Department and division: _____

Description of items: _____

_____

_____

_____

_____

Reasons for disposal: _____

_____

_____

_____

Age of items: _____

_____

Cost data:

Item	Book value	Original cost	Depreciation method used

Description of present condition: _____

_____

_____

Estimated cost to fix item or place in good standing: _____

_____

_____

Approvals:	Title	Yes	No	Signature	Date
	_____	—	—	_____	_____
	_____	—	—	_____	_____
	_____	—	—	_____	_____
	_____	—	—	_____	_____
	_____	—	—	_____	_____

penalty should be made to poor estimators unless they have provided misleading estimates on purpose. As a result of the post-audit, profiles of various departments and their records of over- or underestimating benefits and costs are kept. Some companies found a need to adjust project costs upward by a given percentage for all projects submitted by a given department.

Having enough records to be able to compare the actual to the forecast for a given project is not an easy task, since accounting records are not always kept on a project basis. Accordingly, some companies found it necessary to request the sponsoring department head to personally sign an agreement that sufficient records will be kept to allow post-auditing the results when the project is completed.

Post-auditing a project is done at several stages. The first time a project is post-audited is when it is completely operational, that is, when the plant is operating or machinery and equipment are installed. Since a project may have a life of 10 or more years, actual cash flows for the life of the project can never be determined until the end of that life. Therefore, a project should be audited at its 3rd, 5th, and 10th years, and at 5-year intervals until the end of its projected life. Each audit will not start from scratch but rather will update the notice of completion or the previous post-audit report. Due to the expense involved in auditing a project more than once, sampling techniques may be used to provide an element of unpredictability needed to keep proposal authors honest. The sample should be a representative sample that takes the size of investments into consideration by sampling a higher percentage of more expensive projects and by sampling from each capital expenditure classification.

Surplus Equipment Report

This report is designed to inform different departments of intention to dispose of equipment (see Figure 16). Since one individual's leftovers are another individual's feast, it allows for better utilization of resources and saves in unnecessary expenditures by transfer of unneeded equipment and facilities from one plant to another.

SUMMARY AND CONCLUSIONS

In this chapter many ideas were explored and suggestions were made on how to deal with capital expenditure paperwork from beginning to end. Practices vary to reflect particular circumstances of each company.

The system should be checked at least once every two to three years to find if it is working at various stages of project generation, evaluation, selection, execution, and post-audit. All the paperwork is designed to serve the useful purposes of monitoring, controlling, and effectively managing capital expenditures from beginning to end. If the system is too complicated and excessively slows down processing of requests and implementation of projects, then it needs modification. The system should be the servant, not the master. Making the system work effectively is a never-ending process. However, the returns are worthwhile.

IV

Financing Capital Expenditures

24

Long-Term Cash Forecasting: How to Determine Financing Needs

Lewis J. Altfest

Altfest, Young Associates Inc.

INTRODUCTION

Cash flow is essentially the liquid resources that a business generates after deduction for all its needs. It differs from reported earnings in that it is not offset by depreciation and other noncash charges, and thus contains fewer estimates about how assets are to be used in the future. Cash is a tangible resource that can be employed immediately. Cash flow forecasting or providing for sufficient liquidity to run a business is one of the important decisions facing the corporate executive. Too little liquidity can force the corporation into making ill-timed financing and operational decisions. Too much liquidity can suggest unneeded omission of past profitable investment opportunities and subject public corporations to takeover threats.

Often cash forecasting is not given the recognition it deserves. The author has witnessed a *Fortune* 500 company set a low priority on a long-term cash forecast. Each division had a low-level employee perform the calculation. The figures that followed suggested a large cash deficit. This resulted in a large standby term loan. While the forecast of overall revenues and profits were fairly accurate, the rest of the forecast was off substantially. The company was in the embarrassing and costly situation of disclosing to Wall Street its payments for a standby term loan at a time it was running a huge excess cash flow.

FORECASTING

Long-term forecasting of cash flows should be at the heart of any business. It can be distinguished from short-term projections in being concerned with strategic decision making while short-term forecasting devotes itself to tactical decisions. The amount of time encompassed in a long-term forecast is dependent on the type of company. Some of the factors to be considered are:

The Business Cycle

The natural cutoff for a forecast can be after completion of one entire business turn, particularly if it takes a number of years to do. If, for example, company activities are related to the U.S. business cycle, a four- to five-year period may be used. For a real estate company which intends to build and hold its properties for 10 years, that period is more appropriate.

Technological Developments

The pace of change in the industry can define the time period. The key here is visibility in forecasting—if the industry is expected to shift from one form of doing business to another in about seven years, then that should be the period used.

Important Future Events

Forecasts may best be timed to dates key debt obligations fall due, contracts run out, or key employees are scheduled to retire.

The method or methods of forecasting cash flows are many. Some basic approaches which can be employed follow.

Seat-of-the-Pants Forecasting

This is the simplest method. Management picks a forecast based on its own judgment without employing any detailed analysis. In the absence of any further analysis, the figures can be extremely wide of the mark.

Simple Trend Analysis

Under this method recent past experience is used for projecting future values. The most simple method is to take last year's growth rate and forecast future growth by that same rate. A more involved procedure known as moving averages takes an average past growth rate that is representative and uses it as the projection. Exponential smoothing is like that of moving averages but assigns greater weights to more recent experiences. Trend analysis' advantage is simplicity and low cost. Its disadvantage is a lack of penetrating analysis in projecting future flows.

Regression Analysis

In this method relationships are presented between certain relevant factors. In a simple regression there are just two variables: an independent variable and one that the company is trying to forecast—the dependent variable. The relationship is developed through examination of past data and drawing a line or constructing a formula (by computer or advanced pocket calculator) which best represents the data. An example would be a company whose revenues have on average grown 1½ times that of Gross National Product. Using forecasts of the independent variable GNP, one can find out projected revenues for the dependent variable, company sales. Multiple regression uses a similar approach but employs a large number of dependent variables. The system works best where there are strong relationships which vary relatively little over time.

These three approaches lack the sophistication that is often needed in forecasting. Two systems which are more sophisticated than those mentioned will be described in some detail. One is largely qualitative (based on human judgment); the other is principally quantitative with little need for decision making by individuals.

QUALITATIVE APPROACH

The first is a more traditional judgmental approach which typically involves many of the staff. Top management sets the structure for forecasting future cash flows through establishing policy-level decisions. The planning staff sets the economic and company framework. The operating staff does the company forecast using management guidelines and planning department forecasts. This is done through a series of meetings with representatives from key departments—finance, production, and marketing. The forecast is then reviewed by top management. Each of the major steps in this process will be described separately.

Policy-Level Decisions

Each corporation has its own individual method of operating. Its style comes about through the interaction of the competitive environment and the vision of its management and board of directors. These decisions—made at the highest levels of management—are embodied in a set of corporate guidelines. These guidelines will set the parameters for those who work out the long-term cash forecast. Without these guidelines, varying and even erroneous assumptions can be made for different components of the forecast. A selection of the most important guidelines follow.

Capital Budgeting

The approach the corporation uses in making its internal investment decisions is relevant here. One common alternative is a required rate of return below which the company will not invest. If that is the method used, keep in mind that the rate will be influenced by future interest rates and the market valuation of the common shares. For example, a current required rate of return of 15 percent should be raised substantially if the company expects double-digit inflation, interest rates of over 15 percent and a sharp increase in the cost of raising equity capital. If the company makes investment decisions on the basis of the number of years to recover their investment, or just budgets a fixed sum of money to invest and chooses the most attractive investments within that budget, the need for future forecasting of financial factors isn't as great but still should be taken into account. Whatever the approach, it must be clearly delineated for future usage by the staff.

External Acquisitions

Guidelines on acquisitions policy are needed. Many companies have a goal of a certain percentage of total growth to come from acquisitions. If that is the case, management should indicate the minimum required rate of return so that an estimate can be made of cash flows needed. When calculating returns keep in mind that new additions commonly take a few more years than generally expected to reach targeted levels.

Dividend Policy

Dividends are a major part of corporate cash flow. In most corporations dividends are generally more than what is left over after all cash outlays are planned. The company should have a targeted payout policy or goal for annual growth in the dividend.

Financial Structure

The company's targeted financial structure should be detailed. Thus the current ratio the company is comfortable with should be stated. The relative proportion of long-term debt, leased assets, preferred stock, and common equity should be established even if it requires assumptions about the cost of raising funds for each. The extreme volatility of interest rates suggests that the company should take a conservative approach where possible by having a required minimum of equity at the high end of needs.

Corporate Philosophy

Too often a company operates on a day-to-day "tactical" basis. Top management should formulate the company's goals. Does it want to be the largest in its business? Does it want to have the highest return on equity or grow the fastest? What degree of risk is it willing to undertake to accomplish those goals? These goals must be internally consistent. For example, there is no need to formulate a goal of gaining market share when doing so will require start-up expenses and management is not willing to sacrifice earnings growth for several years. These strategic plans must be made clear to the staff so that they may clearly know the parameters they are working under.

Limitations

What are the realistic limitations on management actions? If the company is a division of a corporation, headquarters management may have established its own broad financial and operational guidelines. Have dissident groups made it more difficult to sacrifice near-term goals for longer-term objectives? In smaller corporations in particular,

565

goals .must be matched with resources. Nonrecognition of limitations can lead to great difficulties. The checkered history of corporations who have expanded into building cable systems and then have had to cut back is a good example of this phenomenon.

THE STRATEGIC PLAN— FORECASTING OVERALL

Before corporate managers can forecast their cash needs, they must understand the environment they are working in. Their requirements would be entirely different if the corporation were anticipating "stagflation"—extended slow growth in the nation's economy with high levels of inflation as opposed to rapid growth, large productivity gains, and a resultant low level of inflation. If management feels uncomfortable with one forecast, it can choose three—optimistic, pessimistic, and most likely. This will help to ensure the sensitivity of projected results to the economic environment. The forecast—as generated by the planning department in large corporations, or outside advisers, or frequently seat-of-the-pants forecasts for smaller ones— starts with general economic projections and works down to specific company plans.

Economic Forecast

The two segments of the forecast are economic growth and the level of inflation. The growth of the economy over the longer term has averaged around 3 percent a year, and inflation since 1970 has averaged about 7 percent. Do you believe these are representative of the future? In the absence of strong feelings about the future, it would be wise to stay fairly close to the past figures. There are a number of good natural economic forecasting services such as Data Resources and Wharton Econometrics that can give you further guidance.

Financial Forecast

The financial forecast is important since most companies will be using debt of some kind, and those that are growing rapidly may wish to raise equity capital as well. The financial forecast tends to follow from the economic forecast, although Federal Reserve policy has a great deal of influence as well. The company should project the level of interest rates prevailing over the cycle. Are the current levels reasonable, or are you expecting higher interest rates due to a high level of inflation and large company deficits? Alternatively, if you are anticipating that the country's economy will grow steadily with low inflation, you should project a decline in interest rates. One method to approximate future long-term interest rates would be to add a premium to the inflation rate for return required to compensate investors for loaning money. A 3.5 percent premium is frequently used. Thus, if a long-term inflation rate of 7 percent were contemplated, U.S. government bonds would be expected to yield 10.5 percent. A further premium would be needed for company risk of default which, depending on individual company factors, could amount to 1 to 6 percent or more. A past comparison of yields on long-term treasuries to your company or similar companies to your own would provide further information on the premium question.

Your forecast of stock market prices and price-to-earnings multiples should relate both to economic growth and interest rates. Where you have no strong feeling you may want to use current price-to-earnings (P/E) multiples and have stock market prices move at your assumed level of growth in the economy. Last, relate your company's price-to-earnings multiple for a public company or the cost of equity capital for public and private companies to the stock market as a whole. The average large public company which has an estimated sustainable return on equity of 15 percent may be used as a guide. Those companies with returns well above this level that have the same risk characteristics would derive a proportionately higher valuation. For example, a company with a sustainable return on equity of 18 to 20 percent above the market would deserve a P/E multiple of 20 percent above the market. If the market were to have a 10 P/E, it would deserve a 12. A similar approach could be used to determine premiums for nonpublic companies.

Industry Forecast

The industry forecast has an equally great impact on your company's prospects as the overall economic forecast. The company should incorporate how its industry (or industries) has grown relative to the economy as a whole and whether it expects this relationship to continue in the future. The level of inflation in the industry should be compared with that for the economy as a whole. Many technology-based industries will have below-average inflation rates. Other labor-intensive, service-based industries may not be able to enjoy productivity gains and have greater than average inflation rates. A comparison of historical relative inflation rates and competitive pressures can be helpful in making future projections.

Company Forecast

Given the level of industry growth, it is possible to forecast the company's growth in revenues. Wherever feasible, the company should target its anticipated future market share. It is important that this figure be realistic, and all key employees should be involved in establishing it. The combination of industry growth and targeted market share will result in internal revenue growth for the company. If, for any reason, pricing policy for the company is to be different than for its industry, it should be incorporated in the revenue growth figure. For example, a company with $5 million in sales has a 5 percent share of a $100 million industry. It expects to have a 10.0 percent share of the industry that in five years will amount to $150 million. Its revenues will grow from $5 million to $15 million. To this growth figure must be added expansion activities, if any. These would include new internal start-up operations and external acquisitions.

PROJECTING EARNINGS

If cash flow is the lifeblood of the company, the most important source of cash is the ongoing earnings of the business. The foregoing strategic plan provides the backdrop. The pro forma income statement integrates this strategic plan into a forecast of sales and cost of sales so as to develop earnings.

Sales

The revenues for the company can be taken directly from the aforementioned strategic plan. Particular emphasis should be placed on the competitive environment that is anticipated. A decision must be made as to whether prices are expected to keep pace with cost increases or whether competition is so intense that margins will erode. Factors such as planned industry capacity additions and competition from outside the industry can be helpful in anticipating this environment.

Cost of Sales

The leading components of cost of sales should be established. Likely increases in labor costs must be arrived at. If labor is unionized and union power has declined in this industry recently, projections should incorporate this factor. Productivity gains through substituting machines for labor should also be calculated. Raw material costs should be calculated with the rate of increase in price stated in relation to the assumed inflation rate for the economy. Outlays for operating overhead should be estimated on the basis of sales and plant expenditures.

Selling, General, and Administrative Expenses

The expenses of doing business should be related to their component factors if possible or the entire S G & A expressed as a percentage of sales. Where expectations are for above-average growth in revenues it may be appropriate to schedule S G & A as a declining percentage of sales.

Depreciation

Depreciation is a noncash charge and should be segregated on the income statement. It is necessary, however, to make an accurate forecast of depreciation charges since it is a deductible expense in calculating actual tax expenditures. Depreciation calculations should be made in conjunction with forecasts of actual capital outlays which are described later.

Interest and Other

Interest costs are related to the level of debt outstanding and the assumed level of rates given in the strategic plan. When calculating other expenses keep in mind that if unforeseen extraordinary costs tend to recur, they should be reserved for in this category.

Taxes

The tax rate is, of course, related to pretax income and should also reflect the level of capital outlays which will provide investment tax credits. Remember that taxes that are not payable currently but are deferred should be separately indicated since they are a noncash charge.

Net Income

As income figures are developed, they should be compared with sales. Note whether profits are projected to grow more rapidly than sales. Projections which indicate significant changes in net margins should be reviewed carefully for reasonableness. Frequently they suggest a flaw in the calculations or a too optimistic forecast.

Forecasted Income Statement

	198_	198_	198_	198_	198_	Cumulative
Sales	—	—	—	—	—	—
Cost of sales						
Labor						
Material						
Overhead						
Total	—	—	—	—	—	—
Selling, general, and adminis- trative expenses						
Depreciation						
Interest expense and other	—	—	—	—	—	—
Total expenses	—	—	—	—	—	—
Pretax income						
Taxes	—	—	—	—	—	—
Net income	—	—	—	—	—	—

THE CURRENT POSITION

The current position consists of all assets and liabilities that are due within a year. The cash available must be sufficient to fund near-term operating needs of the business. The targeted ratio of current assets to current liabilities is an important ingredient in determining the amount of cash that will be maintained for current needs. Generally, a critical factor in this calculation is the level of accounts receivable maintained. If the targeted ratio of current assets to current liabilities is 2:1, and your projections indicate a ratio closer to 1.5:1, additional cash funds will have to be raised to bring the ratio up to desired levels. It is common to break out all major components of the current position and express them as year-to-year changes in positions. Generally, a critical factor in this calculation is the level of accounts receivable maintained. Accounts receivable is most directly related to sales. Therefore, the company's projection of sales should be utilized and compared to credit terms and experience with the "aging" of amounts past due. More and more companies are finding out that their customers are delaying payments on their purchases even though they are in excellent financial condition. In effect, they are using their suppliers as a source

570

of no-cost loans as opposed to high interest rate debt from the bank. If there are any trends in aging or receivables in the company, they should be extended out into the future.

Accounts payable is thought of in the same light as accounts receivable. Accounts payable is also related most directly to sales, with established industry practices and company policy on payment terms as the key determinants. Be aware that if you are anticipating relatively high interest rates in the future, your suppliers could decide to tighten their credit terms.

The other key factor is the level of inventory held. Again, here the level will be most directly related to sales. However, decisions on inventory policy—minimum levels, proposed changes in asset mix—should be taken into account. Keep in mind that actual cash outlays for inventory should be employed since the method of accounting for inventory—LIFO, FIFO, or others—can distort the projection.

Other current items, if significant, such as prepaid and accrued expenses, can be estimated individually or projected as a whole.

STATEMENT OF FORECASTED CASH FLOWS

The income statement provides a statement of change in earnings over a period of time. The balance sheet gives a listing of assets less liabilities as of various points in time. The statement of forecasted cash flows integrates the relevant factors in the income statement and balance sheet that affect cash into one all-inclusive statement. This statement should not be confused with a source and application of funds. The cash flow statement focuses on cash and is not subject to accounting estimates and other items which can distort the status of the company. It is thus the single most important statement in anticipating future needs.

Net income comes from the projected income statement as non-cash charges such as depreciation and deferred taxes. The statement includes the cash needed for current positions as previously described. Capital outlays must be forecasted. These will depend on projected sales, the physical state of current plants, and projected obsolescence factors. Any diversification activities either internally generated or through acquisition must be taken into account. The figures should incorporate an assumed inflation factor for the type of plant being built.

Dividends are related to net income and the company's policy-level decision on payout practice. Debt repayments are a simple function of the amount of debt due and payable by year. By starting with internal sources and uses of cash, the statement clearly separates the ongoing source and uses of cash from operation from external financial

Statement of Forecasted Cash Flows

	198_	198_	198_	198_	198_	Cumulative
Sources						
Net income						
Noncash items						
Depreciation						
Deferrals						
Other net						
Total cash provided	___	___	___	___	___	___
Uses						
Working capital						
Accounts receivable						
Inventory						
Other current assets						
Accounts payable						
Other current liabilities						
Capital expenditures						
Dividends						
Other net						
Total cash used	___	___	___	___	___	___
Internal cash flow	___	___	___	___	___	___
Financing						
Additions to debt						
Repayments of debt						
Additions to common equity						
Other net						
Total cash flow	___	___	___	___	___	___
Cash—Beginning of period						
Cash—End of period	___	___	___	___	___	___
Total cash flow	___	___	___	___	___	___

factors. The cash flow figure developed is a statement of change in cash for the period. This change is used to obtain the forecasted cash figures for the period. Any large increase or decrease in cash can suggest changes in key factors such as capital outlays, financing policy, or cash dividends. Sometimes the changes in policy can be dramatic. One major retail corporation had a relatively conservative historical policy of purchasing its real estate for cash and using relatively little debt to finance it. Others in its industry were less conservative, and many leased their outlets. Its net margins suffered by comparison. However, the company's forecasted statement of cash flow indicated a strong cash flow as less attractive sites with strong asset values were liquidated, an added plus in the eyes of stockholders as reported earnings were scheduled to rise rapidly as many sites became fully depreciated. The net result of this forecast was an intentionally more aggressive expansion policy.

The net of all these figures will give you the corporate cash flow. It should be done individually by year and cumulatively over a 5- to 10-year period. For those companies that are not capital-intensive or that have a high return on equity or low payout policy, the figure may indicate a positive internal cash flow. However, for many companies (either because of choice or necessity) the figures will indicate the need for financing in company's plans. The choice for financing—debt, equity, or leasing—will be a function of targeted balance sheet ratios as well as the projected relative cost of debt and equity. Since planning is for long-term needs, management may want to delay financing plans for favorable times in market cycles.

BOX JENKINS MODEL

The second approach is a quantitative technique. The heart of the system is a Box Jenkins model. This is a particularly sophisticated approach to analyzing past data to get future forecasts. It does not assume any particular pattern in the past data. Through a series of trial-and-error calculations, it comes up with the most attractive model of the ones surveyed. It provides the proper structure for judging good forecast models, estimates the parameters, and then checks to see if the model can be improved.

Steps in the Box Jenkins approach are as follows:

1. Decide on class of models to be introduced.
2. Identify specific model to be tested.
3. Identify most attractive model.
4. Implement model as forecasting technique.

573

Class of Model

The decision on which class of model to use depends on the characteristics of what the company is trying to forecast. If there are key factors that can be identified in comprising sales, then a regression model is best. If there are no closely identified factors but there is a clear trend in the data, moving average models are best. Many times both are present; in that situation a third class of general model combining the two is called the autoregressive moving average model. For example, in forecasting the energy usage one should consider both the trend in energy usage which is being influenced by conservation and specific factors such as growth in the economy that help or hinder energy consumption.

Specific Model

Each model selected is tested against the past data. As mentioned, the Box Jenkins approach has no preconceived notions. The goal is to find the model that explains the data the best—that is, the one that has the fewest differences between models forecasted and actual data. The Box Jenkins computer program will calculate values for your model. The model with the best fit—which has the lower error rate—is selected. If two "best" models fit the data the same way, the simplest one should be chosen.

Implementation

The model is then ready for forecasting. It should be set up by using certain confidence intervals based on past fit of the data. For example, if projecting broadcasting revenues, the forecast might indicate an annual growth rate of +7 percent plus or minus 2 percent. Keep in mind that the further into the future the forecast is made, the wider the confidence interval will become.

Probably the most crucial variable to be forecasted would be sales. Most of the other income statement and balance sheet items tend to be a function of sales. The Box Jenkins approach could be used to develop submodels. Alternatively, if the costs of developing the submodels were too great, regression models could be used for such factors as cost of sales, accounts receivable, etc. The approach taken would be similar to that described under the qualitative method except for the use of the computer for developing the relationships. As a result a full forecast of projected future cash flows can be made based on past relationships and computer modeling.

574

EVALUATION OF QUANTITATIVE VERSUS QUALITATIVE APPROACH

There are advantages and disadvantages to each approach. Factors to be considered are:

The accuracy of the model. Models vary in how well they represent what happens in the past. If the computer model developed by Box Jenkins fits the past data well, it is a strong point for using it.

Use of past as predictor. The quantitative models assume that the past is a good indicator of the future. They have most difficulty with changes such as turning points in trends. Management belief that severe changes are coming in the industry strengthens the case for a more judgmental qualitative approach.

Staff involvement. Forecasts can take up a great deal of time. If management feels that involving key divisions will detract from company day-to-day efforts, then the quantitative case is strengthened.

Objectivity. There is no question that the Box Jenkins "value-free" approach is more objective. If staff biases have been a problem in the past, then a quantitative approach may be best.

Flexibility. Once set up, a computerized model can be altered much more easily than a consensus forecast. If forecasts are expected to be changed fairly frequently, the quantitative approach has an advantage. The approach which should be taken depends on circumstances. Where feasible, use of both qualitative and quantitative approaches is recommended. One can then serve as a check on the reasonableness of the other. If management chooses, the final forecast could be an average of the two approaches.

SENSITIVITY ANALYSIS

Sensitivity analysis is a method for calculating how changes in assumptions on certain factors alters the forecast. It helps to determine which factors are most important in achieving the forecast of future cash flows. For example, for many companies it is important to know what effect a change in the long-term forecast of U.S. economic growth from 4 percent on average to 2 percent would have on forecasted cash flows. For some companies that are highly leveraged, the difference could be 50 percent or more. The goal should be to isolate those factors that

575

have the greatest impact on cash flow. Footnotes to the forecast should indicate how a given change in projections of these factors would effect cash flows. Computer modeling is ideally suited for sensitivity analysis. It allows updating and "what if" forecasting in a relatively simple fashion.

TOP EXECUTIVE REVIEW

Top management started the process by establishing the guidelines. It is incumbent upon them to review the anticipated results. Management should ask what could go wrong. If a quantitative forecasting model is used as well, the two forecasts should be compared carefully and the different results either reconciled or at least the reasons for the differences understood. It is a good idea to review the impact of changes in key factors such as the growth rate in sales on overall results. Where there are large significant uncertainties which result in substantive fluctuations in cash flow, management may request three forecasts—most likely, optimistic, and pessimistic. Seven key things to watch for are:

1. Be careful of qualitative cash flow forecasts based on economic, interest rates, or inflation forecasts that are widely different from the past. Unless your company has a long record of being good forecasters, a good idea is to adjust figures to give significant weight to actual past experience over extended periods of time.

2. Make sure that results make sense to management as a whole. Each segment of the plan may be logically conceived, but if the aggregate results seem unrealistic, the plan should be examined again and more information asked for. If it still doesn't seem reasonable, it should be returned to the staff for reevaluation.

3. Be wary of an overly optimistic staff. Many executives feel they can impress their supervisors by projecting very favorable figures into the future. For example, the marketing staff may be reluctant to forecast a decline in share of market even though one is called for. In this situation the plan should be turned back for revisions or perhaps the pessimistic forecast employed as the most likely.

4. Don't bet the ranch. Have a fallback position should things not turn out the way things are forecasted to. That may include a standby line of credit or expansion policy that is handled in stages and dependent on meeting targeted results.

5. Don't be too influenced by short-term results. It is human nature to extrapolate recent results into the future. Doing so can frequently distort the results anticipated. If a quantitative forecast is being used, make sure the time period selected is representative.

6. Key assumptions should be stated clearly. Those assumptions that have great impact on results should be delineated along with their impact for a given change in forecast. These should be described fully in footnotes to the statement.

7. Provide for periodic review and update. Any forecast, no matter how soundly conceived, grows stale with age. If the forecast is to continue to have relevance, it must be updated to reflect inevitable changes in circumstances. As soon as management feels the forecast cannot be relied on for company needs, it is time to revise it.

The forecast of long-term cash flows compels a company to think beyond the narrow framework of day-to-day transactions. As such, it can provide a guide to correct actions in our rapidly changing economic environment. A serious effort that employs the techniques described herein can place the company at a distinct advantage over its competition.

25

Sources of Funds for Capital Projects: How to Choose the Best Methods of Financing

John F. Childs

Kidder, Peabody & Co. Inc.

INTRODUCTION

*T*he purpose of financial management is to establish policies and take actions so that the company can be supplied with whatever capital is needed for new plant and equipment at the lowest possible cost in order to assist the company in meeting customers' needs and to provide investors at least a fair return.

THE RELATIONSHIP BETWEEN FINANCING AND CAPITAL DECISION MAKING

A decision with regard to a particular project will be affected by the company's ability to finance the project, the effect of the financing on income from the project, and the effect on earnings per share.

However, it is a fatal mistake to have the method of financing play a part in the basic decision as to whether the project should be accepted in the first place. Whether the project should be accepted depends on the return on investment compared with the risk of the project, and risk has to be assessed independently of how the financing is done; otherwise, the basic decision would depend on whether the project was financed with debt, or common, or some other type of security.

Thus, the decision as to whether to do a project may be affected by the required financing, but the primary consideration is the return expected from the project compared with the project profitability goal. This involves the subject of cost of capital and profit goals for project profitability analysis which is outside the scope of this chapter. This chapter will cover how to get the capital.

THE THREE KEY RATIOS IN FINANCIAL PLANNING

In order to make financial decisions to carry out the purpose of financial management, it is essential to establish goals for certain key ratios as a basis of financial planning.

There are three key financial planning ratios. These ratios affect the stockholders' investment through quality, return, and division of return.

Benefit to stockholders	Three key ratios
I. Quality of investment	Long-term debt to total long-term capital. This is debt ratio or leverage. For a bank, the ratio is common equity to assets.
II. Return on investment	Return on beginning common equity.
III. Division of return between cash paid out and reinvested	Dividend payout ratio.

These three ratios are the basis for financial planning because, if they are correct, they:

1. Ensure that the stockholders will be treated fairly.
2. Ensure that all other financial ratios will be correct.
3. Provide the company reasonable access to capital through the securities market at the lowest cost over the long run.

4. Determine the company's ability to grow without the sale of stock, because the growth in common equity depends on the return the company earns and the amount of earnings retained.

Furthermore, return on investment is the basis for new product pricing.

In addition to these ratios for financial planning, a five-year forecast of outside capital requirements is essential. These requirements will affect the financial plan that will have to be developed to keep within the guidelines for the three key ratios.

In this chapter we will only be concerned with the first of the three key ratios, that is, long-term debt to total long-term capital.

LONG-TERM DEBT TO TOTAL LONG-TERM CAPITAL

Four principal sources of capital will show up in a company's statement of sources and uses of funds. One source is developed from revenues in the income statement. It is *cash flow* from noncash expense items such as depreciation and from earnings retained after dividends. The three other sources are developed in the balance sheet from:

1. Liquidation or *sale of assets.*
2. *Short-term borrowings.*
3. *Sale of long-term securities,* such as bonds and stock.

Cash flow from the income statement is limited and varies with earnings; sale of assets is generally not a ready source of capital; short-term borrowings used for capital purposes have to be paid back.

These three sources of capital have to be taken into account in financial planning, but the open door that a company should be able to count on for obtaining capital is the sale of long-term securities. If a company has the ability to issue long-term securities, it will be able to meet maturing obligations and pursue expansion projects as they may arise.

There are two basic types of long-term securities: debt and equity. Long-term debt includes all leases capitalized (including most operating leases) and also bank loans rolled over and not paid off seasonally.

Debt results in leverage; and, in deciding how to finance, a decision first has to be made as to how much leverage is appropriate for a particular company. This decision determines whether financing should be in the form of debt or equity. In making this decision, a company should wish to achieve the following goals:

1. Always be able to raise capital.
2. Raise capital without straining its credit.
3. Raise capital on the cheapest overall basis, that is, the cheapest cost for total long-term capital, debt, and equity combined.
4. Never be placed in a position of having to cut dividends, or being restricted in dividend policy because of unsound financial policy with too much leverage.
5. Have good-quality not "yo-yo" stock.

These goals would seem to be as sacred to a company as motherhood. If this is so, then the question has to be answered as to how a company will be able to achieve them.

Quality of securities determines whether a company is able to sell securities and the rate it will have to pay. Thus, quality is the basis which determines whether a company will be able to achieve these goals. In finance quality is designated by bond ratings. Thus, a company must first decide what bond ratings it wishes to achieve. There are five principal bond ratings to consider: AAA, AA, A, BBB, and BB.

BBB and BB can be eliminated because they include speculative elements, and there are times when such quality would prevent a company from achieving the above five goals.

AAA is only achievable by a few very large, well-situated companies. Therefore, for most companies we are left to choose between AA and A. An AA can only be achieved by a large company. For such a company an AA has real advantages over the long run. The five goals can be achieved.

For the medium-sized and smaller companies, A is as good as can be achieved. Companies with common equity less than $100 million may not be able to achieve an A because of size. Such companies should establish a debt ratio which would result in an A rating if they were larger.

Long-term capital is easily changed in only one direction. The debt ratio can be easily increased but corrected only with difficulty, even under favorable conditions. The effect of financial policy should be tested in the short run, but consideration of future periods is more important when making a final decision. After five years the outlook for a company cannot be foreseen. More capital may be needed, and debt obligations may mature in this period. Equity securities are outstanding indefinitely. A company may run into unforeseen problems in the future, and its long-term capital should have sufficient quality to withstand unforeseeable adversities. This requires financial strength and also financial flexibility, and this consists of financial insurance and financial reserves.

Financial insurance refers to a company's ability to have its bond rating lowered and maintain good-quality credit. A company whose bonds are rated AA clearly has financial insurance.

There are three financial reserves:

1. Short-term borrowing reserve.
2. Long-term borrowing reserve, or the ability to increase debt within a limited range without having the bond rating lowered.
3. Incentive securities such as convertibles and senior securities with warrants.

The list of goals for long-term capital includes the ability to raise capital on the cheapest overall basis. Basically, there are two risks in the securities of a company: the risk of the business itself and a financial risk which is added by having too much leverage or debt so that the other goals cannot be achieved. Adding debt up to the point that a financial risk is not added decreases the overall cost of capital because cheap debt is substituted for equity. Thus, since debt reduces the overall cost of capital when used properly, it should be used to the extent possible without violating the five goals and adding a financial risk.

How much debt a company can have and achieve a good quality depends on all the factors which affect risk: the type of business, the earnings record, the cash flow, the makeup of a company's customers and expenses, etc. An industrial company, for example, would generally have a much lower debt ratio than an electric utility, and an electric utility would generally have a much lower debt ratio than a finance company. And in the industrial field there is wide variation among companies, with a steel company having a lower debt ratio than a consumer products company.

Thus, a company first has to make a thorough analysis and decide on the debt ratio it should achieve in order to assure the appropriate quality. This is really the major decision that a company has to make regarding financial policy because, almost universally, top managements do not like to sell equity because of the immediate dilution of earnings per share. If management has clearly set a debt ratio goal, it will provide the necessary discipline to sell equity when it should do so. Otherwise, it will take the easy way out and sell debt, which ultimately may be adverse for the company in the future and may even result in disaster.

Summary

In summary, debt used properly is good. Debt should be used up to the point that financial flexibility will be preserved so the five goals can be achieved, and no significant financial risk will be added. A company should determine an average and maximum debt ratio policy as a basis for financial planning so that its senior debt will be rated no lower than A and, preferably, AA if circumstances permit. For a limited number of companies, AAA may be the most appropriate goal. A smaller company which is not rated should still attempt to maintain ratios that will give it the equivalent of an A-quality debt if it were larger in size. Thus, having made this decision, consideration next can be given to the specific type of security to sell.

Various Types of Securities

Securities can be classified into two broad groups: debt securities and senior securities. Senior securities include debt securities and all types of equity ahead of the common such as senior equities.

As discussed above, debt securities should be limited so as to meet a company's goal for the key ratio, long-term debt to total long-term capital.

Senior securities should be limited so as not to adversely affect the quality of the common equity with too much leverage ahead of the common. In certain situations it is appropriate to have an equity security such as a preferred stock as part of long-term capital, providing the company has a proper debt ratio and the amount of the senior equity security does not push the common too far out on the limb.

For example, in the electric utility field it is generally accepted that preferred representing 13 percent of total long-term capital is appropriate. Such a security has a lower cost of capital than common and does act as protection for the debt; but, as we have said, it does come ahead of common.

Within these broad classifications of securities, there is a great variety. For example, a few of the types of securities within these classifications are as follows:

583

I. Debt securities
  A. Leases
  B. Mortgages
  C. Mortgage bonds
  D. Unsecured debenture bonds
  E. Unsecured long-term notes
  F. Convertible bonds
  G. Bonds with warrants attached, etc.
  H. Debt with fixed rates
  I. Debt with variable rates

II. Senior equity securities
  A. Preferred stock
  B. Preference stock
  C. Convertible preferred stock
  D. Preferred stock with warrants

III. Common stock

The things that distinguish one security from another are the terms which include maturity, repayment schedule or sinking fund, interest payments—fixed or variable, call feature, and restrictive provisions regarding the issuance of additional debt, the payment of dividends, borrowings by subsidiaries, etc.

Choosing the Right Security

Given below are some of the factors to consider in evaluating a particular security and some examples to illustrate the points.

1. *What is the true nature of the security?* This calls for a thorough analysis and understanding of the nature of the security and its various terms. For example, a debenture plus a warrant supposedly reduces the interest cost and produces a high price for the stock at the exercise price. Nonsense! Analyze the two securities separately, and, as a matter of fact, they will separate when they are sold. The debenture is actually sold at a discount, and the so-called interest savings is the price the company gets for the warrants, giving the holder a call on the common stock at a fixed price far into the future. Ask yourself if you would sell these two securities separately. Probably not, unless you had to as a matter of necessity.

2. *Will it fit the company's requirements to meet the goal for the ratio of debt to total long-term capital?* For example, a convertible may ultimately turn into common; but, if a company needs common, a convertible postpones the time when it will be common, and it will not become common unless the stock goes up—which is always uncertain. Furthermore, a convertible is debt until it converts; and, if the company runs into difficulty, the debt will be a burden. Convertibles do serve a very useful purpose under some circumstances, but they are often badly misused.

3. *How will the terms affect the company's future operations and ability to raise capital?* For example, a mortgage on a building may be available at times at a reasonable rate and may have limited restrictive provisions. However, if the company wishes to sell unsecured debt in the future, the mortgage will be in a senior position to the unsecured debt and to some extent may increase the cost of the unsecured debt.

4. *To what extent does the security provide flexibility so that it can be eliminated if it becomes desirable to do so in the future?* For example, an original issue discount bond and a zero coupon bond generally have no call feature, and the company is locked in until maturity.

5. *To what extent does it depend on forecasting interest rates?* For example, a bond sold with a warrant attached to buy additional bonds in the future is a play on future interest rates, and experienced financial experts will not do financing on that basis because they know that forecasting interest rates cannot be done. The correct rule is finance when the money is needed.

6. *Does it fit sound principles of financing future projects?* For example, an original issue discount bond or a zero coupon bond results in doing financing at today's rates for projects in the future; this is unsound.

7. *What is the relative cost compared with another type of security?* For example, a lease is a form of debt financing and should be compared with a debt financed with exactly similar terms, that is, with the same maturity and repayment schedule of the lease. Also included in the cost analysis should be the loss of residual value with a lease.

8. *Is the security dependent on a tax savings, and what are the chances of a change in the tax law?*

9. *Will it make it more difficult for investors to analyze the company's securities?*

Common Stock

Managements have a strong prejudice against issuing common stock because of the immediate dilution; thus, it may be appropriate to comment on the advantages and disadvantages of raising capital through the sale of common stock if the debt ratio suggests that more common is needed or will be needed within the period of capital planning. The pros and cons of common stock financing are outlined below.

Advantages

1. It builds up the company's ability to sell more debt in the future.
2. It improves the quality of the debt and the equity.
3. Because it reduces leverage, the common dividend is more secure.
4. If in the future there is an adverse stock market, or the company runs into difficulty, it might not be able to sell common stock. Because it is essential to have adequate equity, the idea of a "bird in the hand" is important.
5. It increases the amount of stock in the hands of the public; and, for a closely held company, it may improve the market for the stock.

Disadvantages

1. Earnings per share are not as great after the sale of common stock as compared with the sale of debt. However, there is no ultimate dilution in earnings per share if the same return is earned on the new common as on the old. Furthermore, the earnings per share with less leverage will be higher-quality earnings.
2. If earnings per share increase and market improves, a higher price might be obtained in the future. However, as the book value grows through retained earnings, there would be no benefit to stockholders unless the stock is sold at a higher-percentage premium (or, under certain circumstances, at a lower discount) in relation to book value. Therefore, the test as to the current market price has to be made on the basis of the relationship of the current market price to the current book value compared with the future relationship of estimated market price to estimated future book value.

If a company decides to issue common stock, then a decision has to be made as to the size of the issue.

A rule of thumb for the size of a common offering is as follows:

Comment	Ratio of number of new shares to already outstanding shares	Dilution of earnings per share without any return from new investment
Light offering	1 for 20	4.8%
Average offering	1 for 10	9.1
Heavy offering	1 for 5	16.7

To determine the size of the offering, many factors have to be considered, including:

1. The amount of common to keep the long-term debt to total long-term capital ratio on track to meet the goal ratio in view of the company's existing financial ratios and future capital requirements.
2. The effect of the new offering on dilution of forecast earnings per share.
3. What the market will take. Market conditions and the demand for the particular stock will affect the amount that can be sold.
4. The size of an issue to make it worthwhile to finance. There may be a minimum amount of common that the company should sell to make it worthwhile to do the financing in view of the costs involved.

Short-Term Debt Used for Long-Term Purposes

Another source of long-term capital is short-term debt, such as bank loans and commercial paper, used for long-term purposes. As we have said, such short-term debt used for long-term purposes should be included with long-term capital, and in general it should be used sparingly. When it is used, plans should be developed for repayment. Of course, the credit standing of a company will affect the extent to which short-term debt should be used. For example, an AAA company has such financial strength that it could not be embarrassed by a large amount of short-term debt coming due under adverse conditions, whereas excessive short-term debt might become embarrassing to a financially weak company.

587

CONLUSION

The big decision in deciding how to raise capital is making a firm decision on how much long-term debt is proper for the particular company in view of all the factors which affect the risk of the business. Then, specific steps should be taken which will assure that this goal will be met. This may mean considerable intestinal fortitude to sell common stock under adverse conditions. And, in order to avoid the use of common, too much reliance should not be made on senior equities.

The choice of various securities within the debt security group is a much less important decision. An error in the big decision may mean disaster for a company, whereas an error in the details of choosing a security may not even be noticed.

26

Leasing: How to Evaluate the Costs and Benefits

Nathan Snyder

CBS Inc.

LEASING

Background

*T*he concept of leasing—that is, the distinction between ownership and use of property—is not new. In many societies the ownership of land was restricted to certain social classes. The use of that land, however, was granted to those of lesser stature in return for payment—often in the form of a portion of the crop generated by the land. Thus the land was *leased* by those of wealth and stature to those of inferior economic standing. As to personal property, however, the distinction between ownership and use is a more recent development.

In the middle of the 19th century there evolved the concept of the equipment trust lease. When the railroads of the United States were rapidly spanning the continental United States, the demand for rolling stock was greater than the capital resources that the railroad companies could satisfy. Another source of capital was needed. The confluence of this surging demand for equipment and a supply of capital from a variety of sources led to the formation of trusts that retained the ownership of the rolling stock but entered into contractual agreements with railroads for the use of that property in exchange for the payment of fees or rentals.

The importance of leasing as a method of financing, however, did not flourish until after World War II when the economic growth of the United States intensified. New and creative forms of financing were welcomed as the conservation of working capital was a paramount motivation to allow the development of industry to satisfy the needs of a society that had made wartime sacrifices and was now anxious to satisfy a varied menu of industrial needs.

Leasing, as a method of financing, has been subject to governmental manipulation from time to time through tax legislation. As the depreciation and investment tax credit regulations have been used to stimulate or discourage investment, the lessor—as the *owner* of property—has had to react and adjust investment planning.

Although the opportunity to contract for the use of property without the need to own that property may be an appealing concept, there are economic trade-offs that accompany this option. This chapter will attempt to highlight some of the unique implications to the lessor and lessee as one enters the ever-expanding and dynamic galaxy of leasing.

Types of Leasing

Tax-oriented lease. In many instances leasing becomes an attractive method of financing when the lessee is not in a position to maximize the tax benefits of ownership of the property, while the lessor, often the subsidiary of a bank or industrial company with ample taxable income, is providing "tax shelter" to its parent. In the tax-oriented lease, the lessor generally passes on to the lessee, in the form of reduced rentals, a portion of the economic benefit of the depreciation and investment tax credit associated with the leased equipment. In such a true tax lease the lessor avails himself of depreciation deductions, and the lessee claims the full lease payment as an expense. The investment tax credit may be a negotiated issue to be claimed by the lessor or lessee, but if the lessee is not in a tax-paying position, he will usually pass this benefit on to the lessor in exchange for more favorable terms under the lease. At the end of the lease term, the lessor continues to be the owner of the equipment, unless the lessee has negotiated a purchase option under the lease and has elected to exercise that option.

The lessee who enters into a true tax lease is motivated into that form of transaction because he is seeking the economic benefit that is available by exchanging the tax benefits of accelerated depreciation and investment tax credit for lease rentals that are less costly than the cost of financing the acquisition of the property through a loan. This assumes that the lessee has insufficient tax liability to avail himself of the benefits associated with ownership of property. Obviously the lessee must evaluate any such lease on a discounted cash flow basis and must factor in his cost of capital as well as the cost of acquiring the property at the end of the lease, assuming continued useful life of the property.

Non-tax-oriented lease (conditional sales contract). Although this form of transaction may be referred to as a lease, in fact the "lessee" has all of the attributes of ownership while the "lessor" in fact is reserving to himself a security interest in the property. The characteristics of this type of transaction are that the lessor supplies the full purchase price of the property; the lessee pays to the "lessor" that full price plus an interest rate that relates to the creditworthiness of the lessee for a secured loan, over a lease term that may have little to do with the useful life of the property; and, at the end of the term, the lessee will be entitled to ownership upon the exercise of a bargain purchase option. This purchase option will have no relationship to the fair market value of the property at the time of exercise of the option. Under this type of lease, the lessee is the true owner of the property and for tax purposes he claims the depreciation and investment tax credit and deducts only the interest portion of the rental payments. The lessor treats the transaction as a loan.

The leveraged lease. A leveraged lease is a form of true tax lease that is generally associated with personal property that is substantial in cost. This type of lease involves at least three parties: the lessee, the lessor, and a long-term lender. The leveraged lease attempts to associate the nonrisk portion of the lease with the long-term lender who will seek a lender's return for a position of modest risk. The lender's risk is a blend of the lessee's creditworthiness and the expected realizable value of the equipment in the event foreclosure occurs. The lessor's risk in this type of lease is generally related to the value of the tax benefits, the potential residual value of the property, and the risk of loss of all or a portion of those tax benefits in the event of a default by the lessee and the repossession and sale of the equipment.

In the nonleveraged lease the lessor, as owner, invests the full purchase price to acquire the equipment. In the leveraged lease the lessor will hold title to the equipment and be entitled to the tax benefits of ownership for an investment equal to only 20 percent of the cost of the equipment. The balance of the cost is supplied by a long-term lender, without recourse to the lessor, in exchange for a first lien on the equipment and an assignment of the lease and the rental payments thereunder. The cost of the nonrecourse loan is a delicate blend of the creditworthiness of the lessee and the salability of the property by the lender at any time during the period of the loan at a price that is no less than the outstanding loan balance. With the leveraged lease the lessor derives full ownership tax benefits through only a fraction of the cost of the equipment, but his risk position is significantly magnified. In the event of a default by the lessee, the lessor has no control over the disposition of the equipment. The lender may elect to seek a quick sale which will result in significant loss exposure to the lessor. In such a circumstance the lessor may be inclined to pay off the lender if he feels that he can improve his economic position by controlling the asset.

Lease versus Purchase Decision

The decision whether to buy or lease equipment is related to a variety of factors, each of which may be weighted differently by different potential lessees. Among the factors that would normally be weighed by the lessee are:

Loan indentures. To the extent that most loan indentures limit the amount of additional debt a borrower may incur during the term of the loan, the indenture may be silent regarding lease transactions, or it may treat lease transactions as a separate category, permitting the borrower to finance a certain level of equipment needs through this device. Of course, to the extent that the lease transaction meets the criteria of a capital lease under current accounting standards, then such a lease may be deemed to be a loan for indenture purposes.

Rental deductions. To the extent that the lessee is not able to immediately use the tax benefits of tax depreciation and investment tax credit, the rental payments over the term of the lease become the tax expense. Thus by transferring the tax benefits of ownership to the lessor, the lessee can spread out the tax benefits over a longer period which may more properly reflect his own tax-paying liability. Also as a lessee with a fixed lease term, the lessee will avoid the issue of establishing the appropriate depreciable life of the asset for tax purposes. That becomes the lessor's problem.

Equipment cost fully financed. Although many lessors may call for prepayment of one or more lease rental payments to provide themselves with some cushion, most lease transactions call for the lessor to provide 100 percent of the cost of the equipment. The leasing company will obviously be borrowing all or a significant portion of the funds, generally at an interest cost lower than that which the lessee would pay to borrow those funds. To a significant extent the lessor is dependent on his ability to re-lease or sell the equipment in the event of a default by the lessee. Readily marketable, high-residual equipment will generally command more flexible lease terms than will special-purpose, highly customized, potentially obsolete equipment.

Higher book income. Because net book income is of considerable importance to public companies reporting to stockholders, it is possible that lease payments, as a book expense, may be lower than the combination of interest costs plus depreciation. Obviously, this is related to the interest cost payable by the lessee as well as the depreciable life of the equipment.

Lower state taxes. Because state taxes are often based on an allocation formula that includes property owned in a particular state, the shift of the ownership to a lessor may result in a reduction in state taxes to the lessee without a commensurate increase in taxes to the lessor, depending on the lessor's tax position in the particular state.

Speed of approval. Based on the size of the transaction, many managers are authorized to enter into lease transactions with a less elaborate approval mechanism than is the case with capital outlays. Although this simplified procedure may sound shortsighted on the part of a corporation, there is an element of self-correction to this apparent leniency. To the extent that lease payments are an ordinary expense, the manager is faced with that cost being charged directly to his specific budget, while a capital outlay, supported by centrally borrowed loan funds, may not result in the interest cost and depreciation being allocated to the manager's budget. Thus, although leasing may be a tempting alternative to the manager, the budget impact may be a negative inducement.

Flexibility. Depending on the dominance of the lessee in the negotiation of the terms of the lease, there may be significant potential flexibility and convenience available in terms of cancellation of the lease or exchange of equipment for purposes of upgrading. Often the opportunity to exchange equipment is essential in areas of high technology where obsolescence is a serious risk.

Return on assets. If the lease is not capitalized for accounting purposes, then the asset base of the enterprise, if the asset is leased, will be lower than if the equipment was owned. In that event, obviously the return on assets will be better with a lower asset base; and, to the extent that a shortsighted management permits that type of manipulation, a resourceful manager will avail himself of that benefit.

Sale-leaseback. A fully depreciated asset that continues to have a useful life may be the source of additional funds to an enterprise that is cash short. Because a leasing company will entertain a sale-leaseback at 100 percent of fair market value, while a lender may be more interested in the book value of depreciated assets, a sale-leaseback may be a desirable course of action under the appropriate circumstances. Of course, based upon the nature of the asset, recapture of depreciation will be a relevant consideration.

Disadvantages to a Lessee

Loss of residual. Because lessors are often experts in the aftermarket for the equipment that they lease, they are often the beneficiaries of a significant residual value in the equipment that is the subject of a lease. The lessee, on the other hand, may be more concerned with the short-term economic benefit of the lease transaction and will often forgo the tremendous upside benefit that a generous residual may provide.

Cost. Because the lessor derives his funds from the loan market, he obviously looks for his profit from a combination of tax benefits, residual, and lease rental charges. If the lessee had equivalent access to the loan markets and could have taken advantage of the tax benefits, it is likely that the aggregate economic cost to the lessee on a discounted cash flow basis would have been lower than that available under a lease.

Debt refinancing. Because lessors generally match their assets and liabilities, a lessor will attempt to obtain his financing for a term comparable to that of the lease and may even pledge that lease and the rentals as security for his loan. The lessee will obviously be faced with fixed rental payments for the term of the lease. If interest rates decline he will not be in the position to refinance the lease. On the other hand, if he had relied on debt financing to provide the funds for the purchase of the equipment, it is likely that the debt would either be at a floating rate or he would be in a position to refinance his debt obligation.

Factors to Be Weighed by the Lessor

Yield. Because the lessor is advancing 100 percent of the cost of the equipment and is thereby taking a greater risk, he will generally be the recipient of a higher yield than is available to a lender. Because he usually understands the equipment market, he is in a good position to maximize his return if the lessee defaults and he is forced to repossess the equipment.

Specific security. In the event of the lessee's bankruptcy, the lessor, subject to the rights of a trustee in bankruptcy, may take possession of his equipment, rather than be reduced to the position of a general creditor. Having that right will place the lessor in a preferred negotiating position with respect to lease payments that may be in arrears. Obviously this advantage is illusory if the equipment is obsolete or no longer important with respect to the lessee's business. In that case the trustee will probably disaffirm the lease, and the lessor will be a general creditor with respect to any unpaid rentals.

Residual value. In an inflationary economy where the value of hard assets increases, the lessor is in a position to benefit from the increase in the value of the equipment during the lease term as a result of his retention of the residual interest.

Risk. Because the lessee is often entering into a lease to expand his borrowing ability or because his taxable income is reduced, he probably represents a credit risk of some degree. His ability to maintain the lease payments and the marketability of the equipment are ever-present concerns to the lessor.

Tax. In the event of the sale of the equipment, the lessor must be concerned with recapture penalties associated with the investment tax credit and depreciation.

Legislation. The business of leasing has been the subject of extensive legislation, depending on Congress's perception of the economy from time to time and its perception of the value of shifting tax benefits from lessees to lessors or even the sale of tax benefits to third parties. To the extent that this business has been the subject of legislative attention, it has lacked stability and predictability.

ACCOUNTING FOR LEASES

Capital versus Operating Leases

The most natural and conventional approach to asset acquisition has been via the route of ownership. Profitable companies have enhanced their cash flow, after investing in the asset, through the maximization of tax benefits that are associated with the ownership of capital assets. These benefits are usually accelerated depreciation, investment tax credit, and interest expense deductions associated with the funds borrowed to purchase the asset. When a company is not subject to taxes (usually as a result of unprofitable operations), it cannot avail itself of the aforementioned tax benefits, and leasing provides a vehicle to shift these benefits to a third party—the lessor. To properly evaluate the advantages of one method over the other, a comparison of the cash flow streams available under each of the methods is necessary. This approach should consider the tax liability of the lessee and the costs he is likely to incur through leasing or borrowing. Also the timing of the cash flows associated with each method must be measured. A critical element in this analysis is the quantification of the lost residual value of the equipment to the lessee. Only through a careful discounted cash flow analysis, which properly recognizes the time value of a cash stream, can the lease versus buy analysis be done properly.

Through June 1983, approximately 25 percent of all FASB statements and interpretations that had been promulgated related to the subject of leasing.[1] Statement No. 13 of the Financial Accounting Standards Board places leases into two classifications—operating leases and capital leases. Where a lease is designated as a capital lease, it is more akin to a sale of the equipment from the lessor to the lessee than to a lease. Capital leases fall into three subclassifications: a sales-type lease, a direct finance lease, and a leveraged lease.

SFAS 13 provides that:

> If at its inception a lease meets one or more of the following four criteria, the lease shall be classified as a capital lease by the lessee. Otherwise, it shall be classified as an operating lease.
>
> **a.** The lease transfers ownership of the property to the lessee by the end of the lease term.
> **b.** The lease contains a bargain purchase option.

596

c. The lease term is equal to 75 percent or more of the estimated economic life of the leased property.

d. The present value, at the beginning of the lease term of the minimum lease payments, equals or exceeds 90 percent of the fair market value of the leased property at the inception of the lease. (The fair market value of the property is to be reduced by any investment tax credit retained by the lessor prior to determining the 90 percent base.)[2]

Material Definitions

The understanding and definition of certain of the foregoing terms are critical to the interpretation and analysis of a lease transaction.

The *inception of the lease* is the date of the lease agreement or of the commitment, if earlier. The commitment, if it is relied on as the date of inception, must be in writing, executed by the parties, and contain the principal provisions of the transaction.

The *fair market value of the leased property* is the price that the leased property would be sold for in an arms-length transaction between unrelated parties.

If the subject of the lease is a standard piece of equipment, its fair market value is easily determined by reference to the selling price of the dealer or manufacturer. To the extent that the property is highly customized, ascertaining fair market value without reference to the lease transaction may be more difficult.

The relationship between the lessor and lessee must not be that of a related party. Where significant influence may be exerted by one party upon the other, those parties may be deemed to be related. Thus, a parent and a subsidiary or an existing lender and his borrower would be characterized as related parties.

The determination of fair market value at the inception of a lease is critical to a lessor, not only to establish whether the transaction is a capital lease or an operating lease but, if the transaction is a capital lease, it will be relevant to the subclassification of the lease as a sales type or direct financing lease. A sales-type lease results in a profit or loss to the lessor, determined by the difference between the fair market value and the cost of the equipment at the inception of the lease.

A *bargain purchase option* or a *bargain renewal option* allows the lessee to purchase the property, or renew the lease, as the case may be, at a price or rental sufficiently lower than the fair market value or fair rental value as of the option date so that the exercise of the option is reasonably assured. The determination of whether a bargain purchase or renewal option exists is made as of the inception of the lease.

597

The *lease term* is defined to be the sum of (*a*) the noncancelable term of the lease (this is the term during which the lessee may terminate the lease only upon the occurrence of a remote event, such as the bankruptcy of the lessee, or with the consent of the lessor, or if a new lease covering the sale equipment is entered into between the lessee and lessor or upon payment of an extraordinarily severe penalty); (*b*) any period related to a bargain renewal (this is where the renewal rate is sufficiently below the market rate so that the exercise of the renewal is reasonably assured); (*c*) any period during which a termination by the lessee would impose a severe penalty obligation upon the lessee; (*d*) any period during which the lessee has guaranteed the debt of the lessor; and (*e*) any period with respect to which the lease may be renewed at the lessor's option.

The *estimated economic life* of the leased property is the period during which the property is estimated to be economically usable, assuming normal repair and maintenance and assuming further that it is used for the purpose it was intended at the inception of the lease. This estimate is not intended to be related to the term of the lease.

The *estimated residual value* of the leased property is the estimated fair market value of the property at the end of the lease term.

Minimum lease payments, as to the lessee, represent the sum of the minimum rental payments during the lease term, plus any residual guaranty by the lessee plus any penalty payable by the lessee for failure to renew the lease.

From the lessor's standpoint, the minimum lease payments are those which are the obligation of the lessee, plus any guaranty of the residual value or rental payments beyond the lease term by unrelated third parties.

In determining the relevant payments to be considered during the lease term, there should be included any amounts related to bargain purchase options or bargain renewal options, and any amounts identified as guarantees of a residual value of the leased property.

It should be noted that there is not included in the definition of minimum lease payments any penalty which is of an amount that reasonably assures renewal. This is because the penalty is not likely to be imposed or paid and the lease term is likely to be continued.

If a lease provides for a bargain purchase option and a residual guaranty, only the payments called for during the lease term and the bargain purchase option amount would be included in the calculation of minimum lease payments. Because upon exercise of the bargain purchase option the lessee would become the owner of the property, the residual guaranty to the lessor would no longer be an appropriate consideration.

The *interest rate implicit in the lease* is the interest rate calculated on a discounted cash flow basis which relates the minimum lease payments and the estimated unguaranteed residual value with the fair value of the leased property at the inception of the lease. The fair value should be reduced by the investment tax credit retained by the lessor for purposes of the calculation.

The *lessee's incremental borrowing rate* is the rate that the lessee would have paid in the market at the inception of the lease for the acquisition of sufficient funds to have purchased the leased property.

The determination of the lessee's incremental borrowing rate and the implicit lease rate are important to determine the present value of the cash flow under the lease. In order to properly define the lease as a capital lease, the present value of the relevant cash flow must be equal to or exceed 90 percent of the fair market value of the leased property.

The *initial direct costs of a lease* are those lessor costs that are directly associated with negotiating and concluding the lease transaction. Included in this category would be commissions, salespersons' compensation other than commissions, legal fees, the cost of credit investigations, and the cost of preparing and processing documents. Not included in this category are general administrative costs or the overhead associated with the operation of the leasing activity such as heat, light, and rent for the office facilities. In a sales-type capital lease the initial direct costs are related to the calculation of the sales price and can affect the profit or loss to the lessor. In a direct financing lease these initial direct costs are charged against income by the lessor as they are incurred.

Contingent rentals may sometimes be a part of the lease transaction. This type of rental may be related to the number of hours of usage of the property or may fluctuate depending on an external financial standard such as a price index. For the purpose of calculating minimum lease payments, contingent rentals are excluded and any index relationship is disregarded. Only the index standard in effect at the inception of the lease is considered relevant.

Executory costs under a lease are those costs directly related to the leased property such as insurance, taxes, and maintenance costs.

Accounting Treatment of a Capital or Operating Lease by the Lessee

With these definitions understood it is now appropriate to consider how to identify a lease as a capital lease or an operating lease and the accounting treatment afforded each of these categories.

599

As noted earlier, a lease is deemed to be a capital lease if it meets any one of the following categories:

- The lease transfers ownership to the lessee by the end of the lease term.
- The lease contains a bargain purchase option.
- The lease term equals 75 percent or more of the estimated useful life of the lease property.
- The present value of the lease payments (excluding executory costs) equals 90 percent or more of the fair market value of the property (less the investment tax credit retained by the lessor) at the inception of the lease.

If a lease meets none of the foregoing criteria, it is then classified as an operating lease. The first two criteria, those relating to transfer of title and bargain purchase option, are *always* critical for purposes of classification. The last two criteria are not used, however, if the inception of the lease term falls within the last 25 percent of the total estimated economic life of the leased property.

The application of the four criteria to determine whether a transaction shall be deemed to be a capital lease reflects the basic concept that leases that transfer substantially all of the benefits and risks of ownership should be accounted for as the acquisition of an asset by the lessee with the concurrent incurrence of a liability to pay for that asset.

In order to determine the present value of the minimum lease payments, the lessee is required to use his incremental borrowing rate, unless he can determine the lessor's implicit rate and that rate is less than the lessee's incremental borrowing rate.

If the lease is determined to be a capital lease, the lessee records the transaction as the acquisition of an asset and the incurrence of an obligation in an amount equal to the lower of (*a*) the present value of the minimum lease payments, excluding executory costs, or (*b*) fair market value of the leased property as of the inception of the lease.

The amortization of the asset value booked by the lessee is then based on the method normally used to depreciate an owned asset of similar nature. As to lease payments, a portion is treated as a reduction of the balance sheet obligation that was deemed to have been incurred, and the balance of the payment is treated as an interest expense which is the discount rate that was used in arriving at the present value of the booked asset.

If the fair market value of the asset at the inception of the lease is deemed to be less than the present value of the lease payments (the present value having been determined by using the lessee's incremental borrowing rate), then the interest rate used to amortize the debt obligation would be that rate which would be used to discount the minimum lease payments down to that fair market value.

Because, as noted above, contingent rentals are not deemed to be part of the minimum lease rentals, those payments are charged to expense as incurred, or booked to income as incurred if they result in a reduction of the basic rental payment.

If the lease is properly classified as an operating lease, then rental expense is an ordinary expense charged to the income statement of the lessee over the lease term on a straight-line basis, even if the payments are contractually made on a skewed basis. The modification of the straight-line treatment of rental expense should be considered only if the modified payments more accurately reflect the pattern in which the benefits from the leased property occur. Thus, if the rental payment is based on usage of the equipment, then the expense is properly booked on that basis.

The reporting obligation for capital leases may be properly met by reflecting the gross amount of assets recorded under capital leases by major classes, according to nature or function and the related accumulated depreciation. This information may be combined with comparable information for owned assets as of the appropriate balance sheet date. The offsetting obligation must be identified in the balance sheet as an obligation under a capital lease, with the obligation properly reflected as to its current and noncurrent segment. The amortization on the asset side may either be separately stated or included with depreciation expense of owned assets, with appropriate disclosure of such inclusion being made.

In addition, the financial statements should reflect future minimum lease payments in the aggregate; and, for each of the succeeding five years, there should be shown separately deductions for executory costs and imputed interest. It is important to note that the present value of the minimum lease payments should be equal to the total lease obligation.

As to operating leases having remaining terms in excess of one year, the lessee must disclose, as of the date of the latest balance sheet presented, future minimum rental payments required in the aggregate as well as for each of the five succeeding fiscal years. In addition the lessee must disclose total future minimum rentals under noncancelable subleases. Also, for each period that an income statement is presented, the lessee must identify rental expense consisting of minimum rentals, contingent rentals, and sublease rentals.

With respect to all leases, capital as well as operating, the lessee is expected to disclose any material terms of the lease (such as restrictions on debt or dividends), the terms of any material renewal clause or purchase option, and the methodology for the calculation of contingent rentals.

From the lessor's point of view, there are two special criteria that must be met to properly characterize a lease as a capital lease. Those are (*a*) that the collectibility of the minimum lease payments is reasonably predictable (this test is primarily an ascertainment of the lessee's creditworthiness), and (*b*) that there are no significant uncertainties related to the amount of costs to be incurred by the lessor.

Thus, from a lessor's perspective a lease is a capital lease if it meets any *one* of the four criteria used by a lessee in classifying the lease; plus, the lease must meet *both* of the standards related to (*a*) collectibility of payments and (*b*) certainty of costs. If the transaction results in a manufacturer/dealer profit, it is a sales-type capital lease. Otherwise, it is a direct financing capital lease.

There are a variety of circumstances that will result in the lessee and lessor treating the same lease differently for reporting purposes. Thus, because of the use of a lower interest rate assumption by a lessor, he may determine that the present value of the minimum lease payments exceeds 90 percent of the fair market value. He will then treat the lease as a capital lease, while the lessee—who may have a marginal credit rating—may use a higher borrowing rate to discount the payments. As a result the lessee may determine that the present value of the payments is less than 90 percent of the fair market value of the leased asset and, consequently, will treat the lease as an operating lease. In addition, a lessor may enter into a standard operating lease with a lessee but, as a result of a guaranty of the residual value from an insurance company, the lessor may properly treat the lease as a capital lease. Given the multitude of issues that require judgment in terms of evaluating the criteria and determining whether a lease is an operating lease or a capital lease, it is not unusual that the lessee and lessor will treat the same lease in different fashions. The determination of fair market value, useful economic life, or whether a purchase option price is a bargain price or not represent a few of the areas where reasonable persons may reach different conclusions.

With respect to the determination of the certainty of a lessor's costs under a lease, it may be relevant to note whether the lessor has agreed to maintain the equipment beyond a normal product warranty or beyond the level available by contracting for third-party maintenance, or if the lessor has agreed to replace the equipment if it becomes technologically obsolescent. In those circumstances the lessor is faced with an uncertain and material economic exposure.

Accounting Treatment of a Capital or Operating Lease by the Lessor

Capital leases may be classified as sales-type leases or direct financing leases. Where a manufacturer or dealer offers his customers a leasing arrangement, the characterization of the transaction as a lease should not affect the profit or loss that would otherwise be booked if the property were sold and if the transaction is properly classified as a capital lease. Thus, if the fair market value of the leased property is greater or less than its cost or carrying value, the lessor records the profit or loss at the inception of the lease. With a direct financing lease the cost or carrying value is equivalent to the fair market value of the property and therefore no profit or loss is recorded.

In order to record a sales-type lease the lessor must identify the gross investment in the lease, the unearned income, the sales price, and the cost of the property. The gross investment in the lease is equal to the minimum lease payments (excluding executory costs) plus the unguaranteed residual value of the leased asset. The unearned income is equal to the difference between the gross investment and its present value. This unearned income is amortized over the term of the lease. The sales price is determined by calculating the present value of the minimum lease payments (net of executory costs) determined at the interest rate implicit in the lease. Note that for this calculation the minimum lease payments do not include the unguaranteed residual value. After the determination of the sales price, the profit or loss is determined by charging against this amount the cost or carrying value of the leased asset plus any initial direct costs, less the present value of the unguaranteed residual value.

The estimated residual value should be reviewed on a frequent basis, and any significant and permanent decline should be recorded and charged to income. Increases in value are not recognized.

Unlike a sales-type capital lease, the direct financing capital lease involves no dealer or manufacturer's profit. This is essentially a simple financing transaction. The gross investment is the same as that for a sales-type lease, namely the minimum lease payments, excluding executory costs and the unguaranteed residual value. The amount of the unearned income is equal to the gross investment less the cost or carrying value of the asset. This is subtracted from and reduces the amount of the gross investment. The unearned income is amortized over the lease term to produce a constant rate of return on the net investment. As in the sales-type lease, the residual value should be reviewed frequently, with any decline in value charged to income. Increases in value are not recognized.

An operating lease, on the books of the lessor, reflects the cost or carrying value of the leased asset as part of the property, plant, and equipment account on the balance sheet.

The property is depreciated in accordance with normal depreciation methods, and rents are recognized as income and booked on a straight-line basis unless the provisions of the lease would reflect that the rental is based on usage or another basis that reflects the benefit of the property to the lessee. If the parties merely contract for payments to be skewed without regard to the use of the leased property, these rents will be booked on a straight-line basis. Direct initial costs are customarily deferred and recognized over the lease term in proportion to the recognition of rental income.

A lessor of capital leases must disclose (*a*) the future minimum lease payments to be received with separate deductions for executory costs and accumulated allowance for doubtful accounts; (*b*) the unguaranteed residual; (*c*) unearned income; (*d*) the future minimum lease payments recoverable for each of the next five years; and (*e*) total contingent rentals included in income. A lessor of operating leases must disclose (*a*) cost and carrying amount, if different, and accumulated depreciation of property on lease or held for leasing; (*b*) future minimum rentals under noncancelable leases, both in total and for each of the next five years; and (*c*) the total contingent rentals included in income.

All lessors, capital as well as operating, must describe the leasing arrangements for all leases.

Financial Statements

Set forth below are examples of the financial statements of a lessee of a capital lease and a lessee of an operating lease. It is evident that under the operating lease each monthly payment is a full expense that is charged against revenue, just like any other operating expense. Under a capital lease, however, each monthly payment is split into two separate categories. One portion represents an interest expense, which is charged against revenue in the income statement, and the other portion is a monthly reduction of the balance sheet liability labeled *lease payable*. In addition, because the leased asset has been capitalized, there is a monthly depreciation charge reflected in the income statement. The most significant distinction is that the capital lease results in the asset and liability being reflected on the balance sheet of the lessee; with the operating lease, the only financial statement impact is the recording of the monthly rental as a normal operating expense.

The following financial statements are intended to show the alternative entries for a capital lease and an operating lease.

ZEBRA MANUFACTURING COMPANY
Balance Sheet

	Lessee's point of view	
	Operating lease	*Capital lease*
Assets		
Current assets:		
Cash	$ 4,000	$ 4,000
Accounts receivable	12,000	12,000
Inventory	8,000	8,000
Fixed assets:		
Property, plant, equipment	48,000	48,000
Capital leased equipment.	–0–	58,000
Less accumulated depreciation	(10,000)	(17,000)
Total assets	$62,000	$113,000
Liabilities		
Current liabilities:		
Accounts payable	$ 6,000	$ 6,000
Current portion leases payable	–0–	7,000
Long-term liabilities:		
Bonds payable.	30,000	30,000
Long-term portion leases payable	–0–	44,000
Total liabilities	$36,000	$87,000
Stockholders' Equity		
Common stock (5,000 shares).	$ 5,000	$ 5,000
Retained earnings	21,000	21,000
Total equity	26,000	26,000
Total liabilities and equity.	$62,000	$113,000

ZEBRA MANUFACTURING COMPANY
Income Statement

	Operating lease	Capital lease
Revenue:		
Sales.	$ 200,000	$200,000
Less: Cost of goods sold	(100,000)	(100,000)
Gross profit.	100,000	100,000
Operating expenses:		
Selling	(3,000)	(3,000)
General and administrative	(30,000)	(30,000)
Lease expense	(15,000)	–0–
Depreciation expense	(5,000)	(12,000)
Operating income:		
Other income and expenses:		
Interest expense	(6,000)	(16,000)
Income before taxes:	41,000	39,000
Income taxes 50 percent.	(20,500)	(19,500)
Net income	$ 20,500	$ 19,500

Statement of Changes in Financial Position—Cash Basis

	Operating lease	Capital lease
Sources of cash:		
Operations:		
Net income	$ 20,500	$ 19,500
Add: Depreciation.	5,000	12,000
Total sources	$ 25,500	$ 31,500
Uses of cash:		
Dividends.	(4,000)	(4,000)
Purchase of equipment	(10,000)	(10,000)
Reduction of lease liabilities	–0–	(5,000)
Total uses	$ (14,000)	$ (19,000)
Net cash increase	$ 11,500	$ 12,500

It is interesting to apply several of the customary ratio tests to the foregoing financial statements to understand the impact that the operating lease or capital lease will have.

		Operating lease	Capital lease
Current ratio	$= \dfrac{\text{Current assets}}{\text{Current liabilities}} =$	$\dfrac{24{,}000}{6{,}000} = 4.0$	$\dfrac{24{,}000}{13{,}000} = 1.85$
Quick ratio	$= \dfrac{\text{Quick assets}}{\text{Current liabilities}} =$	$\dfrac{16{,}000}{6{,}000} = 2.67$	$\dfrac{16{,}000}{13{,}000} = 1.23$
Net working capital	$= \begin{array}{l}\text{Current assets}\\ -\ \text{Curr. liab.}\end{array} =$	$\begin{array}{r}24{,}000\\ -6{,}000\\ \hline 18{,}000\end{array}$	$\begin{array}{r}24{,}000\\ -13{,}000\\ \hline 11{,}000\end{array}$
Times interest earned	$= \dfrac{\begin{array}{c}\text{Interest + Taxes}\\ +\ \text{Net income}\end{array}}{\text{Interest}} =$	$\dfrac{47{,}000}{6{,}000} = 7.83$	$\dfrac{55{,}000}{16{,}000} = 3.44$
Debt to equity	$= \dfrac{\text{Debt}}{\text{Equity}} =$	$\dfrac{30{,}000}{26{,}000} = 1.15$	$\dfrac{74{,}000}{26{,}000} = 2.85$
Debt to assets	$= \dfrac{\text{Debt}}{\text{Assets}} =$	$\dfrac{30{,}000}{62{,}000} = 0.48$	$\dfrac{74{,}000}{113{,}000} = 0.65$
Net profit margin	$= \dfrac{\text{Net income}}{\text{Sales}} =$	$\dfrac{20{,}500}{200{,}000} = 0.1025$	$\dfrac{19{,}500}{200{,}000} = 0.0975$
Asset turnover	$= \dfrac{\text{Sales}}{\text{Assets}} =$	$\dfrac{200{,}000}{62{,}000} = 3.22$	$\dfrac{200{,}000}{113{,}000} = 1.77$
Return on assets	$= \dfrac{\text{Net income}}{\text{Assets}} =$	$\dfrac{20{,}500}{62{,}000} = 0.33$	$\dfrac{19{,}500}{113{,}000} = 0.17$
Return on equity	$= \dfrac{\text{Net income}}{\text{Equity}} =$	$\dfrac{20{,}500}{26{,}000} = 0.79$	$\dfrac{19{,}500}{26{,}000} = 0.75$
Earnings per share	$= \dfrac{\text{Net income}}{\text{Total shares}} =$	$\dfrac{20{,}500}{5{,}000} = \$4.10$	$\dfrac{19{,}500}{5{,}000} = \$3.90$

LEGAL CONSIDERATIONS

Uniform Commercial Code

To the extent that a true lease exists between a lessor and a lessee, the provisions of Article 9 of the Uniform Commercial Code do not apply. However, if it is determined pursuant to Section 1-201(37) that although the transaction has been labeled a lease transaction, it is more accurately characterized as a situation involving a retention of title by a seller with the intent of creating a security interest, then the transaction will be subject to Article 9. Section 1-201(37) provides:

> *Security interest* means an interest in personal property or fixtures which secures payment or performance of an obligation. The retention or reservation of title by a seller of goods notwithstanding ship-

ment or delivery to the buyer (Section 2-401) is limited in effect to a reservation of a "security interest."

The term also includes any interest of a buyer of accounts, chattel paper, or contract rights which is subject to Article 9. The special property interest of a buyer of goods on identification of such goods to a contract for sale under Section 2-401 is not a security interest, but a buyer may also acquire a security interest by complying with Article 9. Unless a lease or consignment is intended as security, reservation of title thereunder is not a security interest, but a consignment is in any event subject to the provisions on consignment sales (Section 2-326). Whether a lease is intended as security is to be determined by the facts of each case; however, (*a*) the inclusion of an option to purchase does not of itself make the lease one intended as security and (*b*) an agreement that upon compliance with the terms of the lease the lessee shall become or has the option to become the owner of the property for no additional consideration or for a nominal consideration does make the lease one intended as security.

The seller's retention of title is not always deemed to be a security interest. Rather, such retention of title is *limited* to a security interest if all of the terms of the transaction otherwise indicate that the buyer has acquired ownership of the property. Under the predecessor statute of the Uniform Commercial Code, such a set of facts resulted in a conditional sale.

To be properly deemed a conditional sale under that statute, the buyer had to be obligated to pay an amount substantially equal to the purchase price of the property, and he had to either acquire or have the option to acquire the status of owner of the property.

Although Sections 1-201(37) and 9-102 of the Uniform Commercial Code speak in terms of the "intention" of the parties, the intention of the parties to create a lease will be subverted to the analysis of all of the elements of the transaction. The rights of a third-party creditor of a "purported lessee" is subject to the specific terms of the transaction, not the intent of the lessee and lessor. Obviously, if the transaction is a true lease, the Code does not apply, the lessor has properly retained title to the equipment, and that equipment is not subject to the claims of the creditors of the lessee. If, on the other hand, the transaction is deemed to have created a security interest rather than being a true lease, then the seller is at his peril vis-à-vis creditors of the lessee, if he has not filed the appropriate Uniform Commercial Code documents at the appropriate locations to reflect his "security interest."

As a reflection of caution, many lessors will require the lessee to execute the appropriate Uniform Commercial Code form, and the lessor will retain the right to file those documents at will. Many lessors, however, have resisted such a filing for fear that, even though the filing will generally state that it covers a lease transaction and is not required to be filed, a court might interpret the act of filing as a concession by the lessor that the lease is flawed and that title passed to the lessee with the lessor having nothing more than a security interest.

Why the fuss? What difference does it make? The rights of a lessor and the rights of a secured party are viewed quite differently under the law. While a lessee pays a rental fee which is deemed to be consideration for the *use* of the property, a party who has obtained property subject to the security interest of another party is deemed to have an equity interest in that property. Thus, in the event of a default under a lease, the lessor should be able to enter the lessee's premises (this is subject to a variety of restrictions under the laws of the various states) and reclaim his property. If a bankruptcy trustee has taken over the estate of the lessee, the trustee generally has a right to terminate lease contracts and surrender the property to the lessor, or to ratify the lease and continue to pay the lease rental in exchange for continued use of the property. In a transaction where title is deemed to have been transferred to the lessee, then the lessee is deemed to be paying not for the use of the property but for its equity; and, in the event of a default, the foreclosure and sale of the property by the lessor is subject to the lessee's "equity of redemption." Such a sale must be conducted with the lessee's interests in mind, and any surplus proceeds must be turned over to the lessee.

The case law interpreting Section 1-201(37) distinguishing which transactions are deemed to be leases and which are deemed to be conditional sales is not totally consistent; but as an overview approach it is safe to conclude that in order for a court to classify the transaction as a conditional sale, two essential elements must be evident. First, there must be an obligation between the parties; second, there must be an interest in personal property. If we ascertain the existence of both of these elements and also determine that title retention is involved, then if the recipient of the property is under no obligation to pay an amount substantially equal to the purchase price, the transaction is likely *not* to be deemed to be a conditional sale. It may be a gift, a consignment, a bailment, or a lease.

It is tempting to look to the tax standards and accounting standards to determine whether a transaction should be deemed to be a lease or a conditional sale, and the literature in both of these areas may be helpful. However, the accountants who are quite comfortable with a set of rules that may result in inconsistent conclusions by the lessee and lessor as to whether the transaction is a lease or not do not set a comfortable precedent for the chattel security lawyer looking to counsel his client. Similarly, the intricate standards established for tax purposes are not automatically conclusive for Uniform Commercial Code purposes. The tax considerations that are relevant to the generation of revenue for the government are not necessarily consistent with the interests of a trustee in bankruptcy—who is often the challenger to the characterization of a transaction as a lease, and is seeking to have title to the equipment vested with the "lessee."

Sales and Leasebacks

Although the law generally shows a marvelous adaptability to the world of commerce, many state jurisdictions have on their books statutes that are remnants of an outdated and impractical historical theory related to the "vendor in possession." That theory has been traced back to Twyne's Case, which was decided in England in 1601. The doctrine evolved because a secret sale of property, with the continued use of that property by the seller (as is the case in a sale-leaseback), was deemed to be a fraud on the creditors of the seller. A creditor of the seller in the early days of commerce generally made his commercial judgments on the basis of the property in the possession of his customer. In modern days, when creditors rely on detailed financial statements, this doctrine would appear to have outlived its usefulness. Nevertheless, in many states, unless such a transaction is recorded in the appropriate governmental office, it is deemed to be a fraud upon the creditors of the vendor in possession. The law varies, and in many states the procedures are set forth in detail in statutes, while in other states the common law prevails, and it generally provides that such a transaction raises a presumption of fraud, but that presumption is rebuttable.

A special area with its own rules for filing relates to aircraft. The Federal Aviation Act requires that ownership of aircraft shall be recorded with the Federal Aeronautics Administration. Therefore, if a transaction is intended to be a true lease but ultimately determined to be an installment sale on a "conveyance" within the meaning of the statute, and such conveyance has not been recorded, then the lessor-owner may find that his claim for lease payments may not be secured as against the claim of other creditors.

Product Liability

When a lessor and a lessee enter into a lease transaction for personal property and the property is defective, who shall bear the economic burden of the defect? Shall the lessee be required to continue to pay rent when he has been deprived of the enjoyment of his property? Should the lessor be required to repair or replace the property?

One theory on which a lessor's liability for a defective product may be based is negligence. The tort of negligent misrepresentation may be the basis of liability of a lessor where he has endorsed the product to the lessee for his own economic gain.

In *Hanberry* v. *Hearst Corp.* (276 Cal.App2d 680, 81 Cal.Reptr. 519 (1969) the court said:

> The basic question . . . is whether one who endorses a product for his own economic gain and for the purpose of encouraging and inducing the public to buy it, may be liable to a purchaser who, relying on the endorsement, buys the product and is injured because it is defective and not as represented in the endorsement. We conclude such liability may exist and a cause of action has been pleaded in the instant case. In arriving at this conclusion, we are influenced more by public policy than by whether such cause of action can be comfortably fitted into one of the law's traditional categories of liability.

Although the foregoing decision involved a sale and purchase, the Restatement (2d) Torts §408 applies the logic of that decision to claims for compensation for physical harm. That treatise states:

> One who leases a chattel as safe for immediate use is subject to liability to those whom he should expect to use the chattel, or to be endangered by its probable use, for physical harm caused by its use in a manner for which, and by a person for whose use, it is leased, if the lessor fails to exercise reasonable care to make it safe for such use or to disclose its actual condition to those who may be expected to use it.

The limitation of the negligence theory to damage for physical harm makes the availability of a claim under a warranty theory a most appealing alternative. To the extent that a warranty is a promise that the product will meet certain standards of performance, this is a claim in the nature of a contract and, of course, may be expected to cover claims of economic harm. Because Article 2 of the Uniform Commercial Code is the repository of most of the guidelines for warranty claims, the impediment that must be vaulted is that Article 2 by its title applies to sales. Fortunately, a comment to Section 2-313 of the Uniform Commercial Code is helpful. It provides, in part: "[Warranties] may arise in other appropriate circumstances such as in the case of bailments for hire, the matter is left to the case law with the intention that the policies of this Act may offer useful guidance in dealing with further cases as they arise.''

There is little doubt that if a lessor makes an express warranty to the lessee which is part of the basis of the bargain and upon which the lessee relies, the lessor will be held liable for damages resulting from a breach of that warranty. The matter becomes more difficult in the area of the implied warranties of merchantability and fitness for a particular use. In this area the distinction between (*a*) a merchant/manufacturer who is leasing a product with which he is intimately familiar and (*b*) a finance-lessor is significant. The Code states that the warranty of merchantability is implied only if the seller is a merchant with respect to goods of that kind. The implied warranty of fitness for a particular purpose is deemed to exist only if the buyer is relying on the seller's skill or judgment to select or furnish suitable goods. The Code also provides that:

> a merchant is a person who deals in goods of the kind or otherwise by his occupation holds himself out as having knowledge or skill peculiar to the practices or goods involved in the transaction. Given the clear distinction between a merchant/lessor's familiarity with the product, he is far more likely to be held to have provided the implied warranties of merchantability and fitness than will a finance/lessor.

Generally, a finance-lessor will require that the lease agreement contain a disclaimer of all warranties, express or implied. On occasion the courts have rejected such disclaimers as unconscionable. This has generally been limited to those situations where the lessee's level of sophistication was significantly below that of the lessor.

In recent years, the courts have extended liability to lessors for physical harm to a lessee, even if negligence has not been established. This doctrine of strict liability has evolved as a matter of public policy. To the extent that one person has enjoyed economic gain and his customer has been harmed, the person who has benefited should make the injured person whole. In *Price* v. *Shell Oil Company* (2 Cal.3d 245, 466 P2d 722 (1970) the doctrine of strict liability was directly applied to leases:

> [There is] no substantial difference between sellers of personal property and nonsellers, such as bailors and lessors. . . . [T]he seller or nonseller places [the product] on the market, knowing that it is to be used without inspection for defects. . . . [I]t should make no difference that the party distributing the article has retained title to it. Nor can we see how the risk of harm associated with the use of the chattel can vary with the legal form under which it is held. Having in mind

612

the market realities and the widespread use of the lease of personalty
. . . we think it makes good sense to impose on the lessors of chattels
the same liability for physical harm which had been imposed on the
manufacturers and retailers. The former, like the latter, are able to
bear the cost of compensating for injuries resulting from defects by
spreading the loss through an adjustment of the rental.

In most instances a knowledgeable lessor will protect himself
against the risk by requiring the lessee to obtain product liability insurance naming the lessor as an insured party.

Miscellaneous Legal Issues

Sales taxes. In many states a lessor may file a resale certificate and
avoid the payment of sales taxes upon his acquisition of the property.
The sales tax obligation is deemed to be satisfied by charging a sales tax
on the rentals to the lessee. In Louisiana the most onerous situation
prevails. The lessor pays sales tax upon his acquisition of the equipment and must charge sales tax upon the rental payments, and the
lessee must pay a further sales tax if he purchases the property from
the lessor.

Personal property taxes. Personal property taxes are imposed in
many states, and the economics of a leasing transaction must recognize
this obligation. Although the title holder will be liable to the state taxing
authorities for this tax, it is not unusual for a lessor to require the lessee
to bear the economic burden and to bear the exposure for any increases
in the tax rates during the term of the lease.

Doing business in various states. Use of equipment in a particular
jurisdiction is likely to be related to the overall business activity of the
lessee. In most jurisdictions the combination of an active business
activity with salespeople, telephone listings, offices, and advertising is
clearly sufficient for the company to qualify to do business in that
jurisdiction. The leasing of equipment, as a part of the overall scheme
of doing business, is merely another factor in the overall consideration
of whether such qualification is necessary. On the other hand, as a
lessor of equipment where the only relationship to a particular jurisdiction is the ownership of property located in that jurisdiction, there are
genuine questions as to whether qualification to do business is necessary under the statutes of most states. However, consequences of not
qualifying to do business within a jurisdiction where qualification
would otherwise be necessary are generally the prohibition of using the

613

courts of that jurisdiction to enforce contracts and, in addition, there may be certain penalties involved for such failure. In most states a corporation has the right to "cure" the failure to qualify before suing on a contract. In a few states the contract is void and unenforceable if the corporation did not properly qualify before the contract was entered into.

Specialized issues. Among the more specialized issues to be reviewed by counsel are (*a*) landlord and mortgagee waivers, (*b*) insurance coverage and conditions, (*c*) consequences of bankruptcy of lessee, (*d*) filing of lease under the Uniform Commercial Code, and (*e*) appropriateness of placing ownership plates on the equipment.

TAX CONSIDERATIONS

Critical Elements of the True Lease

With respect to most lease transactions of substantial size, the tax issues are of profound significance in determining the economic results to the lessor and lessee in the transaction. To the lessee, the incidents of ownership that generate tax benefits (namely, depreciation and investment tax credit) are of less significance and importance than they are to the lessor. This may be related to the lessee not being subject to federal income taxes as a result of (*a*) current losses, (*b*) a tax loss carryforward, or (*c*) a tax-exempt status (either a nonprofit or governmental entity). To the extent that the lessor is generating taxable income from other sources, the lessor will be in a position to offer the lessee a lease rate which from a cash flow perspective and from an economic point of view is more favorable to the lessee than his borrowing rate.

Because the tax rules that have been articulated by the Internal Revenue Service to define the true tax lease and the conditional sale are not the ultimate in precision and because they require an evaluation in each instance based on varying facts and circumstances, the risk of an improper classification of a transaction as a true lease (when in fact it is ultimately deemed to be a conditional sale) can result in an economic debacle to the lessor and a windfall to the lessee. Therefore, responsible lessors tend to be relatively conservative in their structuring of leases.

The critical tax issue to be assessed in each lease transaction is whether a sufficient portion of the risks and rewards of ownership have been retained by the lessor so as to qualify him as the owner of the equipment. If the conclusion is that the lessee is the owner, then the transaction is not a true lease but a conditional sales contract, with the lessor now being treated as a lender of funds with a security interest in the equipment (assuming he has complied with the appropriate statutory requirements) but with the investment tax credit and the depreciation associated with the ownership of the equipment redounding to the benefit of the lessee.

The operative section of the Internal Revenue Code that is the basis of any analysis of the true tax lease is Section 162(a)(3), which relates to whether the lessee through his "rental" payments has acquired an equity in the property.

In 1955 the Internal Revenue Service issued Revenue Ruling 55-540, which was an early attempt to synthesize the position of the government and of the courts with respect to the critical elements of the true lease. This ruling set forth a series of tests which "in the absence of compelling persuasive factors of contrary implication [set forth] an intent warranting treatment of a transaction as a purchase and sale rather than a lease or rental agreement."

Those tests are:

1. Portions of the periodic payments are made specifically applicable to an equity to be acquired by the lessee." Thus, an installment sale would be the result if a portion of each rental payment is to be applied to the buildup of an equity interest.
2. "The lessee will acquire title upon the payment of a stated amount of rentals, which under the contract he is required to make." This situation might be the result of having title transfer to the lessee after the payment of a specified number of rental payments, with no purchase option.
3. "The total amount which the lessee is required to pay for a relatively short period of use constitutes an inordinately large proportion of the total sum required to be paid to secure the transfer of title." This provision would apply if the sum of the rental payments plus a fixed purchase option price is equivalent to the purchase price of the equipment, giving effect to the time value of money. In addition, this provision would be relevant if the rental payments (giving effect to the time value of money) are equivalent to a purchase price plus interest, and at the end of the initial rental period, without any transfer of title to the lessee, at the lessee's option, there is a continuation of the lease at a token rental value.
4. "The agreed rental payments materially exceed the current

615

fair market value. This may be indicative that the payments include an element other than compensation for the use of property."

5. "The property may be acquired under a purchase option at a price which is nominal in relation to the value of the property at the time when the option may be exercised, as determined at the time of entering into the original agreement, or which is a relatively small amount when compared to the total payments which are required to be made." This provision does not preclude a fixed price purchase option, which reflects a bona fide estimated future value of the equipment at the end of the lease.

6. "Some portion of the periodic payments is specifically designated as interest or is otherwise readily recognizable as the equivalent of interest."

Since the promulgation of Revenue Ruling 55-540, the courts have focused on the term of the lease. If the lease term is essentially equal to or longer than the estimated useful life of the equipment, it is likely that the court will find that a sale has taken place. On the other hand, if the lessor can show that he anticipated a significant interest in the property at the end of the lease, he is likely to be treated as the owner of the equipment.

Recent Guidelines

In addition to Revenue Ruling 55-540, the Internal Revenue Service has promulgated Revenue Procedures 75-21 and 75-28 which, although intended primarily as guidelines for advance rulings of leveraged leases, are helpful with respect to the structuring of lease transactions generally. Subsequently, Revenue Procedures 76-30 (dealing with limited-use property) and 79-48 (dealing with lessee improvements) have been promulgated. The guidelines contained in these Revenue Procedures may be summarized as follows:

1. It is important that the lessor can establish that he has at least a 20 percent equity interest in the cost of the property. This must remain "at risk" throughout the lease term. The lessor may borrow the funds to establish his equity interest, so long as the lender has recourse to the lessor.

2. The lessee must have no ownership interest or investment in the property.

616

3. If the property is highly customized for the lessee or is essentially a single-purpose property with no utility to any other user at the end of the lease, it is likely that a sale will be deemed to have occurred.
4. The property should be anticipated to have a residual value, at the end of the term, at least equal to 20 percent of its original cost and a remaining useful life equal to 20 percent of its originally estimated useful life.
5. The Internal Revenue Service will challenge a transaction that has no economic substance and is solely intended to create a tax avoidance scheme.
6. The lessor must be shown to have retained some element of the risk of loss from a leasing transaction. If all of the risk is shifted to the lessee, a challenge to the lease status of the transaction is likely.
7. It is important that the lessor be able to establish that, without regard to tax consequences, he will have a profit from the transaction. The profit test, however, is not an onerous one. So long as the lessor's receipts from the transaction (which are likely to be his gross rents plus the estimated residual value at the end of the lease) will exceed his disbursements (which are likely to be his debt service plus other transactional expenses, including direct costs to finance his equity investment) plus the equity investment by as little as one dollar, the test is met.

In one of the most recent cases to be reviewed by the U.S. Supreme Court on the subject of the qualification of a transaction as a true lease for tax purposes (*Frank Lyon Co.* v. *United States* 435 U.S. 561 (1978)), a lengthy opinion does not totally embrace or reject the guidelines. That case took a "facts and circumstances" approach but did not establish new principles with universal applicability to other transactions. Although the Court accepted that case upon a writ of certiorari, which is normally granted in a case of unusual significance, the opinion has not become a significant tool for future planning and decisions. In fact, the tax court concluded that "it is difficult to pinpoint a general legal proposition for which the case stands." (*Belz Investment Co., Inc.* 72T.C. No. 101 (1979))

Notwithstanding the overall scope of the Internal Revenue Service guidelines, in 1982 Congress passed the Tax Equity and Fiscal Responsibility Act of 1982 which resulted in three major liberalizations in the classification and treatment of leases by corporate lessors for agreements entered into after December 31, 1983 (other than public utility property, property of certain formerly tax-exempt organizations, and rehabilitation property). The relevant provisions are:

1. Fixed-price purchase options that are equal to at least 10 percent of the original cost of the property are not to be taken into account in determining whether a transaction is a lease. The fact that the lessor has a contractual right requiring the lessee to purchase the property (a "put" option) in a finance lease will still be taken into account as an adverse factor in determining whether a transaction is a lease or a sale.
2. Limited-use property, other than public utility property, is eligible for lease treatment for leases entered into after December 31, 1983.
3. §38 property (Investment Tax Credit) leased within three months after it is placed in service will be treated as new §38 property.

Proposed Regulations

As of this writing there are proposed regulations from the Treasury Department that are expected to be released for public comment. It is expected that those proposed regulations will expand and ease the definition of a true lease for tax purposes. The momentum for the new proposals is based on an assessment that the existing guidelines create an economic bias in favor of lessors, work hardships on unprofitable lessees who could be helped by more lenient guidelines, and that after 30 years the old guidelines need reexamination to reflect a vastly changed marketplace. It is expected that the new regulations are likely to touch on the following areas:

1. Eliminate the existing cash flow test.
2. Reduce the minimum equity requirement from 20 percent to 10 percent.
3. Reduce the remaining useful life test from 20 percent to 10 percent.
4. Permit lessee loans and third-party guarantees, including letters of credit.
5. Increase permitted lease term to 90 percent of an asset's life from the current 80 percent.
6. Permit fixed-price purchase options to be determined at the commencement of the lease.

The pressure for reduced fixed-price purchase options has come from lessees who have been subject to the present rules which result in the increased value of the leased equipment flowing to the lessor at the conclusion of the lease.

SELECTING THE RIGHT LESSOR

Although the selection of a lessor (by a potential lessee) might appear to be merely a matter of choosing the company that offers the lowest lease rate, there are countless standards that should be considered in addition to the simple economics of the rate. Set forth below are several of the factors that a lessee should focus on before making his final commitment to any one lessor.

1. Is the investment tax credit passed to the lessee?
2. If the investment tax credit is passed on to the lessee, is it immediately passed to the lessee through an election, or through the technique of a rental adjustment with a resulting effect on cash flow?
3. Is a security deposit or downpayment required?
4. Are trustee's fees payable over the lease term? (applicable to leveraged leases)
5. Does the lessor purchase the equipment and add a fee?
6. Does the lessor borrow from the banks of the lessee and diminish access by the lessee to his own credit sources?
7. Are compensating balances required or imputed in the lessor's program?
8. Are premiums applicable upon involuntary loss or destruction of a leased asset?
9. What are the lessor's termination fees?
10. Does the lessor pay vendors' invoices promptly or does it obtain free financing by delaying payments? The cost to the vendor of carrying such financing is passed on to the lessee in a higher acquisition cost of equipment.
11. Is the quoted rate in fact a true simple interest rate or an add-on rate?
12. Does the lessor receive a full month's rent no matter when, during the month, the equipment is delivered?
13. Are finders' fees or commissions payable by the lessee?
14. What are the legal expenses payable by the lessee?
15. What are the renewal options?
16. What are the purchase options?

17. Are rental payments due and payable quarterly or semiannually in advance?
18. Are commitment or "standby" fees required?
19. Are any interim rents payable?
20. Are there additional "administrative fees" above and beyond the lease rate charge?
21. Are some of the competitive lessor's "operating services" mostly fictitious, enabling the lessor to obtain higher charges and fees for services with little or no value to the lessee?
22. Is there any possibility of increased rent during a later period in the lease, or is the rent fully predetermined throughout?
23. Is the lessor financially stable?
24. Does the lessor have a firm commitment from his lenders for the stated lease rate quotation?
25. Will the lease be treated as a true lease from the standpoint of the Internal Revenue Service and loan agreement restrictions?
26. Are there any negative covenants or restrictive requirements in the lease?
27. Are any personal or corporate guarantees required by the lessor?
28. Does the lessor require any additional security by way of pledged collateral?
29. Is the lessor vulnerable to any tax assessment by the Internal Revenue Service?
30. Is there a "hell-or-high-water" clause in the lease agreement making the instrument effectively a debt obligation from the standpoint of lessee's lenders?

DISCOUNTED CASH FLOW ANALYSIS

The measurable costs and benefits of alternative financing methods can be evaluated using discounted cash flow analysis. For example, in comparing a lease to a borrow and buy alternative, the relevant cash flows might include:

	Lease	*Borrow and buy*
Costs	Lease payments	Debt service
		Investment outlay
Benefits	Tax shield from:	Loan principal
	Lease payments	Tax shield from:
		Interest expense
		Depreciation
		Residuals (e.g., salvage value)

Note that these are financial cash flows that exclude operating costs and benefits of the capital project itself. To determine present values of the alternatives, discount the cash flows by the after-tax cost of debt.

NOTES

[1] A. *FASB STATEMENTS*
  i. *SFAS 13*, "Accounting for Leases."
  ii. *SFAS 17*, "Initial Direct Costs."
  iii. *SFAS 22*, "Leases and Tax-Exempt Property."
  iv. *SFAS 23*, "Inception of the Lease."
  v. *SFAS 26*, "Profit Recognition on Sales-Type Leases of Real Estate."
  vi. *SFAS 27*, "Classification of Renewals or Extensions."
  vii. *SFAS 28*, "Accounting for Sales with Leasebacks."
  viii. *SFAS 29*, "Determining Contingent Rentals."

B. *FASB Interpretations*
  i. *FASB Int. 19*, "Lessee Guaranty of Residual Value."
  ii. *FASB Int. 21*, "Leases in Business Combinations."
  iii. *FASB Int. 23*, "Leases of Government Property."
  iv. *FASB Int. 24*, "Leases on Part of a Building."
  v. *FASB Int. 26*, "Purchase of Leased Asset by a Lessee."
  vi. *FASB Int. 27*, "Loss on a Sublease."

[2] FASB, *Statement of Financial Accounting Standards No. 13*, "Accounting for Leases" (Stamford, Conn., November 1976).

621

27

Raising Funds for Capital Projects: How to Arrange External Financing

Charles R. Frank, Jr.

Salomon Brothers

PROJECT FINANCING

Sponsors of capital projects most often finance the projects with their own funds. If a project is large, however, sponsors may not be able to raise all of the required funds on their own credit and may need to supplement the financing from other sources. Some sponsors may have more than enough ability to finance a project on their own, but they wish to preserve their ability to access the debt and equity markets using their own name and credit. In these situations project sponsors may turn to *project financing* in which the sponsors finance only a portion of the project with their own funds. The balance of the debt and equity for the project is raised "without recourse" to the project sponsors; recourse is only to the cash flows generated by the project itself. In project financing the nonrecourse lenders do not sign loan agreements with the sponsors but with a project entity created especially for the purpose of owning or leasing the project assets. Equity investors do not look to the project sponsors for return on their investment but to the rewards of project ownership.

Credit

If a project is financed with recourse to the project sponsors, the investors, whether they be lenders or holders of equity, tend to be concerned only with the credit of the project sponsors. They analyze sponsor's debt/equity ratio, his interest or fixed-charge coverage ratios, his liquidity, and overall business prospects. Investors are usually less concerned with the viability of the project itself. If the project fails, the sponsor is still responsible for paying back his loans with interest and still responsible for paying dividends on equity shares. Unless the project is a very big one relative to the size of the companies sponsoring it, investors are not subject to a great deal of "project risk." Rather, their exposure is to the "credit risk" of the companies sponsoring the project.

In nonrecourse project financing the investors are far more concerned with the credit of the project itself. They will be concerned about the credit of the sponsors as well, since frequently in project financing the sponsors themselves will have contractual relationships with the project, such as offtake agreements, completion guarantees, and supply agreements, which can enhance the credit of the project. But investors will also pay very close attention to three basic indicators of project credit: (1) the ratio of project debt to project equity, (2) project cash flow coverage of debt service, and (3) project liquidity.

The ratio of debt to equity is important because if a project fails, and the assets are sold, the lenders have a superior claim on the assets compared to the equity investors. The higher the amount of equity relative to the amount of debt, the greater is the likelihood that lenders to the project will recover their investment in the project.

Lenders are concerned about debt service coverage because, to the extent that cash is available, lenders are entitled first to receipt of interest and repayments of principal. Equity investors have a subordinated claim on available cash. Lenders, therefore, want to be assured of a relatively high ratio of project cash flow to debt service. The higher the ratio, the less the perceived degree of project risk.

In addition to debt/equity ratios and debt service coverage indicators, project lenders look for indication that the project will not default because of a lack of liquidity. Thus, they want to see that the project has adequate working capital and adequate reserves of cash and cash equivalents at all times.

In some projects equity may be supplemented by quasi-equity or mezzanine financing of one form or another. This may include subordinated debt in which lenders take a subordinated position with respect to senior debt but a senior position with respect to equity; convertible debt in which lenders receive a lower interest rate in return for the right to convert their loans into equity shares; and preferred equity shares which have a subordinated position with respect to debt but a senior position in respect to common equity.

A project financing is far more complex and difficult to arrange than a direct financing by the project sponsors. It also tends to be more expensive. Investors will want to satisfy themselves that the project economics are sound, governmental regulations and controls will not present insurmountable obstacles to the project's success, the project risks are manageable and within limits, and the sponsors provide appropriate support of the project through an equity investment of their own or through meaningful contractual relationships with the project entity.

Project Economics

Good project economics is perhaps the most important consideration in the success of any project financing. The marketability of project outputs and the availability of supply of project inputs need to be assured. Estimated rates of return on total investment must be sufficient to cover debt service and provide an adequate return on equity.

The return on equity for a project can be broken down into two components. First, a project may generate a positive cash flow if revenues are in excess of operating costs. The return deriving from positive cash flow is sometimes called the cash-on-cash return of the project.

Second, most projects typically generate tax credits and deductions in excess of those required to shelter the taxable income generated by the project. These credits and deductions can be used to shelter other income of the equity investors in the project. By taking account of the tax shelter aspects of a project, the rate of return can be substantially higher than the cash-on-cash return. Investors might look for an aftertax rate of return in the range of 10 to 20 percent (a pretax equivalent return of 18 to 37 percent), again depending on the degree of project risk.

Ideally, cash-on-cash and aftertax returns should be estimated assuming that the project takes on no debt. If the equity investors leverage their investments with debt, rates of return can be enhanced, but the risks to the equity investors are increased. Returns from various projects can be compared independently of differences in leverage if rates of return are computed on the basis of 100 percent equity investment.

Sometimes projects do not generate an adequate return on a cash-on-cash basis, but when tax benefits are taken into account, the returns may be more than sufficient. Investors tend to be wary of projects for which rates of return depend mostly on the availability of tax benefits since the investors are especially exposed to the risk of a loss of tax benefits. Furthermore, the U.S. Internal Revenue Service tends to take a dim view of investments motivated solely by tax benefits. By law tax credits and deduction associated with such projects can be disallowed unless it can be established that there are economic motivations for the investment aside from the immediate tax benefits.

Economics are crucial to a project's success even if project sponsors are willing to offer a great deal of support through contractual undertakings with the project entity. If the project economics are poor, the sponsors may eventually begin to look for legal and contractual escapes from their obligation to honor those contracts. In the case of the Washington Public Power Supply System, for example, a large number of small communities signed take-or-pay contracts which were thought to provide adequate credit support for the nuclear project. The affected communities petitioned the state courts and won their case on the grounds that the communities could not legally enter into take-or-pay contracts. The financing of many gas and oil pipelines in the United States is supported by throughput and deficiency agreements which obligate the pipeline sponsors to ship specified amounts through the pipeline at agreed prices or to make up the cash deficiency caused by lower throughput. Recently, a major shipper invoked *force majeure* to avoid its obligations under its throughput and deficiency agreement. In both cases if the project economics had been more solid, the project sponsors may not have been so determined to find a way out of performing under their contracts.

Government Involvement

Project economics can be adversely affected if the project sponsors fail to receive appropriate governmental licenses, permits, and other required official approvals in a timely fashion. Environmental regulations and controls often make projects difficult. Time delays in preparing environmental impact statements and achieving the necessary governmental approvals can have a very adverse impact on the costs of the project and on the rate of return on investment. In the nuclear power industry the safety standards and controls imposed by the Nuclear Regulatory Commission have made many partially finished nuclear projects uneconomic to complete.

Project financings in regulated industries in the United States can be successful only if the tariffs allowed by the relevant regulatory body, typically either a state regulatory commission or the Federal Energy Regulatory Commission, are sufficient to cover operating costs and debt service. A number of pipelines have been financed on the basis of FERC-approved tariffs. Some coal-conversion projects have been or are expected to be financed by reliance on a specially enacted electricity tariff at the state level. Failure of a regulatory body to provide adequate assurances and approvals for the proposed tariff plan, however, can destroy a project's economics.

Sometimes governments will provide subsidies, special tax advantages, or other means of support for projects in fields deemed to be in the public interest. While government supports can be helpful to the success of a project, investors tend to discount the value of supports because the political environment can change very quickly and make the supports no longer tenable. Furthermore, the bureaucratic approvals required to obtain government supports can often be very consuming of managerial time and talent. Many U.S. companies, for example, have made substantial investments in synthetic fuel projects only to be frustrated by the repeated political difficulties experienced by the U.S. Synthetic Fuels Corporation and the difficult requirements of its bureaucracy.

Project Risk

Successful project financing requires not only expectations of adequate rates of return on investment but also an assessment that the risks associated with those rates of returns are not excessive. It is hard to quantify project risks, but one way to approach the problem of risk is to estimate project returns in a worst-case scenario.

Project lenders are usually very sensitive to project risks. Lenders do not have the upside potential that attracts equity investors to projects. They are, therefore, more concerned about getting their loans repaid with interest, even in a worst-case scenario.

Some of the project risks that most concern lenders are the following.

Completion risk. Projects involving complicated or advanced technology run the risk of failing to meet anticipated performance standards. Even projects with a simple technology may take much longer to complete than anticipated. Failure to complete a project by a certain date adds to the cost of the project since interest continues to accrue on outstanding debt. The costs of some of the nuclear projects under construction in the United States, for example, will be inflated more because of interest accrued during construction rather than increases in direct construction costs.

Market price risk. The economics of many projects is highly sensitive to fluctuating prices for both outputs and basic inputs. Many energy and mineral projects have floundered because energy and mineral prices did not sustain the high levels reached in the 1970s. Processing industries such as petroleum and metal refineries, chemical plants, and food processing companies can get squeezed as the prices of the products they produce decline relative to the prices of the raw materials they consume. Projects with relatively high operating costs (including labor, fuel, or raw materials) are especially vulnerable to adverse price movements.

Market quantity risks. For some projects, particularly in regulated industries for which prices are controlled, the risk is great that the market will not absorb the anticipated output or utilize fully the project's capacity. Other projects run the risk that supply of basic raw materials or labor supply may be unreliable.

Operating risk. A project may have been completed on time and at cost, may have excellent markets for its outputs, and may have reliable and relatively inexpensive sources of raw material and other inputs, but the project may fail if the plant does not operate efficiently, requires excessive maintenance and repairs, or is plagued by frequent unscheduled plant outages. The more sophisticated the technology, the more likely the project will be characterized by a high degree of operating risk.

Legal and regulatory risk. Many projects are subject to substantial legal and regulatory risks, including failure to meet environmental quality control standards, obtain appropriate operating permits and licenses, and meet requisite safety standards. Sometimes it may be anticipated that a project will meet all relevant standards at the initiation of construction—but the rules may change and the new rules are applied to the project afterward. This can be especially destructive of a project's economics. Regulatory risks are greatest in those industries whose prices are regulated by governmental bodies. Some regulatory entities are sensitive to the needs of project investors while others are not. Regulatory legislation, regulatory entities, or the political environment in which they operate can change, making it increasingly difficult to obtain prices that can assure an adequate rate of return on capital invested in a project.

Tax risk. The tax benefits associated with investments in projects can be substantial. In the United States investors can receive a tax credit of 10 percent of their total investment. Under the Tax Equity and Fiscal Responsibility Act of 1982 (TEFRA), capital investments are depreciated according to the accelerated cost recovery system (ACRS). Under this system most investments in machinery and equipment are depreciated over five years, as opposed to the previous rule which was based on estimates of useful economic life of the assets (the asset depreciation range or ADR system). The investment tax credits and the ACRS system are very advantageous to project investors; the tax benefits alone can be worth 35 to 40 percent of the total value of the project. Under these circumstances investors are likely to be very concerned about the risk of loss of the tax benefits.

Sponsor Support

It is rare that a project's economics will provide lenders with sufficient comfort that their investment in the project is secure. Lenders will be looking for some form of involvement by the sponsors. One of the most effective forms of involvement is for the project sponsors to make an equity investment in the project. If the project sponsors make a substantial equity investment, the balance of the financing may be raised through project loans without recourse to the project sponsors.

Frequently, however, project sponsors are not willing to make large equity investments in projects but are willing to provide support through contractual undertakings with the project entity. These contractual undertakings can be a substitute for equity and enable a project to be financed with a greater degree of leverage, that is, a higher proportion of nonrecourse debt. Some of the more common forms of contractual undertaking in project financings include the following.

Take-or-pay contracts. In a take-or-pay contract the purchaser of a project's output is committed to pay for the output whether or not the output is produced and delivered. The pricing of the output is usually designed to cover all operating costs plus the cost of servicing debt, regardless of how much the project produces. A take-or-pay obligation is most useful in a capital-intensive project. For all practical purposes a taken or contract party can be as effective in supporting the credit as if the project sponsors were to guarantee the project's debt.

Take-and-pay contracts. A take-and-pay contract (sometimes called a take, if tendered, contract) obligates the purchaser of the project's output to pay only if the project produces and delivers the output. A take-and-pay obligation is considerably weaker than a take-or-pay contract since the project rather than the purchaser takes the risk that the project may not produce. If the technology is simple and the operating risk slight, however, a take-and-pay contract can be effective as a means of credit support.

Requirements contracts. Sometimes project sponsors desire an even weaker form of contractual obligation to take project output. Under a requirements contract the purchaser of the project's output is obligated to take all of his requirements for the output from the project and not from any other seller. If the purchaser does not require the output, he is not obligated to make the purchase, even if the project produces and delivers the output.

Capacity charge pricing. Capital-intensive projects are especially vulnerable to variations in the use of the project's capacity. Therefore, purchasers of the project's output may be charged on a two-part pricing basis. A capacity charge is levied which is independent of the amount of output produced or percentage of capacity utilized. An output charge is also levied but only on the basis of actual output produced and sold or percentage of capacity actually utilized. Two-part pricing schemes are typical of electric power and pipeline projects. In the electric power industry capacity charges are often called demand charges, and output charges are called energy charges. The capacity charge is usually designed to cover the cost of debt service, fixed operating and maintenance expense, and also sometimes a return on equity. The output charge is often designed to cover that portion of operating and maintenance costs which are dependent on the level of output and also sometimes to cover the return on equity.

Fixed and floor prices. In order to reduce some of the market price risk associated with some projects, the output prices may be predetermined or fixed in advance for a period of years. Alternatively, there may be a price floor. If output is sufficient, this assures the project of a minimum revenues stream. If operating costs are not fixed, however, a fixed-price or floor price output contract may be more risky than one in which prices are market determined.

Net cost or net revenue contracts. In a net cost or net revenue contract the project sponsor is obligated to purchase the project's output at a price equal to the net cost of producing the output or to sell an input to the project at a price equal to some percentage of the net revenues generated by the project. In effect, the project sponsor absorbs some or all of the market price risk associated with the project.

Cash deficiency undertakings. Another way for the sponsors to provide credit support for a project is through some form of cash deficiency undertaking. This may take the form of a cash deficiency agreement in which the sponsors agree to make subordinated advances or contribute additional equity to the project if the cash flow generated by the project is insufficient to meet all of the contractual payment obligations of the project entity. Cash deficiency obligations are frequently an integral part of throughput and deficiency agreements used to support pipeline financings. A cash deficiency obligation can take other forms, such as a working capital maintenance agreement or an agreement by a purchaser of project output to make advance payments against future deliveries of output or a provider of basic projects inputs to defer payments for current deliveries of inputs.

Loan guarantees. Sponsors can provide a relatively direct form of credit support for a project undertaking through loan guarantees. Sponsors are often reluctant to guarantee loans because the obligation, while contingent and normally off the balance sheet, must be fully disclosed and is perceived by credit analysts to be a direct charge against the credit of a corporate sponsor. Sponsors may reason that, under these circumstances, it is better to provide equity funds to the project rather than guarantees.

Accounting Aspects

The accounting treatment of a sponsor's support obligation depends: first, on his ownership share of the project; and second, on the nature of any contractual relationships with the project. If the sponsor owns 20 percent or less of the project, his interest in the venture is normally accounted for on a cost basis. That is, the sponsor records his investment on his balance sheet as the lesser of the original cost of acquisition or market value of the investment. If the sponsor owns at least 20 percent and not more than 50 percent of the project, it is normally accounted for on an equity basis. That is, the investment is recorded on the balance sheet on an original cost basis and is increased (or decreased) by the proportionate amount of the joint venture undistributed earnings (or losses), subject to the constraint that the carrying amount of the investment cannot exceed its realizable value. If the sponsor owns more than 50 percent, the assets and liabilities of the joint venture are generally fully consolidated in the financial statements of the sponsor. The economic structure of the ownership percentage must be considered; ownership of 50 percent or less may result in consolidation if, for example, control rests with that party. Even if the equity or cost method is used, however, the sponsor may be required to disclose financial information pertaining to the joint venture if certain materiality tests are met.

The sponsor's contractual relationship with the project entity, whether or not the sponsor has an ownership interest in the project entity, also affects accounting treatment. For example, an obligation to purchase project output is an unconditional purchase obligation according to *Financial Accounting Standard No. 47* if it is an obligation to transfer funds in the future for fixed or minimum amounts or quantities of goods or services at fixed or minimum prices. An unconditional purchase obligation that has all of the following characteristics shall be disclosed in footnotes to the financial statements:

1. Is noncancelable, or cancelable only:
   a. Upon the occurrence of some contingency;
   b. With permission of the other party;
   c. If a replacement agreement is signed between the same parties; or
   d. Upon payment of a penalty in an amount such that continuation of the agreement appears reasonably assured;
2. Was negotiated as part of arranging financing for the facilities that will provide the contracted goods or services or for costs related to those goods or services; or
3. Has a remaining term in excess of one year.

The disclosure shall include:

1. The nature and term of the obligation.
2. The amount of the fixed and determinable portion of the obligation as of the date of the latest balance sheet presented in the aggregate and, if determinable, for each of the five succeeding fiscal years.
3. The nature of any variable components of the obligation.
4. The amounts purchased under the obligation for each period for which an income statement is presented.

Guarantees of debt of the project entity are disclosed as to amount in the footnotes. Cash deficiency agreements and working capital maintenance agreements may be classified as indirect guarantees, in which case they are disclosed as guarantees. Otherwise such obligations, to the extent that they are not fixed and determinable, are not quantified but may be described in the footnotes.

Third-Party Support

If project sponsors are unwilling or unable to provide the credit support necessary to finance a project, it is sometimes possible to obtain some form of third-party credit support. There are three main types of such support: governmental grants and guarantees, bank guarantees or letters of credit, and insurance.

The U.S. government has a variety of loans, grants, and loan guarantee programs such as Title XI ship financing, loans and guarantees by the Rural Electrification Administration, the Department of Energy grants program, grants by the Economic Development Administration, and loans and guarantees of the U.S. Export-Import Bank, the U.S. Agency for International Development, and the U.S. Synthetic Fuels program. Foreign governments have similar support programs; many have particularly aggressive export credit schemes. Multinational governmental organizations such as the World Bank, the International Finance Corporation, and the regional development banks have cofinancing and guarantee programs which can sometimes be of assistance in project financing.

Commercial bank guarantees and letters of credit can be essential in a number of instances. For example, if one of the sponsors is not a creditworthy entity, its obligations may be supported by a bank letter of credit. If the sponsor fails to make an advance under a cash deficiency agreement, the lenders to other sponsors of the project may be able to draw under the letter of credit to satisfy the obligation of the defaulting sponsor. Letters of credit may be issued by a group of banks to support lease rental or debt service payment obligations of the project since the banks may be in a better position to evaluate the project sides than institutional investors in lease equity or institutional lenders to the project.

Insurance can cover a number of risks, including casualty risks and business interruption risks. Surety bonds issued by insurance companies can be used in a fashion similar to bank letters of credit in order to support performance obligations of sponsors or other interested parties such as the engineer and construction firm building the project.

632

Attracting Project Equity

A project sponsor or sponsors may wish to attract other sources of equity into the project for a number of reasons, including the following:

- The sponsor or sponsors may not be able to utilize fully all of the tax benefits associated with the project. They may wish to bring in other equity investors to share in the tax benefits.
- The project may be too large for the project sponsor or sponsors. They may not feel comfortable with providing all of the required equity or contractual support for the project.
- The sponsors may lack certain technical expertise or capabilities needed to construct or operate the project successfully and may wish to bring a partner into the transaction who possesses the requisite expertise.

If the sponsors are looking for a joint venture partner to share in the business risks, then they would most likely be looking for a partner with specific expertise and knowledge of the industry in which the project is located. Typically, project sponsors know well which other corporations would have an interest in their project, and the sponsors would seek out partners on their own. Sometimes, however, they hire investment bankers to help in the search for joint venture partners.

If the sponsors are looking for a partner to share in the tax benefits but not necessarily in all of the business risks involved in the project, then they would look toward either tax-oriented institutional investors or high-income individuals. Tax-oriented institutional investors are typically finance companies associated with commercial banks or industrial companies. These investors are usually interested primarily for the tax benefits associated with investment in the project. They tend to be very reluctant to take project risk and are more like lenders in their aversion to project risk. Tax-oriented institutional investors usually prefer to invest in a project as a lessor of equipment.

High-income individuals are often willing to invest in projects as limited partners. Usually, they tend to be most interested in the tax shelter aspects of the investment, but they are also willing to assume some degree of project risk.

Project Loans

Lenders to projects can be divided into two major groups: commercial bank lenders and institutional lenders such as insurance companies and

633

pension funds. Commercial bank lenders often are willing to lend on a nonrecourse basis to projects, thereby assuming some degree of project risk, but of course they will charge for it by lending funds at a substantial spread over their cost of funds. Commercial banks will typically lend on a floating-rate basis, using either the current bank prime rate, the bank certificate of deposit rate, or the current London Interbank Offered Rate (LIBOR) as the indicator rate. Commercial banks rarely lend beyond 10 years for a project, although in rare instances they may lend 12 or 15 years.

Institutional investors, by way of contrast, are usually more reluctant to assume project risk. They feel more comfortable in lending directly to the sponsors rather than on a nonrecourse basis to the project. They will more often, however, lend on a fixed-rate basis for the term of the loan and will sometimes lend for 15 or even up to 20 or 25 years, depending on the project.

A number of important issues must be addressed in structuring project loans. The loan repayment schedule must be compatible with cash flow generated by the project. Equity investors generally like extended debt repayment terms because they are usually anxious to have access to the project's cash flow. Lenders wish to assure themselves that the equity investors do not withdraw cash early in the project life if the project creditors are left without resources when cash flow is insufficient in the later years to service debt. Thus, debt repayment terms are often structured so that a certain percentage of any excess cash flow must be used to prepay or defease project debt. Alternatively, project sponsors may be subject to clawback provisions under which they are responsible to make cash available later in the project life to the extent that they have taken cash from the project in the early years.

Project debt may be variable rate or fixed rate, depending on the source and the needs of the project. Increasingly, however, currencies in which project revenues and operating costs are denominated may differ. The project sponsors can often borrow, however, in whatever currency provides the best borrowing terms and adjust the currency of denomination through currency swaps.

In the financing of projects, there are a number of structural forms that are very common. These include leasing and partnerships in particular.

Leasing

A lease structure is typically used as a vehicle for attracting tax-oriented equity into a project financing. In a typical lease the tax-oriented equity investors purchase capital equipment by providing a portion of their own funds and borrowing the remainder on a nonrecourse basis to the equity investors. The equity investors claim the investment tax credits and depreciation associated with ownership of the equipment. The equity investors lease the equipment to the project sponsors or a special-purpose project entity established by the sponsors. The sponsors or the special-purpose entity is obligated to make periodic lease payments, usually semiannually, the proceeds of which are used by the lessor to service the nonrecourse debt.

In order to qualify as a lease for U.S. federal income tax purposes and for the equity investors to be entitled to the tax benefits, certain tests must be met, including the following: (1) the lease term should be no more than 80 percent of the estimated useful economic life of the equipment being leased; (2) the residual value of the equipment must be at least 20 percent of the original cost of the equipment; (3) the lessee should not be able to purchase the facilities at the end of the lease term at a bargain price; and (4) the property being leased should not be limited-use property.

The accounting treatment of a lease from the lessee's perspective is based on *Financial Accounting Standard No. 13,* according to which a lease is classified either as an operating lease or as a capital lease. The lease is a capital lease if any one of the following four conditions is satisfied:

1. The present value of the lease rental is 90 percent or more of the fair market value of the leased property at the inception of the lease, less the investment tax credit utilized by the lessor.
2. The lessee has an option to purchase the facility at a bargain price.
3. Ownership of the property is transferred to the lessee at the end of the lease term.
4. The lease term is 75 percent or more of the estimated economic life of the leased property.

If the lease is a capital lease, the present value of the lease rentals is shown as a long-term obligation on the balance sheet of the lessee. If the lease is an operating lease, the present value is not shown on the balance sheet. Instead, the obligation is disclosed in a footnote to the financial statements of the lessee and is quantified in the footnote to the extent that the lease obligation is unconditional.

Normally, lease obligations are commitments to pay periodic, fixed lease rentals over a specified period of time. It is possible, however, to

635

structure a lease agreement so that lease rentals are contingent upon the output or capacity utilization of the project facility. In these circumstances, to the extent that the lease obligation is not fixed and determinable, it need not be quantified on the balance sheet or in a footnote. The contingent lease obligation, however, may need to be described in a footnote.

Partnerships

A frequently used method of organizing a project entity is a partnership. In a partnership the individual partners are entitled to a pro rata share of the tax benefits associated with ownership of the assets. The tax benefits can take the form of tax credits such as the investment tax credit, energy credits, research and development credits, or accelerated depreciation.

The advantage of a partnership structure is that the partnership itself, unlike a corporation, does not pay taxes. A partnership, therefore, is a means of avoiding double taxation.

A partnership may have limited partners as well as general partners. Limited partners have limited liabilities and usually various limitations on their returns as well.

If a sponsor of a project cannot utilize all of the tax benefits associated with the project, there are a variety of techniques that may be used to transfer the benefits to other partners in the project. For example, another sponsor may be better able to utilize the benefits. In this case it may be possible to allocate the tax benefits, as well as the profits and losses, of the partnership in one manner during the initial years of project operation and then to change (flip) the allocation after a number of years. Since tax credits vest after five years and accelerated depreciation benefits often run out after five years, it is usually advantageous to structure the transaction so that the flip occurs after five years. The partners having the ability to utilize tax benefits receive a higher allocation in the initial years and a lower allocation in the later years.

Another often-used technique is to sell limited partnership interests to outsiders, usually high-income individuals with a strong need to shelter income from federal income taxes. The marketing of limited partnership interests is usually done through a retail brokerage establishment. Limited partnership interests may also be sold to institutional investors with a need for tax shelter, but institutional investors typically prefer to invest in leasing arrangements rather than as limited partners in a project joint venture.

V

Implementing a
Capital Project

28

Project Management: How to Move from the Proposal Stage to Project Completion

---

Herbert Berman

ORU Group

INTRODUCTION

A capital project is a long-term investment that either involves installing new facilities or reconditioning old ones. In each case a significant amount of money will be spent. This year business will spend over $300 billion on new plants and equipment. If the past is any indication, capital expenditures could easily reach $600 billion by 1990.

This type of investment demands strict accountability of project costs, especially when project financing becomes more difficult and more costly. Also, the timing of completion of these capital projects is an important consideration because every day the plant is not on-line could mean lost sales and added expenses.

With cost and time so critical to a project, owners can ill afford to delegate project management to others. Yet it happens. Owners typically focus their attention on technical engineering and plant operations while delegating the management of the project to the engineering-construction firms (E/C). This probably occurs because the owners feel the E/C firms must be good managers since they've been doing design and construction for many years. However, there are several complications with this.

First, there is the question of management style. For the capital projects we've worked on, the E/C firm assembles a management team ranging from 20 to 500 key personnel, depending on project size and complexity. These people may never have worked together, may not even know each other, and may use variations of a management system that was used on their most recent project by their project manager. There are bound to be differing management attitudes and styles, which may or may not be consistent with the client's expectation of project management. Second, the E/C firm assembles its team only after it has been given the notice to proceed. The team members will have varying degrees of familiarity with the project. Some have provided technical services during the project development stage. Others have designed similar plants. Still others will be added to the project as time progresses. The learning time to bring the team "up to speed" will usually affect the project schedule. Finally, the owner must realize that E/C firms manage projects based on their own business profitability, rather than minimizing cost and time for the owner. Improved labor productivity and coordination, for example, are not strong components of the E/C management process. Typically, the E/C control systems focus on project progress rather than on identifying problems. So any potential cost deviations or time delays generally tend to be glossed over in their reports. It is because of these factors that the owner (or financial lender) must maintain a management role in the project. The owner must provide direction to the project and cannot delegate to the E/C the responsibility of completing the project on time and within budget.

Project management is managing and directing the timing and quantity of personnel, materials, skills, and knowledge to complete a project in an orderly manner while meeting the objectives in time, cost, and technical results. Project management has two functions: direction and control. For direction the project management group tells the functional experts of engineering, procurement, and construction what is needed (in terms of drawings, equipment, etc.), how many dollars are available for the activity, and when the activity must be completed.

On the control side it measures the course of the project, analyzes the results, and ensures that it proceeds on schedule and within budget.

In Part V, Implementing A Capital Project, we will outline the basics of project management for capital projects, pulling together the many concepts and experiences the ORU Group has assembled over the last 20 years for more than 200 projects. We begin our discussion from the time the project is officially recognized as having merit. This means that the project initiator has already developed a preliminary budget and schedule, has some concept of an organizational structure, and has some general operating policies and procedures. It is important to realize that these four documents are not for presentation purposes only. Once the board of directors has approved the capital appropriations, these documents form the basis for more detailed planning. For a project to have credibility with senior management, new budgets and schedules requesting more money and time extension should not be considered.

Receiving proper attention from the company is only the project's first step. To reach fruition will require coordinating many groups of people and providing effective direction throughout the duration of the project. This is the function of project management.

For modest-sized projects (say, a million dollars) the project manager may perform these tasks alone. However, for larger projects, the project manager needs support in the furnishing of the many project management services. In this respect an experienced professional team is needed. The successful completion of a project is closely related to the skills of the entire team. Therefore, its selection should be given considerable thought.

CHOOSING A PROJECT MANAGER

The activities involved with project management come from a series of interrelated job functions (process design, piping and instrumentation specifications, equipment procurement, site preparation, etc.). A project manager's function is essentially planning these activities over a specific period of time and monitoring them to ensure that the project deadline is met at minimum cost and maximum quality. To do this requires directing, coordinating, and controlling the efforts of the people involved with engineering, procurement, construction, and suppliers.

In this regard it would be helpful if the project manager is familiar with the engineering-construction process and possesses the knowledge of how a plant is designed and built. Most important, the manager must be schedule- and cost-conscious with previous experience in project management and a background in project work.

The project manager takes an active part in the execution of the project and serves as the final approval authority for matters relating to design, plans, progress, and costs. The manager has the responsibility to determine when each project area is complete and has the authority to accept the completed area. Specifically, the project manager has the following duties: organize and plan the project; authorize project work; direct the progress of the work; meet with senior management to report and discuss project status, progress, and changes; identify and establish priorities; and resolve conflicts within the scope of responsibility.

To do this job requires many different skills. The project manager must be a communicator, since he will be dealing with people having many different personalities. In many cases the project manager must exercise his responsibilities involving people over whom he has no authority to manage. In this respect he must be persuasive, receptive, and diplomatic. This applies not only to the groups mentioned above but also to senior management. He is the one person responsible for seeing the project through to completion and is the one to whom top management will look for project information and status.

He must also be a decision maker, one who can analyze and solve problems and then take corrective action. In addition he must be a leader who can understand and be sensitive to people. Often he will be called on to reduce tensions, negotiate difficulties, and motivate others to the achievement of common goals. He will have to handle a lot of different situations. To do this, he will have to be aggressive and convincing, but it also helps to have a bit of humor, humility, and common sense.

As you will see, the scheduling and control of a project is a very complex job. It is full of stress and demands long hours. The project manager will be required to have an intimate knowledge of what is planned and expected when monitoring project progress. He must, therefore, be able to organize and set objectives. Finally, there is a need for objectivity. For the project manager to have credibility with senior management and with the E/C firms, he has to be able to report his findings in a fair and accurate manner. He must not be concerned whether someone looks "bad" or "good" but must focus on what it takes to get the job done right. He must also be ready to accept the blame or credit for his actions. The company's goals must be put ahead of his own career ambitions.

With all this said and done, it looks as though a person would have to be either insane or superhuman to accept this position. However, all is not so bleak. The project manager's first objective is usually to build a multidisciplined team and delegate some of his authority and responsibilities. Team building is an important function and is critical in order for the project manager to be able to keep on top of things. Now let's turn our attention to what actually sets the basis for project management.

DEFINING THE PROGRAM

Program definition essentially involves what work has to be done and who is going to do it. There are four major tasks involved with defining the program:

1. Establish the project strategies.
2. Define the reorganization structure required to meet these strategies.
3. Establish the methodologies necessary for the organization to manage and control the project.
4. Implement these methodologies.

Task 1—Establish Project Strategies

The project strategies establish the ground rules for all the parties involved and include such items as project scope, budget, schedule, and company policies. Project scope sets the boundaries to which the project will be confined. It includes items such as:

1. *Design basis*—capacity throughput, product slate, quality specifications, raw materials, utilities and equipment requirements, range of operating conditions, etc.
2. *Site preparation*—location, land requirements, refurbishing or scrapping of existing equipment, soil testing, foundation requirements, etc.
3. *Contracting policy*—determination of the packaging of purchases and the type of contracts to be used.
4. *Equipment procurement*—list of acceptable vendors, bid evaluation criteria.
5. *Contractor selection*—degree of outside contract work, evaluation criteria for engineering and construction firms.

As engineering work proceeds, some revisions in scope may be advisable, as evident by more detailed study. When revisions are made late in the project, or when the magnitude of these revisions exceed about 10 percent of the initial project cost, serious effects are felt in the

FIGURE 1

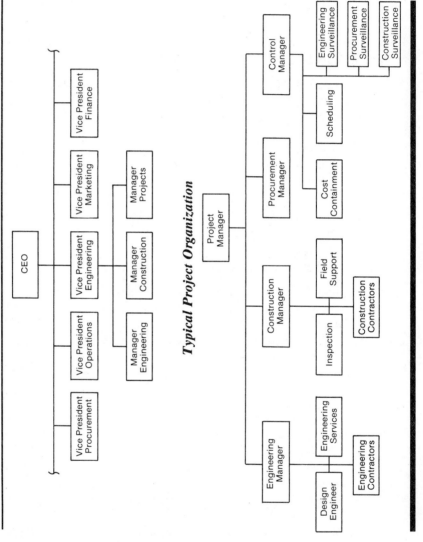

Typical Organization Chart for a Large Company

Typical Project Organization

project schedule. Scope revisions should only be considered within the early stages of engineering. Not to do so will cause scheduling problems in the subsequent construction phase. Excessive revisions or changes when the engineering phase is beyond 50 percent complete should be avoided. Changes during the project are inevitable but can be minimized in advance by a well-defined scope of work.

The *budget* is a reflection of the costs involved with the project scope. Once approved, it becomes a yardstick for measuring cost performance. It should be a definitive estimate of the workerhour requirements, wage and hourly rates, equipment requirements and costs, escalation factors, and costs connected with possible changes and additions to scope.

The *schedule* is a written plan involving the timetable of activities to be accomplished, and it becomes the basis for tracking on-time performance. The schedule should contain the following information:

1. Completion date.
2. Operational dates for individual project areas.
3. Key engineering and construction activities.
4. Critical path(s) that establish the completion date, taking into account the time required for engineering drawing releases, bid invitations, equipment manufacture and delivery, foundation construction, etc.

The company's policies center around the extent of involvement of the owner in the project activities. For example, should procurement be handled in-house or by the contractor, or should there be a project manager and a team or just the project manager and the contracted engineering firm? These policies must be decided early on and will dictate the structure for Task 2.

Task 2—Define Reorganization Structure

It has been ORU's experience that a company's existing operating structure generally will not lend itself to the effective coordination of all project activities. This is essential in order to successfully control time and cost. A project reorganization will delineate managerial responsibilities, reporting relationships, and the overall organization interrelationships. It provides the structure to maintain control over quality, cost, and schedule for each phase of the project (design, procurement, construction, and start-up). An example of how project management fits within an organization is shown in Figure 1. This type of structure does the following:

I. Ensures that project responsibility will focus on one individual who will have the time and perspective necessary to make decisions that incorporate all factors.

II. Provides for a dedicated project control group with responsibility for critical control functions such as:

    A. Developing and maintaining integrated cost and schedule plans.

    B. Conducting the surveillance of engineering, procurement, and construction activities.

    C. Analyzing cost and schedule data and reporting the status, trends, and projections to project management with recommendations for action.

Task 3—Establish Methodologies

The methodologies for managing and controlling the project involve the flow of information and contractual arrangements. A management information system (MIS) provides current and timely information to the owner concerning the project status, progress, and potential problems. An MIS basically establishes a procedure for the flow of information within the organization. The owner must have factual information to judge the project's viability, manage time and money requirements, and influence the activities and emphasis of the E/C firms. The MIS should provide senior management with objective appraisals of project status, commitments, best forecast of operations to date, most likely cost at completion, and realistic cash flow needs.

For the system to work, two things are needed. First, a set of operating policies and procedures must be developed for the control of all design, procurement, and construction activities. These procedures will treat every phase of the project control in regard to organization, administration, document distribution, type and frequency of reports, and management meetings. Second, the degree of involvement by the owner for such items as approval of engineering and construction drawings, bid review, and overtime should be established at the onset of the project. It is important to determine the extent of detailed checking and surveillance since this will affect the team size and the overall cost of the project. A cost/value analysis should be done to completely understand the impact on the project of additional checking by the owner's organization.

Because outside engineering firms, construction firms, and equipment vendors are integral parts of the project, their selection is a significant decision. Let's examine each participant. Earlier, under project scope, equipment procurement was mentioned as an important item. This is because the source, cost, and delivery of material and equipment will affect the project's success. During the early stages of engineering, an acceptable vendor's list is developed, usually based on the owner's preferences. This list will provide the basic source from which to seek vendor quotations on all equipment and bulk materials. As several equipment deliveries will be critical to the schedule, selected vendors will be investigated to determine current shop loads and production capabilities. Unsatisfactory performance can cause certain vendors to be removed from the list.

As for E/C firms, it is necessary to request proposals from several contractors for engineering and construction. The evaluation criteria will be based on the company's prior experience with the firm, the firm's capabilities in similar ventures, location of the engineering offices, fee, and references. The fee is usually based on one of five contracts: lump sum, cost plus, guaranteed maximum, target price, or turnkey. Each of these contracts is described in Figure 2, together with their advantages and disadvantages.

Because contracts are legal documents, the corporate attorney should provide assistance in developing the wording and in administering the contracts once they are signed. It is important to include a clause stating that the owner has the rights to any and all data generated by the E/C firm, such as engineering drawings, workerhour calculations, time sheets, etc. If this is not spelled out in the contract, the owner may end up paying for these items later on. Also, without these data it would be difficult to control the project.

After the E/C firms are selected, the next step is to assign responsibilities to each participant. Representative functions concerning preliminary engineering, final engineering, construction, and start-up are shown in Figure 3, which also delineates owner's and contractors' responsibilities.

Task 4—Implement the Methodologies

The underlying theme of Figure 3 is that project management is the responsibility of the owner. However, the owner will normally need to supplement the project team with specialized consulting services. Those services must be independent of the engineering or contracting firms selected to perform the project activities. In this manner the owner is assured an independent, nonvested support to the project management team.

Because there are several project participants, the owner must actively influence each of them toward the common goal of proper

FIGURE 2

Types of Contracts for Engineering and Construction Firms

Type	Description	Advantages	Disadvantages
1. Lump sum	Agreement to perform the work for a fixed price, regardless of cost to the contractor.	1. Final price is known. 2. Bid evaluation is the one least subject to assumption and judgments, provided the proposals have equal quality. The more exact the design specifications, the easier will be the comparison among bids. 3. Cost risk due to poor productivity borne by contractor. 4. Cost-escalation risk borne by contractor. 5. Risk due to poor subcontractor selection borne by contractor. 6. Least bookkeeping and auditing expense. 7. Requires least amount of owner control.	1. Contractor and owner are in adversary positions. 2. Contractor incentive favors productivity over quality. 3. Contractor incentive favors low-price materials and low-bid subcontractors over quality materials and workmanship. 4. Contractor incentive favors low-price materials over timely delivery, with resultant risk of schedule slippage. 5. Longest process. Design and construction phases are sequential. Contractor not selected until design substantially complete. 6. Advice of contractor not available during design phase. 7. High cost because of contractor assuming the risks.
2. Cost plus	Agreement to perform the work on the basis of actual cost, plus a percentage (or fixed amount) fee for the contractor.	1. Complete plans are not necessary. General contractor can be selected very early in project. 2. Total design-construction	1. Total cost of job not fixed until very late in project. 2. Risk due to price escalation for materials, equipment, and labor borne by owner.

period is reduced since field work is started immediately and continued as design packages are completed and released to the construction contractor.

4. Advice of contractor is available during design period.

5. Owner has maximum input and control of materials, equipment, and subcontractor selection, with minimum contractor resistance.

6. Contractor incentives same as owner's as to quality of materials, equipment, selection of subcontractors and craftworkmanship.

7. Possible lowest-cost approach with effective control.

1. Restores contractor's economic incentives for achieving a higher productivity for all cost factors.

2. Owner has "known maximum cost" at a relatively early point in the project.

3. Guaranteed maximum — Contractor guarantees that the contract cost will not exceed a specified dollar amount. Usually the guarantee is not established until the design has reached a substantial degree of completion.

3. Cost risk due to poor productivity borne by owner.

4. Commercial evaluation of cost-plus proposals is subject to assumptions and judgments, particularly in area of productivity.

5. Contractor's economic incentives for achieving highest productivity and meeting schedule are weaker because of lack of dollar risk.

6. More work for owner in monitoring costs, bookkeeping, and auditing.

7. Early construction start can cause delays or additional expense if the design is changed.

8. Requires extensive owner control to accumulate potential advantages.

1. Contingency and profit factors are higher than any other contract because of the greater economic risk to the contractor.

2. Contractor placed in adversary position with owner. Same disadvantages listed under lump-sum contract.

FIGURE 2 (*concluded*)

Type	Description	Advantages	Disadvantages
4. Target price	A "target price" is established at some point in the contract life. Both underruns and overruns are shared by the owner and contractor, usually on a percentage basis.	1. Establishes contractor incentive for good cost control. 2. Can combine the advantages of a price guarantee from a lump-sum contract with the flexibility in scheduling and project development of a cost-plus contract.	1. Difficulty in establishing an equitable "target" and in setting the rules permitting "target price" adjustments for changes in scope. If many changes can be anticipated, the method loses much of its value. 2. Same as for a cost-plus contract, with the exception of the price guarantee feature.
5. Turnkey	Owner assigns full responsibility to the contractor for engineering design construction cost (and many times for the performance of the plant).	1. Owner's program and engineering staff can work directly and closely on a continuing basis with one contract entity, experienced in both the design and construction process. 2. Construction may be started before plans are complete, which may produce time savings for the entire project.	1. The check-and-balance system in other contracts does not exist under the design-build method. The owner, contractor, and architect/engineer do not interact so that form, convenience, cost of maintenance, and aesthetics may be unduly sacrificed to low initial cost. 2. The burden on the owner to select a qualified contractor/designer is heavier than other types of contract. When the price is guaranteed and particularly where the contract has been let on a competitive basis, the owner must accept a certain lack of flexibility in obtaining desired features of the work and may have to accept details of the final design which he considers undesirable. 3. Owner pays for contractor assuming the risks.

FIGURE 3

Partial List of Responsibilities for Project Management				
Function	*Owner*	*Owner's engineering staff*	*Engineering contractor*	*Construction contractor*
Define project scope of work	X			
Prepare process specifications	X	X		
Acquire necessary permitting	X			
Respond to all legal requirements	X			
Maintain master workorder files	X			
Contract administration	X			
Prepare project plot plans		X	X	
Develop P&I diagrams		X	X	
Prepare mechanical, electrical, and civil/structural specifications and drawings		X	X	
Prepare equipment bid specifications		X	X	
Make technical evaluations on equipment quotations		X	X	
Make purchase recommendations on equipment		X	X	
Review and approve equipment bid specifications		X		
Control finances on project, including forecast and transfer of funds	X			
Generate cash requirements and reports	X			

FIGURE 3 (*continued*)

Function	Owner	Owner's engineering staff	Engineering contractor	Construction contractor
Maintain necessary insurance coverage on project	X		X	X
Develop complete code of accounts	X	X$_a$*		
Develop cost estimates		X	X	
Analyze cost estimates, develop project cost plan, and report on actual costs	X	X$_a$		
Establish cost-surveillance program which encompasses engineering, procurement, and construction	X			
Prepare and distribute progress reports on design and construction		X	X	X
Report project status, progress, and expenditures to upper levels of management	X			
Determine project warehousing needs and establish facilities	X			
Develop and maintain change order procedures		X$_a$		
Determine and establish utility requirements		X	X	
Maintain construction records and files and distribute necessary data	X			

FIGURE 3 (*continued*)

Function	Owner	Owner's engineering staff	Engineering contractor	Construction contractor
Develop procurement control procedures	X			
Receive, tag, and lay down equipment and materials	X			
Prepare and issue equipment/material receiving reports	X			
Expedite delivery of equipment/material	X			
Coordinate purchasing activities, expediting, inspection, and deliveries of equipment/material with all participants	X			
Develop construction surveillance programs	X			
Maintain the proper relations with the local community	X			
Adhere to all safety and health regulations (OSHA)	X	X	X	X
Perform safety inspections and issue reports	X	X_a		X
Maintain medical and first-aid support functions	X			
Maintain site security	X			
Maintain proper labor relations on project	X			X
Control construction equipment usage				X
Control small tool usage and storage				X

FIGURE 3 (*concluded*)

Function	Owner	Owner's engineering staff	Engineering contractor	Construction contractor
Establish and maintain temporary construction facilities				X
Perform field inspections and maintain required quality control		X	X_a	X
Coordinate all project and construction activities with plant operations	X	X_a		
Develop, plan, and coordinate all plant tie-ins	X			
Develop and initiate plant testing, commissioning, and start-up	X	X_a		

* X_a = Assist as required.

project development. Remember, each of the participants is an operating unit in itself, with their own strengths and weaknesses. Each has vested interests which prevent it from sharing troubles until it is too late. By the time the owner learns of them, the opportunity to take corrective action has been lost. An analysis by ORU shows that major project overruns result mainly from inadequate communication among participants. Some objective form of review and surveillance is required that not only isolates problems but also promotes their solution through cooperative action of all project participants. This is the purpose of project control and involves the project manager and the management team.

BUILDING THE TEAM

Since the responsibilities of project management are enormous, one of the first jobs of the project manager is to select the project team. Members of this team can be divided into two groups. The first group provides *management and control information* to the project manager.

654

Its functions include: (1) providing cost-estimating services, (2) developing a realistic and obtainable schedule, (3) ensuring accurate and timely reporting of expenditures and work progress, (4) developing an early warning system for assessing the impact due to cost overruns and schedule slippages, and (5) taking corrective action to get back on track.

The second group provides the special *technical support* necessary to interact with engineering design, procurement, construction, and project start-up. It also ensures that the quality of the technical design and construction meet the owner's process standards and operational requirements.

The project team staffing level will depend on the degree the owner wants to be involved with the details of engineering and construction. As mentioned before, the extent of checking and approving drawings and of reviewing proposals will affect the number of people on the team. The owner must decide early on, when establishing project strategies, what he should do versus what should be left to the contractor. Obviously, the greater the degree of checking by the owner, the more expensive and longer the project takes to complete.

A typical project management team for projects in the $50 to $60 million range would consist of the following people:

- Project manager—1 person.
- Project control—up to 5 people.
- Procurement management—up to 5 people.
- Accounting and clerical—average of 4 people.
- Construction—up to 20 people.
- Engineering—up to 10 people.
- Operations planning.

The staffing shown above will provide for reviews of plant layout and processes, a reasonable amount of spot checking of important detail areas, and general reviews to ensure that the design meets the owner's established standards and operating needs. The placement of the team members would be as follows:

1. *Project control* must transfer to the field offices as soon as they are established. Control people would remain in the engineer's office until the engineering function is completed.
2. *Procurement management* could be located in the office of the contractors performing the procurement function, provided this function has not been assumed by the owner.
3. *Accounting* would be a field operation.

655

4. *Operations* would start in the engineer's office then relocate to the field.
5. The *construction manager* should start with some time in the engineering offices early in the project then relocate to the field as construction starts.

The project team usually includes the following positions: cost engineers, scheduling engineers, project engineers, procurement personnel, and construction surveillance engineers. The *cost engineer* has the responsibility for all cost-surveillance activities for the project. Specific duties and responsibilities include development of an independent cost-measurement base, early identification of cost trends, preparation of cost forecasts and reports, invoice and commitment approvals, and timely completion of all cost-related functions.

The *cost engineer* is responsible for detailed evaluations of the project estimate including scope description, change orders, cost coding, estimating procedures, and project pricing and maintains a close relationship with the accounting department in relation to all cost aspects. While on site the cost engineer will monitor, analyze, and summarize daily activities to ascertain potential cost impacts.

The *scheduling engineer* develops the project plan (an independent plan encompassing all project activities and requirements, which serves as one of the measuring bases), monitors and evaluates the contractor's schedules, and makes progress assessments. The *project engineer* is responsible for the control of engineering and home office activities. Time is divided between the client's office and the contractor's home office, as conditions require. The *project engineer* monitors and assesses worker utilization productivity, effectiveness of supervisors and lead engineers, compliance with schedules and daily work plans, approvals and turnaround times, and effectiveness of support services.

The *procurement person's* responsibilities include determining sources of supply; developing lists of qualified bidders; soliciting and analyzing bids for services, materials, and equipment; assisting contractors, when appropriate, in expediting and inspecting materials and equipment; arranging for inland, ocean, or air shipment; verifying invoices; and preparing damage claims against suppliers. Last, the *construction surveillance engineer* has the responsibility to monitor all field activity. Specifically, this includes evaluating work force levels and productivity, determining effectiveness of contractor's supervisory staff, assessing daily work plans and their execution, commenting on "housekeeping" and safety factors, evaluating site limitations and temporary facilities, monitoring construction equipment utilization, monitoring performance of subcontractors, assessing warehousing and materials handling effectiveness, authorizing change orders and extras, and providing assistance to project start-up and initial operations.

For some companies project management may be a temporary position. Team members are taken from various parts of the organization. It is our experience that unless these people are given full-time involvement, project responsibilities are usually juggled with their normal work load. Each member's priorities will be different. Quite likely, numerous project-related items get pushed aside only to wind up being with the contractor. When this happens, the owner relinquishes project control to an outside party. Soon schedules start to slip, and/or major cost overruns start piling up. To avoid this, members' time should not be split between project and operations work.

In addition to analysis and control, project management also coordinates the flow of progress data and other control information among all project participants and work locations. Specifically, there are three levels of reporting which project management must address:

- Level I : Executive reports
- Level II : Project control reports
- Level III: Detailed reports

FIGURE 4

Three Levels of Reporting for Project Management

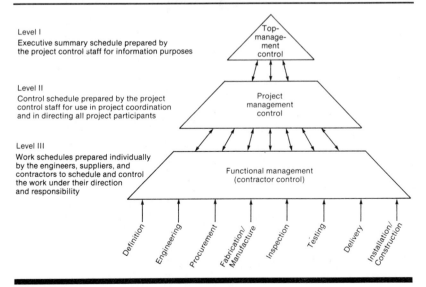

Level I
Executive summary schedule prepared by the project control staff for information purposes

Level II
Control schedule prepared by the project control staff for use in project coordination and in directing all project participants

Level III
Work schedules prepared individually by the engineers, suppliers, and contractors to schedule and control the work under their direction and responsibility

Top-management control

Project management control

Functional management (contractor control)

Definition Engineering Procurement Fabrication/Manufacture Inspection Testing Delivery Installation/Construction

657

FIGURE 5

Responsibilities of Project Management

Improving project performance		Project Performance view of investment
Execution—contractor level (III)	*Tactical—project level (II)*	*Strategic—ownership level (I)*
Improve contractor's abilities to plan, schedule, and execute the project.	Conduct audits.	Ensure schedule compliance.
Analyze project schedules and provide recommendations to contractor.	Make recommendations.	Ensure the integrity of the budget.
Analyze project work plans and submit recommendations to contractor.	Initiate operating audits, work measurements, productivity analysis, schedule compliance, cost containment.	Advise as to the most likely cost and completion date.
Analyze project resource utilization with recommendations to contractor.	Implement alternate work.	Advise actions absolutely required on a strategic basis to engineering, the contractor, management, and the board of directors.
Analyze project cost reports with recommendations to contractor.	Optimize work force utilization.	
	Improve communication.	
	Generate list of problem areas and corrective actions.	
	Expedite solutions.	

The pyramid in Figure 4 shows how these levels are related. Within each level, reporting is done by exception (deviation from plan) to alert management to acute problem areas. Basically, this information system summarizes all the field data from level III so that management in levels I and II can act on problems before the project becomes adversely affected.

The responsibilities of project management can also be summarized using these three levels (see Figure 5). The strategic implications of project cost and schedule are handled at level I. Level II is involved with analyzing the project status and implementing the decisions of senior management. Finally, level III deals with the contractor's everyday schedules and work plans.

The project management team must keep senior management informed on a timely basis on the project status. "No surprises" is the best philosophy. At the same time, the team must constantly be aware of the progress of the engineering, procurement, and construction groups to ensure adherence to the budget, schedule, and quality requirements. To do these things necessitates careful preparation of the schedule and cost reports.

PREPARING THE PROJECT PLAN

Preparing the project plan involves correlating the scope of work with the schedule and cost reports. It is one of the first steps in project management and should be prepared within a few weeks after project approval. The schedule and cost of the project are refined as work progresses and always remain the direct responsibility of the project manager, who must develop realistic time and cost estimates and provide these to each supervisor for their area of activity on the project.

Quite often the owner relies on the general contractor to construct the schedules and issue progress reports. It has been ORU's experience that delegating to the contractor what should be the owner's responsibility often leads to late information which is of little value. The owner needs to be kept up to date. This can only come from the owner originating the schedule, being on the scene, and observing the actual progress. This assures the identification of problem areas and the application of remedies before the project is adversely affected.

Project managers have a variety of tools by which they can plan, monitor, and control the project schedule. These range from bar chart schedules (Gantt charts) to computerized network-based programs. *Bar charts,* while useful for small projects, have several limitations when planning and scheduling a large number of complex activities: they do not show the interrelationships among activities; they cannot define which activities are genuinely critical; they cannot be readily modified when unexpected problems occur; and they cannot indicate a corrective course of action when delays, changes, or other problems arise.

Because of these, we favor *network-based* management techniques. Two network concepts are arrow diagramming and precedence networking. The two are similar but vary in presentation and preparation. Most computer systems will process both methods.

Arrow diagramming is the one we prefer. The details of its construction and analysis can be readily found in scheduling textbooks and management journals. Essentially, it involves determining all the activities or tasks required for project completion and arranging them in a sequence such that no activity can be started until its predecessor(s) has been completed. A time estimate for each activity is given, and the path having the longest duration is the "critical path." This is the one that must be addressed first.

From a project management point of view, the entire purpose of developing a schedule is to have a basis to evaluate progress reports. Project scheduling is usually divided into three parts: (1) an executive-level schedule; (2) a control-level project schedule; and (3) engineer, procurement, and construction detail schedules. The objectives of these schedules are:

1. To provide direction and control of the project.
2. To establish the scope and timing of the overall project.
3. To provide a tool for tracking progress and for developing probable completion times based on trends.
4. To provide a system that drives the project rather than records job history.

In our experience, project schedules usually are not prepared properly. They are too general, cover only the preparer's work (for example, the engineering group and contractor prepare their schedules independently of each other), are not current, and are difficult to read by anyone other than the preparer or technician. Often they do not include time for the owner's approval of vendor's drawings and schedules, for change orders, or for government approval of permits. Without proper planning of the schedule, delays and disruptions are inevitable. Typically, the results are excessive replanning, overstaffing or understaffing of project areas, loss of trained personnel because of erratic staffing, underutilization or shortage of tools and equipment resulting from erratic job programs, disorderly flow of materials, and congestion of work areas.

660

With this in mind, let's proceed with the scheduling process. The control schedule is the first step in the project plan. It sets the milestones and the periods for engineering, procurement, and construction. Early procurement ensures that equipment will be delivered on time to the field, thus avoiding delays in the project. The control schedule must be realistic and tight since time is the most important factor of project control. To avoid work delays, careful scrutiny of the schedule is required to ensure that the following conditions are met:

1. Will initial design be completed prior to procurement?
2. Can engineering meet procurement and construction schedules?
3. Will the flow of materials be consistent with the needs of construction?

After project management prepares this schedule representatives from engineering and construction conduct a thorough review to determine if they can complete the activities within the timeframe allowed.

The control schedule forms the basis for the more detailed schedule of the project, namely the engineering and construction schedules that are prepared and maintained by the E/C firm. These schedules are best prepared using network logic that identifies the critical path of the project. These detailed schedules require the following information as it becomes available:

- Definitive breakdown of work scope.
- Well-defined process requirement.
- Exact number of engineering drawings.
- Equipment and material specifications.
- Concise definition of project responsibilities of the owner and E/C firms.
- Equipment and material delivery dates.
- Outside engineering requirements.

Periodic updates of the detail schedules are performed by the participants and are reviewed by the project management team through (1) Personal contact with project participants, on site and in offices, including visual verification of drawings produced, purchase orders released, and physical progress in the field; (2) incorporation of pending and approved change orders and scope changes.

With these updates the control schedules and networks are recalculated, and a project status report is issued during the regularly held meetings.

Different contractors will utilize certain scheduling levels and omit others. Also, the titles and terminology may differ from one contractor to another. The following is a cross section of the different types of schedules which may be used by contractors on the project.

1. *Objective schedule (as required)*—This is either an abbreviated milestone or bar chart schedule used only for submission with the contractor's proposal. It is rarely utilized after a contract is awarded.

2. *Control schedule by the owner (mandatory)*—This needs to be in network form. It fixes all of the major project start and completion dates. It must be prepared within a few weeks of project award and maintained in a current condition throughout the project duration. It forms the basis for all subsequent schedules and is the driving force for all project schedules.

3. *Engineering and procurement schedule (mandatory)*—This is prepared by the engineering contractor and is used to identify and set durations for this segment of the work. The minimum content should be:

- Engineering design, drafting, procurement, decision points, and tie-ins to construction activities.
- Significant dependencies among activities.
- Key project and milestone events.
- Award of purchase orders by commodity.
- Special equipment and materials.
- Preparation and issue of all subcontracts.
- Client reviews and approvals.
- Vendor print receipts, vendor reviews, and purchase order approvals.
- Model construction and reviews until shipment.

4. *Construction schedule (mandatory)*—Each contractor will prepare their own detailed schedule covering their scope of work during the entire project. This includes all important construction tasks, critical approvals, drawing needs, and equipment deliveries.

5. *Construction 90-day schedule (mandatory)*—This is a segment of the project schedule that details work to be done during the next 90-day period. This can also be a 60-day schedule, updated on a weekly basis.

6. *Construction's weekly work plan (mandatory)*—Field schedulers, with construction supervisors, will issue detailed work plans each week. These are taken from the 90-day schedules and modified to fit field requirements.

During the time the schedule is being prepared, the cost engineer is working on the cost report. Cost analysis is a continuous process throughout the life of the project whereby each element of the job is translated into cost. It provides a precise cost interpretation of design and engineering requirements, furnishes information for bid evaluation, and produces a baseline for project cost control, scope change orders, and cost planning.

Cost control is minimizing the variation between actual cost and the budget or control estimate. The primary function of project cost control is to keep the owner's project and operations management advised of the current cost status of the project. This involves analyzing costs, measuring the progress of work accomplished, and interpreting project trends. Such information develops a predicted total cost at completion, which is then compared to the control budget.

In order to accurately measure and report progress, a reliable basis of work to be performed must be determined. The determination of this base is the responsibility of the cost engineer. The establishment of the work unit is based upon the completion of the following events: project description and scope, preliminary design and engineering, and preliminary equipment and material specifications.

Following these events, the estimator prepares quantity take-offs, applies standard unit workerhours, and adjusts for the expected area productivity. From this workerhour budget a control project schedule is prepared, and crew staffing and labor force loading are established. At this time the total budget for workerweeks or work units to be completed is generated.

The next step is approval of the estimated work units and quantities by the responsible management, engineering, and construction representatives. After this, the cost engineer allocates the budgeted units to specific account codes for cost control and establishes individual budgets containing both work units (or workerweeks) and respective quantities.

Progress in each account is monitored and compared to the budgeted amount. A trend line on forecasted work unit expenditures to completion is also prepared. Reports are then generated to show work unit and quantity expenditures and to forecast work units to be completed.

The summary document for cost control is the monthly report entitled "Project Consolidated Cost Report" and is management's primary source of cost information. (See Figure 6.) This report summarizes the levels of expenditures, commitments to date, total anticipated cost at completion, and probable overruns or underruns. Information

FIGURE 6

| | | | | | | PRELIMINARY FORECAST | | | |
| PROJECT _____ F.S.S. PROJECT CONSOLIDATED COST REPORT PERIOD ENDING _____ CLIENT _____ PAGE ___ OF ___ | | | | | | | | | |

DESCRIPTION	TENTA-TIVE BUDGET	APPVD SCOPE CHANGE	REVISED BUDGET	COM-MITTED	SPENT TO DATE	COST TO COM'L	TOTAL COST FORECAST	+ (-) VARIANCE
TOTALS								

P.A.S.S.®   ORU Group   ©1977 by ORU Group Inc.   FORM _____

for this report is obtained through the engineering and construction surveillances.

First-level control procedures, collectively called construction surveillance procedures, establish control at the source by identifying situations which require corrective action. Examples of first-level controls are:

- Monitoring labor utilization and productivity.
- Monitoring construction equipment utilization.
- Monitoring equipment and material costs.
- Monitoring overtime and average craft rates.
- Monitoring schedule compliance.
- Monitoring equipment delivery schedules.
- Analyzing bids, proposals, and invoices.
- Analyzing material and consumable usages and predicted surpluses.
- Analyzing work methods and crewing.
- Analyzing supervisory effectiveness.
- Preventing scope changes, add-ons, and reworks.

An *intermediate level* of cost control is trending. Trend reporting, or predicting costs, is the vehicle for quantifying the impact of cost control at the first level. It also provides a track record on effectiveness of the corrective actions taken at the first level.

A combination of cost trending, an estimate of work remaining, and knowledge of costs to date establishes the total anticipated cost at completion. Comparing the anticipated cost by line items to the control budget gives project management the basis for action to reduce the total cost and for reallocating the control budget among cost areas.

EXERCISING PROJECT CONTROL

The activities of network diagramming; cost containment; engineering, procurement, and construction surveillance; and reporting all comprise a system called project control. A project control system is used both as a yardstick and an anchor. As a yardstick it measures job progress and efficient use of resources. As an anchor it holds down unwarranted growth of project scope and expenditures. ORU Group has developed a set of services to assist management in the area of project control. We call these services Project Assessment and Surveillance System (PASS), which evolved from many years of project interaction with our clients and contractors.

The PASS services are designed to improve executive decision making. Basically, PASS focuses on five areas: engineering, scheduling, financial, procurement, and construction. Each area generates a series of reports (see Figure 7). By using PASS the project manager, at any point in time, can determine the following: (1) current progress, job status, and assessment of work completed; (2) costs incurred to date; (3) estimated project completion date; (4) changes in project scope; (5) specific areas requiring corrective action for cost and schedule improvement; (6) cost trends for all accounts; (7) estimated costs to completion; and (8) action items requiring immediate attention.

The main thrust of PASS and project control is to ensure timely project completion on or below budget. To do this will require a surveillance system to monitor and control all project work and to relate progress to agreed standards. These standards relate to staff utilization, labor productivity, time, and cost. The elements of project control will be explained in the sections below, using a fictitious gas company as an example.

Engineering Surveillance

The engineering progress monitoring system is oriented around planning work loads, controlling the work flow, and detecting operating

FIGURE 7

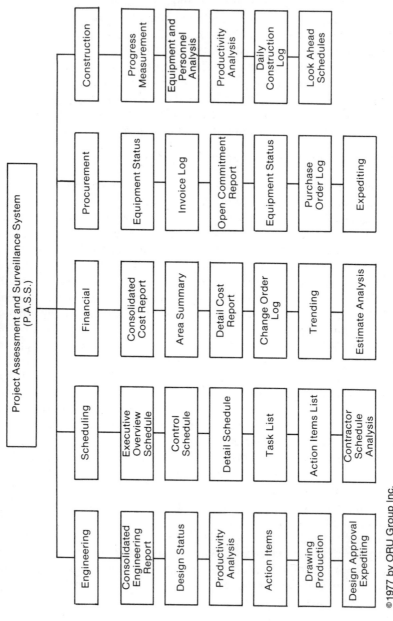

Project Assessment and Surveillance System (P.A.S.S.)

Engineering
- Consolidated Engineering Report
- Design Status
- Productivity Analysis
- Action Items
- Drawing Production
- Design Approval Expediting

Scheduling
- Executive Overview Schedule
- Control Schedule
- Detail Schedule
- Task List
- Action Items List
- Contractor Schedule Analysis

Financial
- Consolidated Cost Report
- Area Summary
- Detail Cost Report
- Change Order Log
- Trending
- Estimate Analysis

Procurement
- Equipment Status
- Invoice Log
- Open Commitment Report
- Equipment Status
- Purchase Order Log
- Expediting

Construction
- Progress Measurement
- Equipment and Personnel Analysis
- Productivity Analysis
- Daily Construction Log
- Look Ahead Schedules

problems. The overall project work requirements are successively broken down, through each level of responsibility, into a series of smaller tasks such that at the level of operation, each member of supervision is controlling the shortest practical increment of work. The system is designed to "control the whole by controlling the parts." It provides predictability in the flow of work and highlights operating problems in sufficient time so that management can take corrective action to make the overall plan succeed.

With the project underway process design is the initial work to be completed, followed by mechanical engineering and drafting. A weekly labor-hour report and the number of drawings completed should be furnished by the engineering department to the project manager, with a copy to the cost engineer. The physical progress of the work is reported and compared weekly with the schedules in order that time and cost to completion can be forecast and controlled. The project engineer is responsible for overseeing the progress and for recommending corrective action. This is done by conducting his or her own sampling of engineering work, analyzing productivity, and developing productivity improvement measures which are discussed with the project manager.

ORU's system of engineering surveillance (ESS) was developed to improve the production of drawings, specifications, design data, and to increase the utilization of personnel. There are several documents used for this surveillance, some of which are:

1. *Consolidated Engineering Report*—This outlines the status of documents and workerhours for each cost account (Figure 8).
2. *Engineering Status*—This is a bar chart showing the actual and scheduled progress for engineering activities (Figure 9).
3. *Work Sample—Engineering Surveillance*—This report is a summary of how many people are engaged in productive activity (Figure 10).
4. *Action Log*—This list shows what work items have to be done, by whom, and by which date. It is issued weekly and serves as a reminder to all participants that prompt attention will ensure progress (Figure 11).

Schedule Control

The scheduling engineer has the responsibility of getting all participants to adhere to the control schedule mentioned earlier. Continual tracking of performance against the plan will ensure smooth progress and avoid completion delays. To do this requires reviewing the actual

FIGURE 8

ESS
CONSOLIDATED ENGINEERING REPORT

PROJECT __Refinery B__   PERIOD ENDING __1-Oct.-82__

CLIENT __Gas Company__   JOB # __999__   ENGR $/WKHR: __36.00__

DESCRIPTION	QTY	QTY CODE	IN PROGRESS QUAN	IN PROGRESS EQV. COMP	COMP. TO DATE PLAN	COMP. TO DATE ACT.	% COMP	FORECAST TOTAL	FORECAST TO DATE	EXPENDED THIS PERIOD	EXPENDED TO DATE	EARNED THIS PERIOD	EARNED TO DATE	% PROD.	MNHRS/ DOCUMENT PLAN	MNHRS/ DOCUMENT ACT.	MAN HOURS TO COMP	MAN HOURS TOTAL REQ'D	% COMP
				DOCUMENT STATUS					RELATED MAN HOURS						INDICES		PROJECT STATUS		
30 Engineering																			
38 Control Systems																			
39 Electrical*																			
42 Environmental																			
45 Structural*																			
SUB-TOTAL																			
SUPPORT																			
Marketing; Accounting; Processing and technical services; Records and information; Cost and estimate; Computer services TOTALS																			

P.A.S.S.®   *Control Areas   ORU Group   ©1977 by ORU Group Inc.   **FORM** _____

FIGURE 9

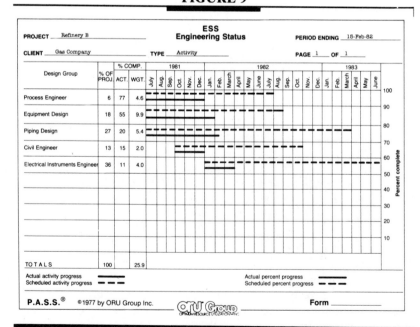

ESS
Engineering Status

PROJECT __Refinery B__   PERIOD ENDING __15-Feb-82__

CLIENT __Gas Company__   TYPE __Activity__   PAGE __1__ OF __1__

Design Group	% OF PROJ.	% COMP. ACT.	% COMP. WGT.	1981 ... 1982 ... 1983 (monthly chart)	Percent complete
Process Engineer	6	77	4.6		
Equipment Design	18	55	9.9		
Piping Design	27	20	5.4		
Civil Engineer	13	15	2.0		
Electrical Instruments Engineer	36	11	4.0		
TOTALS	100		25.9		

Actual activity progress ▬▬▬
Scheduled activity progress ▬ ▬ ▬
Actual percent progress ▬▬▬
Scheduled percent progress ▬ ▬ ▬

P.A.S.S.®   ©1977 by ORU Group Inc.   ORU Group   **Form** _____

668

FIGURE 10

ESS
Work Sample — Engineering Surveillance

LOCATION _New York, New York_   PROJECT _Refinery B_   TIME _9:05_

CONTRACTOR _A B C Engineer_   NAME _John Doe_   DATE _2/5/82_

Description	Assign	Productive	Idle	Total observed	Total productive	Total idle
Process						
Civil/Structural						
Piping/Mechanical						
Electrical Instruments						
TOTAL						

General comments:

P.A.S.S.®
©1977 by ORU Group Inc.   Form _____

ORU Group
OPTIMUM RESOURCE UTILIZATION INC

FIGURE 11

ESS
Action Log

PROJECT ___Refinery B___

PERIOD ENDING 15-Feb-82

CLIENT ___Gas Company___

PAGE ___1___ OF ___1___

Item no.	Date orig.	Description	Resp.	Req. date	Date actual	Comments
1	12/19/81	Provide up-to-date list of construction equipment per Gas Company request	Engr.	1/8/82	2/10/82	Complete
2	12/22/81	Issue detail engineering schedule	Engr.	1/15/82		Late reschedule 2/25/82
5	1/10/82	Issue area 100 PFDs	Engr.	3/5/82		
6	2/10/82	Approve exchanger specs	Gas Co.	3/1/82		
7	2/10/82	Initiate engineering work sampling reports	ORU	2/20/82		
8	2/10/82	Issue 30 percent cost estimate	Engr.	2/20/82	2/16/82	Complete

ACTION NUMBERS WILL NOT BE REASSIGNED IN FOLLOW-UP ISSUES OF AN ACTION LIST, AND AS AN ITEM IS COMPLETED, THAT ACCOMPLISHMENT IS SO NOTED. THE FOLLOWING ISSUE WILL SO NOTE THAT THE ITEM HAS BEEN ACCOMPLISHED AND ELIMINATED FROM THE CURRENT ISSUE.

P.A.S.S.® ©1977 by ORU Group Inc. ORU Group Form _____

physical progress of engineering, procurement, and construction, and the results of the surveillance programs. From this the scheduler issues a project schedule status report to the key managers, highlighting progress and changes in schedule.

At ORU we developed the Project Time Control System (PTCS) to provide direction to all project participants by defining the key milestones that must be met, and to provide the basis for measuring and reporting schedule progress. One of the key documents used for this system is the engineering executive schedule. This gives management an overview of the entire project showing the percent completion for several engineering activities (Figure 12). Another document is the current status of major milestones (Figure 13), which delineates the target date, scheduled completion date, and variances for major project activities.

Procurement Surveillance

When design has reached a suitable stage, solicitation of firm competitive quotations can be started. Equipment items must be specified in sufficient detail to obtain firm bids. To avoid misinterpretation of in-

FIGURE 12

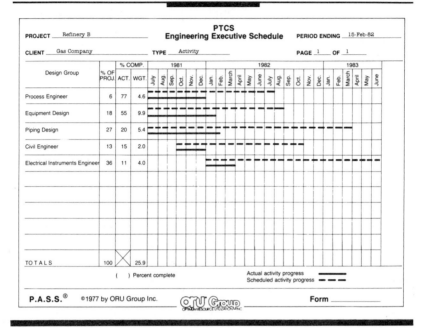

Design Group	% OF PROJ	% COMP. ACT.	WGT.	1981 July	Aug.	Sep.	Oct.	Nov.	Dec.	1982 Jan.	Feb.	March	April	May	June	July	Aug.	Sep.	Oct.	Nov.	Dec.	1983 Jan.	Feb.	March	April	May	June
Process Engineer	6	77	4.6																								
Equipment Design	18	55	9.9																								
Piping Design	27	20	5.4																								
Civil Engineer	13	15	2.0																								
Electrical Instruments Engineer	36	11	4.0																								
TOTALS	100		25.9																								

PROJECT _Refinery B_   **PTCS**   **Engineering Executive Schedule**   PERIOD ENDING _15-Feb-82_
CLIENT _Gas Company_   TYPE _Activity_   PAGE _1_ OF _1_

( ) Percent complete

Actual activity progress ▬▬▬
Scheduled activity progress ▬ ▬ ▬

P.A.S.S.® ©1977 by ORU Group Inc.   Form _____

tent, these specifications must be complete, correct, and consistent. Proper preparation of equipment specifications should result in quotations with identical bases. Purchase orders should be, if possible, on a fixed-price basis, inclusive of escalation and freight. Cost control is important at this level since revisions or corrections can be costly.

The vendor's delivery date is just as important as price. As mentioned before, the material or equipment must arrive during the scheduled construction time frame or it will delay the project. Proper inspection and expediting, including visits to the shop to check the vendor's facilities, will ensure the schedule. The material progress record issued by the expediter indicates to the project manager, the cost engineer, and the field engineer the actual material status.

The person in charge of this activity will provide a plan to assure a cost-effective bidding process, favorable terms and conditions, control of payments, and the expediting of deliveries.

Three reports we find useful for procurement surveillance are:

1. *Equipment Analysis Report*—For each type of equipment, this report lists the number required, number of requests for quotations, and the number of quotations received and on order (Figure 14).

671

2. *Purchase Order Status*—This shows the planned, actual, and forecasted level of purchase orders for each month as a function of the cost (Figure 15).
3. *Procurement Status*—This indicates the procurement history and forecast of each order, including purchase order number, description, vendor, promised delivery, last expediting visit, method of shipping, and scheduled need date.

FIGURE 13

PTCS
Current Status of Major Milestones

PROJECT _Refinery B_   PERIOD ENDING _3-Feb-82_

CLIENT _Gas Company_   PAGE _1_ OF _1_

Items	Target date	Current scheduled completion date	Variance + / − days
Boiler Foundations			
Reactor Structure Unit #9			
Air Cooler, East/West Rack			
Onsite Silos Complete			
Reactor Complete			

P.A.S.S.®
©1977 by ORU Group Inc.   Form _____

ORU Group
OPTIMUM RESOURCE UTILIZATION INC

FIGURE 14

PSS
Equipment Analysis Report

PROJECT Refinery B

PERIOD ENDING 11/13/82

CLIENT Gas Company   CONTRACTOR Engineer C   PAGE 1 OF 15

| Description | Quantity | Request for quotations | | | Quotations | | Percent equip. on order | Remarks |
		No. req'd.	No. issued	Percent issued	No. rec'd	P.O. placed		
Compressors								
Pumps								
Exchangers								
Fab vessels								
Towers								

P.A.S.S.®   ©1977 by ORU Group Inc.   ORU Group   Form _____

Construction Surveillance

The primary concerns of field construction surveillance are isolating the factors that could have an impact on the project schedule or budget, determining alternative methods to lessen the impact, and making recommendations to project management as to the best alternative to implement. The key person involved in this area is the field cost engineer who reports the job progress to the construction manager on a daily basis, and to the home office construction and cost control departments on a regular monthly basis. The main responsibility of the field cost engineer is to write the construction report. The record of workerhours and dollars expended by cost code is developed from the work of the timekeepers and the field accounting staff. Installed quantities, unit costs, final quantities as taken from drawings and invoices, and the final cost forecast are recorded by the field cost engineer. As soon as unusual unit costs appear, the engineer will advise the construction manager. Suitable corrective action should then be taken.

FIGURE 15

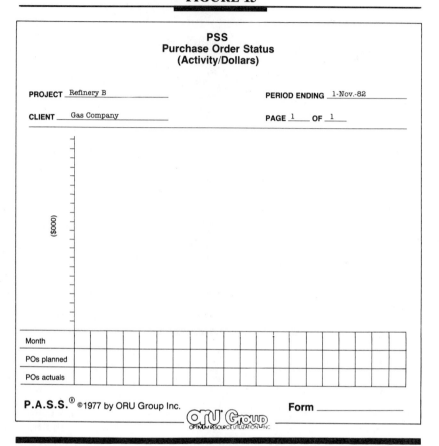

Some of the documents we use for construction surveillance include:

1. *Work Unit Summary*—This shows the total number of work units assigned to a particular construction activity, the total earned, and the percent completed (Figure 16).
2. *Work Sample—Construction Surveillance*—this delineates productive and idle time for various craft people (Figure 17).
3. *Productivity Analysis Summary*—This shows the labor force requirements during the construction phase (Figure 18).

674

FIGURE 16

	CSS Work Unit Summary				

PROJECT __Refinery B__   PERIOD ENDING __5/2/82__

CLIENT __Gas Co.__   TYPE __Cooling Tower__   PAGE __1__ OF __5__

Activity no.	Description	Total work units	Total earned work units	Percent complete
CTO156	Grade cooling tower area			
CTO291	Form and pour cooling tower foundation			
CTO331	Erect cooling tower			
Totals				

P.A.S.S.® ©1977 by ORU Group Inc.   ORU Group   **Form** _____

Two of the most obvious areas where potential for overruns exist are craft personnel and contractor's field staff. For craft personnel typical questions the field engineer should ask are:

- Are crew mixes adequate for maximum efficiency?
- Is the project overstaffed or understaffed? What about crew sizes for specific jobs?
- Are the craftsmen receiving proper work plans each day?
- How is the flow of instructions?
- Is craft supervision at the general supervisor and supervisor levels adequate and efficient?
- How well do the workers perform their tasks?
- Are there any labor relations problems?
- Do the workers have the tools, materials, equipment, and so on necessary to do their work?

The field engineer should also be aware of possible safety hazards and violations of craft labor agreements that could possibly cause a

675

FIGURE 17

CSS
Work Sample — Construction Surveillance

LOCATION __Area 5A__   PROJECT __Refinery B__   TIME __3:22__

CONTRACTOR __Contractor B__   NAME __John Doe__   DATE __1-10-82__

Description	Assign	Produc-tive	Idle	Total observed	Total produc-tive	Total idle
Carpenter						
Ironworker						
Pipefitter						
Welders						
Instruments						
Electrical						
TOTAL						

General comments:

P.A.S.S.® ©1977 by ORU Group Inc. ORU Group OPTIMUM RESOURCE UTILIZATION INC   Form _____

FIGURE 18

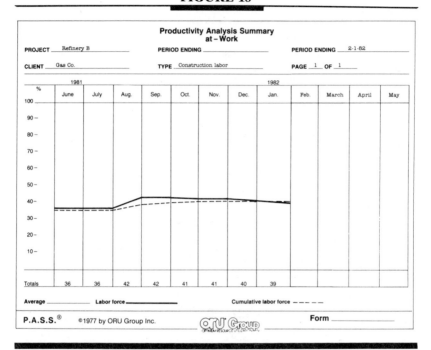

work stoppage or slowdown. Items of this nature should immediately be brought to the attention of the contractor's supervisory personnel.

Several factors relating to the contractor's field staff can have considerable effect on a project's costs and schedules. The effectiveness of these staff members will determine the success of a project. Some of the items to look for are (1) Is the supervisory staff adequate to do the job, or is there a significant overstaffing situation? What is the ratio of field staff to craftsmen? (2) Is the contractor's field organization structured for maximum efficiency? (3) What type of relations exist between the superintendents and craft supervisors? (4) Is there an adequate flow of instructions and other communications to the specific work site? (5) How well do the contractor's personnel work together? (6) How well do they coordinate field activities? (7) How well do they respond to an emergency or a crisis situation? and (8) What role do the labor relations and safety personnel play? Essentially, all of these questions involve determining just exactly how effective the organization is and then making the pertinent recommendations for improvement.

Cost Control

The cost engineer is the key person involved with monitoring project costs in conformity with the budget. The control document is the "Project Consolidated Cost Report." In addition to this report, the cost engineer should develop a program to analyze trend factors that affect project cost; establish a change order control procedure that includes all proposed and approved changes to project cost; provide a current cost to complete, total cost forecast, and variances; and review cost results with key managers.

Reports we use for cost control include:

1. *Cash Flow Schedule*—A plot showing cumulative costs incurred to date versus planned expenditures, and what the forecasted completion costs will be (Figure 19).
2. *Change Order File*—This report describes the equipment changes, assigns a number to them, and indicates whether or not there is a budget adjustment (Figure 20).
3. *Project Change Order*—This is a form showing information required to make a change order (Figure 21).

FIGURE 19

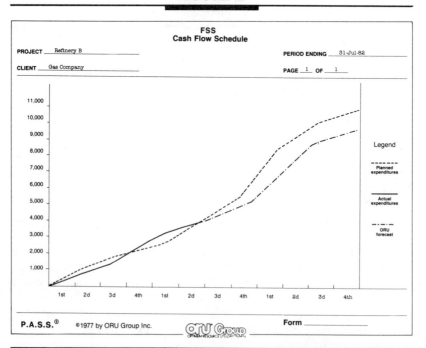

FSS
Cash Flow Schedule

PROJECT ___Refinery B___   PERIOD ENDING ___31-Jul-82___

CLIENT ___Gas Company___   PAGE __1_ OF __1__

Legend

- - - - - Planned expenditures

———— Actual expenditures

— ·· — ·· — ORU forecast

P.A.S.S.®   ©1977 by ORU Group Inc.   ORU Group   Form _____

FIGURE 20

			FSS Change Order File					

PROJECT __Refinery B__   PERIOD ENDING __26-Mar-82__

CLIENT __Gas Company__   PAGE __1__ OF __1__

Major code no.	Area no.	Change order no.	Change order discription	Change order code	Approved change order	Pending change order	Trend	Budget adjustment
003	09	090001	Unit 09 Definitive estimate reduction — complexity					
005	09	090001	Unit 09 Definitive estimate reduction — complexity					

Form _____

P.A.S.S.®   ©1977 by ORU Group Inc.   ORU Group

Meetings

Typically, progress meetings are held regularly with each contractor individually (or jointly) as may be required. These meetings are chaired by the project manager and are the prime vehicle for planning future work; discussing action log items; and resolving disputes, alternative strategies, disruptions, and interferences. Other types of meetings include:

- *Management meetings*—The control team assists the project manager in conducting a weekly management briefing on-site regarding the critical elements of the project relating to cost, time, contractor performance, deliveries, problems, and resolutions.
- *Monthly presentation*—The control team makes a monthly presentation to management on the time and cost aspects of the project.
- *Steering committee*—The control team will also assist the project manager in preparing and in presenting the project cost and schedule status at the quarterly steering committee meetings.

FIGURE 21

Project Change Order

ORU GROUP, INC.	Date		P.V.M. no.	Rev. no.
To:	Project no.		Origination	
Project:			Cost Schedule area	
File reference				

Description of change

=	Unit area	Actv.	Equip. no.	Quan.	Unit	Man-hours	Labor	Material	Subs.	Const. equip.	Const. over-head	Total
+												

Construction and material cost

Direct manhours

Construction fee

Engineering cost

Unit area	Manhours	Rate	Remarks	Total

Engineering cost

Total project change order

Change order classification:
1. Non-discretionary
a. Required to meet project objectives
b. Process modification
c. Changes in Material or Labor Cost
g. Other _____

d. Design modification
e. Vendor modifications
f. Field conditions

2. Discretionary
a. To improve operability
b. Change in scope
c. Other _____

Effect on schedule

Estimating _____ Cost control _____ Scheduling _____

Operator

• Includes sales tax. as applicable

Approved by

Approved by

Client

P.A.S.S.®

© 1977 by ORU Group Inc. ORU Group OPTIMUM RESOURCE UTILIZATION INC   **Form** _____

680

To summarize this chapter, the key points to remember for effective project control are:

1. A control budget.
2. A realistic and tight control project schedule.
3. Budgets disseminated in advance to all individuals with cost responsibilities.
4. Engineering design on schedule, with checks made of drawing quantities versus plan.
5. Material delivery schedules must be maintained.
6. The field cost engineer is essential to field cost control.
7. A regular construction report reflecting installed quantities as well as total quantities to be installed.
8. Planning and scheduling must be based on actual unit costs with full information on job progress from the construction report.
9. Corrective measures must be taken by the project manager when poor unit costs appear on the project.
10. Agreement on the status of project completion must be obtained weekly.
11. Time is the most important factor. All efforts must be undertaken within tight schedules.

EVALUATING BENEFITS

As we have shown, there are many elements to project management: the people, the plan, and the procedures. The owner must devote considerable time and effort to develop each of these parts in order for the system to work. This type of commitment may be difficult to undertake, and usually what happens is that the owner does a half-hearted effort or delegates project management to the E/C firm.

In our experience ineffective project planning and control will increase the cost to owner by 13 to 18 percent of the total project cost. The reason for this is that the owner management generally is preoccupied with long-range planning, leaving the short-range scheduling to others, such as the contractor. Unfortunately, the contractor also manages by long-term goals. The net result is that there is no short-range scheduling at the point of execution. Project control is absent, with resultant drastic cost overruns and schedule slippages.

ORU Group also finds that projects are initiated with a fair amount of optimism, coupled with a lack of control at the point of execution. Things don't always happen as planned. In addition the absence of accurate and "real time" reporting hinders the search into the true problem areas. Previous ORU diagnostic assignments showed that if news was "bad for a client," E/C firms sometimes withheld information on the chance that the situation would correct itself in sufficient time so as not to affect schedules or costs. This "shielding the owner" approach could be acceptable provided action is taken by the contractor in time to remedy the situation; unfortunately, in almost all cases there was a passive, wait-and-see attitude instead of a make-things-happen approach. Having the surveillance and reporting system described earlier will provide accurate information of the true picture. It will also develop a sense-of-urgency environment which will make things happen and maintain the original schedules and cost goals.

A typical breakdown of the types of savings that could result from effective project management for several budgeted items is shown in Figure 22. The range is quite varied; however, ORU has been success-

FIGURE 22

Typical Project Savings through Effective Project Management

Project component	Savings
Home office engineering	6 to 8 percent of engineering cost
Major equipment	2 to 5 percent of equipment costs
Bulk materials	3 to 5 percent of bulk material costs
Subcontracts	3 to 5 percent of subcontract costs
Direct labor	8 to 15 percent of direct labor costs
Indirects	8 to 15 percent of field indirect costs
Construction equipment rentals	7 to 10 percent of equipment costs
Tools, supplies, and consumables	7 to 10 percent of consumable costs
Escalation	15 to 25 percent of estimated escalation costs
Contingency	15 to 30 percent of estimated contingency

ful in recovering between 6 and 10 percent of the total project costs. Other benefits from this type of project management are:

I. Time.
  A. Shorter overall timetables.
  B. Earlier predictability of project costs and schedule completion.
  C. Greater visibility and improved communication of project plans and status through use of various scheduling aids.

II. Cost.
  A. Lower overall project cost.
  B. Emphasis is placed on control measures to be taken during the early phases of project development to realize maximum effectiveness of cost control efforts.
  C. Control and coordination of contractors.
  D. Improved cash forecasting.
  E. Encourages and promotes cost-consciousness in the performance of all work phases.

It is quite likely the project team was assembled on an ad hoc basis, or it may be a newly created division within the organization. If either is the case, the viability of the group will depend on the project's performance. In this regard one final benefit of the management system described in this chapter is to improve the credibility of the team or division with corporate management. Keen attention to detail, interpreting difficulties, and quick resolution of problems are the keys to successful project completion.

29

Capital Budgeting Audits: How to Profit from Experience

Keith B. Ehrenreich

California State Polytechnic University

*C*apital budgeting decisions are among the most challenging decisions executives must make, as these affect the long-term viability of the firm. The organization is committed to actions involving its future flexibility as well as daily operations; a bad decision will impact financial performance, the balance sheet, and firm image. Since capital budgeting is generally based on a set of assumptions regarding rapidly changing technological and financial conditions, the uncertainty and risk in the process add to its challenging nature.

Reviews of the capital budgeting function have great potential to contribute to the financial health of the organization. By evaluating projects in light of initial assumptions and documenting reasons for project performance, the post-audit can make the difference between success and failure in the future, that is, the organization profits from past experience.

A professionally oriented audit, by focusing upon the actual quality of decision making, can reduce management's exposure to long-term risk. Management is continually concerned with the allocation of available resources for projects that promise future returns. What makes this kind of decision so difficult is the high degree of uncertainty inherent in the decision-making process and the long lead times required to get these projects on-line.

The literature regarding how to post-audit a capital budgeting decision is mostly limited to approaches that select and evaluate specific projects. The focus is upon end results or expected performance. The first part of this chapter will discuss guidelines for conducting a post-audit review of projects. Another audit approach is a review which attempts to evaluate the total capital budgeting *process*. This includes, but is not limited to, policy planning, project requirements, project development, accounting, personnel, purchasing, and other activities necessary to bring projects on-line. This latter audit approach may be more valid and useful, depending on the nature, size, and complexity of some capital projects. The latter portion of this chapter discusses this methodology.

PROJECT AUDITS

Postcompletion auditing is not just a matter of learning if a specific project exceeded the predetermined hurdle rate or generated a rate of return in excess of the hurdle rate. It also concerns why the project was selected, what the expected outcomes were, what subsequent capitalization may be necessary, how related expenses were affected, and what were the positive and negative qualitative factors that resulted from the project. Knowing the answers to these and other questions can provide the kind of information which could determine the success or failure of projects and give management feedback as to how and in what ways the capital budgeting process can be made more successful in the future.

Research has revealed several shortcomings in capital budgeting decision making that can be corrected. First, many organizations conduct no post-audits and thus don't take advantage of the learning possibilities an audit creates. Second, some businesses treat each capital budgeting project as a unique investment. While it is quite useful to classify projects as either normal capital investments or special capital investments, by focusing on common characteristics and formalizing the process, learning can be enhanced. Third, management may be reluctant to accept negative findings from postadoption audits and thus fail to make constructive use of negative feedback. Even if current results would be difficult or impossible to improve, the learning should help in the evaluation of future proposals.

The following section will elaborate on audit project objectives with emphasis on a number of decisions to make, that is, what projects to audit, when to audit, who conducts the audit, and what information to audit.

What Projects to Audit

Auditing is not an exercise to be carried out routinely or without regard to cost/benefit considerations. Since auditing is expensive it is probably impractical for all capital expenditures to be audited in most organizations. Very often the bulk of new projects are additions or replacements to existing capital equipment. Systematic sampling of normal capital expenditures and smaller projects would suffice in these instances. Consideration should be given to auditing 100 percent of projects over a predetermined dollar amount and special projects which have characteristics requiring further study. For example, projects with exceptional returns, revolutionary new projects, and/or projects associated with considerable risk would be audited on a comprehensive basis.

In the selection process consideration should be given to the total dollar amount spent per project (materiality), the type of expenditure made, time since the project has been on-line, management requests, and other variables which might be pertinent.

When to Audit

The timing of the post-audit evaluation is an interesting question which requires considerable judgment. If one of the objectives of the audit is to suggest corrective action to management for project implementation, long time delays will mitigate achievement of this objective. However, auditing too early after implementation, usually within 6 to 12 months after completion, may not be realistic because overly generous allowances may be made for many problems on the basis that poor results are short-term ''shake down'' conditions. Gold has expressed concern for early audits as follows:

> These early appraisals often yield overly optimistic findings, however, because generous allowances are made to offset actual shortcomings on the assumption that these are attributable to temporary problems such as excessive maintenance, inadequate labor experi-

ence, or underuse due to incomplete integration with adjacent operations.[1]

The project should be considered for audit sometime after it is onstream and has had an opportunity to be debugged. Gold has additionally recommended that in the use of major technological innovations,
the post-audit appraisals be conducted repeatedly for at least two to
three years after completion. This process would be used to develop
performance trends and demonstrate transitory as opposed to permanent results.

Who Does the Audit

The assignment of responsibility for conducting the post-audit has been
designated to various individuals and groups. The literature on the
subject has specified the originator of the proposal, financial staff members, new MBAs, engineering staff members, and staff from the internal audit department as potential candidates for postadoption appraisals. The problem in selection is the balance between objectivity and the
required technological expertise and project knowledge. Perhaps the
best approach is an interdisciplinary team composed of individuals
who can bring objectivity as well as the requisite expertise. The interdisciplinary team should assume a problem-solving evaluation approach and can adopt a more participatory audit style.

What Information to Audit

Basically, the purpose of conducting a post-audit of a capital project is
to determine whether the anticipated performance goals were reached
and whether this was achieved within the cost instruments initially
specified. Therefore, the audit effect should focus upon gathering information regarding actual project benefits (outcomes) as well as the costs
associated with this project. This process usually includes cash flow
analysis, tax implications of the cash flows, and assessment of the
qualitative cost/benefits. In order to give management information
which will improve future decision making and/or take corrective
action, the auditors must go beyond the accounting components of the
analysis (interest rates, costs, etc.) and dig below the results to find
unforeseen errors in estimating cost savings, profits, productive efficiencies, and other *ex ante* expectations.

Figure 1 summarizes various types of capital budgeting investments, discrepancies which limit profit potential, evidence, and source
data the auditor can use as a starting point.

FIGURE 1

*Types of Capital Budgeting Investments, Discrepancies which
Limit Profit Potential, Evidence, and Source Data the Auditor
Can Use as Starting Points*

Investment	Discrepancy	Evidence	Source data
Costs	Too high	Input costs have risen	Accounting Production
Quality	Inadequate	Competitive deterioration Customer needs Prices down	Accounting Marketing General management
Capacity	Insufficient	Sales exceed capacity Forecasts exceed capacity	Accounting Marketing General management
Replacement	Machinery obsolete	Repair costs Input costs have risen	Accounting Production
New products	Products replaced or added	Market change	Marketing

Figure 2 lists the variables in a typical capital budget and also provides a starting point for the determination of what information to audit. A point to be understood by potential auditors is that some of the information is based upon estimates (for example, economic life projectors, salvage values) and cannot be audited with hard evidence.

AUDIT THE CAPITAL BUDGETING PROCESS

Some capital budgeting decisions might not lend themselves to audit on a project basis. For example, consider a large, diverse company with a substantial demand for internal use of microcomputers for many diverse tasks. Different departments and divisions would probably want different machines and software for their individual needs, but many related problems would develop from this approach, for example, system compatibility, communications, training, service contract costs, and companywide coordination. Therefore, one machine would probably be selected, and this decision would probably be a compromise to

688

FIGURE 2

Variables in Typical Capital Budget

Initial investment—
The necessary amount of funds to begin the project in its first year.

Subsequent capitalization—
Any additional funding over the life of the project.

Related expenses—
Costs not directly attached to the project which will be incurred by other components of the company.

Purpose of project—
A general statement as to the need for the proposed expenditures.

Expected benefits
Monetary—
Cash flow analysis over the years of the project.

Qualitative—
A written analysis of the pros and cons of the project (those factors which cannot be quantitatively defined but should be considered, such as environmental impacts).

Length of construction period—
Time period, also target dates along the way for checking on the progress.

Payback period—
The period of time in which the initial investment will be recovered.

Discounted rate of return—
Using present value techniques, the expected percentage return where inflow equals outflow.

Working capital requirements—
Any additional assets or liabilities which will be incurred outside of capitalized amounts.

Personnel effects—
Increases or decreases in number of people, including positions and when effect is to take place.

Source: Adopted from Richard S. Savich, *Internal Audit of the Budget Process* (Institute of Internal Auditors, 1976).

accommodate as many tasks as possible; and several hundred machines could be involved. To audit this situation on a project basis could cause problems because of the scope, timing, and assessment of benefits associated with the many diverse tasks. An alternative approach would audit the total capital budget process as a management system. The next sections explore some of the factors to be considered when taking this type of audit approach.

The Process

The capital budgeting decision-making process begins with the organization's business strategy and includes the determination of long-term goals and objectives. How the strategy will be administered and implemented is considered. Many firms adopt a formal system to evaluate investment ideas. (See Figure 3.)

FIGURE 3

The Capital Budgeting Process

I. Policy planning
  A. Screening and implementation
  B. Committee
  C. Policy specification
  D. Initial investigation
 	
II. Project requirements
  A. Operations analysis
  B. Output requirements
  C. Alternatives evaluation
 	
III. Project development
  A. Model cash consequences
  B. Rank projects
  C. Financing decided
 	
IV. Top-management review and decision
 	
V. Project implementation
  A. Timetable and dates
  B. Implementation
  C. Control expenditures
 	
VI. Post-audit review
  A. Review project documentation
  B. Perform fact finding
  C. Prepare report

Step I—Policy planning. Most organizations of considerable size establish a formal screening and implementation committee to administer their capital budgeting function. This committee reviews organization strategy and specifies policy guidelines regarding product lines, distribution systems, labor requirements, and sources of capital. During the planning phase they conduct investigations regarding the overall capital requirements of the firm and make feasibility studies of project areas as needed.

Step II—*Project requirements.* This step focuses on a review of present operations and identifies specific outputs required by the organization. The committee members review technical specifications and compare various alternative projects on the basis of their efficiency and effectiveness in accomplishing specific outcomes/goals.

Step III—*Project development.* In this phase of the audit, cash consequences and potentials of the various capital expenditure proposals are evaluated using various quantitative models. The committee ranks the projects in order of most favorable cash benefits. They also identify and evaluate alternative financing arrangements.

Step IV—*Top-management review and decision.* At this point the screening and implementation committee reviews the ranked projects with top management. Sound business judgment is necessary here to capture the complexity, importance, and sheer size of the decision. Top management must be concerned with economic trends, legal and regulatory requirements, competitive conditions, industry characteristics, and evaluations of future developments. The high failure rate of new products, technological obsolescence, and volatile consumer preferences are variables which must be considered and yet are difficult to capture in quantitative analytical models. Imagination, innovation, judgment, and experience all help the decision process.

Step V—*Project implementation.* Once top management has approved the ranking of projects, the implementation phase begins. The important step here is the establishment of a timetable with project start-up dates. Management designates project administrators and gives them specific appropriation budgets to carry out the project. A formal purchasing system controls expenditures, but the implementation committee continues to monitor the appropriations by comparing actual to budgeted amounts. The committee also follows up on cost overruns and watches over the physical progress of projects.

Step VI—*Post-audit review.* The last phase of capital expenditure administration is the post-audit review. This review should identify project failures, inefficiencies, or weaknesses and develop recommendations for management. By identifying problem areas the post-audit review will give management the necessary feedback to implement needed reforms.

The Review

The review or audit of the capital budgeting process has not received a great deal of attention in the business literature. The limited amount of research conducted indicates that such reviews are not currently being performed widely but that where this responsibility is conducted, problems often exist. For example, technological innovations can be extremely complex, and it takes considerable expertise of the auditor to evaluate the effectiveness or results of using these new technologies.

The review of the capital budgeting process should begin by addressing key areas and variables. By assuring that key factors have been identified, assumptions tightened, and internal control is effective, the decision-making process will benefit from past experience. Key areas in the review are:

- Evaluate whether the formal screening and implementations committee has identified the key factors upon which the results of the capital expenditure will depend.
- Evaluate the variables in the financial models developed for project requirements.
- Evaluate the internal control procedures in place during the implementation phase.
- Measure the contribution to overall profit (where feasible) from the various implemented projects and compare with project results.
- Prepare a post-audit review report.

Key factors. The key factors, a set of relevant characteristics which can be delineated from the organization's environment and which are commonly selected for attention, include market conditions, competitive environment, resource availability, technology, economic conditions and trends, government policies and regulations, demographic changes, and social environment.

The auditor must be knowledgeable about the past performance of the firm, the expectations of various groups with interest in the organization's actions, and the capabilities of the business in order to determine whether management has identified the key factors. Additionally, the auditor must assess the validity, reasonableness, and completeness of the assumptions management makes with regard to each key factor. See the Appendix for a list of questions which should be asked during the audit to determine the feasibility and applicability of capital expenditure projects.

As previously mentioned, the cash consequences of various capital projects are assessed by financial models. The auditor must evaluate the data and information used in these calculations because each variable can represent a range of values and important assumptions made regarding the timing of events.

Variables. See Figure 2 for variables included in financial models developed for project requirements. At this point, the audit should not concentrate solely on financial measures but should also include all other changes initiated by the project. Bela Gold, who has conducted considerable research in the area of technological innovations, has suggested looking at quality as well as quantities of inputs and outputs; shifts in worker tasks; product mix and production runs; reject rates; and equipment failure.

Another pertinent point made by Gold concerned the accounting treatment of certain costs associated with capital projects. In the companies researched, the question of revenue versus capital expenditure became relevant to evaluating the project.

> In evaluating the cost effects of technological innovations, result may be heavily affected by decisions concerning whether the following are treated as increases in the investment charged to the innovation or as additions to operating costs: the cost of interruptions to production caused by the innovation; the cost of delays before achieving effective functioning of the innovation, including attendant costs of equipment modifications, debugging, operator training, and trial runs; additional outlays in order to improve the capabilities of the new facilities; and the costs and investments involved in readjusting preceding and subsequent operations in order to improve the capabilities and integration of the encompassing production process. In general, there seems to be a widespread tendency to charge such additional outlays to early operating cost, in respect to which overruns are likely to be regarded sympathetically as virtually inevitable, thereby holding down the investment base to be used in calculating future rates of return.[2]

Internal control. The internal auditors will review, test, and evaluate the internal control system associated with the capital budgeting expenditures. This should ensure that well-conceived projects have not failed during the implementation phase due to lack of control procedures. Internal controls are also important in controlling costs, ensuring that all expenditures are authorized, and safeguarding assets and the accuracy of reports and records.

Contributions. Capital spending programs have the potential to satisfy organization profitability in a variety of ways. For example, capital programs can concentrate on replacement, cost reduction, capacity, quality, expansion, new products, or combinations of these profit factors (see Figure 2). The reviewer reports must be aware of the desired results from projects and reports and review them with this understanding.

Reports. In the post-audit report the auditor should summarize all recommendations dealing with key factors, variables, internal control, and contribution of projects to profits. An overall assessment of the projects audited could be most helpful from the auditee's viewpoint. Identification of strong points and recommendations can help management in assessing strengths as well as improvements needed. Demonstrating possible means of improving results as well as spotting sources of error in the project development phase will result in more effective guidelines for future projects. Appraisals of performance can be sensitive; therefore, the report should focus upon the intent of the evaluation to improve capital budget administration and, hopefully, guide, improve, and assist future capital programs.

The Benefits

Which personnel of the firm should perform the post-audit is a question not adequately answered in the literature. Members of management or persons closely involved with the capital projects are questionable choices when it comes to conducting unbiased reviews. Internal auditors are less connected to the capital projects. Moreover, with a broad knowledge of accounting and finance, they are familiar with methods of developing sound capital budgeting programs. In addition their backgrounds may well include the following potentially vital expertise:

- Knowledge of pro forma balance sheets and income statements to provide insight concerning the impact of investment decisions.
- Insight concerning legal and tax implications of investments.
- Understanding of the mechanics of capital budgeting models including key factors, key variables, and important assumptions.
- Knowledge of the sources of information for the key factors and key variables.
- Experience with report presentation which will communicate findings in the most usable fashion.

CONCLUSION

Successful capital budgeting is important to the financial well-being of most organizations. The post-audit review of capital expenditures is an important element of the process which can improve management's forecasting, evaluation, and decision-making procedures. The fact that such audits are conducted signals the organization that top management is committed to these objectives. The reviews may be accomplished by two audit strategies: the audit of specific projects or of the total capital budgeting process. This chapter has discussed each approach and has stressed many quantitative and qualitative factors that must be considered to ensure effective audits.

NOTES

[1] B. Gold, "Strengthening Managerial Approaches to Improving Technological Capabilities," *Strategic Management Journal,* 1983, pp. 209–20.

[2] Ibid., p. 217.

APPENDIX

Request Phase Questions

1. Is the capital expenditure procedure understood by administration and financial personnel?
2. Is the procedure adequately coordinated by the financial area?
3. If the division developed its own capital expenditure procedure and forms for evaluation and control of appropriations, are they compatible with those of corporate headquarters?
4. Are environmental controls built into capital projects?
5. Are tax considerations listed and computed on capital projects?
6. Are investment tax credits computed on capital projects?
7. Are indirect costs of projects estimated and included in capital proposals?
8. Are outside contractors' costs included?
9. Are start-up and completion dates listed?
10. Is justification of capital expenditures verified for reasonableness after the acquisition of the capital asset?
11. Are capital projects justified in accordance with the procedure (that is, economic justification versus another)?
12. Are discounted cash flow techniques used for capital expenditures?
13. Is the minimum acceptable rate of return known and applied on projects?
14. Is the payback period computed?

15. Is accounting net income shown?
16. Is inflation included in budget figures?
17. Is sensitivity analysis used for capital projects?
18. Are capital projects separated among their proper classifications: Replacement? new product lines? cost efficiencies?
19. What capital projects do not follow normal approval channels? Why?
20. Are rentals included in capital budgets?

Source: Adapted from Richard S. Savich, *Internal Audit of the Budget Process* (Institute of Internal Auditors, 1976).

Appendixes

A

Capital Budgeting Calculations: How to Use a Financial Calculator

Elbert Greynolds

Southern Methodist University

INTRODUCTION

*T*his appendix discusses how to compute the net present value (NPV) and the internal rate of return (IRR) for several common capital budgeting aftertax cash flow patterns. Time line diagrams provide the linkage between the capital budgeting cash flow pattern and the solution. Setting up the problems with time line diagrams facilitates solution with either calculators or computers. All examples of these basic cash flow patterns are solved using two powerful financial calculators: the HP-12C and the Texas Instruments Professional Business Analyst BA-55. A computer solution requires software that is similar to the calculator routines. A suitable software package for the IBM personal computer is listed in the Bibliography along with a reference supporting all mathematical calculations.

All examples assume discrete cash flows, which means that cash flows occur at specified points in time such as the end of months, quarters, or years. Interest rates are also discrete, which means interest is calculated at the *end* of specified time periods such as days, months, or years. Annual interest rates are stated as annual nominal interest rates (ANI percent), where the effective interest rate per compounding period equals the annual rate divided by the number of compounding periods per year (CPY). The number of compounding periods per year can differ from the number of payment periods per year (PY) for multiple cash flow situations. For example, the discount rate can be stated as an annual effective rate with cash flows occurring monthly, or the IRR based on monthly cash flows can be converted to the equivalent annual effective interest rate.

CASH FLOW PATTERNS

Most capital budgeting analyses have one of four fundamental cash flow patterns: (1) one cash outflow and inflow, (2) one cash outflow and level cash inflows plus a residual, (3) uneven cash outflows and inflows, or (4) level cash flows growing at a constant percent rate.

After developing a time line diagram, the cash flows should fit one of the above patterns. The examples shown in this appendix illustrate each of the above patterns.

CONVERTING INTEREST RATES

In the past, capital budgeting analyses often assumed all cash flows occurred at the end of each year with annual compounding of interest. Today, however, the high interest rates involved in capital budgeting analyses preclude such simplifications. Furthermore, calculators currently available allow computing NPVs and IRRs for projects with monthly or quarterly cash flows. For consistency a company should state their discount rate as an annual effective interest rate that can be converted to the appropriate equivalent interest rate per cash flow period before computing NPV. Also, all IRRs should be converted to a common base such as an annual effective interest rate. For these reasons the examples for multiple cash flow analyses include procedures for converting interest rates.

Converting interest rates is simple using the basic compound interest equation.

$$FV = PV(1 + i)^N \qquad \text{(A--1)}$$

$$i = [(FV/PV)^{(1/N)}] - 1 \qquad \text{(A--2)}$$

where

> FV = Future value of amount invested for N periods at i interest rate per compounding period.
>
> PV = Amount invested.
>
> N = Number of compounding periods.
>
> i = Decimal interest rate per compounding period (effective interest rate per compounding period).

The examples below do not show the solution using this equation because the calculator solves for all unknown values in this equation directly with the financial function keys.

Consider Time Line Diagram A–1, where $1 is invested at 18 percent annual with monthly compounding. Because the 18 percent is an

TIME LINE DIAGRAM A–1

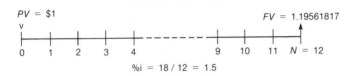

annual nominal interest rate, the effective rate used for compounding is 1.50 percent per month. After one year the interest earned is $0.19561817, and the annual effective interest rate is 19.561817 percent. After determining the annual effective interest rate, you can calculate the equivalent annual nominal interest rate for any number of compounding periods per year. For example, converting the annual rate in Time Line Diagram A–2 to the equivalent rate per quarter

TIME LINE DIAGRAM A–2

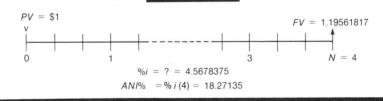

requires the following diagram with the compounding periods expressed as quarters (N equals 4 instead of 12).

By changing the number of compounding periods per year to four for quarterly compounding, and computing the interest rate, the equivalent quarterly interest rate, 4.568 percent, is found. Next, the quarterly rate is multiplied by the number of compounding periods per year to convert it to the equivalent annual nominal interest rate.

In summary, this section shows that an 18 percent annual interest rate with monthly compounding is equivalent to either a 19.561817 percent annual effective rate or an 18.27135 percent annual rate with quarterly compounding. Hence, for calculator solution, remember that the equations used require the interest rate per payment period as an input. So, for situations where the compounding periods per year differ from the number of payment periods per year, simply convert the rate to the equivalent rate per cash flow period and solve for the NPV. But when determining the IRR, the calculator computes the interest rate per payment period, which can be converted into the equivalent rate per compounding period when the compounding and payment periods per year differ.

ONE CASH OUTFLOW AND INFLOW

As indicated on Time Line Diagram A–3, this cash flow pattern matches capital budgeting situations with one cash outflow and inflow.

TIME LINE DIAGRAM A–3

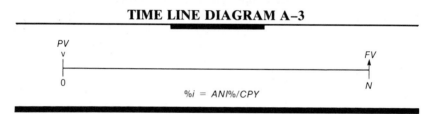

Examples include determining the present value of a future sum such as the salvage value of an asset, the sale value of an asset, or the amount realized from an investment. Other examples include determining the interest rate that makes the cash outlay grow to equal the future inflow (for example, the interest rate earned on a stock sold after 10 years with no dividends paid during the period).

The PV represents the present value of the cash outflow at time 0 (down arrow). Time 0 is the beginning of the first compounding period for discrete compounding. N represents the number of compounding periods, and FV is the cash inflow (up arrow) at the end of the Nth period. The annual nominal interest rate (ANI percent) is divided by the number of compounding periods per year (CPY) to determine the effective periodic compounding or discounting rate. For situations where the first cash flow is an inflow and the last cash flow is an outflow, simply reverse the down and up arrows on the diagram. All inputs necessary for calculator solution are shown on the time diagram.

Example A–1

A company has the opportunity to invest $50,000 in a project that returns $120,000 at the end of six years. Using a 14 percent annual discount rate compounded monthly, compute the investment's NPV. Compute the IRR with monthly compounding and convert it to an annual effective interest rate.

TIME LINE DIAGRAM A–4

Time Line Diagram A–4 shows the NPV as the difference between the present value of $120,000 received after 72 periods and the $50,000 outlay. The effective interest rate per month equals the 14 percent discount rate divided by 12. The total number of compounding periods equals the number of years multiplied by the number of compounding periods per year.

Solving for the IRR, however, requires changing the input values as indicated on Diagram A–5. Here the unknown value is the interest

TIME LINE DIAGRAM A–5

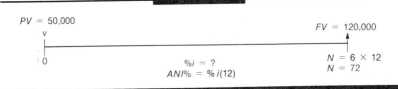

rate. After the effective rate per month is computed, it is multiplied by the number of compounding periods per year to convert it to the annual nominal rate.

Calculator Solution Example A–1

Each calculator's solution steps are shown below. Calculator keys pressed are enclosed in brackets [ ] as shown in the middle column.

703

The procedure is explained in the right-hand column, with the answer shown in the display column. Refer to the manufacturer's owner's manual for detailed explanations of specific calculator features.

HP-12C Keystroke Solution

Procedure	Keystroke	Display
Compute NPV		
1. Clear calculator and set display.	[f] [REG] [f] 2	0.00
2. Calculate and enter total number of compounding periods.	6 [ENTER] 12 [X] [n]	72.00
3. Enter annual discount rate and divide by number of compounding periods per year.	14 [ENTER] 12 [÷] [i]	1.17
4. Enter future value.	120000 [FV]	120,000.00
5. Compute present value.	[PV]	−52,057.76
6. Change sign and subtract outlay cost, to find NPV.	[CHS] 50000 [−]	2,057.76
Compute IRR		
7. Enter outlay as negative amount.	50000 [CHS] [PV]	−50,000.00
8. Compute effective interest rate per compounding period.	[i]	1.22
9. Multiply by number of compounding periods per year for ANI percent.	12 [X]	14.68
10. Compute equivalent annual effective rate.		
a. Enter number of compounding periods per year.	12 [n]	12.00
b. Enter 1 for PV, 0 for PMT, and compute FV.	1 [PV] 0 [PMT] [FV]	0.00 −1.16
c. Enter 1 for n.	1 [n]	1.00
d. Compute IRR as annual effective rate.	[i]	15.71

This project has a $2,057.76 NPV because the present value of the future amount discounted at 14 percent annual with monthly compounding equals $52,057.76, which exceeds the cash outlay of $50,000.

704

TI-BA-55 Keystroke Solution

Procedure	Keystroke	Display
Compute NPV		
1–a. Press Mode key until "FIN" appears.	[ON/C] [2nd] [Mode]	0.00
1–b. Clear calculator and set display.	[2nd] [CLmode] [2nd] [Fix] 2	0.00 0.00
2. Calculate and enter total number of compounding periods.	6 [X] 12 [=] [N]	72.00
3. Enter annual discount rate and divide by number of compounding periods per year.	14 [÷] 12 [=] [%i]	1.17
4. Enter future value.	120000 [FV]	120000.00
5. Compute present value.	[CPT] [PV]	52057.76
6. Subtract outlay cost to find NPV.	[−] 50000 [=]	2057.76
Compute IRR		
7. Enter outlay cost.	50000 [PV]	50000.00
8. Compute effective interest rate per compounding period.	[CPT] [%i]	1.22
9. Multiply by number of compounding periods per year for ANI percent.	[X] 12 [=] [STO] 1	14.68 14.68
10. Compute equivalent annual effective rate.		
a. Enter number of compounding periods per year.	12	12
b. Compute annual effective rate.	[APR>] [RCL] 1 [=]	12.00 15.71

The internal rate of return expressed as an annual nominal interest rate is 14.68 percent with monthly compounding, which is equivalent to an annual effective interest rate of 15.71 percent.

The keystroke procedure shown for computing the annual effective interest rate with the HP-12C calculator used the financial key functions for solution. The TI BA-55, however, uses a special function key for computing the annual effective interest rate for a given annual nominal rate.

ONE CASH OUTFLOW AND LEVEL CASH INFLOWS PLUS A RESIDUAL

Often, a capital budgeting situation involves a cash outlay and a series of level cash flows with a residual or salvage value. Time Line Diagram A–6 illustrates such a cash flow pattern where the level cash flows occur at the end of each payment period.

TIME LINE DIAGRAM A–6

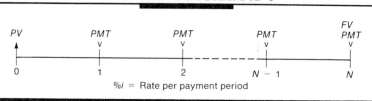

$\%i$ = Rate per payment period

The value used for the interest rate is the effective rate per *payment period,* which often matches the compounding period. For example, cash flows occur monthly and interest compounds monthly. But, as shown in this section, the discount rate can have a compounding period frequency different than the number of payments per year. Solving these end-of-period cash flow patterns with either calculator requires using the [CPT] key on the TI BA-55 and setting the payment switch to [END] on the HP-12C calculator. As before, developing the time diagram determines the calculator inputs. Both calculators' financial key equations assume that the FV occurs at the end of the last *payment period,* as shown in Time Line Diagram A–6.

This cash flow pattern matches capital budgeting analyses where one cash outlay occurs, with level or equal end-of-period cash inflows, and a final extra cash inflow such as a salvage value or residual value. For situations where the payments occur at the beginning of each period and the extra cash flow occurs at the end of the last period, use the [2nd] [DUE] key for solution with the TI BA-55, and use the [BEG] switch for solution with the HP-12C.

Example A–2

A company is evaluating a capital budgeting project that requires a $20,000 outlay. This project will generate savings of $9,000 aftertax at the end of each quarter for 10 years. At the end of the 10 years, the project's assets will generate $50,000 aftertax. Using an annual discount rate of 16 percent with monthly compounding, compute the

NPV. Next, determine the annual IRR with quarterly compounding, with annual compounding, and with monthly compounding. In other words, convert the annual nominal rate with quarterly compounding to the equivalent annual effective rate, and to the equivalent annual nominal rate with monthly compounding.

Calculator Solution

This example illustrates the conversion of interest rates as well as the computing of the NPV and IRR. The procedure shown for the HP-12C calculator uses the financial keys, while the TI BA-55 uses special interest rate conversion function keys.

TIME LINE DIAGRAM A–7

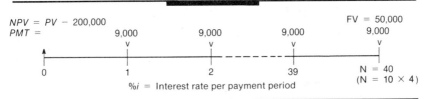

Time Line Diagram A–7 has all necessary inputs for computing NPV except for the interest rate conversions. NPV equals the difference between the computed present value and outlay cost.

Solving for IRR requires entering the cash flows indicated on Time Line Diagram A–8 and computing the interest rate per cash flow pe-

TIME LINE DIAGRAM A–8

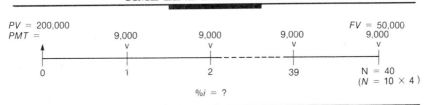

riod. The effective interest rate per cash flow period can then be converted to the equivalent annual effective interest rate or the equivalent rate for any other discrete time period.

HP-12C Keystroke Solution

Procedure	Keystroke	Display
Compute NPV		
1. Clear calculator and set display.	[f] [REG] [f] 2	0.00
2. Compute interest rate per cash flow period.		
a. Enter annual discount rate and divide by number of compounding periods per year.	16 [ENTER] 12 [n] [÷] [i]	1.33
b. Enter 1 for PV, 0 for PMT, and calculate FV.	1 [PV] 0 [PMT] [FV]	−1.17
c. Enter number of cash flow periods per year.	4 [n]	4.00
d. Compute effective rate per cash flow period.	[i]	4.05
3. Calculate and enter total number of level cash flow periods.	10 [ENTER] 4 [X] [n]	40.00
4. Enter level cash flow.	9000 [PMT]	9,000.00
5. Enter future value.	50000[FV]	50,000.00
6. Compute present value of cash inflows.	[PV]	−186,925.78
7. Change sign and subtract outlay cost, to find NPV.	[CHS] 200000 [−]	−13,074.22
Compute IRR		
8. Enter outlay as negative amount.	200000 [CHS] [PV]	−200,000.00
9. Compute effective interest rate per cash flow period.	[i]	3.64
10. Multiply by number of cash flow periods per year for ANI percent.	4 [X]	14.57
11. Compute equivalent annual effective rate.		
a. Enter number of cash flow periods per year.	4 [n]	4.00
b. Enter 1 for PV, 0 for PMT, and compute FV.	1 [PV] 0 [PMT] [FV]	0.00 −1.15
c. Enter 1 for n.	1 [n]	1.00
d. Compute IRR as annual effective rate.	[i]	15.38
e. Enter number of compounding periods per year.	12 [n]	12.00
f. Compute the rate per compounding period.	[i]	1.20
g. Compute annual nominal rate compounded *n* times per year.	[RCL] [n] [X]	14.39

TI-BA-55 Keystroke Solution

Procedure	Keystroke	Display
Compute NPV		
1–a. Press Mode key until "FIN" appears.	[ON/C] [2nd] [Mode]	0.00
1–b. Clear calculator and set display.	[2nd] [CLmode]	0.00
	[2nd] [Fix] 2	0.00
2. Convert interest rate.		
a. Enter number of compounding periods per year.	12 [STO] 1	12.00
b. Enter annual rate and calculate annual effective rate.	[APR>] 16 [=]	17.23
	[STO] [2]	17.23
c. Enter number of cash flow periods per year and compute annual rate compounded *N* times per year.	4 [<EFF]	4.00
	[RCL] 2 [=]	16.21
d. Divide by number of cash flow periods and enter.	[÷] 4 [=] [%i]	4.05
3. Calculate and enter total number of cash flow periods.	10 [X] 4 [=] [N]	40.00
4. Enter level cash flow amounts.	9000 [PMT]	9000.00
5. Enter future value.	50000 [FV]	50000.00
6. Compute present value.	[CPT] [PV]	186925.79
7. Subtract outlay cost to find NPV.	[−] 200000 [=]	−13074.21
Compute IRR		
8. Enter outlay cost.	200000 [PV]	200000.00
9. Compute effective interest rate per cash flow period.	[CPT] [%i]	3.64
10. Multiply by number of cash flow periods per year for ANI percent.	[X] 4 [=]	14.57
	[STO] 1	14.57
11. Compute equivalent annual effective rate.		
a. Enter number of cash flow periods per year.	4	4
b. Compute annual effective rate.	[APR>] [RCL] 1 [=]	15.38
	[STO] 2	15.38
c. Enter number of compounding periods per year, and compute annual nominal rate, compounded monthly.	12 [<EFF] [RCL] 2 [=]	14.39

This project has a negative NPV of −$13,074.22, with a discount rate of 16 percent compounded monthly. As a result, the IRR with quarterly compounding is 14.57 percent, which is equivalent to an annual effective rate of 15.38 percent or an annual rate with monthly compounding of 14.39 percent.

UNEVEN CASH FLOWS

Often, capital budgeting problems involve uneven cash flows when working with aftertax cash flows. The two calculators illustrated in this section have features that ease computation of NPV and IRR for a capital budgeting analysis with uneven cash flows. Specifically, each calculator can compute the NPV and IRR of *Grouped Cash Flows*. As a result, problems where the cash flows remain constant for a period of time and then change are easily solved. The procedure shown for both calculators works for all cases but is not necessarily the most efficient for some cases. But it is effective. Time Line Diagram A–9 illustrates grouped cash flows.

TIME LINE DIAGRAM A–9

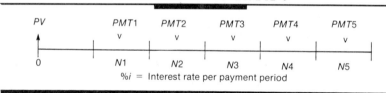

%*i* = Interest rate per payment period

The cash outflow (*PV*) is shown at time 0 above the up arrow. The first cash inflow (*PMT*1) is shown above the line with the number of times this amount occurs in sequence shown below the line. For example, the cash flow is $1,000 and occurs 12 times. Each cash flow or group of cash flows is shown in this fashion. Both calculators will compute the NPV or IRR for such cash flow patterns.

Example A–3

A capital budgeting project requires an initial outlay of $250,000 with the following end-of-month cash inflows. At the end of the final cash inflow period, the project's assets can be sold for $75,000.

Cash flow	Number of months
$ 2,000	1
5,000	8
7,500	12
8,700	24
11,000	6

Compute the NPV, assuming a 20 percent annual nominal interest rate compounded quarterly. Next, compute the IRR and convert the annual interest rate with monthly compounding to the equivalent annual effective rate, and the equivalent annual rate with quarterly compounding.

Calculator Solution

All cash flow inputs necessary for solution of this example are shown on Time Line Diagram A–10.

TIME LINE DIAGRAM A–10

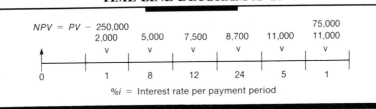

TIME LINE DIAGRAM A–10

Both calculators have special key stroke procedures for entering these cash flows and computing the NPV. Unlike the example involving equal cash flows, the NPV is computed directly by the calculator.

TIME LINE DIAGRAM A–11

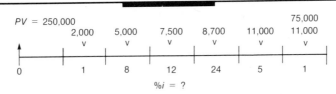

711

When multiple cash flows occur at the same time as in the final period above, they must be added together because the calculators allow only one cash flow amount per time period to be entered.

The cash flow inputs for computing IRR are shown in Time Line Diagram A–11. Actually, as shown in the keystroke solutions, both the NPV and IRR are calculated based on the same set of input values.

HP-12C Keystroke Solution

Procedure	Keystroke	Display
Compute NPV		
1. Clear calculator and set display.	[f] [REG] [f] 2	0.00
2. Compute interest rate per cash flow period.		
a. Enter annual discount rate and divide by number of compounding periods per year.	20 [ENTER] 4 [n] [÷] [i]	4. 5.00
b. Enter 1 for PV, 0 for PMT, and calculate FV.	1 [PV] 0 [PMT] [FV]	−1.22
c. Enter number of cash flow periods per year.	12 [n]	12.00
d. Compute effective rate per cash flow period.	[i]	1.64
3. Enter initial cash outflow.	250000 [CHS] [g] [CFO]	−250,000.00
4. Enter grouped cash flows as indicated on time diagram.		
a. Group 1		
Amount	2000 [g] [CFj]	2,000.00
Number	1 [g] [Nj]	1.00
b. Group 2		
Amount	5000 [g] [CFj]	5,000.00
Number	8 [g] [Nj]	8.00
c. Group 3		
Amount	7500 [g] [CFj]	7,500.00
Number	12 [g] [Nj]	12.00
d. Group 4		
Amount	8700 [g] [CFj]	8,700.00
Number	24 [g] [Nj]	24.00
e. Group 5		
Amount	11000 [g] [CFj]	11,000.00
Number	5 [g] [Nj]	5.00
f. Final group with the salvage value added to the final cash flow.	11000 [Enter] 75000 [+] [g] [CFj] 1 [g] [Nj]	75,000.00 86,000.00 1.00

Procedure	Keystroke	Display
5. Compute NPV of cash inflows.	[f] [NPV]	43,212.54
Compute IRR		
6. Compute effective interest rate per cash flow period.	[f] [IRR]	2.22
7. Multiply by number of cash flow periods per year for ANI percent.	12 [X]	26.67
8. Compute annual rates.		
a. Enter number of cash flow periods per year.	12 [n]	12.00
b. Enter 1 for PV, 0 for PMT, and compute FV.	1 [PV] 0 [PMT] [FV]	0.00 −1.30
c. Enter 1 for *n*.	1 [n]	1.00
d. Compute IRR as annual effective rate.	[i]	30.18
e. Enter number of compounding periods per year.	4 [n]	4.00
f. Compute the rate per compounding period.	[i]	6.82
g. Compute annual nominal rate compounded *n* times per year.	[RCL] [n] [X]	27.26

The key [<>] shown in the keystroke solution below is the "X Exchange Y" key located above the [STO] key on the BA-55.

TI-BA-55 Keystroke Solution

Procedure	Keystroke	Display
Compute NPV		
1–a. Press Mode key until "CF" appears.	[ON/C] [2nd] [Mode]	0.00
1–b. Clear calculator and set display.	[2nd] [CLmode] [2nd] [Fix] 2	0.00 0.00
2. Convert interest rate.		
a. Enter number of compounding periods per year.	4 [APR>]	4.00
b. Enter annual rate and calculate annual effective rate.	20 [=] [STO] [%i]	21.55 21.55
c. Enter number of cash flow periods per year	12 [<EFF] [RCL] [%i] [=]	12.00 19.68

713

Procedure	Keystroke	Display
and compute annual nominal rate.		
d. Divide by number of cash flow periods and enter.	[÷] 12 [=] [%i]	1.64
3. Enter outlay cost as a negative value.	250000 [+/−] [PV]	−250000.00
4. Enter grouped cash flows as indicated on time diagram.		
a. Group 1		
Amount	2000 [2nd] [Frq]	Fr 000
Number	1 [STO] 1	2000.00
b. Group 2		
Amount	5000 [2nd] [Frq]	Fr 000
Number	8 [STO] 2	5000.00
c. Group 3		
Amount	7500 [2nd] [Frq]	Fr 000
Number	12 [STO] 3	7500.00
d. Group 4		
Amount	8700 [2nd] [Frq]	Fr 000
Number	24 [STO] 4	8700.00
e. Group 5		
Amount	11000 [2nd] [Frq]	Fr 000
Number	5 [STO] 5	11000.00
f. Final group with the salvage value added to the final cash flow.	11000 [+] 75000 [=] [2nd] [Frq] 1 [STO] 6	86000.00 Fr 000 86000.00
5. Compute NPV of cash inflows.	[CPT] [2nd] [NPV]	43212.58
Compute IRR		
6. Compute effective interest rate per cash flow period.	[CPT] [2nd] [IRR]	2.22
7. Multiply by number of cash flow periods per year for ANI percent.	[X] 12 [=] [STO] [%i]	26.67 26.67
8. Compute equivalent annual effective rate.		
a. Enter number of cash flow periods per year.	12	12
b. Compute annual effective rate.	[APR>] [RCL] [%i] [=] [STO] [%i]	30.18
c. Enter number of compounding periods per year, and compute annual nominal rate.	4 [<EFF] [RCL] [%i] [=]	27.26

This project has a positive NPV of $43,213 (the small difference between the two NPV answers is due to each calculator using a different number of digits internally for calculations). The annual IRR is 26.67 percent with monthly compounding, which is equivalent to a 30.18 percent annual effective interest rate, which in turn is equal to a 27.26 percent annual rate with quarterly compounding.

CASH FLOWS GROWING AT A CONSTANT PERCENT RATE

Another common capital budgeting situation involves cash flows growing at a constant percent rate over a period of time (for example, cash flows increase by 5 percent each month for four months as illustrated in Time Line Diagram A–12).

TIME LINE DIAGRAM A–12

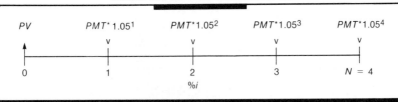

The present value can be computed by manually determining the amount of each cash flow and using the grouped cash flow keys. This, however, is awkward and for a large number of periods exceeds the capacity of the calculators or even many computer programs.[1]

By converting the interest rate, the calculator financial keys can compute either the NPV or IRR for such cash flows. The interest rates are converted using the following equation when solving for the NPV.

$$b\% = \{[(1 + i)/(1 + g)] - 1\} * 100 \qquad \text{(A–3)}$$

The i represents the decimal interest rate per cash flow period, and the g represents the decimal growth rate per cash flow period. The $b\%$ represents the equivalent percent interest rate used for computing the present value. So, for the example above, if the interest rate per cash flow period ($\%i$) is 1 percent, and the growth rate ($g\%$) is 5 percent, then the $b\%$ rate is:

$$b\% = \{[(1 + .01)/(1 + .05)] - 1\} * 100$$
$$b\% = -3.80952$$

The equivalent interest rate is negative because the growth rate is larger than the discount rate. Don't be alarmed: the calculator's financial equations operate with either negative or positive interest rates. In any case the cash flow pattern in Time Line Diagram A–8 is converted to that found in Time Line Diagram A–13.

TIME LINE DIAGRAM A–13

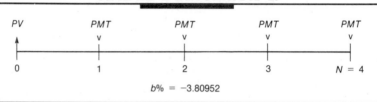

When using this method, however, the payment received at the end of the first cash flow period is compounded by the growth rate. Hence, if the first payment is not compounded, then divide it by $(1 + g)$ before entering the cash flow with the [PMT] key.

Computing the interest rate is simply the reverse of the above procedure, assuming the growth rate is specified. First, compute the interest rate per cash flow period ($b\%$), and then convert to the actual interest rate ($\%i$), assuming a given growth rate ($g\%$) using Equation A–4. The values b and g are expressed as decimals.

$$i\% = [(1 + b) * (1 + g) - 1] * 100 \qquad \text{(A–4)}$$

Example A–4

A company is expecting 8 percent annual increases in maintenance expenses for a particular manufacturing process over the next 10 years. Last year, the annual maintenance expense totaled $5,000. As part of a capital budgeting evaluation, the present value of the maintenance expenses must be computed, assuming a 15 percent discount rate. What is the present value?

First, the equivalent interest rate ($b\%$) is computed, and then the present value is computed using the financial function keys on each calculator.

HP-12C Keystroke Solution

Procedure	Keystroke	Display
Compute present value		
1. Clear calculator and set display.	[f] [REG] [f] 2	0.00
2. Compute equivalent interest rate (b%).		
a. Enter 1 and the growth rate per cash flow period.	1 [ENTER]	1.00
	8 [%] [+]	1.08
	[STO] 1	1.08
b. Enter 1 and the discount rate per cash flow period. Compute (1 + i).	1 [ENTER]	1.00
	15 [%] [+]	1.15
c. Compute b% and enter.	[RCL] 1 [÷]	1.06
	1 [−] 100 [X] [i]	6.48
3. Enter total number of equal cash flows.	10 [n]	10.00
4. Enter level cash flow.	5000 [PMT]	5,000.00
5. Compute present value of cash inflows.	[PV]	−35,975.32

TI-BA-55 Keystroke Solution

Procedure	Keystroke	Display
Compute NPV		
1–a. Press Mode key until "FIN" appears.	[ON/C] [2nd] [Mode]	0.00
1–b. Clear calculator and set display.	[2nd] [CLmode]	0.00
	[2nd] [Fix] 2	0.00
2. Compute equivalent interest rate (b%).		
a. Enter 1 and the growth rate per cash flow period.	1 [+]	1.00
	8 [%] [=]	1.08
	[STO] 1	1.08
b. Enter 1 and the discount rate per cash flow period. Compute (1 + i).	1 [+]	1.00
	15 [%] [=]	1.15
c. Compute b% and enter.	[÷] [RCL] 1 [=]	1.06
	[−] 1 [X] 100 [=] [%i]	6.48
3. Enter total number of equal cash flows.	10 [N]	10.00
4. Enter level cash flow.	5000 [PMT]	5000.00
5. Compute present value of cash inflows.	[CPT] [PV]	35975.32

The present value of the 10 years of maintenance expenses growing at 8 percent annually is $35,975.32, using a 15 percent discount rate.

SUMMARY

Examples contained in this appendix should provide enough guidance for computing the NPV and IRR for a number of capital budgeting situations. Remember that the key for solution is developing time line diagrams and identifying the cash flow pattern.

NOTES

[1] Fortunately, an alternative method is available. For an in-depth treatment, see Greynolds, Aronofsky, and Frame, *Financial Analysis Using Calculators: Time Value of Money* (New York: McGraw-Hill, 1980), pp. 390–94.

BIBLIOGRAPHY

Books

Greynolds, Elbert B., Jr.; Julius S. Aronofsky; and Robert J. Frame. *Financial Analysis Using Calculators: Time Value of Money*. New York: McGraw-Hill, 1980.

Greynolds, Elbert B., Jr.; Kathy A. Kelly; and Steven W. Smith. *Texas Instruments Professional Business Analyst Guide*. Dallas: Texas Instruments, 1982.

Hewlett-Packard. *HP-12C Owner's Handbook and Problem-Solving Guide*. Corvallis, Oreg. Hewlett-Packard Company, 1981.

Computer Software

Ansonn Software, Inc. *Real Estate Tools I*. 2801 N. Surrey Drive, Carrollton, Texas.

B

Capital Budgeting Models: A Software Directory

Mike Kaufman

Corporate Finance Associates

*T*his is a cross-section of commercially available software packages that are useful for one or more capital budgeting applications. Section 1 deals with mainframes and minicomputer software. Section 2 covers software for microcomputers. Information provided:

- Product/publisher
- Applications/price
- Compatible systems
- Comments

Application codes:

1. Strategic planning of capital expenditures.
2. Preparing the capital budget.

3. Initiating an individual project.
4. Financing capital expenditures.
5. Implementing a capital project.

Software vendors should be contacted for complete information on their packages. A directory of the software publishers cited appears at the end of this appendix.[1]

Software directories tend to be ephemeral. This one represents the generation preceding the IBM PC AT and "fully integrated" software (Symphony, Framework, etc.). A key point being made here is that much of the software for capital budgeting is marketed for more general applications. See Chapter 1 for further comments.

---

[1] Sources: Mainframe and minicomputer information based on data furnished by Datapro Research Corporation, Delran, N.J. 08075. Microcomputer information from Datapro and other sources.

Mainframes and Minicomputers

Product Publisher	Applications Price	Compatible systems	Comments
ARIMA I. P. Sharp Associates	1 $1,200/month	IBM 370, 3000, 4300, PCMS	Interactive time series analysis and forecasting.
Business Models Business Model Systems	1 $8,000–30,000	IBM 34, 36, 38, 3000, 4300 Wang VS; HP 3000, NCR 9000; Honeywell DPS6	Financial modeling, planning, and budgeting; over 600 users.
Control Strategist Xerox Computer Services	1, 2 $25,000	IBM 370, 303X, 308X, 4300; DEC:VAX; Honeywell	Consolidations, budgeting, analysis, modeling, forecasting, simulation.
Impact DSS MDCR, Inc.	1 $2,000/month	IBM 370, 3000, 4300; Wang	Planning, reporting, modeling; micro-mainframe compatibility; over 1,000 users.
Insight Insight Software Systems	1 $12–17,000	IBM 34, 38	Financial modeling and reporting; over 350 users.
Capital Project Accounting American Software	2, 5 N/A	IBM 3000, 4300; HP 3000	Capital budget administration and tracking.
CA–Financial Planner Computer Assoc. Int'l	1, 4 N/A	IBM 370, 3000, 4300; HP 3000	Evaluates alternative financing; 900 plus users; micro link, data base link.
CETS Mgt. Science America	5 N/A	IBM 370, 303X, 4300	Tracks capital expenditures (new product).
Capital Program Analysis and accounting McCormack & Dodge	2, 5 N/A	IBM 370, 3000, 4300	Capital budget and project monitoring; PC link.

Product / Publisher	Applications / Price	Compatible systems	Comments
Discounted Cash Flow / Resource Software Int'l	3 / $490	HP 3000	Project feasibility analysis.
Dollar Flow / Cognos, Inc.	4 / $900/month	HP 3000	Financial planning and analysis.
FCS-EPS / EPS	1, 2 / N/A	IBM 370, 303X, 4300 Prime; DEC, HP, etc.	Powerful analytic package; 800+ users.
Financial Ratio Code / Resource Software International	4 / $300	HP 3000	Useful for evaluating financing alternatives.
Fiscal / Rapidata	3 / N/A	DEC 10, 20	Simulation models; also runs on most micros.
IMPACT / MDCR, Inc.	1 / $2,000/month	IBM 370, 303X, 4300; PCMS	Planning, forecasting, analysis.
IFPS / Execucom Systems	1, 2 / $64,000	IBM; CDC; Honeywell; DEC; Prime; HP; Wang	Integrated system—English commands; 700+ users
IRR / Resource Software, International	3 / $250	HP 3000	IRR calculations.
Lease Buy Analysis / Resource Software, International	3, 4 / $400	HP 3000	Uses NPV comparison.
Lease Purchase Analysis / IBM	3, 4 / $34/month	Any Fortran IV IBM	Comprehensive reports.
NY Plan / Mycroshare, Inc.	3, 4 / $5–10,000	DEC:PDP11, VAX; TI 600, 800; Prime	Modeling and capital investment analysis.

Product / Company		Computers	Description
RETURN Automated Analysis	3 N/A	HP 3000; any system using CPM	Menu-driven; interactive IRR calculator; over 10,000 users.
SIMPLAN Simplan Systems	1 $30–70,000	IBM 370, 303X, 4300; PCMs; Prime	Powerful modeling package; planning, forecasting, budgeting.
SPREAD L&L Products	1, 2 N/A	IBM 34, 370; HP 3000; CDC; Data General, DEC	Versatile spreadsheet package; 600+ users.
Easyplan Professional Computer Resources, Inc.	1 $795	IBM 34	Interactive, on-line business planning and modeling; 600+ users.
MSCS McDonnell Douglas	5 N/A	IBM 370, 3000, 4300; CDC; Omega; Itel; DEC	Project scheduling and control.
PAC II AGS Management Systems	5 N/A	Any COBOL system	Project management and planning; 1,000+ users.
PREMIS K&H Computer Systems	5 $2,700/month	IBM 370	Network planning.
Project Planner Para Research, Inc.	5 $3–5,000	IBM 34, 36, 38	Extensive reporting.
Project/2 Project Software and Development	5 N/A	IBM 370; DEC; Sperry	Multiproject capability; 800+ users.
Sunplan II Sun Information Services Company	2, 5 N/A	IBM 370, 3000, 4300; PLMs	Modular project management package.

Microcomputers

Product Publisher	Applications Price	Compatible systems	Comments
Context MBA Context Management Systems	1, 2 $695	IBM PC	Integrated package for information analysis and data management.
Financial Modeling Program	1,4 N/A	Apple II, III; CP/M Systems	Interactive evaluation of financial alternatives.
Lotus 1-2-3 Lotus Development Corporation	1, 2 $495	IBM PC and compatibles	Best-selling integrated spreadsheet, graphics, and data management.
Spread Financial Modeling Lupfer & Long, Inc.	1, 2 $500	IBM PC; PCXT	Modeling, analysis, and forecasting.
Multiplan* Microsoft	1, 2 $375	Apple II, III; IBM PC	Another popular spreadsheet package with some unique features.

	PLAN 80*	CP/M	
	1, 2 / N/A		Financial modeling.
Business Planning Systems			
Milestone	5 / $295	Apple II, III; CP/M Systems	Network analysis for project control.
Digital Marketing			
Project Management Systems (PMS II)	5 / $1,295	CP/M, MP/M, CP/M86 systems	Network analysis.
North America MICA			
Visi Schedule	5 / $300	Apple II, III	Project planning and resource allocation.
Visi Corporation			
AG Statement Spread	4 / $150	Apple II, III	Financial statement analysis.
Financial Systems, Inc			
Economic Analysis Program Group	3 / N/A	TRS 80, I, III; Apple II, III	Decision tree analysis; lease versus buy; IRR.
Institute of Industrial Engineers			

* Not datapro.

PUBLISHERS' DIRECTORY

AGS Management Systems, Inc.
320 Walnut St.
Philadelphia, PA 19106
(215) 265-1550
Telex: 510–6603320

American Software, Inc.
443 E. Paces Ferry Rd.
Atlanta, GA 30305
(404) 261-4381

Automated Analysis
14617 Victory Blvd. #4
Van Nuys, CA 91411
(213) 787-7700

Business Model Systems, Inc.
2625 Butterfield Rd. Ste 103N
Oak Brook, IL 60521
(312) 789-9160
Telex: 230-280051

Business Planning Systems
Two North State St.
Dover, DE 19901

Cognos, Inc.
275 Slater Street, 10th Flr.
Ottawa, Ontario K1P 5H9
(613) 237-1440
TWX: 0533341

Computer Associates International
Computer Associates Building
125 Jericho Turnpike
Jericho, NY 11753
(516) 333-6700
(800) 645-3003

Context Management Systems
23864 Hawthorne Blvd. Ste 101
Torrance, CA 90505
(213) 378-8277
Attn: Martin Mazner, VP Mktg.

Digital Marketing
2363 Boulevard Circle
Walnut Creek, CA 94595
(415) 938-2880
Attn: Hal Miller, Sales Rep.

EPS
1 Industrial Dr.
Windham, NH 0307
(603) 898-1800

Execucom Systems Corp.
P.O. Box 9758
Austin, TX 78766
(512) 346-4980
Telex: 776497

Financial Systems, Inc.
P.O. Box 2012
Kearney, NE 68847
(308) 237-5995

Georgia Tech Research Institute
225 North Avenue, 3rd Flr.
Atlanta, GA 30332
(404) 894-4812
Attn: Elinor Plowden,
Licensing Administration

International Business Machines
Old Orchard Rd.
Armonk, NY 10504
(914) 696-1900

Insight Software Systems, Inc.
One N. Broadway
White Plains, NY 10601
(914) 682-4910

Institute of Industrial Engineers
25 Technology Park
Norcross, GA 30092
(404) 449-0460

I.P. Sharp Associates Ltd.
2 First Canadian Pl. Ste 1900
Toronto, Ontario M5X 1E3
(416) 364-5361
Telex: 065229

K & H Computer Systems, Inc.
P.O. Box 4
Sparta, NJ 07871
(201) 729-6142

L & L Products, Inc.
P.O. Box A-57
Wheeler Professional Park
Hanover, NH 03755
(603) 643-4503

Lotus Development Corporation
55 Wheeler St.
Cambridge, MA 02138
(617) 492-7171
Attn: Marv Goldschmitt,
Dir., Product Mktg.

Lupfer & Long, Inc.
P.O. Box A-57
Hanover, NH 03755
(603) 643-4503

Management Science America, Inc.
3445 Peachtree Rd., N.E. Ste 1300
Atlanta, GA 30326
(404) 239-2000

Microsoft
10700 Northup Way
Bellevue, WA 98004

McCormack & Dodge Corp.
1225 Worcester Rd.
Netick, MA 01760
(617) 665-8200

McDonnell Douglas Automation Co.
P.O. Box 516
St. Louis, MO 63166
(800) 325-1551

MDCR, Inc.
750 Highway 18
East Brunswick, NJ 08816
(201) 257-5700

Mycroshare, Inc.
135 Lake St., South, Suite 209
Kirkland, WA 98033
(206) 822-6074

North America MICA, Inc.
11772 Sorrento Valley Road, Ste 260
San Diego, CA 92121
(714) 481-6998
Attn: E. A. Vanderpool, Pres.

Para Research Inc.
85 Eastern Avenue
Gloucester, MA 01930
(617) 283-3438

Professional Computer Resources, Inc.
2021 Midwest Rd.
Oak Brook, IL 60521
(312) 932-2200

Project Software & Development, Inc.
14 Story Street
Cambridge, MA 02138
(617) 661-1444
Telex: 921415

Rapidata,
Division National Data Corp.
20 New Dutch Ln.
Box 1049
Fairfield, NJ 07006
(201) 227-0035

Resource Software International, Inc.
330 New Brunswick Ave.
Fords, NJ 08863
(201) 738-8500

Simplan Systems, Inc.
300 Eastowne Dr.
Chapel Hill, NC 27514
(919) 493-2495

Sun Information Services Co.
Glenhardie Corporate Center
1285 Drummers Ln.
Wayne, PA 19087
(215) 687-8210

VisiCorp
2895 Zanker Road
San Jose, CA 95111
(408) 946-9000
Attn: Jeff Walden, Public Relations
Mgr.

Xerox Computer Services
5310 Beethoven St.
Los Angeles, CA 90066
(213) 306-4000

727

C

Capital Budgeting in the Public Sector: The MTA Program

David Kessler

MTA Office of the Inspector General, New York City

This appendix is about capital budgeting in the nonprofit sector. How are capital expenditures planned and managed in the world of governmental and not-for-profit bureaucracies? How are capital improvements financed? Finally, how do the two sectors compare in the area of capital planning, and to what extent do the lessons learned in the private sector have applicability in the public sector?

As an example of the problems experienced in the governmental sector and the progress made in improving the processes of capital budget planning and financing, we will review some of the approaches being used at New York's Metropolitan Transportation Authority, which recently embarked on an $8.5 billion five-year program to revitalize the facilities of the New York City subway and bus systems and the Long Island and Metro-North commuter railroads.

COMPARING THE NONPROFIT AND PRIVATE SECTORS

While it is impossible to generalize about the wide variety of planning, financing, and project management techniques used by various levels of government (federal, state, and local), by the wide spectrum of different-sized organizations, and by the quasi-governmental enterprises, George A. Steiner has pointed out a number of characteristics that are unique to government organizations in particular. Among these are:

1. Decision making in government is dominated by politics and not by economic factors, as is the case with most business decisions.
2. Managers in government are influenced by the pressures of interest groups to a much greater extent than managers of private businesses.
3. The missions, purposes, and objectives of government agencies are typically greater in number and less specific than those of business organizations.
4. The criteria for decision making in government have more to do with satisfying the "public good" and with political compromise than with economic factors such as profit and return on investment—and the governmental criteria are less easily quantifiable.
5. Although governments have increasingly used cost-benefit analysis for decision making, the quantitative tools for choosing among alternatives are not as precise and rigorous as in the private sector.
6. The implementation process in government can take years and involve complex reviews at many levels (including citizen participation). This delays improvements and impedes effectiveness since it means that governments are often following outdated priorities.[1]

On the other hand, through cost-effectiveness techniques and by applications of the concept of Planning-Programming Budgeting Systems (PPBS), governments have used analytical methods to allocate funds among alternative programs. The development of PPBS, in which a government's budget comprises the costs and outputs associated with the functions it performs or the programs it operates (rather than on a line-item-by-line-item basis), is generally credited to former Secretary of Defense Robert McNamara and his associates ("the whiz kids") at that agency during the mid-1960s. It is a powerful tool that

729

encompasses many elements of business strategic planning. In addition, state and local governments have developed long-range plans for water resource systems, land use, health-care systems, and transportation.

During the past 15 years or so, governments have increasingly had to present their capital improvement plans to the public. This is due to the following developments:

1. The need to seek financing outside of the annual budget process. Most state and local governments borrow money on a regular basis through government-backed bond issues, or they establish quasi-independent agencies or authorities which are empowered to borrow from investors. Prospective lenders require plans, project information, and revenue streams before making their commitments.

2. Federal capital grant programs. The federal government requires a great deal of detailed planning in connection with its capital grant programs in areas such as highway construction, mass transit, sewage treatment plants and other environmental improvements, health care, and education facilities.

3. National infrastructure needs. There is a growing public awareness and discussion regarding the need to repair and rehabilitate the nation's infrastructure. There have been articles on the "infrastructure problem" in the popular press, and there have been several recent studies of the problem, all pointing to the sharp downward trend in investment in infrastructure renewal. The result has been that governments at all levels have been called upon to respond to the growing public concern with plans to close the funding gap and to improve the increasingly dangerous condition of some public facilities.

A recent study by Morgan Guaranty Trust Company analyzed the trends in public facility expenditures over a period of three decades. The trend in capital investment in recent years has been sharply downward compared with the earlier periods (see Table C–1).

The study projected a short fall in investment of $500 billion for 1980 to 1985. A large portion of this represents an investment lag in transportation facilities.

Five-Year Capital Improvement Program of the Metropolitan Transportation Authority (MTA) in New York

In 1982, New York's Metropolitan Transportation Authority (MTA) embarked on a massive rehabilitation program for subways, buses, and commuter railroads in the 12-county New York region. By making

TABLE C–1

Changes in Net Stock of Public Structures			
	Annual average percent change in net stocks 1950–80*	Current percent trend* projected 1980–85	1985 infrastructure gap ($ billion—1972)
Buildings			
Schools	1.6%	−0.4%	$ 47.4
Hospitals	2.6	0.2	8.4
Other	5.0	1.6	37.3
Highways, streets, bridges	1.0	0.0	45.9
Conservation and development	5.5	1.3	10.0
Sewer	4.4	3.1	15.2
Water	2.8	1.7	7.3
Other†	3.7	2.5	10.7
Total	2.4	0.7	$182.2

* Trends adjusted for school population change and interstate highway completion.

† Includes public transit and airports.

capital revitalization a top priority, this program is reversing a long-time negative trend in the public transportation system and is restoring the New York metropolitan region's transit system (the nation's largest) to a state of good repair.

By any measure the MTA has put into motion unprecedented innovations in planning, processing, financing, and monitoring of transit capital improvement programs. The unique approach used by MTA to develop and finance the $8.5 billion five-year program will undoubtedly be adopted by other transit and nonprofit agencies. Moreover, the management of the capital program has become a model for transit agencies throughout the United States. It is therefore useful to analyze the major changes in management, legislation, funding, and procedures that are producing dramatic and continuing benefits.

THE MTA'S TRANSPORTATION SYSTEM

Each weekday approximately 5.6 million riders use the subways, buses, and commuter rail lines under the jurisdiction of the Metropolitan Transportation Authority. Nearly 3.4 million of these passengers travel on the New York City subway system—almost the equivalent of the entire population of Chicago.

The operations of MTA extend over some 685 miles of subway track, 999 miles of city bus routes, 1,024 miles of commuter rail track, and 745 miles of suburban bus routes. MTA carries about one out of every three persons who use public transit in the United States. The Authority operates more rail passenger cars than Amtrak and all of the other transit systems in the country combined. In addition every day 700,000 vehicles traverse the Authority's two tunnels and seven bridges.

MTA's subways, buses, and commuter rail lines carry people through New York City and take passengers from Long Island and the northern counties to work, study, shop, and be entertained in the urban center. The commuter lines and suburban buses also move passengers between towns and take "reverse commuters" to work from the city to the suburbs.

MTA, a New York State-chartered public-benefit corporation, operates its services under a common Board of Directors through these affiliated agencies:

- New York City Transit Authority (NYCTA)
- Manhattan and Bronx Surface Transit Operating Authority (MaBSTOA)
- Staten Island Rapid Transit Operating Authority (SIRTOA)
- The Long Island Rail Road Company (LIRR)
- Metro-North Commuter Railroad Company
- Metropolitan Suburban Bus Authority (MSBA)
- Triborough Bridge and Tunnel Authority (TBTA)

MTA also provides service under contract on New Jersey Transit's Hoboken–Port Jervis and Pascack Valley Lines.

Through its facilities MTA's responsibility extends to New York City's five boroughs as well as seven suburban counties: Dutchess, Putnam, Westchester, Orange, Rockland, Nassau, and Suffolk. This 4,000-square-mile area has a population of 11.4 million.

THE PROBLEM IN 1979

Mirroring the city of New York's fiscal crisis, MTA was itself in the throes of a severe fiscal and operational crisis during the 1970s. A series of developments produced an unparalleled threat to the continued safe and reliable operations of some of the city's transit system.[2]

The system was in a state of poor repair, and everyone who used it could see that it was deteriorating at an accelerating rate. Trains broke down more and more frequently. On-time performance suffered. Many trains and buses never made it out of yards and shops, leaving gaping shortages in the amount of equipment minimally necessary to serve customers during the morning rush hour. The peak of adversity was reached in early 1982 when there were as many as 100 10-car trains short for the morning rush hour. See Table C–2 for some of the key operating trends.

How had responsible elected officials and transit executives allowed such neglect of the plant and equipment valued at $55 billion in replacement terms in 1980, jeopardizing the region's economic well-being?

The politics of transit is a dominant factor, naturally. The study of these aspects would provide a fertile field for political scientists; this is beyond the scope of this appendix. Interested readers are referred to *The Politics of Urban Regional Development* by Michael N. Danielson and Jameson W. Doig for a discussion of mass transportation and the limited capabilities of government

We want to focus on the capital planning and budgeting process. The historical perspective is necessary in order to understand the significance of the MTA's Five-Year Capital Improvement Program in terms of its funding and its scope. The changes that have taken place have successfully begun to reverse the trend of deterioration of the capital plant. This together with the speeding of the funding and processing of capital projects is contributing to more effective and efficient transit capital planning in the New York region.

The MTA's approach can serve as a model for the nonprofit sector. It relies not only on cutting red tape and improving the levels of funding, but it draws upon some of the features used in the private sector (see Figure C–1).

It is instructive to use illustrations involving the New York Transit Authority, the largest and most complex of all of the MTA agencies. The TA processes have been studied in great detail, and there is ample documentation of past problems. The Metro-North Commuter Railroad, on the other hand, was under the direct control of Conrail until January 1983, and capital improvements were the responsibility of that organization.

The Long Island Rail Road is a much smaller organization than the Transit Authority and did not experience the same kind of difficulties with disinvestment and bureaucratic red tape as the Transit Authority.

The following is a description of the process and funding as it existed in 1979.

733

TABLE C-2

Operating Trends
New York City Transit Authority*

Fiscal year	Nominal fare	Real fare (1967 $)	Total revenue ($ millions)	Subsidies and taxes ($ millions)			Miles between equipment failures	
				Federal	State	City	Subway	Bus TA/MaBSTOA
1978	$.50	25.1	1,257	127	70	70	13,470	978/400
1979	.50	22.9	1,287	85	91	88	10,960	803/319
1980	.60	25.1	1,422	151	146	72	8,210	718/315
1981	.75	28.5	1,702	128	227	74	6,640	756/329
1982	.75	28.0	1,977	106	293	110	7,161	1,086/463
1983	.75	25.6	2,238	89	481	92	8,663	1,044 (both)
1984	.90	30.5	2,597	83	555	92	8,830	1,114 (both)

* NYCTA changed to calendar year basis beginning in 1983.
Sources: (1) NYCTA Transit Fact Book.
(2) NYCTA Monthly Financial Report.

The Capital Budget Process

The New York City Transit Authority's capital budgeting and approval process had four phases and lasted over three years on the average. Roughly 40 percent of the process was devoted to program development, budgeting, design, and contract award activities by the Transit Authority itself. Budget and contract review and approval by outside agencies accounted for the remaining 60 percent.

FIGURE C–1

Transit Authority Capital Budget Development and Approval Process

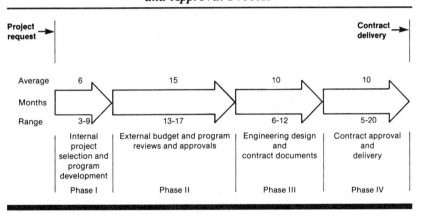

Ten Transit Authority departments played a significant role in requesting, prioritizing, and selecting projects for the annual program, and *over 35 government agencies, legislative bodies, and community groups participated in the external review and approval of the annual capital budget* and program. (See Table C–3.) Some of these outside groups exercised decisive control over individual projects and their funding.

Here is how one study described the process for obtaining and using transit funds:

> (It) defies understanding and delays improvements. Many agencies at all levels of government claim decisive roles, and the cross-currents among plans, "annual elements," federal grants, state and local appropriations, and authorization to spend the money are complex. *It appears that only a few people fully comprehend what is going on.* (emphasis added).[3]

TABLE C–3

External Review Agencies

1. New York City Transportation Coordinating Committee.
2. Tri-State Regional Planning Commission (the federally recognized metropolitan planning organization).
3. Transit Authority.
   a. Program management.
   b. Fiscal management.
4. New York City Office of Management and Budget (local government).
5. Borough boards in each of New York City's five boroughs.
6. Community Planning Boards (55 local districts).
7. New York City Council (elected city legislators)
8. New York City Board of Estimate (consists of top elected city executives).
9. Mayor of the city of New York.
10. New York City Department of City Planning—Transportation Division.
11. New York City Department of Transportation.
12. New York City Planning Commission.
13. New York City Comptroller.
14. New York State Department of Transportation.
15. New York State Division of the Budget.
16. U.S. Urban Mass Transportation Administration.
17. MTA Staff and MTA Board (external to the NYC Transit Authority).

The Rapid Transit Department of the Transit Authority initiated the majority of the capital projects.

Prior to 1980, the staff resources to develop and process budget requests were scarce. Individual project requests were prepared by personnel responsible for day-to-day operations. A small capital budget staff in the office of the head of Rapid Transit analyzed capital needs and priorities. Because this group lacked enough staff and data resources, information provided by operating departments was not sufficient for evaluation of project requests; most decisions were made judgmentally. The absence of documented justification may have led to poor judgments regarding project priorities. In any event, it most assuredly caused problems during the funding approval process.

Priorities were based on judgments involving age of equipment, useful life, and safety problems. There was no procedure for systematic evaluation based on the performance benefits of capital investments. In addition, although the Transit Authority had an established management by objectives programs, there was no attempt to relate capital improvement programs to system goals. However, until 1980 the number of project requests satisfying the judgmental criteria annually exceeded available funding.

Funding Levels

In 1979, transit capital funding levels were inadequate and limited, to a large degree, by the amount of funds provided through federal grants.

Because the City of New York owned the subway and bus plants, equipment, and track systems, it was legally responsible for the funding of capital improvements. In the 1960s the city provided the Transit Authority with an average of approximately $100 million a year for its capital program. Prior to the advent of federal grants in 1964, there were no other sources of capital funds. In 1967 the state received voter approval for a $2.5 million transportation bond issue, of which $600 million was to be allocated for the Transit Authority (the entire amount was to be expended for new routes).

The capital construction program of the Transit Authority as of 1980 relied largely on federal funding, with the local matching share being provided by the state (through its executive budget) and the city (through its capital budget). The total dollar amount of grants approved for the Transit Authority, including the required local matching share, averaged about $280 million between 1975 and 1980 (including $60 million in capitalized operating funds).

Prior to the advent of the MTA's Five-Year Capital Improvement Program, then, the sources of funds for the annual capital program were:

1. *Federal Capital Grants* (UMTA Sections 3 and 5)—required a 20 percent local match.
2. *Federal Aid to Urban Systems* (FAUS)—capital assistance to cities for highways and transit; required a 75 percent local match.
3. *Federal Interstate Highway Transfer*—state can transfer interstate authorization to transit; New York State has two projects: Westway and Long Island Expressway widening; New York State has not requested transfer.
4. *Port Authority Local Share*—for bus-related projects only.
5. *New York State*—1967 State Bond Issue; direct state appropriation: Commuter Railroad, and 1979 Accelerated Transit Program.
6. *City of New York Local Share.*

By 1980 it was clear that mass transit capital needs, both to modernize and expand the system, far exceeded the available resources

737

and that the federal government would not provide New York with anywhere near the amount required.

At the same time, it should be noted, the level of operating subsidies provided by federal, state, and city sources was approaching $600 million annually, and there was no permanent solution in sight to the problem of providing a sure and certain source of funds to meet operating requirements. In the face of a chronic state of near solvency, the MTA should not be expected to find additional funds to make the capital improvements.

HOW THE CAPITAL PROGRAM DEVELOPED

At the time Richard Ravitch accepted the MTA chairmanship in 1979, he recognized that he faced a staggering task: initially, to avoid a major collapse in service; and, ultimately, to restore the system to a state of good condition so that the public could receive the quality of service that it is entitled to and so that the regional economy could remain viable.

A number of studies had set forth the capital requirements of the system. Notwithstanding estimated capital replenishment needs of over $1 billion per year (based on an estimated replacement cost of MTA's transit assets of $55 billion in 1980 dollars), the MTA had been spending less than $280 million a year.

Ravitch immediately commissioned a new analysis to update the previous studies. The staff report, entitled *Capital Revitalization for the 1980s and Beyond (1980),* showed a projected need for $14 billion, for the TA and the commuter railroads, over a 10-year period.

With this needs assessment in hand, Ravitch tackled three other needs in connection with capital improvements:

1. To propose new mechanisms for raising funds beyond the existing federal, state, and local sources.
2. To provide improvements in the way in which capital priorities are set.
3. To speed up the process by which capital projects are planned, reviewed, and funded.

Ravitch brought forth innovative proposals based largely on his experience as a private businessman. And he worked tirelessly with federal and state legislators and with key members of New York's financial and business community to sell his ideas.

Among his proposals were the following.

Funding

1. The surpluses from bridge and tunnel tolls (MTA Triborough Bridge and Tunnel Authority) had helped defray mass transit operating deficits for years. Now it was proposed that the TBTA be authorized to borrow money for transit capital improvements, using some surpluses to back up its borrowing capacity.

2. The MTA should be permitted to use its own farebox revenues to back up revenue bonds, thus establishing the principle that the replenishment of infrastructure, or depreciation of fixed assets, should be treated as an operating expense.

3. State appropriations should be pledged to support the sale of bonds, with the MTA contracting to provide service in return for the state funds.

4. The federal government should be permitted to enter into long-term contracts with agencies such as the MTA, instead of providing annual contributions. This would give MTA the ability to borrow substantial amounts of money based on these contracts.

5. The federal tax laws should be changed to allow MTA to enjoy indirectly the tax credit benefits that are directly applicable to equipment used by private transit companies. Private enterprises can obtain the benefit of a 10 percent investment tax credit when they purchase new equipment. The owner of new equipment leased to private companies can also obtain the benefit of the investment tax credit. Ravitch asked, Why can't federal and state laws be changed to do away with the inequity that makes these benefits available to private companies which lease equipment to *public agencies?*

He estimated that the MTA would be paying only 80 percent as much in rent for equipment as it would have to pay in debt service to purchase the equipment outright. In terms of impact on the MTA's capital needs, this would mean the equivalent of one subway car free for each four purchased.

Setting Priorities

Although ensuring safety of operating would always remain the number one priority, Ravitch suggested several changes so that the process of setting priorities could be made more explicit and rational, and so that the process could be understood by the public.

He made some tough decisions. Specifically, he called for a halt to the emphasis on new routes, recommending orderly conclusion of just a few key projects.

He also established "commodiousness of the system" as being important to the passengers; and, therefore, station improvements would receive a somewhat higher priority than they had previously received.

In one of his key moves, Ravitch directed the MTA staff to address the competing needs of each component part of the system and to develop guidelines and priorities concerning which rehabilitation projects should be addressed first. This would be based on an understanding of the improvement in the quality of service realized in relation to the impact of projects on maintenance and labor costs. It also entailed gaining an understanding of the consequences of a failure to spend money in areas that may appear to be of relatively low priority. On a year-to-year basis, these decisions would be reviewed and revised continuously.

In the absence of standard business methodologies for ranking projects, the MTA developed the *Capital Value Matrix* (see Table C–4) to assume the best use of funds and to assist in establishing relative priorities. The priority-setting process consisted of three steps: (1) an estimate of existing and new funding, (2) a priority evaluation system, and (3) a detailed list of projects within estimated costs. The NYCTA matrix form is shown in Table C–4. The Commuter Rail Matrix is similar in concept and logic except that it places a slightly higher rating on passenger service and environment.

Eight factors were considered in assigning a priority, or matrix value, to a project—safety, reliability, security, maintainability, passenger service/environment, economics/cost, control, public interest, and employee interest.

Each of the eight factors can have one of four degrees of impact— critically important, very important, important, no impact.

Numeric values were assigned to each of the eight factors. They range from 10 for safety to 4 for employee or public interest. Values are also assigned to the degree of impact: 5 for critical, 3 for very important, 1 for important, and 0 for no impact.

To use the matrix, one would first identify the project or program and the capital cost. Then, going down the list of factors, one must determine the degree of importance for each factor. The appropriate value for each factor is entered in the space on the right-hand column in the weight value column.

After each factor has been considered the weighted values are added to produce a total value. The total value is the matrix value or priority rating.

The matrix provides for consideration of negative impact by allowing negative values to be assigned to category III—important needs.

The matrix analysis is only one part of an overall program review process that takes into account economic appraisals as well as other considerations. For instance, one question that is asked is: "Does this program serve all those who have a community of interest? Most important, there is overriding concern with whether a project contributes to the entire program working as a whole. Issues addressed in this regard include:

- Does one program's success depend on another's?
- Can all the components be accomplished within the five-year period?
- Can service continue to be provided while this program is underway?

Based on the combination of funding availability and the final rating of projects, MTA developed lists of projects in program categories. Included were back-up projects that would be advanced only should a level of funding higher than anticipated become available. These project lists reflected what were believed to be realistic expectations for construction scheduling and projected inflation over the construction period. Each year's program level was designed to represent the value of commitments (that is, contracts) that would be entered into in that year. Program priorities also suggested what areas could be curtailed if funding was reduced.

Streamlining the Process

To deal with the red tape and bureaucratic delays involved in the planning and funding process, Ravitch proposed eliminating the time-consuming reviews and approvals by various New York City legislative bodies and mayoral agencies, and suggested that state funds should go directly to MTA by program category instead of appropriations to the State Transportation Department.

He asked that federal grants be awarded early in the federal fiscal year and that the MTA and the Urban Mass Transportation Administration set overall MBE goals, dispensing with time-consuming project-by-project evaluation.

Finally, he directed the staff to implement many of the recommendations of Booz-Allen & Hamilton contained in the 1979 *MTA Management Study,* Task 1.[4]

TABLE C–4

Capital Value Matrix—NYCTA/SIRTOA

Program/Project:
Capital Cost:

Factor	Existing needs						Weighted value
	Category I Critically important needs	Value	*Category II Very important needs*	Value	*Category III Important needs*	Value	
Safety	Avoid serious injuries to individuals (See note 4)	+50	Remedy hazardous conditions involving large numbers.	+30	Otherwise improve safety.	Value ±10	
Reliability	Reduce MDS; meet service requirements; maintain operations	+45	Reduce numerous disruptions; provide vital support; maintain operations.	+27	Otherwise improve reliability.	±9	
Security	Reduce major crimes; implement major policies.	+35	Reduce other crimes affecting passengers.	+21	Otherwise improve security.	±7	

Need		+35		+18		±7
Maintainability	Replace components which are not maintainable.	+35			Parts difficult obtain; special inventories required.	±7
Passenger services/environment	Relieve unreasonable overcrowding of services.	+30	Relieve unpleasant conditions affecting large numbers.	+18	Otherwise improve service and environment.	±6
Economics/cost control	Cost effective.	+30	Ratio of cost savings to capital cost between 0.5 and 1.0.	+18	Otherwise reduce system cost and avoid cost increase.	±6
Political/public interest	Directives; persistent criticism; mandated.	+20	Considerable criticism.	+12	Some interest.	±4
Employee interest	Union contract, remedy degrading conditions.	+20	Interest resulting in improved productivity; remedy inadequate working conditions.	+12	Improve employee facilities and work environment.	±4

Total value _____

Prior to selecting the proper weighted values refer to the detailed description of needs on the following pages.

1. The numbers represent weighted values for each need.
2. The value for a factor shall be zero when a proposal does not have any impact on the needs within that factor.
3. An asterisk (*) next to the total value indicates the project does not satisfy critically important needs.
4. In the event that safety is exceptionally critical, the safety portion of the matrix is to be +100.

THE TRANSPORTATION ASSISTANCE AND FINANCING ACT OF 1981

In 1981 state legislation was introduced at MTA's request to provide new funding and to accomplish many of the reforms in the capital budget process that Chairman Ravitch sought. Many of the approval steps required by statute were removed; and, following passage of this act, funds would be provided directly by the MTA, subject to state audit.

Equally important, the law allowed the MTA to raise its own capital through the state and local financing methods mentioned previously.

To recap, these are the borrowing mechanisms made possible by the act:

- TBTA Revenue Bonds secured by the toll income of the TBTA.
- Special NYS Service Bonds secured by future streams of capital assistance from the state of New York.
- Transit Facilities Revenue Bonds secured by the passenger revenue of the transit systems themselves.

In addition to the new state-approved mechanism for obtaining capital funds, several additional funding mechanisms recommended by Chairman Ravitch were approved. These included:

1. Sale-leaseback agreements (safe harbor leasing).

The Reagan administration actively supported the MTA's tax proposals for the sale and leaseback of transit rolling stock. Congress enacted the latter measures as part of the Economic Recovery Tax Act of 1981.

The concept of "safe harbor" leasing, as it is named, has some unique features as it is applied to transactions involving the sale of buses or railcars to an investor. The principal distinction is that the benefit can be achieved by a sale of the *right of tax depreciation* by the leasee to the leasor without transferring title. The transit authority retains the title and the obligation to maintain the property and insure it against risk of loss.

The investor owns the right to take depreciation on transit vehicles, as well as to deduct interest payments in the early years. Only one cash payment representing some 10 to 25 percent of the value of the property is made at the commencement of the lease.

744

2. Increased funds from Port Authority of New York and New Jersey.
3. The right to negotiate contracts for the purchase of buses.
4. Vendor financing (MTA-vendor loan agreements at favorable terms).

At the same time, the MTA gained acceptance of its proposals on gaining long-term commitments of UMTA funds that could be pledged to bondholders or to contractors.

Because of the large amount of investment funding for capital projects made possible by these new funding sources, for the first time it was possible to develop a long-term approach to transit capital improvements. The new funding sources were expected to generate some $3.4 billion over five years and, taken together with existing sources, a total capital program totaling more than $7 billion was planned.

MTA CAPITAL PROGRAM REVIEW BOARD

As part of the capital program streamlining process and to satisfy legislative oversight and monitoring requirements, the Transportation Systems and Financing Act of 1981 provided for a unique review procedure.

The act established an MTA Capital Program Review Board (MTACPRB) composed of appointees of the governor, New York State Senate and Assembly leaders, and the mayor of the City of New York. The purpose of the Capital Program Review Board is "to ensure that the capital programs to be undertaken and financed pursuant to the act are not inconsistent with sound transportation planning and fiscal policies."

All capital program plans were to be submitted to the MTACPRB for one-time approvals. There are actually two capital program plans: one containing the program for NYC Transit Authority and the other for the facilities of the MTA's Commuter Railroads.

The MTA's Five-Year Capital Plan was approved by the MTA Board of Directors in July 1982 and by the MTACPRB, who also monitors the capital program.

In support of the MTA program, six supplemental actions were required by the Capital Review Board as follows:

1. Refiling of the Five-Year Capital Plan approximately one year after initial approval. This would provide an opportunity to make technical changes, revise commitment schedules, and, by mutual agreement, to make certain changes in the program.

745

2. Service standards. Within one year, the MTA was required to provide to MTACPRB a method for measuring improvements in the performance and service resulting from the implementation of the plans, including a description of service standards to be met during the life of the acquired rolling stock.

3. Car maintenance plan. Also within one year, the MTA had to file a description of how acquired rolling stock was to be maintained and served so as to assure maximum service improvements.

4. Service plan and sufficiency studies. The MTA would have to answer the question: What are the operations of the MTA going to look like over the short, intermediate, and long-range periods?

5. Capital facility evaluation. The condition and life-cycle costs of all facilities to be constructed would be reported to the Capital Review Board.

6. Industrial engineering review. The MTACPRB required industrial engineering reviews of maintenance activities to "assess requirements relating to work flows, locations of key component maintenance functions, inventory accessibility, mechanical enhancements, and other physical constraints that limit the achievements of higher output than existing maintenance forces."

MTA FIVE-YEAR CAPITAL IMPROVEMENT PROGRAM (AS REVISED IN APRIL 1983)

The original MTA Five-Year Program was approved in December 1981. It provided for a total of $7.2 billion in capital projects.

In April 1983 the MTA Board of directors approved a $1.3 billion expansion of the program. The increased funds were made possible through the federal five-cent-a-gallon gasoline tax, lower than expected interest costs (permitting the sale of additional MTA bonds), and money previously appropriated but unallocated. Table C–5 shows the highlights of the current program (in 1983 dollars).

The emphasis in the program is consistent with the four primary goals originally established by Chairman Ravitch:

Reestablish and maintain reliable operations on the existing subways, buses, and commuter railroad lines. This includes a rational replacement cycle for trains and buses, rehabilitation of existing passenger vehicles (such as fixing defective subway car doors), improve-

746

TABLE C–5

MTA Five-Year Capital Program Funding Plan
($ millions)

	Transit system	Commuter railroad system
Federal	$2,315	$ 534
State	212	270
Local	604	—
Port Authority of New York and New Jersey	92	—
MTA Transit Facilities Revenue Bonds and Party Obligations	1,542	—
MTA Commuter Facilities Revenue Bonds	—	388
MTA Service Contract Bonds	407	219
MTA Service Contract Payments	107	58
TBTA	643	429
Lessor Equity	394	106
Parking Bonds	—	30
Other	173	19
Total	$6,489	$2,053

Proposed Expenditures
($ millions)

	Transit system	Commuter railroad system
Cars—new, rebuilt/rehabilitated	$2,085	$ 509
Buses	339	—
Passenger stations	573	217
Track	392	28
Line equipment	140	—
Line structures	237	171
Signals and communication	454	152
Power and power equipment	296	191
Electrification/extension	—	232
Shops, yard, and depots	1,342	429
Service vehicles	63	—
Security	20	4
New routes	171	—
Emergency/miscellaneous	343	121
SIRTOA	34	—
Total	$6,489	$2,053

Source: Amendment to Capital Program dated 8/25/83.

ments in shop and yard maintenance facilities, and providing additional rail cars (and seats) to commuters who now stand for the length of their trips.

Ensure long-term survival of the existing transit systems and their safe, reliable operations at reasonable cost. This means making funds available to repair and upgrade the infrastructure and vital components.

Other improvements to the existing systems. These improvements include a more reliable operation, a more commodious environment for the passengers, increasing commuter rail system capacity, and advancing such commuter railroad programs as electrification and interlocking modernization.

Advance "new routes" projects already underway (Transit Authority only). Existing new route programs were to be brought to an orderly conclusion.

SALE OF MTA REVENUE BONDS

The first sale of Transit Facility Revenue Bonds was completed in October 1982. These $250 million in bonds are backed by all gross revenues of the subway and bus systems, including passenger revenue, subsidies, and special taxes.

The MTA commissioned extensive engineering and economic studies in preparation for the sale of these bonds. An estimated total of $1,845,000,000 is expected to be sold.

A study by the consulting engineering firm of De Leuw, Cather and Company of New York established the need for the capital improvement projects and concluded that the program would reestablish reliable transit service and ensure the system's long-term survival if the proposed projects were funded in the amounts and at the times scheduled and if there was timely approval by the appropriate governmental entities.

An independent economic feasibility study by Charles River Associates of Boston concluded that it was reasonable to expect the following economic consequences as a result of the capital program:

1. Sufficient revenues can be generated from the farebox to cover the projected net operating and maintenance cost of the system as well as the debt service on bonds and parity obligations proposed to be issued to finance the capital program, under widely varying assumptions on subsidy funding from all levels of government, including the elimination of all general operating subsidies.

2. The higher fares necessary to cover the system's net operating and maintenance costs and projected debt service requirements associated with the capital program, even in the event that all general operating subsidies are eliminated, are within the capacity of the city economy to pay. Such increases in transit fares are not expected to impact adversely the city economy to an extent that would materially affect the ability of the Transit Authority and MaBSTOA to generate the necessary revenues from the farebox.

3. The improved system operation attributable to the implementation of the capital program, as documented in the De Leuw engineering audit, can be expected to result in increases in system ridership and in regional economic activity, particularly over the five-year implementation period of the capital program.

Based on these analyses and additional conditions and representatives contained in the official statement prepared by the MTA's bond counsel, Moody's Investors service gave a quality rating of Baa to the proposed new issue bonds. This was thought to be a highly favorable rating for the first sale of transit bonds for which farebox revenues were pledged as backing.

HIGHLIGHTS OF THE MTA FIVE-YEAR CAPITAL PROGRAM

By the end of 1983, $3.9 billion had been committed to contract.

In operation, under construction, or planned for the New York City Transit Authority are new, air-conditioned buses and cars; modernized subway stations; upgraded car maintenance facilities, signal, and track work; security programs for trains, station, and yards; and new bus depots.

Rehabilitation programs include retrofitting older subway cars with air conditioning, modernizing doors, installing new air brakes, improving communications and signal systems, instituting noise-abatement procedures, refurbishing stations, modernizing shops, and renovating power substations.

The purchase of new rolling stock, representing about one third of the dollar value of the program, became the subject of serious debate during the program review procedure. Several planners agreed that it was better to rebuild existing subway cars than to purchase new ones. The decision was made to favor new equipment purchases rather than to depend on rebuilding poorly maintained old cars whose life expectancy when rebuilt was uncertain. Some $371 million was, however, allocated for rehabilitating more recent subway cars; and $29.4 million was earmarked for similar work on Metro-North Commuter cars.

Guidelines for new equipment specify simplicity and practicality. The 1,375 subway cars now being manufactured are mechanically less complicated than most of the later-model cars currently in operation; they also feature graffiti-resistant stainless steel exteriors. Approximately 250 new cars were in service by early 1985.

The purchase of the new cars, together with the rehabilitation of existing cars, is expected to improve performance and reliability. The 1987 goal for MDBF is over 15,000 miles, and the subway fleet size is expected to drop by about 350 cars to 5,963 cars by 1987.

Similarly, the 1981 bus fleet consisted of 4,560 buses, including a spare ratio of 26 percent. The long-term goal is to reduce fleet size to 4,000 and to maintain within that number a spare ratio of 16 percent. By mid-1983 2,300 new buses had been placed in service. By 1986, this number will have grown to approximately 3,000.

The next two highest dollar categories of TA spending are for track and signal work and for the rehabilitation and new construction of yards, depots, and shops.

The importance of the projects involving signals, track, and contact rail was underscored in 1983 when train derailments became a serious problem for the Transit Authority (20 derailments of trains in service during the year). Over 500 areas were "red-tagged" and slated for priority improvement. The TA's capital program for track work is $374 million.

A large investment is being made in yards and shops to improve working conditions for employees, increase productivity, and to ensure that all trains and buses will be stored in secure locations where they cannot be vandalized.

Of the 20 bus depots owned by NYCTA, 18 are being rebuilt, replaced, or overhauled. Four new depots are planned, and work has begun on two of them.

A key new element of the capital program is the allowance of $100 million for the purchase and installation of automated card readers for subways and buses. Once established, a system of fare cards will yield substantial benefits for the MTA, not the least of which will be the virtual elimination of fare cheating, which costs the MTA an estimated $35 million each year.

The capital program is also bringing substantial improvements to the Long Island Rail Road, including new cars and equipment, rebuilt stations, and upgraded maintenance and storage facilities.

The first of 174 new M-3 electric cars are scheduled to start regular runs in early 1984. All the cars will be in service by 1985. More than 200 diesel coaches are being improved, with new seats and sound-absorbing wall coverings.

On Manhattan's west side, a huge lay-up yard is under construction, slated for completion in 1985. In conjunction with signal, switch, and track improvements now being made, it will increase rush-hour train capacity by 25 percent at Pennsylvania Station, LIRR's Manhattan terminus.

Penn Station, the world's busiest terminal, is undergoing renovations—the first in 30 years undertaken for passenger comfort—that are bringing more air conditioning, a new public address system, escalators for the disabled, direct access to the IND subway, improved access from the IRT subway, and new street entrances from Eighth Avenue.

New maintenance and repair shops for diesel and electric cars are under construction in Queens. And the lines between Huntington and Northport and Hicksville and Ronkonkoma are being electrified to provide a faster, smoother trip.

With respect to the Metro-North Commuter Railroad—long-neglected by its previous operator, Conrail—the requirement to replace equipment and facilities is enormous. For example, $190 million was required to replace poorly operating power stations.

On the upper Harlem electrification in outlying Westchester and Putnam counties has been extended 28 miles, from North White Plains to Brewster North. The faster, more efficient service began in early 1984.

For the New Haven line specifications have been prepared and manufacturers have submitted proposals for the design and construction of up to 100 new electric cars.

The sprawling, outmoded Harmon shop, which services electric and diesel trains, is being rebuilt and expanded, as are other shops and yards. And throughout the Metro-North system, power and signal equipment, switches, and tracks are being upgraded.

Commuters in the New York region will continue to benefit from Ravitch's accomplishments for many years to come.

PROGRAM MANAGEMENT PROCESS

Managing a capital program as large as the MTA's would be impossible without new program planning and management tools. The MTA's new capital program management process includes the future development of new strategic planning activities, the MTA's new Capital Program Tracking System (CENTRAK), an annual capital budget for every MTA agency, and the MTA Performance Planning and Reporting System. The transition to this new process is not yet complete, and it will require additional improvements and refinements.

Each of the new elements is briefly described below.

Long-Range Planning

In conjunction with its operating agencies, the MTA and the operating agencies are developing a strategic planning activity to prepare five-year strategic operations plans. These five-year plans will eventually include long-range goals and objectives, service and performance standards, projections of future financing, strategies to improve productivity, service configuration, and evaluation of service performance.

This strategic planning effort involving the staffs of MTA, TA, LIRR, and M/N, will provide a context for considering a host of inter-related issues including finance, service quality and distribution, capital requirements, productivity and efficiency, fare collection and fare structure, legal issues, and marketing and management issues.

The planning agenda is a complement to the efforts directed toward system revitalization. Now that the successful implementation of the capital program has reversed the long-term trend in disinvestment in the transit facilities, the MTA has to come to terms with the issues mentioned above.

Capital Program Tracking System (CENTRAK)

MTA's CENTRAK is an on-line, user-oriented management information system that was specifically tailored to MTA's needs but can be easily adapted for other transit systems as well as government agencies in general. The system is basically designed to handle any type of capital, maintenance, or procurement program involving the tracking of contracts, personnel, and materials. At MTA, the restoration program was the catalyst for CENTRAK, but the system will also be used for a variety of functions such as the scheduling and tracking of maintenance work by railroad labor and routine procurement. Multiplications, Inc. is developing and installing the computer software system.

CENTRAK provides MTA management with the ability to determine, on a uniform basis for all capital projects in the five-year program, the current status of every project and to track procurement activities (design and construction contracts and purchase of materials), real estate acquisitions, change orders, contract payments, and force account work associated with each project. In this manner project slippages and/or cost overruns are quickly identified, and remedial action can be taken. CENTRAK, in short, provides an early warning system, allowing project delays to be handled before they become major problems.

CENTRAK also aids in the development of master schedules for each project and detailed schedules for specific project tasks. In addition the system pinpoints who is responsible for the various activities required to complete each project, allowing MTA management to determine whether an individual or a group is performing properly. This clear assignment of responsibilities enables MTA and the operating agencies to provide project managers with a great deal more flexibility regarding use of funds allocated to projects.

CENTRAK can provide management with special reports whenever necessary, such as a complete listing of the progress of work done by a particular contractor, as well as standard reports for outside funding sources. The system also assists in the processing of paperwork required for the five-year program, in part by centralizing all relevant project information in a common computer data base.

Beyond the benefits associated with the Five-Year Capital Program, CENTRAK is facilitating general purchasing and procurement procedures. Also, it has enabled the Transit Authority to consolidate 17 separate engineering management information and capital project-related systems into one interactive system.

Annual Capital Budget

The annual capital budget cycle has been revised. While MTA has not developed a uniform, rigorous methodology for determining project acceptance and for routing various projects in accordance with traditional investment criteria, there are standard formats that inform the MTA Board regarding the purpose of each project, its impact on service, and its impact on operating expenses.

Figure C–2 shows how the annual capital budget cycle relates to the planning and operating budget cycles.

The capital program rationale for each program element in the Transit Authority's new capital budget addresses the areas listed below:

- What need or system deficiency does the proposed program of work seek to address?
- How will the capital program of work effect the department's program and element goals over the five-and-one-half-year period, in measurable terms?

753

FIGURE C–2

NYCTA Annual Planning and Budget Cycles for 1984

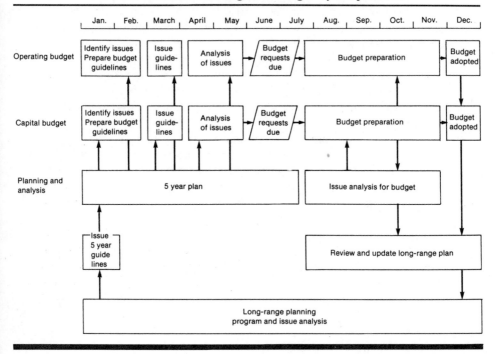

- What is the basis for proposing replacement and improvement projects for each category of capital investment projects?
- What is the anticipated impact of this program of work on cost/savings, productivity, labor needs?

A copy of the Capital Program Control Document is shown in Figure C–3.

Performance Measurement

As a means of measuring the success of the Five-Year Capital Program, the MTA Board of Directors established a performance planning and reporting system that provides MTA management at several levels, leading up to the Board of Directors, with a process for setting performance goals for and measuring the actual performance of the

FIGURE C–3

Capital Project Control Document	Part A

Department:

Planning no.:   PSE no.:
PGM element: NIA cat.:

Program DESC: track

1. Dept. recommendation:
   Project continuation   ____
   Project revision   ____
   Project cancellation   ____
   New project 7/83-12/86 ____
   New project 1/87-12/88 ____

2. Project description: Track and contact rail replacement, various locations

3. Location:
   Borough_____
   Transit line _____
   Subsection _____
   Other_____

4. General project purpose:
   ____Add/Expand
   ____Fac/Eqp Replace
   ____Fac/Eqp Improve

   ____Operating savings
   ____Revenue enhancement
   ____Other:_____

5. TA priority
   Supported by project:
   ____Safety
   ____Reliability
   ____Security

   ____Passenger service/environment
   ____System efficiency
   ____Employee environment

6. General project priority:
   ____Essential
   ____Level I discretionary
   ____Level II discretionary
   ____Level III discretionary

7. Schedule:

	Cap budget	Updates
Proposed		___/___
Design		___/___
Construction award		___/___
Completion		___/___

8. Estimated cost ($millions):

	Cap budget	Updates
Bid price		_____
TA labor		_____
Construction administration		
Property		
Utilities		
Contingency		
Cost code		

9. Related projects:

10. Contractors (check if yes):
   Design consultant   ____
   Construction contractor   ____
   Inspection consultant   ____

11. Project report (check if yes):
   Received____ Date___/___/___
   Approved without change ____
   Comments appended   ____

12. Project manager:

   Signature:

   Date___/___/___

13. Contacts: operating dept. _____ Phone_____

FIGURE C–3 (*concluded*)

```
                    Capital Project Control Document                    Part B

Project_____

Department _____      Element description _____

Element no. _____      _____

Planning no. _____      _____

 In order to complete the Project Justification, respond to the following outline in detail.

 1.  If the Department is recommending revisions or cancellations of an existing project, or proposing a new
 one, explain the reasons (Part A, 1).

 2.  If updates to the schedule or estimated costs (Part A, 6-7) were made, explain the source of the
 information and the reasons for the updates.

 3.  What departmental problem or need is this project designed to solve or meet? How was this project
 chosen? What analysis supports this choice?

 4.  What are the anticipated benefits from the completion of this project? How will these benefits be
 measured?

 5.  What are the results of any economic cost studies (e.g., net present value) that justify this project?

 6.  What will be the impacts on operating costs, manpower and work scheduling from the completion of this
 project? When will these impacts be felt?

 7.  Identify and describe other projects which are significantly related to this project (Part A, 8), e.g., zone
 and line contracts, phased projects, dependent projects, etc.

 8.  What would be the consequences if this project were delayed or cancelled?
```

MTA operating agencies, both in terms of service offered and effectiveness of that service.

The process of planning performance goals takes place annually as part of the agency capital and operating budget requests. So, the achievement of service improvements will thereby be related to the associated costs and the impact on the MTA budget.

The MTA has also developed comparisons of performance that existed prior to the commencement of its Five-Year Capital Program and the levels that the MTA hopes will be achieved (see Table C–6). Some of the key capital program performance indicators and their definitions are the following:

1. *New York City Transit Authority—Rapid Transit Division Key Location Throughput* is the percentage of in-revenue service train trips operating past key points during a given time period, irrespective of the track (local or express) on which the train is operating. This includes the number of gap trains that are dispatched mid-route to mitigate the impact of delays. The key points are generally entrances to the central business district or key stations within the central business district.

- *Terminal abandonments* are the number of scheduled trains, per day, that are not put into service because a sufficient number of trains are not available when they are needed.
- *En route abandonments* are the number of trains, per day, taken out of service for any reason after they leave their originating terminal.
- *Delays due to defective car doors* is defined as the number of trains arriving later than four minutes at the terminal or abandoned en route due to mechanical operating problems or electrical signal indicator problems on car doors.
- *Percent of cars air conditioned* is defined as the proportion of the car fleet that contains air-conditioning units.
- *Percent of air-conditioning units in working condition* is the proportion of cars with air-conditioning units that have units actually operating at any point in time.
- *Number of stations modernized* represents the number of stations provided with a more attractive and convenient environment through the scheduled capital modernization. This number is to be compared both with the 465 stations that are part of the TA's system and with the proportion of passengers who will utilize the modernized stations.

2. *New York City Transit Authority Surface Division.*

- *Trips scheduled* is defined as the number of bus trips scheduled to operate on all routes during a given period of time.
- *Trips canceled at origin* is the number of trips that are canceled before a bus leaves its depot.
- *Trips canceled en route* is the number of trips that are canceled for all reasons once a bus has departed from its depot.

3. *Long Island Rail Road and Metro-North Commuter Railroad.*

- *Number of standees over 20 minutes (east of Jamaica)* represents the number of passengers required to stand for trips of over 20 minutes due to lack of passenger car seat capacity.
- *Clearance times at Penn station platform* (A.M peak) are empirical measurements taken periodically of the time it

takes a passenger to leave the platform area once his or her train has arrived at Penn Station.

- *Ratio of revenue car miles to empty car miles* is a measure of the extent to which "deadhead miles" (nonrevenue service) impact on service reliability and operating costs. As this ratio decreases, more cars are available in the right place at the right time at less movement cost.

- *On-time performance* is defined as proportion of peak-period trains that make their scheduled stops and arrive at the terminal within five minutes of their scheduled or general order in effect. The scheduled terminal is defined as the final scheduled stop in revenue service.

TABLE C–6

Summary of Performance Goals

	1981	1987
New York City Transit Authority		
Throughput (percent of schedule)	89%	98%
Terminal abandonments (trains)	190	30
En route abandonments (trains)	140	65
Delays due to defective car doors	10,000	4,500
Percent of cars air-conditioned	48%	74%
Percent of air-conditioning units working	88%	95%
Station modernization	—	78*
Bus trips scheduled	21 million	21 million
Bus trips canceled at origin	314,000	22,000
Bus trips canceled en route	257,000	121,000
	1981	**1986**
Long Island Rail Road		
Clearance time from Penn Station platform to concourse level	11 minutes	6 minutes
Number of standees over 20 minutes A.M. peak	5,300	3,600
Ratio of revenue car miles to empty car miles	17.1%	10.4%
On-time performance A.M. peak	80%	90%
Average length of peak-period delay	11.2 minutes	8.0 minutes

* Number of modernization from total number (465) of stations.

Conclusion

One of the most important lessons learned from the MTA experience is that, for the public and private sectors alike, strong leadership is required to implement a long-range program successfully. The leadership qualities that Richard Ravitch brought to the MTA were not very different from those that Lee Iacocca brought to Chrysler. Each had a vision of what had to be accomplished, and each developed innovative and creative approaches to achieving their goals. What's more, their objectives were clear to the public, the stockholders, or the riders, and to the governmental and regulatory communities.

In the public sector, with the emergence of a new transit capital planning and funding process, it almost seems as if the impossible has been accomplished—the breaking down of traditional political resistance and negative altitudes toward altering institutional forms in order to achieve long-range goals.

The MTA, under Richard Ravitch's leadership, has proved that public sector managers will respond as enthusiastically and as capably to the development and implementation of long-range plans as private sector managers. They merely had to have the same advantages of an assured, adequate flow of funds and a framework for speedily processing capital plans and projects.

The MTA and its constituent agencies hired experienced long-range planners to continue to roll forward current five-year plans, subject to modifications and amendments. The Transit Authority has prepared its first updated capital needs estimates since the advent of the MTA Five-Year Capital Improvement Program.

TA planners and engineers have estimated the continuing cost of bringing their system to a state of good repair, and they also have developed an ongoing normal replacement program based on analyses of the useful lives of various system elements and estimated replacement costs. The 1984 through 1993 capital investment needs total an estimated $11.8 billion in 1983 dollars, of which $2.7 billion is being provided by the current 1982–86 program.

The commuter railroads are involved in similar efforts.

These plans will have to be reviewed by the MTA Capital Program Review Board, the state legislature, and outside agencies, as well.

Regular planning cycles, such as those proposed in Figure C–4, will go a long way toward ensuring continued funding and widespread support and transit capital revitalization.

In the final analysis it was the marketplace discipline demanded by private sector investors that required the MTA to give consideration to the type and quality of services offered, and the efficiency of their

FIGURE C–4

Existing and Proposed Capital Planning Review and Approval Frameworks

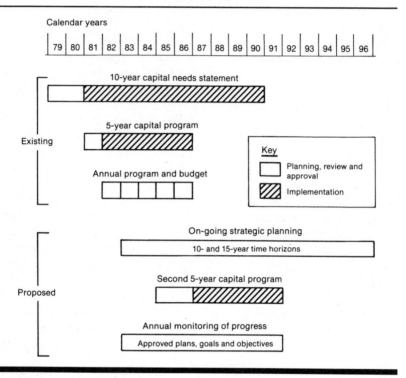

delivery as well, to pay closer attention to financial and operating results, and, finally, to develop a high-quality long-range plan for accomplishing improvements.

These procedures may not be applicable to all public agencies or even to all transit agencies. There are significant political hurdles to overcome. However, it seems likely that other cities will have to confront the same types of infrastructure problems as New York; and, if so, they may be willing to pay closer attention to the kinds of planning and financial innovations used by the MTA.

FIGURE C-5

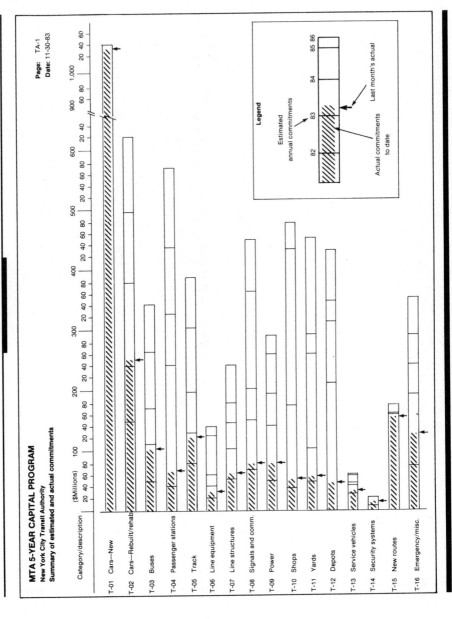

MTA 5-YEAR CAPITAL PROGRAM
New York City Transit Authority
Summary of estimated and actual commitments

Page: TA-1
Date: 11-30-83

Category/description

($Millions)

T-01 Cars—New
T-02 Cars—Rebuilt/rehab.
T-03 Buses
T-04 Passenger stations
T-05 Track
T-06 Line equipment
T-07 Line structures
T-08 Signals and comm.
T-09 Power
T-10 Shops
T-11 Yards
T-12 Depots
T-13 Service vehicles
T-14 Security systems
T-15 New routes
T-16 Emergency/misc.

Legend

Estimated annual commitments

Last month's actual

Actual commitments to date

EXCERPT FROM CENTRAK
PROGRESS REPORT

FIGURE C–6

Summary of Project Highlights and Current Delays

Purchase 325 IRT cars:
The contract for the purchase of 325 IRT cars with Kawasaki Heavy Industries became effective 4/12/82. Cost with escalation (revised 10/83 to reflect actual invoices, payments, and project schedules as of 9/83) is $302,290,000. Delivery of an 11-car test train was scheduled for 12/83, and the last of the 325 cars by 4/85. The first car of the 11-car test train was received on 8/19/83. The remaining 10 cars that make up the 11-car test train were delivered on 10/5/83 and 10/6/83. *Testing of individual cars has been completed and the 30-day 10/11-car train test was started on 11/25/83.* The last of the 325-car order is now anticipated to be received in 1/85.

Purchase 225 BHT/IND cars
The contract for the purchase of 225 BHT/IND cars with Westinghouse-Amrail became effective 11/24/82. Cost with escalation (revised 10/83 to reflect actual invoices, payments, and project schedules as of 9/83) is $244,120,000. Under the terms of the contract, a 10-car tent train is scheduled for delivery in 1/85, and all cars are to be delivered by 5/86.

Purchase 825 IRT cars
The contract for the purchase of 825 IRT cars with Bombardier became effective on 11/15/82. Cost with escalation (revised 10/83 to reflect actual invoices, payments, and project schedules as of 9/83) is $808,170,000. Under the terms of the contract a 10-car test train is scheduled to be delivered by 12/84 and all cars by 10/87. The present schedule is 11/84 and 9/87, respectively.

Current Delays
None.

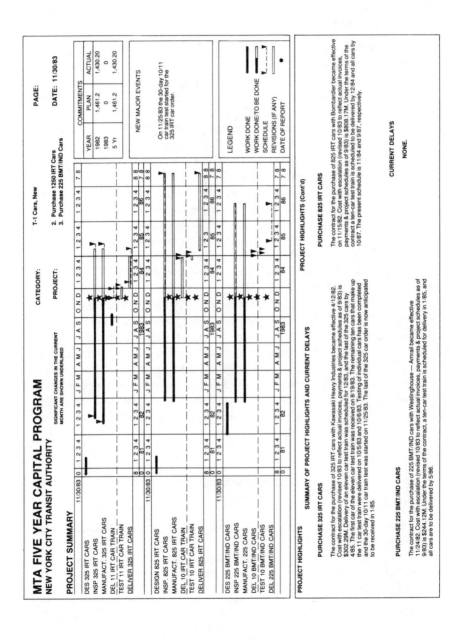

MTA FIVE YEAR CAPITAL PROGRAM
NEW YORK CITY TRANSIT AUTHORITY

CATEGORY: T-1 Cars, New

PROJECT:
2. Purchase 1250 IRT Cars
3. Purchase 225 BMT/IND Cars

PROJECT SUMMARY

SIGNIFICANT CHANGES IN THE CURRENT MONTH ARE SHOWN UNDERLINED

(Schedule bars, rows:)
DES 325 IRT CARS
INSP 325 IRT CARS
MANUFACT. 325 IRT CARS
DEL 11 IRT CAR TRAIN
TEST 11 IRT CAR TRAIN
DELIVER 325 IRT CARS

DESIGN 825 IRT CARS
INSP. 825 IRT CARS
MANUFACT. 825 IRT CARS
DEL 10 IRT CAR TRAIN
TEST 10 IRT CAR TRAIN
DELIVER 825 IRT CARS

DES 225 BMT/IND CARS
INSP 225 BMT/IND CARS
MANUFACT. 225 CARS
DEL 10 BMT/IND CARS
TEST 10 BMT/IND CARS
DEL 225 BMT/IND CARS

COMMITMENTS

YEAR	PLAN	ACTUAL
1982	1,461.2	1,430.20
1983	0	0
5 Yr	1,461.2	1,430.20

NEW MAJOR EVENTS

On 11/25/83 the 30-day 10/11 car train test started for the 325 IRT car order.

LEGEND

WORK DONE
WORK DONE/TO BE DONE
SCHEDULE
REVISIONS (IF ANY)
DATE OF REPORT

PROJECT HIGHLIGHTS

SUMMARY OF PROJECT HIGHLIGHTS AND CURRENT DELAYS

PURCHASE 325 IRT CARS

The contract for the purchase of 325 IRT cars with Kawasaki Heavy Industries became effective 4/12/82. Cost with escalation (revised 10/83 to reflect actual invoices, payments & project schedules as of 9/83) is $302.29M. Delivery of an eleven car test train was scheduled for 12/83, and the last of the 325 cars by 4/85. The first car of the eleven car test train was received on 8/19/83. The remaining ten cars that make up the 11 car test train were delivered on 10/5/83 and 10/6/83. Testing of individual cars has been completed and the 30-day 10/11 car train test was started on 11/25/83. The last of the 325 car order is now anticipated to be received in 1/85.

PURCHASE 225 BMT/IND CARS

The contract for the purchase of 225 BMT/IND cars with Westinghouse — Amrail became effective 11/24/82. Cost with escalation (revised 10/83 to reflect actual invoices, payments & project schedules as of 9/83) is $244.12M. Under the terms of the contract, a ten-car test train is scheduled for delivery in 1/85, and all cars are to be delivered by 5/86.

PROJECT HIGHLIGHTS (Cont'd)

PURCHASE 825 IRT CARS

The contract for the purchase of 825 IRT cars with Bombardier became effective on 11/15/82. Cost with escalation (revised 10/83 to reflect actual invoices, payments & project schedules as of 9/83) is $808.17M. Under the terms of the contract a ten-car test train is scheduled to be delivered by 12/84 and all cars by 10/87. The present schedule is 11/84 and 9/87, respectively.

CURRENT DELAYS

NONE.

HOW TO INTERPRET THE SCHEDULE BAR CHART

The bar charts included in this report show project schedules at a summary level. The most significant activities for the project are displayed. Included among these are major procurement efforts, contractor performance, and summary construction activity. Other information may be shown depending upon the particular project conditions.

It should be noted that the accuracy of the information shown on the schedule represented by the bar chart varies with the current stage of development for each project (that is, conceptual planning, final design, construction in progress, etc.). A schedule based on conceptual planning information could therefore change dramatically, as more information becomes available (for example, when a project progresses from the conceptual planning stage to the design stage).

The bar chart schedule is comprised of two sections: the summary activity descriptions on the lefthand side, and the graphical schedule display on the right side. The schedule symbols are placed in the display area. The calendar is variable: monthly for the current period, quarterly for the succeeding years, and yearly for the first year and the last two years. As the capital program progresses, the monthly area will be shifted to the right, yielding a "moving lens" effect.

The schedule symbols which appear in the display area are described in the legend below. They show schedule data as follows: work completed—a solid rectangle; scheduled completion of work in progress—an unshaded rectangle; the schedule—a pair of triangles; changes to the schedule—an unshaded rectangle; the date of the report—a vertical line of stars.

NOTES

[1] George A. Steiner, *Strategic Planning: What Every Manager Must Know* (New York: MacMillan, 1979).

[2] A very liberal 1968 labor agreement provided early retirement benefits after only 20 years of service, which encouraged many experienced maintenance workers to leave the Transit Authority within a very short time. Also, operating funds were tight at the onset of the fiscal crisis, and in 1977 a decision was made to virtually abandon preventive maintenance—vehicles were being repaired only after they actually broke down. Not only maintenance but also capital spending became inadequate, due not only to the fiscal crisis but also because a disproportionate share of rather meager funds were being poured into construction of new or expanded routes—hence, planning to provide more service in the future to a dwindling ridership base. In short, poor planning and short-sighted handling of a labor negotiation exacerbated the situation.

³ Richard A. Chudd, David Schoenbrod, and Ross Sandler, *A New Direction in Transit* (New York: New York City Planning Commission, December 1978).

⁴ The state of New York retained Booz-Allen & Hamilton (BAH) to conduct a comprehensive analysis of specific management issues at the MTA. The work was conducted between May 1978 and August 1979 by BAH and two subcontractors—System Design Concepts, Inc. and London Transport International Services. Focusing on the TA and LIRR, the consultants developed implementable recommendations in 13 task areas. The recommendations covered cost reduction, improving operational effectiveness and efficiency, improving management systems, and improving planning and capital investments practices. See *The MTA Management Study*, prepared for the MTA by Booz-Allen & Hamilton, January 1980.

BIBLIOGRAPHY

Books

Steiner, George A. *Strategic Planning: What Every Manager Must Know.* New York: MacMillan, 1979.

Official Statement, Transit Facilities Revenue Bonds Series A. Prepared by Mudge Rose Guthrie & Alexander, Bond Counsel, October 15, 1982.

Metropolitan Transportation Authority: Finances of Mass Transit Services in New York City. Bear, Stearns & Co.; Public Finance Department Research Report, 1983.

Published Studies and Technical Papers

Chudd, Richard A.; David Schoenbrod; and Ross Sandler. *A New Direction in Transit.* New York: New York City Planning Commission, December 1978.

Morelli, Anthony. *Economic Cost Study Program for Capital Investment Decisions.* New York City Transit Authority Task Force of the Economic Development Council, July 28, 1982.

Summary of Completed Projects. New York City Transit Authority Task Force of the Economic Development Council, September 1, 1983.

Strategic Planning Manual. NYCTA Task Force of the Economic Development Council, December 13, 1982.

Municipal Credit Report, No. 344, Metropolitan Transportation Authority. Fitch Investors Service, October 5, 1982.

Municipal Credit Report, Metropolitan Transportation Authority. Moody's Investors Service, October 13, 1982.

Downey, Mortimer L. "Generating Private Sector Financing for Public Transportation." Presented at American Public Transit Association, October 1983.

Speeding the Funding and Processing for the Transit Capital Program. Prepared for the NYC Department of City Planning by Systems Design Concepts, Inc., October 27, 1983.

Periodicals and Newspapers

On the Move. Published by MTA for employees.

Special Issue: Capital Program, October 1981.

"Capital Program Expansion Approved," May 1983.

Special Issue: Capital Program, Winter 1983.

MTA Reports. Published by MTA for riders.

Special Issue: Capital Program, January 1982.

Empire State Report

Special Supplement on the MTA's Five-Year Capital Program, December 1981, pp 517–532.

Special Supplement on the MTA's Five-Year Capital Program: An Update, January 1983.

Special Supplement on the MTA's Five-Year Capital Program: An Update, January 1984.

Sandler, Ross. *"MTA: Light at the End of the Tunnel?"* December 1983, pp 6–12.

Other Periodicals

"The Transit Issue." *New York Affairs* 7, no. 3, New York University, 1982.

Jurow, Steven; and Ross Sandler. "Transit: Keeping the Customer Satisfied." *New York Affairs* 6, no. 4, New York University, 1981, pp. 57–69.

Shedd, Tom. "Five-Year MTA Program Moves ahead in New York." *Modern Railroads,* November 1983, pp 26–32.

Downey, Mortimer L.; and Amy Linden. "We're Not WPPSS, Says MTA." *Investment Dealers Digest,* October 18, 1983, pp 14–15.

Derrick, Peter. "New Financing Ideas May Help Bring back Polish to Transit in Big Apple." *Mass Transit,* April 1982, pp 10–14.

—————. "Space-Age Computers to Keep MTA Project on Track." *Mass Transit,* November 1982, pp 16–22.

"Outlook 84: In New York Capital Revitalization Is Priority." *Passenger Transport,* October 24, 1983, p 45.

MTA Internal and Documents

Metropolitan Transportation Authority. *Submission to the MTA Capital Program Review Board for Long Island Rail Road, Metro-North, New York City Transit Authority, Staten Island Rapid Transit Operating Authority,* September 25, 1981.

_____. *The Capital Program of the MTA Transit Systems and the MTA Commuter Rail Systems as Approved by the MTA Capital Program Review Board,* August 25, 1983.

_____. *Sale and Leaseback of Buses and Commuter Rail Cars* (Confidential), October 12, 1981.

The MTA Management Study. Prepared for the MTA by Booz-Allen & Hamilton, January 1980.

MTA Memoranda

From David Z. Plavin to MTA Board Members. "Recommendation for an MTA Capital Project Tracking System—CENTRAK," April 9, 1982.

From J. M. Kaiser to MTA Agency Budget Directors. "Actions Required in Support of the MTA Five-Year Capital Program," August 12, 1982.

From Mortimer L. Downey to members of the finance committee. "Capital Program Funds," April 7, 1983.

From Mortimer L. Downey to Stephen Berger. "NYCTA Capital Budget—July–December 1983," June 6, 1983.

From Mortimer L. Downey to members of the MTA Board. "Amendment to the MTA Capital Plan," July 12, 1983.

Summary Report
> Task IA: Capital Planning Analysis, NYCTA.
> Task IB: Capital Planning Analysis, LIRR.

New York City Transit Authority. *Ten-Year Capital Needs Assessment: 1984–1993,* November 28, 1983.

_____. *Instructions for the Preparation of the Five-Year Plan: Fiscal Years 1984 to 1988,* August 6, 1982.

Richard Ravitch Speeches

Statement on accepting chairmanship of the MTA, November 21, 1979; on capital revitalization agenda, November 1980.

Testimony before the Senate Banking Committee Subcommittee on International Finance and Monetary Policy (on purchase of subway cars from Bombardier of Canada), July 22, 1982.

Remarks before Association for a Better New York on status of capital program and automatic fare collection, March 2, 1983.

Legislation

State of New York S. 6928, A 8912; An Act to amend the public authorities law, in relation to providing, for the financing of an emergency capital program for the Metropolitan Transportation Authority, June 16, 1981.

Index